Public Relations Writing and Media Techniques

W9-CBF-156

SEVENTH EDITION

Dennis L. Wilcox
San Jose State University

Bryan H. Reber
University of Georgia

PEARSON

Boston Columbus Indianapolis New York San Francisco Upper Saddle River
Amsterdam Cape Town Dubai London Madrid Milan Munich Paris Montréal Toronto
Delhi Mexico City São Paulo Sydney Hong Kong Seoul Singapore Taipei Tokyo

Editor-in-Chief, Communication:
    Karon Bowers
Editor: Ziki Dekel
Marketing Manager: Blair Zoe Tuckman
Supplements Editor: Corey Kahn
Senior Digital Editor: Paul DeLuca
Digital Editor: Lisa Dotson
Associate Managing Editor:
    Bayani Mendoza de Leon
Production/Project Manager:
    Raegan Keida Heerema
Project Coordination, Text Design, and
    Electronic Page Makeup: Integra

Cover Designer/Manager: Nancy Danahy
Cover Art: (From top to bottom)
    ©Nikhil Gangavane/Dreamstime LLC;
    Greenpeace life ring in Cancun, Mexico/
    Newscom; ©Allen Fredrickson/Newscom;
    ©SuperStock/Alamy
Senior Manufacturing Buyer: Mary Ann
    Gloriande
Printer/Binder: Courier
    Corporation–Westford
Cover Printer: Lehigh-Phoenix Color/
    Hagerstown

Credits and acknowledgments borrowed from other sources and reproduced, with permission, in this textbook appear on the appropriate page within text or on pages 527–528.

Library of Congress Cataloging-in-Publication Data
Wilcox, Dennis L.
    Public relations writing and media techniques / Dennis L. Wilcox, Bryan
H. Reber.—7th ed.
        p. cm.
    Includes bibliographical references and index.
    ISBN-13: 978-0-205-21167-8
    ISBN-10: 0-205-21167-4
    1. Public relations—United States.   2. Public relations—United States—
    Authorship.   I. Reber, Bryan H.   II. Title.
    HM1221.W55 2013
    808'.066659—dc23
                                                            2011040970

Copyright © 2013, 2009, 2005, 2001 by Pearson Education, Inc.

All rights reserved. Manufactured in the United States of America. This publication is protected by Copyright, and permission should be obtained from the publisher prior to any prohibited reproduction, storage in a retrieval system, or transmission in any form or by any means, electronic, mechanical, photocopying, recording, or likewise. To obtain permission(s) to use material from this work, please submit a written request to Pearson Education, Inc., Permissions Department, One Lake Street, Upper Saddle River, New Jersey 07458, or you may fax your request to 201-236-3290.

10 9 8 7 6 5 4 3 2 1—CRW—14 13 12

www.pearsonhighered.com

ISBN 10:   0-205-21167-4
ISBN 13: 978-0-205-21167-8

Contents

Preface   xvi

PART ONE The Basics of Public Relations Writing

» CHAPTER 1 Getting Organized for Writing   1

The Framework of Public Relations Writing   1
Writing Is Only One Component   1   ·   Writers as Communication
Technicians   2

The Public Relations Writer   3

TIPS FOR SUCCESS   Writing Is One of Six Skills   3
Objectives   4   ·   Audiences   4   ·   Channels   5

Preparation for Writing   6
Computers   6   ·   Reference Sources   7

Research: The Prelude to Writing   13
Search Engines   14

TIPS FOR SUCCESS   Useful Websites for Public Relations Writers   15
Electronic Databases   16

Writing Guidelines   17
Outlining the Purpose   17

TIPS FOR SUCCESS   Need Information? Use a Database   18
Sentences   19   ·   Paragraphs   20

TIPS FOR SUCCESS   How to Improve Your Writing   20
Word Choice   21   ·   Active Verbs and Present Tense   22   ·   Imagery   22

Errors to Avoid   23
Spelling   23   ·   Gobbledygook and Jargon   23   ·   Poor Sentence
Structure   24   ·   Wrong Words   25   ·   Redundancies   25   ·   Too Many
Numbers   26

TIPS FOR SUCCESS   What's in a Word? Will You "Accept" or "Except"
the Challenge?   26

TIPS FOR SUCCESS   How Dating Advice Can Make You a Better Writer   27
Hype   28   ·   Bias and Stereotypes   28   ·   Politically Incorrect Language   29

iii

» **CHAPTER 2** Becoming a Persuasive Writer   32

Persuasion: As Old as Civilization   32

The Basics of Communication   33
Sender 33 · Message 33 · Channel 34 · Receiver 34

Theories of Communication   34
Media Uses and Gratification 34 · Cognitive
Dissonance 35 · Framing 36
TIPS FOR SUCCESS Why Writing Fails to Persuade   36
Diffusion and Adoption 37 · Hierarchy of Needs 38

Factors in Persuasive Writing   40
Audience Analysis 40
TIPS FOR SUCCESS How to Be a More Persuasive Writer
and Speaker 41
Source Credibility 42 · Appeal to Self-Interest 43 · Clarity of the
Message 44
TIPS FOR SUCCESS Appeals That Move People to Act   44
Timing and Context 45 · Symbols and Slogans 45 ·
Semantics 45 · Suggestions for Action 46 ·Content and Structure 46
PR CASEBOOK Emotional Appeals Humanize an Issue   48

Persuasive Speaking   51

Persuasion and Propaganda   52

The Ethics of Persuasion   53
TIPS FOR SUCCESS An Ethics Test for Public Relations Writers   54

» **CHAPTER 3** Finding and Making News   59

The Challenge of Making News   59

What Makes News   60
Timeliness 60 · Prominence 62
TIPS FOR SUCCESS Celebrate! It's National Bagel Day   63
Proximity 64 · Significance 65 · Unusualness 66 ·
Human Interest 66 · Conflict 67 · Newness 68

How to Find News   69
Internal News Sources 69 · External News Sources 70

How to Create News   70
Brainstorming 72 · Special Events 72

TIPS FOR SUCCESS   32 Ways to Create News for Your Organization   73

Contests 74 · Do 75 · Don't 75 · Polls and Surveys 76 ·
Top 10 Lists 77 · Product Demonstrations 77

TIPS FOR SUCCESS   How to Conduct a Credible Survey   78

Publicity Stunts 79

PR CASEBOOK   A Baskin-Robbins Publicity Stunt Retires Flavors
            with Style   80

Rallies and Protests 81 · Personal Appearances 83 · Awards 83

» **CHAPTER 4** Working with Journalists and Bloggers   87

The Importance of Media Relations   87

The Media's Dependence on Public Relations   88

Public Relations' Dependence on the Media   89

Areas of Friction   90

Complaints about Public Relations Personnel 90 · Complaints about
Journalists and Bloggers 91 · Working with Journalists 92

TIPS FOR SUCCESS   Working with Bloggers   93

Media Interviews 94

PR CASEBOOK   The Ethical Dilemma of Being a Spokesperson   95

TIPS FOR SUCCESS   Nine Tips for a Spokesperson   98

TIPS FOR SUCCESS   Alternatives to Saying "No Comment"   100

News Conferences 99 · Teleconferences and Webcasts 102 ·
Media Tours 103 · Previews and Parties 104 · Press
Junkets 105 · Editorial Board Meetings 107

A Media Relations Checklist   108

Media Etiquette 110

TIPS FOR SUCCESS   Correcting Errors in News Stories   110

Crisis Communication   112

PART TWO Writing for Mass Media

» **CHAPTER 5** Writing the News Release   117

The Backbone of Publicity Programs   117

The Value of News Releases   118

Planning a News Release   119

The Basic Questions   119

The Basic Components of a News Release   120

TIPS FOR SUCCESS   Is Your Release Newsworthy?   120

Letterhead   121 · Contacts   122 · Headline   123 ·
Dateline   124 · The Lead   124 · Body of the Text   128 ·
Description of the Organization   129

TIPS FOR SUCCESS   A News Release by the Numbers: A Quick Guide   129

TIPS FOR SUCCESS   How to Write Executive Quotes   130

TIPS FOR SUCCESS   Rules for Writing a News Release   132

News Release Formats   133

The Traditional News Release   133 · The Online News Release   133 ·
The Multimedia News Release   137

» **CHAPTER 6** Preparing Fact Sheets, Advisories, Media Kits,
and Pitches   142

Expanding the Publicity Tool Kit   142

Fact Sheets   143

Media Advisories   146

Media Kits   150

The Traditional Media Kit   150 · The Digital Media Kit   152

Pitching a Story   154

Researching the Publication   154

PR CASEBOOK   A Good Pitch Can Get You on Jay Leno   155

The Email Pitch   157

TIPS FOR SUCCESS   Pitches That Help Reporters Do Their Job   157

The Telephone Pitch   159 · The Twitter Pitch   160 · The Follow-up   160

TIPS FOR SUCCESS   How to Successfully Pitch Bloggers   161

TIPS FOR SUCCESS   How to Get Your Pitch Noticed   162

» **CHAPTER 7** Creating News Features and Op-Eds   165

The Value of Features   165

Planning a News Feature   166

Ways to Proceed   167

Types of Features   169

Case Study   169 · Application Story   170

TIPS FOR SUCCESS   How to Write a Case Study   170

Surveys and Research Studies   171 · Backgrounder   173 ·
Personality Profile   173 · Historical Piece   174

TIPS FOR SUCCESS   How to Write the Personality
Profile   174

Parts of a Feature   175

The Headline   175

TIPS FOR SUCCESS   How to Write a Great Feature Story   176

The Lead   177 · The Body   178

TIPS FOR SUCCESS   How to Personalize a Lead Paragraph   178

The Summary   180 · Photos and Graphics   180

Placement Opportunities   182

Newspapers   182 · General Magazines   182 · Specialty/Trade
Magazines   182

Writing an Op-Ed   183

TIPS FOR SUCCESS   How to Write the "Perfect" Op-Ed   184

Letters to the Editor   185

» CHAPTER 8 Selecting Publicity Photos and Graphics   190

The Importance of Publicity Photos   190

Components of a Good Photo   191

Technical Quality   192

TIPS FOR SUCCESS   How to Take Product Photos That Get
Published   192

Subject Matter   193 · Composition   194 · Action   196 ·
Scale   197 · Camera Angle   197 · Lighting and Timing   198 ·
Color   199

Working with Photographers   199

Finding Photographers   200

TIPS FOR SUCCESS   Photo Advice from the Experts   200

Contracts   201 · The Photo Session   201 · Cropping and
Retouching   202 · Ethical Considerations   202

Writing Photo Captions   203

Creating Other Graphics **205**

Charts 205 · Diagrams 206 · Renderings and Scale Models 206 · Line Drawings and Clip Art 206

Maintaining Photo and Art Files **207**

Distributing Photos and Artwork **207**

» **CHAPTER 9** Radio, Television, and Online Video **211**

The Wide Reach of Broadcasting **211**

Radio **212**

Radio News Releases 213

TIPS FOR SUCCESS How to Write a Radio News Release **214**

Dressing For A Successful Interview **215**

Audio News Releases 216 · Public Service Announcements 218 · Radio Media Tours 223

Television **223**

Video News Releases 224 · The New Trend: B-Roll Packaging 227

TIPS FOR SUCCESS The Jargon of Writing for Video **227**

PR CASEBOOK B-Roll Drives Shell's Eco-Mileage Competition **229**

Public Service Announcements 231

PR CASEBOOK Water Campaign Taps media with PSAs **232**

Satellite Media Tours 232

TIPS FOR SUCCESS Guidelines for a Successful SMT **235**

Talk Shows and Product Placements **236**

Talk Shows 237 · Magazine Shows 239 · Product Placement 240

TIPS FOR SUCCESS The Ideal Talk Show Guest **240**

TIPS FOR SUCCESS Guidelines for Product Placement on Your Favorite TV Show **242**

Radio Promotions 243 · Community Calendars 243

Film Features and Online Video **244**

Features for Cable 244 · Online Video 245

TIPS FOR SUCCESS How to Make a Good Video **246**

» **CHAPTER 10** Distributing News to the Media **250**

Reaching the Media **250**

Media Databases 251 · Editorial Calendars and Tip Sheets 253

Distribution of Materials   255

Email   255

TIPS FOR SUCCESS   Selecting a Distribution Channel   256

Online Newsrooms   257   ·   Newswires   259

PR CASEBOOK   Online Newsrooms: A Fortune 500 Scorecard   260

Mobile Applications   263   ·   Twitter   264   ·   Feature Placement Firms   265

TIPS FOR SUCCESS   How to Write a Food Feature   267

Photo Placement Firms   268   ·   Mail   269   ·   Fax   269

» **CHAPTER 11** Avoiding Legal Hassles   272

A Sampling of Legal Problems   272

Libel and Defamation   274

The Fair Comment Defense   274   ·   Avoiding Defamation Suits   275

Invasion of Privacy   276

Employee Newsletters   276   ·   Photo Releases   276   ·   Product Publicity and
Advertising   277   ·   Media Inquiries about Employees   277   ·
Employee Blogs   278

TIPS FOR SUCCESS   Can Facebook Get You Fired?   279

Copyright Law   280

TIPS FOR SUCCESS   How to Use Copyrighted Material for Fun
and Profit   281

Fair Use versus Infringement   282

TIPS FOR SUCCESS   Don't Plagiarize: It's Unethical   282

Photography and Artwork   283   ·   Work for Hire   283   ·   Use of Online
Material   284

Trademark Law   284

The Protection of Trademarks   285   ·   The Problem of Trademark
Infringement   287

TIPS FOR SUCCESS   Trademarks Require a Capital Letter   288

Misappropriation of Personality   289

Regulatory Agencies   290

The Federal Trade Commission   290

TIPS FOR SUCCESS   FTC Guidelines for Publicizing Products   291

The Securities and Exchange Commission   292   ·   The Federal Communications
Commission   294   ·   The Food and Drug Administration   294

Working with Lawyers   295

PART THREE Writing for Other Media

» **CHAPTER 12** Tapping the Web and Digital Media 299

The Internet: Pervasive in Our Lives 299

The World Wide Web 300

TIPS FOR SUCCESS Traditional Media versus New Media 301

Writing for the Web 303

TIPS FOR SUCCESS Writing for a Website 305

Building an Effective Website 306 · Making the Site Interactive 307 · Attracting Visitors to Your Site 308 · Tracking Site Visitors 310 · Return on Investment 311

The Basics of Webcasting 311

The Value of Social Media 312

Tapping into Listservs 313 · Using RSS to Distribute and Manage Information 313 · The Explosion of Blogs 314

TIPS FOR SUCCESS How to Write a Blog 316

TIPS FOR SUCCESS IBM's Guidelines for Employee Blogs 319

Making Friends on MySpace and Facebook 320 · YouTube: King of Video Clips 322

TIPS FOR SUCCESS Making Your Facebook Page a Winner 323

PR CASEBOOK PepsiCo Uses Social Media to Build Brand Awareness and Support 324

Flickr: Sharing Photos 325 · Twitter 326 · Texting and Wikis 327

TIPS FOR SUCCESS How to Increase Retweets 328

Podcasts: The Portable Medium 330 · Mobile Media 333

The Continuing Role of Traditional Media 334

» **CHAPTER 13** Newsletters, Brochures, and Intranets 340

The Value of Print Publications 340

The Balancing Act of Editors 341

A Mission Statement Gives Purpose 342 · Making an Article Schedule 343

Newsletters and Magazines 344

Meeting Audience Interests 344 · Design 345 · Format 345

TIPS FOR SUCCESS   Story Ideas and Packaging Tips for Newsletters   346

Layout   347

TIPS FOR SUCCESS   How to Create Great Publications   349

Photos and Illustrations   350   ·   Headlines   351   ·   Lead
Sentences   352

Online Newsletters   353

Intranets   354

TIPS FOR SUCCESS   Lessons in Good Intranet Design   356

Brochures   357

Planning   357   ·   Writing   358

TIPS FOR SUCCESS   Basic Brochure Design 101   358

Format   359   ·   Paper   361   ·   Type Fonts   362   ·   Ink and
Color   363   ·   Finding a Printer   364

Annual Reports   364

TIPS FOR SUCCESS   How Much Will It Cost?   365

Planning and Writing   367   ·   Trends in Content and
Delivery   368

» **CHAPTER 14** Writing Email, Memos, and Proposals   373

The Challenge of Communication Overload   373

Email   374

Purpose   375   ·   Content   376   ·   Format   377

TIPS FOR SUCCESS   Mind Your Email Manners   378

Memorandums   379

Purpose   379   ·   Content   379   ·   Format   380

Letters   380

Purpose   381   ·   Content   382

TIPS FOR SUCCESS   How to Write Efficient Letters   382

Format   383

Proposals   384

Purpose   384   ·   Organization   384

TIPS FOR SUCCESS   How to Write a Position Paper   386

Proposals by Public Relations Firms   387

PR CASEBOOK   Zipcar Picks Weber Shandwick through
RFP Process   389

» **CHAPTER 15** Giving Speeches and Presentations   392

The Challenge of the Speaking Circuit   392

The Basics of Speechwriting   393

Researching the Audience and Speaker 393   ·   Laying the Groundwork 393   ·   Writing the Speech 395

PR CASEBOOK   A Systematic Approach to Speechwriting   396

The Basics of Giving a Speech   398

Know Your Objective 398

TIPS FOR SUCCESS   How to Introduce a Speaker   399

Structure the Message for the Ear 400   ·   Tailor Remarks to the Audience 400   ·   Give Specifics 401

TIPS FOR SUCCESS   Keep Your Audience in Mind   401

Keep It Timely and Short 402   ·   Gestures and Eye Contact 402

Visual Aids for Presentations   403

TIPS FOR SUCCESS   Nonverbal Communication Speaks Volumes   404

PowerPoint 405   ·   Prezi 407

Other Speech Formats   408

Panels 408

Speaker Training and Placement   409

Executive Training 409   ·   Speaker's Bureaus 410   ·   Placement of Speakers 411   ·   Publicity Opportunities 412

TIPS FOR SUCCESS   The Speech as News Release   413

» **CHAPTER 16** Using Direct Mail and Advertising   417

The Basics of Direct Mail   417

Advantages of Direct Mail 418   ·   Disadvantages of Direct Mail 419

Creating a Direct Mail Package   419

Mailing Envelope 420   ·   The Letter 420   ·   Brochures 423

TIPS FOR SUCCESS   How to Write a Fundraising Letter   423

TIPS FOR SUCCESS   How to Do a Direct Mail Package   424

Reply Card 425   ·   Return Envelope 425   ·   Gifts 425

The Basics of Public Relations Advertising   426

Advantages of Advertising 426   ·   Disadvantages of Advertising 427

TIPS FOR SUCCESS   Effective Online Ad Elements   428

Types of Public Relations Advertising   **429**

Image Building   429   ·   Investor and Financial Relations   429   ·   Public
Service   431   ·   Advocacy/Issues   433   ·   Announcements   433

Creating a Print Ad   **434**

Headline   434   ·   Text   434   ·   Artwork   434   ·   Layout   435

TIPS FOR SUCCESS   Getting the Most from Your Ads   435

Working with an Ad Agency   **436**

Other Advertising Channels   **436**

Billboards   436

PR CASEBOOK   U.S. Census Bureau Targets Millennials   887

Transit Panels   437   ·   Buttons and Bumper
Stickers   437   ·   Posters   438   ·   T-Shirts   438   ·
Promotional Items   439

PART FOUR Managing Programs and Campaigns

» **CHAPTER 17** Organizing Meetings and Events   441

A World Filled with Meetings and Events   **441**

Staff and Committee Meetings   **442**

Group Meetings   **443**

Planning   443

TIPS FOR SUCCESS   How to Plan a Meeting   444

Registration   447   ·   Program   447

Banquets   **449**

Working with Catering Managers   449

TIPS FOR SUCCESS   Making a Budget for a Banquet   450

PR CASEBOOK   A Fundraising Gala: The Nitty-Gritty   451

Logistics and Timing   452

Receptions and Cocktail Parties   **453**

Conventions   **454**

Planning   454   ·   Program   455

TIPS FOR SUCCESS   Online Invites Make It Easy to RSVP   457

Trade Shows   **458**

Exhibit Booths   459   ·   Pressrooms and Media Relations   460

Promotional Events   461

Using Celebrities to Boost Attendance   462

TIPS FOR SUCCESS   Corporate Sponsorships Require Strategic
Thinking   462

Planning and Logistics   464

Open Houses and Plant Tours   465

TIPS FOR SUCCESS   How to Plan an Open House   468

» **CHAPTER 18** Planning Programs and Campaigns   471

The Value of a Written Plan   471

Developing a Plan   472

Gathering Information   472   ·   Analyzing the Information   474

Elements of a Plan   474

Situation   474

TIPS FOR SUCCESS   Components of a Public Relations Plan   475

Objectives   476

PR CASEBOOK   Winery Creates a "Goode" Job through
Social Media   477

TIPS FOR SUCCESS   How Public Relations Helps Fulfill Marketing
Objectives   480

Audience   481   ·   Strategy   481   ·   Tactics   482   ·
Calendar   483   ·   Budget   485   ·   Evaluation   486

Submitting a Plan for Approval   487

TIPS FOR SUCCESS   Do You Have a Winning Campaign?   488

» **CHAPTER 19** Measuring Success   491

The Importance of Measurement   491

Program Objectives   493

Measurement of Production/Distribution   494

TIPS FOR SUCCESS   Media Clippings Remain Most Popular
Measurement Tool   494

PR CASEBOOK   A Frito-Lay Campaign Meets Its Objectives   495

Measurement of Message Exposure   497

Media Impressions   497   ·   Advertising Value Equivalency   498   ·   Systematic
Tracking   499   ·   Monitoring the Internet   500   ·   Requests and 800
Numbers   502

TIPS FOR SUCCESS   How to Measure the Impact of Social Media   502

Cost per Person   503   ·   Event Attendance   503

Measurement of Audience Awareness   504

TIPS FOR SUCCESS   A Major Goal of Campaigns: Create Awareness   504

Measurement of Audience Attitudes   505

Measurement of Audience Action   506

Evaluation of Newsletters and Brochures   507

Content Analysis   507   ·   Readership Surveys   508   ·   Article Recall   508   ·
Advisory Boards and Focus Groups   508

Writing a Measurement Report   509

Index   512
Photo Credits   527

Preface

The seventh edition of *Public Relations Writing and Media Techniques* continues its reputation as the most comprehensive "how-to" text on the market. It will give you a complete tool kit for writing and creating a full range of public relations materials for distribution through traditional media and what are now known as "new media." In addition, it's the only major PR writing text that provides entire chapters on how to plan events, compose publicity photos, write news features, and measure the success of a campaign.

It is a user-friendly text written in plain English that contains clear, step-by-step guidelines illustrated by multiple examples from actual award-winning public relations programs conducted by many well-known organizations.

Although the emphasis is on the "nuts and bolts" of effective public relations writing and techniques, the text also provides the conceptual framework and broader context of how the tactics of public relations fit into the entire public relations process—research, planning, communication, and evaluation. The idea is to ensure that you not only know *how* to write public relations materials, but also understand *why* they are written from the standpoint of furthering organizational objectives.

The many updates, revisions, and additions to this new edition reflect today's work in public relations. Perhaps the most significant changes in this edition concern the rise of tablets, e-readers, mobile-enabled smartphones, and apps that have significantly changed how public relations writers think and work. The rise of blogs and other social media such as Facebook, Google+, Twitter, and YouTube has also challenged and created new opportunities for public relations practitioners.

This edition, more than any other comparable introductory writing text, tells you how to work in the rapidly changing digital environment. It's more than a textbook; it's a handy reference book that students will constantly use on their first job and current practitioners will use as an expert resource.

New in the Seventh Edition

The fundamentals of public relations writing remain the same, but how materials are formatted and distributed is constantly evolving. Since the last edition, for example, the iPad and smartphones have revolutionized how millions of people receive their information. There has also been major growth in Twitter, an explosion of apps, and increasing use of QR codes to package and convey information in a totally mobile-enabled society.

The increasing array of available media platforms is a bonanza for public relations specialists but also presents two challenges to today's students and current practitioners. One challenge is to constantly keep up with the latest device or new social networking site. The second challenge is to understand how all these new developments can be applied in public relations to more effectively communicate with a variety of increasingly segmented audiences.

No book, including this one, can possibly reflect today's constantly evolving technology and media environment, but this textbook will give you a solid foundation about the basic concepts of public relations writing and media techniques. This new edition will also give you a good overview of how traditional media and the "new media" are converging and being used daily by public relations practitioners to plan, organize, and execute a variety of communication programs. The following sections outline the contents and what is new in the seventh edition.

Expanded Information on Key Aspects of Today's Public Relations Practice

This edition offers new and expanded treatment of numerous topics. Some examples include:

- » The use of iPads, tablets, and e-readers by public relations writers (Chapter 1)
- » How framing theory helps writers determine story angles and themes (Chapter 2)
- » Techniques for brainstorming creative ideas for stories and events (Chapter 3)
- » The stress and occasional ethical dilemma of being a spokesperson (Chapter 4)
- » Use of SEO (search engine optimization) to write online news release headlines (Chapter 5)
- » Writing executive quotes that sound authentic (Chapter 5)
- » Using Twitter to "pitch" a news story (Chapter 6)
- » Lessons from *The Wall Street Journal* on how to write a personalized lead on a news story (Chapter 7)
- » The popularity of infographics to portray information in an attractive way (Chapter 8)
- » The trend for B-roll packages to replace scripted visual news releases (Chapter 9)
- » Techniques for shooting video that can be distributed through YouTube or intranets (Chapter 9)
- » The use of mobile-enabled devices, apps, and QR codes for distribution of publicity materials (Chapter 10)
- » New FTC guidelines on product endorsements by bloggers and celebrities (Chapter 11)
- » The risk of employees getting fired for posting negative comments about their employer on social networking sites (Chapter 11)
- » Expanded information about Twitter, apps, and mobile-enabled content (Chapter 12)
- » The use of online newsletters to reach employees, consumers, and members (Chapter 13)
- » Intranets as an employee communication channel (Chapter 13)
- » Writing proposals offering public relations services, often called RFPs (Chapter 14)

» Preparing PowerPoint slides and using Prezi (Chapter 15)
» Writing and preparing direct mail packages for fundraising by charitable groups (Chapter 16)
» Online reservation systems for events (Chapter 17)
» Incorporating social media tactics in public relations campaigns (Chapter 18)
» Measuring the impact of social media (Chapter 19)

How-To Checklists for the Aspiring Writer

Every chapter has new and revised TIPS FOR SUCCESS boxes that offer students and current practitioners checklists on how to write various materials and conduct basic media relations techniques. Such checklists provide step-by-step directions and help readers grasp basic concepts that are discussed and elaborated upon in the chapter. The following are some examples from the almost 80 checklists in the book:

» How dating advice can make you a better writer (Chapter 1)
» An ethics test for public relations writers (Chapter 2)
» 32 ways to create news for your organization (Chapter 3)
» How to work with bloggers (Chapter 4)
» How to write executive quotes (Chapter 5)
» Pitches that help reporters do their jobs (Chapter 6)
» How to write a personality profile (Chapter 7)
» How to take product photos that get published (Chapter 8)
» Guidelines for product placement on your favorite TV shows (Chapter 9)
» How to select the best distribution channel for your material (Chapter 10)
» Can Facebook get you fired? (Chapter 11)
» How to write copy for a website (Chapter 12)
» Lessons in good intranet design (Chapter 13)
» How to write a business letter (Chapter 14)
» How to introduce a speaker (Chapter 15)
» How to write a fundraising letter (Chapter 16)
» How to make a budget for a banquet (Chapter 17)
» How to write a public relations plan (Chapter 18)
» How to measure the impact of social media (Chapter 19)

New PR Casebooks to Stimulate Interest and Insight

Students can better grasp a concept if it is illustrated with a practical example from the "real world." The extensive use of examples is a highlight of this text in two ways.

First, every concept throughout the book is followed by a practical example. Second, a more in-depth summary of a particular campaign is given in a "PR Casebook" that helps students understand how various techniques complement each other in a campaign. Some new cases include the following:

» Emotional appeals humanize an issue (Chapter 2)
» A Baskin-Robbins publicity stunt retires flavors with style (Chapter 3)
» The ethical dilemma of being a spokesperson (Chapter 4)
» A good pitch can get you on Jay Leno (Chapter 6)
» B-roll drives Shell's eco-mileage competition (Chapter 9)
» Water campaign taps media with PSAs (Chapter 9)
» Online newsrooms: A Fortune 500 scorecard (Chapter 10)
» Pepsi uses social media at SXSW (Chapter 12)
» Zipcar picks Weber Shandwick through RFP (Chapter 14)
» A systematic approach to speechwriting (Chapter 15)
» U.S. Census Bureau targets millennials (Chapter 16)
» Winery creates a "Goode" job through social media (Chapter 18)
» A Frito-Lay campaign meets its objectives (Chapter 19)

New and Revised Exercises at the End of Each Chapter

A popular feature is exercises at the end of every chapter. These skill building activities provide students with practical assignments that can be done individually or in a group to reinforce the techniques they have learned in each chapter.

Quotes from Leading Professionals

New quotes from leading professionals are highlighted in each chapter. These short, pithy statements give the essence of a professional's insights and wisdom on a particular concept or technique. This approach is much more readable than the short narrative or Q&A with a professional featured in some texts.

A New Coauthor

Dr. Bryan Reber, associate professor of public relations at the University of Georgia, makes his debut as coauthor of this textbook. He teaches a variety of public relations courses at the University of Georgia, including public relations writing, and has 15 years of professional experience in the field. He regularly publishes his research in academic journals and serves as a public relations consultant to a variety of public relations firms and other organizations. Dr. Reber is constantly in contact with professional practitioners and also has a sensitive understanding of what students need to know if they are to succeed in the field.

Organization of the Book

The text is written and organized so instructors can easily mix and match chapters that suit their students' needs. It's also adaptable for either a semester or quarter course and can even be divided for two courses. The first course could cover the fundamentals of basic writing and how to prepare publicity materials for traditional media and online news sites. The second course would then focus on controlled or sponsored media, including preparing materials for newsletters, brochures, presentations, and websites. The book is divided into four parts:

> Part One: The Basics of Public Relations Writing
> Part Two: Writing for Mass Media
> Part Three: Writing for Other Media
> Part Four: Managing Programs and Campaigns

Part One: The Basics of Public Relations Writing

This section introduces students to the basic framework of today's public relations practice and the role of the public relations writer. **Chapter 1** reviews the basic concepts of good writing, errors to avoid, and what resources are needed. **Chapter 2** continues with the components of persuasive writing, provides a brief overview of major communication theories, and ends with the ethical responsibilities of the public relations writer. **Chapter 3** helps students think strategically and creatively about what makes news. Traditional journalistic values are emphasized, but students are also told how to brainstorm ideas to generate news through special events, contests, and even stunts. **Chapter 4** is about effective media relations—how public relations personnel work with journalists and bloggers for everyone's mutual benefit. How to communicate during a crisis also is covered.

Part Two: Writing for Mass Media

The focus of this section is on how to prepare basic materials for distribution to traditional mass media outlets and online news sites. **Chapter 5** thoroughly details the structure and format of the news release. Attention is given to writing and formatting digital news releases, including multimedia ones, that are distributed via email, websites, and wire services. **Chapter 6** continues the process by detailing how to prepare fact sheets, media advisories, and media kits. Particularly valuable is a detailed section on how to "pitch" journalists a story. **Chapter 7** focuses on the writing of news features, such as personality profiles and product-application stories. The writing of opinion pieces, such as op-eds, is also discussed. **Chapter 8** examines the elements of good publicity photos and infographics, which often make a story more attractive to editors. It also offers suggestions on how to work with photographers and how to write photo captions. **Chapter 9** is about writing news releases for radio and television. The mechanics of video news releases (VNRs) and B-roll packages are explained, as well as how to book guests on talk shows and conduct a satellite media tour. The chapter ends with tips on how to produce a video for YouTube or a company intranet. **Chapter 10** is a detailed examination of how to use media databases and distribute public relations materials a number of ways, including via email, online newsrooms, wire services, social media, mobile devices, apps, and even QR codes. The pros and cons of each method are discussed. **Chapter 11** provides a legal framework for preparing materials. Attention is given to libel, privacy, copyright, trademarks, and governmental regulatory agencies such as the Federal Trade Commission (FTC).

Part Three: Writing for Other Media

A major aspect of public relations is writing for "controlled" or "sponsored" media; in other words, media that don't have external gatekeepers who filter the organization's messages. **Chapter 12** is about effectively using the Web and digital media. The construction and maintenance of websites are discussed. The chapter also examines how to use webcasts, blogs, podcasts, apps, and social networking sites such as Facebook, YouTube, and Twitter in public relations campaigns. **Chapter 13** offers information on how to write and design print and online newsletters and brochures. The writing format for company intranets, as well as annual reports, is also discussed. **Chapter 14** offers students tips on email etiquette, how to write a business letter, and how to organize a proposal offering public relations services. **Chapter 15** is about how to write and give speeches and presentations. Guidelines for PowerPoint and Prezi are provided. **Chapter 16** is about preparing direct mail pieces, primarily for nonprofit organizations, and the key elements of public relations advertising. Other media such as billboards, transit panels, and event T-shirts are discussed.

Part Four: Managing Programs and Campaigns

This section gives students the broad picture and helps them understand how the multiple tactics throughout the textbook are integrated into a coherent program or campaign. **Chapter 17** is about planning meetings and events. Detailed steps are given for organizing a banquet, planning a convention, setting up a trade show, and selecting a celebrity for a promotional event. **Chapter 18** presents the essential elements of a public relations campaign, providing the information needed to integrate various strategies and tactics into an effective campaign. The steps for how to write a public relations plan are given. **Chapter 19** explores the various ways that the success of a campaign can be measured.

Student Learning Tools

Each chapter of *Public Relations Writing and Media Techniques* includes several learning tools to help students better understand the concepts and give them the practice they need to apply what they have learned. In each chapter, you will find:

Chapter opening preview. A chapter overview that specifically tells students what they will be able to do after reading the chapter.

"Tips for Success" boxes. Step-by-step guidelines on how to do various tactics and techniques discussed in the chapter.

PR Casebooks. Summaries of actual public relations programs that show the practical application of various communication tactics.

Skill Building Activities. Suggested assignments that help students apply what they have learned from the chapter.

End-of-chapter summary. Concise summary of major concepts in brief sentences.

Media Resources. Readily accessible books, print articles, and online postings suggested for additional reading.

Websites. URLs for organizations mentioned in the text so students can access more information about a particular program or campaign.

Supplements

Instructors and students have a variety of tools available to them that will help make teaching and learning with *Public Relations Writing and Media Techniques* easier.

Instructor's Manual and Test Bank

The Instructor's Manual includes chapter outlines, sample syllabi, learning objectives, class activities, and discussion questions. The Test Bank includes several hundred multiple-choice and True/False questions. Available for download through our Instructor's Resource Center at www.pearsonhighered.com/irc (access code required).

MyTest Computerized Test Bank

This flexible, online test generating software includes all questions found in the test bank, allowing instructors to create their own personalized exams. Instructors can also edit any of the existing test questions and even add new questions. Other special features of this program include random generation of test questions, creation of alternate versions of the same test, scrambling of question sequence, and test preview before printing. Available at www.pearsonmytest.com (access code required).

PowerPoint Slides

This text-specific comprehensive package consists of a collection of lecture outlines and graphic images keyed to every chapter in the text. The PowerPoint slides can be downloaded from our Instructor's Resource Center at www.pearsonhighered.com/irc (access code required).

MySearchLab with Pearson eText

MySearchLab is an interactive website that features an eText, access to the EBSCO ContentSelect database, and step-by-step tutorials which offer complete overviews of the entire writing and research process. **MySearchLab** is designed to amplify a traditional course in numerous ways or to administer a course online. Additionally, **MySearchLab** offers **course specific tools** to enrich learning and help students succeed.

eText: Identical in content and design to the printed text, the Pearson eText provides access to the book wherever and whenever it is needed. Students can take notes and highlight, just like a traditional book. The Pearson eText also is available on the iPad for all registered users of MySearchLab.

MediaShare: A cutting-edge video upload tool that allows students to upload presentations of campaigns for instructors and classmates to watch (whether face-to-face or online) and provide online feedback and comments. Customizable rubrics can be attached for further evaluation and grading purposes. Grades can be imported into most learning management systems. Structured much like a social networking site, MediaShare can help promote a sense of community among students.

Online Quizzes: Chapter quizzes test student comprehension, are automatically graded, and grades flow directly to an online gradebook.

Flashcards: Review important terms and concepts from each chapter online. Students can search by chapters or within a glossary and also access drills to help them prepare for quizzes and exams. Flashcards can be printed or exported to your mobile device.

Chapter-specific Content: Each chapter contains Learning Objectives, Chapter Summaries, Quizzes, and Flashcards. These can be used to enhance comprehension, help students review key terms, prepare for tests, and retain what they've learned.

To order the printed version of this book with MySearchLab access at no extra charge use ISBN 0-205-84394-8.

Learn more at www.mysearchlab.com.

Acknowledgments

We would like to thank those who reviewed previous editions and made many suggestions that have been incorporated into this revision: Claire Badaracco, Marquette University; Lora J. DeFore, Mississippi State University; Donn Silvis, California State University, Dominguez Hills; and Brenda J. Wrigley, Michigan State University. And a special thanks to the following educators who provided input for the sixth edition: Jeanne Allison, University of Missouri, St. Louis; Coy Callison, Texas Tech University; Kirk Hallahan, Colorado State University; Johnathan M. Marlow, Howard Payne University; Winston Mitchell, City University of New York, Medgar Evers College; Donnalyn Pompper, Temple University; and Erin E. Wilgenbusch, Iowa State University.

About the Authors

Dennis L. Wilcox

Dr. Wilcox is professor emeritus of public relations at San Jose State University and former director of the School of Journalism & Mass Communications. He is also the lead author of two other popular textbooks, *Public Relations Strategies and Tactics* and *Think: Public Relations*.

He is an accredited (APR) member of the Public Relations Society of America (PRSA) and is also in the organization's College of Fellows, recognizing his lifelong contributions to the profession. Wilcox is a former chair of the PRSA Educator's Academy and the public relations division of the Association for Education in Journalism & Mass Communications (AEJMC). Among his many awards is PRSA's "Educator of the Year," the Xifra-Heras Award from the University of Girona (Spain), an award of excellence from the Public Relations Society of India, and an honorary doctorate from the University of Bucharest for his many contributions to global public relations education and to advancing the profession.

Wilcox is currently active in the International Public Relations Association (IPRA) and is a member of the Arthur W. Page Society, an organization of senior public relations executives. He now travels extensively as a speaker and consultant in Europe, South America, and Asia. His philosophy, to quote St. Augustine, is "The world is a book, and those who do not travel read only a page." He can be reached at denniswilcox@msn.com.

Bryan H. Reber

Dr. Reber is associate professor of public relations at the University of Georgia, Grady College of Journalism and Mass Communication. He teaches introduction to public relations, management, and writing. On the graduate level, Reber teaches management, persuasion, campaign research, and public opinion.

Reber's research focuses on public relations theory, practice, pedagogy, and health communication and has been published in the *Journal of Public Relations Research, Journalism and Mass Communication Quarterly, Journal of Health Communication, Public Relations Review*, and *Journal of Broadcasting and Electronic Media,* among others.

Reber regularly presents his research at national and international academic conferences. He is the coauthor of *Gaining Influence in Public Relations* and THINK *Public Relations*. He worked for 15 years in public relations at Bethel College, Kansas, and has conducted research for the Sierra Club, Ketchum, and the Georgia Hospital Association, among others. He can be reached at reber@uga.edu.

Getting Organized for Writing

>> After reading this chapter, you will be able to:

» Understand the importance of writing in the public relations process

» Know the difference between being a public relations writer and working as a journalist

» Have a good understanding of the equipment and reference tools needed for writing

» Be familiar with the capabilities of search engines and digital databases

» Recognize common errors to avoid in spelling, sentence structure, and the use of sound-alike words

The Framework of Public Relations Writing

The focus of this book is on the most visible aspect of public relations—the writing and distribution of messages in a variety of formats to multiple media channels and platforms. To the uninitiated, this activity is the sum and substance of public relations. For them, PR stands for "press release," which has historically been the most common publicity technique. Because of this, it's necessary to first establish the framework in which public relations writing takes place.

Writing Is Only One Component

It's important to realize, however, that the preparation and distribution of messages is only one part of the public relations process. Public relations work is actually composed of four core components: *research*, *planning*, *communication*, and *evaluation*. Public relations writing is part of the communication component, which only occurs after research has been conducted and extensive planning to formulate the goals and objectives of a campaign has taken place. Planning also involves the selection of audiences to be reached, the key messages to be distributed, and the strategies that should be used to ensure the overall success of the program or campaign.

It's also important to know the difference between strategies and tactics. Strategies are statements of direction. A strategy, for example, might be to use multiple media outlets to reach women between the ages of 18 to 30 to make them aware of a new cosmetic on the market. In a public relations campaign, each strategy is made operational through a list of tactics.

A tactic, for example, might entail the writing and placement of feature articles and "new product" reviews in appropriate women's magazines. Such a tactic might even specify how many product news releases and features would be written and what "angle" would be used in each one. Other tactics might include placing a celebrity spokesperson on a television show that reaches women in the target audience, posting a YouTube video, creating a Facebook page, and setting up a Twitter feed.

Writers as Communication Technicians

Public relations writers and media placement specialists are responsible for implementing all of the above tactics in a campaign or program. They, by definition, fulfill a "technician" or "tactical" role. They are the "production" staff who write the news releases, formulate the feature stories, and contact the television show producer to make a "pitch" for the company's spokesperson to appear as a guest to talk about the product.

> *The use of fact and emotion in a story is critical—particularly in public relations. In a world cluttered with messages competing for audience time and attention, our messages and stories require both elements to be effective.* Kevin Dugan, founder of the Bad Pitch Blog

It is important to note that a public relations writer usually prepares material for possible use in the news columns of newspapers or on broadcast news and magazine programs. Such placement is called "earned media" because, unlike advertising that is purchased, public relations materials are only used if journalists and editors decide the information is newsworthy. Chapter 3 explains in more detail the process of finding and creating news.

The role of writer and technician is the standard entry-level position in public relations, but some in the public relations field have been writers and media relations experts for most of their careers. This is because most positions in public relations at corporations or public relations firms are at the technician or tactical level. A speechwriter or an editor of an employee newsletter, for example, may be a skilled technician by definition, but he or she is also a highly prized professional who receives a good salary because of his or her expertise.

There is a distinction, however, between the duties performed by a technician and those of a public relations manager. Professor David Dozier of San Diego State University, who has done considerable research on roles in public relations, says, "Managers make policy decisions and are held accountable for public relations outcomes," whereas "technicians carry out the low-level mechanics of generating communication products that implement policy decisions made by others."

This is not to say that professional practitioners don't fulfill both manager and technician roles. A professional may primarily be a manager but also be deeply involved in preparing a media kit or arranging a special event. By the same token, a public relations writer in an organization with limited staffing may primarily be a technician but also be involved in the planning of an entire campaign. The Tips for Success below outlines additional skills that a public relations writer should possess.

As you can see, the total framework of public relations is much more than just "press releases." Such materials are important, but they are only one highly visible manifestation of the entire public relations process. With this framework in mind, we begin our discussion about public relations writing and media techniques. At the end of the book, we will return to the managerial aspects of public relations with chapters on campaign planning and program evaluation.

The Public Relations Writer

Although the public relations writer and the journalist share a number of common characteristics in their approach to writing, the public relations writer differs in objectives, audiences, and channels.

Tips for Success   Writing Is One of Six Skills

The ability to write is one of the six essential skills for a successful career in public relations. Dennis L. Wilcox and Glen T. Cameron summarize the essential skills in the 10th edition of their textbook, *Public Relations Strategies & Tactics.*

Writing skill.   The ability to put information and ideas on paper clearly and concisely is essential. Good grammar and spelling are vital. Misspelled words and sloppy sentence structure are unacceptable.

Research ability.   Arguments for causes and products must have factual support instead of platitudes. A person must have the persistence and ability to gather information from a variety of sources, as well as to conduct original research by designing and implementing opinion polls or audits. Researching audience needs and perceptions is important.

Planning expertise.   A public relations program involves multiple communication tools and activities. You need to be a good planner to coordinate everything and keep on budget.

Problem-solving ability.   Innovative ideas and fresh approaches are needed to solve complex problems or to make a public relations program unique and memorable.

Business/economics competence.   A public relations person must understand business and the economics of the "bottom line." He or she must understand that all communications activity must support the business objectives of the organization.

Social media expertise.   Understanding traditional media is still important, but today's practitioners must also have social media savvy. They need to know how to use podcasting, search engine optimization, email outreach, Web content management, and social media such as Twitter and Facebook to advance organizational objectives.

Objectives

A journalist is usually employed by a news organization to gather, process, and synthesize information for the primary purpose of providing news to the organization's subscribers, viewers, or listeners. A hallmark of professional reporting is to present information in a fair and balanced manner.

The public relations writer, in contrast, is usually employed by an organization that wants to communicate with a variety of audiences, either through the news media or through other channels of communication. These organizations may include corporations, government agencies, environmental groups, labor unions, trade associations, or public relations firms that provide information on behalf of clients.

The writer's purpose is advocacy, not objectivity. The goal is not only to accurately inform, but also to persuade and motivate. Edward M. Stanton, former chairman of the Manning, Selvage & Lee public relations firm, once described public relations activity in *Public Relations Quarterly* as "working with clients on strategy and messages, and then delivering these messages to target audiences in order to persuade them to do something that is beneficial to the client."

Professor Robert Heath, coauthor of *Rhetorical and Critical Approaches to Public Relations*, points out that the role of advocate is a time-honored one. It goes back 2,000 years to Aristotle, who conceptualized the term *rhetoric*—the ability to determine what needs to be said and how it should be said to achieve desired outcomes. Heath writes that rhetoric "entails the ability and obligation to demonstrate to an audience facts and arguments available to bring insight into an important issue."

Hence, all public relations writing should begin with the question, "How does this help the organization achieve its objectives?" For example, "Does the news release contain the key messages about the product and how it can benefit customers?" In the case of a newsletter for an organization, there might be several objectives. Akron Children's Hospital, for example, started *Inside Children* as a way of reaching single-family households with children and family incomes of $30,000 or more within its 17-county service area. The objectives of the newsletter, published three times a year, were:

1. To generate business by building awareness for various departments and programs.
2. To recruit participants for various pediatric drug and clinical trials.
3. To generate requests for more information from the hospital's referral telephone line and the website.
4. To distribute various parenting and child health materials to interested parents.

Audiences

The traditional journalist writes for one audience—readers, listeners, or viewers of the medium for which he or she works. Newspapers, magazines, radio, and television are usually defined as "mass media," because the audience is very broad and its members have little in common.

The public relations writer, however, may write for numerous, specialized audiences—employees, community leaders, customers, teenagers, seniors, women, various ethnic and racial groups, travelers, governmental regulatory agencies, investors, farmers, and many others. Effective public relations writing requires careful definition of the audience and its composition so that information can be tailored to its interests and concerns. A public relations writer performs research constantly to determine the audience's needs, concerns, and interests. Armed with this information, the public relations writer can write a more persuasive message. The concepts of public opinion and persuasion are discussed in Chapter 2.

Channels

Journalists, by nature of their employment, primarily reach their audiences through one channel, the medium that publishes, broadcasts, or posts their work on websites. The public relations writer, with many specific audiences to reach, will probably use many channels. Indeed, public relations writers must not only determine the message, but they must also select the most effective channel of communication.

In many cases, the channel might not be any of the traditional mass media. The most effective channel for the tailored message may be direct mail, a pamphlet, an organizational newsletter, a video, a poster, a special event, or even the Internet via online newsletters, chat groups, websites, blogs, podcasts, or even email. In most cases, a combination of channels is selected to achieve maximum message penetration and understanding. This important concept is illustrated throughout this book by showing how organizations have used multiple media channels for a single project or campaign.

Preparation for Writing

It is essential for the public relations writer to have a workspace that includes a computer and a printer, Internet access, and a reference library.

Computers

Public relations professionals spend much of their working day in front of a computer. One survey of independent public relations practitioners, many of whom work from home, found that they spend about 70 to 80 percent of their day on the computer.

A computer enables you to use sophisticated word processing software programs that permit maximum flexibility to write, edit, format, insert artwork, and merge information into a complete document. Word processing packages such as Microsoft Word or MacWrite have built-in dictionaries for checking spelling and grammar plus other features, such as a thesaurus, page preview, search and replace, word count, pagination, and editing functions. These tools substantially reduce the time needed for revisions and rewrites.

The type of computer you use is a matter of personal choice. The first decision is whether you want a desktop or a laptop. Public relations writers who are in the same office on a daily basis often prefer a desktop, because they can generally get more memory and hard disk space for less money than with a comparable laptop. In addition, they like the idea of using large monitors, rather than the smaller ones found on a laptop.

FIGURE 1.1 Today's laptops remain the most versatile tool for public relations writers and practitioners because they are portable and have good memory and storage capacity, decent-sized screens and keyboards, several USB ports, and a built-in webcam and Wi-Fi.

Others, particularly students and professionals who travel frequently, prefer laptops because of their portability and flexibility. In many cases, professionals have it both ways. They have a laptop that serves as the CPU (central processing unit) that can go on the road with them, but they also use the laptop in the office, connecting it to a standard keyboard and a larger monitor. Figure 1.1 shows a product publicity photo of a new laptop model.

The second choice is whether to buy an Apple or a Windows PC. Both have their advocates. The PC crowd likes the idea that about 90 percent of the desktops and laptops sold in the United States are still Windows based, and more software applications are available because of this large market. PCs, in general, are also cheaper than Apple products and easier to repair, because many standardized components are common to all PC brands.

Apple devotees, however, remain undaunted. They cite product reviews that say Apple machines are faster, better, and far less prone to malicious viruses than Microsoft's operating system. In addition, Apple has considerably narrowed the compatibility gap with PCs. Many people also like the slick, modern design of Apple products.

Cost can be a factor. Walt Mossberg, technology editor of *The Wall Street Journal*, wrote in mid-2011 that a good-quality Windows laptop could be purchased for about $500, but the leading brands with a 13-inch screen and good battery life cost about $800. In contrast, a basic Apple Mac starts at $999. A decent netbook costs about $350 to $500, but they have the disadvantage of having less memory and storage space. In addition, many users find that the keyboards and screens are somewhat small for constant use as your primary computer.

"Laptops still win for intensive work like creating long documents, or doing anything that requires precision and benefits from a physical keyboard. They also are more compatible with printers and external disks." Walter Mossberg, technology editor of *The Wall Street Journal*

Netbook sales declined in 2011 with the advent of the iPad and other tablet machines that were quite adequate for such purposes as Web browsing, email, social networking, and accessing and posting photos, video, and music. The iPad2 and tablets were less useful, however, for such tasks as writing long documents and doing presentations because they had no standard USB ports and moving files into and out of them was difficult. In addition, the virtual keyboard is not ideal for extensive writing. New generations of the tablet no doubt will have improved capabilities.

Working professionals, recognizing the rapid pace at which new computer and software products come to market, often recommend that you buy the most powerful computer and collateral equipment you can possibly afford. In 2011, experts were recommending that you buy a computer with a minimum of 4 gigabytes (GB) of memory and a 250-GB or larger hard drive. Mossberg, for example, recommends 320 GB.

Reference Sources

A reference library is a must for any writer. Basic sources should be part of your book library, but they can also be in the format of a software program or an online resource. The key point is to have references that quickly give you instant access to a body of knowledge and enable you to confirm basic factual information.

Encyclopedias — The world's most popular general reference source is Wikipedia (www.wikipedia.org), which is regularly among the top 10 visited sites on the Internet, with more than 350 million visitors every year. The site has 18 million articles, including 3.6 million articles in English. Wikipedia is unique in several ways. First, it is an online encyclopedia that is free. Second, it is written by thousands of volunteers who post and edit entries. Traditionalists still express some concern about the accuracy of information without the benefit of qualified experts certifying the entries, but Wikipedia has gained stature and greater acceptance as a legitimate source in recent years. Another online encyclopedia is www.britannica.com, which requires a subscription fee.

> **❝Wikipedia already has more visitors than the online** New York Times, *CNN, and other* **mainstream sites.❞** The Economist

Dictionary — The most common reference book is an up-to-date dictionary, and many writers keep a paperback version handy for a fast check instead of taking the time to log on to the Internet or bring up a software version. A popular paperback choice is the *Oxford Pocket Dictionary and Thesaurus*, which includes other references such as a handy list of countries and their capital cities.

Public relations writers and journalists also like *Webster's New College Dictionary*, the *American Heritage Dictionary of the English Language*, and the *Concise Oxford English Dictionary*. According to Ragan.com, a public relations newsletter, the first two ". . . not only define but they also provide an array of useful information: geographic and biographic entries, abbreviations, a list of colleges and universities, measurement conversion tables, foreign words and phrases, forms of address, etc."

The most extensive dictionary is the *Oxford English Dictionary* (OED), which contains more than 600,000 word definitions. But the number of words in this 20-volume set probably makes it more dictionary than anyone can absorb. There's also an online edition, but a subscription costs about $300 annually unless you can piggy-back on the subscription held by your city or college library.

Stylebook — A writer's reference library should contain several stylebooks. All writers, on occasion, puzzle over a matter of punctuation, subject–verb agreement, or the use of passive or active voice. Strunk and White's *The Elements of Style* has saved numerous writers from embarrassment over the years, but other grammar and style texts are also available. For example, Diana Hacker has written a number of books on writing style and grammar, which are readily available through Amazon.com.

In terms of journalistic writing, the most widely used stylebook is the *Associated Press Stylebook and Briefing on Media Law*, available in print form or online. It is used by most weekly and daily newspapers in the United States, and it is updated and revised on a periodic basis. In addition, there's even an AP Stylebook Twitter feed (#APStyle) for instant updates. The following are some recent AP style updates regarding the Internet:

Apps: Names of apps (applications) are capitalized.

BlackBerry: Capitalize the second B because it is a trademarked name.

blog: Lowercase.

cell phone: Two words without a hyphen, but many publications use one word.

disc: Use this spelling if you are using a term such as *videodisc*. However, a *hard disk* is located in your computer.

e-book or **e-commerce**: Lowercase and use a hyphen.

email: Lowercase and one word.

FAQ: Acronym for "frequently asked questions," a format often used to summarize information on the Internet.

high-tech: Never *hi-tech*.

home page: Two words and not capitalized.

Internet: First letter capitalized. *Net* can be used in later references.

intranet: A private network inside a company or an organization. Unlike *Internet*, it is lowercase.

IT: Acronym for *information technology*; spell it out in a story.

OK: Can use as OK'd. Do not use *okay*.

online: Lowercase and one word.

podcast: Lowercase.

Web: Always capitalized.

website: Lowercase and one word. Names of websites are capitalized.

PowerPoint: One word with a capital P in the middle.

Twitter: Always capitalize as a trademarked name, but lowercase *tweet*.

wiki: Lowercase, but *Wikipedia* is a proper noun.

World Wide Web: The shorter term, "the Web," is acceptable.

The New York Times Stylebook is also widely used. Writers who cover business or prepare news releases about business topics often use *The Wall Street Journal Stylebook*.

These manuals enable you, as a public relations writer, to prepare materials in the writing style used by most newspapers. They cover such topics as capitalization, abbreviations, punctuation, titles, and general word usage. For example, there is a trend to combine words that were once written separately or hyphenated; hence, the proper style is now *software*, *database*, *lifestyle*, *teenager*, *spreadsheet*, *website*, and *non-profit*. Organizations also develop their own stylebooks for employee publications.

You most likely will need to be familiar with several kinds of stylebooks depending on your writing assignment.

Media Directories — A major activity of a public relations writer is contacting journalists and sending news releases to the media. It is therefore important to have lists of publications, names of editors, and addresses readily available. Local directories of media outlets are often available from the chamber of commerce, the United Way, or other civic groups. Metropolitan, state, or regional directories also exist.

Probably the most comprehensive online media database is CisionPoint PR software platform (www.us.cision.com). It claims to offer almost 1 million media contacts, outlets, and editorial (news) opportunities. Cision also publishes *Bacon's Media Directories*, available online and in print form. *Bacon's Newspaper/Magazine Directory* provides information on (1) all U.S. and Canadian daily newspapers, (2) about 22,000 trade and consumer magazines, (3) news services and syndicates, (4) ethnic newspapers and magazines, and even (5) college and university newspapers. The *Bacon's Radio, TV, and Cable Directory* lists about 40,000 broadcast outlets and provides profiles on news, talk, public affairs, and topical shows.

Both Cision and its Bacon's online media database allow a public relations writer to build targeted media lists by beat, market, demographics, media type, country, and audience. In addition, the company offers a database of over 5,000 magazine and newspaper *editorial calendars*. According to Cision, a public relations writer can use this database to find out when publications are planning special issues around a holiday, a specific industry, annual product roundups, or major trade shows. Another service is profiles of influential contacts in specific industries, including their interests and how to approach them with a story idea.

Another popular media directory is BurrellesLuce (www.burrellesluce.com), which also has a comprehensive online media database that includes many of the same services as Cision and Bacon's. Its media database includes over 76,000 media outlets in North America and 380,000 staff listings with their contact preferences.

There is also Media Pro, published by *Bulldog Reporter* (www.infocomgroup. net/mediaPro), which claims to have the names and profiles of 90,000 "influential" journalists at 12,000 "top" newspapers, broadcast stations, websites, and blogs. For freelance writers on a budget, Gebbie's *All-in-One Media Contacts Directory* (www.gebbieinc.com) has 24,000 listings available in print or as text files that can be imported to your computer. There is also the DowJones Media Manager (www .dowjones.com), which gives basic contact information and profiles on journalists and bloggers. Figure 1.2 shows a sample online listing.

The major advantages of online media databases is that they provide the ability to build a media distribution list, print labels, and even send news releases by email. Many also offer media monitoring, enabling practitioners to match actual news coverage against a distribution list so they can evaluate their efforts. Other firms, such as Vocus (www.vocus.com), offer similar services as well as the ability to track media clips generated by news releases. Media directories are discussed at greater length in Chapter 10.

Professional Publications — Standard references should be supplemented with subscriptions to professional periodicals. It is important for the professional writer

Search Alerts Analyze **Engage**
Dashboard | **Contacts** | Outlets | Opportunities | Briefing Book | Activities

Walter S. Mossberg   Options

"Personal Technology" Columnist
The Wall Street Journal - Washington Bureau
Regional bureau
1025 Connecticut Avenue, N.W. Suite 800
Washington DC 20036-5477 United States

Phone: +1 202 862-9287
Fax: +1 202 862-6657
Email: mossberg@wsj.com
Web Site: http://www.wsj.com
Contact By: E-mail

📧 Send Message

Technology Reporter
The Wall Street Journal Radio Network
Network
1025 Connecticut Avenue, N.W. Washington DC
20036 United States

Phone: +1 202 862-9287
Fax: +1 202 862-6657
Email: mossberg@wsj.com
Web Site: http://www.wsjradio.com
Contact By: E-mail

📧 Send Message

Co-Executive Editor
All Things Digital - The Wall Street Journal
Print/online
200 Liberty Street World Financial Center Room 200
New York NY 10281 United States

Phone: +1 202-862-9287
Email: mossberg_mailbox@allthingsd.com
Web Site: http://allthingsd.com
Contact By: E-mail

📧 Send Message

Personal Technology Reporter
Fox Business Network
Network
1211 Avenue of the Americas New York NY 10036-

Publications   **Web News**

Sort by: Relevance | Date ▼   Next »

1. Más opciones para quien busca una computadora
    The Wall Street Journal Americas, 11/6/2009, 934 words, (Spanish)
    Los nuevos sistemas operativos de Microsoft y Apple amplian la oferta; una guía básica
    para no perderse Ahora que tanto Microsoft como Apple han lanzado nuevas versiones de
    sus sistemas operativos, Windows 7 y Snow Leopard, respectivamente, ...
    Document: WSJAES0020091106e5b600002

2. Motorola's Droid Is Smart Success For Verizon Users
    The Wall Street Journal, 11/5/2009, 942 words, (English)
    Verizon Wireless customers tend to love the company's fast 3G network. But many tech-
    oriented Verizon loyalists gripe about the carrier's high-end smart phones, which haven't
    matched the cachet and versatility of the Apple iPhone sold by ...
    Document: J000000020091105e5b50001j

3. Mossberg's Mailbox
    The Wall Street Journal, 11/5/2009, 563 words, (English)
    [Technology columnist Walter S. Mossberg answers readers' questions] Q: I have just
    bought a new computer with Windows 7, and not only can't I download Outlook Express, I
    can't even find it. Is it there? Where?
    Document: J000000020091105e5b50001a

4. Motorola's Droid is smart success for Verizon users
    The Wall Street Journal Europe, 11/5/2009, 936 words, (English)
    Verizon Wireless customers tend to love the company's fast 3G network. But many tech-
    oriented Verizon loyalists gripe about the carrier's high-end smart phones, which haven't
    matched the cachet and versatility of the Apple iPhone sold by ...
    Document: WSJE000020091105e5b5000w

5. Mossberg's Mailbox; Technology columnist Walter S. Mossberg answers
    readers' questions
    The Wall Street Journal (Online and Print), 11/5/2009, 567 words, (English)
    Q: I have just bought a new computer with Windows 7, and not only can't I download
    Outlook Express, I can't even find it. Is it there? Where?
    Document: WSJO000020091104e5b500byl

6. Más opciones para quien busca una computadora
    The Wall Street Journal Americas, 11/4/2009, 934 words, (Spanish)

Discovery Pane

∧ **Companies**   Export

Apple Inc   32
Microsoft Corpor... 22
Motorola Inc   8
Google Inc.   5
AT&T Inc   4
Cake Financial C... 3
Florida Associat... 3
Verizon Wireless   3
HTC Corporation   2
Research In Moti... 2

∧ **Industries**   Export

Software   7
Computers/Electr...   5
Computer Hardware   5
Motor Vehicle Pa...   4
Applications Sof...   3
Investment Advice   2
Unit Trusts/Mutu...   1
Financial Invest...   1
Mobile Communica...   1
Automobile Navig...   1

∧ **Keywords**   Export

snow leopard
operating system
answers readers
web site
mossberg answers
columnist walter
windows xp
technology columnist
windows pcs

FIGURE 1.2 Online media databases provide extensive information on how to reach publications, broadcast outlets, Internet sites, and even detailed information about journalists. This example, from the DowJones Media Relations Manager database, gives background information on Walter Mossberg, the influential technology columnist for *The Wall Street Journal*.

to keep up with developments in the field and to learn about new techniques that can improve the writing, production, and distribution of public relations material.

A number of Web-based news sites and publications cover the public relations field. The leading news sites that post information on a daily basis are *PR Daily News Feeds* (www.prdaily.com), *Ragan's Daily Headlines* (www.ragan.com), *PRWeek* (www.prweekus.com), PRSA's *Issues and Trends* (www.prsa.org), and *O'Dwyer's Daily News Briefing* (www.odwyerpr.com). *Ragan's Daily Headlines* and PRSA's site, for the most part, aggregate news stories and provide links to the original source.

Newsletters include *PR Reporter*, *PR News*, *Jack O'Dwyer's Newsletter*, *Bulldog Reporter*, and *Communication Briefings*. The latter is an excellent source of information about writing techniques. *PRWeek* posts its weekly edition online (www.prweekus.com) but also publishes a monthly magazine for subscribers. The Public Relations Society of America (PRSA) also produces a monthly tabloid newspaper, *Public Relations Tactics*, filled with many "how to" articles. Several of these publications are shown in Figures 1.3 through 1.6.

Magazines about the public relations field include the *Ragan Report*, which focuses on writing techniques and media relations. There are also *Public Relations Strategist*, published by PRSA, and *Communication World*, published by the International Association of Business Communicators (IABC). You can subscribe to these publications or receive them as part of your annual membership fees. Another magazine is *O'Dwyer's Communications & New Media*. The two major scholarly publications in the field are *Public Relations Review* and the *Journal of Public Relations Research*, which are published quarterly. The websites of a number of publications are listed in the Tips for Success on page 15.

In addition to articles about trends and issues in the field, these magazines also carry advertisements for companies that specialize in services such as news release distribution, media monitoring, photography, podcasts, and video news releases.

FIGURE 1.3 *PRWeek.* This publication comes out monthly in print form, but also has an online daily update and a more expanded weekly posting. It covers the activities of public relations firms, campaigns, trends, and issues in the industry.

FIGURE 1.4 *Public Relations Tactics.* This monthly tabloid is published by the Public Relations Society of America (PRSA). Its focus is on professional development, practical tips for conducting public relations, and trends in the field.

Blogs. — Many of the online news sites and publications mentioned above require paid subscriptions or membership in an organization, but a great deal of current information about public relations practice is also available for free through blogs. Technorati (www.technorati.com), for example, lists almost 3,000 blogs devoted to public relations and related topics.

Some of the best-known blogs that generate the most readership are as follows:

» A Shell of My Former Self by Shel Holtz (blog .holtz.com)

» 6AM by Richard Edelman (Edelman.com/ speak_up/blog)

FIGURE 1.5 *O'Dwyer's.* This online weekly newsletter is supplemented by an online daily briefing and a monthly magazine in print form. It has links to a large number of other sites and has an archive of public relations resources available to subscribers.

FIGURE 1.6 *Ragan Report.* This monthly is supplemented by a daily online posting of four or five major stories, primarily about effective writing and media relations skills. *Ragan.com* also operates a popular website, *PR Daily News Feeds,* that aggregates stories about public relations from a variety of publications and blogs.

» The Daily Lark by Andy Lark (thedailylark.com)

» The Flack by Peter Himler (theflack.blogspot.com)

» Communications Conversations by Arik Hanson (arikhanson .com)

» Defining the Convergence of Media and Influence by Brian Solis (briansolis.com)

» Spin Sucks by Gini Dietrich (spinsucks.com)

» Mashable (mashable.com)

» DannyBrown.me by Danny Brown (dannybrown.me)

As with everything else on the Web, blogs come and go, so it's a good idea to check with some professionals in the field about current listservs or blogs focusing on public relations and marketing communications. They can also offer insight into what forums offer the most information and value.

Discussion Groups — A cheap and efficient form of professional development is available through joining a discussion group. A number of Usenet groups (a global system of discussion areas called *newsgroups*) and listservs are devoted to public relations. You can review the possibilities simply by doing a topic search on Google, Yahoo!, or MSN. Such groups may be sponsored by public relations firms, individuals, or public relations groups, such as PRSA and IABC, for their members. Another listserv group open to anyone is prbytes@yahoogroups.com.

A number of Twitter chats also enable public relations writers to connect and communicate with other professionals in the field. One primarily for students is *#PRStudChat;* it brings students, educators, and professionals together on a monthly basis. Other recommended Twitter groups include *#Commschat, #PR20Chat, #SoloPR, #Journchat, #MeasurePR, #IMCChat, #u30pro,* and even a monthly Hispanic PR chat at *#HPRChat.*

LinkedIn also has several public relations groups. Some of the groups with the most followers in mid-2011 were *MarketingProfs* (9,800 members) and *PR News Group* (5,400 members). In addition, there was *HAPPO* (1,000 members), a discussion primarily about job hunting and salaries. Facebook pages for various publications and blogs also offer the opportunity for discussion. Some pages in mid-2011 that were popular among public relations writers included *Ragan. com, PRWeek, PR News, PR on Facebook, Danny Brown, Edelman Worldwide,* and *PR Job Watch.*

Current Events and Trends — Writing often starts with a creative idea and a good understanding of the world around you. Many public relations employers screen job applicants by administering a current events quiz to ascertain the scope of their interests and intellectual curiosity. Employers require outstanding writing skills, but they are also looking for a second dimension in a public relations writer: knowing what to write about. A person who reads newspapers and magazines on a regular basis often gets story ideas for his or her client or employer, which will be discussed in Chapter 3.

Thus, aspiring public relations writers should make it a habit to read the local daily and at least one daily with national circulation. Online dailies include *The Daily* on iPad, *Huffington Post*, the *Daily Beast*, or *Politico*. Print and online editions of the *New York Times*, *The Wall Street Journal*, or even the *Financial Times* are good for in-depth news analysis and commentary. Weekly newsmagazines such as *Time*, *Newsweek*, and the *Economist* also provide in-depth coverage of current issues. Nationally syndicated public affairs programs on radio and television are also good sources of current event knowledge and interpretative analysis. National Public Radio (NPR), for example, has extensive news and commentary throughout the day.

Many people get all their news and entertainment from television. You should know what is being presented to the public for several reasons. First, media coverage sets the agenda for people's thinking. Second, watching the national and local news will show you what kinds of stories are used and how they are handled. Other programs, especially talk shows, will teach you what sorts of stories get on the air and indicate the kind of audience that tends to watch such programs.

> **❝**I like to get my information from various sources across the ideological spectrum. I'll read through the New York Times, the Economist, and the Huffington Post, but also Politico, Drudge Report, The Wall Street Journal, the Financial Times, the Sun, and Fortune. **❞** Paul Taaffe, chairman and CEO of Hill & Knowlton, in an interview with *PRWeek*

In sum, paying attention to current events and the thoughts of opinion leaders pays several dividends. First, it makes you a well-informed person, and hence more attractive to employers for public relations writing jobs. Second, knowing the public's concerns helps you construct more salient messages for your target audience. Third, current events and subjects of popular books often provide a "news hook" for obtaining media acceptance of your material.

A company making security locks for computer files, for example, was virtually ignored by the media until news stories about hackers breaking into national security systems made national headlines. And publicists for food products have long recognized that information about the health benefits of a product will attract more media attention. Using current public and media interests as a "news hook" for generating publicity is discussed further in Chapter 3.

Research: The Prelude to Writing

An essential first step to any public relations writing task is the gathering of relevant information. The process is called *research*, and it can take many forms.

In some cases, all the facts will be readily available from a client or employer. All you need to do is pick up some background materials, ask a few questions, and start writing. More often than not, however, the information you need to understand the subject thoroughly and write a well-crafted piece requires some digging.

Let's assume you are given the assignment of writing a news release about a new product. One of your first contacts, no doubt, will be the vice president of marketing, who will give you the general details about the price and availability of the product. In order to understand better the benefits or capabilities of the product, however, you may need to interview someone in the company's research and development (R&D) department who was responsible for developing the product.

You may stop there in your inquiries, or you may decide to do some research on the potential market for the product and how you might position the product against the competition. One way to do this is to research competing products on the market to determine why your product is different or better. You may also want to contact some experts in the field by email or telephone to get their assessment. Their comments, if they give permission, could be included in your news release as a form of endorsement for the new product. On another level, you might talk with some consumers to find out what would convince them to try the product. Is it price, convenience, brand reputation, or reliability?

Public relations writers are constantly looking up information, whether for a news release or for background on what kinds of issues and trends might affect a current employer or prospective client. Fortunately, a virtual universe of information is available to you at the click of a mouse. Thanks to the information revolution, two valuable resources are available: Internet search engines and electronic databases.

Search Engines

Search engines make it possible for you to simply type in a keyword or two and click "Go." Within a few seconds, the computer screen shows all the links that the search engine has found relating to the topic. The hard part is checking out the promising links, because the search engine may have found several hundred possibilities.

Google is the most widely used online search engine. It processes about 10 billion queries a month, which is about two-thirds of the searches made on the Internet. Microsoft's Bing and Yahoo! each handle about 15 percent of Internet searches. It's worth noting that the fourth most used search engine in the world is Baidu, which is based in Beijing. Its use will continue to rise as China becomes even more Internet connected. A listing of useful websites for public relations writers is shown in the Tips for Success on page 15.

In general, it is a good idea to use several search engines, because all of them have different strengths and weaknesses. Peter Meyers, writing in *The Wall Street Journal*, assessed the most popular search engines. He thought Google was best for news, images, and general Web searches. He noted, "Google has the broadest range of solid tools and did the best job of distinguishing between ad-supported results and real ones."

Yahoo!, according to Meyers, excels in its Yellow Pages listings, particularly if you live in a major metropolitan market. MSN's Bing gets high ratings for its stem-searching

Tips for Success   Useful Websites for Public Relations Writers

Public relations requires research and facts. Here's a sampling of sites on the Internet where you can find information.

General Information

www.highbeam.com: Provides full-text articles from multiple sources, including newspapers, newswires, magazines, etc.

www.pollingreport.com: Compilation of findings from surveys regarding trends in public opinion.

thomas.loc.gov: Site of the Library of Congress and the starting point for legislative and congressional information.

www.infoplease.com: Online almanacs on various topics from business to history and sports.

www.biography.com: Backgrounds on current and historical figures.

www.acronymfinder.com: Definitions of acronyms, abbreviations, and initials.

www.howstuffworks.com: Descriptions, diagrams, and photos that show how devices work.

www.statistics.com: Statistics from government agencies and other sources on a range of subjects.

www.ipl.org: The Internet Public Library; a University of Michigan site that gives links to all kinds of sources, from dictionaries to writing guides to newspapers.

resourceshelf.freepint.com: A favorite among reference librarians.

www.salary.com: Salaries in all fields, including public relations.

www.norc.org/GSS+website: General Social Survey, which examines social trends in the United States.

Public Relations

www.about.com: Provides multiple guide sites. Site offers articles, directories, forums, etc.

www.pr-education.org: An aggregation of PR-related sites, resources and services.

www.businesswire.com, www.prnewswire.com, www.prweb.com: News releases by company and industry.

tweepml.org/Starter-Pack-for-PR-Students/: Useful Twitter feeds for PR students to follow.

www.prmuseum.com: The (online) Museum of Public Relations houses information on early pioneers in the field.

www.workinginpr.com: Public relations jobs and salaries by classification and geographical area.

Organizations

www.awpagesociety.com: Arthur W. Page Society

www.pagecenter.comm.psu.edu: Arthur W. Page Center at Pennsylvania State University

www.egpr.uncc.edu Center for Global Public Relations, University of North Carolina at Charlotte

www.prfirms.org: Council of Public Relations Firms

www.globalalliancepr.org: Global Alliance for Public Relations and Communication Management

www.instituteforpr.com: Institute for Public Relations (IPR)

www.iabc.com: International Association of Business Communicators (IABC)

www.ifea.com: International Festivals and Events Association (IFEA)

www.ipra.org: International Public Relations Association (IPRA)

www.niri.org: National Investor Relations Institute (NIRI)

www.plankcenter.ua.edu: Plank Center for Leadership in Public Relations at the University of Alabama

www.pac.org: Public Affairs Council

www.prsa.org: Public Relations Society of America (PRSA)

www.prssa.org: Public Relations Student Society of America (PRSSA)

www.annenberg.usc.edu/sprc: Strategic Public Relations Center at the University of Southern California Annenberg School for Communication

> *" Cheap, fast global communication, online commerce, the ability to find answers to almost any question on the Web using a search engine and the many wonders of the Internet are all underpinned by the widespread availability of inexpensive, powerful PCs. "*
>
> *The Economist*

tool and its automatic searches for all variations of a word. Yahoo! gets more good reviews for news searches that also look for audio and visual video clips.

The most important part of your search for information is choosing the right keywords. You should be as specific as possible to make sure you don't get a display listing hundreds of pages. Nouns make the best keywords.

The *Associated Press Stylebook* gives some additional tips for a search:

» Use uncommon words that identify your topic. Unusual proper or technical names are good. Avoid words with dual meanings.

» Use several keywords at a time, or even phrases. You can use two or three different phrases.

» Use synonyms. You might find different information with "attorney" instead of "lawyer."

» Use connecting words such as AND, OR, or NOT. Syntax varies with search engines, so check the help page if you are not sure how to structure these queries. Some search engines, for example, want you to put quotes around a phrase to limit a search. For example, a search for "site: apple.com iPod" will only provide links that appear on official Apple Web pages.

The editors of the *Associated Press Stylebook* make a final, cautionary point. They say, "Do not mistake the Web for an encyclopedia, and the search engine for a table of contents. The Web is a sprawling databank that's about one quarter wheat and three-quarters chaff. Any information you find should be assessed with the same care that you use for everything else."

Electronic Databases

The second valuable source of information, which is often more comprehensive than various websites, are electronic databases that provide in-depth information and full texts of published articles. Many of these databases, such as Lexis/Nexis and Factiva, are available online, and many organizations subscribe to their services. Another approach is to simply use your local city or campus library; many libraries provide free access to multiple reference databases.

One popular database is *Academic Search Premier*, which provides the full text for almost 5,000 publications, including more than 3,600 academic journals. It is said to be the world's largest multidisciplinary database. The majority of full-text articles are available as searchable PDFs. A similar database is ABI/Inform Complete. A favorite of public relations writers is *ProQuest Newsstand*, which is the full text of U.S. and international news sources in newspaper and periodical formats. An online database for mobile and iPad users is Zinio.com, which allows you to access a large number of magazines while you're sipping your latte at Starbucks.

Advertising agencies, public relations firms, and marketing departments regularly consult another electronic database, *Simmons Study of Media and Markets*. It reports research data on lifestyles, media behavior, and brand preferences of the American consumer by gender, age, and household income.

In sum, if you need in-depth information about any topic—from the biography of a business executive to market conditions in Zambia—an electronic database is a good source. See the Tips for Success on page 18 for a listing of popular databases.

Writing Guidelines

The ability to write well is essential for work in public relations. Countless client surveys and interviews with public relations employers confirm that good writing is at the top of their list of expectations. J. Ronald Kelly, senior vice president of Cohn & Wolfe public relations, makes the point:

> The majority of our entry-level work requires good, basic writing skills. I simply do not have the time to teach grammar, spelling, punctuation, subject–verb agreement, and use of active verbs, lead writing, inverted pyramid style, etc. And as you know, time is money in an agency setting. Therefore, I seek graduates who can contribute to the bottom line from the first day. I need people who have good mastery of basic writing skills.

Outlining the Purpose

Before beginning any writing assignment, take the time to ask yourself some key questions. Public relations counselors Kerry Tucker and Doris Derelian suggest six basic questions:

1. What is the desired communication outcome? In other words, what do we want our audience to do or not do?
2. Who is our target audience? Defining your audience in terms of age, gender, and educational level helps set the framework of the message.
3. What are our target audience's needs, concerns, and interests?
4. What is our message? Do you want to inform or persuade?
5. What communication channel is most effective?
6. Who is our most believable spokesperson?

Answering these questions goes a long way toward helping you determine the content and structure of your message. Regarding questions 2 and 3, Julie Story Goldsborough, president of a Kansas public relations firm, says, "I try to delve into the minds of the readers. What is the main benefit to them? What do they want to know about the subject?"

Tips for Success Need Detailed Information? Use a Database

Although "Googling it" is a highly popular way of finding information, it's not always the best way to find in-depth information. Both students and professionals should take advantage of the many electronic databases that are available at the city or university library. The following are a few databases that libraries commonly subscribe to that you may find useful:

ABI/Inform Complete. Full-text articles from standard magazines and scholarly journals in business and economics.

Academic Search Premier. Full text of about 5,000 publications, including more than 3,600 academic journals. It's the world's largest multidisciplinary database.

Alt-PressWatch. Full text of newspapers and other periodicals representing the alternative and independent press.

AP Images. Photos, images, and audio files from the Associated Press.

Associations Unlimited. Basic information on more than 455,000 associations and nonprofit groups at the international, national, state, and local levels.

Business Source Complete. Full-text content for scholarly business journals, including profiles for the most-cited authors in the database. Full-text content includes major reference works, case studies, market research reports, country reports, and company profile.

Communication & Mass Media Complete (CMMC). Provides full text and abstracts for almost 400 journals. It includes 3,000 author profiles.

CQ Researcher. Gives background information on current and controversial issues. Includes pro and con arguments, bibliography, contacts, and future outlook.

Economic Census. Profiles the U.S. economy from the national to local level. Includes reports for individual states, zip codes, and by broad market sectors.

Ethnic Newswatch. Full text of newspapers, magazines, and journals of the ethnic, minority, and native American press. English and Spanish publications are indexed.

Factiva. General news about companies and business topics from newspapers, magazines, and trade journals from almost 120 nations.

Global Market Information Database (GMID). Provides data on industries, countries, and consumers on a worldwide basis. Includes full-text market reports, comments from expert industry and country analysts, and sources for more information.

Lexis/Nexis Academic. Complete text of newspapers, magazines, newswires, TV transcripts, and trade publications.

ProQuest Newsstand. Full text of stories in U.S. and international publications, including the *New York Times* and the *Times of London*.

Simmons Study of Media and Markets. Information and research on lifestyles, media behavior, and product preferences of U.S. consumers by gender, age, and household income.

The next step is to outline question 4 more fully—what is the message? Usually, an outline includes major topics, and minor topics within each major topic. One approach to outlining is to list the major message points as major topics. For example, you might have one to three key points that you want to communicate in a news release or a feature story. Under each of these headings, jot down a list of the facts, statistics, and examples you will give to support the major point.

Once the objectives and content of the message are determined, the next challenge is to compose a succinct, well-organized document that uses all of the rules of grammar, punctuation, and spelling correctly. Entire books are available that are devoted to composition, and you should refer to the list of additional resources at the end of the chapter. However, here are a few general guidelines you should keep in mind as you prepare to write public relations materials. (See the Tips for Success box on page 20 for further tips on how to improve your writing.)

Sentences

Sentences should be clear and concise. Long, compound sentences slow the reader down and often are difficult to understand. In general, a sentence containing 25 to 30 words is difficult even for a college-educated audience. This does not mean that all sentences should be 8 to 10 words long; you should strive for a variety of lengths, with the average sentence being about 15 to 17 words.

In many cases, a complex sentence simply contains more words than necessary. Take this bloated sentence, for example: "They have assisted numerous companies in the development of a system that can be used in the monitoring of their customer service operations." Revised, this sentence is more concise and easier to understand: "They have helped many companies develop systems for monitoring their customer services operations."

Communication Briefings has compiled a list of word savers that can help keep sentences concise and on course. You should shorten the common wordy phrases on the left to the single words on the right when writing or editing copy:

a great number of	many
at this point in time	now
come to a realization	realize
despite the fact that	although
due to the fact that	because
for the purpose of	for, to
give approval of	approve
of the opinion that	believe
owing to the fact that	because
since the time when	since
take under consideration	consider
until such time as	until
with the exception of	except for
would appear that	seems
as to whether	whether

Paragraphs

Short paragraphs are better than long ones. A review of a daily newspaper shows that the journalistic style is short paragraphs averaging about six to eight typeset lines. Lead paragraphs in news stories are even shorter—about two or three lines.

Tips for Success   How to Improve Your Writing

Writing is hard work. It takes a good understanding of basic English composition, plenty of practice, and a lot of rewriting and editing to produce interesting and readable copy. The following are some good tips adapted from an article by Katie Badeusz that appeared in Ragan.com.

Be Clear

Don't use technical terms and convoluted sentence structures. If it's not written clearly, nothing else will matter because people won't understand it.

Use Action Verbs

Verbs are the basis of good writing. Instead of using weak verbs such as *utilize* or *optimize*, use visual verbs such as *plunge*, *hover*, *reveal*, and *rebound*.

Apply Active Voice

Avoid writing in passive voice. Sentences in active voice are more concise and direct because fewer words are needed to express action. Noun–verb construction is best. Say "He made a mistake," not "Mistakes were made."

Avoid Jargon

Don't exclude readers by using words that are not familiar to them. If you must use jargon, limit the number of terms you use, and don't forget to define them.

Focus on People

Writing about processes, programs, and policies is boring because they often lack the human element. For better understanding and readership, explain programs by focusing on the people affected.

Don't Neglect the First Paragraph

An enticing first sentence or paragraph attracts readers. The writing should be short, punchy, and to the point. A good question to ask yourself when writing a lead is "What is this story about?" Answer that question in a creative, inviting way.

Include Quotes

Too many quotes, particularly from executives and officials, are too long-winded and full of jargon. Avoid losing readers by incorporating quotes that sound authentic and reflect what a person might say in a normal conversation.

Write with Your Ear

You can improve your writing by reading it out loud to hear what actually works in terms of rhythm and pacing. If you find yourself gasping for air as you read through a long, convoluted sentence, break it into several sentences or use more punctuation.

Allow Yourself to Write Crap

Don't write perfect sentences in your head. Let your thoughts go and then fix them. Good writing involves rewriting. Take a break and come back to your manuscript to reorganize your thoughts, move things around, and do it again.

Take Chances

Writing is a creative process. Think outside the box and ask yourself questions such as "Why should I care about this?" "So what?" and "Why should my readers care about this?" also are good questions. And don't forget to have fun. If you enjoy writing the story, it's likely that your audience will enjoy reading it.

Public relations writing should follow the same guidelines. Short paragraphs give the reader a chance to catch a breath, so to speak, and continue reading. Long paragraphs not only tax the reader's concentration but also encourage the reader to "tune out."

Remember that the paragraph on your computer screen is even longer when set in a newspaper column only 2 inches wide. Your 8 lines become 12 lines in a newspaper or magazine. A typical paragraph contains only one basic idea. When another idea is introduced, it is time for a new paragraph.

Short, punchy paragraphs are particularly important for online news releases and newsletters. According to a study by Sun Microsystems, it takes 50 percent more time for an individual to read material on a computer screen. Consequently, according to Michael Butzgy, owner of a New York communications firm, people need key information in short, digestible chunks. How to structure a news release is discussed in Chapter 5.

Word Choice

College-educated writers often forget that words common to their vocabulary are not readily understood by large segments of the general public. General-circulation newspapers, aware that a large percentage of their readers have not been to college, strive to write news stories at the fourth- to sixth-grade level.

If your target audience is the general public, remember that a short word—one with fewer syllables—is more easily understood than a longer one. *Communication Briefings* gives the following list of "stately," multisyllable words and some shorter, more reader-friendly options:

"Stately" Word	Reader-Friendly Word
frequently	often
majority	most
regulation	rule
subsequent	future
reiterate	repeat
approximately	about
additional	more
fundamental	basic
individual	person
requirement	need
accomplish	achieve
characteristic	trait
initial	first
additional	more
residence	home

More complex words, of course, can be used if the target audience is well educated. Most readers of *The Wall Street Journal*, for example, are college graduates, so the writing is more complex than that found in a small-town daily.

Also, if the target audience is professionals in a field such as law, education, science, or engineering, the standard for word choice is different. Educators, for example, seem to like elaborate expressions such as "multiethnic individualized learning" or "continuum."

Scientific writing, too, is loaded with esoteric words. Newspaper editors often complain that they receive news releases from high-technology companies that are so full of jargon that neither they nor their readers can understand them. Of course, if your audience is engineers, you can use specialized words and phrases. Good writing, however, requires that you simplify the message as much as possible.

Active Verbs and Present Tense

Verbs vitalize your writing. Don't sacrifice verbs by burying the action in nouns or adjectives. You will boost clarity and add vigor to your writing by stripping away excess words around a verb. A sentence using active voice is also more direct and usually shorter than a passive sentence. Here are some examples:

> *Original statement:* Our consultants can assist you in answering questions about floor treatments.
>
> *Revised statement:* Our consultants can answer your floor treatment questions.
>
> *Original statement:* There is a considerable range of expertise demonstrated by the spam senders.
>
> *Revised statement:* The spam senders demonstrate a considerable range of expertise.
>
> *Original statement:* It was determined by the committee that the report was incomplete.
>
> *Revised statement:* The committee decided that the report was incomplete.

Use of present tense also improves writing. It is better to write "The copier *delivers* 100 copies per minute" than to write "The copier *will deliver* 100 copies per minute." In most public relations writing, particularly news releases, use present and active tense as much as possible. In quotations, for example, it is better to write " 'The copier is being shipped next month,' *says* Rowena Jones, sales manager." Doesn't this sound better than " 'The copier *will be* shipped next month,' *said* Rowena Jones, sales manager"?

Imagery

Strong visual descriptions are better than generalized statements. Writing that Coca-Cola is sold in many nations or marketed internationally does not have much impact on the reader. A stronger image is created if you write that Coca-Cola is now sold on all continents and is readily available to two-thirds of the earth's population. Or, as Coca-Cola stated in a recent annual report to stockholders: "If all the system's customers lined up along the equator, a thirsty consumer could purchase a Coca-Cola every 16 feet."

Visual descriptions can even be used to portray the wealth of Bill Gates, one of the world's richest people. One writer came up with the following imagery: "If Mr. Gates' fortune were converted to dollar bills, it would take 296 747s to fly the pile from Microsoft's Redmond, Wash., headquarters to New York. And once there, the loot would cover every square inch of Manhattan, not just once, but six times." One also gets a better image of the international space station when a writer says it's the length of a football field.

Errors to Avoid

Errors in your writing will brand you as careless, unprofessional, and inconsiderate of your audience. Errors also call into question the credibility of the entire message. Professional writing requires attention to detail and repeated review of your draft to catch all potential errors.

Spelling

Credibility is sacrificed when spelling errors appear in public relations materials. For example, one news release for a company that offered a spell-checking program included the nonwords "tradmark" and "publishere." Naturally, the company was embarrassed about the typos—especially after *The Wall Street Journal* poked fun of the company on page 1. We can only guess at how much these typos cost the company in sales and consumer confidence.

Time magazine does know the actual cost of a spelling error. Some years ago, *Time* ran a cover headline reading "New Plan for Arms Contol." More than 200,000 covers were printed without the "r" in the word "control" before the error was discovered. The presses were stopped and the error was corrected; putting the "r" back in "control" cost the magazine $100,000. Of course, there are always chuckles when someone writes about "pubic relations" instead of "public relations."

> ❝*Employing improper grammar, no matter how good the content, is detrimental to your credibility. Why should I trust a word you write if you don't know how to write it?*❞
>
> Jon Gingerich, editor of *O'Dwyer's Newsletter*

Gobbledygook and Jargon

Every occupation and industry has its own vocabulary. Telephone executives talk about "LATAs" and "attenuation rates." Cable people talk about "pay-to-basic ratios," and even public relations professionals talk about "mug shots," "ANRs," "VNRs," "boilerplate," and "evergreens." All too often, businesspeople slip into a pattern of bloated terms, gobbledygook, and clichés. Things don't get "finished"; they get "finalized." An event didn't happen "yesterday"; it occurred "at that point in time." There are also useless phrases such as "for all intents and purposes," "thinking outside the box," "real-time," and everything being a "groundbreaking" event. Other jargon and buzzwords to avoid are shown in Figure 1.7.

All these terms and acronyms may be fine if professionals are talking to each other or sending material to an industry publication, but they should be avoided in news releases and other messages to the public. Public relations consultant Joan Lowery, writing in *Communication World*, says, "Knowingly or unknowingly, jargon

Buzzwords to eliminate

model(s) social media expert
integrated viral
resolve value added
moving forward
telemarketing 24/7
interactive
free leverage
extra value
synergy
culture
change branding
thinking out of the box

Source: The Creative Group   By Nick Galifianakis

FIGURE 1.7 Everyone has a tendency to use "buzz-words" that tend to become meanignless through over-use. This infographic from "Public Relations Tactics" gives a list of words and phrases that you should avoid in your writing.

has become the lazy man's way to avoid wrestling with how to communicate clearly, concisely, and with passion to others who may not understand the concepts that some of us live and breathe each day." She also encourages public relations writers to always ask, "So what?" This forces executives, as well as engineers, to understand that the news release to the daily newspaper should skip all the technical details and concentrate on how the new product benefits the consumer.

Broadcast news veteran David Snell adds that public relations writers need to "de-geekify" their superiors. In an article for *The Strategist*, he writes, "To function with maximum efficiency, the public relations person needs to be the 'Outsider's Insider'; the person who understands the jargon, but maintains an active memory of the level of ignorance brought with them to the job." In other words, the public relations writer must always ask the question, "Will someone unfamiliar with this profession or industry be able to easily understand the message?"

As a wordsmith, you should also be cautious about the organization's executives selecting names of projects and programs that could become somewhat embarrassing if the public begins using the abbreviation or acronym instead of the full name. You can easily imagine the acronym for Franklin University College of Knowledge or the Flood Assistance Relief Team. Or perhaps the acronym for Sears Home Improvement Training?

Poor Sentence Structure

The subject and the words that modify it often become separated in a sentence, causing some confusion about what exactly is being discussed. Here are some examples from news stories:

Police will be looking for people driving under the influence of alcohol and distributing pamphlets that spell out the dangers of drunken driving.

The proposed budget provides salary increases for faculty and staff performing at a satisfactory level of 2 percent.

The student was charged with possession and consumption of an opened beer can, which is against university rules.

Poor sentence structure can also lead to embarrassment. A company newsletter, detailing an employee's illness, once reported: "Jeff was taken to the hospital with what was thought to be thrombus phlebitis. After spending a restless night with a nurse at the hospital, the results were negative."

Wrong Words

A good writer not only checks spelling, but also verifies the meaning of words. An Associated Press (AP) story once told about a man who had inherited a small scenic railroad from his "descendants," who had started it in the nineteenth century. The writer meant "ancestors" but used the wrong word. Another publication also used the wrong word when it reported "The iPhone: a High-Tech Coupe for Consumers." The actual word is "coup."

More mistakes involve the usage of "it's" and "its," "effect" and "affect," or "there" and "their." A common error is using the pronoun "their" when referring to an impersonal object such as a company. Thus, you need to write "Starbucks announced *its* (not *their*) new blend of coffee." You, however, could use *their* if you instead refer to individuals, such as "Starbucks executives announced *their* new blend of coffee."

Sound-alike words often give writers the most trouble. Such words sound alike and are similar in spelling but have different meanings. Although it might be somewhat humorous to read that a survey is "chalk full" of information (instead of "chock-full"), a company's management team is doing some "sole" searching (instead of "soul searching"), or an employee was in a "comma" (instead of a "coma") after a car accident, such mistakes are the mark of a careless writer. See the Tips for Success on page 26 for the sound-alike challenge.

> **" Use spell-check as a starting point, but never use it as a substitute for a thorough proofreading. "** Joseph Priest, editor of online communications at Ketchum, New York

Spell-checker software, unfortunately, will not catch any of the errors just described because all the words are spelled correctly. Thus, it's the responsibility of the writer to know the actual meaning of various sound-alike words and use them properly in a sentence. The second responsibility of the writer is to do a more thorough job of proofreading. Mignon Fogarty, writing in *Ragan.com*, suggests several methods: (1) read your work backward, (2) read your work out loud, (3) always read a printed version of your work, and (4) read the copy with a fresh perspective after taking a break.

Redundancies

Another major error in writing is redundancy. It is not necessary to use the word "totally" to modify a word such as "destroyed," or "completely" to modify "demolished." Many writers also say that something is "somewhat" or "very" unique. "Unique," by definition, means one of a kind; either something is unique or it isn't. In addition, it's often unnecessary to write "*Both* President Obama and Vice President Joe Biden will attend" because *both* is implied when you name them.

Other redundant words crop up when using terms like DVD *disc* or ATM *machine*, since DVD is a digital video disc and ATM means automated teller machine.

See the Tips for Success on page 27, which outlines how dating advice can make you a better writer.

Too Many Numbers

People can digest a few figures but not a mass of statistics. Use numbers sparingly in your writing, and don't put too many in a single sentence. Avoid such constructions as "During 2012, the corporation acquired 73 companies in 14 nations on five continents to achieve revenue of $14.65 billion, up $3 billion from the $11.65 billion in 2011." Consider the following tips for using numbers:

» Write "$92 million" instead of "92,000,000 dollars."

» Use a comma to separate thousands, such as in 571,200 miles. For millions, use a decimal, such as 38.5 million.

» Provide a readily understood comparison. Few people will instantly grasp the size of a new warehouse that is 583 feet long, but they will immediately form an image if you say that it's about the length of two football fields.

+

Tips for Success   What's in a Word: Do You "Accept" or "Except "the Challenge?

The following is a list of words that are frequently confused and often used incorrectly. Do you know the difference between these similar-sounding words? Do a self-test and write a sentence using the correct word.

accept, except	less, fewer
adapt, adept, adopt	lose, loose
affect, effect	may, might
callow, callous	negligent, negligible
canvas, canvass	peak, peek, pique
compliment, complement	pore, pour
disinterested, uninterested	proceed, precede
dominant, dominate	principal, principle
desert, dessert	site, cite
ensure, insure, assure	stationery, stationary
farther, further	there, their, they're
foreword, forward	precedent, precedence
imply, infer	adverse, averse
implicit, explicit	antidote, anecdote
its, it's	

- » Check your math. The price of something can go up more than 100 percent, but it can never go down more than 100 percent.
- » Don't use "over" when referring to an amount. The proper terms are "more than," as in "More than 5,000 people attended the event."
- » Spell out "percent" instead of using the "%" sign in more formal writing, such as a news release.
- » Spell out numbers smaller than 10.
- » Don't use two numbers next to each other. It's confusing to read "12 13-year-olds."

Tips for Success   How Dating Advice Can Make You a Better Writer

Some of the guidelines for attracting a new love are also applicable for making you a better writer. Lindsey McCaffrey, an Ottawa-based communications/public relations consultant, posted six tips on *Ragan.com*.

Avoid too much information

Don't overwhelm your date with information about yourself; it's a real turnoff. What does your audience need to know? What will leave them wanting more and motivate them to have a second date?

Don't talk about relationships gone bad

Unhappy customers? Product defects? Share snippets if you're asked, but don't volunteer this information freely. Save the negative stuff for another day.

Be yourself

Show personality, but don't go overboard. Keep the exclamation marks to a minimum. Don't bellow in ALL CAPS. Don't try too hard to make people like you.

Dress for the occasion

Would you wear tattered jeans to a fine restaurant? Or a tuxedo to a diner? Tailor your writing to the place and time. Don't make a sales pitch in a news release.

Keep your drinks to a minimum

There is no excuse for sloppiness. Your writing should be crisp, clean, and—most important—coherent.

Order the steak

Men aren't attracted to women who only order salad. How does this apply to writing? People want substance over style. So, go for the steak because it sizzles.

Hype

You can ruin the credibility and believability of your message by using exaggerated words and phrases. When Sharp Electronics Corporation introduced a new hand-held device, the news release called it "the next true revolution in man's conquest of information." Other companies often describe their products as "first of its kind," "unique," "a major breakthrough," and even "revolutionary," which tends to raise suspicion among journalists.

Indeed, some buzzwords crop up in news releases so frequently that they become meaningless. Public relations strategist Adam Sherk ran a day's output of news releases through PRFilter, a website that aggregates news releases, and found that *leading* was used 776 times and *solution* was used 622 times. Other words in the top 10 of excessive use were *best*, *innovative*, *leader*, *top*, *unique*, *great*, *extensive*, and *leading provider*. In sum, try to be more creative in your writing instead of relying on the standard buzzwords that everyone else is using. The writing of news releases is detailed in Chapter 5.

Bias and Stereotypes

Stereotypes often creep in as a writer struggles to describe a situation, group, or person. How often have you seen a writer describe a woman with such adjectives as "pert," "petite," "fragile," "feminine," "stunning," "gorgeous," "statuesque," or "full-figured"? How about "blond and blue-eyed"? Would you describe a man as a "muscular, well built 6-footer with sandy hair and blue eyes"?

In general, avoid descriptive terms of beauty or physical attributes and mannerisms whenever possible. In most cases, such descriptions have no bearing on the story and can be considered sexist. For example, one Chicago company was criticized for describing its president in a news release as "a tall, attractive blonde who could easily turn heads on Main Street but is instead turning heads on Wall Street."

You should also avoid any suggestion that all members of any group have the same personal characteristic, be it ambition, laziness, shrewdness, guile, or intelligence. Don't suggest that some characteristic sets an individual apart from a stereotyped norm either. For example, it is inappropriate to write, "John Williams, who is black, was promoted to senior vice president." Nor would you write, "Linda Gonzales, a U.S. citizen, will serve as assistant treasurer." In both cases, you are implying that these individuals are exceptions to some norm for their ethnic group.

Avoid gender bias by using non-gender-related words. Awareness of the irrelevance of an employee's gender is why airlines now have "flight attendants" instead of "stewardesses" and why the U.S. Postal Service hires "mail carriers" instead of "mailmen." It also is unnecessary to write that something is "manmade" when a neutral word such as "synthetic" or "artificial" is just as good. "Employees" is better than "manpower," and "chairperson" is more acceptable than "chairman." Some terms may seem difficult to neutralize—"congressperson," "businessperson," and "waitperson" don't exactly trip off the tongue. However, with a little thought, you can come up with appropriate titles, such as "legislator," "executive," and "server."

You should avoid messy constructions such as "he/she" or "his/her" that make for difficult reading. Another word can be used in most cases. If you make the noun in question plural, the pronoun "their" or "them" will serve nicely. For example, you can write, "When customers request a brochure, tell them . . ." In other cases, you can use words such as *personnel, staff, employee, worker, person,* or *practitioner* to describe both men and women in the workplace.

Politically Incorrect Language

Beyond avoidance of stereotypes, there is an ongoing controversy about what constitutes *politically correct* (commonly called "PC") language. In today's world of diversity at all levels of national life, there is increased sensitivity about what words and images are used to describe minorities and other groups of people. The terms "handicapped" and "crippled," for example, are considered insensitive, so such terms as "mobility impaired" or "physically disabled" are now used. As for holidays, most retailers have sales during the "holiday season" to avoid the use of "Christmas," which may offend non-Christian groups.

You must also be sensitive to words describing ethnic groups. Today's writers use "Asian American" instead of the pejorative "Oriental." The term "Hispanic" is now common, but "Latino" raises some criticism. Some women say it is sexist because the "o" in Spanish is male. "Afro-American" is a generally accepted term, and the term "black" is also widely accepted by African Americans and the media. Language and its connotations are constantly changing. The public relations writer must be aware of the changes and make decisions based on such factors as sensitivity to the audience, accuracy, and clarity of communication.

Summary

The Framework of Public Relations

» Public relations writing and media placements are accomplished within the framework of the complete public relations process—research, planning, communication, and evaluation.

» Public relations personnel who write news releases and other materials fulfill a valuable role as technicians because they implement and execute the tactics of a public relations program.

The Public Relations Writer

» Public relations writing is similar to journalism in that both strive to provide accurate, credible information. They differ with respect to objectives, audience selection, and the variety of media channels that are used.

Preparation for Writing

» A desktop or laptop computer is the preferred device for public relations writers. Tablets and other devices such as the iPad are less versatile for extensive writing and transferring of files.

» A basic dictionary and ready access to an online encyclopedia are important reference tools.

» The most widely used stylebook for journalistic writing is the *Associated Press Stylebook.*

» Media directories are available in print and CD formats, but online databases are most popular because they can be updated on a daily basis.

» Public relations writers should keep current in the field by reading professional publications. They should also read a local daily, a nationally circulated daily or online site, and weekly newsmagazines.

» Blogs and Twitter feeds about public relations and marketing communications are another way to keep up with developments in the public relations field.

Research: The Prelude to Writing

» Search engines such as Google, Yahoo!, and MSN's Bing help public relations writers find information on the Internet.

» Electronic databases such as Academic Search Premier and Lexis/Nexis are good for gathering in-depth information and full-text articles.

Writing Guidelines

» All public relations writing starts with the basic steps of determining the purpose and content of the message.

» Public relations writers should work as "translators" of organizational jargon

so messages can be understood by the public.

» Writers should strive to create strong images that make information more clear and interesting to the reader.

» Always write in active, present tense whenever possible.

Errors to Avoid

» Writers must pay close attention to spelling, grammar, and sentence structure to gain credibility with the reader. Writers should always strive for brevity and clarity. Bloated sentences and jargon should be avoided.

» There are many sound-alike words. Writers must know the meaning of similar words and use them correctly in a sentence.

» Hype and exaggerated claims ruin a message's credibility.

» Writers should be sensitive to words and terms that can be considered sexist or racist.

Skill Building Activities

1. Select a topic, such as public relations, and look it up on Wikipedia. Compare the information with that from another online encyclopedia, such as *Britannica*. How are the entries similar? How are they different? Which entry, in your view, is the most complete and credible?

2. Go to the library and review several media directories that are provided in the reference section. Or, if possible, make arrangements with a public relations firm to be shown the online media databases it uses. Compare and contrast the various directories (databases).

3. Read an issue of a trade publication in the public relations field. You may choose such publications as *PRWeek*, *PR Tactics*, *O'Dwyer's PR Report*, or the

Ragan Report. You can also go online, using the URLs listed on pages 11 and 12; however, note that full access to the articles on some sites is only available with a paid subscription.

4. Several public relations blogs were mentioned on pages 11 and 12. Visit at least three of them. What aspects of each blog were interesting to you?

5. Visit the websites of several public relations organizations, such as PRSA, IABC, IPRA, and so on. Explore their various links and pages. Write a short report on what you found. The URLs are in the Tips for Success on page 15.

6. Select a topic that interests you and "Google it." In addition, use at least two digital databases available in

your library (see box on page 18) to find information on the same topic. What are the pros and cons of using a search engine versus using a library database?

7. Review the Tips for Success box on page 26. Can you write a sentence correctly using each of these sound-alike words?

8. Select a topic of interest to you and do a search on Google, Bing, and Yahoo!. What was the difference in the search results?

Media Resources

Associated Press Stylebook (2011). New York: Associated Press.

Baron, D. (2009, March). "Writers: What's on Your Bookshelf?" *Ragan Report*, 5.

Doyle, S. (2010, August). "Required Reading: Blogs and Twitter Feeds That Communication Pros Need to Bookmark." *PRWeek*, 42–46.

Fogarty, M. (2010, September). "If You Miss One Typo, Will All the Rest of the Typos Know?" *Ragan Report*, 3–4.

Gingerich, J. (2011, February). "Watch Your Grammar! 20 Writing Tips for PR Pros." *O'Dwyer's*, 36–37.

Gray-Grant, D. (2010, November 8). "Top 25 Grammar and Language Mistakes." Retrieved from www.ragan.com.

Hanson, A. (2011, January 11). "Five LinkedIn Groups for PR Pros." Retrieved from www.ragan.com.

Kennedy, M. (2011, February 11). "Eleven PR Blogs You Need to Read in 2011." Retrieved from www.ereleases.com/prfuel.

Moser, M. (2011, April 5). "Ten Guidelines for Writing Numbers and Numerals." Retrieved from www.ragan.com.

Mossberg, W. (2011, April 21). "Picking Out a Laptop in the Brave, New World of Tablets." Retrieved from www.online.wsj.com.

Nichol, M. (2011, February 4). "Seven Examples of Passive Voice (And How to Fix Them)." Retrieved from www.dailywritingtips.com.

Porter, J. (2011, January 20). "Tools No PR Pro Can Live Without." Retrieved from www.blog.journalistics.com.

Porter, J. (2010, December 28). "The Best PR Blogs Out There." Retrieved from www.blog.journalistics.com.

Ramage, J., Bean, J., and Johnson, J. (2011). *Allyn & Bacon Guide to Writing*. New York: Longman, 6th edition.

Reinalda, R. (2010, May). "Comma Chameleon: How It Changes the Color of Your Meaning." *Ragan Report*, 4–6.

Whaling, H. (2011, November 4). "The PR Pro's Guide to Twitter." Retrieved from www.mashable.com.

Becoming a Persuasive Writer

>> After reading this chapter, you will be able to:

» Understand the basic elements of communication

» Apply theories of communication to writing a persuasive message

» Consider the various factors that shape a message or speech

» Understand the use and abuse of propaganda techniques

» Recognize the ethical responsibility of crafting persuasive messages

Persuasion: As Old as Civilization

In their daily work of crafting messages that will persuade and motivate people, public relations writers are following a tradition that goes back at least 2,000 years. The ancient Greeks made *rhetoric*, the art of using language effectively and persuasively, part of their educational system. Aristotle, for example, was the first to set down the ideas of *ethos*, *logos*, and *pathos*, which translate roughly as "source credibility," "logical argument," and "emotional appeal," respectively.

These three elements of persuasion are still relevant today, and Professor Robert Heath of the University of Houston makes the point that

> ...public relations professionals are influential rhetors. They design, place, and repeat messages on behalf of sponsors on an array of topics that shape views of government, charitable organizations, institutions of public education, products and consumerism, capitalism, labor, health, and leisure. These professionals speak, write, and use visual images to discuss topics and take stances on public policies at the local, state, and federal levels.

Indeed, public relations, marketing, and advertising personnel constantly craft messages to change attitudes and opinions, reinforce existing predispositions, and influence people to buy a product, use a service, or support a worthy cause. Consequently, you need to understand the basic elements of communication and the complex process of how individuals respond to different messages. In an age of information overload, you must constantly analyze public attitudes and shape persuasive, credible messages that cut through the clutter.

You need to keep asking questions. How do you appeal to self-interests? Which spokesperson has the most credibility? What information is most salient to the target audience? What is the most effective communication channel? What are my ethical responsibilities as a writer?

This chapter summarizes some communication theories applicable to public relations writing and what social science research tells us about the way people receive, interpret, and act on information. It also provides guidelines about how to make your writing—whether it's on behalf of the Sierra Club or General Electric—more persuasive. Later in the chapter you'll learn about the ethical guidelines and professional standards that should guide the content of your writing.

The Basics of Communication

To communicate is to make known—to project ideas into the minds of others. This process depends on four basic elements: a *sender*, a *message*, a *channel*, and a *receiver*. If all these elements are present, there will be communication. Because your purpose is to persuade, you want to communicate your ideas to a particular group of people—those who can help or hinder your organization in attaining its objectives. The following chart summarizes the basic communication process from a public relations perspective.

Sender

- » The sender is the organization that prepares and distributes the message.
- » Every organization has different publics, divergent interests, and its own values.
- » A writer must have a thorough knowledge of the organization and its organizational objectives, such as selling a product, providing a service, or educating the public about an issue or cause.

Message

- » Planning starts with deciding what the key message is and what you want the recipient to think, believe, or do about it.
- » A thorough knowledge of audience characteristics helps shape a message that is relevant to their interests, desires, and needs.
- » The message must be clearly expressed and in words that are understandable to the audience.
- » Benefits to the audience should be the focus, not benefits to the organization.

Channel

» Organizations have multiple channels available to them. They may include traditional mass media, websites, social media, brochures, newsletters, videos, and events. Every medium has its advantages and disadvantages.

» The characteristics of the audience determine what medium or combination of channels should be used. College-age women use different media than senior citizens.

» It is essential to know the format of each medium. Television requires visuals and short **soundbites.** A website requires strong graphics and interactive links.

Receiver

» Messages are most effective when tailored to a specific, well-defined audience that has similar characteristics in terms of gender, age, income, education, etc.

» In public relations and marketing, there is no such thing as the "general public." Instead, there are groups of **"publics"** that may be defined as customers, suppliers, employees, community leaders, or investors. Each requires different kinds of information about the organization and its products, services, or policies.

Theories of Communication

There are numerous theories about how messages are conceptualized and how recipients filter and evaluate such messages. The following is a brief summary of the theories that you will find most useful in formulating messages and understanding how individuals process information.

Media Uses and Gratification

Recipients of communication are not passive couch potatoes. The basic premise of uses and gratification theory is that the communication process is interactive. The communicator wants to inform and, ultimately, motivate people to act on the information. Recipients want to be entertained, informed, or alerted to opportunities that can fulfill their needs.

Thus, people are highly selective about what messages catch their attention and meet their needs. The role of the public relations writer, then, is to tailor messages that are meaningful to the target audience.

A good example is how Burson-Marsteller tailored messages on behalf of the National Turkey Federation to generate year-round sales. The public relations firm used a psychographics model developed by SRI International, a research organization. The model, known as VALS, has several lifestyle typologies:

» *Survivors and sustainers* are at the bottom of the hierarchy. Generally, members of this group have low incomes, are poorly educated, and are often elderly. These people eat at erratic hours, consume inexpensive foods, and seldom patronize restaurants.

» *Belongers* are family oriented and traditional and tend to be lower- or middle-income people.

» *Achievers*, the uppermost level of the VALS scale, are often college-educated professionals with high incomes. They are also more experimental and open to new ideas.

By segmenting the consumer public into these lifestyles, Burson-Marsteller selected appropriate media for specific story ideas. An article placed in *True Experience*, a publication reaching the "survivors and sustainers" group, was headlined "A Terrific Budget-Stretching Meal" and emphasized bargain cuts of turkey. *Better Homes & Gardens* was used to reach the "belongers," with articles that emphasized tradition, such as barbecued turkey as a "summer classic" on the Fourth of July. The "achievers" were reached through *Food and Wine* and *Gourmet* magazines, with recipes for turkey salad and turkey tetrazzini.

By identifying the magazines that catered to these three lifestyle groups and tailoring the information to fit each magazine's demographics, Burson-Marsteller was able to send an appropriate message to each audience. The result was increased turkey sales on a year-round basis.

Cognitive Dissonance

People will not believe a message, or act on it, if it is contrary to their predispositions. This is the crux of Leon Festinger's theory of cognitive dissonance. In essence, it says that people will not believe a message contrary to their attitudes and existing opinions unless the communicator can introduce information that causes them to question their beliefs.

Dissonance can be created in at least three ways. First, the writer needs to make the public aware that circumstances have changed. Oil companies, for example, say that the era of cheap gasoline is over because a rising middle class in such nations as India and China also have cars and are now competing with U.S. drivers for the available supply. Second, the writer needs to provide information about new developments. Public perceptions about China making unsafe toys changed somewhat when Mattel finally admitted that it recalled 18 million toys because of design flaws, not manufacturing problems. Third, the writer should use a quote from a respected person that the public trusts. Chevron, for example, attempts to overcome unfavorable public attitudes about its "green" initiatives by getting endorsements from respected leaders in the conservation and environmental movement.

In many cases, public attitudes can be changed by presenting facts that counter the public's perceptions. A good example is what happened to the lowly potato when the diet industry demonized the vegetable as a fattening, high-carbohydrate food. One survey, for example, showed that almost 25 percent of female heads of households believed that potatoes were fattening. The U.S. Potato Board and its public relations firm, Fleishman-Hillard, countered this perception by pointing out that potatoes have positive nutritional benefits because they are a good source of vitamin C and potassium, are low in calories, and are sodium free. As a result of the campaign, a positive shift occurred in public perceptions about the potato as a nutritious vegetable, increasing potato consumption. Unfortunately, many other campaigns are not as effective because the message is poorly conceived and written. See the Tips for Success below to find out why messages often fail to persuade.

Framing

Historically, the term *framing* was used to describe how journalists and editors select certain facts, themes, treatments, and even words to "frame" a story in order to generate maximum interest and understanding among readers and viewers. For example, how media frame the debate over health care and how to cut the federal deficit plays a major role in public perceptions of the problem. Many people, because they lack specific knowledge and experience about an issue, usually accept the media's version of reality.

+

Tips for Success   Why Writing Fails to Persuade

Many product news releases and marketing brochures don't persuade because key components are missing. Dianna Huff, a business-to-business marketing writing specialist, gives 10 reasons why marketing materials often remain unread:

Emphasis on the company instead of the customer.   It's all right to tell customers about your company and its great manufacturing facility, but it's important to tell customers how it benefits them. Do they get a better product or service? Lower prices? Faster turnaround?

All features, no benefits.   Don't let engineers write your copy. Focus instead on how your product or service will benefit your customers.

Copy that fails to say, "What's in it for me?"   Stay away from generalities. Be specific about how the product or service will help the consumer save money, do things easier, or enhance his or her quality of life.

Too much jargon.   Make sure phrases and sentences are not corporate or engineering lingo. Translate concepts into basic English.

Redundancies.   Are you using the same words or phrases in several places? Edit them out or use other words.

No call to action.   The number one rule in promotional writing is to tell potential customers what you want them to do. Pick up the phone? Visit the website? Visit a store? Buy the product?

Copy not addressed to target audience.   Try to picture a person who represents your audience and write directly to him or her.

Failure to nail down messaging.   Don't use vague, meaningless phrases about the product or service. Keep asking management about specific benefits, how the product differs from the competition, etc.

Poor grammar.   Yes, people do notice.

Failure to edit or proofread.   Ask others to also proofread copy. They will no doubt find typos you have missed.

Framing theory also applies to public relations because, according to more than one study, about half of the content found in the mass media today is supplied by public relations sources. Indeed, Kirk Hallahan of Colorado State University says that public relations personnel are essentially *frame strategists*, because they construct messages that "focus selectively on key attributes and characteristics of a cause, candidate, product, or service." This framing, in turn, is echoed in the context and content of stories that the mass media disseminate.

> " *These days, 'spin' is more likely to mean ensuring the story is told in a way that's meaningful to the audience rather than twisting a client's response to an issue to make them look good.* " Shel Holtz, on his blog, a shell of my former self

The issue of bottled water is a good case study in framing. The $12 billion bottling industry, of course, "frames" bottled water as being better than tap water, a healthy alternative to sodas, and a part of an active lifestyle. Activist groups, such as the National Resource Defense Council (NRDC), frame the consumption of bottled water as environmentally irresponsible because the transport of bottled water from exotic places such as Fiji generates greenhouse gases, a primary cause of global warming. In addition, plastic bottles not only require oil to make, but an estimated 2 billion pounds of plastic bottles are now clogging landfills. Public relations personnel on both sides, including the tap water filter manufacturers, work very hard to influence how the media frame the issue in their news coverage.

Political candidates, of course, constantly work to frame issues that support their viewpoint. The national debate about pension reform for public employees is an example. Advocates for reform frame the issue in the media as one of cutting the high cost of benefits to taxpayers. Unions and their supporters, however, frame the issue in terms of an assault on the rights of employees to participate in collective bargaining and to be fairly compensated.

Diffusion and Adoption

The diffusion theory was developed in the 1930s and expanded on by Professor Everett Rogers of Stanford University. It holds that the process of acquiring new ideas has five steps:

1. **Awareness.** The person discovers the idea or product.
2. **Interest.** The person tries to get more information.
3. **Trial.** The person tries the idea on others or samples the product.
4. **Evaluation.** The person decides whether the idea works for his or her own self-interest.
5. **Adoption.** The person incorporates the idea into his or her opinion or begins to use the product.

In this model, the public relations writer is most influential at the *awareness* and *interest* stages of the process. People often become aware of a product, service, or idea through traditional mass media outlets such as newspapers, magazines, radio, and television. Indeed, the primary purpose of advertising in the mass media is to create awareness, the first step in moving people toward the purchase of a product or support of an idea.

At the interest stage, people seek more detailed information from such sources as pamphlets, brochures, direct mail, videos, meetings, and websites. This is why initial publicity to create awareness often includes an 800 number or a website where people can get more information.

Family members, peers, and associates become influential in the trial and evaluation stages of the adoption model. Mass media, at this point, serve primarily to reinforce messages and predispositions.

A person, however, does not necessarily go through all five stages of adoption with any particular idea or product. A number of factors affect the adoption process. Rogers lists at least five:

» **Relative advantage.**   Is the idea better than the one it replaces?
» **Compatibility.**   Is the idea consistent with the person's existing values and needs?
» **Complexity.**   Is the innovation difficult to understand and use?
» **Trialability.**   Can the innovation be used on a trial basis?
» **Observability.**   Are the results of the innovation visible to others?

You should be aware of these factors and try to formulate messages that address them. Repeating a message in various ways, reducing its complexity, taking competing messages into account, and structuring the message to the needs of the audience are ways to do this. Another aspect of adoption theory is that some people are predisposed to be *innovators* and early adopters, whereas others, known as *laggards*, won't adopt an idea or product until it is well established. Public relations campaigns often are directed toward the early adopters, also known as *influentials* or *catalysts*, to launch a new product.

Apple's introduction of the iPhone and the iPad is an example of successfully reaching early adopters and opinion leaders. Apple's hard-core fans, dubbed "iCultists," stood in line for hours for bragging rights to be the first among their friends to have the device. They, in turn, provided the impetus for extensive media "buzz" that encouraged the *early majority* to buy several million iPhones and iPads in succeeding months.

Hierarchy of Needs

The hierarchy of needs theory has been applied in a number of disciplines, including communication. It is based on the work of Abraham H. Maslow, who listed basic human needs on a scale from basic survival to more complex needs:

» **Physiological needs.**   These involve self-preservation. They include air, water, food, clothing, shelter, rest, and health—the minimum necessities of life.
» **Safety needs.**   These comprise protection against danger, loss of life or property, restriction of activity, and loss of freedom.

FIGURE 2.1 *Early adopters,* known as iCultists, stand in line for hours to purchase an Apple product. Here, Alex Shumilov from Moscow shows off his iPad2 after becoming the first customer to buy one at the Apple store in New York. He, and all the others who were standing in line behind him, are the catalysts for extensive media coverage and publicity that create a buzz about a new product, which fuels even more sales to the *early majority.* In the three days after the iPad2 launch, about 500,000 units were sold.

» **Social needs.** These include acceptance by others, belonging to groups, and enjoying both friendship and love.

» **Ego needs.** These include self-esteem, self-confidence, accomplishment, status, recognition, appreciation, and the respect of others.

» **Self-actualization needs.** These represent the need to grow to one's full stature after all other needs are met. Individuals may learn a new language for the fun of it, volunteer for a cause, or travel.

The campaign for the National Turkey Federation, mentioned earlier, is a good example of the application of Maslow's concepts. Low-income people got an economical recipe that satisfied basic physiological needs. However, the fancy recipes in upscale magazines were designed to meet the ego and status needs of people not worried about food costs.

Advertising is particularly adept at tapping Maslow's hierarchy. An ad for a new car, for example, often emphasizes economic, safety, social, and ego needs. For the Baby Boomer who just turned 60, an ad for an expensive sports car often appeals to self-actualization needs. The main point is to understand that your audience is looking for messages that satisfy needs. If you can identify and articulate those needs, you are well on your way to being a persuasive writer.

Factors in Persuasive Writing

Your purpose is to persuade your target audience. Your message may be delivered in one way, a few ways, or many ways. Techniques for getting your messages into the mass media are detailed in later chapters. As you work on message content, however, keep in mind the concepts of (1) audience analysis; (2) source credibility; (3) appeal to self-interest; (4) clarity of the message; (5) timing and context; (6) symbols, slogans, and acronyms; (7) semantics; (8) suggestions for action; and (9) content and structure. See the Tips for Success on page 41 for how to become a persuasive writer.

Audience Analysis

A message, as already stated, must be compatible with group values and beliefs. People who commute by car, for example, become more interested in carpooling and mass transit when the message points out the increasing cost of gas and how gridlock increases every year.

Tapping a group's attitudes and values in order to structure a meaningful message is called *channeling*. It is the technique of recognizing a general audience's beliefs and suggesting a specific course of action related to audience members' self-interests. In this example, the incentive to participate in carpooling or mass transit offers more motivation than the more abstract concept of saving the environment.

Communicators must have a thorough understanding of their audiences, and they must stay very current with the media being used by these audiences. Jerry Swerling, director of the USC Annenberg Strategic Public Relations Center

Professor emeritus James Grunig of the University of Maryland says audiences can be defined as either passive or active. *Passive audiences* have to be lured into accepting your message. Consequently, messages directed to them need to be highly visual, use catchy themes and slogans, and contain short messages. A number of communication tools provide this format: dramatic pictures and graphics, billboards, radio and television announcements, posters, bumper stickers, buttons, and special events that emphasize entertainment.

Active audiences, in contrast, are usually aware of the product, service, or idea. They have reached the second stage of the diffusion process—*interest*—and are seeking more detailed information. Appropriate communication tools for them include brochures, in-depth newspaper and magazine stories, detailed websites, videos, seminars, speeches, and trade shows. Indeed, research shows that visits to websites often are driven by stories in the traditional mainstream media.

In most cases, the competent communicator acknowledges the existence of both passive and active audiences by preparing a number of messages that vary in content and structure. A daily newspaper may receive an attractive publicity photo with a short

Tips for Success   How to Be a Persuasive Writer and Speaker

A number of research studies have contributed to our understanding of the persuasion process. Listed below are key findings that provide insight into how to create and distribute persuasive messages.

+ A persuasive message must be personally relevant to the audience. Otherwise, they will ignore it.

+ Convey the message in a setting and environment where the audience feels the most comfortable. That's why organizations use Facebook pages or iPhone Apps to reach teenagers and young adults.

+ Use multiple communication channels. The impact is far greater when a message reaches people in a number of different forms.

+ Maintain consistency so that the basic content is the same regardless of audience or context. Then tailor that content to the specific audience as much as possible.

+ Cite and quote individuals perceived as experts by the audience.

+ A celebrity or an attractive model is most effective when the audience has low involvement. A well-known celebrity or an attractive model attracts attention to a message that would otherwise be ignored.

+ Repeat the key point, in different ways, throughout the message.

+ Positive appeals are generally more effective than negative appeals, in terms of both retention of the message and actual compliance with it.

+ Brief, simple messages on television or in a Web video tend to have more persuasive impact than those seen in print because "seeing is believing." Print media, however, are more effective for conveying detailed, lengthy information.

+ Television and radio messages tend to be consumed passively, whereas the print media more fully engage the individual's attention.

+ Strong emotional appeals and the arousal of fear are most effective when the audience has some minimal concern about or interest in the topic.

+ Highly fear-arousing appeals are effective only when some immediate action can be taken to eliminate the threat.

+ Individuals in an audience have different preferences. Some prefer fact-based information while others prefer emotional arguments. Ideally, both approaches should be included in the message.

+ With highly educated, sophisticated audiences, logical appeals using facts and figures work better than strong emotional appeals.

+ Messages are more persuasive if they are balanced in terms of presenting two sides of an issue.

+ Like self-interest, altruism can be a strong motivator. Men are more willing to get physical checkups for the sake of their families rather than for themselves.

caption, whereas a specialized trade publication might get an in-depth news release detailing the product's features. On another level, a customer assessing the corporate website may review a product or service by clicking on multiple links. The strategy of developing multiple messages for a variety of media platforms is emphasized throughout this book.

Source Credibility

A message is more believable to an audience if the source has credibility, which is why writers try to attribute information and quotes to people who are perceived as experts. Indeed, *expertise* is a key element in credibility. The other two elements are *sincerity* and *charisma*. Ideally, a source will have all three attributes.

Steve Jobs, founder of Apple, was a good example. As CEO before his death in 2011, he was highly credible as an expert on Apple products and considered a high-tech visionary. In countless news articles and speeches, he came across as a personable, laid-back "geek" in a designer T-shirt and jeans who was passionate about the company's products.

Not every company has a Steve Jobs, nor is that necessary. Studies, such as the annual Edelman Trust Barometer, show that certain occupational groups have more credibility with the public than others. In its 2011 report, Edelman found that 70 percent of the survey respondents thought academic experts were the most credible, followed by 64 percent who would trust a technical expert within the company. About 55 percent would trust a financial or industry analyst, but only 50 percent would trust the CEO.

In other words, you need to evaluate the message and the audience to determine the most appropriate spokesperson. For example, if you are writing a news release about a new product for a trade magazine, perhaps the most credible source to quote would be the company's director of research and development. This person is credible because of his or her specialized knowledge and expertise. If the news release is about a company's fourth-quarter earnings, however, the most credible person to quote in the news release would be a financial or industry analyst.

Source credibility also can be hired. The California Strawberry Advisory Board, for example, quotes a home economist in its news releases, and this individual appears on television talk shows to discuss nutrition and demonstrate easy-to-follow strawberry recipes. The audience for these programs, primarily homemakers, not only identifies with the representative but also perceives the spokesperson to be an expert.

Here's a sampling of hired experts who have been quoted and have provided media interviews for various public relations campaigns:

» A veterinarian for a campaign by Novartis Animal Health to launch a new arthritis drug for dogs

» Two professors of nutrition for a campaign by Frito-Lay to tell the public that its potato chips are now made with sunflower oil, a "good" fat

» A celebrity interior designer for a campaign by Olympic Paints and Stains to position itself as a home decorating brand

» A well-known food expert in the African American community for a campaign by Lawry Seasoned Salt to show how its product line enhances this ethnic group's favorite recipes

FIGURE 2.2 Olympic skier Lindsey Vonn is a popular endorser of many products because she is attractive and an Olympic champion. When she and other athletes compete, their uniforms are a virtual billboard of brand names. Vonn's cap, for example, prominently shows the Red Bull logo. Celebrities add glamour and tend to attract readers or viewers who would not ordinarily consider the product or service.

Celebrities often are used to call attention to a product, service, or cause. Celebrities, as already noted, attract passive audiences to a message. The sponsor's intent is to associate the person's popularity with the product and thus give it more "glamour." This is called *transfer*. Celebrity endorsements are often used in the marketing world, and athletes are particularly popular. In 2011, male Olympic champions (Shaun White, Apolo Anton Ohno, and Michael Phelps) were the top male endorsers, as well as NBA basketball star Shaquille O'Neal and NFL quarterback Peyton Manning. The top female athletes, according to rankings, were tennis star Venus Williams and Olympic skater Lindsey Vonn.

Prestige events and Hollywood celebrities also attract audiences to a message. This is why Kodak chose the Academy Awards to highlight its new dual-lens digital camera. The company's objective was to position itself as a lifestyle brand among women who take their cues from the world of celebrity. In addition to giving cameras with a diamond monogram to the five Best Actress nominees, Kodak also preselected celebrities, such as Keira Knightley, to take photos of other celebrities attending an Oscar movie-viewing party at a swank restaurant in New York. The resulting photos were distributed to the media and generated hundreds of stories.

Not all celebrities need to be Hollywood stars or even famous athletes. Again, it depends on finding the appropriate, credible spokesperson for the situation. The Kansas City Health Department had a much less glamorous assignment—educating the gay community and sex workers about the risk of syphilis and the availability of free testing. Flo, a local celebrity drag queen, was chosen as a spokesperson because she was widely accepted in the gay and straight communities. According to Fleishman-Hillard, the public relations firm handling the campaign, "She possessed the ability to take sensitive topics, such as syphilis, and motivate people at risk to take action. Her personality and credibility gave far more exposure to the issue than a straight public health message would have received."

Appeal to Self-Interest

Self-interest was mentioned in connection with both Maslow's hierarchy of needs and audience analysis. A public relations writer must at all times be aware of what the audience wants to know.

Writing publicity for a new food product can serve as an example. A news release to the trade press serving the food industry (grocery stores, suppliers, wholesalers, and distributors) might focus on how the product was developed, distributed, and made available to the public, the manufacturer's pricing policies, or the results of marketing studies that show consumers want the product. This audience is interested in the technical aspects of distribution, pricing, and market niche.

You would prepare quite a different news release or feature article for the food section of a daily newspaper. The consumer wants information about the food product's nutritional value, convenience, and cost and wants to know why the item is superior to similar products. The reader is also looking for menu ideas and recipes that use the product. The Tips for Success on page 44 provides a list of common message themes that appeal to an audience's self-interests.

Clarity of the Message

Communication, as already stated, does not occur if the audience does not understand your message. It is important to produce messages that match the characteristics of your target audience in content and structure.

A bar association once thought it was a great idea to produce a brochure to help motorists understand liability in an accident. However, by the time the committee of lawyers added all the legalese, the brochure became useless as an aid to the general public.

One solution to this problem is to copy-test all public relations materials on the target audience. Another solution is to apply readability and comprehension formulas to materials before they are produced and disseminated. Most formulas are based on the number of words per sentence and the number of one-syllable words per 100 words. In general, standard writing should average about 140 to 150 syllables per 100 words, and the average sentence length should be about 17 words. This is the reading level of newspapers and weekly newsmagazines such as *Time*.

+

Tips for Success   Appeals That Move People to Act

Persuasive messages often include information that appeals to an audience's self-interest. Here is a list of persuasive message themes that author Charles Marsh compiled for an article in IABC's *Communication World*:

Make money	Satisfy curiosity	Save money	Protect family
Save time	Be stylish	Avoid effort	Have beautiful things
More comfort	Satisfy appetite	Better health	Be like others
Cleaner	Avoid trouble	Escape pain	Avoid criticism
Gain praise	Be individual	Be popular	Protect reputation
Be loved/accepted	Be safe	Keep possessions	Make work easier
More enjoyment	Be secure		

Timing and Context

Professional communicators often say that timing is everything. In the earlier example about car commuters, it was pointed out that the best time to talk about carpooling and mass transit to owners of sport utility vehicles is when there is a major increase in gas prices. Another good context is when the state highway department releases a study showing that the average commute on a congested highway from point A to point B now takes 20 minutes longer than it did last year. Both of these situations are good examples of keying messages around events and related news stories that provide a context for your message.

Your message also must arrive at a time when it is most relevant to the audience. If it is too early, your audience might not be ready to think about it. April is not the time to talk about new facilities at a ski resort, but October might be just right. Cruise ships also distribute news releases and travel features about tropical destinations as the temperature drops in the Midwest and on the East Coast. Information about a new software program for doing taxes is relevant in the weeks before the April 15 deadline, but the news value drops after this date. News about a new club would get attention from single, young professionals almost any time.

Symbols and Slogans

The Red Cross (known as the Red Crescent in the Middle East) is well known throughout the world. The name is totally unenlightening, but the symbol is recognized and associated with the care and help given by the organization. Flags are symbols. Smokey the Bear is a symbol. Even the Nike Swoosh is a familiar symbol on a global scale. You are not likely to produce a symbol that will become world famous, but, if at all possible, you should try to find something graphic that symbolizes a given organization. This is called *branding*, and corporations often spend millions to establish a symbol that immediately means reliability and quality to a consumer.

Slogans can be highly persuasive. They state a key concept in a few memorable and easily pronounceable words. The American Revolution had the rallying cry of "No taxation without representation," and today's corporations are just as slogan conscious.

Nike tells us to "Just Do It" and McDonald's assures us that "You Deserve a Break Today." Coca-Cola wants us to have "The Pause That Refreshes," and MasterCard talks about things that are "Priceless." Perhaps one of the most successful slogans of all time is DeBeers' assurance that "A diamond is forever." If you can come up with a slogan that expresses the essence of what you are trying to promote, it will help you attain your objective.

Semantics

The dictionary definition of words may be clear and concise, but there is another dimension to words—the connotative meaning to various individuals and groups of people. The study of meaning given to words and the changes that occur in these meanings as time goes on is the branch of linguistics called *semantics*.

For example, consider the evolution of the word "gay" in American society. The word was traditionally defined as merry, joyous, and lively. Thus, in the nineteenth century, we had the "Gay Nineties" and people often referred to bright colors or sprightly music as "gay." By the 1920s and 1930s, however, "gay" started being applied as a code word for prostitutes, who were said to be in the "gay life." Today, "gay" is only used in the context of the homosexual community.

By the same token, the terms "pro-life" and "pro-choice" have very definite connotations to certain groups of people. "Affirmative action" means opportunity to some and exclusion to others. The controversy over politically correct language was cited in Chapter 1. Even the expression "politically correct" has different connotations to different groups of people. To some, it is derogatory, an attempt by radical groups to censor freedom of expression. To others, the concept stands for equality and an effort to eliminate sexism and racism.

To write persuasively and to influence target audiences, you must be sensitive to semantics. The protracted argument between the Republicans and the Democrats over Medicare funding is a good example. The Republicans say they want to "preserve, protect, and strengthen" the program, whereas the Democrats say such rhetoric is just code words to disguise legislation that will lead to major "cuts" in funding. The issue is again a matter of framing.

Suggestions for Action

Persuasive writing must give people information on how to take action, and the suggestions must be feasible. A campaign by a utility provides a good example. If the company really wants people to conserve energy, it must provide them with information about how to do so. The suggestions may be as simple as turning the thermostat down to 68 degrees, wearing sweaters in the house during the winter months, or purchasing a roll of weather stripping to place around the windows and doors. All these suggestions are within the capability of the utility's customers.

However, if the suggestion is to insulate your house thoroughly, this might not be feasible for consumers with limited incomes. In this case, the utility might accompany the suggestion with a special program of interest-free loans or a discount coupon to make it easier for customers to take the recommended action. In this way, the suggestion becomes feasible to thousands of homeowners.

Environmental organizations, to use another example, make a point of providing information on how to contact your legislator to support or oppose pending legislation. They provide not only the legislator's email address, but also a sample letter that you can copy or adapt. In many cases, you are encouraged to sign an online petition or post a comment on the official's Facebook page or Twitter account.

Content and Structure

People are motivated by theatrics and a good story. They are moved by bold action and human drama. Your message should go beyond cold facts or even eloquent phrases. If you can vividly describe what you are talking about—if you can paint word pictures—your message will be more persuasive.

A number of techniques can make a message more persuasive; many of these have already been discussed. The following is a summary of some additional writing devices.

Drama — Everyone likes a good story. This is often accomplished by graphically illustrating an event or a situation. Newspapers often dramatize a story to boost reader interest. Thus, we read about the daily life of someone with AIDS, the family on welfare who is suffering because of state cuts in spending, or the frustrations of a middle-class family facing eviction from their home because they couldn't pay the balloon mortgage payments. In the newsroom, this is called *humanizing the issue*.

> **❝At the end of the day, regardless of the means by which your message was communicated, did it reach the target audience(s) in an understandable fashion with a clearly expressed call for action?❞** Kirk Hazlett, associate professor, Curry College

Drama, or human interest, is also used in public relations. A good example is how Harden & Partners used the human interest element when Covenant House opened in Oakland, California. The basic news was that the nonprofit organization was opening a new multipurpose shelter to serve homeless and at-risk youth in the San Francisco Bay area. Such an announcement lacks drama, but the story became more interesting when a human interest element was added. Journalists were given the names of some Covenant House residents who had agreed to be interviewed. Consequently, a front-page story in the *Oakland Tribune* started this way: "For Marcus, the bed and the hot food he found at Covenant House gave him a chance to rejuvenate and get his life organized. 'You can't think when you are hungry,' said the 22-year-old Missouri native, one of the dozen or so homeless young people who began staying at the new youth shelter in Jack London Square last week."

Relief organizations, in particular, attempt to humanize problems to galvanize public concern to attract donations. Saying that nearly 2 million people in Sudan's Darfur region have become homeless doesn't have the same emotional impact as describing a young mother in a refugee camp sobbing over the lifeless form of her 11-year-old daughter who was raped and then murdered by a Janjaweed militia that also burned down her village. Readers and viewers can identify with the mother's loss, which graphically illustrates the need for aid. Large numbers alone are impersonal and generate little or no emotional involvement. See the PR Casebook on page 48 for an example of an emotional appeal by a nonprofit agency.

A more mundane use of dramatizing is the application story that is sent to the trade press. With this technique, sometimes called the *case study technique*, a manufacturer prepares an article on how an individual or a company is using its product. Honeywell Corporation, for example, provides a number of application stories about how offices and businesses have saved money by installing Honeywell's temperature-control systems. More examples of the application story are found in Chapter 7.

Statistics — Although numbers can be cold and impersonal, they also can convey objectivity, largeness, and importance in a credible way. For some reason, people are awed by statistics. For example, Toyota, seeking to portray itself as an important contributor to the American economy, once placed ads in major metropolitan dailies that used impressive numbers. One ad stated, "Over the last 5 years Toyota in America has purchased $20 billion in parts and materials from 510 U.S. suppliers. Today, more than half the Toyota vehicles sold in America are built at our plants in Kentucky and California."

PR casebook

Emotional Appeals Humanize an Issue

A basic approach for many fundraising letters is to humanize the problem with a strong emotional component.

The American Society for the Prevention of Cruelty to Animals used a letter that starts with a story about an abused dog named Brutus. It follows up with his rescue by ASPCA and gives facts and information about the organization's efforts to rescue hundreds of animals from abuse.

The four-page letter ends, of course, with a note about Brutus being back to "his happy handsome self" and requests the reader's help in saving dogs like him. The following is the first page of the fundraising letter. It starts with an introductory note in large type that states:

The 5 pound chain was so tight it had turned into a deadly noose. The wound was so deep it was nearly to the bone. No food. No water. Locked in a yard, alone and covered with feces. Brutus had only a few days to live.

The letter continued:

"You wouldn't treat a dog that way."

No, you and I wouldn't. But too many people would—and do. Brutus's story is sadly not unique or unlike the multitudes of others the ASPCA Humane Law Enforcement Team witnesses day in and day out.

By the time a neighbor called us about Brutus, the dog was nearly dead. Empowered by law to investigate cases of cruelty and seize abused animals, our ASPCA Humane Law Enforcement Agents entered the backyard. Brutus was too weak to bark or even stand up. In the place of a collar was a 5 pound chain that was so tight it was embedded into his neck. He was so emaciated that you could count every single rib on his weak, dehydrated body.

The Agents knelt down, speaking gently to Brutus. They didn't want to frighten him so they moved very slowly—and at first, they didn't pet him.

Then they saw it. Brutus was wagging his tail. He was barely moving, but yes—the poor, sick dog was saying, "Welcome, friends!"

Brutus was rushed to the ASPCA Bergh Memorial Animal Hospital where he was examined by expert veterinarians who immediately discovered the severity of his abuse and the gaping wound where his collar should have been. Several major surgeries were required to close the wound and repair the tissue around Brutus's neck. While he went through rehabilitation for his injuries, our certified behaviorists spent time showering Brutus with the love, affection and socialization skills he had lived without for so many years.

Brutus's abuser was charged with animal cruelty, and now Brutus is eagerly waiting for a new loving home.

Such numbers can be effective, but a writer should use them sparingly. A news release crammed with statistics tends to overwhelm the reader. Consequently, efforts are often made to dramatize statistics in a way that paints a more vivid picture for readers and viewers. Gun control advocates, for example, say that 13 children are killed daily by guns in the United States—the equivalent of 365 Columbine High School killings each year. Antismoking advocates describe the number of deaths each day attributed to smoking as the equivalent of two loaded 747s crashing every day. On a less horrific note, Kimberly-Clark said it sold 4.5 billion rolls of toilet paper annually—enough to stretch from the earth to the sun. One can also dramatize statistical percentages by putting them in terms that people can readily understand. For example, one MIT professor was quoted as saying, "You can take a flight every day for 21,000 years before you would be statistically likely to be in a fatal plane crash."

Surveys and Polls — The public and the media express a great deal of interest in what might be called popularity ratings. During a presidential election campaign, various polls and surveys about who is ahead and why seem to dominate coverage. People are also interested in what product ranks number one in cost or satisfaction or what airline is first in service or legroom.

Polls and surveys are related to the persuasion technique called the *bandwagon*. The idea is to show overwhelming support for a particular idea or product by saying that "four out of five doctors recommend..." or that "Most voters support..." Consequently, everyone should get on the "bandwagon."

Various organizations use polls and surveys as a way of getting media publicity and brand recognition. A mattress company once did a poll on how many people slept in the nude. Gillette launched a campaign urging young men to shave more often by citing an online survey that only 3 percent of women liked scruffy men. The possibilities are endless, and the use of surveys as publicity opportunities is elaborated upon in Chapter 3.

Examples — A general statement becomes more persuasive when a specific example can clarify and reinforce the core information. A utility company, when announcing a 5 percent rate increase, often clarifies what this means by giving the example that the average consumer will pay about $5 more per month for electricity. The railroad industry, competing with the trucking industry, gives the example that moving freight by train is three times more fuel efficient than using trucks. A school district fighting for more funds could bolster its case by giving examples of overcrowded classrooms, high teacher/student ratios, and poor student achievement compared to wealthier school districts.

Testimonials — A testimonial is usually a form of source credibility that comes from individuals who have directly benefited from using a product, program, or service. Thus, a happy consumer is quoted in a news release or an advertisement about how much he or she likes a particular product or service. A university might use favorable quotes from outstanding alumni about the value of their education. A celebrity on a television talk show might say that a particular drug helped her cope with severe migraine headaches. Another form of testimonial are consumer websites such as Trip Advisor or YELP where individuals often post favorable comments about restaurants, hotels, and other products or services.

Some testimonials are indirect, but powerful. The American Cancer Society may have a woman in her 50s who is dying of lung cancer do a testimonial about the dangers of smoking. Mothers Against Drunk Driving (MADD) might feature a medical doctor talking about the effects of three drinks on a driver's perceptions. Or, it might feature a young woman who is the victim of a drunk driver talking about the many months of hospitalization and plastic surgery that she had to endure.

Endorsements — The endorsement is a variant of the testimonial. Advocacy on behalf of a product, service, or event is often called *third-party endorsement* because often there is no personal connection, as in a testimonial, to what is being endorsed. One form of endorsement is the proclamation by a mayor, governor, or even the president endorsing the celebration of a particular day or week. Thus, we have officials proclaiming "Red Cross Day" or "National Library Week." The U.S. president even proclaims "National Heart Health Month" to help raise public awareness about heart disease. In almost all of these cases, some organization has requested the proclamation as part of its public relations strategy.

> *"Popularization happens when you get credible third parties to speak for your brand, and that is something PR can do extremely well."* Scott Keogh, chief marketing officer of Audi

A second kind of endorsement is generated by media. These endorsements can come through editorials, product reviews, surveys, news stories, and even blogs. A daily newspaper may endorse a political candidate or a community cause, review restaurants and movies, or even compile a reader survey ranking the best pizza joints. Popular bloggers can make or break a new product by posting favorable or unfavorable reviews. Magazines endorse products by giving "seals of approval" that can be touted by the winning companies. *Allure* magazine, for example, has "Best of Beauty" awards in two categories: beauty products chosen by readers and those chosen by the magazine's editors with the help of beauty experts. *Allure*'s "endorsement" pays dividends for many companies. Becca, a maker of a high-end crème blush, saw its sales triple after winning an award.

The third kind of endorsement is statements by experts, credible organizations, and celebrities; these usually involve payment or some other kind of financial arrangement. Thus, a well-known medical specialist may publicly state that a particular brand of exercise equipment is best for general conditioning. Organizations such as the American Dental Association, the National Safety Council, and even a group called Cosmetic Executive Women also endorse a variety of products and services.

Celebrities, of course, endorse all kinds of products and services for a fee. Indeed, they often make more money in endorsements than from what they actually do for a living. The primary purpose of using celebrity endorsements, as already noted, is to add glamour and attract passive audiences that ordinarily would not pay attention to information about a particular product or service. But the cost isn't cheap. Nicole Kidman got $5 million for 2 minutes of airtime endorsing Chanel No. 5, and Madonna charged designer Donatella Versace $12 million to endorse a spring collection.

A new concept is the Twitter endorsement. Canadian teen singer Justin Bieber told 100,000 of his followers about his experience flying Air New Zealand and pronounced it a "great airline." Shaquille O'Neal told his more than 2 million followers about his endorsement deal with Enlyten, an electrolyte strip brand, and continued to tweet about the company along with all the other products he has endorsed.

Emotional Appeals — Persuasive messages often play on our emotions. Fundraising letters from nonprofit groups often use this writing device, as demonstrated in the letter from the American Society for the Prevention of Cruelty to Animals (ASPCA) in the PR Casebook below. Another fundraising letter, one from the Marine Mammal Center in California, began as follows:

> How could someone?
>
> She was just 5 months old, a feisty sea lion pup practicing what sea lions do best—fishing. But this time the fish she swallowed had a hook in it. She was yanked violently from the sea and left dangling from the end of a fishing rod. Then someone aimed a high-powered crossbow and fired a metal arrow point-blank, directly into her neck.

Such "stories" can elicit strong emotions and galvanize public opinion, but they can also backfire. If the appeal is too strong or shocking, it tends to raise people's ego defenses, and they tune out the unpleasant message. The key is to relieve the stressful situation by providing a happy ending. In the case of the ASPCA and Marine Mammal letters, the animals were successfully rescued.

Fear arousal is another form of emotional appeal. Many public service information campaigns use this approach. First, a question is raised. An example is "What would happen if your child were thrown through the windshield in an accident?" or "What would happen to your wife and children if you died of a heart attack?" Second, a relatively simple solution is given to relieve the emotional anxiety. A young mother is told that her baby should always be placed in a secured infant seat. Or, the husband might be encouraged to regularly exercise or even buy more life insurance. Moderate fear arousal, accompanied by a relatively simple suggestion for avoiding the situation, is considered an effective persuasive technique.

Psychologists say the most effective emotional appeal is one coupled with facts and figures. The emotional appeal attracts interest, but logical arguments also are needed. See additional tips about persuasion concepts below.

Persuasive Speaking

Psychologists have found that successful speakers (and salespeople) use several persuasion techniques:

» **Yes–yes.** Start with points with which the audience agrees to develop a pattern of "yes" answers. Getting agreement to a basic premise often means that the receiver will agree to the logically developed conclusion.

» **Offer structured choices.** Give choices that force the audience to choose between A and B. College officials may ask audiences, "Do you want to raise taxes or raise tuition?" Political candidates ask, "Do you want more free enterprise or government telling you what to do?"

» **Seek partial commitment.**   Get a commitment for some action on the part of the receiver. This leaves the door open for commitment to other parts of the proposal at a later date. "You don't need to decide on the new insurance plan now, but please attend the employee orientation program on Thursday."

» **Ask for more, settle for less.**   Submit a complete public relations program to management, but be prepared to compromise by dropping certain parts of the program. It has become almost a cliché that a department asks for a larger budget than it expects to receive.

A persuasive speech can be one sided or offer several sides of an issue, depending on the audience. A series of studies by Carl Hovland and his associates at Yale conducted in the 1950s determined that one-sided speeches were most effective with persons favorable to the message, whereas two-sided speeches were most effective with audiences that might be neutral or opposed to the message.

Persuasion and Propaganda

No discussion of persuasion would be complete without mentioning propaganda and the techniques associated with it. According to Garth S. Jowett and Victoria O'Donnell, in their book *Propaganda and Persuasion,* "Propaganda is the deliberate and systematic attempt to shape perceptions, manipulate cognitions, and direct behavior to achieve a response that furthers the desired intent of the propagandist." Its roots go back to the seventeenth century, when the Roman Catholic Church set up the *congregatio de propaganda* ("congregation for propagating the faith"). The word took on extremely negative connotations in the early twentieth century as a result of World Wars I and II, when competing sides accused each other of using "propaganda" to further their military objectives.

Some critics have even argued that propaganda, in the broadest sense of the word, also includes the advertising and public relations activity of such diverse entities as Exxon and the Sierra Club. Social scientists, however, say that the word *propaganda* should be used only to denote activity that sells a belief system or constitutes political or ideological dogma. Advertising and public relations messages for commercial purposes, however, do use several techniques commonly associated with propaganda. The following are the most common:

» **Plain folks.**   An approach often used by individuals to show humble beginnings and empathy with the average citizen. Political candidates, in particular, are quite fond of telling about their "humble" beginnings.

» **Testimonial.**   A frequently used device to achieve credibility, as discussed earlier. A well-known expert, popular celebrity, or average citizen gives testimony about the value of a product or the wisdom of a decision.

» **Bandwagon.**   The implication or direct statement that everyone wants the product or that the idea has overwhelming support; for example, "Millions of Americans support a ban on assault rifles" or "Every leading expert believes global warming is a significant problem."

- » **Card stacking.**   The selection of facts and data to build an overwhelming case on one side of the issue while concealing the other side. Critics of the Beijing Olympics, for example, emphasized China's record on human rights, but didn't mention that the quality of life for most Chinese has risen dramatically in the past 20 years.
- » **Transfer.**   The technique of associating the person, product, or organization with something that has high status, visibility, or credibility. Many corporations, for example, pay millions to be official sponsors of the Olympic Games, hoping that the public will associate their products with excellence.
- » **Glittering generalities.**   The technique of associating a cause, product, or idea with favorable abstractions such as freedom, justice, democracy, and the American way. American oil companies lobby for drilling in the Arctic wilderness or the Gulf Coast to keep "America energy independent." Other groups opposed to immigration reform or foreign imports use the rallying cry of "American jobs for Americans."

A student of public relations should be aware of these techniques to make certain that he or she doesn't intentionally use them to deceive and mislead the public. Ethical responsibilities exist in every form of persuasive communication; guidelines are discussed next.

The Ethics of Persuasion

Robert Heath, coauthor of *Rhetorical and Critical Approaches of Public Relations*, writes, "A theme that runs throughout the practice and criticism of public relations is its ability to influence what people think and how they act." He continues:

> Even when practitioners' efforts fail to establish their point of view or to foster the interests of their sponsors and influence stakeholders, their comments become part of the fabric of thought and over time add to societal beliefs and actions. Practitioners create opinions, reinforce them, or draw on them to advocate new opinions and actions.

To many observers, persuasion is a somewhat unsavory activity that distorts the truth and manipulates people. The public distrusts professional "persuaders," and the media often refer to public relations people and political consultants as *spin doctors*. Yet persuasion is an integral part of society. Everyone uses words and visual symbols to share and evaluate information, shape beliefs, and convince others to do or think things. The ancient Greeks recognized rhetoric, the "science of persuasion," as worthy of study and an essential part of public discourse.

In sum, persuasion is not a nasty concept. It does not have to be manipulative, propagandistic, or full of half-truths. Thomas Collins, manager of public affairs for Mobil Oil Company, sounded this theme when he addressed the annual meeting of the Public Relations Association of Indonesia. He said:

> PR counselors must ensure the messages we create, package, and target are efficient and cost-effective, but they must also be believable. This requires that the images we engineer reflect the reality of our clients' existence. We reject deliberate fabrication

because bogus images pollute the public mind and do not serve the public interest, and ultimately undermine the trust we seek.... The essential ingredient underlying any successful relationship is trust.

A large measure of public trust, which Collins just described, comes from telling the truth and distributing accurate information. A core value of the Arthur W. Page Society, a group of senior communication executives, is to tell the truth by providing an accurate picture of the company's character, ideals, and practice.

> **What people in PR have to understand is not only do you have the facts on your side, you have to know how to communicate them.** Peter Pitts, senior vice president of Manning, Selvage, & Lee

The IPRA has a core tenet in its charter that states, "Each member shall refrain from subordinating the truth to other requirements." And the PRSA states, in part, "We adhere to the highest standards of accuracy and truth in advancing the interests of those we represent and in communicating with the public." On a more practical note, *PRWeek* writer Anita Chabria simply says, "Do make sure your statements are accurate. The press will pick up on even innocent mistakes as potential lies." See the Tips for Success below for a model regarding personal ethics.

Tips for Success   An Ethics Test for Public Relations Writers

Persuasive efforts require an ethical framework for decision making. Professors Sherry Baker of Brigham Young University and David Martinson of Florida International University have developed a model they call the TARES test. Public relations writers should test their persuasive communication against five basic moral principles:

1. *Truthfulness.* Are you just telling the literal truth and not the whole story? "Truthfulness (material and substantial completeness) is essential to ethical persuasion."

2. *Authenticity.* Are you intentionally deceiving or manipulating others for the practitioner's or client's self-interest? "A good test for authenticity is whether the practitioner is willing to openly, publicly, and personally be identified as the persuader in a particular circumstance."

3. *Respect.* Are you giving respect to your audience as persons of dignity and intelligence? "Respect for others includes facilitating their ability to be informed and to make good choices."

4. *Equity:* Are you taking advantage of the public's lack of knowledge or information about a topic, a product, or an idea? "The equity/fairness principle requires, for example, that practitioners avoid fashioning persuasive messages in such a manner as to play upon the vulnerabilities of a particular audience."

5. *Social responsibility:* Are your persuasive efforts serving the broader public interest? "Ethically proactive practitioners find ways to make positive contributions to the common good as an integral part of achieving their basic professional objectives."

Thus, it can be seen that public relations writers are, by definition, advocates in the marketplace of public opinion. It is their professional and personal responsibility, however, to be persuasive, using techniques that are forthright, truthful, and socially acceptable. Professor Richard L. Johannesen of Northern Illinois University lists the following persuasive techniques that should be avoided in persuasive writing:

» Do not use false, fabricated, misrepresented, distorted, or irrelevant evidence to support arguments or claims.

» Do not intentionally use specious, unsupported, or illogical reasoning.

» Do not represent yourself as informed or as an "expert" on a subject when you are not.

» Do not use irrelevant appeals to divert attention or scrutiny from the issue at hand. Among the appeals that commonly serve such a purpose are "smear" attacks on an opponent's character, appeals to hatred and bigotry, innuendo, and "God" or "devil" terms that cause intense but unreflective positive or negative reactions.

» Do not ask your audience to link your idea or proposal to emotion-laden values, motives, or goals to which it is not actually related.

» Do not deceive your audience by concealing your real purpose, your self-interest, the group you represent, or your position as an advocate of a viewpoint.

» Do not distort, hide, or misrepresent the number, scope, intensity, or undesirable features of consequences.

» Do not use emotional appeals that lack a supporting basis of evidence or reasoning and would therefore not be accepted if the audience had time and opportunity to examine the subject itself.

» Do not oversimplify complex situations into simplistic, two-valued, either/or, polar views or choices.

» Do not pretend certainty when tentativeness and degrees of probability would be more accurate.

» Do not advocate something in which you do not believe yourself.

It is also clear that as a writer of persuasive messages the public relations writer is more than a technician or a "hired gun." Responsibility to a client or an employer should never override responsibility to the profession, the law, and the public interest. This is discussed further in Chapter 11.

However, writers often lack the technical and legal expertise to know whether information provided to them is accurate. Robert Heath explains, "In this regard, they are uneasy partners in the public relations process. They are often given information regarding managerial or operating decisions or practices that they are expected to report as though it were true and just."

This does not excuse writers from ethical responsibility. Heath continues:

The problem of reporting information that they cannot personally verify does not excuse them from being responsible communicators. Their responsibility is to demand that the most accurate information be provided and the evaluation be the best available.

Summary

Persuasion: As Old as Civilization

» Persuasion is part of the human fabric and has been around since the ancient Greeks.

» The Greek concept of *ethos*, *logos*, and *pathos* is known today as source credibility, logical argument, and emotional appeal.

» Public relations writers spend most of their day crafting and disseminating messages that will persuade and motivate people.

The Basics of Communication

» The basic communication model has four elements: sender, message, channel (medium), and receiver.

» Multiple channels should be used to communicate a message in order to reach the largest audience.

» In public relations, there is no such thing as the "general public." Messages are designed for specific publics or audiences that are segmented by interests, gender, education, income, etc.

Theories of Communication

» Several useful theories provide insight as to how people are persuaded and motivated. Public relations writers should be familiar with such theories as (1) media uses and gratification, (2) cognitive dissonance, (3) framing, (4) diffusion and adoption, and (5) hierarchy of needs.

» Mass and directed media messages are most influential in the awareness and interest stages of the adoption process. Opinion leaders and peers are influential in the later stages.

» Public relations writers, as part of message design, use the technique of framing—selecting certain facts, situations, and a context that are then disseminated by the media.

Factors in Persuasive Writing

» A number of factors are involved in preparing persuasive messages. They include (1) audience analysis, (2) source credibility, (3) appeal to self-interest, (4) clarity of message, (5) timing and context, (6) use of symbols and slogans, (7) semantics, and (8) suggestions for action.

» A communicator recognizes that there are two kinds of audiences—passive and active (information seeking)—and plans messages and communication channels accordingly.

» Some persuasive writing devices are the use of (1) drama and human interest, (2) statistics, (3) surveys and polls, (4) examples, (5) testimonials, (6) endorsements, and (7) emotional appeals.

» Endorsements are part of establishing credibility for a message. There are several kinds of endorsements: (1) proclamations by civic officials, (2) editorials and product reviews by the media, (3) statements by trade or professional organizations, and (4) celebrity spokespersons.

» Emotional appeals and fear arousal are most effective when accompanied by suggestions and solutions for solving the situation.

Persuasive Speaking

» Persuasive speaking techniques include (1) using yes–yes, (2) offering a structured choice, (3) seeking partial commitment, and (4) asking for more, settling for less.

» Highly educated audiences or those who are neutral or opposed to the topic are most persuaded by two-sided argument.

Persuasion and Propaganda

» Some common techniques of propaganda include (1) plain folks, (2) testimonial, (3) bandwagon, (4) card stacking, (5) transfer, and (6) glittering generalities. All, to some degree, are also used in public relations writing.

The Ethics of Persuasion

» Persuasion should not be manipulative and misleading. It should be based on truthful information and the presentation of facts and ideas in the marketplace of public discussion.

Skill Building Activities

1. A state university, facing major cuts in its public funding, wants to persuade the state legislature and the taxpaying public to not make any budget cuts. Use drama, statistics, surveys and polls, examples, testimonials, endorsements, and emotional appeals to make a persuasive argument.

2. The concept of channeling is discussed in terms of tailoring messages to audience self-interests. A city zoo wants to increase memberships and donations. Identify the message theme you would use for the following audiences: (a) business and industry, (b) teachers, (c) parents, (d) senior citizens, and (e) conservation groups.

3. Public relations and advertising practitioners often use experts and celebrities to build credibility and acceptance for the product. Select (1) an expert endorser and (2) a celebrity that you would use for each of the following situations: (a) lightweight luggage, (b) suntan lotion, (c) a laptop computer, (d) hiking boots, and (e) a high-end outdoor gas grill.

4. The text points out that passive audiences and active (information-seeking) audiences require different kinds of messages and media channels. Given this situation, what kinds of messages and media would you use to reach passive audiences about National Breast Cancer Awareness Month? By the same token, what information and media channels would you use to satisfy active audiences?

5. The TARES model on page 54 suggests that public relations practitioners should consider five moral principles when they communicate with the public. Here's a practical situation: A student accuses the swim coach of forcing her to have sex with him. The coach claims the encounter was consensual, but the student is threatening to file a rape charge unless the university takes action. The administration, in order to avoid unfavorable publicity, convinces the coach to resign by giving him a $100,000 separation agreement. The director of university relations tells you to write a news release that the coach has voluntarily resigned to "explore new challenges" and that the university "appreciates his fine work building the swim team." No other details are mentioned. Would the news release meet the principles outlined in the TARES test?

Media Resources

Baldwin, J. H., Perry, S. D., and Moffitt, M. A. (2004). *Communication Theories for Everyday Life*. Boston: Allyn & Bacon.

Bowen, S. A. (2007). *Ethics and Public Relations*. Retrieved from Institute for Public Relations website: www.instituteforpr.org.

Cialdini, R. (2001, October). "Harnessing the Science of Persuasion." *Harvard Business Review* (HBR 72-79

Damon, D. (2010, May 9). "Applause, Please, for Early Adopters." *New York Times*, BU6.

Frymer, A. B., and Nadler, M. K. (2010). *Persuasion: Integrating Theory Research and Practice*, 2nd edition. Dubuque: Kendall/Hunt Publishing.

Hansen-Horn, T. L., and Neff, B. D. (2008). *Public Relations: From Theory to Practice*. Boston: Allyn & Bacon.

Lee, S. T., and and Cheng, I. H. (2011). "Characteristics and Dimensions of Ethical Leadership in Public Relations." *Journal of Public Relations Research*, 23(1), 46–74.

O'Quinn, K. (2009, February). "The Elements of Persuasion: Three Principles That Will Strengthen Any Appeal." *Public Relations Tactics*, 20.

Perloff, R. (2010). *The Dynamics of Persuasion: Communication and Attitudes in the 21st Century*, 4th edition. Clifton, NJ: Taylor & Francis.

Smith, T. (2011, February 16). "Improving Your Written Communication Skills." Retrieved from Little Things Matter blog, www.littlethings.matter.com/blog.

Finding and Making News

3

» **After reading this chapter, you will be able to:**

» Understand the key factors that make information newsworthy

» Find news in your organization

» Harness creativity and brainstorming techniques

» Apply various strategies and tactics that generate news coverage

---

The Challenge of Making News

A major purpose of many public relations programs is to provide information to the media in the hope that it will be published or broadcast. The resulting coverage is called *publicity*. The public relations writer who writes and places stories in the media is commonly referred to as a *publicist*.

Effective publicists need to know three things. First, they must be thoroughly familiar with traditional journalistic news values. Second, they must know where to find news and how to select the angle that will be most interesting to journalists and the public. Third, they must be problem solvers and come up with creative publicity tactics that effectively break through a forest of competing messages. These topics are the subject of this chapter.

Indeed, the publicist must navigate at least four obstacles on the way to generating coverage in the news media. The first obstacle is media gatekeepers. Reporters and editors decide what information qualifies as news and is worthy of being published or broadcast. Only one sentence or paragraph of the news release that you spent hours on may be used or, more often than not, the entire release might be thrown away.

The second obstacle is the incredibly shrinking news hole. The increasing migration of advertising to the Internet, for example, has caused most daily newspapers and many magazines to reduce the number of pages in each issue, which has also affected the amount of space available for news and features. This, in turn, has increased the competition for getting material published, because publications literally receive hundreds of news releases and story ideas every day.

The third obstacle is the fragmentation of traditional mass media, and it is no longer possible to reach the larger public through a single medium or digital platform. That means that today's public relations writer must be adept at preparing and packaging publicity materials in a variety of formats—for print, broadcast, video, direct mail, email, and the Web. Increasingly, interactive social media sites are being used (see Chapter 12).

Information overload is the fourth obstacle. In today's world of 24/7 news, everything from suburban weeklies to cable channels, online networks, and websites compete for an individual's attention. As a consequence, your organization's news may never even get the audience's attention.

Overcoming these obstacles can be a daunting task for any publicist responsible for informing, persuading, and motivating various audiences on behalf of an employer or client. You can take several steps, however, to make your efforts more effective. These include (1) understanding news values, (2) targeting the right media with your information, (3) thinking continuously about the interests of the readers or listeners, (4) keeping in mind the objectives of the client or employer, and (5) exercising creativity in thinking about how to present information that will meet the requirements of media gatekeepers.

What Makes News

Students in news writing classes are taught the basic components of what constitutes "news." Publicists must also be familiar with these elements if they are to generate the kind of information that appeals to *media gatekeepers*. The following is a brief overview of traditional news values from a public relations perspective.

Timeliness

Timeliness may be the most important characteristic of news. By definition, news must be current. A publicist can make a story angle timely in four ways.

Provide Immediate Notification — One way to make news timely is to announce something when it happens. An organization should contact the media as soon as an event occurs. This might be the announcement of a new CEO, the merger of two companies, the launch of a new product or service, or even the settlement of a labor dispute. Such items are fairly routine and don't require much creativity, because the emphasis is on providing the basic facts. A delay in conveying this kind of information, however, could result in a news item being rejected as "old news."

Relate Messages to Breaking News — A second approach is providing information or story ideas that relate to an event or situation that is already being extensively covered by the news media and the topic of public discussion. A good example is how a tax and financial planning firm, Gilman Ciocia, used the U.S. government's announcement of a tax stimulus package to issue a news release reminding people that they had to complete their tax returns in order to get a rebate check. Even scandal can provide a publicist with a timely opportunity. While the media were having a field day covering the revelations that Governor Eliot Spitzer of New York was a client of a high-end prostitution service, publicist Michael Darden successfully arranged to have his client, couples expert Rich Hammons, appear on the *Oprah & Friends* XM satellite radio show.

> " *In the public relations business, the name of the game is finding a hook that links your press release to the news.* " Joshua Harris, reporter for *The Wall Street Journal*

Another tactic is to relate the organization's products or services to another event that has national recognition and interest. Kimberly-Clark and its public relations firm, Ketchum, used this approach to publicize its toilet tissue by capitalizing on the effects of America's potty break during the halftime of the Super Bowl. The company used former player and coach Mike Ditka to be a spokesperson and sponsored an essay contest, "Share Your Cloggiest Moment." The efforts generated considerable media coverage, and 98 percent of the media placements mentioned that Scott Bath Tissue dissolves four times faster than the leading brand—something to consider for Super Bowl fans racing to the bathroom during the long commercial breaks.

An organization, however, must be careful not to capitalize on a conflict or natural disaster that is dominating the news. Kenneth Cole, a shoe designer brand, was roundly criticized for insensitivity when its publicist posted a tweet relating to the Egyptian revolution that overthrew the government. The text was "Millions are in uproar in #Cairo. Rumor is they heard our new spring collection is now available online at http://bit/KCairo-KC." Tweeters wasted no time lambasting the company, and one joked that the company probably would have sent the following tweet after Hurricane Katrina devastated New Orleans: "People from New Orleans are flooding into Kenneth Cole stores!"

Tap Ongoing Issues and Controversies — At other times, a topic or issue generates media and public interest over a period of weeks and months. For example, health care issues continue to hold media interest, so pharmaceutical firms tailor their news releases around the idea that new "wonder drugs" are a cost-effective way to reduce hospital stays. Travel publicists also successfully place articles in travel magazines about how to save money on a European vacation when the dollar sinks to new lows against the euro.

Global warming and environmentalism also get frequent media coverage. First Act, one of the world's leading makers of musical instruments, successfully placed a story with the *Los Angeles Times* about its "green guitars" during the annual convention of the International Music Products Association in that city. Indeed, positioning a product as environmentally friendly seems to generate more media coverage. H.J. Heinz Company, for example, switched to a new type of bottle that ordinarily would not generate much media interest. The company, however, positioned the new bottle as more "green" because it used Coke's plant-bottle technology. As a result, about 260 news articles were generated.

Relate Messages to National Holidays — A fourth approach is offering information linked to holidays that are already on the public agenda. Auto clubs and insurance companies, for example, have excellent placement success with articles about safe driving just before the Labor Day and July Fourth holiday weekends, when millions of Americans take to the road. Even April Fool's Day can be used as a hook. Mr. Handyman International, for example, used the day to send a news release not to be "fooled" by handyman scam artists when hiring professionals to do home improvements. It cautioned homeowners not to fall for such pitches as "I have a special offer that's good only for today."

Halloween is another timely holiday. The American Academy of Ophthalmology issued a news release warning that "some ghoulish things can happen to your eyes" unless you take some precautions. The same theme was sounded by the American Optometric Association, which said that masks can be very scary if they limit your peripheral vision. Of course, the American Association of Orthodontists, which knows about candy and teeth, sent out a news release about the "tricks treats can play" and offered orthodontic tips.

At Thanksgiving, Butterball Turkey achieves a publicity bonanza by operating a Turkey Talk-Line and website (www.butterball.com), which is used by about 200,000 novice cooks each year. Information about Butterball's hotline, plus articles about how to cook a turkey, receives considerable print and broadcast coverage. One story that usually gets media pickup is a summary of what questions callers ask. One common question is "What is the best way to thaw a turkey?" And almost 20,000 people asked that question in a recent year.

Christmas is the major season for purchasing children's toys, so the media are receptive to news releases from toy manufacturers about new products on the market. Duracell capitalizes on the holiday gift-giving season with its annual "Duracell Kids' Choice Toy Survey." It publicizes a "Top 10" toy list based on a survey of children in YMCA afternoon programs. Ameritech used the holiday season to release publicity material about its home security systems, which will protect all of those packages under the tree. The American College of Gastroenterologists reminded people to see a doctor if all the holiday food and drink cause stomach problems.

Trade groups and nonprofits also designate national days, weeks, and months as a news angle. See the Tips for Success on page 63.

Prominence

The news media rarely cover the grand opening of a store or anything else unless there is a prominent person with star power involved. For example, a bank might use a music or film celebrity from the 1960s to open a new branch to attract senior citizens as customers. Home Depot got publicity mileage by having Brad Pitt appear at a news conference to talk about the company's partnership with Pitt and Global Green to rebuild New Orleans.

Beauty queens still attract attention too, even in New York City. When the city inaugurated its 311 number to answer citizen questions about such mundane things as how to recycle trash, Miss Universe was enlisted to make a call and ask a question about a swimming pool's hours of operation. The *New York Times* carried a photo of the 18-year-old beauty queen from the Dominican Republic talking on the phone and devoted 16 column inches to the new service. The headline: "Miss Universe Dials 311 (Don't Ask for Her Number)."

Tips for Success   Celebrate! It's National Bagel Day

National organizations and trade groups often designate a day, a week, or even a month to focus on a cause, an industry, or even a product. February 10 happens to be National Bagel Day, so bagel manufacturers use the opportunity to publicize the merits of their product.

Bruegger's Bagels, for example, conducted a survey among its Facebook fan base to find out about their favorite bagels. Anyone filling out the survey got a coupon for three free bagels on February 10. The result was that (1) store traffic doubled, (2) more than 70,000 people redeemed the coupon, and more than 200,000 bagels were given away. In addition, there was TV coverage in 14 markets and more than 200 stories ran in local newspapers.

If a special day, week, or month is well organized and promoted, it can provide a focal point for media coverage on an annual basis. Breast Cancer Awareness Week, for example, was started more than 20 years ago by ICI Pharmaceuticals with the assistance of its public relations firm, Burson-Marsteller. The week is still going strong with a coalition of 17 organizations supporting a variety of educational efforts and events during the designated week. As a result of continued media coverage, the majority of American women now recognize the phrase "early detection."

However, experts say Breast Cancer Awareness Week is an exception in a very crowded field. "Clients often think these national days are a fantastic way to get publicity when in fact it is one of the least interesting kinds of news you can present to the media," says Audrey Knoth, vice president at Pennsylvania-based Goldman & Associates.

Echoing Knoth's thoughts is Reg Henry, a columnist at the *Pittsburgh Post-Gazette*. He notes, "The Awareness Month industry has proliferated to such an extent that observances often overlap and the result is almost nobody is aware of anything." Making his point is a partial list of designated weeks from Chase's Calendar of Events (www.chases.com) for the first week of May. The list includes: (1) Be Kind to Animals Week, (2) National Family Week, (3) Reading Is Fun Week, (4) Teacher Appreciation Week, (5) Astronomy Week, (6) National Wildflower Week, and (7) National Nurses Week. After all that, it's no wonder that May 7 is designated as the "Great American Grump Out."

If you insist on creating a special day, week, or month for your client, *PRWeek* suggests the following tips:

+   Do have an educational component or call to action.

+   Do make sure the campaign has a human element.

+   Do find credible experts and partners for the media to interview.

The presence of movie stars, rock stars, and professional athletes at special events invariably draws crowds and the media, but an organization can attract media coverage by using other kinds of prominent people as well. An immunization clinic for low-income children usually gets first-page coverage if a governor, or even a mayor, pays a visit. A former astronaut or a retired Olympic medalist visiting a local high school also generates media interest. The National Education Association (NEA), shown in Figure 3.1, kicks off its annual Read Across America program every year with prominent individuals such as First Lady Michelle Obama.

> **❝❝If a celebrity doesn't show up to an event or party, what will the media write about?❞❞**
>
> Lori Levine, founder of Flying Television, a talent booking and brokering firm

Many events, of course, don't have the high-priced glamour of Brad Pitt or the high public visibility of a First Lady, but you can still gain from the use of officials and other well-known individuals in quotes and pictures. One common tactic is the award photograph. Organizations often honor prominent individuals, which attracts media coverage. Even photographs of an organization's national president giving an award can generate publicity in local media.

Note that prominence is not restricted to people; it also extends to organizations. Large multinational corporations such as ExxonMobil and Wal-Mart automatically get more media attention, because they control so many resources and affect so many lives. If you work for a smaller, less prominent company, you will have to try much harder to get media coverage.

Proximity

Surveys have shown that the news releases most acceptable to media gatekeepers are those with a local angle. These stories, often called **hometowners,** are custom tailored for an individual's local newspaper or broadcast station by emphasizing the local angle in the first paragraph of the news release. One study, by Professor Linda Morton at the University of Oklahoma, found that 36 percent of hometown releases from a major university were published as opposed to less than 10 percent of the generalized news releases.

FIGURE 3.1 Many events get good media coverage because prominent people attend them. The National Education Association (NEA) always kicks off its annual Read Across America program with prominent individuals. Here, First Lady Michelle Obama (right) watches the arrival of the Dr. Seuss Cat in the Hat character along with Librarian of Congress James Billington (left) and U.S. Education Secretary Arne Duncan.

Obviously, the local angle has strong news value. Whenever possible, it is important to "localize" information by including local dealers, retailers, and other area representatives in a news release for a particular city. A case in point is the announcement that the Dr Pepper/Snapple Group pledged $15 million to build or fix 2,000 playgrounds over three years. Such an announcement doesn't generate much interest, but a new playground in a particular town or small city would probably generate considerable coverage in the local media.

Today it is easy to localize news releases and to tailor them to specific kinds of media by using software applications that can automatically merge the names of local people into a news release. An insurance company, for example, may announce that 150 of its agents nationwide qualified for induction into the "Million Dollar Roundtable" in sales. The publicist would localize this event by using software to insert the names of individual agents into the lead paragraph of the news release. Thus, a newspaper editor in Lexington, Kentucky, would receive a news release that begins, "Denise Smith of Lexington, an agent for Northwestern Mutual Insurance Company, has been inducted into the company's 'Million Dollar Roundtable.' " The names of the other 149 agents, who live elsewhere, would not be mentioned. Hometown news releases are discussed further in Chapter 5.

Another form of localizing is highlighting various aspects of a person's background in different publications. In the case of Denise Smith, various audiences would be interested in her achievement. For example, the weekly newspaper in the small town where Denise graduated from high school needs a news release that mentions Denise's parents, her graduation year, and the fact that she was president of the senior class. In contrast, the suburban weekly in Lexington would appreciate a paragraph giving her business address and noting the fact that she is the past chair of the local planning commission. A trade newspaper covering the insurance industry would be more interested in a news release that details her professional career.

In sum, always keep the local angle in mind when you write a news release. This often requires additional research and writing, but the resulting media coverage is worth the effort. As news correspondent Mort Rosenblum once wrote, "A dogfight in Brooklyn is bigger than a revolution in China."

Significance

Any situation or event that can affect a substantial number of people is significant. Global warming continues to be a hot topic, so to speak, but the concept and the scientific debate about the problem are somewhat abstract to the public. Publicists for environmental groups have worked to make the topic more significant to the average person by focusing on a popular consumer item.

The Natural Resources Defense Council (NRDC), for example, points out that consuming bottled water is not environmentally friendly because it takes oil to make all of those plastic bottles and only a quarter of them are ever recycled. The result is about a billion pounds of plastic bottles clogging landfills every year. In addition, the transport of bottled water contributes to greenhouse gases, a major source of global warming. The transport of a case of bottled water from Fiji to Los Angeles, for example, produces about 7 pounds of greenhouse gases on its 5,500-mile journey.

The major media coverage of the NDRC's "Think Outside the Bottle" campaign has, of course, become a significant issue for the $11 billion American bottled water industry. Bottlers such as Coca-Cola are publicizing their efforts to make thinner, more ecologically correct plastic bottles, but publicists from manufacturers of tap water filters also are finding renewed media interest in their products.

In judging significance, you must know not only *how many* people will be affected but also *who* will be affected. A major task, of course, is to convince media gatekeepers that the issue, product, or service is significant to their readers, listeners, or viewers. In sum, be prepared when the journalist says, "So what?"

Unusualness

Anything out of the ordinary attracts press interest and public attention. The presence of a giant inflated King Kong hugging an office building in Portland to promote the Oregon lottery is certainly unusual. So is a 75-foot birthday cake in the shape of a snake that the San Diego Zoo made to celebrate its 75th year of operation. Even the National Education Association (NEA) got media coverage for its Read Across America campaign by staging events with a costumed Dr. Seuss character.

Many products are pretty ordinary, so it's always a challenge for a publicist to think of something "unusual" that will attract media interest. Heckel Consumer Adhesives, the parent company of the Duck brand of duct tape, decided on a series of unusual events featuring the tape. One such effort was inviting students to design prom dresses made of duct tape. That led to a duct tape fashion show in New York where all the designer dresses were fashioned out of duct tape. The company also exhibited a giant American flag made entirely of multicolored duct tape in New York on Flag Day.

Melanie Amato, director of advertising and research for the Heckel Company, told *PRWeek* that all Duck brand public relations efforts have to involve four elements the company wants the brand to convey: They have to be fun, they have to project friendliness, they must display resourcefulness, and they have to be imaginative. Such efforts have made the Duck brand the number-one brand in the United States.

The opening of a new bank branch also falls into the category of less than exciting news. The typical ribbon cutting won't cut it, so to speak, so publicists need to be more creative in thinking up something more unusual. Colorado-based Peter Webb Public Relations came up with a winner for Safeway Select Bank in Phoenix with a campaign called "Cold Hard Cash." The firm capitalized on Phoenix's high summer heat by creating 10 ice sculptures fashioned into various shapes, such as computer terminals, grocery bags, and dollar signs. Frozen inside each sculpture was a cash prize; $10,000 was divided among the sculptures. More than 400 people registered, and 10 got the chance to melt their ice blocks and take home whatever cash they could get their hands on by rubbing away the ice. The *Arizona Republic* ran a front-page business story and photo of the event, and the three network affiliates also covered the event.

Human Interest

People like to read about other people. That is why the news media often focus on the lives of the rich and famous and why *People*, *USWeekly*, and *OK!* magazines are such a success. The love lives of movie stars and the antics of rock singers provide constant grist for the tabloids and the mainstream media.

Interest in people, however, is not restricted to celebrities. A journalist may focus on the plight of one family on welfare to illustrate the problems of the entire social services system. Television news, which tries to explain complex issues in a minute or two, often uses the vehicle of personalizing an issue by letting one individual or family speak. Indeed, people would rather listen to the problems of a welfare mother in her own words than view a series of bar charts showing the decline in state and federal funding for social services.

Public relations writers also have opportunities to humanize stories. Here are some examples:

» A university graduates 10,000 students every spring, but the news release focuses on an 80-year-old grandmother who is graduating with her daughter and her granddaughter.

» A company that manufactures a voice-activated cellular phone for disabled people prepares a feature article about how the phone helps one disabled Iraq war veteran.

» A brilliant research engineer for a computer company is the subject of a company feature story that is sent to the trade press.

» A food bank, after getting permission, gives the names of clients to a reporter who wants to interview some of them for a story on how the agency has helped them.

» *The Wall Street Journal* is approached about doing an in-depth profile on the first woman CEO in the company's history.

» A food and cooking channel is approached for an interview with a restaurant chef who will demonstrate an easy-to-do recipe for calorie counters.

Conflict

When two or more groups advocate different views on a topic of current interest, this creates news. Indeed, reporters often fuel the controversy by quoting one side and then asking the other side for a comment.

Organizations get coverage when they state a position or viewpoint regarding a local or even international controversy. Labor disputes between management and employees, for example, are often accompanied by competing media interviews, news releases, and picket lines, as shown in Figure 3.2.

Organizations, groups, and individuals also receive media coverage for stating various opinions about such ongoing controversies as global warming, illegal immigrants, universal health care, the price of gasoline, and increased automobile fuel efficiency. Managed health care and patient rights, for example, were supported by such groups as the American Medical Association and the Trial Lawyers of America, but strongly opposed by insurance companies and the United States Chamber of Commerce.

In sum, publicists should be aware of ongoing public issues and conflicts to determine if their clients or employers should publicize a particular viewpoint or perspective on the issue. A publicist, however, must first assess whether the particular issue is relevant to the organization. Rising gasoline prices may not be particularly relevant to a chain of restaurants, but they may be highly relevant to delivery services such as UPS, FedEx, or even local pizza parlors that deliver.

FIGURE 3.2 Conflict is a basic news value so various groups stage demonstrations to publicize their cause. In this situation, Wisconsin teachers march through the rotunda of the state capitol to protest pending legislation that would revoke collective bargaining rights for state workers.

Newness

Advertising and marketing people say that the two words they find most useful are "new" and "free." You will seldom use "free," but you should constantly search for something "new." Any news release announcing a new product or service has a good chance of being published if you can convince a journalist that it is truly "new." Apple's iPhone and iPad, for example, generated thousands of articles and blog posts when they were introduced. New, updated models of these products, however, receive considerably less media coverage.

New uses for old products are the basis of most food publicity. There is nothing new about potatoes, walnuts, yams, or avocados; yet food editors steadily publish new recipes for these and scores of other foods. A growing trend is relating food to health. James Cury, executive editor of Epicurious (www.epicurious.com), told *O'Dwyer's PR Newsletter* that he likes food publicists who can relate their products to such buzzwords as "organic," "clean," and "sustainable."

Publicists for new products often work to have reviews of the product published in leading publications. A favorable product review by Walt Mossberg in *The Wall Street Journal* is the Holy Grail for the high-tech consumer goods industry. By the same token, a review or product mention on Epicurious or in *Food & Wine* is highly sought by the food and restaurant industry.

One note of caution: Journalists and bloggers are somewhat distrustful of claims that a product or service is "new." In many cases, the only thing "new" about a product is the packaging; from an editor's point of view, that is not "new" enough. High-technology companies have also raised reporter suspicions about new products that often turn out to be what cynical reporters call "vaporware."

How to Find News

Now that you understand what constitutes traditional news values, you should have a good framework as you approach the process of finding news.

Internal News Sources

The first step in finding news is to become totally familiar with the organization you represent. One way to learn about an organization is to do research. This involves looking at a variety of sources, including the following:

» **Important papers.** Policy statements, annual reports, organizational charts, position papers, research reports, market share, sales projections, and biographies of top managers.

» **Periodicals.** Current and past issues of employee newsletters and magazines, plus Intranet archives.

» **Clipping files.** Published articles and online postings about the organization and the industry. Use Google alerts to compile mentions about the organization or the industry across the spectrum of articles, social media postings, and blogger comments.

» **Other materials.** Copies of the organization's brochures, speeches, PowerPoint presentations, videos, and sales material.

In addition to reviewing all of these sources, you must also play the role of roving reporter. Talk to a variety of people, ask a lot of questions, and constantly be on the lookout for something new or different. Most news stories don't come to you; you have to seek them out. Most people have no clue whether an event or a situation is newsworthy, so you must be alert to clues and hints as well as hard facts.

A new process or technique may be just business as usual to a production manager, but it might lead you to several possible stories. For example, AlliedSignal received news coverage for a new fiber by pointing out that it could be used in automobile seat belts to slow the movement of a passenger's upper body in a collision. The company publicist did two things to make this story newsworthy. First, she related the new fiber to a use that the public could readily understand. Second, she arranged and distributed an interesting photo that showed the manufacturing process.

A change in work schedules may affect traffic and thus be important to the community. Personnel changes and promotions may be of interest to editors of business and trade papers. A new contract, which means hiring new employees, might be important to the regional economy. By the same token, the loss of a major contract—and its implications for the employees and community—also qualifies as significant news.

External News Sources

Ideas on how to get your organization into the news can come from almost any source. For example, you might attend a Rotary Club meeting and hear a speaker talk about the national need to train more engineers in the computer sciences. That might spur you to investigate how the problem affects your employer or client. This, in turn, might lead to the idea that you could generate some media coverage by telling the media what your company is doing about the problem, such as providing college scholarships or even recruiting engineers from other nations. Or perhaps you might offer the media an interview with the company president, who can articulate some solutions to the problem. In sum, you must continually train yourself to think about how a news event relates to your organization or client.

An example is what the Department of Child and Family Services of New Hampshire did when the media reported that a newborn baby had been abandoned. The day the story hit, Renee Robertie, communications director of the agency, notified all state dailies, radio stations, and television stations the options a mother experiencing a crisis pregnancy would have if she were to call Child and Family Services. This got an immediate media response, and there were many stories of the "What a mother can do" type, which prominently featured the agency's services. Robertie adds, "The key to success is being prepared so when something like this happens, you are able to step in as the voice of authority and provide reporters with good data and soundbites at a moment's notice."

Another source of story ideas are publications and blogs covering the public relations industry. They often include results of surveys indicating what the "hot" topics are in the media. A national survey of newspaper editors by News USA found, for example, that the topic of health care generated the most interest. Other topics of media interest included retirement strategies, medicine, environment, food, education, consumer issues, recreation, and finance. A survey of food editors by another firm indicated that low-fat and fat-free recipes were "hot" topics.

How to Create News

There is no hard-and-fast definition of what is news. A Hearst editor once declared, probably with more truth than he realized, "News is what I say it is." It's also true that most "news" is created by individuals and organizations that plan activities and events for the purpose of creating public awareness to inform, persuade, and motivate.

Historian Daniel Boorstin even coined the term **pseudoevent** to describe events and situations that are created primarily for the sake of generating press coverage. Some classic examples of the pseudoevent are the Miss America pageant, the Academy Awards, and the Super Bowl.

The Miss America contest was a creative solution by a publicist hired by the Atlantic City Chamber of Commerce, which wanted to extend the summer tourist season past Labor Day. The contest was not only good for business in Atlantic City, but it also provided the American public with a form of entertainment.

The Academy Awards, another American institution, also had its beginnings as a publicity stunt. It was begun in 1929 by the movie industry to garner media attention and also increase movie attendance during the Depression. Today, the Academy Awards has grown into a $100 million industry that not only continues to increase box office revenue for winning films, but also serves as a showcase for celebrities, jewelers, designers, and even caterers.

The Super Bowl is essentially a pseudoevent invented by the National Football League (NFL) in 1961. As in the case of the Miss America pageant, it was originally designed to extend the professional football season and increase revenues. The event generates considerable hype and media coverage. In 2011 more than 110 million people watched the XLV game (Roman numerals is part of the hype) as two American teams vied for the "world" championship.

Although the term *pseudoevent* has a somewhat negative connotation, the main point is that such events are considered legitimate news if they also meet the standards of traditional news values. A news conference by Apple executives announcing a new product, for example, may be carefully planned and staged, but it also provides useful information to the media and consumers. A product launch of a new cleaning product from Clorox, in contrast, requires considerable creativity to generate media attention.

Indeed, such creativity and vision are essential attributes for work in public relations, but such things are difficult to teach and even more difficult to learn. Hal Lancaster, author of the "Managing Your Career" column in *The Wall Street Journal*, says creative people share some common traits: "keen powers of observation, a restless curiosity, the ability to identify issues others miss, a talent for generating a large number of ideas, persistent questioning of the norm, and a knack for seeing established structures in new ways."

> **❝ PR firms of the future will still need creative people capable of generating brilliant ideas. ❞**
> Miles Nadal, CEO of MDC Partners

Judith Rich, now a Chicago-based creativity consultant and former vice president of Ketchum, gives some tips for developing your creative instincts. Writing in PRSA's *The Strategist*, she offers the following:

» Look at things with new eyes.

» Hear with new ears. Listen to the world outside of yourself for a change.

» Ask questions and start learning from people you might not usually consider as resources.

» Stop saying or thinking "No." Be more open to possibilities.

» Keep things in perspective and, at the same time, try to expand your horizons.

» Don't be put off by rules that may not even exist. Don't limit your thinking.

» Get excited about ideas that may change the way you do business.

» Inspiration comes easiest to a rested mind. Escape, on occasion, from the daily grind.

» Record ideas whenever they occur.

» Don't just look for information and ideas in the "normal" places.

» Draw heavily on personal resources—remember the content of your dreams. Your unconscious may sometimes solve your conscious concerns.

Brainstorming

Public relations firms such as Ketchum generate creative ideas by conducting **brainstorming** sessions. The point of such a session is to encourage everyone to express any idea that comes to mind. An idea may be totally impractical and off the wall, but no one is allowed to say "it won't work" or "that's a stupid idea." This inhibits creative thinking and people's willingness to participate.

All ideas, regardless of their merit, can be placed on a flip chart or whiteboard. As the team looks at all the ideas, new ideas that combine and refine the original list are usually generated. Another approach is to have everyone write down the three ideas they believe are best, based on feasibility, cost-effectiveness, and timeliness. Those ideas receiving the most interest and enthusiasm are then thoroughly discussed and shaped into a comprehensive campaign.

> ❝Brainstorming should never be a struggle to find one great idea. It's about coming up with as many ideas as possible in a short amount of time.❞ Sam Harrison, author of *IdeaSpotting: How to Find Your Next Great Idea*

A good example of how brainstorming can lead to a creative program is PETCO. The objective of the brainstorming session was to create an event that would attract customers but also raise PETCO's brand on a national level. A brainstorming session by the public relations staff finally came up with the idea of hosting a Chihuahua race—not exactly a breed associated with racing. The team publicized the races at various stores and also put race footage on YouTube and on PETCO's website. In addition, the original idea was expanded to taking dogs on the road, holding races in TV studios and parking lots in partnership with dog-rescue groups and local humane societies.

You, too, can create news in a variety of ways. See the Tips for Success on page 73 for a list of 32 ways to generate news. The next several pages highlight various tactics for making news: (1) special events, (2) contests, (3) polls and surveys, (4) top 10 lists, (5) stunts, (6) product demonstrations, (7) rallies and protests, (8) personal appearances, and (9) awards.

Special Events

Any number of events are created or staged to attract media attention and make the public aware of a new product, service, or idea. This goes back to the concept of the "triggering event" that becomes the catalyst for individuals to adopt new ideas or modify their behavior.

It is less certain, however, what exactly constitutes a "special event." Some say that any event that is out of the ordinary is "special," whereas others say that any event can be "special" if the organizers are particularly creative at organizing it. At times, things that occur on a routine basis can become the focus of media coverage if some creativity is exercised. A new store may quietly open its doors for business, or it can have a "grand opening" with a celebrity cutting the ribbon and a circus in the parking lot.

The opening of a new museum or facility usually requires special event planning to ensure attendance and media coverage. The International Civil Rights Center & Museum in Greensboro, North Carolina, was opened on the 50th anniversary of the historic event in which four black students sat at a "whites-only" counter in a local Woolworth's store. The public relations team from RLF Communications (1) organized pre-opening activities with the city and local groups, (2) produced a public service announcement, (3) announced the opening festivities on Twitter, Facebook, and YouTube, and (4) conducted media tours for journalists. The opening event drew 3,000 spectators and about 200 members of various media. The result was more than 700 broadcast stories and multiple print articles, as well as 11,000 new followers on Facebook. How to plan an event is the focus of Chapter 17.

New product launches are also often accompanied by special events, launch parties, and activities. When J. K. Rowling's *Harry Potter and the Deathly Hallows* was released, bookstores around the world hosted midnight parties the night of the release complete with games, costumed customers, and music. Borders, for example, reported that 800,000 people attended the parties at its locations around the world. A party atmosphere is usually present in Apple stores on the first day of sales for a new iPhone or iPad, when the media converge on the first person to buy the new product. See Figure 2.1 on page 39.

Major long-term campaigns are often launched with an event. Dow Chemical's campaign to raise public awareness about the lack of access to clean water for one billion people started with an event during the start of Earth Week in 2010. A 6K

Tips for Success   32 Ways to Create News for Your Organization

1. Make a statement about a breaking news event.
2. Cooperate with another organization on a joint project.
3. Tie in with a newspaper or broadcast station on a mutual project.
4. Conduct a poll or survey.
5. Issue a report.
6. Tie in with a celebrity endorsement or appearance.
7. Take part in a controversial issue.
8. Arrange for a testimonial.
9. Arrange for a speech.
10. Make an analysis or prediction.
11. Tie in with a charity or a cause.
12. Hold an election.
13. Announce an appointment.
14. Celebrate an anniversary.
15. Issue a summary of facts.
16. Tie in with a popular movie.
17. Make a trip.
18. Make an award.
19. Hold a contest.
20. Pass a resolution.
21. Appear before a public body.
22. Organize a special event.
23. Issue a top 10 list.
24. Release a letter you received (with permission).
25. Adapt national reports and surveys for local use.
26. Stage a debate.
27. Tie in to a well-known holiday.
28. Honor an institution.
29. Organize a tour.
30. Inspect a project.
31. Become part of a trend.
32. Issue a commendation.

run (the average distance many women and children walk each day to fetch water) was held in 200 cities and 81 nations to raise public awareness about the issue and Dow's water and environmental efforts. In addition, a series of concerts and educational activities complemented the run. The event led to 3,000 media placements in 40 nations, 20,000 tweets, and 40 million Facebook mentions.

Anniversaries also are events. Major milestones in the age of a product, an institution, or a service are often a catalyst to generate media coverage. Detroit, for example, held a year-long celebration of its 300th birthday, and a resort hotel in Florida celebrated its 75th anniversary by inviting all the couples married there back for a three-day celebration. The Museum of Art in Dallas celebrated its 100th anniversary by keeping the museum open 100 hours straight for a series of events occurring at all hours of the day. Hershey's celebrated its centennial by unveiling the world's largest Hershey's Kiss during a gala event at the company's headquarters (see Figure 3.3).

San Diego's Seaport Village celebrated its 30th anniversary by having 30 contestants ride a 115-year-old carousel for 30 hours for a chance to win $10,000. The carousel was used because it was the focal point of the village, but additional activities such as live music, magic shows, radio giveaways, and street entertainers also took place while Seaport businesses remained open for the entire 30 hours. The campaign generated about 45 media placements, including on CNN, and visits to Seaport's website increased 93 percent. Parking revenues even increased 45 percent during the 30-hour period.

Creating a compelling special event is more art than science. However, reporter Anita Chabria of *PRWeek* says an event or a publicity stunt should do more than grab media coverage. She writes, "While their wacky or weird imagery may draw camera crews quicker than an interstate pile-up, the end result is that consumers receive a message about the brand identity."

FIGURE 3.3 Special events can also include publicity stunts. Hershey's celebrated the 100th anniversary of its Kisses Chocolate brand at a gala event in which it unveiled the world's largest piece of chocolate. The 12-foot-high structure weighing 30,540 pounds was certified by *Guinness Book of Records* representative Jane Boatfield (left), who attended the unveiling.

Contests

The contest is a common device for creating news. In fact, it is often advised that "if all else fails, sponsor a contest." There are contests of every kind. At the local level, the American Legion sponsors high-school essay contests on citizenship, and Ford dealers enthusiastically sponsor safe-driving contests for teenagers. There are also numerous Elvis look-alike contests, tractor pulls, beauty pageants, and eating contests.

Here are some examples of successful contests:

» Kimberly-Clark, as a way of promoting its toilet tissue as a tie-in with the Super Bowl (described earlier), sponsored an essay contest on the topic "Share Your Cloggiest Moment." The winner received $25,000 to "Flush Your Worries Away."

» Pepsi, instead of spending $20 million on advertising for the Super Bowl, sponsored an online contest where nonprofit organizations who got the most votes received grants ranging from $5,000 to $250,000 for projects. For example, the high school band in Cedar Park, Texas, got $25,000 for new uniforms by getting the town's residents to vote for the project. Other competitors for grants turned to their personal networks on Facebook and Twitter to gain support, which extended the Pepsi brand.

» Nikon, seeking to expand its brand reputation in digital video, created an online video contest that encouraged people to submit a short "Day in a Life" themed video. The top 50 videos were then showcased on the Nikon website. *PRWeek* noted, "A great way to demonstrate the product benefit and generate user content." The contest generated 2,200 submissions, 500,000 visits to the Nikon website, and more than 7,000 social media followers.

» Mattel generated more than one million online votes in a contest to choose a new career for Barbie. The winning career was computer engineer, which was announced in a news conference at the 2010 New York Toy Fair. The campaign stressed career aspirations for women, and it caused a 144 percent sales increase for the "I Can Be" line. Barbie's new career generated hundreds of print and broadcast stories, as well as 450,000 Facebook fans.

» Intel has sponsored the annual Intel Science Talent Search competition since 1998 to encourage high school students in the sciences. Forty high school seniors are named as finalists, and the top winner receives a $100,000 scholarship.

Publicists and organizations, however, are warned that sponsoring a contest takes a great deal of planning and legal considerations. David Ward, a reporter for *PRWeek*, gives these tips:

> **❝ The hardest thing is to convince the media that your contest or sweepstakes is going to deliver real informational interest as opposed to pure commercialism. ❞** Julie Hall, vice president of Schneider & Associates

DO

» Get your planning done early. There are a lot of regulations and details.

» Get some well-known celebrities involved to establish credibility and interest with the media.

» Think local, especially when you get down to finalists. Most outlets love stories on locals who do well.

DON'T

» Go it alone. Hire experts to help you run the contest or sweepstakes.

» Worry about the size of the prize. Even million-dollar prizes don't attract media attention.

» Go to media too often unless they are cosponsors. The same outlet won't cover the launch, the finalists, and the winner. Spread various angles around to various media.

Polls and Surveys

The media seem to be fascinated by polls and surveys of all kinds. Public opinion is highly valued, and much attention is given to what the public thinks about issues, lifestyles, political candidates, product quality, and so on.

Author Peter Godwin, writing in *The New York Times Magazine*, says the public's fascination with polls and surveys is "a uniquely American trait—a weakness for personal comparative analysis." He continues, "It's the reason we devour surveys about success, weight, love, family and happiness. And why not? Political polls tell us only how one candidate is faring against another. Polls about other people's personal lives let us gauge how we're faring relative to our friends and neighbors."

Given this media and public interest, many organizations are willing to oblige by conducting polls and surveys on a range of topics. Larry Chiagouris and Ann Middleman, in a *Public Relations Quarterly* article, say that "publicity-driven research" is one of the most effective ways for an organization to get media coverage and position itself as a market leader. In addition, surveys have high credibility because quantitative data is perceived as accurate. It should be noted, however, that not all surveys are created equal. Online surveys, in particular, are less reliable and scientific because respondents self-select themselves to participate.

Here are some examples of polls or surveys that have generated media coverage:

» HP Labs analyzed 16.2 million tweets on 3,361 topics during a 40-day period and found that the traditional media (newspapers, magazines, radio, TV) drives more Twitter trends than do bloggers. An earlier study found that most blogs draw their primary content from traditional news sources rather than each other.\

» Cheapflights.com (www.cheapflights.com) conducted a survey on its blog site about airplane etiquette. It found that 2,000 respondents thought the incessant talker embodied the most offensive behavior. Ranking a close second was the person who immediately reclines his or her seat—into your lap. Third was the armrest hog, which tied with the carry-on luggage champ who tries to stuff suitcases in the overhead rack.

» Celebrity news site OMG! and Yahoo! conducted a Mother's Day poll (http://omg.yahoo.com) of 2,000 adults to find out what famous moms are hot and who's not. Angelina Jolie got the highest number of votes for the title of hottest celebrity mom, but Sandra Bullock got the nod as the mom that most respondents would like as their own mom. Hillary Clinton, however, was considered the best mom to go to for advice, and Penelope Cruz won the top spot for the best post-baby body. On the negative side, parents selected Britney Spears as the celebrity mom they would least likely have as a babysitter.

» Sex and romance are popular topics for surveys and polls. Even Euro RSCG Worldwide PR issued a 22-page report titled "Love (and Sex) in the Age of Social Media" based in part on an online survey of 1,000 Americans. It concluded that "the Internet is the most powerful erogenous zone the world has ever known." Among its findings, which found their way into many media stories, are some of the following stats: (1) Forty-one percent of the male and 28 percent of the female respondents said it was possible to have a romantic relationship with someone on the Internet, (2) the majority of men and women believe online dating has become a mainstream activity, (3) sixty-two percent of the men and 65 percent of the women think the Internet has made it easier for people to cheat on their partners, and (4) "more men than women think it's possible to have romantic or erotic relationships on the Internet."

Nancy Hicks, a senior vice president of Hill & Knowlton, says surveys and polls can be marvelous publicity opportunities if a few guidelines are followed. In an article for *PR Tactics*, she suggests:

» **The topic** should be timely, have news value, and fit the needs of the organization.
» **The research firm** should be one that has credibility with journalists. That's why many commissioned surveys are done by the Gallup Organization or similar nationally known firms.
» **The survey questions** should be framed to elicit newsworthy findings.

Hicks also suggests paying attention to how the material is packaged for the press. "The lead in the news release should feature the most newsworthy findings, not what is of most interest to the sponsoring organization," says Hicks.

Media kits, discussed in Chapter 6, should include background information on the organization and on the research firm, a summary of the major research findings, and simple charts and graphs that can be easily reproduced as part of a news story. See the Tips for Success on page 78 for more information on how to conduct and report the results of a survey or poll.

Top 10 Lists

A good alternative to polls and surveys is to simply compile a "top 10 list." Fashion trade groups announce the "Top 10 Best Dressed Women," and environmental groups compile lists of the "Top 10 Polluters." Newspapers and magazines also get into the act by compiling a list of the "Top 10 College Basketball Players" or the "Top 10 Newsmakers" of the year.

Briggs & Stratton, a leading manufacturer of lawn mowers and other outdoor power equipment, builds its brand identity with an annual list of the "Top 10 Lawns in America." And the American Kennel Club gets publicity for announcing the 10 top dog breeds in the United States. The Labrador retriever has been the most popular dog in the United States for a number of years, but the Yorkshire terrier is now in the number two spot, beating out the golden retriever and the German shepherd.

There are endless possibilities for top 10 lists. The California Association of Winegrowers issued a news release on Earth Day, for example, giving the "Top 10 Reasons California Wines Are an Eco-Friendly Choice." A San Francisco public relations firm even got 8 inches in *The Wall Street Journal* for its "Top 10 Most Humiliating Public Relations Gaffes of the Year." First place went to the District of Columbia Housing Authority, which issued a news release about a drug bust the night before the raid was planned. The dealers heard about it on the radio and failed to make an appearance.

Product Demonstrations

The objective of a product demonstration is to have consumers or media representatives actually see how a product performs. Auto manufacturers do "product demonstrations" by inviting journalists to test-drive a new model. Hotels and resorts invite travel writers to spend a weekend at the facility. Food companies do demonstrations by getting representatives on cooking and home shows. Weber Grills, for example, hires well-known chefs to give tips on talk shows about the proper way to barbecue.

A product demonstration can take many forms. PetSmart publicized a grand opening of a store by offering its pet grooming services to some of the local Humane Society's grubbiest guests and then putting them on display for adoption. It was a win-win situation. The idea clearly demonstrated the value of its grooming services and also placed the new store in a favorable light because of its community outreach. Groupon took another approach. It demonstrated its daily online "deals" by having a contest to select an individual (20,000 applied) who would use only "Groupons" to travel around the United States for one year.

Tips for Success   How to Conduct a Credible Survey

A survey of topical interest can generate considerable publicity for an organization. Mark A. Schulman, president of a market research and opinion polling firm in New York, offers these tips in an article for *O'Dwyer's PR Report*:

+ Choose a topic that captures the interest of key targets and the media.
+ Results must not appear to be self-serving. Journalists look for balance. Don't shy away from some negative findings.
+ Find the story hook in advance by doing some preliminary research, often through focus groups.
+ Choose a sample size that will be credible. Don't skimp on sample size and undercut the project's appeal to media outlets. Sample the appropriate target groups.
+ Put a human face on the percentages. Sprinkle some respondent quotes into the report.
+ Plan your media strategy at the beginning of the process, not as an afterthought. Build excitement in the survey by including in the press kit some additional background material and sources to help the press build the story. Provide a list of outside experts who can be interviewed.
+ Provide key press contacts with an advance peek in exchange for premium coverage.
+ Don't sit on your data. Release it quickly. News events can make even the best study stale.
+ Release all the results, not just the ones that are favorable to your client.
+ Guidelines for release of survey results are issued by the American Association for Public Opinion Research (www.aapor.org) and the Council of American Survey Research Organizations (www.casro.org). You should always include information on the method of interview, the number of people interviewed, dates, and the exact question wording. Journalists may not use this information in their stories, but it gives them confidence that the survey findings are credible.

On occasion, a product demonstration is built around a social setting or junket. A cosmetic company, Styli-Style, introduced its newly designed flat makeup pencil at a New York champagne bar. It hired a celebrity makeup artist to demonstrate the various colors and to also apply makeup to the various journalists and guests attending the event. And Procter & Gamble introduced its new Head & Shoulders HydraZinc shampoo by taking editors to Arizona where they could experience the benefits of the zinc-rich desert landscape. Briefings included a celebrity stylist and a P&G research scientist to highlight the benefits of the HydraZinc formula. The result was articles about the new shampoo in such publications as *Elle*, *Shape*, and *Redbook*.

Publicity Stunts

Journalists often disparage publicity stunts, but, if they are highly creative and visual, they often get extensive media coverage. One popular theme is doing something that qualifies for the Guinness World Records. Some examples:

» Baskin-Robbins made the world's largest ice cream cake (5.5 tons) in one of the hottest spots on earth, Dubai, to celebrate International Ice Cream Month.

» Hidden Valley Ranch salad dressings sponsored the world's longest salad bar in New York's Central Park. It took 17,000 pounds of vegetables to make the salad, which, of course, was topped with Hidden Valley's Original Ranch dressing.

» Kraft Foods' Oreo brand set a Guinness world record by achieving 114,619 Facebook "likes" to a single posting in a 24-hour period. Oreo has the third-largest Facebook community of any brand worldwide with 16 million–plus fans in more than 20 nations.

Achieving a world record to generate publicity for a brand seems to be popular among corporations. Guinness World Records is actually a business that consults with organizations to figure out what records they can set for their brands and products. The process costs about $5,000 and includes having a judge verify the accomplishment as well as brainstorm other ideas for establishing some sort of world record.

> **❝ You need something that is fun and irresistible to get people's attention. ❞**
>
> Kathy Carliner, senior vice president of Golin Harris

Other kinds of stunts can be staged with a bit of creative thinking. A classic example is how the Queensland Tourist Authority (Australia) generated worldwide publicity for months by soliciting applicants for the "Best Job in the World." It was a six-month stint as a caretaker of an island on the Great Barrier Reef that included a $100,000 salary and a three-bedroom villa with a pool. The "job" attracted 34,000 applicants from practically every nation in the world who auditioned via video clips, which also found their way onto YouTube and other social media sites.

The eventual winner, a 34-year-old man from England, kept the publicity going by blogging about his experience, posting video updates, and conducting media interviews about living in "paradise." The campaign, which the Queensland Tourist Authority estimated to be worth about $130 million in publicity, was so successful that it received the Grand Prix award in public relations at the International Advertising Festival in Cannes, France.

In another example, a German software firm celebrated its listing on the New York Stock Exchange by converting a block of New York's financial district into a "beach party." It took 60 tons of sand, 5,000 beach balls, and several volleyball nets to accomplish the transition. Because of the visual element, the company received more extensive coverage than just a short paragraph on the business page. See the PR Casebook below to read about a publicity stunt by Baskin-Robbins.

Publicity stunts don't have to be elaborate or expensive, however. NBC's Oxygen Media, for example, wanted to raise awareness for its reality show, *Hair Battle Spectacular,* so it held a fantasy hair-sculpting competition in Times Square. And the Opera Company of Philadelphia created a mob gathering of 600 singers who mingled with regular shoppers at Macy's but burst out singing Handel's Hallelujah Chorus exactly at the stroke of noon. Greenpeace and other activist groups are also fond of staging publicity stunts because they give a highly visual element to their cause. See Figure 3.4 for a Greenpeace "performance" at a world conference on climate change.

Some publicity stunts, however, are not well conceived and become public relations blunders. In Florida, for example, an unemployment agency spent more

PR casebook

A Baskin-Robbins Publicity Stunt Retires Flavors with Style

Ice cream flavors come and go, so it's not exactly newsworthy. Baskin-Robbins and its public relations firm, Schneider Associates, solved this problem when the company decided to use a publicity stunt in 2010 to retire five flavors just before National Ice Cream Day on July 15th.

It was the company's 65th anniversary year, so Baskin-Robbins used the usual 65 retirement age to retire five flavors in a celebration at the company headquarters. The event consisted of a group of employees walking retired flavors down a pink carpet and placing them in an armored truck, which drove them to rest in a "deep freeze."

A satellite feed of the event included the company's executive chef talking about the history of each retired flavor. Public relations staff aggressively pitched the story to media markets in California, Chicago, and New York, where Baskin-Robbins had the most stores. National consumer media and food bloggers were also targeted. In addition, outreach was done via Facebook and Twitter and a video was posted on YouTube.

The result was stories in print media such as the *Chicago Tribune* and broadcast mentions on programs such as *World News* with Diane Sawyer and *CNN Express News.* Conan O'Brien tweeted about the flavor retirement and Jimmy Fallon and Craig Ferguson mentioned the story in their opening monologues. Most important, there was a "significant spike" in store traffic and sales during the week of the event.

Julie Hall, executive vice president of Schneider Associates, told *PRWeek* that the publicity stunt was successful because "...it engaged Baskin-Robbin employees and created visually powerful photos and video coverage to drive media coverage."

FIGURE 3.4 Greenpeace often engages in publicity stunts to generate media attention. Volunteers, for example, constructed a large life ring on the beach in Cancun, Mexico, during an international conference on global warming. It symbolized the need to rescue delegates from drowning in a sea of political self-interests and to support international agreements to limit the causes of global warming.

than $14,000 on superhero red capes for the unemployed as part of a "Cape-A-Bility Challenge" public relations campaign to defeat a cartoon character, "Dr. Evil Unemployment." Florida officials and taxpayers were not amused. In another situation, a little-known rock band, the Imperial Stars, staged an impromptu concert in the middle of a Los Angeles freeway, blocking several lanes of traffic. The LAPD and furious drivers were also not amused.

Rallies and Protests

A rally or protest generates news because one of the traditional news values, discussed earlier, is conflict. Some rallies involve thousands of protestors, such as a series of rallies throughout the United States to protest proposed legislation restricting the legal status of Hispanic immigrants. On a more modest scale, even a group of local high school students holding a rally protesting the firing of a favorite coach generates media interest.

Other groups use demonstrations as a tactic to publicize their cause. The Save Darfur Coalition, for example, organizes small groups of protestors to "picket" the offices of financial institutions and corporations that have investments in Sudan. They carry signs about companies condoning genocide and show graphic photos of victims.

Few television stations or newspapers can resist covering such rallies or protest demonstrations, each of which has high news value from the standpoint of human interest and conflict. Moreover, a rally or protest is highly visual, which is ideal for television coverage and newspaper photographs.

Although television often gives the impression that demonstrations are somewhat spontaneous events, the reality is that they are usually well planned and organized. The manuals of activist groups, for example, give guidelines on everything from contacting potential participants via an email network to appointing "marshals" who will ensure that the protestors won't destroy property or unnecessarily provoke police confrontations. The idea is to make a statement, not create a riot that will damage the organization's cause.

When planning a protest or demonstration, the media should be contacted in advance to ensure coverage. More than one rally has been rescheduled to accommodate the media. Prominent people and celebrities, if possible, should be asked to join the march or give a talk at a rally. Prominence, as activists know, is another important news value.

On a humorous note, Gillette capitalized on the media's tendency to cover protests. It organized a fake protest movement called the "National Organization of Social Crusaders Repulsed by Unshaven Faces (NoScruf)" to counter the trend of the unshaven look among young men. A group of young women were hired to do a mock demonstration in New York, complete with banners, bullhorns, and fake underarm hair to give the message, "We won't shave until you do." The effect was so real that a CNN producer on his way to work called in a news crew to cover it. See Figure 3.5 for an example of another Gillette publicity stunt.

FIGURE 3.5 Publicity stunts are primarily created to generate news. A key element is creating a stunt that is highly visual and lends itself to television or YouTube distribution. Gillette, for example, staged an event in New York's Times Square to promote its new Fusion razor by having future hall of famer pitcher Pedro Martinez (center) congratulate the two winners of the Fusion ProGlide "Ultimate Summer Job" contest.

Personal Appearances

Two kinds of personal appearances generate news. The first is the kind where the publicity is incidental to something else. The second is the appearance where the publicity is the only objective. Most typical of the first type is the situation where someone makes a speech to an organization. If the president of the XYZ Company addresses the local chamber of commerce, he will be heard by all who attend the meeting.

The audience for the speech, however, may be greatly increased if the media are supplied with copies of the speech, a news release, or several soundbites. As a general rule, every public appearance should be considered an opportunity for news both before and after the event. And, of course, there should always be an effort to get reporters to attend the meeting and get the story themselves.

Appearances where publicity is the sole objective take several forms. One is an appearance on a local radio or television talk show. There are numerous opportunities for appearing on such shows. For example, more than 1,000 radio stations (out of 10,000) in the nation now emphasize talk instead of music.

Talk shows with a national audience include *Meet the Press* and the *Today* show. The American Fly Fishing Trade Association (AFFTA), for example, scored a coup by getting on three major television shows in a three-day period. First was the *Late Show with David Letterman*, where Sister Carol Anne Corley ("The Tying Nun") enlightened the host about some of the finer points of the sport. The next morning, two AFFTA representatives—clad in boots, waders, and vests—garnered prime time in front of the *Today* show window in New York's Rockefeller Plaza. Chapter 9 discusses how to get on such shows.

Another approach is the media tour. Increasingly, this is done via satellite and the Internet to save travel time and costs. A **satellite media tour (SMT),** explained further in Chapter 9, is essentially the process of placing a spokesperson in a television studio and arranging for news anchors around the country to do a short interview via satellite. It is the same process that news programs use to get reports from their correspondents in the field.

Awards

Last, but not least, you can create news for your organization by giving and receiving awards. The California Pharmacists Association (CPhA), for example, inducts several outstanding pharmacists into its Hall of Fame every year at its state convention. By honoring these individuals, the organization also creates the opportunity to send a news release to the inductees' local newspapers, generating even more media coverage. The entertainment industry has numerous annual awards that are nationally televised, such as the country music awards shown in Figure 3.6.

At the local level, organizations give any number of awards. The YMCA honors the "Outstanding Woman of the Year," the chamber of commerce names the town's "Outstanding Business Owner of the Year," and even the local college honors the "Graduate of the Year" and the "Alumnus of the Year." If an organization receives an award, that also can generate news. Intel, for example, sent out a news release announcing that it was ranked number one in the "100 Best Corporate Citizens" list by *CRO*, a magazine for corporate responsibility practitioners.

FIGURE 3.6 Awards are often an opportunity to generate publicity for an organization or an industry. That's why we have the Academy Awards or even the annual Academy of Country Music Awards. Here, Dave Haywood, Hillary Scott, and Charles Kelley of Lady Antebellum show their awards for top vocal group and album of the year for "Need You Now."

At times, however, an award can be more hype than substance. The Hollywood Walk of Fame, sponsored by the Hollywood Chamber of Commerce, is somewhat suspect. The impression is that a celebrity gets a "star" embedded in cement because he or she has achieved something. The reality is that no "star" gets considered unless a film studio agrees to pay $15,000. In other words, the "award" often boils down to being part of a publicity campaign to bolster a star or promote an upcoming movie.

Summary

The Challenge of Making News

» A major objective of many public relations programs is to generate publicity for the employer or client.

» Publicity, however, is not an end in itself. It is a means to help achieve organizational goals and objectives.

What Makes News

» Publicists should thoroughly understand the basic news values of

(1) timeliness, (2) prominence, (3) proximity, (4) significance, (5) unusualness, (6) human interest, (7) conflict, and (8) newness.

» A national holiday or special week can be a "news hook" for media coverage.

How to Find News

» The first step in preparing publicity is to become thoroughly familiar with the company or organization through use of internal documents and interviews. Use of external sources, such as media and Web coverage, also is recommended.

» A public relations writer should constantly monitor current events and situations that may affect the organization and provide opportunities for publicity.

» The public relations writer's job is to identify story and news opportunities in developments and information that

regular employees of the organization may perceive as just "routine" activities.

How to Create News

» Problem-solving skills and creativity are required to generate publicity. One way to get creative ideas is through brainstorming with colleagues.

» Some tactics for generating news include (1) special events, (2) contests, (3) polls and surveys, (4) top 10 lists, (5) stunts, (6) product demonstrations, (7) rallies and protests, (8) personal appearances, and (9) awards.

» Polls and surveys, despite their questionable scientific basis, are popular with Americans if they are about topics that attract their interest—such as romance, sex, and money.

» Dull or routine developments and announcements can generate more media coverage if they are packaged as a publicity stunt.

Skill Building Activities

1. A popular local Mexican restaurant is celebrating its 10th anniversary next year. What activities and special events would you recommend to attract more customers and generate media coverage?

2. Surveys indicate that the topic of health generates a lot of media interest. How would a manufacturer of vacuum cleaners use this "hook" to generate some publicity for the company and its products?

3. A beer company is interested in doing some sort of poll or survey that would generate media coverage. What would you recommend?

4. An architectural firm likes the idea of creating a "top 10 list." What ideas do you have for such a list?

5. A major drugstore chain has developed a new App that provides free mobile health messages to pregnant women and moms. How would you generate media interest and publicity for this new service?

6. Organize an in-class brainstorming session to generate ideas about how the women's soccer team at the university can get more media coverage. Alternatively, conduct a brainstorming session on how you would organize a campus campaign to make students more aware of the dangers of binge drinking.

7. A national pizza chain is celebrating its 25th anniversary and wants to create a highly visual publicity stunt that will attract media coverage. What would you recommend?

Media Resources

Allen, K. (2011, February 26). "The Magic Word That Turns Non-stories into News." Retrieved from PRDaily, www.prdaily.com/main/articles.

Austin, C. (2009, January). "Fueling a Culture of Creativity." *Communication World*, January–February, 21–23.

"Bad Publicity: Better to Be Reviled than Ignored." (2011, February 26). *The Economist*, 70.

"Fifty Top Publicity Stunts." (2009, January). Retrieved from Taylor Herring Public Relations Blog, www.taylorherring.com/index.

Harrison, S. (2009, May). "Be Inspired to Innovate: Five Steps to Up Your Odds for Bigger and Better Ideas." *Communication World*, January–February, 17–19.

Hopper, J. (2010, March). "And the Survey Says... How to Create Surveys for PR Stories." *Public Relations Tactics*, 16.

Iny, D. (2011, May 12). "21 Ways to Create Compelling Content When You Don't Have a Clue." Retrieved from www.copyblogger.com.

Lewis, T. (2010, November 22). "Baskin-Robbins Gives Flavors the 'Deep Freeze.'" Retrieved from *PRWeek*, www.prweekus.com.

Nadal, M. (2010). "Talent Will Still Drive Tomorrow's PR Agency." *PRWeek*, 25.

Nolan, B. (2010, November 10). "How to Get Great PR for Your Event." Retrieved from Brooke Nolan's blog, www.brookenolan.com.

Rich, J. (2007, Spring). "Waiting for Inspiration: Why You Need to Be Prepared to Be Inspired." *Strategist*, 12–13.

Verlee, E. (2010, December). "Fifteen Ways Little Companies Can Get Media Coverage." *Ragan Report*, 15–16.

Working, R. (2011, February 14). "Sweet-Talking the Press: 5 Ways to Woo Journalists with Holiday-Themed Pitches." Retrieved from www.ragan.com/main/articles.

Working with Journalists and Bloggers

》》 After reading this chapter, you will be able to:

» Understand the importance of media relations

» Recognize that public relations personnel and journalists/bloggers are mutually dependent on each other

» Be familiar with the areas of friction that arise between public relations staff and journalists

» Establish a good working relationship with journalists and bloggers

» Understand how to be a spokesperson for an organization and organize a news conference or media tour

» Understand the daily etiquette of interacting with journalists and bloggers

» Effectively communicate in a crisis

The Importance of Media Relations

Media relations is a core activity in public relations work. Although public relations work now includes many other functions such as reputation management, communications strategy, community relations, and even crisis management, most surveys show that public relations personnel in organizations and public relations firms spend a large percentage of their time on media relations.

A survey by *PRWeek*, for example, found that media relations was the number one activity performed by corporate public relations departments. Another study by Corporate Communications International (CCI) found that media relations was a key function in 100 percent of the departments surveyed. Similar surveys of public relations firms also show that media relations is a major source of client billings. Indeed, public relations personnel are the primary contact between the organization and the media. Consequently, it is important to discuss the concepts of effective media relations and how to establish a good working relationship with journalists working in traditional and online media.

This chapter explores the symbiotic relationship between publicists and journalists from several perspectives. First we explore how publicists and journalists depend on each other. Then we examine various complaints and pet peeves

> **"*Media relations is the crux of all PR. It is about getting your clients in—and keeping your clients out of—the press.*"** Ray Kerin, executive director of media relations for Merck, as quoted in *PRWeek*

that public relations practitioners and journalists have about each other. The chapter concludes with guidelines for giving effective media interviews, organizing news conferences, conducting media tours, and handling crisis situations. By keeping these guidelines in mind, you will be able to build trusting and productive relationships with journalists.

The Media's Dependence on Public Relations

The reality of mass communications today is that reporters and editors spend most of their time processing information, not gathering it. And, although many reporters deny it, most of the information that appears in the media comes from public relations sources, which provide a constant stream of news releases, features, planned events, and tips to the media. Even Gary Putka, the Boston bureau chief of *The Wall Street Journal*, once admitted that "a good 50 percent" of the stories in the newspaper come from news releases.

A number of surveys and analyses of media content over the years have documented the media's reliance on public relations. One such study goes back to 1973, when L. V. Sigal wrote *Reporters and Officials: The Organization and Politics of Newsmaking*. He found that almost 60 percent of the front-page stories in the *New York Times* and the *Washington Post* came through routine bureaucratic channels, official proceedings, news releases and conferences, and other planned events. Just 25 percent were the products of investigative journalism. Sigal explained, "The reporter cannot depend on legwork alone to satisfy his paper's insatiable demand for news. He looks to official channels to provide him with newsworthy material day after day."

> **"*In a lot of ways, PR people do the legwork of journalists—feeding them stories and sources, and doing research.*"** Sheldon Rampton, research director of PRWatch, as quoted in the *New York Times*

More recent surveys bear out Sigal's original findings. *PRWeek* conducted a national survey of journalists and found that almost 60 percent used news releases "all the time" or "often." Another survey by Arketi Group found that 90 percent of the business journalists surveyed used industry sources and news releases to get basic information and story ideas. A third study by Bennett & Company found that 75 percent of the journalists surveyed said they used public relations sources for their stories. Organizational websites that usually include links to news releases and other publicity material are used by about 95 percent of journalists, according to a 2010 *PRWeek* survey.

All this amounts to what O. H. Gandy calls "information subsidies" to the press. In his book, *Beyond Agenda Setting: Information Subsidies and Public Policy*, he explains that material such as news releases constitutes a "subsidy," because the source "causes it to be made available at something less than the cost a user would face in the absence of a subsidy." In other words, public relations materials save media the time, money, and effort of gathering their own news. As one editor of the *San Jose* (CA) *Mercury News* once said, publicists are the newspaper's "unpaid reporters."

Today, traditional print and broadcast media have become even more dependent on public relations sources because newsroom staffs have drastically declined in recent years due to major drops in revenue from advertising. The American Society of News Editors reports that the number of reporters and editors has declined 35 percent since 2007, and the Pew Research Center reports that the number of broadcast journalists is now less than half of what it was in the peak employment period during the 1980s.

Many journalists, however, continue to deny any reliance on public relations sources. Denise E. DeLorme and Fred Fedler comment on this in a *Public Relations Review* article that offers a historical analysis of journalist hostility to public relations. They write:

> In one contradiction, journalists wanted information to be easily available, yet resented the men and women who made it available. By the mid-twentieth century, journalists were dependent upon PR practitioners for a large percentage of the stories appearing in newspapers. But admitting their dependence would shatter cherished ideals. Journalists were proud of their ability to uncover stories, verify details, and expose sham. Thus, they were unlikely to admit their dependence, lack of skepticism, failure to verify, and failure to expose every sham.

Public Relations' Dependence on the Media

The purpose of public relations, as mentioned throughout this book, is to inform, to shape opinions and attitudes, and to motivate. This can be accomplished only if people receive messages constantly and consistently. Consequently, public relations heavily relies on a variety of established media channels to (1) efficiently distribute information to millions of people, and (2) validate the credibility and value of the information to the public.

Efficient Distribution — The traditional media, even in the Internet age, continue to be cost-effective channels of communication. They are the multipliers that enable millions of people to receive a message at the same time. Thousands of newspapers and magazines, plus hundreds of radio, television, and cable outlets, enable the public relations communicator to reach large audiences over a widespread geographical area. *The Wall Street Journal*, for example, has a daily circulation of 2.1 million in contrast to a much more fragmented, smaller audience using a variety of news websites. The multiplier effect of traditional media is also evident in terms of the Internet. Research shows most blogs draw their primary content from stories in traditional media, and that mainstream media influence topic trends that dominate Twitter feeds. HP Labs, for example, found that "...social media behaves as a selective amplifier for the content generated by traditional media."

Validation of Information — The media's power and influence in a democratic society are based on the idea that reporters and editors serve as independent filters of information. They are generally perceived as more objective than public relations people, who represent a particular client or organization. This is important because the media, by inference, serve as third-party endorsers of your information.

Media gatekeepers give your information credibility and importance by deciding that it is newsworthy. The information is no longer from your organization, but from the *New York Times*, *The Wall Street Journal*, or CNN. Indeed, many public relations professionals talk about this as **earned media** because their message has "earned" the trust of media gatekeepers who publish or broadcast it as "news" at no cost to the organization. Advertising, in contrast, is called **paid media** because an organization buys space to distribute its messages in exactly the format that it specifies.

> **"** *The PR industry has been built on the knowledge that* earned media, *traditionally the most influential driver of customer behavior, is gold.* **"** Mark Hampton, CEO of Blanc & Otus, in *PRWeek*

Areas of Friction

The working relationship between public relations practitioners and journalists is based on mutual cooperation, trust, and respect. That doesn't mean, however, that the relationship is always smooth and free of friction. As in any relationship, each group has some pet peeves.

Complaints about Public Relations Personnel

Poorly Written Material — Journalists and popular bloggers receive hundreds of news releases every week. A significant percentage of them are poorly written. Often they (1) sound like an ad in paragraph form, (2) contain too many hype words such as "revolutionary, "cutting edge," and "state-of-the art," (3) don't include anything newsworthy, and (4) contain verbose sentences and paragraphs instead of concise, brief information.

Shotgun Distribution — A major sore spot for many editors and journalists is the large number of news releases they receive that reflect a total ignorance of a publication's format and content. Many reporters label such news releases as nothing but spam, and some get so irritated that they "blacklist" the senders to block any further messages from them.

Lack of Access — Journalists and bloggers often have difficulty contacting a public relations representative for an organization. Far too many organizational websites don't provide links to the public relations department or the names of press contacts with their email and phone numbers. News releases also raise ire when only the contact for the public relations firm is listed and not the contact person for the organization. At other times, reporters complain about corporate telephone trees that lead to voice-mail hell, or that public relations reps don't return calls or respond to an email query in a timely manner.

Trash and Trinkets — Journalists tend to resent the gimmicks that often accompany news releases and media kits. T-shirts, coasters, caps, paperweights, pens, and mugs are often sent, but *PRWeek* columnist Benedict Carver says these items are dull and overdone: "Everyone has 50 mugs and T-shirts." Journalists and bloggers also receive other items as part of a new product publicity kit; a new style of light bulb might be accompanied by a lamp, or an oversized sneaker might be sent with the announcement of a new line of shoes. Most journalists say such gimmicks are a waste of time and money because they don't really make the information more interesting or newsworthy. Matt Lake, a senior editor at CNET, an online publication, is even more blunt: "These things are really stupid."

Taking "No" for an Answer — Persistence is considered a plus in the public relations business, but journalists complain that many publicists don't understand the word "no." They resent being continually called or contacted about a topic or story idea.

Getting to the Point — Journalists are constantly working under deadline and don't have time for long chats and discussion. They get irritated with public relations representatives who can't get to the point in the first 30 seconds of a phone call or in the first two lines of an email.

Complaints about Journalists and Bloggers

Constant Flux — There is constant late-breaking news so journalists and editors are often indecisive as to whether a story about your organization or client will actually be used. Editors or bloggers may agree to use a story, but then change their minds if something else comes up that is more interesting. A reporter may even write a story, or a broadcaster interview a source, but space and time limitations often mean that the story will be axed at the last minute. Such indecision, although understandable, is annoying to publicists who often spend much time and energy to get a story placement.

Failure to Contact the Organization — Journalists, in a hurry to meet deadlines, often fail to contact your organization for a comment even though the story is directly related to the organization's policies, products, or services. Public relations personnel are also annoyed when a reporter calls at the last minute and wants an immediate off-the-cuff statement. Such an approach often forces an organization to say "no comment" because it hasn't had time to prepare an answer.

Lack of Preparation — Journalists and bloggers often fail to do their "homework" on the organization or the industry. This irritates public relations personnel who must bring a journalist up to speed on basic facts readily available on the website. It also annoys executives who are taking their valuable time to sit for an interview, only to have the reporter display a lack of knowledge about the company or industry and an inability to ask intelligent questions.

Bias — Some reporters already have a preconceived opinion about a story before they even check the facts. Consequently, their line of questioning is merely to reinforce their own predispositions and they won't let countering information dissuade them from writing that story.

Sensationalism — Competition among all media is extremely intense; there's always pressure to attract readers and viewers with stories that simplify complex issues, concentrate on the negative, and emphasize the highly visual aspects of conflict. Consequently, public relations personnel often complain that the protest demonstration or the highly inflammatory rhetoric of criticism often gets more coverage than the viewpoint of the organization being attacked. To them, the concept of fairness and balance has been compromised.

Advertising Influence — Although mainstream news periodicals and daily newspapers generally keep a high wall between the news and advertising department, this is not always the case in the trade press and among specialized magazines. Beauty, fashion, auto, and home decorating magazines, for example, are well known for running fashion layouts and other features that prominently promote their advertisers.

Indeed, a *PRWeek* survey of public relations practitioners in 2010 found that 38 percent of respondents had received news/editorial coverage (pay for play) as a result of purchasing advertising. And 33 percent of the journalists, in the same survey, reported that "coverage is influenced slightly by advertising." Almost 10 percent said coverage was "influenced heavily" by advertising. This raises troubling questions about journalistic ethics and integrity. If the public increasingly takes a skeptical view of what they read and hear, the value of the media as objective, independent sources of information is compromised. Thus, messages from organizations won't have the same impact and believability that the media now bestow on such messages.

Name Calling — Many journalists often disdain public relations as just covert advertising, deception, and manipulation. They call all public relations people "flacks," which is a derogatory term for a press agent. They are quite convinced, says Mickie Kennedy, CEO of eReleases, that "...the PR guy is the devil that's there to manipulate the facts or keep them from getting the real story." Although all occupations have their share of bad apples, including journalism, public relations professionals say that such blanket name calling impedes mutual respect and cooperation. How many journalists, for example, would resent being called a "hack"?

Working with Journalists

There will always be areas of friction and disagreement between public relations people and journalists, but that doesn't mean they can't have a solid working relationship based on mutual respect for each other's work. Indeed, one definition of *public relations* is that it is the building of relationships between the organization and its various publics, including journalists.

Press interviews, news conferences, media tours, and other kinds of gatherings provide excellent opportunities to build these working relationships. They are more personal than just distributing information and helping reporters get direct answers from news sources. Indeed, regular one-on-one contact with journalists helps the organization accomplish the objectives of increasing visibility, consumer awareness, and sales of services or products. The key is preparation. As book author Dick Martin points out, "In dealing with the press, as in any other business dealing, preparation is compulsory." The following discussion will provide tips and techniques to make sure that you and your organization's executives are prepared to interact with journalists and bloggers. In addition, see the box below for more tips on how to work with bloggers.

Tips for Success   Working with Bloggers

The blogosphere has had a significant impact on traditional media relations. The influence of the blogosphere means that public relations professionals now include bloggers—or citizen journalists—in their media relations outreach efforts.

According to Aaron Heinrich and Adam Brown of Ketchum, writing in PRSA's *The Strategist*, "Creating an outcome favorable to our companies or clients will mean creating a relationship with a blogger or podcaster in the same way we have relationships with members of traditional media."

Indeed, key bloggers are finding themselves being courted with the same intensity as regular journalists. The American Petroleum Institute (API), for example, organized teleconference briefing sessions for bloggers on gasoline prices and other oil industry issues. Weber Shandwick works with about 20 influential food bloggers on behalf of food industry clients. And General Mills invited 30 "mommy" bloggers to its headquarters for a two-day event to bake in Betty Crocker's kitchen and taste new products.

❝*Bloggers are not interested in you, your company, or how cool you think you are. They are interested in their readers. Your pitch should be about their audience and how you can bring value to them.*❞ Lisa Barone, in her blog, Social Media

A number of organizations now invite bloggers to news conferences and special events. An example is IMG, the organizer of New York Fashion Week. It now issues 10 percent of its press credentials to fashion bloggers. Building relationships with bloggers, however, takes time, because they are more independent and wary of using public relations materials. Here are some tips for working with bloggers:

+ Do your homework. Use research tools, such as Technorati and Google Blog Search, to create a short list of blogs in your subject or industry area that have the most influence and followers.

+ Read posts and comments on the blog to gauge readership and the blogger's personality.

+ Begin posting comments on the blog about topics being discussed. As *The Wall Street Journal* notes, "Some bloggers may need to see that you are a regular reader in order to take your pitch seriously."

+ Tailor your approach in subject matter and tone. Some blogs are extremely casual, whereas others are more formal in tone.

+ Don't blanket bloggers with untargeted, irrelevant pitches and releases. They will consider it spam and many will criticize you online.

+ Regularly monitor blogs for mentions of your client or organization. A number of sites, such as Google Alerts and Bloglines, can do this. A mention is an opportunity for you to post a comment.

It's wise to keep in mind that blogs often have a major influence on coverage by the mainstream press. In a study conducted by Brodeur and Marketwire, 62 percent of the journalists surveyed said blogs had a significant impact on the "tone of discussion" in news reporting. The same study found that almost 30 percent of the journalists had their own blogs, either a personal one or as part of their job. Another study by the Arketi Group found that almost 60 percent of journalists say they sometimes get story ideas from blogs.

FIGURE 4.1 A spokesperson's life is a series of media interviews. Most interviews are fairly low-key and with one or two reporters. However, when there is widespread media interest, it can become fairly intense as a hoard of journalists ask you blunt questions and stick a forest of mics in your face as multiple camera flashes blind you. Here, publicist Steve Whitmore talks to the press about the arrest of singer Christina Aguilera in Los Angeles on charges of being drunk in public.

Media Interviews

A major job responsibility in media relations is to be the spokesperson. You are the human face of the organization, the person quoted in the print media or giving the 30-second statement on television. Many media interviews are one-on-one but, at times, you may be speaking before a forest of microhones, which can be somewhat intimidating (see Figure 4.1). You must correctly reflect the official stance of the organization, but that can also raise some concerns about professional ethics if you are asked by your employer or client to provide inaccurate or misleading information. See the PR Casebook on page 95.

There are many tip lists on how to be a spokesperson, but some points are worth noting here. First, if a reporter calls to request an interview, you should interview the reporter first. Some common questions are:

» Who are you?
» What is the story about?
» Why did you call me?
» What are you looking for from me?
» Who else are you speaking with?
» Are you going to use my comments in your story?
» When is the story going to run?

By asking such questions, you can decide if you are qualified to answer the reporter's questions or whether someone else in the organization would be a better source. You may also decide that the context of the story is not appropriate for your organization and decline to be interviewed. For example, the reporter may ask you to comment on some topic that has nothing to do with your organization.

PR casebook

The Ethical Dilemma of Being a Spokesperson

One duty of public relations practitioners is to serve as the organization's official spokesperson. What they tell the media is not considered their personal opinion, but management's response or stance on an issue or situation. Lauren Fernandez, a public relations professional who also blogs about the field, says, "As PR professionals, we represent a client, brand, and organization."

The ethical challenge comes, however, when spokespersons are asked to say things on behalf of management that are misleading and even untrue. In such a situation, many practitioners take the approach that they are only the messenger and are not responsible for the accuracy of the message. Other practitioners, however, say their own values and credibility are on the line as a spokesperson and it's unethical to intentionally distribute false or misleading information.

Apple Computer is an example of the use of the messenger approach. A spokesperson told the media in 2009 that CEO Steve Jobs was taking a six-month leave of absence to correct a "hormonal imbalance." That was only partially true; Jobs actually took the leave to get a liver transplant in Memphis. In another situation, the spokesperson for large insurance firm AIG was criticized for defending the company's decision to spend $300,000 for an executive retreat at a luxury resort barely one week after receiving $85 billion in bail-out funds from the government.

Media spokespeople do, however, resign when they feel that they have been misled by their client or employer. Joel Sawyer, communications director for South Carolina Governor Mark Sanford, resigned after he lost considerable credibility by telling the media that the governor was hiking on the Appalachian Trail when, in fact, Sanford was in Argentina having an affair. When reporters asked about reports that the governor was seen boarding a plane at the Atlanta airport, Sawyer flatly denied them. Upon returning after five days, Sanford admitted the affair and apologized to the citizens of South Carolina. The State Ethics Commission, in charging him with ethics violations, noted that Sanford "directed members of his staff in a manner that caused them to deceive and mislead the public."

The communications director and the press secretary of New York's Governor David Paterson also resigned after the governor was involved in a scandal charging that he used his influence to suppress charges of domestic violence against one of his closest aides. Peter E. Kauffmann, the communications director, announced that he could no longer "in good conscience" continue to serve because he had come to doubt the truthfulness of what Governor Paterson wanted him to say about the allegations. Several weeks later, press secretary Marissa Shorenstein walked away from her $154,000 job, telling the New York *Daily News*, "Throughout my career, I have performed my duties professionally and with integrity basing my actions on what I believe to be true at the time." Her friends told the *Daily News* that she resigned because the governor "duped her into playing a role in covering up the explosive domestic case against another top aide."

(continued)

The role of spokesperson raises some ethical questions for you to think about. What would you do as a spokesperson if a client or employer gave you information that proved to be false or misleading? Would you justify your actions by saying that you were only the "mouthpiece" or would you quit? Is there anything you could do between these two extremes?

Source: Wilcox, D., and Cameron, G. (2012) *Public Relations Strategies & Tactics,* 10th edition. Boston: Allyn & Bacon, 82–83.

❝ *There is no such thing as the 'perfect question.' It's your job as a spokesperson to transition or 'bridge' from the reporter's question to your message.* ❞ Brad Phillips on his blog, Mr. Media Training

One danger in a telephone interview is that you may be caught off guard and will not have time to formulate your thoughts. Before you know it, you and the reporter are chatting away like old friends about a number of topics. This is fine, but do remember that your name and a quote will probably appear in the article or as a soundbite on a newscast. It may be used accurately, or it may be completely out of context.

The following tips, compiled from a number of sources, give advice on how to handle media interviews and be an effective spokesperson. More tips are given on page 98.

- » Determine, in advance, what key point or message you want to convey on behalf of the organization or client.
- » Answer questions, but link them to your key message whenever possible.
- » Anticipate questions and plan answers. Be totally familiar with facts, figures, and details that will help you sound credible.
- » Prepare for the worst. Think of every question that might possibly be asked, reasonable or unreasonable. Then prepare answers for each.
- » Use examples and anecdotes. Don't tell half-truths. Don't exaggerate. Don't brag about your organization or its products or services.
- » Be quotable. Say it briefly, clearly, and directly, in 30 seconds or less.
- » Speak conversationally and use personal anecdotes when appropriate.
- » Don't let reporters put words in your mouth. Rephrase their words, avoiding negative ones.
- » Don't lie. If you know information that's not appropriate to give out at that moment, say so.
- » Never say "no comment." It conveys the impression that you are hiding information or are guilty of something. Try to give the reporter a reason you can't comment, and

offer alternative information if appropriate. See the Tips for Success box on page 100 for more on how to avoid saying "no comment."

» There is no such thing as "off the record." Assume anything you say will appear in print or be broadcast.

» Don't answer hypothetical questions.

» Don't speak ill of the competition or other individuals.

» Dress and act appropriately. Don't distract your listeners with defensive nonverbal language, such as crossing your arms.

» Watch for loaded questions. Take time to think. Don't repeat a derogatory remark; shift to another subject.

» Always answer positively. It's the answer that counts, not the question.

» Watch your attitude. Don't be arrogant, evasive, or uncooperative. Don't argue. Don't use jargon. Don't lose your temper.

» Avoid memorizing your statements, but do use notes for reference. Speak from the public viewpoint; it is the public's interest that is important. Look at the interviewer when he or she is asking a question, but face the camera when you are answering a question being recorded by a television crew.

» Be cooperative, but don't surrender. Watch for presumptive questions: "Why are you resisting the efforts to control pollution?" "Why do you charge such outrageous prices?" Deny the statement and shift to another topic.

» If a question is unfair or too personal, say so and refuse to answer. You are not required to answer every question.

» Don't challenge figures unless you know for certain they are wrong. Remember that there are too many ways to cite statistics.

» Discuss only activities and policies that lie within your area of responsibility.

» Admit that you don't know the answer if that is the case. If you promise to provide more information later, make sure you do.

» Smile. Be as relaxed and informal as possible. A humorous remark may be used if it is appropriate, but don't be facetious; you might be misunderstood.

Other media training experts have added to and elaborated on this list. One common suggestion is to provide reporters with company background materials in advance. This will help them get facts and names correct. Body language is important. Be confident and relaxed, always look a reporter in the eye, keep your hands open, and smile and lean forward when you're talking. The idea, says Stephen Rafe of Rapport Communications, is to be assertive and avoid being defensive, passive, submissive, or aggressive.

Grooming and dress are also important in a television program or videos posted on organizational websites or even YouTube. Men should wear suits or sports jackets that have muted colors and avoid white shirts or flashy ties. Pale blue, gray, or tan shirts with no noticeable pattern are best. In today's world, however, more casual dress is often the uniform; it depends on the person's position (computer guru or corporate CEO) and the interview format. For any television appearance, the producer may suggest some makeup. This should not be resisted; even the nation's presidents have used it. Women should dress conservatively in dresses or suits. Makeup should be the kind that is normally worn for business. Any jewelry that dangles, jingles, or flashes should be avoided. If you're in the entertainment business and appearing on *The Late Show with David Letterman,* all this advice can be ignored.

Tips for Success   Nine Tips for a Spokesperson

Have you just become a spokesperson for an organization? Brad Phillips, in his Mr. Media Training blog, gives these pointers that you "...absolutely, positively, need to know."

1. **Develop a message.**   Jot down the three most important phrases or sentences you want to communicate to the audience.

2. **Repeat, repeat, repeat.**   You should articulate at least one of your messages in every answer. Don't parrot them verbatim, but communicate the central idea of a message in each response.

3. **Transition.**   There's no such thing as the "perfect" question. It's your job to transition or bridge from the reporter's question to your message.

4. **Don't make a new friend.**   If things are going well in the interview, resist the temptation to think of the interview as a casual conversation with a "friend." You will venture away from your key messages and make a mistake. The journalist may legitimately be friendly—but he or she is not your friend.

5. **Speak everyday English.**   Don't use jargon-filled language. When speaking with general audiences, use words a bright 12-year-old would understand. It's the language of *USA Today,* not *The Wall Street Journal.*

6. **Don't bury your lead.**   When answering a question, don't lead up to your conclusion. Give the most interesting part of your answer, or your "lead," first. If you don't start with the key message or "lead," the reporter may cut you off before you have a chance to say it.

7. **Be your most engaging self.**   Don't be a robotic spokesperson, which bores everyone. Be your passionate self; gesture, convey warmth, and smile.

8. **Speak 10 percent louder than usual.**   Television usually has a muting effect. In order to sound like yourself, boost your volume a bit; it usually helps to animate your body language too.

9. **Watch your tone.**   If you feel defensive, you will look defensive. Welcome tough questions as an opportunity to correct the record. Even if you have an imperfect answer, the audience will be more inclined to believe your response.

Source: Phillips, B. (2011, February 11). "Nine Practical Tips for a Spokesperson." Retrieved from www.prdaily.com.

News Conferences

A news conference is a setting where many reporters ask questions. It is called by an organization when there is important and significant news to announce, news that will attract major media and public interest.

Bulldog Reporter, a media relations newsletter, gives the following list of instances appropriate for news conferences:

» An announcement of considerable importance to a large number of people in the community is to be made.

» A matter of public concern needs to be explained.

» Reporters have requested access to a key individual, and it is important to give all media equal access to the person.

» A new product or an invention in the public interest is to be unveiled, demonstrated, and explained to the media.

» A person of importance is coming to town, and there are many media requests for interviews.

» A complex issue or situation is to be announced, and the media need access to someone who can answer their questions.

In other words, don't use news conferences to make routine announcements that are self-explanatory and don't require elaboration. A better approach is to just distribute a news release or post the information on the organization's website or Intranet.

Scheduling a News Conference — The news conference should be scheduled at a time that is convenient for the reporters—that is, with an eye on the deadlines of the media represented. In general, Tuesday, Wednesday, or Thursday mornings are best for dailies and broadcast media. This allows sufficient time for reporters to get stories in the next morning's daily or on the 6 P.M. news. If the primary audience is the trade press—reporters representing publications in a particular industry—late afternoon news conferences may be more convenient.

Avoid weekends, as well as major holidays. Most media operate with skeleton staffs on these days and don't have the personnel to cover news conferences. Also, avoid news conferences after 5 P.M. Major newspapers and broadcast outlets are unionized, and they prefer not to pay reporters overtime. Another consideration is to schedule the news conference on a day when there are no other major news conferences by other organizations. The Associated Press (AP) bureau in major cities often maintains a "day book" of upcoming events, including news conferences that have already been scheduled.

Selecting a Location — A location for a news conference must meet several criteria. First, it must be convenient for the media invited and be relatively close to their places of work. Hotels, conference centers, and even corporate headquarters can be used. Second, the room selected must have the necessary electronic facilities to accommodate reporters from print, broadcast, and digital media. Any site should be tested to ensure excellent signal strength for cell phones and Internet access.

A third criterion, particularly for news announcements that have high impact and widespread interest, is for the organization to use a facility that accommodates technical

+ Tips for Success   Alternatives to Saying "No Comment"

Most media guidelines emphasize that public relations personnel should always be helpful to and cooperative with the media. However, there are times when the best course of action is to not answer a reporter's question. Instead of saying "no comment," however, you should explain why you can't respond to the question.

Betsy Goldberg of Waggener Edstrom Worldwide offers some tips in an article written for *Public Relations Tactics*. She says that no practitioner should feel compelled to answer a question, particularly if (1) it's not your area of expertise, (2) your organization is not prepared to reveal details at the present time, (3) the issue is before the courts, and (4) government and financial regulations prohibit you from talking about the subject.

Ron Levy, former president of North American Précis Syndicate, adds two more reasons: (1) the question deals with proprietary information that would benefit competitors and (2) the question violates the privacy of employees.

In general, Goldberg believes journalists will understand if you follow three steps: (1) I can't discuss that, (2) here's why I can't discuss that, and (3) this is what I can discuss.

staff and equipment to provide a live video feed of the news conference for journalists in other cities. When the music industry announced a new copyright protection plan to allow music to be distributed on the Internet, 2,500 journalists and industry experts received press materials and heard the announcement online through their personal computers. Only 25 reporters actually attended the event, which was held in New York City. Another consideration is to have several smaller rooms reserved nearby for exclusive interviews with a company representative after the general news conference.

You should make the room available 1 or 2 hours in advance so reporters and crews can set up. You should have a general seating plan to make sure that the equipment doesn't obstruct the view of reporters who are attending. An elevated platform for TV cameras in the back of the room is helpful. See Figure 4.2, which shows a news conference in Japan about the damage to nuclear power plants after a major earthquake and tsunami in 2011.

Invitations — The invitation list should include all reporters, and even influential bloggers, who might be interested in the announcement. It is better to invite too many than to omit some who may feel slighted.

Invitations take various forms, depending on the event and the creativity of the public relations person. The standard approach is a personal invitation via email sent to a particular journalist or blogger. A second approach, commonly used, is a media advisory (discussed in Chapter 6) that is sent to a number of media contacts at the same time or even posted on an electronic newswire. A third method is a more formal invitation that is sent via first-class mail or FedEx. This approach is often

FIGURE 4.2 A news conference is held when there is an issue or event of widespread public interest and reporters are seeking clarification or more information. Officials of the Tokyo Electric Company held multiple news conferences to give reporters updates on the Fukushima nuclear power plant that was devastated by a massive earthquake and tsunami in Japan. Such news conferences are not neat and tidy; notice the array of electronic and recording equipment on the floor as the three executives talk into multiple microphones.

used for events and new product announcements. A fourth approach is the stunt. When Swatch invited reporters to a news conference announcing a new line of divers' watches, it had people in SCUBA gear deliver aquariums containing invitations.

If the news conference will also be broadcast live via satellite to reporters in various cities, a satellite distribution firm will send a media advisory. SGI, for example, held such a news conference when it announced a joint business venture with movie producer Steven Spielberg. Apple regularly used live satellite feeds whenever Steve Jobs gave a news conference about a new product. Use the telephone or email if the conference is being scheduled on short notice, which often occurs in the wake of a natural disaster. In any case, the invitation should state the time and place, the subject to be discussed, and the names of the principal spokespeople who will attend.

Invitations to news conferences about new product launches and other major corporate announcements should be sent 10 to 14 days in advance and should be marked "RSVP" so that you can make appropriate decisions regarding the size of the meeting room, the number of media kits needed, and what special equipment will be required. Reporters are notorious for not responding to RSVPs, so it is standard procedure to phone or email them several days before the event and encourage their attendance.

Handling the Conference — It is important that a news conference be well organized, short, and punctual. It is not a symposium or a seminar. A news conference should run no more than an hour, and statements by spokespeople should be relatively brief, allowing reporters time to ask questions.

You should brief your employer or clients on what they are going to say, how they are going to say it, and what visual aids will be used to illustrate their announcement. Reporters should receive copies of the text for each speech and other key materials such as PowerPoint presentations, charts, executive bios, and background materials. These are often given to reporters in the form of a media kit, discussed in Chapter 6.

It's also important to establish ground rules for the conduct of the news conference. Usually, brief opening statements are made, followed by a Q&A session. If there are many attendees, it might be wise to consider the format of one question and follow-up per person. This ensures that more people can ask a question rather than having one or two reporters dominate the session. The other consideration is to keep on track. Reporters often take the opportunity to ask oddball questions that distract from the stated purpose and objectives of the new conference.

Coffee, fruit juice, and rolls can be served prior to the opening of a morning news conference. Avoid trying to serve a luncheon or cocktails to reporters attending a news conference. They have deadlines and other assignments and don't have time to socialize.

After the Conference — At the conclusion of the news conference, the spokespeople should remain in the room and be available for any reporters who need one-on-one interviews. This can be done in a quiet corner or in a room adjacent to the site.

As the public relations person, you should be readily accessible during the remainder of the day in case reporters or bloggers need more information or think of other questions as they prepare their stories. You should know where the spokespeople are during the day and how they can be reached, just in case a reporter needs to check a quote or get another.

Another duty is to contact reporters who expressed interest but were ultimately unable to attend. You can offer to email them the materials from the news conference and, if you have recorded the news conference, offer video excerpts or audio soundbites. Another possibility is to arrange a one-on-one interview with one of the spokespeople. In media relations, as stated previously, service is the name of the game.

Teleconferences and Webcasts

A news conference can also be held via phone (teleconference) or video (Webcast). The technology is simple: a speakerphone hookup or a video streamed via the Internet or a satellite dish. According to a survey by the National Investors Relations Institute (NIRI), almost 75 percent of *Fortune* 500 companies use large-scale conference calls to announce and disseminate quarterly financial results. In addition, NIRI estimates that one in three U.S. businesses uses teleconferences with journalists at least once a month.

A teleconference or Webcast can be effective for several reasons. First, it is a cost-effective way to interact with reporters on a somewhat one-to-one basis. Second, it is convenient for the media. Rather than taking time to travel to and from a news conference, reporters can participate from their desks. Third, conference calls and Webcasts can generate more "attendance" by journalists in other cities.

Here are some guidelines for holding a teleconference or Webcast:

» Invite reporters and key bloggers to participate in advance.

» The teleconference or Webcast should last no more than 45 to 60 minutes.

» Remember time zones when scheduling such an event.

Media Tours

An alternative to the news conference, which is held in one location, is the media tour. It can be via satellite, which is discussed in Chapter 9, or it can be a series of personal visits to multiple cities and a number of media outlets throughout the region or the nation. Although the ultimate purpose of any media tour is to generate news coverage for the client or employer, there are two kinds of media tours. The first has the immediate objective of generating media coverage. The second is focused on providing background and establishing a working relationship.

Generating Coverage — If the goal is to generate coverage, a spokesperson goes on a media tour and is booked on locally produced broadcast shows in various cities. The publicist also will arrange local print media interviews. This concept, already mentioned in Chapter 3, capitalizes on the idea that a "local" angle often gets more media attention.

A good example of how this works is a marketing communications program conducted on behalf of Step Reebok, an adjustable device for step training. The objective was to promote the product and physical fitness in general. Rich Boggs, founder of Sports Step and creator of the adjustable step, was an ideal spokesperson. He was once an overweight, three-pack-a-day smoker who completely changed his lifestyle and now has a strong commitment to health and fitness.

Boggs went on a 14-city media tour to promote step training and his product. Because physical fitness was topical and trendy, he was able to get on 24 different TV news and talk shows, 4 of which were national. He also gave 21 radio interviews and was the subject of more than 20 newspaper feature articles. The media tour, a key element in an overall marketing communications program, led to a 45 percent increase in sales of Step Reebok. A comparable advertising campaign would have cost almost $750,000.

Relationship Building — The second purpose of a media tour is of longer range in terms of results. An organization's officials visit key editors for the purpose of acquainting them with the organization and what products or services it provides. This, in today's jargon, is called a **desktop tour**, because it takes place at the editor's or reporter's desk. In reality, it usually takes place in a conference room or at a local Starbucks. Unlike the first kind of tour, which focuses on the general media, these tours primarily involve publications that cover specific industries. At times, a desktop tour is also used to reach financial analysts who track a specific industry and make stock recommendations.

It would be difficult to get representatives from national business and trade publications to visit the offices of a small company. Yet by taking the president, the director of public relations, and perhaps the chief financial officer to the publication, it is possible to arrange for a one-on-one meeting with the editors. Your presentation may not result in a story immediately, but you will have laid the groundwork for future coverage.

The Role of a PR Firm — Public relations firms often are hired to arrange media tours. Their job is to (1) schedule appointments with key editors; (2) conduct media training for the organization's spokespeople; (3) prepare an outline of key talking points; (4) make airline, hotel, and local transportation arrangements for each city; and (5) prepare a briefing book about the background of the editor and the publication that will be visited. Of course, an account executive from the public relations firm goes on the media tour and coordinates all the logistics.

Previews and Parties

Three basic situations warrant a press preview or party: (1) the opening of a new facility, (2) the launch of a new product, and (3) the announcement of a new promotion for an already established product.

Journalists are often invited to tour a new facility before it is open to the general public. This allows them to prepare stories that will appear one or two days before the grand opening. From a public relations standpoint, this kind of coverage helps generate public awareness of the new facility and often increases opening-day crowds. Theme park Dollywood, for example, invited the press to preview a new ride called "River Battle" before the ride opened to the public. The invitation, sent to reporters via first-class mail, noted, "Media check-in begins at 9 a.m. at Dollywood's front gate. Please present this invitation for complimentary parking. Lunch will be served. RSVP by April 4th to dollywoodsvp@dollywood.com."

Press previews are routine for a new corporate headquarters, hospital wings, shopping malls, department stores, restaurants, and even the opening of new plays. See Figure 4.3 on page 105 for a media invitation sent via email for the opening night of a new play.

Demonstrations of new products also lend themselves to press previews. This is particularly true in high technology, where sophisticated products can be put through their paces by the engineers who developed them. Many companies have a press preview of their products just before a major trade show. The advantage is that reporters from all over the country are already gathered in one place. New campaigns for old products also generate their share of press previews and parties. The Champagne Wine Information Bureau, for example, invited food and wine journalists to a tasting at the Bubble Lounge in New York to kick off Champagnes Week, a nationwide promotion.

Previews may also include a cocktail party or a dinner. One national company combined a press preview of its new headquarters building with a party that included cocktails and dinner. This kind of event falls into the category of relationship building and networking. It allows company executives to mingle and socialize with reporters in a casual atmosphere. Ultimately, this helps executives feel more relaxed when a reporter they already know wants to interview them for a story. Unlike news conferences, press previews are often held after "working hours," when reporters are not on deadline. Chapter 17 further discusses special event planning.

Press Junkets

A variation on the press preview is the press tour. In the trade, such events are also called **junkets**. Within the travel and tourism industry, they are called **fam trips**, which is shorthand for *familiarization tour*. By whatever name, they usually involve invitations to key reporters, bloggers, and experienced freelance writers for an expense-paid trip to witness an event, view a new product, tour a facility, or visit a resort complex. Figure 4.4 shows a fam trip for a cruise ship line.

Here are some examples of press tours:

» Joe Boxer Corporation took 150 fashion and lifestyle reporters on an all-expense-paid weekend trip to Reykjavik, Iceland, to unveil its new line of underwear and pajamas.

FIGURE 4.3 The media are often invited to attend a preview of an attraction or facility before it is open to the general public. Invitations are sent by first-class mail or emailed to selected journalists inviting them to attend. This is the email invitation sent by the San Jose (CA) Repertory through its public relations firm, PRX, to entertainment journalists and bloggers in the San Francisco Bay Area.

» Weber-Stephens Products took 25 journalists on a four-day trip to the Bahamas to launch its new line of charcoal and gas grills.

» Ford Motor Co. took 14 auto editors and journalists on a five-day trip to France, where it was unveiling a new model at the Paris auto show.

» The Australian Tourist Commission regularly invites groups of travel writers "down under" to acquaint them with the country's natural wonders.

FIGURE 4.4 An important tool in travel promotion is the press junket. Travel writers are taken as guests to inspect a destination such as a resort complex or even a new ship. Royal Caribbean, for example, invited journalists to take a tour and even a short cruise on its new *Oasis of the Seas.* Many resulting stories focused on the sheer size of the ship—longer than four football fields, with a capacity of 6,300 passengers and 2,100 crew members.

Although all-expense-paid junkets are a well-established practice, journalists remain somewhat divided about the ethics of participating in them. Some feel the acceptance of free trips is a corrupting influence on journalistic freedom. Some large media organizations, such as the *New York Times, Conde Nast Traveler,* and *USA Today,* even have policies against free trips. They see no reason why a reporter has to travel all the way to Iceland for the unveiling of a new underwear line. Other organizations, such as the *Chicago Tribune* and CNN, will not accept expense-paid trips but will pay a discount "press rate" on airfares and hotel rooms if they think the tour is sufficiently newsworthy. Still other media outlets, smaller and less wealthy, have no qualms whatsoever about accepting free trips.

As a consequence, public relations people must carefully consider all aspects of sponsoring a junket and determine whether the cost is justified in terms of potential benefits. One of the most important things to remember, says Andrea Graham in *O'Dwyer's PR Services Report,* "is that a sponsored trip is not accepted in exchange for a rave review. It's simply a means of facilitating a writer's research." In other words, there is no guarantee that a story will be written or that it will be positive.

To be effective and generate good media relations, a press tour must be well planned and organized. There must be a legitimate news angle, and it should not be just a vacation with plenty of free food and booze. Lavish entertainment and the giving of expensive gifts are frowned upon in the ethics code of the Society of Professional Journalists (SPJ) and the Public Relations Society of America (PRSA).

Arranging media tours and junkets is not as glamorous as many people might think. Your job as a public relations staffer is to take care of virtually everything—airline tickets, press kits, itineraries, hotel rooms, local transportation, event tickets, menus, and even special requests from somewhat jaded journalists who expect first-class treatment. According to Teri Grove, owner of a Denver firm specializing in travel tourism, "Hosting a press trip is extremely labor intensive, since no detail can be overlooked during the trip, from the moment guests are greeted at the airport to their departure."

Editorial Board Meetings

The key editors of a newspaper or a magazine meet on a regular basis to determine editorial policy. Your client or employer, on occasion, may wish to meet with them as part of an overall strategy of developing long-term relationships. Editors usually are long-term employees of a publication.

Joan Stewart, writing in *PR Tactics*, says there are five reasons for meeting with an editorial board:

1. You want the newspaper's support for a cause or issue.
2. You're about to announce a sensitive and possibly controversial news story and want to meet with the board before the story appears to provide background and context so that the publication can do a better job of reporting the story.
3. The newspaper has been printing unfavorable editorials about you, and you want to present your side in hopes it will change its perspective.
4. You feel the newspaper has been treating you unfairly in its news stories, and you've gotten nowhere with the reporter or junior editors.
5. You want to introduce your new CEO to the board for a "getting-to-know you" session.

In general, you contact the editorial page director (phone call is best) and request a meeting with the publication's editorial board. Most editors want a tightly written, one-page letter outlining who you represent, what issues you would like to cover, and why your representatives are the best qualified to discuss the issue. Don't weigh down your first letter or email with a media kit or other background information.

Once you have an appointment, you should develop a message that focuses on three or four key points. You should also decide in advance what you want to accomplish in the meeting. Do you simply want the editors to know about your viewpoint so it can perhaps be incorporated into future news stories and editorials, or do you want them to write an editorial supporting you?

The best approach is to have a well-informed senior person from your organization give the presentation. This may be the company president, but it can also be an expert in a particular field, such as law, accounting, environmental standards, technology, etc., depending on the issue. In general, your role as the public relations person is not to give the presentation, but to make arrangements for the meeting, prepare the background materials, and help your spokesperson prepare for it.

Here's a list of tips from the experts for meeting with editorial boards:

» Conduct a practice session before the meeting, responding to difficult questions; it helps to know something about previous editorial positions.

» Take no more than three or four people. Well-known experts with credentials are great as long as they can explain their views simply.

» Don't expect more than a half-hour. Make your presentation brief and to the point, so there is sufficient time for Q&A.

» Bring the same materials you would have sent had there been no meeting.

» Leave DVDs at your office (they won't watch them).

» Offer to submit an op-ed piece if the editors do not adopt your position.

» Write a follow-up note offering further information and the names of third-party experts who can be contacted.

Ann Higbee, managing partner at Eric Mower and Associates, sums up the value of editorial boards. She writes, in *Public Relations Tactics*, "Building good working relationships with the editorial board can help your organization get credit for the positive things it does and lays the groundwork for public understanding in tough times."

A Media Relations Checklist

Many checklists and guidelines for dealing effectively with the media have been compiled. Most of them are well tested and proven, but you must always remember that there are no ironclad rules. Media people are also individuals to whom a particular approach may or may not be applicable. Here's a list of commonsense guidelines, many of which will be familiar to you from earlier chapters:

» **Know your media.** Be familiar with the publications, broadcast media, and blogs that cover your organization or industry. Know their deadlines, news format, audiences, and needs. Do your homework before contacting them.

» **Limit your mailings.** Multiple news releases are inefficient and costly, and they alienate media gatekeepers. Send releases only to media that would have an interest in the information.

» **Localize.** Countless surveys show that the most effective materials have a local angle. Take the time to develop that angle before sending materials to specific publications.

» **Send newsworthy information.** Don't bother sending materials that are not newsworthy. Avoid excessive hype and promotion.

- » **Practice good writing.** News materials should be well written and concise. Avoid technical jargon and hype.

- » **Avoid gimmicks.** Don't send T-shirts, teddy bears, balloon bouquets, or other frivolous items to get the attention of media gatekeepers.

- » **Be environmentally correct.** Use digital media for distribution as much as possible. Save trees.

- » **Be available.** You are the spokesperson for an organization. It is your responsibility to be accessible at all times, even in the middle of the night. Key reporters should have your office and cell phone numbers.

- » **Get back to reporters.** Make it a priority to make a quick response to any media inquiries. One survey of journalists found that this was the number one rule to establishing a good working relationship with reporters.

- » **Slow down.** When talking on the phone to a reporter, slow down to ensure that he or she can keep up while taking notes.

- » **Answer your own phone.** Use voicemail systems as a tool of service, not as a screening device. Reporters (like other people) hate getting bogged down in the electronic swamp of endless button pushing.

- » **Be truthful.** Give accurate and complete information even if it is not flattering to your organization. Your facts and figures must be clear and dependable.

- » **Answer questions.** There are only three acceptable answers: "Here it is," "I don't know but I'll get back to you within the hour," and "I can't discuss this now because…" "No comment" is *not* one of the three alternatives.

- » **Avoid "off-the-cuff" remarks.** Don't say anything to a reporter that you would not wish to see in print or on the air.

- » **Protect exclusives.** If a reporter has found a story, don't give it to anyone else.

- » **Be fair.** Competing media deserve equal opportunity to receive information in a timely manner.

- » **Help photographers.** Facilitate their work by getting people together in a central location, providing necessary props, and supplying subjects' full names and titles.

- » **Explain.** Give reporters background briefings and materials so that they understand your organization. Tell them how decisions were reached and why.

- » **Remember deadlines.** The reporter must have enough time to write a story. One good rule is to provide information as far in advance as possible. In addition, don't call a reporter at deadline time.

- » **Praise good work.** If a reporter has written or produced a good story, send a complimentary note. A copy to the editor is also appreciated.

- » **Correct errors politely.** Ignore minor errors such as misspellings, inaccurate ages, and wrong titles. If there is a major factual error that skews the accuracy of the entire story, politely request a correction. See Tips for Success on page 110 for steps to take when the media get it wrong.

Media Etiquette

The points above constitute the core of effective media relations, but here are some additional tips about basic media etiquette that should be observed. Failure to do so often leads to poor media relations.

Follow-up Phone Calls — Don't call a reporter or an editor and say, "Did you get my news release?" Such an inane question is only a weak attempt at making another

+

Tips for Success   Correcting Errors in News Stories

News coverage isn't always objective, factual, or accurate. Mistakes happen, and it is likely that you or your employer will have complaints on occasion about inaccurate and unfair news coverage. The following are some approaches you can take:

+ **Ascertain the facts.**   Analyze the offending article or broadcast news segment. What exactly is inaccurate, incomplete, or unfair about it? An organization's executives often think any article that doesn't praise the organization is unfair and biased, so having a neutral party review the story can often temper such perceptions. At other times, the damaging effect of the inaccuracy or distorted headline is somewhat minor. As public relations counselor Fraser Seitel says, "Don't sweat the small stuff."

+ **Talk to the reporter.**   If the error is significant, contact the reporter to politely discuss factual errors, not subjective differences of opinion or interpretation. In many cases, the reporter will voluntarily correct the information in subsequent articles or broadcasts. Many newspapers also print corrections under the rubric of a clarification.

+ **Write a Response.**   In print journalism, write a letter to the editor or an op-ed (discussed in Chapter 7) to give the organization's point of view. If it's a blog, post a comment as part of the topic thread. Don't repeat the original error or chastise the reporter for sloppy work; just articulate the correct information.

+ **Talk to the editor.**   If you don't get satisfaction from the reporter and the complaint is a major one, you may wish to contact the editor to ensure that he or she is aware of your complaint. If you believe that the reporter consistently writes unfavorable stories about your organization or client, it's a good idea to request a meeting with the reporter and the editor.

+ **Go public.**   An old adage holds that you should never pick a fight with anyone who buys ink by the barrel; nevertheless, many companies take the offensive and make every effort to inform key publics about their side of the story. Letters can be sent to community opinion leaders, employees, or even stockholders, depending on the story. Social media can also be used, or you can purchase advertising to rebut the allegations.

+ **File a lawsuit.**   The last resort is to file a lawsuit if legal counsel believes that the newspaper or broadcast outlet has intentionally distorted the truth. A threatened libel suit often encourages the media outlet to print a correction or an apology. A lawsuit also gets media coverage, which gives the organization a platform to inform the public about inaccuracies in the original story.

pitch for its use. Some publicists strongly defend callbacks as an obligation to their employer or client, but surveys continue to show that such calls are a major irritant to journalists. However, if your boss still insists, it's better to call or email a reporter to offer some new piece of information or a story angle that may not be explicit in the news release. It then becomes an information call instead of a desperate plea to read the release and use it. It's also OK to do a follow-up phone call if you're offering an exclusive story and you need to know if the reporter is interested before contacting other journalists.

Recording Interviews — Many public relations practitioners now routinely record all interviews with reporters to establish a record of what was said. They also request that the reporter record any interview to check the accuracy of his or her notes. In any event, it is important to inform the reporter that a recording is being done and get permission. During the conversation, it is suggested that you again repeat that the conversation is being recorded to ensure a record of notification is captured. There are often state laws regarding recording, so practitioners should be familiar with them.

Off-the-Record Comments — Forget it. There is no such thing in the digital age of smartphones, Twitter, and instant uploads to Facebook or YouTube. Even if a reporter agrees to interview "off the record," editors may not honor such an agreement if they can scoop the competition. Never say anything to a reporter, even after the formal interview is ended, that you would not want to see on the evening news or posted on a blog or Twitter.

Story Approval — Journalists have no obligation to share their story with you before it is published or broadcast, so don't ask. You may, however, offer to review the accuracy of key facts and quotes to help the reporter write his or her story. Some reporters appreciate the offer, particularly if the topic is complex, but others will decline.

Exclusives — On occasion, a public relations strategy is to offer a media outlet the opportunity to be the first with an important story. In general, prestige publications and blogs are approached with exclusives because other media will follow their lead. The key point is that an exclusive should be offered to only one outlet at a time. In some cases, a company will offer more than one exclusive about various aspects of a new product, such as the iPad. In such cases, all recipients should be aware of the other exclusive being offered. For good media relations, exclusives should be offered on a regular basis to a variety of publications to avoid the perception that only one particular news organization is favored by the organization.

Lunch Dates — Don't invite a reporter to lunch unless the purpose is to discuss a possible story or to give a background briefing on some upcoming event. You need to be well prepared to give concise information and answer questions because reporters don't have time for idle chitchat and long lunches. Give the reporter or blogger the opportunity to select the restaurant and determine whether it's appropriate for you to pay the bill. Daily newspapers, in particular, have policies forbidding reporters from accepting free meals and hospitality.

Gift Giving — Many organizations give reporters a souvenir for attending a preview or party. However, it is not wise to give expensive gifts because it raises questions of "influence buying." In any case, the gift should be available at the door, and reporters should be given the option of taking the gift or bypassing it. Gifts aren't necessary to generate a good working relationship, but a personal note or card thanking a reporter or blogger for his or her fine work on a particular article or post goes a long way in cementing a continuing, positive relationship.

> **"** *If it's worth over $20, I can't accept it. If it's worth under $20, it's crap and I don't want it.* **"** Associated Press editor responding to a question about receiving gifts from public relations personnel

Payola — Almost everyone in public relations and the media agrees that bribery is unethical, but variations of the "pay for play" theme are often tried. Anne Taylor Loft, for example, invited bloggers to cover its summer collection and offered gift cards to the bloggers who wrote about the event online. The value of the gift card was not disclosed until after the bloggers submitted their posts, so it was implied that the most flattering posts would probably receive the biggest gift cards. In another example, a publicist emailed media that she would be happy to send a $20 gift certificate as a "thank you" for mentioning her client's new product. Such tactics are tacky and totally unacceptable. Even the FTC has a rule that bloggers must disclose any payments or free products. See Chapter 11 for information about avoiding legal hassles.

Crisis Communication

A good working relationship with the media is severely tested in times of crisis. All the rules and guidelines stated previously about working effectively with the press are magnified and intensified when something out of the ordinary occurs and thus becomes extremely newsworthy. There are many dimensions of what constitutes a crisis for a company or an organization. Kathleen Fearn-Banks, in her book *Crisis Communications: A Casebook Approach*, says, "A crisis is a major occurrence with a potentially negative outcome affecting the organization, company, or industry, as well as its publics, products, services, or good name."

Here is a sampling of major crises that have hit various organizations:

» Facebook's corporate reputation took a beating when it was disclosed that it hired a public relations firm to do a secret campaign against Google on issues of privacy.

» JetBlue received negative publicity and thousands of phone calls from irate passengers when a Valentine's Day snowstorm in the Midwest stranded thousands of passengers. The airline was faulted for not adequately responding to the situation.

» The Florida tourist industry faced a major crisis when the BP oil spill in the Gulf of Mexico caused a massive decline of hotel reservations and tourists in the state.

» Mattel Toys had to recall millions of its products because Chinese subcontractors had used lead paint on many of the toys, which could cause toxic poisoning.

These situations, no matter what the circumstances, constitute major crises because the reputation of the company, industry, or product is in jeopardy. Economic survival is at stake, and a company can lose millions of dollars overnight if the public perceives that a problem exists.

The key to successful dealings with the media during a crisis is to become a credible source of information. The following points are worth noting:

» Get to know the journalists in your area before a crisis hits. That way, they will already know something about you and your company, and you will have an idea of how they work.

» Appoint a spokesperson whom the media can trust and who has authority to speak for the company. It also is a good idea to designate one spokesperson, so that the organization speaks with one voice.

» "No comment" fuels hostility. Even a simple "Can I get back to you?" can be misconstrued as evasive.

» Set up a central media information center where reporters can obtain updated information and work on stories. You should provide telephone lines and Internet connections so reporters can talk with their editors or send email messages. Provide computers for their use. Provide food and transportation if necessary.

» Provide a constant flow of information through news briefings and postings on the organization's website, Twitter feed, or even Facebook page even if the situation is unchanged or negative. A company builds credibility by addressing bad news quickly; when information is withheld, the cover-up becomes the story.

» Be accessible. Provide after-hours phone numbers and carry a cell phone with you at all times.

» Keep a log of media calls, and return calls as promptly as possible. A log can help you track issues being raised by reporters and give you a record of which media showed the most interest in your story.

» A crisis or bad news spreads like a wildfire on social media. An organization must constantly monitor the social media and respond within minutes with information and updates to be an active participant in the "conversation." An emphasis on transparency is vital.

> **❝ The level of transparency that a crisis demands—since the advent of micro-blogs and online forums—is dramatically greater than before. The more you share information on social networks to build transparency, the better. ❞** Rriya Ramesh, head of social media practice at CRT/tanaka, writing in the *Ragan Report*

» Be honest. Don't exaggerate, and don't obscure facts. If you're not sure of something or don't have the answer to a question, say so. If you are not at liberty to provide information, explain why.

These guidelines reflect plain common sense, but when a crisis hits, it is surprising how many organizations go into a defensive mode and try to stonewall the media. Jack-in-the-Box, for example, violated the tenets of crisis communications in the first days of reported food poisonings. The company initially said "no comment" and then waited three days to hold a news conference, at which the company president tried to shift the blame to the meatpacking company. A better approach would have been to (1) take responsibility, (2) offer compensation and an apology to the victims, and (3) assure the public that the company was taking steps to ensure that the situation would never happen again.

David Vogel, a business professor at the University of California in Berkeley, says, "There are two principles: accept responsibility and take action." Even if the organization is a victim, such as the Florida tourism industry dealing with BP's oil spill, it is important to be proactive in terms of what is being done about the problem and to reassure potential tourists about the industry's efforts to clean up all the beaches to ensure the safety and enjoyment of the public.

Summary

The Importance of Media Relations

» Media relations is the primary function of most public relations departments and counseling firms.

» A good working relationship with journalists and bloggers helps ensure that an organization's messages about its products, services, and policies are communicated to the public.

The Media's Dependence on Public Relations

» Journalists depend on public relations sources such as news releases and organizational websites for most of the information used in their stories.

» The constant flow of information from public relations sources is a form of "subsidy" to the media because no media outlet has enough staff to cover all the news and events that occur.

Public Relations' Dependence on the Media

» Public relations personnel rely on traditional and digital media to provide an efficient and cost-effective system for the dissemination of messages to millions of people.

» Media coverage is a form of third-party endorsement that messages from organizations are credible and newsworthy.

Areas of Friction

» Although media and public relations personnel are mutually dependent upon each other to do their jobs, each side has complaints and pet peeves about the other.

» The most common complaints journalists have about public relations people involve (1) poorly written material, (2) shotgun distribution of irrelevant material, (3) inaccessible public relations staff, (4) too many gimmicks such as T-shirts and coffee mugs, (5) not taking "no" for an answer, and (6) inability to get to the point in a concise manner.

» Public relations personnel complain that journalists (l) constantly change their minds about using a story, (2) don't contact the organization for a comment,

(3) fail to do their "homework" before doing an interview or story, (4) occasionally show bias, (5) engage in sensationalism, (6) allow advertising to influence news coverage, and (7) jeopardize mutual respect by calling public relations people "flacks."

Working with Journalists

» Spokespersons are the public face of an organization and the organization's major contact with the media.

» Spokespersons must be skilled communicators and be able to articulate an organization's point of view.

» News conferences should be held only if there is significant news that lends itself to elaboration and questions from journalists. News conferences can also be held via teleconferences or Webcasts.

» Media tours involve travel to major cities and setting up appointments with local media outlets. One purpose is to generate coverage; another is to acquaint editors with your product or services.

» Previews and parties are acceptable ways of giving executives and reporters a chance to know each other better. Gifts are not necessary.

» Press tours, often called *junkets*, should be used only if there is a legitimate news story or angle. Avoid junkets that simply wine and dine journalists.

» A meeting with a publication's editorial board is a good way to establish rapport and long-term relationships.

A Media Relations Checklist

» There are many guidelines for how to conduct effective media relations. The bottom line is to be accurate, truthful, and provide outstanding service.

» Don't irritate reporters by asking, "Did you get my news release?" Also, don't ask to see an advance copy of the story or when a story will be published.

» If you need to set the record straight, begin with the reporter who wrote the story.

Crisis Communications

» Crisis communications is a test of excellent media relations. You need to immediately provide the media and social media with information and constant updates.

» Organizations must be transparent and honest with the public in order to maintain credibility.

Skill Building Activities

1. Do a content analysis of your local daily newspaper to determine the number and percentage of news articles that probably originated from news releases, news conferences, interviews with organizational spokespersons, a press preview, or a media tour. Construct a chart and write a summary of what you found.

2. You have been hired to organize a news conference for Target Stores, which is announcing a major expansion into the Florida market. Outline and describe

the steps for organizing this news conference. The resulting plan should be a blueprint of the entire event, including selection of the site, use of visual aids, list of invitees, and arrangements for the conference to be streamed as a webcast to reporters throughout the state.

3. *Business Week* has decided to write a news feature about your company's innovative approach to conserving energy and reducing greenhouse gases in its manufacturing plants. A reporter and

photographer will be visiting the company headquarters in 10 days. What should you, as director of corporate communications, do to prepare for their visit?

4. The Foster Company operates a chain of clothing stores. Poor earnings and incompetent management have caused the company to declare bankruptcy, but a new CEO has been able to rebuild the brand and make the company profitable again. It's time to let the financial and trade press know about the turnaround. What kind of media tour would you

organize for the CEO? Prepare a memo giving the logistics of a tour, including the media to be contacted.

5. Blogs are now part of the media landscape. Your client makes moderately priced bicycles used for leisure and weekend exercise. The company doesn't have a large advertising budget, but it thinks publicity (and sales) could be generated through blogs devoted to leisure bike riding. Do some research and compile a list of five blogs that would be interested in receiving postings and other information from the manufacturer.

Media Resources

Barone, L. (2010, December 28). "Five Dos & Donts for Getting Blog Coverage." Retrieved from www.smallbiztrends.com.

Jin, Y., and Liu, B. (2010). "The Blog-Mediated Crisis Communication Model: Recommendations for Responding to Influential External Blogs." *Journal of Public Relations Research* 22(4), 429–455.

Kennedy, M. (2011, March). "Ten Ways Journalists and PR Pros P*** Each Other Off." *Ragan Report*, 13.

Kennedy, M. (2010, November 11). "Ten Tips for Success Using Help a Reporter Out." Retrieved from www.ragan.com.

McCown, A. (2011, January). "Stones from the Public, Crisis in the Glass House." *O'Dwyer's Report*, 14.

Morris, E. (2010, April). "Media Survey 2010: News Update." *PRWeek*, 30–35.

Phillips, B. (2011, March 9). "Five Ways to Avoid Being Misquoted." Retrieved from www.prdaily.com.

Phillips, B. (2011, February 26). "Nine Practical Tips for a Spokesperson." Retrieved from www.prdaily.com.

Phillips, B. (2010, November 12). "Seven Things to Do When the Media Get It Wrong." Retrieved from www.ragan.com.

Ramesh, P. (2011, March). "The 10 Commandments of Social Media Crisis Management." *Ragan Report*, 22–23.

Rudawsky, G. (2011, April 21). "'Off the Record' No Longer Applies; Five Crucial Reminders for PR Pros." Retrieved from www.prdaily.com.

Shuffler, J. (2010, December 9). "Comm Pros Adjust to New Realities of Blogger Relations." Retrieved from www.prweekus.com.

Wilkens, S. (2011, April 1). "Three Blogger Relation Blunders to Avoid." Retrieved from www.prdaily.com.

Writing the News Release

»   After reading this chapter, you will be able to:

» Appreciate the value and importance of the news release

» Ascertain when and if a news release should be written

» Be familiar with the basic components of a news release

» Write a basic news release

» Understand the basic format of email and multimedia news releases

---

The Backbone of Publicity Programs

The news release, often called a *press release* by the older generation, has been a staple of the public relations business for more than a century. Indeed, the basic template used today goes back to 1906 when Ivy Lee, a leading pioneer in the development of the public relations field, wrote a news release for the Pennsylvania Railroad. Today, the news release is still the backbone of almost every public relations plan that requires extensive media outreach. There are, however, two sobering facts. First, various studies have found that between 55 and 97 percent of all news releases sent to media outlets are never used. Second, there is massive competition for the attention of reporters and editors.

Feature Photo Services, for example, estimates that daily newspaper editors receive about 2,000 news releases a day. In addition, many reporters say they receive several hundred on an average day. Many come via snail mail, but the majority is now sent via email and electronic distribution services such as Business Wire and PR Newswire. Each of these services distributes about 20,000 news releases a month to media outlets around the world.

Given the odds, this means you must do three things if your release is to stand a chance of being published. First, you must follow a standardized format. Second, you must provide information that will interest the audience. And third, your material must be timely. As Wikipedia notes, a news release is "...for the purpose of announcing something claimed as having news value."

This chapter outlines how to prepare news releases that will meet these criteria. The focus is on describing the various types of information that can be the subject of a news release and outlining the basic components of a news release. In addition, this chapter will show you how to format the standard, traditional news release and how the format is somewhat different for online news release that are emailed to journalists and bloggers or posted on a Web page. A third format is the multimedia news release that embeds photos, video, and social media links in the basic news release.

The Value of News Releases

So why write a news release? The primary reason, of course, is to help achieve organizational objectives. News releases, when they form the basis of stories in the news columns of newspapers and magazines or are part of a TV news hour, create awareness about ideas, situations, services, and products. A new product on the market, or an appeal for Red Cross blood donations, is brought to the attention of the public. A manufacturer of a potato-chip maker, for example, sold out its entire stock after the *New York Times* included parts of a news release in an article about new kitchen gadgets.

News releases are also cost effective. Almost any organization, from a garden club to IBM, can create and distribute news releases at nominal cost compared to the cost of buying advertising. There is also the factor of credibility. News releases appear in the news columns of newspapers, and studies consistently show that people consider information in a news story to be much more believable than an advertisement. In one such study, the Wirthlin Group surveyed a sample of 1,023 adults. Almost 30 percent of the respondents said that a news article would affect their buying decisions, whereas only 8 percent indicated that an advertisement would.

News releases also continue to serve the needs of the media because (1) they are a major information source of story ideas for journalists and bloggers, and (2) they are the basis of many news stories. It has already been noted in Chapter 3 that public relations sources account for a large percentage of published or posted news stories. Even the UK website Churnalism.org found in a 2011 study that more than half the news reported by mainstream media had its origins in material (including news releases) distributed by public relations practitioners. The website editors were even more shocked to find out that many releases were published verbatim or with only minor changes.

> **"**A recent survey of journalists by Atlanta PR firm Arketi Group found news releases are used by 90 percent of business journalists as sources for story ideas. **"** Craig McGuire, *PRWeek*

Indeed, the humble news release is still alive and well despite pronouncements by various social media gurus that it is a relic of the stone age and a "dreadful animal that should be put out of its misery" in the age of Twitter, Facebook, YouTube, and blogs. Even journalists disagree with the latter assessment. Gregg Litman, senior news producer of WCCO-TV, told blogger Arik Hanson, "... We still need information/text to save, forward in office, give to reporters, and use as a reference." Many public relations practitioners also disagree that the news release is dead. Here are some other comments posted on www.ragan.com:

"I'm a PR professional working for clients in manufacturing and trade press editors still appreciate receiving press releases and images, albeit via email."

"The news release is alive and well. With smaller newsrooms and fewer reporters, we are seeing more publications printing them word for word."

"We have many publications that are not on Facebook or Twitter, and the release is the only way they get info. Even if we pick up the phone, they still want to see a release. And we see many weeklies and micro media printing our releases verbatim."

Planning a News Release

Writing a news release requires the tools and equipment described in Chapter 1. The following sections discuss the selection of paper, some fundamentals about word processing a release, and the style you should follow. But before writing anything, the public relations writer should complete a planning worksheet.

The Basic Questions

Your planning worksheet should answer the following questions:

» What is the subject of the message? What is the specific focus of this release?

» Who is this message designed to reach? For example, is it aimed at local citizens, or is it mainly for executives in other companies who read the business page and might order the product?

» What is in it for this particular audience? What are the potential benefits and rewards?

» What goal is the organization pursuing? What is the organization's purpose? Is it to increase sales of a product? Position the company as a leader in the field? Show company concern for the environment?

» What do you want to achieve with the news release? Is the objective to inform, to change attitudes and behavior, or to increase attendance at a local event?

» What key messages should this news release highlight? How can they be tailored to the format of a specific publication and its readers?

These questions enable you to select and structure the content of a news release from a public relations perspective. The release can still meet the journalistic goal of presenting information objectively and in correct newspaper or broadcast style, but it must also be carefully crafted to include key messages. This kind of planning is the major difference between writing as a journalist and writing as a public relations professional.

At the same time, however, you must think like a journalist. Journalists' primary criterion for using a news release is whether the information would be interesting to their readers or viewers. They could care less about your efforts to "accomplish organizational objectives" or even position the company as a leader in the field.

Consequently, you should also review the six questions in the Tips for Success below to determine if your news release is really newsworthy. In many cases, the answer probably would be a definite "NO."

In terms of format and content, a news release should be the same as a news story. Many of the same rules apply, including the news values discussed in Chapter 3. Like a journalist, a public relations writer needs to include the five Ws and one H: *who*, *what*, *when*, *where*, *why*, and *how*. If you have the answers to these questions at your fingertips, you are ready to begin. In addition, you need to be thoroughly familiar with the *Associated Press Stylebook*. It's the standard reference for writing news releases because most American newspapers use "AP style" or some variation of it. If a news release conforms to AP style, it makes the work of reporters and editors much easier.

The Basic Components of a News Release

The news release has six basic components: (1) letterhead, (2) contacts, (3) headline, (4) dateline, (5) lead paragraph, and (6) body of text. A seventh element, often included at the end of a news release, is a standard statement giving basic background

+

Tips for Success   Is Your Release Newsworthy?

A news release must be written to help an organization accomplish its objectives, but the effort is often wasted if the information is not interesting or relevant to journalists and their audiences. Susan Young, a producer of a video series about publicity techniques, says public relations writers should ask themselves these six questions:

1. **Who** gives a crap? If you can answer this question, your response belongs in the headline or subject line. Hint: Relatives don't count.

2. **What** makes my story outshine the other 372 that crossed the desk of the reporter or blogger today? Hint: Pitch purple snowflakes.

3. **Where** would my story fit in the reporter's world? Hint: Relevance rules.

4. **When** is this most important? Today, tomorrow, next Tuesday? Hint: Yesterday = snore.

5. **Why** would anyone sitting in their den in Utah, driving on I-95 in Florida, or bowling next to my dad in New Jersey want to pay attention to this story? Hint: Connect with emotions and the human factor.

6. **How** can this story help other people? Hint: It's not about buying your book or hiring you to train execs.

Source: Young, S. (2011, February 9). "Deciding What's News: Six Questions to Determine If Your Story Is Newsworthy." Retrieved from www.getinfrontcommunications.com.

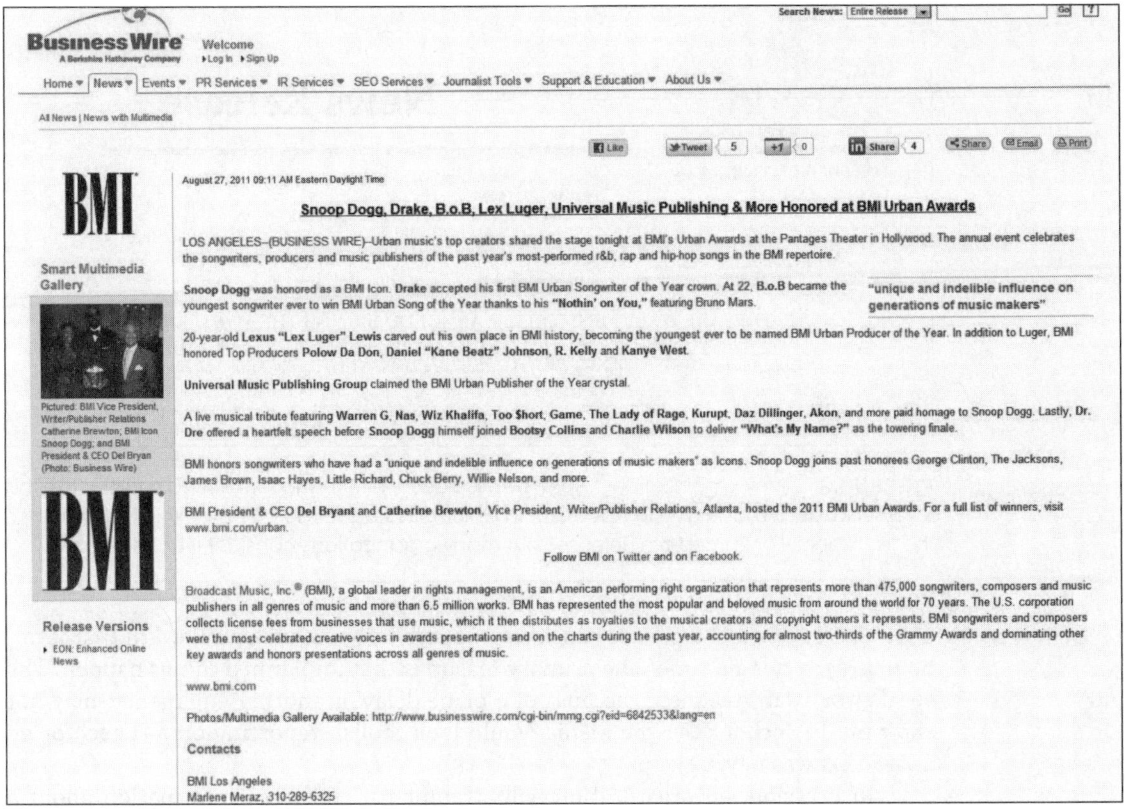

Search News: Entire Release

Business Wire
A Berkshire Hathaway Company

Welcome
Log In Sign Up

Home News Events PR Services IR Services SEO Services Journalist Tools Support & Education About Us

All News | News with Multimedia

Like Tweet 5 +1 0 Share 4 Share Email Print

BMI

Smart Multimedia Gallery

Pictured: BMI Vice President, Writer/Publisher Relations Catherine Brewton; BMI Icon Snoop Dogg; and BMI President & CEO Del Bryan (Photo: Business Wire)

BMI

Release Versions

- EON: Enhanced Online News

August 27, 2011 09:11 AM Eastern Daylight Time

Snoop Dogg, Drake, B.o.B, Lex Luger, Universal Music Publishing & More Honored at BMI Urban Awards

LOS ANGELES--(BUSINESS WIRE)--Urban music's top creators shared the stage tonight at BMI's Urban Awards at the Pantages Theater in Hollywood. The annual event celebrates the songwriters, producers and music publishers of the past year's most-performed r&b, rap and hip-hop songs in the BMI repertoire.

Snoop Dogg was honored as a BMI Icon. **Drake** accepted his first BMI Urban Songwriter of the Year crown. At 22, **B.o.B** became the youngest songwriter ever to win BMI Urban Song of the Year thanks to his **"Nothin' on You,"** featuring Bruno Mars.

"unique and indelible influence on generations of music makers"

20-year-old **Lexus "Lex Luger" Lewis** carved out his own place in BMI history, becoming the youngest ever to be named BMI Urban Producer of the Year. In addition to Luger, BMI honored Top Producers **Polow Da Don, Daniel "Kane Beatz" Johnson, R. Kelly** and **Kanye West**.

Universal Music Publishing Group claimed the BMI Urban Publisher of the Year crystal.

A live musical tribute featuring **Warren G, Nas, Wiz Khalifa, Too $hort, Game, The Lady of Rage, Kurupt, Daz Dillinger, Akon,** and more paid homage to Snoop Dogg. Lastly, **Dr. Dre** offered a heartfelt speech before **Snoop Dogg** himself joined **Bootsy Collins** and **Charlie Wilson** to deliver **"What's My Name?"** as the towering finale.

BMI honors songwriters who have had a "unique and indelible influence on generations of music makers" as Icons. Snoop Dogg joins past honorees George Clinton, The Jacksons, James Brown, Isaac Hayes, Little Richard, Chuck Berry, Willie Nelson, and more.

BMI President & CEO **Del Bryant** and **Catherine Brewton**, Vice President, Writer/Publisher Relations, Atlanta, hosted the 2011 BMI Urban Awards. For a full list of winners, visit www.bmi.com/urban.

Follow BMI on Twitter and on Facebook.

Broadcast Music, Inc.® (BMI), a global leader in rights management, is an American performing right organization that represents more than 475,000 songwriters, composers and music publishers in all genres of music and more than 6.5 million works. BMI has represented the most popular and beloved music from around the world for 70 years. The U.S. corporation collects license fees from businesses that use music, which it then distributes as royalties to the musical creators and copyright owners it represents. BMI songwriters and composers were the most celebrated creative voices in awards presentations and on the charts during the past year, accounting for almost two-thirds of the Grammy Awards and dominating other key awards and honors presentations across all genres of music.

www.bmi.com

Photos/Multimedia Gallery Available: http://www.businesswire.com/cgi-bin/mmg.cgi?eid=6842533&lang=en

Contacts

BMI Los Angeles
Marlene Meraz, 310-289-6325

FIGURE 5.1 This release, distributed by Business Wire on behalf BMI, shows the basic format and components of an online news release that can be easily emailed to journalists and bloggers.

information about the organization. The news release shown in Figure 5.1 illustrates these basic components.

Letterhead

The first page of a news release is usually printed on an organization's letterhead. The letterhead often gives the name of the organization, its address, telephone number, and website.

Many organizations tailor a letterhead specifically for news releases. The Shedd Aquarium in Chicago, for example, has a letterhead with its logo on the left and the words "News Release" on the right. The aquarium also uses the terms "For Immediate Release," but many publicists say this is just a somewhat meaningless tradition in today's digital world of instant 24/7 news. See Figure 5.2.

That may be true, but there are times that a writer will request a specific release time. For example, you may write: "For Release after 9 P.M. January 16." This

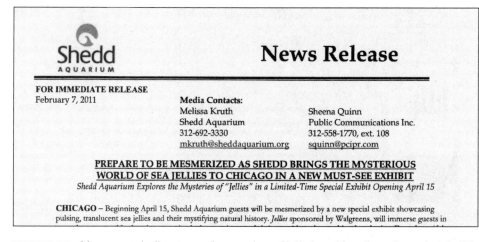

FIGURE 5.2 Many organizations use a "news release" letterhead for all media materials. This letterhead, used by the Shedd Aquarium in Chicago to announce a new exhibit, also uses the traditional "For Immediate Release," but many organizations consider it unnecessary.

often occurs when the release concerns a speech by someone or an award that is announced at a certain time. The primary reason is that unplanned things happen. The speaker or award recipient, because of a plane delay or another emergency, may not show up. In such a case, the media would look foolish reporting on a speech or an award that was never given.

On occasion, an organization will attempt to "embargo" information about a major new product until a formal announcement at a news conference or a meeting. Apple Computer, for example, often sends advance material to the media but with the understanding that they won't publish or broadcast it until the official unveiling at MacWorld or a similar venue. But, of course, leaks always occur. In general, publicists use the embargo sparingly—usually in the case of announcing a major new product, a merger between two major companies, or a change in executive leadership.

Contacts

All news releases should provide a contact person reporters can reach if they have questions or need more information. When a contact is given on a news release, it is assumed that he or she is knowledgeable and qualified about the subject of the news release.

It's also important that the person be readily available to take phone calls and respond immediately to email inquiries. Reporters often complain that the contact is impossible to reach, or doesn't seem to know anything more than what is already stated in the news release. So, if you are listed as a contact, make sure you are thoroughly prepared and can respond almost immediately. Many stories never see the light of day simply because a reporter couldn't reach a contact before the publication's deadline.

The name, telephone, and email address of a contact person are usually given at the top of the traditional news release, but contact information is often provided at the end of online news releases. The idea is to not clutter up the beginning of a news release with such information—and make sure the headline is the most dominant visual. Some examples of a contact listing:

Jim Christensen, HP

+1 408 447 1678

Jim.christensen@hp.com

Rhonda Markos, 407-444-7073

rimarkos@national.aaa.com

Twitter: @AAASafety

If a public relations firm has prepared the release, it's customary to also provide the name and contact details of the staff person handling the account. See Figure 5.2, showing the news release letterhead from Shedd Aquarium. If the news release is distributed nationally, or even internationally, it often is a good idea to also provide an after-hours number to accommodate time zone differences.

Headline

The purpose of the headline is to give a journalist a quick indication of what the news release is about. Headlines are supposed to give the "bottom line"—the most newsworthy aspect of the story—because surveys show that 8 out of 10 people (including journalists) will read headline copy, but only 2 out of 10 will read the rest. Headlines should be factual, devoid of hype, and to the point.

> **"On the average, five times as many people read the headline as read the body copy. When you have written your headline, you have spent 80 cents of your dollar."** David Ogilvy, a legend in the advertising business

Most news releases, particularly product-related ones, carry a brief headline. This usually appears in boldface and in a slightly larger type than that used in the body of the news release. Thus, if the body is in 12-point type, the headline often is in 14- or 16-point type.

Here are some examples:

Merck Develops New Drug for Asthma Sufferers

Comcast Donates $250,000 to Tornado Relief Efforts

Southwest Airlines Names New Vice President of Cargo & Charters

Increasingly, news releases include a second headline, known as a *subhead*. This provides additional key information to journalists and editors, because they scan virtually hundreds of news releases in a short amount of time. See Figure 5.3 to see how McCormick & Company effectively used a secondary headline. Here are some other examples of using a subhead:

Lady Gaga Tops Forbes' Celebrity 100 Power List

Justin Bieber, Katy Perry, Natalie Portman and Mark Harmon Are Among Notables

AAA and the League of American Bicyclists Gear Up to Promote Safety

Recent Data Show the Average Age of a Bicyclist Killed in a Traffic Crash Is 41

Parents: Are Your Grads Ready for the Real World?

National Survey Finds College Grads Likely to Fall Through Gaps in Health Insurance Coverage

Note that these headlines are written in the active present tense. Avoid past tense; it gives the impression that the news item is not timely. Another tip is to use only 8 to 10 words in a headline so Google News and other aggregators such as Digg can easily index your news release by word and topic to facilitate search queries by journalists and the public. There's also the fine art of selecting key-words for a headline to take advantage of *search engine optimization* (SEO). This is discussed in greater detail on page 133 in the section about writing online news releases.

Dateline

The dateline, in all capital letters, appears at the start of the lead paragraph, which is discussed in the next section. The dateline is simply the city where the release originated. You don't have to mention the state if the city is a major one, but smaller, less familiar cities and towns usually include the state. For example, a news release might be datelined RICHMOND, VA, or MANCHESTER, NH, whereas CHICAGO or SAN FRANCISCO can stand alone.

After the name of the city, the date of the release is often given. For example, a complete dateline would be as follows: ST. LOUIS—February 8, 2012. If a news release is being distributed to other nations, however, it's wise to use the day first, followed by the month and the year (8 February 2012), which is the pattern used by almost every nation except the United States. By spelling out the month, the date is clear whether you use the U.S. style or the international method. If you simply write, "2/8/12," there can be confusion. Are you saying "February 8" (U.S. style) or "August 8" (international sequence)? The date of a news release can also be placed in small type above the headline. Those who favor this approach say a date should not clutter up the lead paragraph.

The Lead

The most important part of any release is the **lead** paragraph. In one to three sentences, you must give the reader the basic details of the story or entice the reader to read the second paragraph. Marvin Arth, author of *The Newsletter Editor's Desk Book*, says the trick to good lead writing is to focus immediately on the most newsworthy or interesting point and to reserve other details until later in the story.

Unfortunately, three common mistakes are often made. One is to write leads crammed with too much information. The result is an elongated lead paragraph of 9 or 10 lines that tends to turn off journalists and readers because such a mass

CONTACTS:
Laurie Harrsen
McCormick & Company, Inc.
410/527-8753
Laurie_Harrsen@mccormick.com

Ginny Brocker
Weber Shandwick
312/988-2025
GBrocker@webershandwick.com

**MCCORMICK ANNOUNCES GRILL MATES® AND LAWRY'S®
FLAVOR FORECAST® 2011: GRILLING EDITION**
Grilling Experts Identify Key Trends and Flavors for the Season

HUNT VALLEY, Md. (April 26, 2011) - What's influencing popular flavors on the grill this summer? Big spice profiles, regional American twists, adventurous global inspirations and new tart-sweet combinations will be stoking the fires for a delicious grilling season - as shown in the new **McCormick® Grill Mates® and Lawry's® Flavor Forecast® 2011: Grilling Edition.**

An expanded arsenal of ingredients, techniques and tools has become the modern grillmaster's badge of honor. As the art of grilling continues to evolve, 73 percent of today's grillers say they are looking for the latest trends and techniques. In fact, three quarters of them like to layer flavors and ingredients.[1]

"We see the growing obsession with bolder and more exciting tastes reach a fever pitch during grilling season," said Mary Beth Harrington of the McCormick Kitchens. "There's a real willingness to try new flavors and preparations. For example, now that grillers are confident in a 'basic' grilled steak, they're adding big flavor with a zesty balsamic marinade and serving it sliced over a colorful salad, with a sweet and tangy blueberry dressing."

The **McCormick Grill Mates and Lawry's Flavor Forecast 2011: Grilling Edition** has identified four trends that are firing up flavor this season:

---

[1] Grilling Attitude & Usage and Segmentation Study, deKadt Marketing and Research, Inc. 2010.

FIGURE 5.3 News releases often have a major headline and a secondary headline. This allows busy journalists and bloggers to immediately understand what the news release is about. The tactic also emphasizes the organization's key message. This release, by McCormick & Company, is in the traditional, double-spaced format. See the same release in an online format in Figure 5.4

of words in one paragraph is visually unattractive to the average person. The second is flowery adjectives. This is particularly true in the tourism and entertainment industry. One news release for a Caribbean resort had a lead paragraph that used such terms as "a hidden gem in paradise" with rooms featuring "breathtaking ocean views," "fabulous outdoor pools," and the "world's most incredible cave diving."

The third mistake is a lead paragraph of 9 or 10 lines filled with technobabble. Here is an example of the first four lines of an eight-line lead paragraph:

> Applied Micro Circuits Corporation, a global leader in embedded Power Architecture processing, optical transport, and storage solutions, announced its two new versions of its successful family of Rubicon products that enable low cost Carrier Grade Ethernet services over Metro and Core SONET/SDH and OTN networks.

Inexperienced writers, even those not writing a high-tech release, often clutter up a lead paragraph with unnecessary words and a tangle of information that is difficult to digest. Here is an example:

> Evergreen Community College is pleased to announce a Medical Career Education Expo to be held this Saturday, March 29, 2012, from 10 A.M. until 4 P.M. Both Richmond campuses, South Side at 800 Moorehead Park Drive and West End at 2809 Emerywood Parkway, will be participating in this exciting event.

This lead is cluttered in several ways. First, it's not necessary to give the year; this is assumed. Second, there are unnecessary "hype" words such as "pleased to announce" and "this exciting event." Third, two locations and addresses are given that would be better placed in a subsequent paragraph.

Clutter also occurs when a writer tries to put too many of the five Ws and one H in the lead paragraph. The solution is to put only the most important element of the story in the lead paragraph. The other Ws, or the H, can be woven into the succeeding paragraphs. Here are examples of leads that emphasize only one element:

» **Who:** Recording artist Lisa Atkinson will lead a sing-along and entertain preschool children.

» **What:** "Fire, Earth, and Water," a major exhibit of pre-Columbian sculpture from the Land Collection, opens Friday.

» **When:** November 15 is the last date for filing claims for flood damage caused by . . .

» **Where:** A golden retriever has won Best of Show honors at the 90th Golden Gate Kennel Club Dog Show.

» **Why:** Farnell of Britain will merge with Premier Industrial of Cleveland. The deal, valued at $2.8 billion, is an effort to consolidate the worldwide distribution of electronics equipment.

» **How:** Flextime, the system that permits employees to set their own starting and stopping times, has reduced labor turnover at Kellogg Enterprises by . . .

Several types of leads are possible. They are the (1) straight summary lead, (2) informal lead, and (3) feature lead. The type of lead used often depends on the subject matter. If you are making an announcement, a straight summary lead is preferred. Here are some examples:

» United Airlines today announced that Richard B. Hirst has been named senior vice president of corporate affairs and general counsel.

» More than 25,000 grocery workers in the Baltimore-Washington area represented by the United Food and Commercial Workers Union (UFCW) have reached a tentative agreement with Giant Foods and Safeway.

» The American Red Cross and the Greater Cleveland Business Planning Association (BEPA) will host a series of extreme crisis communications seminars, led by communications expert Bruce Hennes.

» Forty high school seniors today were named finalists for the Intel Science Talent Search. The competition, called the "junior Nobel Prize," is America's oldest and most prestigious high school science competition.

> *Aside from the news item itself, the most important parts of a news release are the headline and the first paragraph.*
>
> Ron Consolino, columnist for the *Houston Chronicle*

The second type of lead is the informal lead, which often provides factual information but in a more informal way. Such leads are often used for publicizing community events or reporting the results of surveys, which are timely but not exactly "hard" news. Here are some examples:

» The sky will be ablaze with the crackle of scale-model machine-gun fire this weekend at the Hill Country Air Museum in Morgan Hill.

» A new national survey finds as parents celebrate their child's graduation, they and their children may not be prepared for all the "real world" costs. When asked if their child had a medical emergency or needed health care while uninsured, only 44 percent of parents say they would pay for their child's expenses, while 39 percent would offer to share the cost or teach the child how to take out a loan. (news release from Aetna, an insurance company)

» The results are in!!! The Tooth Fairy Poll from Securian Dental Plans reports an increase in the current average "gift" U.S. children receive from the Tooth Fairy. Children receive an average of $2.09 per tooth, which is up from last year's gift of $1.71—a 22 percent increase. Tooth Fairy gift amounts range from a low of five cents to a high of $50 per tooth.

The third type of lead is the feature lead, which raises the reader's interest. Essentially, the lead is a "hook" that encourages the reader to read the second paragraph for more information. Feature leads are often used for news releases that are sent to specialized sections of a daily newspaper, such as the travel, auto, lifestyle, and food sections. These news releases, which are also discussed in Chapter 7, are topical but are not as time sensitive as announcement releases. Here are some examples:

» One hundred years ago, Italian immigrant Amedeo Obici "cracked the nut" on how to deliver fresh-tasting peanuts when he established Planters, known today as America's grandest nut company. This year, Planters marks 100 years of history, heritage, and delivering consistently fresh-tasting nuts with a year-long anniversary celebration.

» A transatlantic trip to Naples, Italy, is no longer necessary to dine on the best lasagna, which instead can be found in Naples, Florida, at the namesake Italian restaurant, Naples Tomato.

» Things are getting green in St. Louis—and we're not talking about the foliage. St. Patrick's Day is practically upon us and the Gateway City is gearing up to celebrate its Irish heritage in grand style. St. Louis has a rich history and strong connection to the Emerald Isle—and we're not afraid to show it.

» What makes maps so hypnotic? Is it their endless detail that magically draws us in? The worlds of possibilities they offer as they take us on vicarious journeys? The connection to a moment in history? Their sometimes dazzling beauty? (news release from the Field Museum in Chicago on an exhibition of maps)

The mechanics of a lead paragraph are relatively simple. Always keep these guidelines in mind to help readers quickly understand the information:

» Use strong declarative sentences.
» Use 25 words or less for the first sentence of a lead.
» Keep the number of dependent clauses to a minimum.
» Never start a lead paragraph with a prepositional phrase such as "At a meeting held…"
» Keep the lead paragraph limited to a maximum of three to five lines.
» Rewrite any sentence that is more than three lines long.

For a quick guide to remembering all these numbers, see Tips for Success on page 129.

Body of the Text

The journalistic "inverted pyramid" is the template for the body of a news release. Essentially, it means that the most important information is the apex of the pyramid and other information or details are given in descending order of importance. The top of the pyramid is always the lead paragraph, which has just been discussed.

There are three reasons for using the inverted pyramid structure that puts the most relevant information in the first one or two paragraphs of a news release: (1) if the editor or reporter doesn't find something interesting in the first few lines, he or she won't use the story; (2) editors often cut the bulk of a news release so it's wise to have the most important information at the start; and (3) most people only read headlines and perhaps the first paragraph or two of a news story .

Tips for Success · A News Release by the Numbers: A Quick Guide

Experts recommend that you keep the following numbers in mind when writing a news release:

+ A news release should focus on only one topic.
+ Headlines should be a maximum of 65 to 70 characters, or about 8 to 10 words.
+ Use 25 words or less in the first line of a lead paragraph.
+ A lead paragraph should be no more than three to five lines.
+ Paragraphs in the body of a news release should be three to six lines.
+ Break up any sentence that runs more than three lines.
+ The standard paragraph at the end of the release describing the organization should be 100 words or less.
+ The maximum length of a standard news release should be 400 words or less.
+ An online news release should be 200–250 words or less.

The inverted pyramid has three parts, says Jeremy Porter, founder of the Journalistics.com blog:

Part One: The opening paragraph or lead, where you give the "must have" information to convey your key message

Part Two: Additional information that is helpful, but not necessary. This can be information that elaborates on the key message and provides supporting information. Quotes from an executive are often used; see Tips for Success on page 130 to learn how to write such quotes.

Part Three: The least important information that is "nice to have" but not "need to have" stuff

You should write paragraphs that are three to six lines long; any longer than this affects readability and the reader's incentive to even bother. There is no rule that news releases should be a specific length, but most writers strive to tell their stories in one or two pages, or fewer than 400 words. Other experts say that an online news release should be even shorter—about 200 to 250 words. The mechanics of online releases will be discussed shortly.

Description of the Organization

The last part of a news release is a standard paragraph that provides basic background information about the company so reporters get some idea about the

Tips for Success   How to Write Executive Quotes

+ A quote from a company executive is often included in a news release and, in many cases, the quote is the creation of the public relations writer. This is usually not a problem because the executive usually approves the quote and the news release before it's distributed.

+ A bigger problem, however, is that the quote doesn't add much to the news release because (1) it's mostly hot air, (2) it's a cliché that could be used in any news release, or (3) it's filled with corporate jargon.

+ Personnel promotions tend to generate the most meaningless quotes. The vice president of operations for Southwest Airline, for example, was quoted in one release as saying, "This is a well deserved promotion for Matt, who has shown his leadership and vision by increasing the breadth, scope, and profitability of our award-winning Cargo service." In other releases, executives are quoted about being "excited" or "pleased" about a new product, expansion, or merger.

+ Corporate jargon also creeps into executive quotes. In a Bank of America release, an executive is quoted as saying, "The company has systematically leveraged every aspect of green building practices throughout their entire workplace building stock to help them standardize their energy efficiency and activate their carbon reduction goals." Do people really talk like this?

+ Lauren Edwards, writing in the *Ragan Report*, notes, "Unfortunately, most companies squander an opportunity by slapping quotation marks on either side of canned messaging. Credible? No. Compelling? No. Likely to induce the MEGO (My eyes glaze over) effect? Yes.

+ So what's the answer to writing executive quotes? First, make sure your quotes actually say something that a real person might say. In other words, the quote should be conversational and in plain English. Second, make sure the quote provides information or additional insight to the topic being discussed.

+ A good example is a release by Campbell Soup Company about a program to help feed people in partnership with May's National Stamp Out Hunger Drive. The company's partner, Social Reality, is quoted in the news release, saying that the campaign, "allows consumers to get involved and make a difference with just the click of a button. Everyone joining the cause generates a one pound donation. Not only are we generating donations, we're bringing new, loyal consumers to Campbell's, who might have not known about their philanthropic partnerships. It's a win-win."

+ HP also effectively used an executive quote to elaborate on and reinforce its message about its new Skyroom video conferencing system. The release quotes the vice president of the workstations group saying, "Finally, video meetings with genuine eye contact and natural human interaction are as easy as starting an instant messaging connection."

organization's size and purpose, particularly if the organization is not a household name. This standard paragraph, up to 100 words, is often called **boilerplate** in the jargon of the field.

"The most valuable of all talents is that of never using two words when one will do."
Thomas Jefferson

Information that can be included in a boilerplate statement is: (1) market position, (2) aspiration, (3) size, (4) scope of business activity, (5) geographic coverage, and (6) company core values. Other information might include a listing of trademarked names used in the release. This alerts the reporter to what products and services must be capitalized. Thus, there will be a notation such as "Windows is a U.S. registered trademark of Microsoft Corp." The following are some examples of company boilerplate statements:

About Mayo Clinic

Mayo Clinic is a nonprofit worldwide leader in medical care, research, and education for people from all walks of life. For more information, visit www.mayoclinic.org/about and www.mayoclinic.org/news.

About HP

HP creates new possibilities for technology to have a meaningful impact on people, businesses, governments and society. The world's largest technology company, HP brings together a portfolio that spans printing, personal computing, software services and IT infrastructure to solve customer problems. More information about HP (NYSE:HPQ) is available at http://www.hp.com.

About Google, Inc.

Google's innovative search technologies connect millions of people around the world with information every day. Founded in 1998 by Stanford Ph.D. students Larry Page and Sergey Brin, Google today is a top web property in all major global markets. Google's targeted advertising program provides businesses of all sizes with measurable results, while enhancing the overall web experience for users. Google is headquartered in Silicon Valley with offices throughout the Americas, Europe, and Asia. For more information, please visit www.google.com. Google, Google Apps. Google Docs, Google Calendar, and Google Talk are registered trademarks of Google, Inc.

About Ore-Ida

The Ore-Ida brand is the most trusted and popular name in the frozen potato and onion business. As the nation's leading marketer of frozen potatoes since 1952, people count on the Ore-Ida brand for quality, great-tasting, convenient foods families love. Heinz produces a variety of Ore-Ida frozen potato and onion products, including: Steam n' Mash Potatoes, Golden Fries, Golden Crinkles fries, Steak Fries, Tater Tots potatoes, Hash Browns, Ultimate Baked, Onion Rings, and the most recent introduction of Sweet Potato Fries.

See the Tips for Success on page 132 for more "rules" on how to write an effective news release.

Tips for Success   Rules for Writing a News Release

All news releases should be "news centered." Here is a list of guidelines primarily from Schubert Communications, a Pennsylvania public relations firm, but also supplemented with other sources:

+ Use short, succinct headlines and subheads to highlight main points and pique interest. They should not simply be a repeat of the information in the lead-in paragraph.

+ Don't use generic words and phrases such as "the leading provider" or "world-class" to position your company. Be specific; use phrases such as "with annual revenues of."

+ Don't describe products using phrases such as "unique" or "total solution." Use specific terms or examples to demonstrate the product's distinctness.

+ Use descriptive and creative words to grab an editor's attention, but make sure they are accurate and not exaggerated.

❝Press releases aren't dead, but a poorly written news release is a waste of time for both the company and the reader. ❞ Jenn Riggle, associate vice president and social media leader, CRT/Tanaka

+ Don't highlight the name of your company or product in the headline of a news release if it is not highly recognized. If you are not a household name, focus on the news instead.

+ Tell the news. Focus on how your announcement affects your industry and lead with that rather than overtly promoting your product or company.

Localize whenever possible. A local news angle trumps a generic news release.

+ Critique your writing by asking yourself, "Who cares?" Why should readers be interested in this information?

+ Verify all facts and statistics that you are using. Provide attribution for credibility.

+ Don't use lame quotes. Write like someone is actually talking—eliminate the "corporatese" that editors love to ignore. Craft quotes that provide additional perspective or information, not clichés about how "how excited we are about a product" or "how pleased we are to get the contract."

+ Target your writing. Create two different tailored releases that will go out to different types of media rather than a general release that isn't of great interest to either group.

+ Look for creative ways to tie your announcement in to current news or trends.

+ Write simply. Use contractions, write in active voice, be direct, avoid paired words like "clear and simple," and incorporate common action-oriented phrases to generate excitement. Sentences should be no longer than 25 or 30 words.

+ Follow the *Associated Press Stylebook* and specific publications' editorial standards for dates, technical terms, abbreviations, punctuation, spellings, capitalization, etc.

+ Proofread for spelling, grammar, and punctuation errors. Don't rely exclusively on a spell-checker.

+ Don't overdo it. It's important to write colorfully, to focus on small specific details, to include descriptions of people, places, and events, but do not write poetry when you want press.

+ Don't be formulaic in your news release writing. Not every release must start with the name of the company or product. Break out of the mold to attract media attention.

+ Don't expect editors to print your entire release. Important information should be in the first two paragraphs.

+ Be accessible at all times to answer any follow-up queries from reporters and bloggers.

News Release Formats

The Traditional News Release

The standard news release, as pointed out at the beginning of the chapter, has been around for more than a century with only minor changes to its original format. Essentially, it's a double-spaced document on 8.5- by 11-inch paper that is mailed or faxed to newspapers and broadcast media Today, they continue to be used by many organizations and civic clubs despite pronouncements by social media gurus that they are "relics of the stone age."

> ❝*Journalists, especially those who sit on those panels where they hate on PR people, usually say how much they despise them, but as soon as you speak to them about a news story, they ask 'Do you have a press release?'*❞
>
> Jackson Wightman, in a post on www.prdaily.com

One only needs to review the stacks of news releases that still arrive by snail mail at newspaper offices around the country, or even the media kits (discussed in Chapter 6) that are still being produced in paper form. As one publicist explains, "Our job is to offer the information in any format that the journalist or media outlet desires." For example, even if you visit a corporate newsroom on the Web you will find any number of traditional double-spaced news releases posted on the site that can be downloaded by journalists and the public.

Standard margins for a traditional news release are 2 inches from the top of the page and about 1.5 inches from each side and the bottom of the page. If you have a letterhead, start writing copy about 2 inches below it. See Figure 5.3 on page 124 for an example of a standard news release distributed by McCormick & Company.

Some other formatting rules for a traditional release are as follows:

» Use 10- or 12-point standard type. Courier and Times Roman are popular fonts because they are easy to read. Avoid "squeezing" copy to fit on one page by reducing the size of type: This is self-defeating.

» Don't split sentences or paragraphs between pages.

» Never hyphenate a word at the end of a line. Unjustified right margins are acceptable.

» Number the pages of a news release.

» Place a *slug line* (a short description) at the top of each page after the first one. This identifies the story in case the pages get separated.

» Write "more" at the end of each page if the news release continues.

» Use "###" at the end of your news release. This has replaced the old journalistic "-30-"

The Online News Release

Although the traditional news release is still used, particularly among weekly newspapers in small towns across the nation, the vast majority of news releases today are prepared for distribution by email or via electronic distribution services such as BusinessWire. In fact, most surveys shows that up to 90 percent of journalists prefer to receive news releases via email. See Figure 5.4 for an example of an online news

Flavor Forecast 2011 GRILLING EDITION

NEWS RELEASE

McCormick Announces Grill Mates® and Lawry's® Flavor Forecast® 2011: Grilling Edition

Grilling Experts Identify Key Trends and Flavors for the Season

Recipe & Product Image Gallery:

Recipe & Product Images

More Info:

Press Release Printer-Friendly PDF

Grill Mates Fact Sheet

Lawry's Fact Sheet

Recipes by Flavor Pairing:

Smoke & Craft Brews

Mustard & Sweet Onion

Fiery Peppers & Grilled Corn

Paprika & Orange

Balsamic & Blueberry

HUNT VALLEY, Md. (April 26, 2011) – What's influencing popular flavors on the grill this summer? Big spice profiles, regional American twists, adventurous global inspirations and new tart-sweet combinations will be stoking the fires for a delicious grilling season – as shown in the new **McCormick® Grill Mates® and Lawry's® Flavor Forecast® 2011: Grilling Edition.**

An expanded arsenal of ingredients, techniques and tools has become the modern grillmaster's badge of honor. As the art of grilling continues to evolve, 73 percent of today's grillers say they are looking for the latest trends and techniques. In fact, three quarters of them like to layer flavors and ingredients.[1]

"We see the growing obsession with bolder and more exciting tastes reach a fever pitch during grilling season," said Mary Beth Harrington of the McCormick Kitchens. "There's a real willingness to try new flavors and preparations. For example, now that grillers are confident in a 'basic' grilled steak, they're adding big flavor with a zesty balsamic marinade and serving it sliced over a colorful salad, with a sweet and tangy blueberry dressing."

The **McCormick Grill Mates and Lawry's Flavor Forecast 2011: Grilling Edition** has identified four trends that are firing up flavor this season:

- **The New Tart 'n Sweet** – The American palate is waking up to the uplifting excitement of sour ingredients. Grill-side, these foods find invigorating partners in fruits and naturally sweet flavors.

- **Regional American Fire** – Unique local ingredients and proud regional techniques are gaining a new level of acclaim and influence.

- **Hot, Hotter, Hottest!** – From earthy ancho to smoky chipotle to the red hot pop of cayenne – grillers are creating dynamic taste experiences by mixing and matching heat and flavors.

- **Flames of Adventure** - Backyard chefs of all skill levels are more willing than ever to try something new on the grates. With daring flavor combinations and a hunger for excitement, they're exploring new global frontiers at the grill.

CONTACTS:

Laurie Harrsen
McCormick
410/527-8753
Email

Ginny Brocker
Weber Shandwick
312/988-2025
Email

www.flavorforecast.com

Flavor Forecast®
2011 Grilling
Edition Printer-
Friendly
PDF

Flavor Forecast®
2011 Report
Printer-Friendly
PDF

FIGURE 5.4 McCormick & Company prepares news releases in various formats to accommodate the needs of the media and social network sites. Figure 5.3 shows the traditional news release, and this is the online version. It's a single-spaced format with a number of photos embedded that journalists can easily download to complement the story. The company also formats news releases for mobile distribution, which requires narrow margins to fit the screen of a smartphone.

release posted in the newsroom of McCormick & Company's website. Compare this with the same information posted as a standard news release, shown in Figure 5.3.

The basic components of the traditional news release are still present, but email releases have several format differences:

» Copy is now single-spaced instead of double spaced.

» The ideal length is 200 to 250 words instead of up to 400 words.

» The emphasis is on brevity so journalists see most of the release on one screen without having to scroll.

» The subject line in the email, instead of the release headline, becomes the most important factor in determining whether a recipient clicks "open" or "delete."

» Contact information is often given at the bottom of the email release instead of at the top.

» A quote in larger type is often highlighted in the body of the news release.

» A photo or logo is often embedded in the release for possible use with the story. See Figure 5.5.

B. L. Ochman, writing in *The Strategist*, suggests that you should "think of the electronic news release as a teaser to get a reporter or editor to your website for additional information." He makes the following additional suggestions:

» The subject line must, in a few words, say exactly what the news release is about. Don't be too "cute" or vague.

» Use bullets to convey key points.

» Write only two or three short sentences in each of the five paragraphs.

FIGURE 5.5 Anyone for a brewpub burger? News releases often include photos and other graphics to complement the story. McCormick & Company, which makes a variety of spices, often includes high-resolution photos and recipes in its online news releases to highlight how its products are used. Chapter 8 further discusses the production and use of publicity photos.

» Above the headline, or at the bottom of the release, be sure to provide a contact name, phone number, email address, and URL for additional information.

» Never send a release as an attachment. Journalists, because of possible virus infections, rarely open attachments unless they know and trust the source.

Ochman concludes, "Write like you have 10 seconds to make a point. Because online, you do."

The Vital Need for SEO — News releases distributed online are only effective, however, if the writer carefully uses what is known as **search engine optimization (SEO)** techniques. Essentially, SEO is the process of selecting keywords for the news release that make the content easily retrievable if a journalist or even a consumer conducts a search on Google, Bing, or Yahoo!. Another aspect is using one or two keywords within the first 65–70 characters of the headline and in the first two paragraphs of your news release because search engines, like us, read from top to bottom.

A cruise line, for example, might want to publicize its "eco-friendly" tours but most people would probably use the term "green cruises" in a search. Therefore, the cruise line should use "green" as a keyword in its news release. Or a university may want to publicize a major fundraising campaign as part of its "University Advancement" activities, but most people don't use this somewhat jargonized term. So the university should probably use "fundraising" "donations" or "gifts" as a keyword in the news release headline and in the body of the story. The headline might say, "Ohio State Launches Major Fundraising Campaign for Donations." Anyone using the words "Ohio State" and "Donations" or "Fundraising" would probably come across the news release in a search.

> **"From press materials to the blog posts that we recommend our clients write, we always keep an eye on SEO because Google is the place where everyone starts these days."** Todd Defren, principal with Boston-based Shift Communications

So how do you know what keywords would generate the most search results for you? Fortunately, Google has some tools that give you guidance. One tool is *Google's AdWords*, which gives you insight into what phrases are searched most frequently. Remember that informal words are used most frequently by people, so avoid industry jargon and product service names as keywords.

The *Google External Keyword* tool is also helpful because it lists other words associated with a major keyword and how much they are searched. The strawberry industry may decide to issue a news release about Valentine's Day recipes, but not many searches are done on this topic. However, "Valentine's Day ideas" gets thousands of searches, so perhaps a good news release headline might be "Need an Idea for Valentine's Day? Try a Recipe Using Fresh Strawberries."

Google Trends is also a good tool to find out when to issue a news release. In the case of Valentine's Day, the data available from Google indicate that people don't really start searching for Valentine's Day ideas until the first part of February, so your strawberry recipes news release should probably be sent to journalists and bloggers at that time instead of sometime in January.

The Multimedia News Release

SEO also plays a major role in the multimedia news release, which is also referred to as a *social media release* (SMR). These releases, pioneered by the major electronic distribution services, such as Business Wire, PR Newswire, PRWeb, and Marketwire, now make it possible to embed a news release with high-resolution photos/graphics, video, and audio components. In addition, these services have teamed up with search engines such as Google, Yahoo!, and MSN to promote maximum exposure of the news release.

An SMR, for example, will include social media tags so the content can be circulated through Digg, Technorati, Delicious and other social bookmarking sites to increase search engine rankings of the release and to drive targeted traffic to the organization's website. Other links will be to blogs, an organization's on-line newsroom, and even a space where readers can post comments about the news release. In other words, the SMR has expanded the audience beyond just the traditional media outlets.

Marketwire, in particular, has added services to address social media. According to Craig McGuire in *PRWeek*, "The service includes social bookmarks and tags, news channel distribution, audio headline summaries, search-engine-friendly permalinks, social video hosting on Photobucket, photo hosting on YouTube, and more." According to Paolina Milana, vice president for Marketwire, "Social media releases are generally formatted so information is easy to scan, utilizing bullets and lists of ready-made quotes instead of dense text." See the components of Marketwire's social media release in Figure 5.6.

> **Whereas PR professionals used to target journalists to get a story placed, a social media press release is about targeting three different people: journalists, bloggers, and most importantly consumers. It needs to make sense to all of them individually.** Brian Solis, coauthor of *Putting the Public Back into Public Relations*

The following are some tips for preparing SMRs:

» Include links to pages where multiple instances of your keywords/key phrases reinforce your message.

» Place keywords in headlines and first paragraphs.

» Distribute a release through a service that carries hyperlinks to downstream sites such as Yahoo!, Google, Digg, Facebook, and Twitter.

» Be judicious with links. Too many links will confuse journalists and draw focus away from key messaging.

» Use high-resolution multimedia that can be easily downloaded.

» Be selective about photos and videos; make sure they complement the key message.

Multimedia news releases, of course, are touted as being much more effective than the less sophisticated email release that only has text and perhaps one embedded photo. PRNewswire, for example, claims that its multimedia news releases get almost 80 percent more views than the standard email release and that readers are

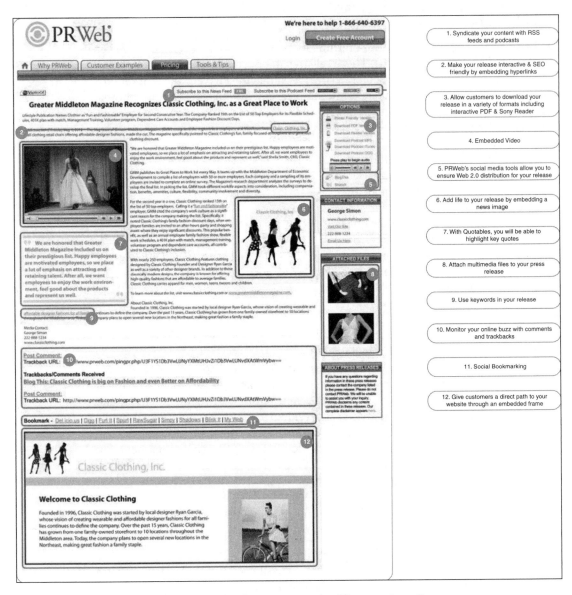

FIGURE 5.6 This PRWeb graphic highlights the components of the smart media news release. The annotations on the side of the sample news release show the placement of such tools as multimedia, embedded hyperlinks, social media tags, blogs, and newsroom links. These news releases are designed to directly reach consumers through search engine optimization and make the information readily accessible on any number of Internet sites.

3.5 times more likely to share the multimedia release with friends. The SMR also fulfills the prediction of Manny Ruiz, president of Hispanic PR Wire, that "the press release of the last century is dead." He enthusiastically adds, "In its place is a dynamic service that is more of an interactive marketing tool, more relevant and compelling for journalists; the difference is it's not only for journalists."

This may be true, but it's still worth remembering that the vast majority of news releases, even those carried by the electronic distribution services, are still basic releases about mundane activities that don't require photos, videos, or audio components. There's also some evidence that SMRs are not that popular with most journalists. One survey, conducted via Twitter, found that almost 75 percent of the respondents actually preferred a news release as text in an email.

Consequently, public relations staff often prepare an email text version and a multimedia version of the same news release. One firm, for example, distributed a one-page email release that only provided the client's Web page, where reporters could get information. The second release was formatted so reporters could click on links to (1) photos and **video clips**, (2) the client's YouTube channel, (3) the client's micro site about the product, (4) the iTunes App store, and (5) the client's Facebook page.

More discussion of placement and distribution is provided in Chapter 10, "Distributing News to the Media."

Summary

The Backbone of Publicity Programs

» News releases are a basic element of almost every publicity plan. When published or broadcast, they can raise public awareness and influence decision making.

» The media are flooded with hundreds of news releases. To beat the odds and get space or time, your release must be newsworthy, timely, and well written.

The Value of News Releases

» News releases are a cost-effective way of informing the media and the public about an organization's products, services, and operations.

» Journalists and bloggers rely on news releases as a source of information on which to write stories and cover events.

Planning a News Release

» Planning worksheets and answering the five Ws and one H are the basic first steps in writing a news release.

» An effective news release must also be newsworthy from the standpoint of why a journalist or the public would be interested in the information.

» A news release follows the same rules and format of a journalistic news story; it should conform to Associated Press (AP) style.

The Basic Components of a News Release

» The news release has six components: organization name, contacts, headline, dateline, lead paragraph, and body of text. A seventh component can be a standard paragraph, often called *boiler-plate,* at the end of the news release that provides basic information about the organization.

» Contacts listed on a news release should be knowledgeable about the topic and highly accessible to reporters who call for more information.

» Lead paragraphs summarize the basic story in five lines or less. Feature leads should arouse interest and encourage people to keep reading or listening.

» Don't try to get all five Ws and one H (who, what, when, where, why, and how) in the lead paragraph. Choose the most important one or two elements.

» Write news releases that will appeal to editors and their audiences. Too many releases please the client or employer but violate journalistic standards.

» News releases are highly structured pieces of writing. Use inverted pyramid style, with the most important facts first.

» Keep news releases factual. Avoid puffery and hype.

News Release Formats

» There are three basic formats: (1) the traditional news release, (2) the online news release, and (3) the multimedia release.

» The traditional news release is double spaced and often distributed via mail or fax to media outlets.

» The online release is now the predominant format; it is a single-spaced document with an ideal length of 200–250 words. It is sent to journalists via email or can be downloaded from the "press-room" of an organization's website. If emailed, the subject heading must be concise and clear to attract attention.

» The multimedia release is also called the *social media release* (SMR) and includes embedded photos, videos, and links to other websites and information.

» Search engine optimization (SEO) is the process of carefully selecting keywords that can be indexed by search engines such as Google. The best keywords are those that an average person would use when conducting a search.

Skill Building Activities

1. There is a list of six questions on page 120 that a writer should answer before writing a news release. Answer these questions as if you were preparing a news release for the following situations:

   a. A new play is opening at the city's professional repertory theater.

   b. A food company is introducing a completely fat-free potato chip.

   c. The local Red Cross chapter is kicking off its annual drive for blood donations.

2. Study the lead paragraphs of stories in the daily newspaper. Find three examples of each of the following: (a) a straight summary lead, (b) an informal lead, and (c) a feature lead. Note in what sections of the newspaper that you found the various kinds of leads, such as local news, lifestyle, business, travel, etc.

3. The point is made that the most important information should be in the lead of a news release. There can, however, be some question about what information is the most newsworthy. A company, for example, is planning to announce a $150 million overhaul of its information technology (IT) infrastructure at its headquarters in Charlotte, North Carolina. The project will also require the hiring of 100 new IT personnel. If

you were writing the lead for this news release, would you emphasize the $150 million overhaul or the creation of 100 new jobs? Explain your answer.

4. The websites for HP, Google, Ore-Ida, and Mayo Clinic are given on page 131 as part of the company boilerplate at the end of a news release. Go to these websites and visit each company's "pressroom" to review various news releases. Write a short memo about the content, subject matter, and format of the news releases you find.

5. Electronic distribution services post hundreds of news releases every day. Go to BusinessWire (www.businesswire .com) or PR Newswire (www.prnewswire .com) and scroll through the news releases posted on a particular day. What is your impression?

6. Write a standard news release for your college newspaper about the upcoming meeting of a student organization that has invited a well-known author to speak on campus. Follow the guidelines in the chapter regarding the six basic elements of a news release. At the end of the release, include a brief description of the organization.

7. Convert the news release written in question 6 to the format of (1) an online news release, and (2) a multimedia news release.

8. A company has made a major breakthrough in producing solar panels that are cost effective and produce twice as much energy as anything on the market. Use *Google Trends, Google Adwords*, and *Google External Keyword* to help you write a news release that would use keywords that would help people find this news release on the Web if they did a search.

Media Resources

Dubois, L. (2010, November 22). "How to Write a Social Media Release." Retrieved from www.inc.com/guides.

Grieb, J. (2011, January). "Make Your Press Release Boilerplate Sizzle." *The Ragan Report*, 15–16.

Hanson. A. (2011, February 8). "Is the Press Release Really Dead?" Retrieved from www.arikhanson.com.

Junker, D. (2010, May). "Move Beyond the Pyramid: Finding a Natural Order for Your News Release." *Public Relations Tactics*, 16.

Kennedy, M. (2010, November 29). "Five Things to Check before Sending Your Next Release." Retrieved from www.ragan.com.

Porter, J. (2011, March 20). "Eight Tips for Writing Press Releases That Journalists Read." Retrieved from www.prdaily.com.

Riggle, J. (2010, November 19). "Are Executive Quotes Killing Press Releases?" Retrieved from www.ragan.com.

Sebastian, M. (2011, March 24). "Social Media News Release: Five Examples to Inspire You." Retrieved from www.prdaily.com.

Smallwood, L. (2011, February 17). "PR Magnetism: Five SEO Tips for Writing Client Copy That Attracts." Retrieved from www.paratuscommunications.com.

Strong, F. (2010, December 16). "How to Write a News Release That Gets Attention." Retrieved from www.problogger.net.

Wightman, J. (2011, March 3). "Seven Gripes about the Press Release—from Someone Who Writes Them." Retrieved from www.prdaily.com.

Wilson, M. (2011, May 2). "Multimedia News Releases Grab 77 Percent More Views, Report Says." Retrieved from www.ragan. com.

Wylie, A. (2011, March). "Anatomy of a 21st-Century News Release: Five Tips That Work." *Public Relations Tactics*, 7.

Preparing Fact Sheets, Advisories, Media Kits, and Pitches

» After reading this chapter, you will be able to:

» Write a basic fact sheet about an event, an organization, or a product

» Prepare media advisories that alert journalists to story opportunities

» Understand the function and contents of a media kit

» Pitch story ideas to journalists and bloggers

Expanding the Publicity Tool Kit

As discussed in the previous chapter, the news release is the backbone of most publicity programs. This chapter explores several other basic publicity tactics that are regularly used to encourage and facilitate media coverage. They include (1) fact sheets, (2) media advisories, and (3) media kits. A fourth tactic that requires a great deal of skill is persuading journalists to write a story about your client or employer.

Fact sheets. These are one-page background sheets about an event, a product, or even the organization. They are formatted in outline or bullet form and may be distributed with a news release or even be part of a media kit. A fact sheet enables journalists to quickly access basic facts about an organization, a product, or event.

Media advisories. Often called *media alerts*, their purpose is to give the basic details (who, what, where, when, why) of an event to encourage media attendance and coverage. Assignment editors use media advisories to assess the newsworthiness of the event and to assign staff to attend.

Media kits. This tool is frequently called a *press kit*. It contains a variety of materials, such as news releases, fact sheets, photos, and short videos that are often assembled for major events and the introduction of new products/services. The purpose of a media kit is to provide a variety of information in one place for the convenience of journalists.

The pitch. When a public relations person contacts a reporter or blogger on a one-to-one basis to "sell" a story idea, it is called making a *pitch*. Contact may be made by email, phone, or even text message or Twitter. The purpose of a pitch is to convince a journalist that your "news" is really newsworthy and should be published or broadcast.

Fact Sheets

Fact sheets are essentially "crib sheets" for journalists. If they are writing about a corporation, for example, they may want to include its annual revenues or even the number of its employees. Or perhaps they will want to add the actual weight and size of a new e-reader to their story. Such facts may not be in the news release, but an accompanying fact sheet often serves as a "cheat sheet" giving them instant access to the information. There are three kinds of fact sheets: (1) event or exhibit announcements, (2) company profiles, and (3) product specifications.

Event or Exhibit Announcements — A fact sheet for an upcoming event, exhibit, or even trade show would use boldface headings to give such basic information as:

» Name of event

» Its sponsor

» Location

» Date and time

» Purpose of event

» Expected attendance

» List of prominent people on program

» Any unusual aspects that make the event newsworthy

The "event" may be a community-wide activity, such as a Jazz Festival, but it could also be the grand opening of a facility for homeless youth. In another situation, the Field Museum of Chicago prepared a basic fact sheet about the opening of a new exhibit on maps. The fact sheet gave (1) the dates of the exhibit, (2) the number of maps on display, (3) a short description of some rare maps on exhibit, (4) hours of the exhibit, (5) admission fees, (6) the museum's address and telephone numbers, and (7) the corporate sponsors.

> "Fact sheets, background materials, and other supporting documents should be made available in a format that is easy for the journalist to recognize and access." Gary Glenn, eNR/NewsWire One

Another Chicago institution, the Shedd Aquarium, used several fact sheets to provide background information on a new exhibit on sea jellies. One fact sheet gave some "Fun Facts" about sea jellies that journalists could use in their stories. One bulleted item, for example, noted "Jellies' mouths are not only used for eating, but also to eliminate waste and reproduce." Another bullet mentioned that a jelly's body is composed of 95 percent water. See Figure 6.1 on page 144.

Shedd
AQUARIUM

Fact Sheet

FOR IMMEDIATE RELEASE

Media Contacts:

Melissa Kruth
Shedd Aquarium
312-692-3330
media@sheddaquarium.org

Roger Germann
Shedd Aquarium
312-692-3265

Jellies Fun Facts

- Despite their name, jellies are mostly made out of the same material that their homes are -- water. A jelly's body is composed of 95 percent water.

- Unlike most animals, jellies do not have bones, brains, eyes or a heart. Instead, they rely on their nervous system to detect and respond to various stimuli.

- Their adaptability has allowed the species to survive for over 500 million years, according to scientists.

- Jellies' mouths are not only used for eating, but also to eliminate waste and reproduce.

- Jellies are known to lay thousands of eggs per day.

- One jelly can eat enough to double its weight each day.

- Sea nettles rarely travel alone. These jellies house hitchhiker animals, such as juvenile cancer crabs, in their bell.

- Upside-down jellies are expert gardeners. These jellies grow a garden of algae on the sea floor, their bodies facing the sun in order to give it plenty of light. The algae use that light to produce food to sustain the jellies.

- With toxins that are harmful only to their prey, blue blubber jellies are the main ingredient in a local delicacy in China, called rubber band salad. Diners describe them as being crispy, but elastic.

- Adult moon jellies, or medusas, usually live three to six months, although medusas more than a year old have been recorded. They can live up to two years in an aquarium setting, and the polyps can live several years.

- Sea nettles are valuable protectors to oyster populations. Sea nettles are known to wipe out entire colonies of comb jellies, which regularly prey on oyster larvae. Additionally, sea nettles can catch oyster larvae, but cannot digest them, instead spitting them out undigested and unharmed.

For a limited time at Shedd Aquarium, *Jellies*, sponsored by Walgreens, will immerse guests in an underwater world of rarely seen animals that survive—and thrive—without bones, blood, or brains. *Jellies* runs through May 28, 2012.

#

FIGURE 6.1 Fact sheets can be compiled on almost any subject. This one, distributed by Shedd Aquarium in Chicago for its sea jellies exhibit, gives some "fun facts" about the animals that are 95 percent water. Note that bullets are used to give factoids that journalists may select to include in their stories.

Company Profiles — A second kind of fact sheet is a one-page sheet giving key facts about an organization. This is also referred to as a *corporate profile.* Typical headings may include:

» Organization's full name and headquarters address

» Products and services produced

» Markets served

» Annual revenues

» Stock market ticker or symbol

» Number of employees

» Name of CEO

» Position in the industry

» Name of public relations person and contact information

Of course, organizations vary in how they prepare their profiles. The profile for Southwest Airlines, for example, uses these subheads in descending order: (1) Name of CEO, (2) Headquarters Address, (3) About the Company, (4) Daily Departures, (5) Employees, (6) Stock, (7) 2011 Financial Statistics, (8) Cities Served, (9) Fleet, (10) Top Ten Airport Departures, (11) Fun Facts, (12) Distinctions, and (13) Recognitions. A company profile for Morton's Steakhouse is shown on page 146.

Product Specification Sheets — The third kind of fact sheet is simply a summary of a new product's characteristics. A fact sheet for a company's new snack product, for example, might give such details as (1) nutrition information, (2) the production process, (3) pricing, (4) availability, (5) convenience, and (6) how it serves a consumer need. A good example of such a fact sheet is one by McCormick & Company about its various spice flavors for grilling, which is shown on page 147.

Technology companies have more detailed spec sheets about new products. Hewlett-Packard (HP), for example, uses a two-page approach when it introduces a new computer or printer. The first page of the spec sheet for its new TouchSmart PC gives consumers bullet points in plain English about its capabilities and major selling points. The second page, however, gives technical specifications about its operating system including its processor, hard drive, memory, video graphics, refresh rate, wireless connectivity, etc.

A variation on the traditional fact sheet is information presented in a question-and-answer format. This format, often used on websites, is called an **FAQ**. This is the acronym for "frequently asked questions." HP, for example, supplemented its Internet news release on a new printer with an FAQ that answered typical consumer questions about the new product. When you write an FAQ, try to place yourself in the shoes of the consumer who is hearing about the product for the first time. What questions would you ask? FAQs on websites also give consumers, as well as editors, the opportunity to click various links (video, audio, photos, product specifications) to get even more information about a product.

THE STEAKHOUSE

June 04, 2010 07:40 AM Pacific Daylight Time

Company Profile for Morton's Restaurant Group, Inc.

—(BUSINESS WIRE)—Morton's Restaurant Group, Inc. is the world's largest operator of company-owned upscale steakhouses. Morton's steakhouses have remained true to our founders' original vision of combining generous portions of high quality food prepared to exacting standards with exceptional service in an enjoyable dining environment. As of June 3, 2010, the Company owned and operated 76 Morton's steakhouses located in 64 cities across 27 states, Puerto Rico and five international locations (Hong Kong, Macau, Mexico City, Singapore and Toronto), as well as Trevi, our Italian restaurant, which is located next to the 'Fountain of the Gods' at The Forum Shops at Caesars in Las Vegas, NV. Please visit our Morton's website at www.mortons.com.

Company:	Morton's Restaurant Group, Inc.
Headquarters Address:	325 North Lasalle Street, Suite #500 Chicago, IL 60654
Main Telephone:	312-923-0030
Ticker/ISIN:	MRT(NYSE)/US6194301015
Type of Organization:	Public
Industry:	Restaurant
Key Executives:	CEO: Christopher J. Artinian CFO: Ronald M. DiNella
Public Relations Contact:	Roger J. Drake
Phone:	312-923-0030

FIGURE 6.2 Another kind of fact sheet is the corporate or organizational profile. This one gives a brief overview of Morton's restaurant group, which has steak houses in 64 cities. Such fact sheets are useful to journalists who may be unfamiliar with an organization and the scope of its activities.

Media Advisories

Media advisories are also called *media alerts* because they tell assignment editors about upcoming events that they might be interested in covering from a story, photo, and video perspective. The most effective advisories don't just announce an upcoming event but also take the time to list possible (1) story angles, (2) interview

NEW McCormick® Grill Mates®
Product Fact Sheet

Master the Flame. Master the Flavor.
Offering authentic grilling flavor with a modern twist, **Grill Mates** seasoning blends, marinades and rubs make it easy to create masterpieces that are sure to make you the ultimate grill master.

Tapping into the latest trends, these new products focus on regionally-inspired barbecue favorites, along with spicy and alcohol-infused flavors designed to complement food without overshadowing the natural flavor of the meat.

Varieties:

Fiery 5 Pepper Blend: A daring blend of coarsely ground ancho, chipotle, cayenne, black peppers and roasted chile peppers that brings new dimensions of heat.

Backyard Brew Marinade: An alcohol-infused marinade pairing the full-bodied flavor of beer with garlic, savory herbs and spices.

Carolina Country Marinade: A tart and tangy, Carolina-inspired blend of mustard and spices.

Cowboy Rub: An adventurous blend of coarsely ground peppers and coffee gives meat a bold and flavorful crust that seals in juices.

Package/Price:

Carolina Country; 1.12 oz., and **Backyard Brew Marinades**, 1 oz.; $1.19 per package.
Cowboy Rub; 4.12 oz; $2.89 per jar.
Fiery 5 Pepper Blend; 3 oz; $1.99 per bottle.

Availability:

Look for all varieties of **Grill Mates Products** in the spice or seasoning mix aisle of supermarkets nationwide.

For More Info:

For more information, visit **www.grillmates.com** or contact:

Contacts:

Laurie Harrsen
McCormick & Company, Inc.
410/527-8753
Laurie_Harrsen@mccormick.com

Ginny Brocker
Weber Shandwick
312/988-2025
gbrocker@webershandwick.com

FIGURE 6.3 Publicists usually prepare a fact sheet for a new product. This one, for McCormick & Company, provides the basic information about its new spice flavors that can be used in grilling. The format is easy to read, and it gives a website for more information. In addition, two media contacts are given if reporters and bloggers have a question or want more information.

possibilities, and (3) visual elements that would interest photographers and television crews.

The most common format uses short subheads followed by one or two descriptive sentences. A typical one-page advisory might contain most or all of the following elements:

» Date

» Headline announcing the event or situation

» Contact person's name, phone, email (can also be listed at end of advisory)

» Brief description of the event or story idea

» The appropriate five Ws and one H of journalism—who, what, when, where, and why, plus how

» Interview opportunities

» Visual elements for possible photos and video

» Brief paragraph giving background of sponsoring organization

A typical media advisory is the one from NYU Stern shown in Figure 6.4. The advisory was about graduation convocation and the name of the keynote speaker. It provides the who, when, and where elements, additional background information about the convocation, and how to RSVP or request a copy of the keynoter's address.

Another example of a media alert for an event is the "World's Longest Salad Bar," a publicity stunt in New York's Central Park sponsored by Hidden Valley Ranch dressings. It was written in such a way that local reporters knew the details of "when" and "where," and television stations in other cities knew how to get video footage and soundbites via satellite.

Media alerts are also used to announce the time and location of a scheduled news conference or a visit of a prominent person or government official. When the secretary of the U.S. Department of Health and Human Services visited a clinic in New Orleans, a basic news advisory gave the what, when, where, and the HHS media contact. Increasingly, news conferences are often webcast so reporters in other cities can "attend" without having to actually travel to the location. In such cases, the media advisory lets reporters know how and when they can sign on to the webcast. Advisories also are sent regarding satellite media tours by experts and celebrities (see Chapter 9 for more on satellite media tours).

Another kind of media advisory lets reporters and editors know about an interview opportunity. Korbel Champagne Cellars, for example, let journalists know that its "marriage proposal" expert was available for interviews during a 2-week period in July. The "interview opportunity" even suggested five other timely topics that he could discuss. Korbel also sent print media and broadcast stations in the Dallas area an advisory that a Dallas couple was one of the three finalists in its "perfect proposal contest." Also made available to the press was a photo of the actual marriage proposal on the stage of the Palace Theatre in New York where "Aida" was playing. And finally, the advisory let the editors know that the couple was available for interviews.

NYU
STERN

May 10, 2011 07:20 AM Pacific Daylight Time

Janet L. Robinson, President & CEO of The New York Times Company, to Keynote NYU Stern School of Business 2011 Graduate Convocation

NEW YORK--(BUSINESS WIRE)--NYU Stern

Who: Janet L. Robinson, President & CEO of The New York Times Company
        Keynote Speaker, NYU Stern's 2011 Graduate Convocation ceremony

When: May 19, 2011, 1-5pm

Where: Jacob K. Javits Convention Center of New York – Javits Center North
        11th Avenue between 39th & 40th Streets, New York, NY

Additional Information on NYU Stern's 2011 Graduate Convocation

- "The Change, The Challenge, The Choice" themes this year's keynote address:
  Ms. Robinson will challenge graduates to make hard choices and embrace new strategies critical for success in today's global and digital economy.

- Ms. Robinson will share her leadership experiences at The New York Times Company during a critical transition for the publishing industry – from traditional to digital media platforms.

- For more than a decade, NYU Stern has offered special and co-curricular programming in Entertainment, Media & Technology.

About NYU Stern

New York University Stern School of Business, located in the heart of Greenwich Village, is one of the nation's premier management education schools and research centers. NYU Stern offers a broad portfolio of academic programs at the graduate and undergraduate levels, all of them informed and enriched by the dynamism, energy and deep resources of the world's business capital.

To RSVP to NYU Stern's Graduate Convocation ceremony or to request a copy of Ms. Robinson's remarks, please contact Carolyn Ritter in Stern's Office of Public Affairs at critter@stern.nyu.edu or 212-998-0624.

Contacts

NYU Stern
Carolyn Ritter, 212-998-0624
critter@stern.nyu.edu

FIGURE 6.4   A media advisory, or media alert, is sent several weeks in advance to let editors and reporters know about an upcoming event. An advisory is usually organized around the journalistic five Ws and one H to give editors a quick overview of the event details. An advisory may also give some suggestions for photo or video opportunities that help assignment editors plan coverage.

Media Kits

A **media kit,** also called a *press kit*, is usually prepared for major events and new product launches. Its purpose is to give editors and reporters a variety of information and resources that will make it easier for reporters to write about the topic.

A basic media kit may include (1) a main news release; (2) a news feature; (3) fact sheets on the product, organization, or event; (4) background information; (5) photos and drawings with captions; (6) biographical material on the senior executive; and (7) several short brochures. All materials should be clearly identified; it's also important to prominently display contact information, such as email addresses, phone numbers, and website URLs.

The Traditional Media Kit

The traditional media kit, before the digital revolution, consisted of a 9- by 12-inch folder with four sides—a cover, two inside pages (often with pockets to hold news releases, etc., in place), and a back cover displaying the organization's name, address, and website address. Another common feature was a slot inside to hold the business card of the media contact. Folders could also include slots for CDs.

An example of a traditional media kit is the one distributed by the Field Museum in Chicago when it opened its "Maps: Finding Our Place in the World" exhibit. A print version of the media kit was sent to major media. The kit also included a CD that contained all of the basic print material plus 30 high-resolution photos that could be downloaded as jpeg files. The kit and the CD contained the following material:

» About 30 photographs of rare maps and globes on display, with captions
» The main news release about the exhibit
» A media advisory announcing a media preview two days before the public opening
» A description of the exhibits in each of the seven galleries, dubbed a "walk-through"
» A feature on the technologies used for mapping today
» Short background stories about the rare maps and globes being exhibited
» A schedule of public lectures and gallery programs
» Texts of radio public service announcements (PSAs) about the exhibits

A more creative approach was taken by Crayola some years ago. It created a colorful media folder to publicize its 25-city bus tour celebrating the 100th anniversary of the company. The package was a self-mailer that unfolded into a large round sheet 2 feet in diameter that featured artwork in a rainbow of crayon colors. The packet included a colorful news release (localized for each city) and two backgrounders. It also included an interesting piece of trivia: "Since 1903, more than 120 billion crayons have been sold throughout the world. End to end they would circle the earth 200 times." Planter's peanuts also created a 100th anniversary media kit, which is shown in Figure 6.5.

FIGURE 6.5 A traditional media kit is usually in an attractive folder. Planters, however, celebrated its 100th birthday by preparing a media kit that reflected the company's business. The media kit was a large can that replicated its well-recognized product tins. Inside, the theme was continued by a spiral-bound anniversary booklet in the round shape of an open can of peanuts. The kit also contained a tin of peanuts. The kit generated more than 1,000 placements, including coverage on the *Today* show and in the *New York Times*. Radio stations in 46 states mentioned the anniversary, and 178 television stories were produced throughout the year. Planters and its public relations firm, Weber Shandwick, received a bronze anvil from the Public Relations Society of America (PRSA) in the category of press/media kits.

Traditional printed media kits are still used, but they are rapidly declining in use because organizations find it more cost effective and convenient to distribute the same information via CDs, email, flash drives, and online newsrooms. Digital press kits, also

❝*The days of a thousand press kits are gone. Instead, well-designed online press kits can have an ongoing shelf life with constantly updated content.*❞ Tom Becktold senior vice president of marketing, Business Wire

known as *electronic press kits (EPKs),* are also more versatile than traditional printed media kits because they can include multiple pieces of information in a variety of formats (text, video, photo, audio, animation, etc.). All this gives the journalist much more flexibility and choice than does the traditional printed kit.

But pronouncements about the death of media kits in print form, like those condemning traditional news releases, may be somewhat exaggerated. Many journalists still prefer the convenience of scanning a media kit in print form because it's less hassle and faster than opening up a series of digital files on a CD or a flash drive. Consequently, many organizations and public relations firms continue to produce and distribute both a printed kit and a CD or flash drive, often in the same package.

The idea, again, is to provide whatever format the particular editor or journalist wants. Echoing the argument for both print and electronic versions is Glen Stone, public affairs manager at the Toronto Board of Trade. He told *PRWeek*, "I give electronic information to journalists via email and in kits, but my kits always include paper versions of the essentials so that reporters, particularly radio reporters who have 24 deadlines a day, have something they can use immediately."

The Digital Media Kit

Most organizations today, however, have gone digital with their media kits. Digital media kits offer several advantages in addition to being cost effective. One advantage is that they expand the potential audience. Traditional media kits were sent only to media outlets. Today's media kits, if well designed, have the potential of reaching a wider audience of consumers, bloggers, online forums, and other websites via social media tags and RSS feeds.

Other advantages include (1) storage and filing simplicity, (2) ease in forwarding materials to others, (3) faster access to company or public relations contacts, and (4) elimination of newsroom clutter. Kelly Brooks, marketing communications manager for Coca-Cola, offers another reason why reporters covering events, such as the Olympics, prefer EPKs. She says, "Reporters would rather use a Web-based tool when it's convenient for them than lug around a bulky kit."

A digital kit, of course, should have the same components as the traditional print version. Craig McGuire of *PRWeek* explains, "There should be a well-written, fact-filled description of the subject, as well as product/event sheets, press releases regarding newsworthy items, bios, and backgrounders on key subjects, testimonials, articles from archives, perhaps a calendar or itinerary, and always a contact sheet."

McGuire adds, however, that the major change is how all these materials are presented. Digital kits have the technical capacity to enrich content by offering a gallery of outstanding photos, embedding hyperlinks to websites, or even providing video demonstrations of how a product works. Electronic Arts (EA), for example, effectively shows entertainment reporters and editors simulations from its various video games. Movie studios use websites and flash drives to promote new films by providing film clips, interviews with the stars, and production facts.

Various platforms are used for digital media kits. The California Academy of Sciences, for example, distributed a CD to the media to publicize its "Life: A Cosmic Story" exhibit at its new Morrison Planetarium. The CD contained (1) 16 high-resolution photos, (2) a video trailer with a link to more YouTube videos, (3) a basic news release about the exhibit, and (4) a bio about the director of the planetarium. Another media kit, about an exhibit of snakes and lizards, is shown in Figure 6.6. The Shedd Aquarium in Chicago also used a CD format in the past, but now just posts its media kits in the organization's newsroom on its website.

Flash drives are now replacing CDs for many organizations. HP, for example, uses a flash drive embedded in a format about the size of a business card (see Figure 6.7). The media kit for its new TouchSmart PR, for example, contained the following items: (1) two news releases, (2) a fact sheet and spec sheet, (3) multiple photos of the new computer from various angles, and (4) a short video with the chief designer describing the innovations built into the new PC. In another media kit about the use of HP notebooks in the film, *Sex in the City 2*, the media kit included several scenes from the movie.

FIGURE 6.6 Today's media kits, also commonly called *press kits*, are usually in digital format. The California Academy of Sciences used a CD format to distribute a media kit to the press about a new exhibit about snakes and lizards. Providing a CD or posting a media kit online is economical and enables multimedia content such as photos, short videos, and links to more information.

FIGURE 6.7 Flash drives are even more portable and cost efficient than CDs, so a number of companies such as HP now use this platform for media kits. The HP approach is to embed the flash drive in a package about the size and thickness of a business card. The extra space gives the flash drive more bulk but also provides the opportunity to clearly portray the brand and give a key message such as "The computer is personal again." The photo shows the flash drive extended for use in a USB port.

Pitching a Story

Public relations personnel spend a lot of time and energy preparing materials such as news releases, fact sheets, and even media kits. These efforts, however, don't amount to much unless they can convince editors or reporters that a particular story is newsworthy and relevant to their readers or viewers.

A lazy approach, of course, is to simply distribute the publicity materials and let nature, so to speak, take its course. Editors, as already noted, review hundreds of news releases and media kits every day and select the few that interest them. A more efficient approach, however, is for publicists to make a **pitch** directly to the media gatekeeper if a particular situation or story angle is more "special" than just a routine news release.

Media kits, in particular, often include a short, personalized letter to the editor that is considered a pitch for using the material. One publicist for an author of a kosher cookbook, for example, included a short letter in a media kit that let editors know that high-resolution photos of recipes and publicity photos of the author were available on a particular website. In addition, the letter ended with an offer to set up a personal interview with the book author.

As you might guess, there is considerable competition to get the attention of an editor or broadcast producer. According to Ragan.com, a typical example is *Barron's*. Richard Rescigno, managing editor of this influential business weekly, gets about 30 to 35 phone calls from public relations people each week. In addition, he receives more than 200 "pitches" by mail and email every week. Rescigno estimates that only 1 or 2 percent of all the ideas that are pitched actually result in stories. Another 5 percent serve as supporting material for larger stories. "PR people have to have a high tolerance for rejection," he told Ragan's reporter.

That's the bad news. The good news is that many other journalists get most of their story ideas from pitches by publicists. The leading tech columnist of the *New York Times,* David Pogue, told Ragan.com (www.ragan.com) that about 60 to 70 percent of his columns come from pitches. However, the rate of rejection still remains quite high. Pogue receives about 150 email pitches daily. Some examples of pitches that have generated major media coverage are given on page 155.

Given these statistical odds, it is important that you understand the components of an effective pitch that will substantially increase your odds for getting a story published or broadcast. A good pitch has three phases: (1) researching the publication or broadcast show, (2) writing the email or letter and making the call, and (3) following up.

Researching the Publication

Perhaps the most important component is the first phase—doing your homework. Pitches must be customized to a particular journalist, editor, and publication. There is no such thing as a "one size fits all" pitch that is appropriate for all media. Visa or MasterCard, for example, might pitch to a bride's magazine a story about the challenges of a young couple combining their finances. In contrast, a story might be pitched to the AARP monthly magazine about how senior citizens can reduce credit card transaction fees while traveling abroad.

PR casebook

A Good Pitch Can Get You on Jay Leno

A good, timely pitch often leads to major publicity for a product or service. Konami Digital Entertainment, a leading game publisher, was able to get its new *Karaoke Revolution Glee* game featured on Jay Leno's *The Tonight Show* by pitching the show's producers.

The company's public relations firm, Bender Helper Impact, found out that *Glee* star Kevin McHale was going to be Leno's guest, so it pitched the producers about including the new game as part of the interview. The firm made several calls to the show's producers, but a decision wasn't made until the afternoon of the show.

The result was that Leno held up the game box for the camera for about 20 seconds while McHale talked about his niece's interest in it. Although it was only a small part of the segment, the exposure on the very week the game hit the stores helped propel consumer interest in the game. *The Tonight Show* was a good choice, according to the public relations firm, because it has viewers that tend to buy a lot of gifts for kids and teens.

A good pitch was also responsible for generating publicity on *Huffington Post* and in *People Magazine*.

In the case of *Huffington Post*, Herradura tequila and its public relations firm, Formula PR, pitched the story idea of a writer visiting the Herradura hacienda in Mexico to see how the super-premium tequila was produced. The public relations firm got the idea because the writer had already done a travel piece on Sonoma County wines. The *Huffington Post* was the ideal publication for such a pitch because it reaches a high-end audience through its lifestyle and travel coverage. The result was that readers of the *Huffingon Post* became aware of the brand and other alcohol-related publications and bloggers also picked up the story.

People magazine also responded well to a pitch by Stratacomm public relations on behalf of its client, Navistar. The magazine is known for its heart-warming stories so the story idea was that Navistar, a manufacturer of military and commercial trucks, took steps to keep employees on the payroll after an economic slowdown by having them do volunteer work at local community nonprofits in Huntsville, Alabama. The magazine's editors thought the story was a good fit, but only as an exclusive story that would be first featured in the magazine. Given *People's* large circulation, this was acceptable to Navistar with the understanding that other media outlets could do follow-up stories. Right after the story hit the newsstands, for example, ABC and CNN also did a story on Navistar's commitment to its employees.

Lynn Lipinski, a senior media specialist for GCI public relations in Los Angeles, writes in *Public Relations Tactics*, "You must... familiarize yourself with the publication's style, format, readership, deadlines, and regular features. Media guides (such as Cision or Burrelles) can provide the basic information about a publication, but the only way to truly know if it is right for your client is to read it."

Even publications that appear to focus on the same subject matter often don't have the same audience characteristics. Tripp Whetsell, a New York public relations counselor, writes in *Public Relations Tactics*, "Even if you're pitching the same story about prostate cancer to *Esquire*, *Men's Journal*, and *GQ*, doesn't automatically assume that the content is the same just because all three are men's magazines." The same goes for broadcasting; Fox News targets 30- to 40-year-olds, whereas CNN draws viewers with an average age of 60. Blogs also have different audiences, and the box on page 157 gives some good tips about pitching them.

> "In the end, you're not going to get coverage unless you're a match for what the outfit is looking for." David Pogue, technology columnist for the *New York Times*

Lipinski adds, "Read articles written by the reporter you are pitching. Familiarize yourself with the reporter's style, interests, background, and regular beat." One method for doing this is to use a service such as Dow Jones Media Relations Manager, which profiles journalists and what they write about. An example is given in Chapter 1, page 10. At the same time, she urges would-be writers of pitch letters to be aware of current issues, business trends, and societal issues, so they can angle their pitch within the framework of a larger picture. If the company is expanding by purchasing smaller companies, perhaps the story can be pitched from the angle that it is an example of consolidation in a particular industry.

> "Sommeliers make a living pairing wines with foods that bring out the essence of each flavor. PR professionals are no different; we pair our client's products and services with publications and media outlets that serve a readership who find value in their content. Thus, the trick to a perfect pitch is crafting a message that displays a profound understanding of that publication's value and their audience's essence." Regine J. Nelson, principal of Allure Marketing Communications

Editorial calendars also help public relations writers make a timely pitch to a journalist.

Newspapers and magazines, in particular, usually post a list of topics and special issues planned for each week or month of the year. A newspaper, for example, may have a special section on holiday gift giving in November, so that's a publicity opportunity for a client or employer to pitch an article about its product as the "perfect gift" for Christmas. By the same token, a travel magazine may be doing a special section on the Caribbean scheduled for January, so a resort in Costa Ria may want to pitch a story about its newly remodeled property. Media databases such as Cision, Burrrellles and Vocus provide compilations of editorial calendars that can be easily accessed with a few clicks. Another good resource is Help a Reporter Out (HARO), which enables journalists to query public relations sources for information. See the box on page 157.

In sum, knowledge of the publication and the demographics of its audience are crucial to a successful pitch. David Pogue of the *New York Times* expresses the frustration of many journalists. He told Ragan.com, "I get the idea that a lot of PR people inherit some database and they just blast everything to the whole list and I cannot tell you what a waste of time that is. It just turns the busy journalists against the person, that firm, and that client."

The Email Pitch

Once you've done your research and have ascertained what kind of pitch would be most appropriate for a particular publication, broadcast show, or even blogger, the next step is to write a succinct, attention-grabbing memo or email. As Richard Rescigno of *Barron's* notes, you have about 60 seconds (either in an email or a telephone call) to grab an editor's interest.

David Pogue of the *New York Times*, for example, prefers short email pitches. One of his favorites, which resulted in a story, was "David, my client sells a laptop that can be dropped from 6 feet, get dunked in water, and survive 300-degree heat. Let me know if you're interested." Another attention-getting pitch that resulted in a story was, "David, I see you've been covering digital cameras a lot. Wondering if you'd be interested in one that shoots underwater and costs less than $100? Press release below. Contact me if you have any questions."

Therefore, the first rule of a pitch is brevity—less than a page or a screen. Second, Whetsell's advice regarding good writing should be followed: "Your sentences should be clean, sharp, and to the point. Your syntax, as well as your spelling, should be flawless. Don't give journalists a reason not to take you and your clients seriously by being sloppy."

Third, a pitch should have an enticing lead. That means that you should avoid beginning a pitch with something trite such as "I'm writing to inquire if you would be interested in a story about…" That's a good way to turn off an editor. See the Tips for Success below for more tips on writing pitches that get noticed.

The Ragan Report has published several articles on how to write pitches and create great opening lines. Here are some examples of opening lines that generated media interest:

» "How many students does it take to change a light bulb?" (story about a residence hall maintenance program operated by students who receive financial aid)

» "Would you like to replace your ex-husband with a plant?" (story about a photographer who is an expert at removing "exes" and other individuals from old photos)

Tips for Success   Pitches That Help Reporters Do Their Job

Not all pitches have to be what salespeople term "cold calls." On many occasions, journalists are seeking information and names of people to interview for a particular story.

One of the oldest services that match reporter queries with public relations sources is ProfNet, which is operated by PRNewswire. It offers a direct way for public relations personnel to list experts in the organization they represent, and to also be on the alert for a pitching opportunity to meet a reporter's specific needs.

ProfNet is available only on a subscription basis, but two free services that match reporters with public relations sources are Reporter Connection and Help a Reporter Out (HARO). The latter is the larger of the two, with 100,000 sources and about 30,000 registered journalists. HARO fields about 200 queries daily, and it sends out a list of reporter queries three times a day via email and Twitter.

» "Our CEO ran 16 Boston Marathons…and now he thinks we can walk a mile around the river." (story about a CEO leading employees on a daily walk instead of paying for expensive gym memberships or trainers)

» "You are cordially invited to the Dirtiest Event in Boulder." (story about staging a coal-dumping event to show people how much fossil fuel it takes to heat an average house. The slightly "smutty" approach worked; major dailies and television stations covered the coal dumping)

» "For almost 25 years, Jack Osman has been drinking shots of oil. He also sings songs about such foot-tapping topics as breakfast and grease. And sometimes, just for fun, he cooks down ground beef to find out its fat percentage." (pitch about the availability of a nutrition professor to give media interviews on diet and health)

As these examples show, a pitch should immediately raise curiosity or get to the point as soon as possible. Here is a letter written by Michael Klepper, owner of a New York public relations firm, that netted 8 minutes on NBC's *Today* show.

Plastics!

How can we get rid of them? Some environmentalists say we can't. Ralph Harding says we can. He is executive vice president of the Society of Plastics Industry. He has just returned from Europe where they easily dispose of plastics in modern incinerators.

I'll call you in a week to see if the *Today* show would be interested in talking to him.

Klepper, who has written hundreds of pitch letters in his career, adds, "The pitch letter should be newsy, not groveling. It shouldn't read 'respectfully submitted' or 'I need this one' or 'my client is breathing heavy.' You are never asking for a favor; you are submitting good, topical, newsworthy material that is directed to a decision maker."

Email Subject Lines — The vast majority of pitches today are sent to editors, reporters, television producers, and bloggers via email. Consequently, probably the most important aspect of the pitch is the subject line. If it doesn't generate interest and curiosity on the part of receivers as they quickly scan hundreds of emails, it's deleted without a second thought. The challenge of coming up with a good subject line requires a lot of creativity on the part of the publicist. Ragan.com compiled a list of creative subject lines that generated media stories. Here are some examples:

» "Call it a display of Howly Muttrimony sealed with a sniff." (story about a dog wedding at a shopping center staged as a benefit for an animal rescue group)

» "The Man Who Will End iPod Whiplash." (story about an engineer who created a new technique for searching music online)

» "Wearing Prada Can Be the Devil for Your Spine." (story from a hospital involved in spinal therapy about women injuring their spines by lugging around ever-larger designer handbags)

» "Weather to Pack Sunscreen or an Umbrella." (story about a new online weather service and its trip planner services)

- » "Veggies for Dessert? Blue Cheese Gelato!!" (story about new fruit and vegetable flavors for an ice cream store chain)
- » "New Book Says Hormones May Be Making You Fat." (story about a weight-loss program authored by a chiropractor)

Not all subject lines, however, need to be creative and clever. An informative subject line, such as "Free Public Hurricane Seminar Tomorrow Night at Nauticus," satisfies the keyword requirement and tells the receiver exactly what the story is about. As Margo Mateas, president of the Public Relations Training Company, writes in *PR Tactics*, "Writing a powerful media pitch doesn't take a lot of words. It takes a lot of thought and planning. Put your effort into being succinct and concise, and it will pay off."

> **" Use the subject line to open the door, and the first two or three sentences to kick the door open and get invited in. "** Gordon Deal, host of *The Wall Street Journal This Morning* broadcast news show

The Telephone Pitch

Despite the popularity of email, it still remains somewhat impersonal and easy to ignore. Consequently, a case can be made for actually picking up the phone and having a real-time conversation with an editor or journalist. As Susan Balcom Walton and Nick Kalm explain in *Public Relations Tactics*, "Pitching a story face-to-face, or at least voice-to-voice, can help develop stronger journalist relationships, greater preparation and knowledge of your subject, and greater flexibility during the pitch."

Calling a reporter or editor requires the same preparation that goes into preparing a written pitch. You need to thoroughly research the publication, broadcast outlet, or blog so you are totally familiar with the content and demographics of its audience. You also need to use media databases, which often give short profiles of editors and reporters so you have some familiarity with their interests and even pet peeves. It's wise to figure out when to call so it doesn't interfere with deadline pressures. If you call when a reporter is under a deadline, you most likely will receive a quick brush-off.

Before making the call, prepare a brief outline or script of what you will say in the first 30 seconds. You should give your name and organization/client before starting and, in one or two sentences, explain what you are calling about. Get to the point; don't try to exchange mundane openers such as "How are you today?" or "I was wondering if you would be interested in a story about XYZ's new widget." It's much better to give the story angle up front and why it would be of interest to readers or viewers.

Walton and Kalm add that you need to say why the story is significant and how it fits into other stories/trends already being covered by the publication, broadcast outlet, or website. As freelance writer Amy Gunderson observes, "Good pitchers think about the larger implications. They are always thinking 'What's the angle?' They are always thinking like journalists." At the same time, listen to what the journalist is telling you. Don't be an insistent telemarketer and ignore the message that he or she is not interested.

Melvin Helitzer, author of *The Dream Job: Sports Publicity*, says a pitch should have the following six elements:

- » Enough facts to support a full story
- » An angle of interest to the readers of that specific publication

- » The possibility of alternative angles
- » An offer to supply or help secure all needed statistics, quotes, interviews with credible resources, arrangements for photos, and so on
- » An indication of authority or credibility
- » An offer to call the editor soon to get a decision

The Twitter Pitch

The new medium on the block is Twitter, and many journalists and bloggers can now be reached by tweeting. Pitching a story idea via a tweet, however, has its distinct challenges. The major one is that you only have 140 characters to make a coherent pitch, so it requires considerable writing skill to make every word count.

There are some other steps involved. First, you need to do your homework in terms of identifying journalists and bloggers who have a Twitter account and want to be contacted by tweets. One way to do this is to use MediaOnTwitter. Publications also are beginning to place their staff's Twitter handles on their website and media databases such as Cision are also including Twitter addresses for various journalists. Another approach: Google the reporter's name.

> *Pitching media on Twitter is like pitching media anywhere else. It's not easy. It takes research, a smart and relevant pitch, and impeccable PR and writing skills.* Maya Wasserman, senior account executive at Bailey Gardiner public relations

The next step is to develop a relationship with the reporter. According to Maya Wasserman, a senior account executive at Bailey Gardiner, "Journalists are much more likely to accept a pitch from a PR person with whom they already have a relationship." She suggests that you begin building a relationship by retweeting them, replying to their questions, and commenting on their blog posts or articles.

Once a relationship is established, you are now ready to make a pitch. Since the message is only 140 characters, many publicists include a link to more information or background in their tweet. The same rules apply to both pitches by Twitter and email and phone pitches. The story idea must be relevant to the reporter's or blogger's interests, and it must be relevant to the media outlet's readers or viewers. See the Tips for Success on page 161 for guidelines on how to pitch bloggers.

The Follow-Up

The advantage of a telephone call, of course, is that you get instant feedback. If you have emailed, faxed, or even mailed a pitch to an editor or broadcast producer, it is important to follow up. It is not good enough to end a pitch by asking a reporter to call you with any questions. A better approach is what Julie Schweigert of Edelman Worldwide wrote at the end of her pitch letter for Korbel's "perfect proposal contest." She takes the initiative in a nice way by writing "I will contact you next week to follow up, but in the meantime you can reach me at 312/233-1380 with any questions." Remember, in public relations, keep the ball and the responsibility for follow-up in your court.

In your follow-up, the reporter may ask you to send more information. If that is the case, make sure you provide all the information within 24 hours. You should also ask how the reporter would like to receive the information—by email, fax, U.S. mail, or special messenger. Reporters all have their own preferences.

Reporters and editors can also be quite blunt and tell you in no uncertain terms that they aren't interested. Or they may be more polite and say they have already done

Tips for Success   How to Successfully Pitch Bloggers

The "blogosphere" is now part of the media landscape; media databases (discussed in Chapter 1) now track the contact information and coverage areas of bloggers who have gained a national audience. Therefore, in addition to pitching stories to traditional media, a savvy publicist also needs to include bloggers in order to reach the widest possible audience.

Pitching a blogger, however, has its perils. Unlike traditional media, which just ignore an off-base pitch, bloggers will gleefully post critical comments about the quality of your pitch and even make snide remarks about your intelligence. Consequently, it's critical to do your homework before you pitch a blogger. Kevin Dugan, co-founder of Bad Pitch Blog (www.bad pitch.blogspot.com), suggests six questions that public relations professionals should ask themselves before aiming a pitch at key bloggers:

1. **Have you read more than the blog's most recent posts?**   A blogger's most recent posts might not be representative of his or her overall interest in topics and issues.

2. **Have you searched the blog for relevant product/service/industry terms to see if they have already been mentioned?**   You should be aware of what the blogger has already said about you or your organization. "If they are already covering you, you have a conversation opener for your pitch," says Dugan.

3. **Have you subscribed to the blog's RSS feed or email delivery system?**   This makes it easier for you to follow a blog and tailor a pitch around something that is already being discussed.

4. **Have you left a comment on the blog that continues a discussion and is unrelated to your pitch?**   Blogs are designed to start conversations about a subject. Become a participant in the discussions so that you will have a relationship with the blogger before you make the pitch.

5. **Have you looked at posts and links from the blogger's home page to find out how he or she wants to be pitched?**   Knowing a blogger's preferences and guidelines goes a long way in delivering a pitch that will be considered.

6. **Have you sent the blogger an email unrelated to your pitch?**   If you leave a public comment, Dugan says, "You should come up with another reason to introduce yourself to the blogger."

Dugan, interviewed by Ragan.com, says building relationships with bloggers comes first and pitching comes second. He even suggests that you develop media contacts on social networking sites such as LinkedIn and Facebook. These sites, Dugan warns, are for building relationships—not making a pitch.

Tips for Success   How to Get Your Pitch Noticed

Most surveys show that journalists prefer to be pitched by email, but what steps can you take to ensure that your email pitch is relevant and on target? The following tips are adopted from a post by Jeremy Porter on his blog, Journalistics:

Attention-Grabbing Subject Line

Use a quick, descriptive subject line that leaves no question what your pitch is about.

Avoid common words in junk mail or spam such as "free" and "congratulations."

Don't use exclamation marks!!!

Keep It Personal

+ Show that you know what the journalist writes about and that you've done your homework.
+ Never cut and paste a pitch or use mail merge software to switch out names and details.

Keep It Brief

+ Get to the point in the first or second sentence.
+ Keep your pitch to three to five sentences.
+ If you have a lot of information to share, link a few key resources from the pitch.
+ Keep rewriting the pitch until it's down to as few words as possible.

What Do You Want?

+ Say exactly what you want from the journalist. Are you offering an interview, an exclusive, or just providing background for future consideration?

Ask What You're Doing Wrong

+ If a journalist is unresponsive or says no, ask what would make your pitch more interesting or compelling.
+ Ask if there's something you should keep the journalist in the loop about in the future.

Where Did You Get an Email Address?

+ Verify the reporter's preferred email address; don't just rely on a standard media database.

Never Mass Distribute

+ Try to avoid PR software and news distribution services that are built for mass distribution.
+ Pitching a large number of journalists at the same time, by cutting and pasting, is why journalists often complain about PR people and their pitches.

Give Them More Than They Need

+ Most journalists like to talk to multiple sources or organizations for a story. Provide additional resources, statistics, and research that might interest them.
+ Include links to related articles or some other nugget of information.
+ Never send attachments, however, unless the reporter has specifically requested them.

Picture This

+ Offer photos and infographics that support your story idea.
+ Include links to a variety of images and file formats available for download.

Best Time of Day to Send Your Pitch

+ There is no best or worse time, but midday (10 A.M. to 2 P.M.) seems to be popular.

Be Courteous

+ Be polite to journalists, regardless of how you are treated.
+ Say "please" and "thank you."
+ Regularly read what journalists write; you'll double the success rate of your pitches.

a similar story recently, so they are not interested at the moment. But you can impress them, and even change their minds, if you have done your homework and can say accurately why your story is different from the last three articles about similar subjects.

Follow-up, however, often means that you graciously accept "No" for an answer. Don't keep pitching the idea or arguing with the editor over the merits of the story; it is better to cut your losses and keep the door open for future pitches to the same editor. You must continually develop good, productive relationships with the reporters you typically pitch; you won't win all the time, but you will improve your batting average by remaining cordial and gaining trust as a good resource person. The box on page 162 gives additional tips on how to make a successful pitch.

Summary

Expanding the Publicity Tool Kit

» Public relations staff, in addition to preparing news releases, are also responsible for preparing other publicity materials such as fact sheets, media advisories, and media kits.

» Another tactic in the publicity tool kit is called the "pitch." Public relations personnel constantly "sell" story ideas to reporters and bloggers.

Fact Sheets

» Fact sheets are a brief outline of an event, an organization, or a new product.

» The purpose is to place basic and supplemental information at the editor's or journalist's fingertips.

Media Advisories

» Media advisories, also called *media alerts*, tell assignment editors about an upcoming event. They often suggest photo, video, and interview opportunities.

» Media advisories about upcoming events typically include the journalistic who, what, when, where, why, and how in outline form.

Media Kits

» Media kits, also called *press kits*, are packets of material that may include

news releases, photographs, feature stories, fact sheets, position papers, backgrounders, and brief biographical sketches.

» The traditional media kit in print form is still used, but today's kits are primarily in digital form.

» Digital media kits, also called electronic press kits (EPKs), are distributed in several ways: CD format, flash drive, or online through an organization's website.

» Digital kits are cost effective and versatile. They often include audio soundbites, high-resolution photos, video clips, and product demonstrations.

Pitching a Story

» The purpose of a pitch letter is to convince editors and reporters to cover an event or do a story. Pitches to editors must be brief, raise interest, and come immediately to the point.

» Pitch letters are customized to each editor based on the publication's content, demographics, and circulation.

» Email pitches must have succinct, creative subject lines. A telephone pitch requires the same preparation as writing a memo or sending an email pitch.

Skill Building Activities

1. Select a local nonprofit organization or a company and write a basic fact sheet about it.

2. The Minnesota Zoo is opening a major exhibit about insects on May 1. A variety of "bugs" from around the world will be included in the exhibit, but the major attraction will be a walk-through butterfly garden where a thousand butterflies will be feeding, resting, and emerging from cocoons. Write a media advisory (alert) inviting the media to the opening and make some suggestions about interview, photo, and video opportunities.

3. The Minnesota Zoo exhibit on insects will have thousands of live bugs on display. Write an email pitch to the lifestyle editor at the *Minneapolis Tribune* to do a story on the exhibit. Also, write another email pitch to the assignment editor at the leading television station in the Twin Cities.

4. A microbrewery, started five years ago by a young couple, has now reached the point in production and sales that enables it to expand its distribution to the entire West Coast. Your public relations firm is hired to get media coverage by pitching story ideas to various publications. First, compile a list of possible story angles that could be pitched. Second, do some homework and match the story ideas to specific kinds of publications most likely to be interested in your pitch.

5. The Hard Rock Hotel and Casino in Las Vegas has completed an $800 million renovation project and wants to attract new business from men and women aged 21 to 49. A media kit needs to be written and produced to start generating coverage and "buzz" about the renovated facilities. Write a memo outlining what materials would be included in a digital media kit.

Media Resources

Bannon, S. (2010, December 28). "Pitch Perfect—Improving Your Chances of Earning Positive Media Coverage." Retrieved from The Bannon Blog, www.bannoncommunications.com.

Handley, A. (2010, August). "Nine Steps for Smarter Pitches and Getting Your Story Covered." *Ragan Report*, 18–19.

Levco, J. (2011, January 19). "From David Pogue: Keys to Pitching Him and Other Journalists." Retrieved from www.ragan.com.

Nelson, R. (2011, January 15). "Pitch Perfect: The Art of Media Pitching." Retrieved from ThePRtibit blog, www.theprtidbit.blogspot.com.

Porter, J. (2010, December 9). "Thirteen Ways to Keep Your Pitch from Getting Deleted." Retrieved from Journalistics blog, www.blog.journalistcs.com.

Porter, J. (2009, January 29). "What's the Best Way to Pitch Bloggers?" Retrieved from Journalistics blog, www.blog.journalistics.com.

Young, S. (2010, July). "Ten Keys to Pitching Your Story and Getting Publicity." *The Ragan Report*, 17–18.

Young, S. (2010, November 11). "How to Pitch Your News Story to *The Wall Street Journal*." Retrieved from www.getinfrontcommunications.com.

Creating News Features and Op-Eds

7

» After reading this chapter, you will be able to:

» Recognize the value of features as a publicity tactic

» Plan a news feature

» Be familiar with the type of features that can be written

» Write a news feature

» Place a feature in the appropriate publication

» Write an effective op-ed or letter to the editor

The Value of Features

Perhaps the best way to show the value of news feature stories is to contrast them with basic news releases. The news release emphasizes the timely disclosure of basic information about situations and events. The **feature story,** in contrast, can provide additional background information, generate human interest, and create understanding in a more creative and imaginative way.

Consider, for example, the appointment of a new company president. The news release will give the basic information in one or two paragraphs. It will give the new president's name and perhaps a brief summary of her professional career—all pretty dry, routine stuff. A feature article, however, could give the new president a human dimension. It would focus on her philosophy of management, college experiences, hobbies and interests, and vision of the future. Such an article might run 750 to 1,000 words instead of two paragraphs.

Features are considered "soft news" rather than "hard news." In journalistic terms, this means that features are not as time sensitive as the "hard" news of quarterly earnings, mergers and acquisitions, contracts, expansions, and layoffs. They entertain, provide background, and give consumer tips. They often show up in the specialty sections of the daily newspaper—entertainment, food, business, real estate, automotive, technology—and most of them originate from public relations sources.

Feature stories come in all sizes and shapes, but all of them have the potential to (1) provide more information to the consumer, (2) give background and context about organizations, (3) provide a behind-the-scenes perspective, (4) give a human dimension to situations and events, and (5) generate publicity for standard products and services.

> *Feature news has an indefinite shelf life, and can be used by the media when it's needed, not just when it's distributed.*
>
> Business Wire

Regarding the last point, many products are not particularly newsworthy and would never get coverage if a feature writer didn't exercise some creativity. Think of the lowly potato. It would seem that no self-respecting editor would be interested in a news release from the National Association of Potato Growers. However, a feature directed to the food editor can generate coverage and also increase sales of potatoes. Some possible features might discuss (1) potatoes as a source of vitamins, (2) potatoes as a low-cost addition to daily nutritional needs, and (3) creative recipes using potatoes as an ingredient. Another possibility is a short history of the potato, its origins, and its economic impact.

Indeed, evidence suggests that feature materials are becoming increasingly popular with newspapers and magazines. A survey of trade editors conducted by Rhode Island–based Thomas Rankin Associates, for example, found that more than half of the editors wanted more case histories and technical "how-to" features from public relations sources. Mike Yamamoto, managing editor of CNET, says, "The future of media is a greater concentration on the feature story as a branding vehicle. The challenge for the media is to capture audiences with a unique presentation of information."

The new interest in feature articles, particularly by print media, no doubt is related to where people get their news. Radio, TV, and the Internet now provide the instant "hard" news, so many newspapers are shifting their focus to publishing more in-depth stories on news events and features that provide consumer tips. A readership study by the Newspaper Association of America and the American Society of Newspapers, for example, found that feature-style writing increased reader satisfaction, was easier to read than the traditional inverted-pyramid news approach, and even made it more "fun" to read the newspaper.

The concept of publishing consumer tips and "news you can use" is referred to as **service journalism**. The key component of service journalism is to demonstrate how a person can use the information to do such things as (1) save time, (2) make more money, (3) save money, or (4) get something free. In other words, what's in it for me?

If public relations professionals keep this axiom in mind, the print media will be more than happy to use their material.

Planning a News Feature

Coming up with a feature idea takes some creative thinking. There are three things to keep in mind. First, you have to conceptualize how something lends itself to feature treatment. Second, you have to determine if the information would be interesting to and useful for a particular audience. Third, you must be sure that the feature helps achieve organizational objectives. Does it position the organization in a favorable light? Does it encourage the use of a particular product or service? At the same time, a news feature cannot be overcommercialized to the point that it sounds like an ad.

Good feature writers ask a lot of questions. They need a natural curiosity about how things work and how things are related to each other. If the company has just produced a new video game, for example, you would find out exactly how the game was developed. By asking questions, you might find out that a 19-year-old computer "nerd" invented the game, or that a new technology was used to create "real-life" animated effects. In each case, you have a potential feature. A story about the inventor would make interesting reading, but so would a story about how the new computer technology could be applied in other fields.

News events and issues can also trigger ideas for feature stories. If media attention is being given to global warming and greenhouse gasses, perhaps you can develop a feature on how your company is using new technologies to reduce its carbon footprint. The possibilities are limited only by your own imagination and creativity.

Ways to Proceed

Once you have a feature idea, there are four ways you can proceed. The most common approach is to write a general feature and distribute it to a variety of publications in much the same way as news releases are sent or posted on the organization's website. A similar method is to have a feature service distribute it for you in various formats, ranging from straight text to more elaborate layouts that include headlines, photos, and stories already prepared for newspaper columns and pages. Such layouts are called *camera-ready* in the trade, and a good example is shown in Figure 7.1. Distribution by feature service firms is discussed further in Chapter 10.

In most cases, such features are topic-specific and are sent to the editor in charge of a particular section. A feature on the lowly potato is sent to the food editor, but a feature on a new smartphone goes to the business or technology editor. A feature on how to have a beautiful green lawn, of course, goes to the garden editor. In a more sophisticated version of this approach, newspapers in the same circulation area will receive different features and photos about the same subject. This way, editors know the material is somewhat exclusive to them and won't show up in a competing publication.

The second approach is to write an exclusive feature for a specific publication. In this case, you need to target a publication that reaches your selected audience, be they engineers, architects, educators, or purchasing agents. You also need to review several issues of the publication to determine the topics it has covered and the style used in similar articles.

Once you are familiar with the publication, phone the editor, outline the subject in about 60 seconds, and ask if he or she would be interested. You can also send a brief email. Carol Haddix, food editor of the *Chicago Tribune*, says the ideal public relations professional "just sends a note explaining his or her idea in a way that is phrased to interest me."

FIGURE 7.1 Feature releases are often distributed in camera-ready format, which means that they are already set up in regular newspaper columns, complete with a headline and even photos. All an editor has to do is insert the article into the page. This service feature, prepared and distributed by Family Features, was for The UPS Store.

The reason for the short phone call or email (called a *query*) is to determine if there is enough interest to justify writing an exclusive feature. Perhaps the editor has recently run several features much like the one you have in mind. Or the editor might suggest another story angle that would appeal to more readers.

Other editors, particularly those for popular magazines, will ask you to submit a *proposal* that outlines the entire article and explains why the magazine should publish it. A proposal should include the following points:

» Tentative title of the article

» Subject and theme

» Significance. Why is the topic important? Why should readers know about it?

» Major points

» Description of photos and graphics available

The third approach is not to write the feature at all. Instead, you give a journalist a story idea that he or she might want to develop on his or her own. In other words, you phone or email the person and make a pitch, which was discussed in Chapter 6. If the journalist is interested, you can offer to help by sending background information, providing photos and other artwork, and even setting up interviews with potential sources for the story.

The advantage of this approach is that the publication's staff actually writes the story. Thus, the publication has invested time and money in the story and is more likely to publish it. The disadvantage is that you can't always control how the story will be developed and whether it will advance organizational objectives.

The fourth approach is simply to post the feature on your organization's website for possible downloading by journalists and consumers. Hewlett-Packard (HP), for example, has a link on its online newsroom (www.hp.com) simply titled "feature stories." Other placement opportunities for features are discussed later in this chapter.

Types of Features

There is no formal classification of feature stories and no practical limit to the variety of stories that can be written. Whenever you find something that can be made interesting to some segment of the public, it may be the beginning of a feature. Some ideas are obvious, but many more can be developed if you hunt for them. Among the most frequently seen features are (1) case studies, (2) application stories, (3) research studies, (4) backgrounders, (5) personality profiles, and (6) historical pieces. These categories are not mutually exclusive, and the lines between them often blur, but some familiarity with them will help you understand the range of possibilities.

Case Study

The **case study** is frequently used in product publicity. Case studies often tell how individual customers have benefited from a company's product or service or how another organization has used the product or service to improve efficiency or profits. In other words, case studies are a form of third-party endorsement or testimonial that helps illustrate the acceptance or popularity of a particular service or product in the marketplace.

Organizations providing various services often use the case study feature. One company, Great Date, distributed a feature release that related the stories of two men who found love and happiness after signing up with the matchmaking service. The founder of the service is quoted later in the feature as saying, "Jim is typical of many male clients who want a professional matchmaker to help them. In just the last month, we have worked with a 40-year-old never-married surgeon, a 38-year-old real estate lawyer, and a 48-year-old stockbroker whose wife had died of cancer several years ago." The idea, of course, is to encourage readers to relate the service to their own needs by showing "typical" clients who are benefiting from its services.

> **Case studies are an essential aspect of many PR programs, providing rich information on the value and strength of a company's offering.** Catherine M. Wolfe, director of marketing services, Toshiba America Medical Systems

In October, at the beginning of the skiing season, Great Date issued another feature titled "Skiers Turn to Professional Matchmakers." The angle was timely, and again the feature gave several case histories of men and women finding love on the slopes thanks to the efforts of the matchmaking firm. In sum, the skiing angle was yet another way to package the same message, but with a seasonal focus.

Technology may not be as interesting as finding love, but HP develops a number of features to demonstrate the versatility and durability of its many products. In one case study, for example, the company explains how Nissan uses HP computer equipment to monitor prototype electronic engine-control systems in its racing cars. The story quotes a Nissan executive as saying, "Our jobs are simplified knowing that the engine computer will perform up to specifications under severe race conditions. With HP's help, we can get down to the business of winning races."

A word of caution about case studies: Although most customers and organizations are flattered that you want to use them in a case study about your products and services, you should always ensure that they have given permission and have approved the feature story—in writing. See the Tips for Success below for more tips on how to write a case study.

Application Story

The *application story* is similar to the case study. The major distinction is that the **application story** focuses primarily on how consumers can use a product or a service in new and innovative ways. The advantage to the organization is that it can show multiple, practical applications of a product or service over a period of time, which generates increased consumer awareness and usage.

> **"** *A succession of application stories about customers utilizing the same product in different ways can show varied uses for a product or service.* **"** Donna St. Jean Conti, owner of St. Conti Communications

Much food publicity consists of application stories—new recipes or new variations on familiar ones. The food pages of newspapers carry many such features. There's nothing new about apples, walnuts, beef, or even artichokes, but the producers and distributors of such commodities regularly send the media new recipes and ways of preparing such foods. Most of these features are accompanied by mouth-watering, high-resolution color photos that entice consumers to try the recipes that, in turn, generate sales for the ingredients. See Figure 7.2 on page 171 for a typical food publicity photo.

Another approach is to give consumers tips and advice that relate to an organization's products and services. Homewood Suites, for example, issued a

Tips for Success   How to Write a Case Study

A satisfied customer is the key to writing a case history that shows how a company's product or service was used successfully. G. A. "Andy" Marken, president of Marken Communications, offers a list of questions that a public relations writer should keep in mind:

+ What can be told about the company, its place in the industry, its size, and other details?

+ Why did the company first need the products or services in question?

+ Who was involved in the application?

+ What did the products or services do for those people? What can they do now, as a result of the products or services, that they couldn't do before?

+ How does the solution save time and money and add quality?

+ Could the company get the same results with a competitive solution? If not, how does this solution provide savings that couldn't otherwise be achieved?

+ What is the customer contact protocol? Who should clear and approve the article?

feature story titled "Taking Your Kids—and Visiting Colleges." It was distributed in March by Business Wire just as the "season" started for parents and high school seniors to visit various prospective colleges. The application story was a list of 10 tips by a travel expert for "visiting colleges with your kids." One tip: "Whenever possible, leave the younger siblings behind. They'll be bored." Another useful tip: "Move on if you arrive on campus and your child refuses to get out of the car."

Gold's Gym also generates publicity and name recognition by sending reporters features on fitness topics ranging from how to get in shape for bikini season to reducing the "tire" found on many middle-aged men. The opportunities for offering consumer tips are boundless and are limited only by the writer's imagination. An orchid farm issued a feature story by offering the tip that men could really impress their significant others by skipping the roses on Valentine's Day and giving a potted orchid instead. According to the feature, an orchid is really a "babe magnet for the clueless guy."

FIGURE 7.2   Food features are made more attractive with mouth-watering photos of prepared dishes. This photo from Boggiato Produce, Inc., features its romaine lettuce as part of a shrimp tempura recipe that was made available to food editors. A CD media kit contained numerous recipes and corresponding high-resolution photos.

Surveys and Research Studies

Surveys and polls, as well as scientific **research studies,** can provide opportunities for features. This is particularly true if the survey is about some aspect of contemporary lifestyles or a common situation in the workplace. Water Pik, for example, commissioned a research firm to do a "Sexy Smile Survey," which found that "6 in 10 Americans would be most disturbed by their partner not brushing or flossing his or her teeth for a week, as compared to only 24 percent who would be most perturbed if their significant other passed on wearing deodorant."

Residence Inn, a chain owned by the Marriott Corporation, got extensive coverage with a research study about the effects of long business trips on female managers and executives. The feature concentrated on the research finding that women feel more productive and stimulated by extended business trips than men, who report feeling lonely and bored. The feature went on to quote psychologists, female executives, and Residence Inn managers about the findings of the study. According to Marriott, women now comprise 31 percent of all business travel "roomnights."

Research studies can also have seasonal themes. For example, Yahoo! used St. Patrick's Day as a news "hook" to distribute its survey of "Alcohol in America." The survey of 2,000 Americans indicates that the most popular drinking holidays, in descending order, are (1) New Year's Eve, (2) Christmas, (3) Fourth of July, (4) St. Patrick's Day, and (5) Thanksgiving. In addition, the most popular drink was red wine, followed by vodka and beer. Another Yahoo! survey feature, which helps spread its brand name, is shown in Figure 7.3 on page 172.

YAHOO!

March 29, 2011 07:12 AM Pacific Daylight Time

New Yahoo! Mail Study Shows Americans' Dependency on Email and DOs and DON'Ts for Digital Communications

--(BUSINESS WIRE)--More than ever before, people rely on digital communication, such as email, instant messaging (IM), and texting to stay connected and get things done. And our evolving online behavior reveals a lot about our habits and values. A new survey conducted by Yahoo! Mail shows the average adult is highly invested in email, regularly using 3 email accounts — 2 for personal use, and 1 for work use. The Yahoo! survey also finds a growing number of adults are "hooked" to their email, with 2 in 3 adults checking their email as soon as they wake up, up from only 41% last year.

The new survey, which polled over 2,000 people in the United States, asked in-depth questions about email accounts and acceptable email behaviors. The key findings include:

- **People Have Multiple e-personalities:** Yahoo! found that adults are heavily invested in email with the average person having a total of about 3 email accounts, all of which are checked on a regular-basis.

- **Breaking up is still hard to do:** 13% of adults think it is appropriate to end a relationship via email, IM, text. The study also shows that men are more likely than women to end a relationship via email, IM, text.

- **We are snoops:** 1 in 5 people admit to having read their significant other's email without their knowledge.

- **Email Appetizer:** The majority of adults check email very frequently, with 48% checking their inboxes during meals.

- Bonjovilover23@yahoo.com, **You're being judged:** Many adults, especially women, have negatively judged someone based on an email, grammatical errors, or even an email address.

- **The clock is ticking:** Most adults believe there is a finite period of time in which someone can respond to an email. When it comes to personal mail, 86% of adults think an email should not go more than a week without a response.

- **Personal Life at Work:** 68% of adults check personal email while at work.

- **iAppreciate it:** 70% of adults believe it's OK to send "Thank You" cards/notes for gifts via email.

- **First email, then driver's license:** 81% of adults would allow their child to have their own email account before the age of 15

If you're interested in speaking to someone about the study and/or digital etiquette please let us know.

Contacts

Yahoo! Corporate Communications
Becky Auslander, 212-381-6909

FIGURE 7.3   Surveys are always popular topics for news features. Yahoo! builds brand awareness by conducting various surveys throughout the year. This feature gives the results, in bullet form, of how much Americans depend on email in their daily lives. In fact, almost 70 percent of the respondents regularly check their personal emails while at work.

Backgrounder

There are several kinds of **backgrounders.** One focuses on a problem and how it was solved by an organization or a product. Often there is some historical material and an opportunity for injecting human interest into the story. One example is a story on the reclamation of strip-mined land and how a coal company restored an area to productive use for farming.

Another kind of backgrounder explains how a technology or product has evolved over the years. A good example is a feature about the evolution of the Global Positioning System (GPS), which is based on a network of satellites circling the earth. The company that supplies road data to in-car navigation systems is NAVTEQ, which is not exactly a household name. A feature was distributed about how the company generates the data used by MapQuest, Google, and almost all GPS systems. It's a fascinating story about two-person teams literally driving millions of miles a year recording "navigation attributes."

Cisco Systems, which had developed a new technology for enhancing global teleconferencing, issued a backgrounder on the problems and challenges of creating a global "virtual team" that could meet as if all the team members were in the same room. As the feature states, "Advances in communication technologies have not only created new opportunities to reach new markets and suppliers, but also a workplace that is becoming virtual, with team members located around the world."

Personality Profile

People like to read about people, particularly if they are celebrities. A review of any magazine newsstand is a graphic confirmation that the "cult of personality" is alive and well. Such **personality profiles** are highly readable because they "humanize" the celebrity by giving a glimpse of what's behind the curtain, so to speak.

Profiles of "movers and shakers" also are popular in the business press. Cover articles in *Fortune* magazine often profile the lives and management philosophies of successful CEOs. Other profiles of prominent executives can also be found in such publications as *BusinessWeek, Forbes, The New Yorker, Financial Times,* and *The Wall Street Journal.*

In most cases, these profiles are written by journalists with, quite often, a strong assist from public relations personnel who (1) "sell" the idea of a profile, (2) make the executive available, (3) provide background information, and (4) even arrange photo shoots.

Another approach is writing a profile of the CEO that can be used in media kits and posted on the organization's website. A media kit for Boston Beer Company, producers of the Samuel Adams brand, includes a two-page, single-spaced profile of its founder, Jim Koch. In it, readers get a sense of Koch's values and philosophy about making beer. We also learn that he has three degrees from Harvard, taught adventure skills for Outward Bound, and told his dad that he wanted to start a brewery. To which his dad responded, "You've done some dumb things in your life, but this is just about the dumbest."

A person doesn't have to be a CEO, however, in order to qualify for a personality profile. Any number of employees in any organization would make interesting profiles because they have an unusual job or an interesting hobby or have distinguished themselves in some way. A San Francisco company, for example, once distributed a feature on the new manager of the company's Vietnamese Service Center because the woman had a compelling story about her escape from war-torn Vietnam. For more tips on how to write a personality profile, see the box below.

Historical Piece

Anniversaries, major changes, centennials, and many other events lend themselves to **a historical piece.** Significant milestones may present an opportunity to report on the history of the organization, its facilities, or some of its people. Stressing the history of an organization lends it an air of stability and permanence. The public can logically deduce that if an organization has lasted "that long," it must have merit.

Planters, discussed in Chapter 6, used its 100th anniversary to distribute features about the founder of the company, Italian immigrant Amedeo Obici, who started the company in 1906 after observing a person eating peanuts and dropping the shells behind him. That led to Obici's idea to sell fresh roasted peanuts without the shells. The rest is history, so to speak. The Hershey Company celebrated the 100th anniversary of Kisses Chocolates by issuing a feature about the evolution and unique packaging of the product.

One doesn't have to wait for a century, however, before writing a historical feature. American Girl products, for example, prepared a feature titled "Hip, Hip, Hooray—It's Our 25th Birthday!" The feature discussed the growth of the company

Tips for Success   How to Write the Personality Profile

Public relations writers are often asked to write a profile of a key executive. Ragan.com gives the following tips on how to enhance the writing of a personality profile:

+   **Give the "essence."** Tell the reader who the profile subject is and why he or she is interesting.

+   **Take some chances.** A profile is an interpretation, not an official biography. Give the reader a picture of your subject as you see him or her.

+   **Get a different view.** Try to see the world through the subject's eyes. A profile works when you understand a person's motivations.

+   **Don't write in chronological order.** Most people are more interesting at 40 than they are at 4. Don't begin at the beginning. Write about what makes your subject interesting now.

+   **Make your subject reflect.** Ask profile subjects to evaluate themselves, describing good points and bad, high and low points.

+   **Don't focus on work alone.** Don't limit your profile to a piece about somebody's job. Try to see the whole person who goes home after work and has an interesting hobby.

+   **Describe, describe, describe.** Paint a picture of your subject. Is he or she serious, jovial, upbeat? What kind of personality does the person exhibit under stress, or at play?

(20 million dolls and 135 million books sold) and its various milestones through the years. One factoid: The company has received an estimated 5 million letters and emails from girls and parents. Of course, the feature also announced that a "Deluxe-Edition Historical DVD" was going on sale.

Another example of a historical piece is a 200-word feature distributed by Fisher Nuts titled "The Humble Peanut Has History as Essential Food." The release begins, "Having nurtured the dawn of civilization in the Amazon River basin, the peanut moved on to support European explorers as early as the 15th century." Historical features are also a staple of tourism publicity. The Alaska Division of Tourism distributes features about the history of the state to encourage visitors. One article was titled, "Following 19th-Century Russians Across Alaska." The lead paragraph was: "Visitors to Alaska who have forgotten their American history are quickly reminded that the 49th state was once a Russian colony. One reminder is the large number of Russian names sprinkled across the map."

Lowe's also used a historical theme to celebrate Thomas Edison's 164th birthday and the invention of the light bulb to make the point that it's the first major retailer to offer consumers an LED bulb that will last 22 years—"just long enough to see a baby graduate from college."

Parts of a Feature

The formatting of a feature is similar to that of a news release. You should use the organization's letterhead and give the standard information such as contacts, headlines, and datelines. The following sections detail the components of a feature news release, and additional tips are given in the Tips for Success on page 176.

The Headline

"Newspaper and broadcast editors pick daily from over 10,000 releases online and on paper," says Ron Levy, the founder of North American Precis Syndicate, but you can get hundreds of placements if you use headlines that "editors find delightful and charming."

"Headlines are vital," says Steven Gossett, editorial manager of PR Newswire's feature news unit. He suggests headlines of 20 words or less and to use the name of the organization or product if it is well known. If your client or employer isn't a household name, then the next best approach, says Gossett, is to tell what's new, unusual, different, or important about your product, service, or organization.

There are two kinds of headlines that you can use. The first is the informational headline, which gives the crux of the story. Some examples are:

» Travel Tips: Travel Insurance Offers Peace of Mind on Family Vacations

» Expert Advice for Buying Power Tools as Gifts

» Good News for Caffeine Lovers: Study Shows Caffeinated Beverages Hydrate Like Water

» New Yahoo Study Shows Americans' Dependence on Email

» Rawlings Offers Expert Tips on Gearing Up for Baseball

The informational headline works well for the results of surveys or when the organization is offering advice and tips (10 tips seem to be the standard) on how to purchase a product, book a cruise, or even improve your wardrobe. Essentially, these headlines make the promise of a "reward" for consumers by helping them save money, buy a good product, achieve better health, or prevent illness. Verizon, for example, got extensive media placements by sending out a news feature offering tips on how to help a child succeed in the classroom.

The second kind of headline is one that uses a play on words, alliteration, or a rhyme to raise the curiosity of the editor or the consumer. Here are some examples of word play:

Work and Money Problems Are One Big Headache (Tylenol)

The Good the Bad and the Bubbly—Celebrating Safely (American Academy of Ophthalmology)

Tips for Success   How to Write a Great Feature Story

An organization may get more media exposure by doing a feature story instead of a straight news release. Fred Ferguson, head of PR Newswire's Feature News Service (www.prnewswire .com), offers the following advice on how to write a feature news release:

+ Grab the editor's attention with a creative headline that tells the story.

+ Tell the same story in the first paragraph, which should never be cute, soft, or a question.

+ Support the lead with a second paragraph that backs it up and provides attribution. Place the product and service name at the end of the second paragraph so it becomes less advertorial.

+ Try to keep all paragraphs under 30 words and to three lines. This makes it easier for editors to cut to fit available space, holds the reader's attention, and is attractive in most page layouts.

+ Do not excessively repeat the name of the product or service. It dilutes the value of the story.

+ Forget superlatives, technobabble, and buzzwords. Instead, tell consumers why they should care.

+ Never say anything is the first or the best, express an opinion, or make claims unless you directly attribute them to someone else.

+ Avoid using a self-serving laundry list of products or services.

+ Discard a telephone number acronym in favor of numerals. It makes it easier for consumers to make a telephone call for more information.

+ Don't put the corporate name in all capital letters. It violates AP style.

+ Don't give a standard paragraph about the organization at the end of the article.

New Parents Need the Scoop on Cat Litter (a new cat litter product)

Help Your Teen Put His Best Face Forward (a new acne medicine)

See Your Way Through the Next Power Outage (a new flashlight)

New National Water Gardening Group to Dive into Deep End on Important Issues (a new water conservation group)

Whatever your choice of headline, whether it is an informational one or one that generates curiosity, make sure it grabs the interest of editors and readers. Philips Norelco's Bodygroom feature, for example, merely stated, "Look Better Naked." And Banfield Pet Hospital had many more placements via a NewsUSA distribution with a feature titled "Tired of Doggy Breath? Prevention Is Key to Protect Pets from Oral Disease." Doesn't that sound more interesting to the average reader than a straight headline announcing "Oral Disease Prevention in Pets"?

The Lead

News releases usually have a summary lead that tells the basic facts in a nutshell. The name of the organization is in the lead, and readers will get the key information even if the summary is all they read.

In contrast, the purpose of the lead in a news feature story is to attract attention and get the reader interested enough to read the entire article. A good lead requires creativity on the writer's part because it must intrigue people and appeal to their curiosity. A lead is a promise; it tells people that they will learn something that will be beneficial to them. Here are some creative leads that generate interest, give information, or promise a benefit:

» Many home improvement enthusiasts will tell you that new tools are at the top of their wish lists. But for those with little knowledge of power tools, shopping for them can be an intimidating and confusing experience. (a feature release by Dremel, a manufacturer of power tools, that gives five tips on shopping for power tools)

» More and more men and women, who are regular skiers, are turning to professional matchmakers to find affluent companions who are also skiers. (a feature release by Great Date Now, a matchmaking service)

» Tired of staying up all night assembling your kids' holiday gifts? Does the thought of deciphering lengthy, complicated instructions make your skin crawl? If so, you're not alone. (a feature release by Huffy Sports Company about a "no tools" portable basketball hoop stand)

Notice that these leads are brief and concise. Most experts recommend a lead paragraph of no more than 30 words. A good lead also focuses on the most unusual part of the story. A lead introducing a machine that builds curbs without forms could start with these words: "The formless curber lays concrete curbs without the use of expensive forms." This statement is factual and true, but the feature would be much more interesting if it started like this: "It's just like squeezing toothpaste out of a tube."

The Wall Street Journal, in particular, is famous for using anecdotal leads in its feature stories. See the Tips for Success box below for more information.

The Body

Chapter 5 pointed out that news releases use the inverted pyramid format, presenting the most important facts first and elaborating on them in the succeeding paragraphs. It also pointed out that news releases should be 200 to 400 words.

The feature story, in contrast, doesn't need to follow the inverted pyramid approach, but it does need to be somewhat concise. Food sections in the newspaper, for example, tend to use features that are 200 to 750 words long. Business Wire, which distributes features on behalf of clients, recommends a six-paragraph story of 400 words or less. Features distributed by North American Precis Syndicate (NAPS) usually have a length of 250 to 400 words. In other words, less is better. In addition, tips should be in bullet form, not numbered. An example of a feature using bullets is shown on page 179.

Feature stories usually include the following:

» Direct quotes from people

» Concrete examples and illustrations

» Basic statistics or research findings

+ Tips for Success   How to Personalize a Lead Paragraph

The Wall Street Journal is famous for using the anecdotal lead in its page one features, usually in the lower section of the front page. Essentially, an anecdote is a short account of an entertaining or interesting incident experienced by an individual that begins a story about a broader topic, issue, or trend.

A good example of the anecdotal lead is one that was used for a story about the efforts of the nudist resort industry to attract a younger audience. Indeed, membership in the two largest nudist groups has been flat or declining for years.

The reporter, however, personalized the lead paragraph and attracted readers with the following anecdote:

On a recent Friday morning, Jessi Bartoletti arrived at the Sunsport Gardens Nudist Resort here in a T-shirt and shorts. By evening, the 19-year-old had stripped down to a string of purple Mardi Gras beads and was dancing around a bonfire with about 200 young nudists, many of them first-timers.

"I don't think I've ever felt this free," Ms. Bartoletti yelled over pounding drums.

That's good news to the nudist resort industry, which is desperate for young nudists like Ms. Bartoletti to augment its clientele of graying baby boomers.

The article then went to on quote nudist association officials and to discuss various efforts by nudist resorts to attract a younger audience.

Mobile Apps That Go On Vacation With You

(NAPSI)-Increasingly, consumers are using their smart-phones for everything from getting timely information about one-of-a-kind sales to booking restaurant reservations.

Now, savvy travelers visiting South Carolina can also use their smartphones to get real-time information about accommodations and events when on vacation.

Mobile apps offering visitor information and special deals have been launched by a number of destinations in the "Palmetto State" in an effort to give visitors a focus and timeliness they can't get from standard guidebooks.

Here are some examples:

• Voted the "Friendliest City" by Conde Nast Traveler magazine, Charleston has the reputation for being one of the top wedding destinations in the country. The city boasts numerous wedding-friendly venues, vendors, planners, caterers and florists. The Charleston Wedding Planner mobile app is designed to help a bride navigate her way through all the options. And, to keep things current, free updates are available about every eight weeks.

• The app for the official guide to the South Carolina National Heritage Corridor's Lowcountry region can direct visitors to a wide variety of attractions. The Lowcountry has much to offer, including sources of antiques, arts and crafts centers, bird-watching areas, canoe/kayak outings, African-American history tours, local foods, military history trails, historic districts, national forests and national, state and local parks.

• The history of Beaufort and the surrounding Sea Islands dates back almost 500 years, and the destinations and area accommodations reflect that rich history. Some of the most vibrant and well-preserved history in the area is also known for its Gullah culture. The Gullah are known for preserving their African linguistic and cultural heritage. The Beaufort mobile app offers timely text and photos on attractions such as these, as well as fishing and eco-tours and the area's annual shrimp festival.

To learn more, visit the website at www.DiscoverSouthCarolina.com.

Edisto Beach State Park has an oceanfront campground on a palmetto-lined beach that's famed for its shelling.

Charleston's Battery offers a picturesque combination of Southern architecture and historic monuments to the city's past.

Download high-resolution, print_quality graphic and MS Word document

Word Count: 330

Copy/Paste HTML Article

FIGURE 7.4 A hallmark of a good feature story is providing information and tips that help consumers in their daily lives. This feature promotes tourism in South Carolina by letting potential visitors know that they can get information about sites to visit via mobile apps. The feature, prepared by NAPS distribution services, is 330 words and uses bullets in a highly readable format. A photo is also provided for downloading.

» Descriptive words that paint mental pictures

» Information presented in an entertaining way

If a feature does run longer than 400 words, insert subheads. The subheads, which often are boldfaced, indicate the major sections of the story. They should also provide information, however. Instead of saying something vague such as "Economical," it is better to write "More Economical Than Similar Products."

The body of the story essentially delivers the reward promised in the lead.

The Summary

In many cases, the summary is the most important part of the feature. It is often quite brief, but it must be complete and clear. Essentially, it is the core message that the writer wants to leave with the reader. Abundant Forests Alliance, for example, ended a feature on Christmas trees by stating the two key points: Recycle your "real" Christmas tree and make Christmas presents out of this year's tree by making holiday potpourri or sachets out of the dried needles.

It's also important to provide sources of more information and product information. Abundant Forests added, "For more Green Tips for the holiday, visit www.abundantforests.org." A feature story on tourist sites in South Carolina ends with "To learn more, visit the website at www.DiscoverSouth Carolina.com."

Photos and Graphics

A feature story is often accompanied by photos and graphics to give it more appeal. Food producers typically send mouth-watering color photos of prepared food. See Figure 7.2 on page 171 see how a lettuce and vegetable producer used such a product photo.

Media outlets also like **infographics,** computer-generated artwork that attractively displays simple tables and charts. *USA Today* pioneered the use of infographics, and newspapers around the nation now use them with great frequency. A key finding of MCI's "Meetings in America" survey, for example, was chosen by *USA Today* for its front-page "USA Snapshot" series. It was a simple bar chart giving the primary reasons why people get stressed about business travel. Leading the list was "time away from family" with 75 percent. Only 20 percent reported stress filling out expense reports. Chapter 8 gives more information about photos and graphics.

Features have also become multimedia in scope. Stories can be illustrated with photos, audio, video, or podcasts, which broaden their visibility and online life. Distribution services such as Business Wire, PR Newswire, NAPS, and MarketWire can facilitate these add-ons, and Figure 7.5 on page 181 shows a NAPS feature that includes a photo that can be downloaded. Photos can also be offered on an organization's website. An HP feature story on using its applications and products to create wedding invitations and programs, for example, included six photos and even had a space where readers could post comments about the article. Feature stories, like news releases, can also be embedded with a URL and Technorati tags to better reach blogs and other online sites such as Facebook. This is discussed further in Chapter 12.

Brides Say "I Do" To Fashionista
Weddings On Frugalista Budgets

(NAPSI)-Brides on a budget can get great advice from television personality and celebrity event designer Samantha Goldberg, who says, "Before purchasing, brides give careful thought to their 'I Do' list of areas where they don't want to skimp, such as ring bling, the dress and honeymoon, but more and more brides-to-be search for creative ways to accomplish this task."

Bridal-Bliss-on-a-Budget Advice

Goldberg, the celebration expert for Party City, goes on to suggest ways to cut costs without compromising style:

• Start with Sophistication: Invitations set the tone with guests, so be sure they coordinate with the event's theme.

• Spice Up Centerpieces: While splurging on flowers may be a must, adding flair to the arrangements with inexpensive accessories, such as candles or crystals, can complete the look and save money.

• Get Creative: Think outside the box for the theme or color scheme. Choose a festive theme such as a red-carpet Hollywood party, Hawaiian luau or Mexican fiesta. With thousands of party supplies, including more than 100 party themes, Party City can be a great resource for any themed occasion.

• Don't Forget the Bling: Bling out the bachelorette party with decorative items and don't forget the bridesmaids with tiaras, sashes, faux gigantic diamonds…a bachelorette can never have too much bling.

Learn More

For more budget-savvy tips, visit www.PartyCity.com or stop by one of the more than 600 stores nationwide.

Elegant dinnerware that matches everything from place cards to invitations can be easy and inexpensive to have at your wedding.

Celebrity event designer Samantha Goldberg says brides-to-be can cut wedding costs without compromising style.

Download high-resolution, print_quality graphic and MS Word document

Word Count: 263

FIGURE 7.5 A news feature doesn't need to be long; this one is only 263 words. Key tips are given in bullet form and provide a teaser to encourage people to visit the PartyCity website for even more tips on how to plan a wedding without breaking the bank. This feature was also prepared by NAPS distribution services and includes a photo that can be downloaded.

Placement Opportunities

Your challenge is to figure out what kind of publication would be most interested in your feature story. It may be only one particular trade publication, or it may be all weekly newspapers in the country. See Chapter 10 for a discussion of databases that can help you make that decision.

In general, placement opportunities for the print media include newspapers, general-circulation magazines, specialty/trade magazines, and internal publications. Placement opportunities for broadcast media are discussed in Chapter 9; opportunities for online media are discussed in Chapter 12.

Newspapers

The primary use of features generated by public relations personnel is in the special sections of daily newspapers. The food section is a popular place for manufacturers and producers of food products, and the automotive section gets its fair share of features from Ford, General Motors, and Toyota.

Weekly newspapers are not as specialized, but editors are always on the lookout for features that affect the average citizen. The Internal Revenue Service, the Social Security Administration, and even producers of grass seed often get space because they give tips to the public about how to save on taxes, file for Social Security, or grow a great lawn.

General Magazines

Although it can be argued that there is no longer any such thing as a "general" magazine, we use the term to mean "popular" magazines such as *Glamour*, *Cosmopolitan*, *Travel & Leisure*, and *People*.

These magazines usually have their own staffs and regular freelancers who write features, but they do rely on public relations sources for ideas and information. Thus, *Seventeen* magazine might carry an article about the difference between suntan lotions and sunscreens. Most of the information would probably have originated with a sunscreen manufacturer that hired a public relations firm to create publicity and increase sales to female teenagers.

Specialty/Trade Magazines

There are two kinds of magazines in this category. The first is magazines that serve particular interest and hobby groups. There are magazines for golfers, surfers, car buffs, stamp collectors, scuba divers, joggers, gardeners, and even soap opera fans. The list of hobbies and interests is endless.

The second category is publications that specialize in a specific trade, industry, or business. There are, for example, about 3,000 publications that cover all aspects of the computer industry. Many of these publications are extremely technical and are usually read by computer nerds or individuals involved in the development and manufacture of high-tech products. A feature on how a company solved a particular technical problem or made a breakthrough on a new design for a chip, however, would be of interest.

Whenever your organization has something bearing on a special field of interest, there may be a theme for a feature—and it is possible to write more than one feature on the same subject. With a new line of golf clubs, one story might tell how the line was developed under the guidance of a well-known player; another might deal with unusual materials and manufacturing techniques; and a third could describe the experiences of several golfers with the new clubs. Each of these stories might be placed in a consumer magazine for golfers or find a home in a magazine covering the golfing industry.

Writing an Op-Ed

The term *op-ed* literally means "opposite the editorial page." The concept originated at the *New York Times* in 1970 and has now spread to many major newspapers and magazines across the country. The purpose of **op-ed** articles is to present a variety of views on current news events, governmental policies, pending legislation, and social issues.

From a public relations standpoint, op-ed pieces provide an excellent opportunity for individuals and organizations to reach an audience of readers who also tend to be opinion leaders or, in the jargon of the industry, "influentials." Indeed, if an organizational executive wants to become a spokesperson or what is now referred to as a "thought leader" for a particular industry or cause, public relations counsel often recommends writing one or more op-ed pieces.

This was the case in Minneapolis when a former mayor was asked by a development company and its public relations firm to write an op-ed piece supporting the immediate opening of a $134 million entertainment complex in the downtown area. About the time the complex was ready to open and tenants were preparing to move in, a political controversy about the wisdom of building the complex in a tight economy started to surface. Even the City Planning Commission was threatening to call public hearings and delay issuing occupancy permits.

McCafferty Interests, the developer of the complex, sought the services of Carmichael Lynch Spong to devise a strategy to get the project back on schedule and to dampen the "political bickering." The firm's recommendation was to place an op-ed in the *Minneapolis Star Tribune* under the byline of the former mayor, who was a strong supporter of the project.

The op-ed reached an estimated audience of 2.3 million residents in the Twin Cities, and it turned the tide in terms of public support for the project. The *Star Tribune* also wrote an editorial supporting the project after the op-ed piece was published, and even the City Planning Commission changed its mind. Due to these efforts, the complex opened on schedule.

Universities and think tanks such as the Brookings Institution and the Hoover Institution also make considerable use of op-ed pieces. The objective is to gain visibility for an institution and establish its experts as "thought leaders" in a particular field. The public relations department of Washington University in St. Louis, for example, got 426 placements in one year by sending op-ed articles written by 62 faculty members.

The op-ed pages of the *New York Times*, *The Wall Street Journal*, the *Financial Times*, and the *Washington Post* are the best known and the most prestigious in terms of placement. They regularly carry op-eds written by ambassadors, former presidents, CEOs of major corporations, senators, and a host of other prominent or influential people. The competition is steep; *The Wall Street Journal* receives about 500 to 700 op-ed articles a month and has space for only a few of them.

Your employer or client may not be a former ambassador or a CEO of a global company, but that should not discourage you from submitting op-ed pieces to these newspapers and to other U.S. dailies. Editorial page directors are always looking for fresh insights from anyone who has expertise or a new perspective on a particular topic of current public concern. David Shipley, op-ed editor of the *New York Times*, says it best: "We look for timeliness, ingenuity, strength of argument, freshness of opinion, clear writing, and newsworthiness." Indeed, op-eds must have a current news angle to fulfill the journalistic requirement of timeliness. For more tips on how to write an op-ed, see the Tips for Success box below.

In addition, you should not overlook the trade press. Publications that serve a particular industry or profession also use commentaries and short opinion articles. A company's head of research or the vice president of human resources might have something to say that would be interesting to the readers of these publications.

Tips for Success   How to Write the "Perfect" Op-Ed

+ Daily newspapers prefer articles of about 400 to 750 words, which are about three double-spaced pages.

+ Concentrate on presenting one main idea or a single theme.

+ Have a clear editorial viewpoint. Get to your point in the first paragraph and then proceed to back up your opinion.

+ Use facts and statistics to add credibility to what you say. Double-check your facts before using them. John Budd, chairman of The Omega Group, says, "Ratio of opinion to fact should be about 20 percent to 80 percent."

+ Don't ramble or deviate from your principal points. An op-ed is not an essay that slowly builds to its point.

+ Use short, declarative sentences. Long, complex sentences and paragraphs cause readers to tune out.

+ Be timely. The article should be about a current social issue, situation, or news event.

+ Avoid the use of "I" in stating your opinion. Write in journalistic third person.

+ Use active verbs; avoid passive tense.

+ Describe the background of the writer in the cover letter to the publication. This helps editors determine the person's qualifications.

+ Don't do a mass mailing of an op-ed piece. Standard practice is to offer the piece to one publication at a time.

+ Query editors before sending an op-ed; it will save you time and energy.

Public relations writers often do the initial work of drafting an op-ed for a client or employer. Another way to approach it is to ask a person for notes from a recent speech. Speeches to organizations are often recycled as op-eds to newspapers.

Op-eds, by definition, are short and to the point. The most effective in terms of placement are 400 to 750 words, which are about three to four word-processed pages, double-spaced. Various publications establish their own guidelines for length. The *Atlanta Journal and Constitution* prefers 200 to 600 words, whereas the *Washington Post* wants submissions of 600 to 700 words. The *New York Times* suggests 650 words.

> **The whole point of an Op-Ed is to illuminate the issue in a new way. It isn't just opinion; it's an opinion grounded in facts, data, and research.** Henry Miller, chief operating officer, Goodman Media

Such restrictions in length mean that you must write well in terms of organization and conciseness. Jennie Phipps, in an article on how to write an op-ed for *PRWeek*, gives the basic format:

> Start with a catchy lead paragraph that is about 30 words. Use the second 35- or 40-word paragraph to explain further what you said in the first graph. The third graph is the nut graph—that's the place where you make your point, preferably in a sentence or two. Use the next half-dozen or so paragraphs to support your point—logically and with verifiable statistical information and quotes from experts. Banish the phrase "I think" altogether. Throw in humor whenever possible. Wrap it all up with a concluding graph that clearly ties back to the nut graph.

This is good advice, but there are some other guidelines to keep in mind. As in pitch letters, you need to do some homework on the audience and geographic reach of the targeted publication. It is also wise to read the editorial pages of the publication and find out, either from the newspaper or a media directory, how op-ed submissions are handled. Some editorial page directors prefer an email or fax query outlining the subject of the proposed op-ed piece and the author's credentials. Others simply want a brief phone call and a pitch in 60 seconds or less.

If the editor is interested, he or she will most likely ask you to submit the op-ed for consideration. This gives you the "green light" to proceed with this particular publication, because you at least have an editor's commitment to review the piece. This is important, because an op-ed should be submitted to only one publication at a time; it is not like a news release that is distributed to numerous publications.

In fact, publications "lock up" exclusive rights by paying op-ed authors, even if they are CEOs or millionaires in their own right. The *New York Times*, for example, pays $450+, and *USA Today* pays $300+. Smaller dailies often pay less or nothing at all.

Letters to the Editor

The next best thing to an op-ed article is a published letter. **Letters to the editor (LTEs),** are generally shorter than op-ed pieces. They focus primarily on rebutting an editorial, clarifying information mentioned in a news story or column, or adding information that might not have been included in the original story. And, unlike an op-ed article that is often arranged in advance, letters to the editor are submitted without any prior consultation with editors. A good example of a letter to the editor published in the *New York Times* is as follows:

Danger: Hookah Smoke
Re "Putting a Crimp in the Hookah" (front page, May 31)

Lawmakers looking to ban hookah bars are on the right track. Hookah smoking has gained popularity among young people partly because of the mistaken notion that it is safer than cigarette smoking. It is not. Hookah smokers may actually inhale more tobacco smoke than cigarette smokers do because of the large volume of smoke they inhale in one smoking session, which can last as long as 60 minutes.

Hookah smoke contains high levels of toxic compounds, including tar, carbon monoxide, heavy metals and cancer-causing chemicals, and hookah smoking is linked to cancer, heart disease, and other serious illnesses. Hookah smoke is addictive, like other tobacco.

The pipes used in hookah bars may also spread infectious diseases. People using hookahs are at higher risk for hepatitis, and are more likely to develop herpes lesions on their mouths.

Clean indoor-air laws should include all forms of smoking, including hookahs.

O. Marion Burton,
President
American Academy of Pediatrics,
Columbia, S.C.

There is limited space for letters, so you should follow closely any guidelines that the publication has established. Most newspapers and magazines publish these guidelines as part of an LTE page. The *San Jose (CA) Mercury News*, for example, has the following policy: "Letters of up to 125 words will be considered for publication. All letters must include a full name, address, and daytime phone number, plus any affiliations that would place your opinion in context."

"*Focus on clearly and concisely making a simple point by using examples, anecdotes, and data.*" Chris Birk, director of communications for VA Mortgage Center.com

Many of the op-ed guidelines apply, but here are some that relate directly to letters:

» Keep it short. A letter of 200 words or less has a much better chance of being published.

» Be temperate and factual. Don't call the editor or the author of an article names or question their integrity.

» Identify the subject in the opening paragraph. If your letter is in response to a specific article, refer briefly to the article and the date it appeared.

» State the theme of your letter in the second paragraph. Do you agree, disagree, or want to clarify something?

» The next several paragraphs should give your viewpoint, supported by convincing facts, examples, or statistics.

» Close. At the end of your letter, give your name, title, organization, and telephone number. Publications often call to confirm that you wrote the letter.

In many cases, an organization will encourage its supporters or donors to write a letter to the editor to promote a cause or issue, or even rebut some unfavorable news coverage.

Summary

The Value of Features

» News feature writing requires right-brain thinking—intuition, image making, and conceptualization.

» A feature story can generate publicity for "ho-hum" products and services. It also can give background, context, and the human dimension to events and situations.

» Features and background stories are part of a trend in the print media to do what is called *service journalism*—"news you can use." Consumer tips are popular topics for features.

Planning a News Feature

» Feature writing uses the "soft-sell" approach. The name of the organization, the product, or the service should appear only once or twice. Stay away from hype and provide editors with information that is factual and informative.

» A good feature writer is curious and asks a lot of questions. He or she can conceptualize and see possibilities for the development of a feature article.

» There are four approaches to feature writing: (1) distribute a general feature to a variety of publications; (2) write an exclusive article for a publication; (3) interest a freelancer or reporter in writing

a story; and (4) post feature articles on the organization's website.

Types of Features

» There are six kinds of features: (1) case study, (2) application story, (3) survey and research study, (4) backgrounder, (5) personality profile, and (6) historical feature. Features can also be a blend of several types.

Parts of a Feature

» Feature stories are formatted much like news releases in terms of using letterheads, contacts, headlines, and datelines.

» The headline must be creative, and the lead paragraph must arouse interest to encourage the reader to read the next paragraphs.

» A feature story must be concise; most are under 400 words.

» A feature should use extensive quotes, concrete examples, highly descriptive words, and information presented in an entertaining way.

» Photos and graphics are an integral part of a feature story package.

Placement Opportunities

» There are numerous placement opportunities for feature articles in specialty newspaper sections (food, real estate, auto, etc.), general-circulation magazines, special-interest magazines, and business and trade magazines.

Writing Op-Eds and Letters to the Editor

» Op-ed pieces are an opportunity to portray the organization and its executives as "thought leaders" on a particular subject or issue of current public interest.

» Op-eds must feature strong writing, use facts, and be concise, only about 400 to 700 words.

» Letters to the editor usually are written to comment on, add information, or rebut an article or editorial that has already been published. Most letters should be 200 words or less to improve chances of publication.

Skill Building Activities

1. Review the contents of your local daily for a week and compile a scrapbook of feature articles you find in the categories of (a) case study, (b) application story, (c) research story, (d) backgrounder, (e) personality profile, and (f) historical piece. In addition, identify the company or association that probably sent the release to the newspaper as part of its publicity efforts. A good place to look for such features will be the specialty sections of the newspaper, such as food, lifestyle, auto, business, real estate, and so on.

2. A feature article can be written on almost any subject. Write a 200- to 400-word feature for one of the following organizations:

   a. a paint manufacturer
   b. the Florida orange industry
   c. a national chain of fitness centers
   d. a national hotel chain
   e. a national restaurant chain

   Remember that the information should be useful to prospective customers and appeal to editors.

3. Select a business executive or the head of a charitable organization in your community and write a personality profile about him or her. An alternative is to write a personality profile on a university professor or administrator who has just received a major honor or award.

4. The state legislature is considering a 10 percent increase in tuition at public universities. Draft an op-ed for the president of your university's student government opposing the tuition hike. The audience is readers of the town's daily newspaper.

5. The local business daily has profiled the owner of a successful public relations firm. In the interview, she is quoted as saying, "You don't need a degree in journalism or public relations to work in the field. I have a B.A. in English and worked my way up from a secretary's job." You're majoring in journalism or public relations. Write a letter to the editor (200 words or less) disagreeing with her assessment.

Media Resources

Birk, C. (2011, January 3). "Good Press: 6 Steps to Writing Killer Op-Eds and Commentaries." Retrieved from www.openforum.com.

Friedlander, E. (2010). *Feature Writing: The Pursuit of Excellence,* 7th edition. Boston: Allyn & Bacon.

Guiniven, J. (2008, October). "Keeping the Op-Ed Effective in Today's Media Climate." *Public Relations Tactics*, 6.

Kent, C. (2009, September). "Pitching Op-Eds in the Internet Age: Changing the Rules for Landing on the Opinion Page." *Ragan Report*, 26–27.

Ragan, M. (2009, November). "How to Write an Anecdotal Lead: Use Real-Life Stories to Attract Readers." *Ragan Report,* 6–7.

Ward, D. (2009, March 2). "Battle Intensifies for Spot on Op-Ed Page." *PRWeek*, 11.

Working, R. (2011, May 26). "Nine Tips for Writing an Intriguing Executive Bio." Retrieved from www.ragan.com.

Working, R. (2011, April 8). "Four Steps to Firing Up Your Writing with an Anecdotal Lead." Retrieved from www.ragan.com.

Selecting Publicity Photos and Graphics

8

» After reading this chapter, you will be able to:

» Understand the importance of publicity photos

» Know the components of a good photo

» Work with professional photographers

» Write a photo caption

» Create other graphics

» Set up photo and graphic files

» Distribute photos and artwork

The Importance of Publicity Photos

Photographs and graphics are important components of news releases and feature stories. They add interest and variety, and they often explain things better than words alone.

Helen Dowler, director of photo services at PR Newswire, told *O'Dwyer's PR Services Report*, "Images should be an integral part of every PR plan. Photos alone, or with a press release, will increase interest in a story. In fact, if your picture illustrates a story well, it can be the deciding factor for an editor on whether to report on a story or someone else's." Indeed, one survey of 200 journalists by PWR New Media found that 80 percent of the respondents were either "much more likely" or "likely" to cover a story if it included high-resolution images.

Today, the digital revolution has made it relatively easy to provide photos and graphics to the media almost instantly via the Internet. Thom Weidlich, a reporter for *PRWeek*, explains: "These days, seemingly nothing could be simpler than supplying a newspaper, magazine, or other publication with a needed photo; just attach a JPEG to an email and whisk it through cyberspace."

This chapter explores the elements that make a good publicity photo or graphic and explains how to prepare the material for media consideration. Its purpose is not to make you a professional photographer, but to give you a better working knowledge of what constitutes a good photo and how to work with photographers to achieve maximum media placement results.

Components of a Good Photo

The adage says that a picture is worth a thousand words. A picture in a newspaper or magazine often takes the same space as a thousand words, but it has much more impact. Studies have shown that more people "read" photographs than read articles. The Advertising Research Foundation found that three to four times as many people notice the average one-column photograph as read the average news story. In another study, Professor Wayne Wanta of the University of Missouri found that articles accompanied by photographs are perceived as significantly more important than those without photographs.

> **Motion and still images are valuable. Somebody might not read the story, but they'll recall the images.** Amanda Watlington, owner of a marketing consulting firm

This also applies to graphics, which will be discussed later in the chapter.

Publicity photos, however, are not published if they are not high resolution and if they do not appeal to media gatekeepers. Although professional photographers should be hired to take the photos, the public relations writer often supervises their work and selects the photos best suited for media use. Therefore, you need to know what makes a good publicity photo.

Product photos are particularly challenging. One approach is to simply show the product, such as a new computer, in a stark background so it is highlighted. HP, for example, provides such photos to the trade press; an example is shown in Figure 8.1. Another approach is to show someone actually using the product. Yet another approach is to "sex it up" with an attractive model standing next to the product. Samsung, for example, distributed a publicity photo for its new 3D television with several attractive Korean models in tight-fitting dresses, sitting on a desk around the computer.

Food publicity has its own particular challenges in terms of making a product look savory in a photo. Some tricks are to use motor oil in place of syrup and mashed potatoes instead of real ice cream, use hair spray on produce, and even use brown shoe polish on raw meat to portray a well-grilled hamburger. More tips on taking product photos are on page 192.

FIGURE 8.1 Product photos are often taken with a plain background so the product is highlighted. This photo, showing HP's new TouchSmart PC, was distributed as part of a media kit about the new product. Such photos are often used in the trade press and in specialty sections of a newspaper, such as the technology or business page.

Technical Quality

The technical quality of a photo is very important. Indeed, a common complaint of editors is the poor content and technical quality of publicity photos. They look for the key elements of good contrast and sharp detail so the photo reproduces well on everything from glossy magazine pages to cheap newsprint. You must also consider that photos are often reduced in size or, on occasion, enlarged when they are published. If they have good resolution to begin with, they will hold their quality.

Back in the days before the digital revolution, the traditional approach was to submit photos on 35mm slides or even on glossy paper. Today, professionals use digital cameras, and the traditional process of taking photos on film, developing the film, and making prints has practically disappeared except in art photography.

Although the process of taking photos has changed radically, the key elements of a good photo remain the same. Digital photos must have high resolution and sharp detail to be used. Online media, for example, are willing to sacrifice quality for the speed of download, so they typically use images at 72 dpi (dots per inch).

+

Tips for Success How to Take Product Photos That Get Published

+ Show the product in a scene where it would logically be used. If it is used in an office, show it in an office.

+ Clean up the area where the picture is to be taken. Remove any litter or extraneous items. Repaint if necessary.

+ If people are in the picture, be sure that they are dressed for the situation. They should wear the kind of clothing that they would wear while using the product.

+ Put perspective into the photo so viewers will know how big the item is. For example, show a hand, a person, or a pencil.

+ Use a top-of-the-line digital camera to ensure maximum quality and resolution.

+ Don't accept anything but the best in photographs. They have a potential shelf life of 5 years; many may be used by others to illustrate books or brochures. Give them quality.

+ Take at least two photos—vertical and horizontal—of each new product. This makes them adaptable to a variety of situations. When possible, show the product in use. Application stories need illustrations.

+ If there are other products in the picture, be sure that the new one is in the dominant position.

+ The setting should be realistic, with everything hooked up and ready to go.

+ Every picture must have an identifying caption.

+ Be sure that the background contrasts with the product. Make the product stand out.

Print publications, however, require much higher resolution, and 300 dpi is a minimum. Distribution services such as NewsCom and Feature Photo Service distribute publicity photos in a 300-dpi JPEG or GIF format to accommodate the needs of almost any publication—from monthly glossy magazines to small weekly newspapers.

Subject Matter

There is a wide variety of subjects for a publicity photo. On one level, there are somewhat static photos of a new product or a newly promoted executive. On another level, photos are used to document events such as a groundbreaking or a ribbon-cutting ceremony.

Trade magazines, weekly newspapers, and organizational newsletters often use the standard "grip and grin" photo of a person receiving an award, a company president turning the first shovel of dirt on the site of a new building, or the traditional "ribbon-cutting" ceremony to open a new store. These shots have been a traditional staple of publicity photos for years, and there is no evidence that they are going out of fashion even in the digital age. At the same time, you should be aware that such photos can be quite boring, and editors want more unusual or artistic material.

Award photos nearly always present a problem. In many ways, they are somewhat of a cliché, showing the typical "grip and grin" format. It is relatively easy to violate the concepts of newsworthiness, action, and central focus as awardees merely look at the camera while holding their check or trophy. Award photos, however, are a fact of life and still get published in local newspapers and even in national publications if the individuals are celebrities. You can make such photos more interesting, however, if the subjects are showing some emotion (even a smile would help) and you just show a close-up instead of a person's full figure. See Figure 8.2 on page 194 for a typical award photograph from the Country Music Awards ceremony.

> **An award shot that doesn't show emotion just dies. It's boring. Get people to yell and scream or hold up a peace sign—it will bring some life to it.** Suzanne Salvo, owner of Salvo Photography

There is also the problem of the large group photo. Organizations love group photos of everyone who attended the seminar or received an outstanding service award. A group photo may be legitimate when you want to give a souvenir of a particular meeting or conference or provide documentation for a specialized publication, such as a fraternal or alumni magazine. However, pictures of this kind should not be sent to general-circulation newspapers and magazines.

A better approach, if you want media coverage, is to use the local angle. Take small group photos of individuals from a particular city and send them to local dailies or weeklies. In general, you should show activity in a picture: people talking to each other, looking at a display, or shaking hands with a notable person in an informal pose. The people should not be lined up, looking at the camera.

FIGURE 8.2 It is always a challenge to make award photos interesting. One good tip is doing a close-up photo that concentrates on the people's faces. Here Neil Perry, Kimberly Perry, and Reid Perry from the musical group The Band Perry receive an award at the Academy of Country Music Awards in Las Vegas.

A common composition is to show three people all talking or listening to a fourth person who is at the left of the picture. This fourth person may be a keynote speaker, the president of an organization, or someone who has just received an award. Such a composition can provide a focus and add some interest, but even these pictures are somewhat of a tired cliché. In a group situation, it is extremely important to take down the names and titles of people as they are photographed. This will make your job much easier later on, when you have to write the caption, which will be discussed in another section. Don't rely on memory—yours or anyone else's.

Composition

We have already discussed ways to compose photographs of groups. Inherent in all this is the concept of keeping the photo simple and uncluttered. A look at the family album will illustrate the point. We have Aunt Minnie and Uncle Oswald looking like pygmies because the family photographer also wanted to include the entire skyline of New York City. Consequently, Aunt Minnie and Uncle Oswald are about 35 feet from the camera.

In most cases, the photographer should move into, not away from, the central focus of the picture. If the purpose is to show a busy executive at his or her desk, the picture should be taken close up so that the subject fills most of it. Sufficient background should be included to provide context, but it is really not necessary to show the entire surface of the desk—including the disarray of papers, picture of spouse and kids, and paperweight from a recent convention. All of this conflicts with what the viewer is supposed to focus on in the picture.

Another reason for moving in on the subject and minimizing the background or foreground is to achieve good composition. That picture of Aunt Minnie and Uncle Oswald also shows the Empire State Building growing out of Uncle Oswald's head.

Experts have made the following suggestions about composition and clutter:

» Take tight shots with minimal background. Concentrate on what you want the reader to get from the picture. A good example of a tight shot is shown in Figure 8.3.

» Emphasize detail, not whole scenes.

» Don't use a cluttered background. Pick up stray things that intrude on the picture.

» Try to frame the picture.

» Avoid wasted space. There should not be a large gap between an object, such as an award, and the person's face. In the case of a group picture, people should stand close to each other.

» Ask subjects wearing sunglasses to remove them.

All this advice is logical, but there may be times when the background plays an important role. If the purpose of the photo is to show someone in his or her work setting, it is important to capture a sense of the person's environment. A photo of a manager in management information systems, for example, might show him or her surrounded by three or four computers and a stack of printouts. Phil Douglis, a widely known photographic consultant, calls it the "environmental portrait." He continues, "Such portraits blend posed subjects with their supporting context to symbolize jobs, capture personalities, and ultimately communicate something about them to readers."

FIGURE 8.3 A strong, appealing, well-composed photo focuses on the subject and minimizes the background. This photo, distributed by Intel to publicize its annual Science Talent Search, highlights one of the high school finalists tinkering with his research project to improve the precision of atomic clocks.

Action

Action is important because it projects movement and the idea that something is happening right before the reader's eyes. A picture of someone doing something—talking, gesturing, laughing, running, operating a machine—is more interesting than a picture of a person standing still and looking at the camera. Douglis says, "Interactive exchanges are the most productive form of communication. Photojournalism is an ideal medium for visually expressing how people communicate interactively with each other."

America's amateur photographers have filled the nation's family albums with pictures of Aunt Minnie and Uncle Oswald in rigid, formal poses, staring blankly, but a quick look through your daily newspaper will not turn up this kind of shot. Prize-winning news photographs bear out that action and interaction among people are the key elements in successful photography. In other words, take pictures of people doing something or interacting with others—not just staring at the camera. A good example is the photo on page 64 in Chapter 3 showing celebrities at a National Education Association (NEA) gathering to kick off the "Reading Across America" campaign.

With some thinking, an action photo can be taken of almost any situation. Professional photographers recommend, however, that the best "action" photos are those taken when the subjects are being spontaneous and are not conscious of the camera. Consequently, photographers will often take multiple shots over a period of several minutes to get the best facial expressions and portrayal of more natural interaction.

However, sometimes a straight head-and-shoulders portrait is exactly what is needed. For example, a press release announcing a promotion or the new president of a club or organization is often accompanied by what is referred to as a *mug shot*. See Figure 8.4 for a typical example. Such photos are used for organizational newsletters and sent to the business section of a local daily for use as a thumbnail in a brief paragraph about the individual's promotion or hiring.

You should not conclude, however, that all good pictures must suggest overt action. Some of the greatest photos have been character studies of people whose faces

FIGURE 8.4 Organizations usually distribute a short news release and a photo to announce the promotion of an executive. These head-and-shoulder photos, also known as "mug shots," are commonly used in business publications. The caption is simply the name of the individual and perhaps his or her new title. This photo, distributed by Business Wire, is of Jeff Weikert, who was appointed vice president of sales for RewardsNow.

reflected their happiness at having won an award, their intense concentration on a critical issue, or their sorrow at having lost an election.

Scale

With inanimate objects, it is important to consider the scale. The picture should contain some element of known size so that the viewer can understand how big or small the object is. With large machines, it is common and effective to place a person in the picture. This helps the viewer estimate the approximate size of the picture's subject. A good example is the person standing beside Panasonic's new 155-inch high-definition plasma screen in Figure 8.5.

When smaller things are photographed, the scale guide is even more important. This also offers an opportunity to provide drama and adds the news value of novelty. For example, a new computer chip from Intel was photographed beside a penny—and the chip was even a bit smaller. In another situation, a manufacturer of a memory card illustrated its capacity by showing a person holding the card, surrounded by a pile of papers and brochures that could be placed on the card.

Camera Angle

Interest can also be achieved through the use of unusual camera angles. Starbucks illustrated its decision to carry Naked Juice (100 percent juices and smoothies) in its 7,000 outlets using the perspective of the camera inside the refrigeration unit looking out, capturing an employee framed at the door reaching in to get a bottle of the product. See Figure 8.6.

Another approach is the extreme close-up that emphasizes shapes and patterns. A photo of a new mainframe computer isn't very interesting, so it's important to look at the situation and come up with an interesting angle that makes a better photo. IBM, for example, chose to show the unusual angle of a technician assembling part of a module that was part of the

FIGURE 8.5 Showing scale and size is important in many product publicity photos. The size of Panasonic's new 150-inch HD plasma screen is better understood by having a person stand beside it. The large image of the panda, which fills the entire screen, is also attention getting and illustrates a key feature of the product—picture clarity.

FIGURE 8.6 An unusual angle can make even a bottle of fruit juice more interesting. This publicity photo, distributed by the Naked Juice Company, shows the perspective of looking out of the refrigeration unit and focuses on a person reaching in to get a container. This element of "action" in the photo elevates a ho-hum product picture into something much more interesting.

new supercomputer. See Figure 8.7 on page 199 for the publicity photo that was made available to the media.

Some other camera angles commonly used are (1) shooting upward at a tall structure to make it look even taller, (2) taking an aerial shot to give the viewer a chance to see something that might otherwise be unnoticeable, and (3) using a fisheye lens to capture a 180-degree image.

Lighting and Timing

Indoor pictures often require more than a flash on a camera. Depending on the subject, a photographer may have to use supplemental lighting to remove or enhance shadows to highlight a key element—a person's face, a product, or some aspect of the background. Even simple product photos, where the background is plain white or black to ensure that the product stands out, require considerable lighting expertise.

Outdoor photos also have their challenges. In general, outdoor pictures taken in the morning or late afternoon are better for contrast than pictures taken at midday. Of

FIGURE 8.7 Mainframe computers are big square boxes that are really dull to look at, let alone photograph for publicity purposes. IBM solved the problem by focusing on the assembly of the computer, using an unusual camera angle that emphasized shapes and the human element.

course, the photographer can use a flash to lighten dark areas.

Selecting the location or setting of a picture is important if you want good, sharp results. For example, if you know that the people involved will be wearing light colors, you should not use a white background. Conversely, don't select a dark background if your photo subjects will be wearing dark clothing. In both cases, the result will be "floating heads," because the clothing will blend into the background. In all situations, you want to strive for high contrast between the background and the individuals being photographed.

Color

Before the digital age, most publicity photographs were produced in black and white because they were economical, versatile, and acceptable to most publications. However, color photographs are now the industry standard and used by all kinds of publications as printing technology has become more sophisticated and less expensive. If a publication plans to use black-and-white photos, color photos can easily be converted. Most of the photos in this book, for example, were originally in color.

Everything that has been said about composition and quality should be underlined in relation to color pictures. To be used, they must be outstanding in both interest and technical quality.

Working with Photographers

It is important to use a skilled photographer with professional experience. Too many organizations try to cut corners by asking an employee with a point-and-click digital camera or even an iPhone to take pictures. Often, the public relations writer is also asked to take the photos. This may be all right for the company newsletter, but publicity photos sent to the media must be extremely high quality if they are going to be competitive with the thousands of other photos that are readily available.

It will cost more money to hire a professional photographer, but at least you won't end up with pictures that are dull, poorly composed, and generally unusable. Another reason is that it's better business practice to use a professional who has formal training in visual communications. He or she is experienced and uses high-quality equipment, which usually produces much better results. Your job, as the public relations professional, is to figure out the purpose of the photograph and its objective. It's the photographer's job to figure how to accomplish the objective from a visual perspective.

Finding Photographers

You should have a file of photographers, noting their fees and particular expertise. If you have no such file built up, you might consult colleagues to find out if they can make any recommendations. If you are unfamiliar with a photographer's work, ask to see his or her portfolio. This is important, because photographers are skilled at different things.

A good portrait photographer, for example, may not be good at photographing special events. A news photographer, by contrast, may be an expert at special events but unable to take good product photographs. In sum, you should find the best photographer for each kind of job.

+

Tips for Success   Photo Advice from the Experts

The following 10 tips were given by three photo experts at a workshop sponsored by MediaLink/WirePix at the National Press Club in Washington, D.C. The list was originally compiled by Jerry Walker for *O'Dwyer's PR Report*.

1. Remember that photographs, even for publicity, are not advertising. Make sure you identify the news value of the story you want to illustrate.

2. Wire services like AP get a thousand or more photos a day. Your photo needs to tell a story quickly and creatively and have real news value to make the cut.

3. Capture images that tell your story at a glance. If your story is you're donating money to build homes for the homeless, get a photo of people building homes, not a "grip and grin" check presentation.

4. Write a complete and proper caption. Don't be misleading.

5. Identify the audience you are trying to reach. Photos for newspapers and trade publications are different than those for annual reports or brochures.

6. Get stories out in a timely fashion. Day-of-event photos are important. Use a respected distributor who is experienced with newsroom operations.

7. Try to create photos that have a shelf life and can be used for other projects down the road.

8. If you are organizing a press event, make sure you provide the media, both print and broadcast, with a visual opportunity. Talking heads at the podium are not visual.

9. Don't try to overbrand the photo. It should look spur-of-the-moment, even if it isn't.

10. PhotoShop is a wonderful tool. Don't abuse it by altering reality in your photos.

Three experts at a workshop sponsored by MediaLink/WirePix say that public relations professionals should always ask a prospective photographer two questions before hiring him or her: (1) Can you show me examples of other similar photos you have taken? and (2) What contacts do you have with the media and how will you help me distribute the photo once it has been shot? More advice about publicity photos is on page 200.

Contracts

Any agreement with a photographer should be in writing. A written document helps you to avoid misunderstandings about fees, cost of materials, and copyright ownership of the images.

A letter of agreement with a photographer should cover the following matters:

» What is the photographer's professional fee for taking pictures? Is it on a project basis or based on an hourly fee?

» How are out-of-pocket expenses, such as meals, mileage, lodging, etc., handled while on assignment? Does the photographer get a daily per diem or submit receipts?

» What will be delivered upon completion of the assignment? Will it be a digital file on CD or a website?

» Who will supervise the photographer? Will you or someone else in the organization help the photographer set up shots?

» Who will retain the images? Under copyright law, photographers retain ownership unless the signed agreement gives full ownership and control to the organization commissioning the work.

» Does the organization have unrestricted use of the photograph, or does it have to get permission from the photographer each time it wants to use the shot?

» Can the photographer sell images to outside parties, or does the organization want exclusive use?

Ideally, you want to sign agreements with photographers that give unrestricted, exclusive use of all images. But be prepared to pay more for the photographer's services if that is the case.

The Photo Session

You will save time and money with regard to the photo session if you plan ahead.

» Make a list of the pictures you want. For pictures of people, arrange for a variety of poses.

» Know who you need, where and when you need them, and what props will be required.

» Notify people whose pictures are to be taken. Get releases, if needed (see Chapter 11).

» Be sure that the location for the photo session is available, clean, and orderly.

- » Consider lighting. Will the photographer have everything needed, or should you make preparations?
- » Have everyone and everything at the right place at the right time.
- » Tell the photographer what you need, not how to do the job.

It's also a good idea to let individuals know that a photo shoot takes time; even a photo of an executive may take an hour or so to get the best results.

Cropping and Retouching

In most cases, the quality and composition of the photos can be improved through editing. The two primary techniques for editing photos are cropping and retouching. **Cropping** is editing the photo by cutting off parts of the picture that you don't want. Eliminating parts of the photo provides a tighter focus on the key elements. A photo of the CEO talking to a major stockholder, for example, may also include the waiter clearing a table at one side. It is relatively easy to "crop out" the waiter and any other surrounding background. In addition, it's usually a good idea to crop photos from the waist up. No one needs to see the shoes that the person is wearing.

The second technique, **retouching,** is usually done to alter the actual content of the photo. Let's assume that the photo just mentioned was taken in such a way that a basket of flowers on the stage behind the CEO looks like it is planted on top of his head. In such a situation, cropping may not be the answer, because it also would scalp the top of the CEO's head. The solution, of course, is to simply eliminate the flowers through "airbrushing," or digital manipulation.

Today, even amateurs can use software such as Adobe Photoshop to crop and retouch photographic images at will. Too much "red eye"? No problem. Is the background a bit dark or the sky not blue enough? With a few keystrokes, the problem is solved. Indeed, amateur photographers armed with digital cameras and software programs can manipulate and improve the quality of their photos with relative ease. Even expert photographers rely on Photoshop to electronically create the perfect picture.

Ethical Considerations

Cropping and retouching are common practices in photography, but there are increasing ethical and legal concerns about the boundaries of altering photographic images. An original photograph, for example, can be scanned or downloaded. An editor can then use photo editing software to make any number of alterations. For example, a person's dark suit can be changed to a light tan, and a shadow on a person's face can be removed. The editor can also change the background from a plain wall to an oak bookcase or even a desert by merging the photo with another one stored in the computer's memory. An output device generates the new image on a printed page.

Advertising and public relations people often use photo editing tools to enhance the quality of publicity photos. Thus, a company's board of directors is shown in front of the production line, even though the original photo was taken in a studio. Or, a new product is enhanced by blacking out the background and putting more light on the actual product.

The examples presented thus far are relatively harmless, but news editors continue to express deep concern about additional liberties that may be taken. A Chinese photographer, for example, received considerable international criticism for taking a photo of China's new high-speed train to Tibet crossing a trestle, and then doctoring it by adding a herd of rare antelope peacefully grazing nearby. The idea, of course, was to visually show how the train had not disturbed the wildlife habitat. One media critic said, "It's the perfect propaganda photo."

> " In PR advocacy, you can choose whether to use photographs. If a photo doesn't meet your needs, don't use it. But once you decide to use it, don't alter it. " Carri Jenkins, director of communications, Brigham Young University

As a public relations professional, you should be concerned about the digital manipulation of photos. You have a professional responsibility to honor the original photographer's work and not make alterations that would violate the integrity of the original photo.

When does a cosmetic correction become a violation of the photographer's copyright—or even an outright deception? Would you, for example, use a composite photo to show gender and racial diversity in your organization? If an altered photo misleads and deceives the public in a significant way, do not use it.

Susan Balcom Walton, a professor of public relations at Brigham Young University, suggests that public relations firms and departments should have a photo manipulation policy. Such a policy can be formed, she says, by first asking three questions:

1. Does the image alter reality?
2. Does the image intend to deceive in any way?
3. Has anything in the image been manipulated to imply endorsement of, or agreement with, your organization's views when that might not have been the photographer's or subject's intent?

Writing Photo Captions

All photos sent to the media need a **caption**. This is the brief text under the photo that tells the reader about the picture and its source. However, a caption is not a description of the photo. Some novice caption writers make the mistake of writing, "Pictured above..." or "This is a picture of..." or "Jane Doe is shown talking to..." Don't write the obvious; write to provide context and additional information not readily apparent from looking at the picture.

Most captions, when they accompany a news release, are two to four lines long. In fact, one study by Gallup Applied Science showed that two-line captions are the most effective. This guideline, however, does not apply to **photo news releases**. PNRs, as they are called, are simply photos with longer captions that are distributed to the media without any accompanying news release—the caption tells the entire story.

According to Deborah S. Hauss, writing in *PRWeek*, "Photo news releases enable PR pros to get pictures out more quickly and stand out amidst a sea of written press releases.... Sometimes all it takes to capture the media's attention is a visually compelling image and a short caption."

Regular captions and PNRs are written in the active, present tense. Don't write "The park gates were opened by Mayor Jones"; say instead, "Mayor Jones opens the park gates." Here are the first sentences of several photos used in this chapter that illustrate the use of active, present tense:

» "Nathaniel Hipsman, 17, of Marietta, GA, a finalist at the Intel Science Talent Search (STS) displays his research ..." (Figure 8.3)

» "Panasonic displays its 150-inch HD plasma, which it says is the world's largest, at the Consumer Electronics Show (CES) in Las Vegas, Nevada." (Figure 8.5)

» "An IBM technician assembles a 'multi-chip' module at the company's Poughkeepsie, NY, plant." (Figure 8.7)

A caption for a head-and-shoulders picture of a person (a mug shot) can be even shorter. The caption may be just the person's name. For full identification, you can also add the person's title and company; for example, "Douglas M. Schosser, director of finance, Associated Banc-Corp."

Captions for publicity photos of new products should include a key selling point. For example, the caption for a new Dell PC made the point that the product is primarily designed for medium and small businesses.

There is some argument about stating "from left to right" in a photo caption. To many people, this seems redundant, because people read copy—and probably scan photographs—from left to right anyway. If there are two or three people in the picture, it is assumed that you are identifying them from left to right. You can also indicate identity by the action taking place in the picture—for example, "John Baroni presents Nancy Southwick with a $5,000 scholarship at the annual awards banquet."

In general, the most important person in the photograph should be the first person at the left side of the picture. This ensures that this person is mentioned first in the photo caption. The most important person may alternatively be in the center of the picture, surrounded by admirers. In this case, you can write, "Sharon Lewis, the singer, is surrounded by fans after her concert in Denver." Any reader should be able to figure out which person in the picture is Sharon Lewis.

However, the use of "left," "right," and "center" is perfectly acceptable if clarity is achieved. Here is the caption used under a photo of the top three winners of Intel's Science Talent Search competition:

First place winner Shivani Sud, 17, of Durham, NC (Center); second place winner Graham Van Schaik, 17, of Columbia, SC (Right); and third place Brian McCarthy, 18, of Hillsboro, OR (Left) celebrate winning the Intel Science Talent Search. Intel Chairman Craig Barnett presented the top winners with college scholarships of $100,000, $75,000, and $50,000, respectively. These top award recipients were chosen from an applicant pool of more than 1,600 American high school seniors.

Creating Other Graphics

Photographs are not the only art form that you can use for publicity purposes. Charts, diagrams, renderings and models, maps, line drawings, and clip art are widely used. Many of these visuals can be formatted on your own computer using Microsoft Office, PowerPoint, or other software applications, but you should also consider using graphic artists and commercial illustrators. This is particularly true if you are preparing what is known as **infographics** for distribution to the media, which requires simple and well-designed, colorful graphics.

Charts

The primary reason for using charts is to make figures understandable. There are three basic charts for this purpose, and each seems to work best for certain kinds of information.

> » **Pie chart.** Ideal for showing what part of a total is used for each of several purposes. An organization may use such a chart to show how a budget or revenues are divided.
> » **Bar chart.** Ideal for showing comparisons between years in such things as income, population, sales, and prices.
> » **Graph.** Somewhat like a bar chart, but better suited for showing changes over a long period of time. A simple graph may track sales and profits in relationship to each other.

Today, charts are being dressed up with graphics so that they are more appealing and easier to understand. Reading a copy of *USA Today* makes the point. Instead of showing a simple bar chart or graph, an attempt is made to incorporate representations of the subject into the chart. Some examples of infographics are shown in Figures 8.8 and Figures 8.9.

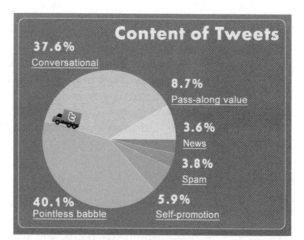

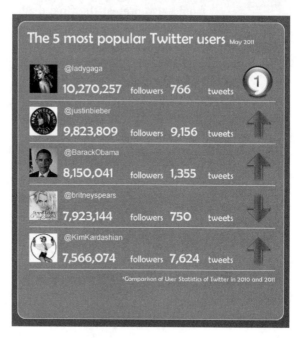

FIGURE 8.8 Infographics that attractively portray data and statistics are now widely used by publications and social network sites. This shows some facts and figures about Twitter. (Copyright by Sebastiaan Laan, InfographicsArchieve.com)

FIGURE 8.9 Percentages can be portrayed in interesting ways by using some creativity and visual elements to give readers an easy way to understand information. This infographic displays the various reasons why individuals stop following brands on Twitter.

Infographics can be prepared using Microsoft Office applications or more sophisticated software in Adobe's Creative Suite. Large dailies usually have their own graphics departments and make their own infographics. However, many smaller dailies and thousands of weeklies lack such capabilities and often are interested in receiving simple, colorful charts in addition to high-resolution photos.

Diagrams

Diagrams are most valuable in showing how something works. How an engine works, how an accessory should be attached, or how a product can be used can all be made clearer with a diagram.

In planning diagrams, you should not only check with the engineers, but you should also pretest the final diagram on potential readers for comprehension and understanding. The key to effective artwork, particularly diagrams, is simplicity.

Renderings and Scale Models

A rendering is an architect's drawing that shows how a finished structure will look. Increasingly, such artwork is being produced by computer drawing programs or photo editing software.

Photos of scale models are also used to give readers a thorough understanding of what is being built or renovated. Both renderings and scale models are widely used in news and feature stories about construction projects. Simple maps showing the location of a construction site or a new freeway ramp, for example, often accompany architectural drawings and photos. The availability of such artwork often makes the difference between a major news story and a brief mention.

Line Drawings and Clip Art

Cartoons are a form of line art, but most people think of line art as drawings of symbols, designs, and objects. These drawings are still made by artists using paper and ink, but the process is now available to almost anybody with a computer.

Barnaby Feder, a *New York Times* reporter, summarizes the state of the art as follows:

> Today's PC graphics programs typically come with hundreds or even thousands of stored images, called clip art, which users can put into their graphics as building blocks. Photographs, shots from video clips and animation can be pasted in as well. Users can also choose from virtually infinite varieties of color and quickly change perspectives, shading, overlapping images and other features.

Adobe's Creative Suite includes stored **clip art** and the tools needed to create line drawings. Clip art can be ordered on CD or even downloaded from the Internet. Microsoft Office and Word Works also feature clip art. Another source of design templates and stock photos is Google Images (images.google.com). Line drawings and clip art are used primarily for organizational advertisements, leaflets, brochures, and newsletters.

Maintaining Photo and Art Files

A properly indexed photo and illustration file is a necessity. Without this, negatives, digital images, or artwork can be inaccessible for future use. The long-term employee who knows where everything is located and can remember the situation will eventually retire or take another job. In other words, don't rely on the collective memory of individuals to keep track of photos and artwork.

Digital photos should be stored on the organization's file server with readily identifiable tags. Corporate files may be identified by names such as "J. Jones, Chairman," or topical areas such as "Employee Recognition Banquet," "Grand Opening of Lansing Store," or "Scale Model of Springfield Office Bldg."

It is important to place all pertinent data in the file or a logbook. This may include (1) the date of the event; (2) when the photo was taken; (3) the location; (4) releases from people portrayed; (5) complete names and titles of people shown; and (6) the name and address of the photographer, including any restrictions on the use of the picture. A good file, which includes dates, will help you avoid the embarrassment of using outdated photos that show current employees at a much younger age or using photos of personnel who have left the organization.

Distributing Photos and Artwork

Digital technology makes it relatively easy to distribute photos and other artwork. However, several approaches are used. The first approach is to simply email a news release or an advisory to specific journalists or editors and let them know that you have photos and artwork if they are interested. You can offer four different formats: (1) a thumbnail, (2) a slightly bigger preview image, (3) a low-resolution version, and (4) a high-resolution (300 dpi) one.

An editor, for example, may just want to preview thumbnails and then order a specific photo. The main point to remember is to never send an attachment (photos or anything else) to an editor unless you are specifically asked to do so. The proliferation of viruses means that no editor will open an attachment unless he or she personally knows and trusts you.

A variation of this approach is to simply list a website in the news release where editors can download the photos and artwork. In many cases, journalists are given a special URL or link that allows them to access high-resolution photos that are not readily available to the general public. HP, for example, requires media to register for access to its "library." Ryan Donovan, HP's director of corporate media relations, told *PRWeek*, "You want to protect the brand so you have to know how those images that represent the brand are being used."

Another approach is to use an electronic distribution service such as Business Wire, PRNewswire, MarketWire, or Feature Photo Service. Editors receive daily feeds from these services that let them know what's being distributed and, with a few clicks, can download any story or related photo to their computers. In many cases, photos and graphics are embedded in the news release so editors can preview a thumbnail. If they like it, they can download a high-resolution copy with a few clicks. The concept of the multimedia news release was discussed in Chapter 5.

These distribution services also archive past stories and photos. This makes it easy for an editor to review all of the news releases and photos that Intel, for example, has distributed over a period of several years. Newscom is a particularly valuable resource; it maintains a searchable database of over 20 million images, graphics, and text from more than 100 photo agencies, wire services, and freelance photographers. Access to Newscom, however, is restricted to registered users and licensing fees are usually required.

Distribution, of course, also occurs online via social networking sites such as Facebook. It is important to tag photos (as well as news releases) with keywords so search engines can index them.

Summary

The Importance of Publicity Photos

» Photographs and graphics add appeal and increase media usage of news releases or features.

» Digital cameras are now used for publicity photos; such photos can be taken and distributed almost instantly.

Components of a Good Photo

» A public relations writer should be familiar with the elements of a good publicity photo: quality, subject matter, composition, action, scale, camera angle, lighting, and color.

» Publicity photos should be sharp, clear, and high contrast.

» Photos should be creative. Traditional pictures of "ribbon cuttings" or awards no longer work.

» An award photo should have no more than three or four people in it. Save the large-group shot for the photo album.

» Photos with action and informality are more interesting than rigid, posed shots.

Working with Photographers

» Use professional photographers if you plan to send materials to news organizations.

» Sign contracts with photographers to clarify such issues as how their images will be used and who owns them.

» Crop photographs to remove clutter and get a tighter focus on the main subject.

» The altering of a photo can raise ethical issues if it misrepresents the original photo.

Writing Photo Captions

» Photo captions are short, use present tense to describe the action, and provide context.

» A photo and a somewhat longer caption can serve as an entire news release.

Creating Other Graphics

» Charts, diagrams, maps, etc., should be simple, colorful, and uncluttered.

» Portraying data in a colorful infographic is a good way of relaying statistical information.

Maintaining Photo and Art Files

» It is important to keep a well-organized photo and graphics file for reference purposes.

» Files or logs should include dates, events, and names of people in the photo.

Distributing Photos and Artwork

» Photos and graphics can be distributed by email, CDs, websites, and electronic news wires.

» Never send an attachment (photo or otherwise) to a reporter or editor unless specifically asked to do so.

Skill Building Activities

1. News releases and features are more attractive to editors if photos are enclosed. Describe the type of photo(s) you would use to illustrate the following situations.

   a. The appointment of a new company president

   b. An announcement that a 22-story hotel will be built

   c. A story about the opening of a new microbrewery

   d. A "how-to" feature on how to get organized

   e. A feature on the growth and success of a local pizza chain

   f. A feature about the ethnic diversity of a college campus

   g. A production of "Mamma Mia" by the local repertory theater

2. Product publicity photos pose a major challenge because it takes creativity to make a product look interesting. What kinds of publicity photos would you recommend for the following products?

   a. An electric frying pan

   b. A new portable GPS navigation system for cars

   c. A tablet computer

   d. A golf cart

   e. Nonfat potato chips

   f. An improved solar panel

   g. A new e-reader

3. A local food bank is having a grand opening of its new facilities, including the traditional ribbon cutting by city officials and an open house for

the community. Describe the types of publicity photos that could be taken of this event to ensure media interest and acceptability. After you decide on the type and content of some photos, write a caption for each one.

4. A civic organization is honoring five outstanding citizens at its annual banquet. Describe how you would organize and compose publicity photos of this event that would be acceptable to the local newspaper.

5. Charts and graphs are more attractive if some creativity is used. A bottled water company wants to show how much water a person needs per day based on the person's weight and activity level. Create a rough draft, either freehand or on a computer, of an infographic that would show this data in an attractive way.

Media Resources

Burns, H. (2008, February 25). "Photography 101: An Editor's Crash Course." Ragan.com (www.ragan.com),

Elliott, A. (2010, November 3). "Ten Essential Websites for iPhone Photographers." Retrieved from www.mashable.com.

Kobre, K. (2008). *Photojournalism: The Professional Approach.* St. Louis: Focal Press, 6th edition.

Miller, L. (2010, July 10). "Four Techniques for Spicing Up Corporate Photos." Retrieved from www.ragan.com.

Nolan, B. (2011, May 9). "Eight Tips for a Perfect Press Photo—That Wins Coverage." Retrieved from www.prdaily.com.

Nolan, B. (2010, December). "Eight Tips for Using Photos in PR Pitches." *The Ragan Report*, 13–14.

Pearcy, A. (2011, March 20). "Eight Tricks of the Food Photography Trade." Retrieved from www.prdaily.com.

Sebastian, M. (2011, April 21). "Five Tips for Improving Your Corporate Photos." Retrieved from www.ragan.com.

Sweetland, B. (2008, January 15). "Captions That Say Exactly Nothing." Retrieved from www.ragan.com.

Radio, Television, and Online Video 9

» After reading this chapter, you will be able to:

» Understand the broad reach of radio and television

» Script a radio audio news release and do a PSA

» Script a storyboard for a television news release

» Book guest appearances on radio and television talk shows

» Do product placements in popular television shows

» Prepare videos for YouTube and other social media

The Wide Reach of Broadcasting

Radio and television offer many opportunities for public relations writers who want to reach both mass and specialized audiences effectively. Online video is also a well-established media platform, reaching millions of people. At least 3 billion videos are viewed every day on YouTube, which is discussed in greater detail at the end of the chapter.

Radio reaches about 95 percent of adults over the age of 18 on a daily basis, with a total estimated audience of about 235 million. A study by Edison Media Research found that college graduates aged 25 to 54 listen to the radio almost 16 hours a week. Radio is particularly strong among Hispanics, the largest and fastest growing minority in the United States; families tune in an average of 24 hours a week. Teenagers also are big listeners, primarily through online sites. According to research by Arbitron, about 85 percent of Americans aged 12 to 18 also listen to radio over the course of a week.

Television has the single largest audience of all media, including social networking sites. Facebook, for example, dominates the Web, but it still doesn't have the reach of a major television network. According to comScore, a research firm, Facebook attracted more than 151 million unique users in October of 2010, staying on the site for 42 billion minutes. However, CBS attracted almost 240 million viewers in the same month who spent 210 billion minutes watching the network's programming. Of course, a large percentage of Americans also surf the Internet while watching TV.

Americans watch an average of 35 hours of TV per week, according to Nielsen research, as opposed to an average of 8.5 hours a week spent on the Internet, excluding the use of email. In addition, broadcast TV stations and cable networks are the first place that about 80 percent of Americans go for late-breaking news, according to the nonprofit Television Bureau of Advertising. Local television news, in particular, tops all other sources

> *The traditional media is always going to be on the menu. The trick is trying to maximize impact with new media tools.*
>
> Joe Case, public relations officer for Nationwide

of news. The bureau survey also found that 71 percent of the respondents relied on TV to learn about products and brands. Other studies have found that traditional media, including television, are the major driver of consumer traffic to websites.

Radio and television continue to thrive in the Internet age because their content has expanded to other digital platforms. More than 40 million people, for example, listen to radio weekly via the Internet, satellite radio, or iPod/MP3 players. Television programs are also widely downloaded to computers, tablets, and smartphones. Consequently, public relations personnel need to pay close attention to broadcast media in order to maximize publicity for a client or employer.

Writing and preparing materials for broadcast outlets, however, requires a special perspective. This chapter explains how to write for the ear, integrate audio and visual elements into a script, and harness the power of satellite and digital communications to conduct media tours that can reach a global audience. It also tells you how to get your spokesperson on broadcast talk and magazine shows.

Radio

Radio lacks the glamour of television and the popularity of the Internet, but it's a cost-effective way to reach large numbers of people in various age, ethnic, and income groups. Radio can be heard almost anywhere. It is the only mass medium that can reach millions of Americans as they commute to and from work in their cars. In addition, the miracle of the transistor brings radio to mail carriers on their routes, carpenters on construction sites, homeowners pulling weeds in their gardens, and exercise enthusiasts working out at a gym or jogging.

> *Radio's power comes from its accessibility. People can listen to radio in almost any location—at home, the car, or work—and it remains a free medium for users.* David Beasley, marketing manager at News Generation, a public relations firm specializing in radio

Approximately 13,500 radio stations are on the air in the United States, ranging from low-powered outlets operated by volunteers to large metropolitan stations audible for hundreds of miles. In addition, radio stations are increasing their audience reach through the Internet. An estimated 2,000 stations now have an Internet presence, and many are concurrently broadcasting and webcasting their programming. The station's format often determines the nature of the audience. There are "top 40" stations for teenagers, all-news stations for commuters, classical stations that appeal to an older and better-educated group, and stations that play "adult contemporary" for aging baby boomers. One popular format is "country," which reaches a variety of age and occupational groups.

A public relations practitioner should study each station's format and submit material suitable to it. There is little sense in sending information about senior citizen recreation programs to the news director of a hard rock FM station with an audience made up primarily of teenagers. You can determine the demographics of a station by consulting radio and television directories or by contacting the station's advertising and marketing department. One common source of advertising rates and demographic data is published by Standard Rate and Data Services. See Figure 9.1 for an example of a typical broadcast listing from Cision's online database.

Radio News Releases

Although radio station staffs often find themselves rewriting print releases to conform to broadcast style, the most effective approach is to send news releases that are formatted for the medium. Radio is based on sound, and every radio release must be written so that it can be easily read by an announcer and clearly understood by a listener.

Format — There are several major differences between a radio release and a news release prepared for print media. Although the basic identifying information is the same

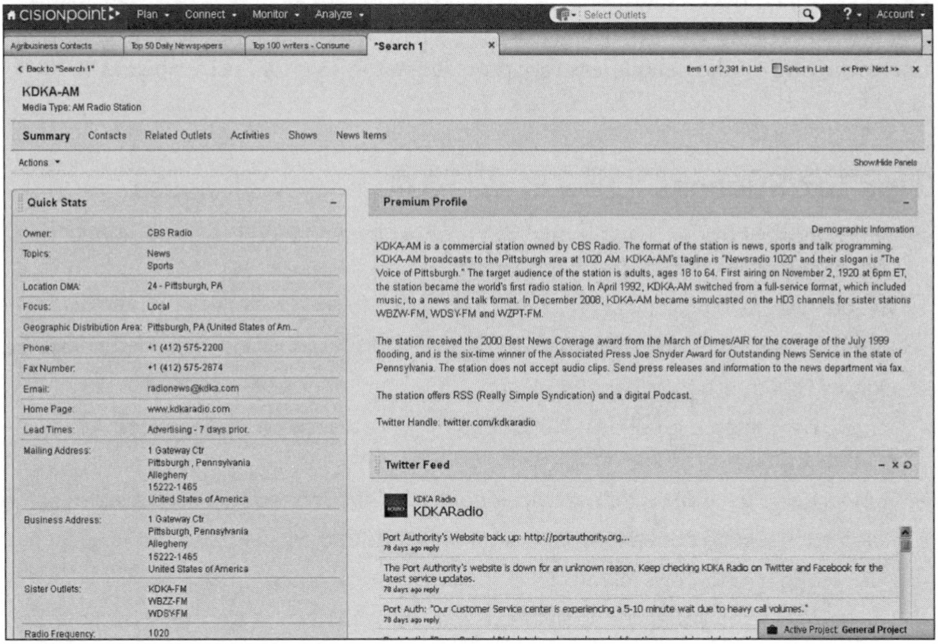

FIGURE 9.1 A publicist has more success placing materials on the radio or television if he or she knows the format and demographics of the station. Armed with such information, the publicist can tailor the material and also find out who should be contacted. This is an excerpt of a radio station listing from a Cision media database. Such databases also let publicists know how the station prefers to receive information.

(letterhead, contact, subject), the standard practice is to write a radio release using all uppercase letters in a double-spaced format. You also need to give the length of the radio release. For example, "RADIO ANNOUNCEMENT: 30" or "RADIO ANNOUNCEMENT: 60." This indicates that the announcement will take 30 or 60 seconds to read.

The timing is vital, because broadcasters must fit their messages into a rigid time frame that is measured down to the second. Most announcers read at a speed of 150 to 160 words per minute. Because word lengths vary, it is not feasible to set exact word counts for any length of message. Instead, the general practice is to use an approximate line count. With a word processor set for 60 spaces per line, you will get the following lengths:

> 2 lines = 10 seconds (about 25 words)
>
> 5 lines = 20 seconds (about 50 words)
>
> 8 lines = 30 seconds (about 75 words)
>
> 16 lines = 60 seconds (about 150 words)

There are also differences in writing style. A news release for a newspaper uses standard English grammar and punctuation. In a radio release, a more conversational style is used, and the emphasis is on strong, short sentences. In fact, you can even write radio copy using incomplete or partial sentences, as you would do in a normal conversation. This allows the announcer to draw a breath between thoughts and the listener to follow what is being said. An average sentence length of 10 words is a good goal. More tips on writing a radio news release are provided in the Tips for Success below.

Tips for Success   How to Write a Radio News Release

+ Time is money in radio. Stories should be no longer than 60 seconds. Stories without actualities (soundbites) should be 30 seconds or less.

+ The only way to time your story is to read it out loud, slowly.

+ Soundbites should be short—about 15 words or less—and capture your most important point.

+ Convey your message with the smallest possible number of words and facts.

+ A radio news release is not an advertisement; it is not a sales promotion piece. A radio news release is journalism—spoken.

+ Announcers punctuate with their voices; not all sentences need verbs or subjects.

+ Releases should be conversational. Use simple words and avoid legal-speak.

+ After writing a radio news release, try to shorten every sentence.

+ Listeners have short attention spans. Have something to say and say it right away.

+ Never start a story with a name. While listeners are trying to figure out who the person is, they forget to listen to the sentences that follow.

Source: News Broadcast Network, New York

Here is an example of a 60-second news feature distributed by North American Precis Syndicate (NAPS) for Timex:

DRESSING FOR A SUCCESSFUL INTERVIEW : 60 SECONDS

THE RIGHT OUTFIT IS AN IMPORTANT PART OF MAKING THE BEST

FIRST IMPRESSION AT A JOB INTERVIEW. BUT WHILE SOME

INTERVIEW-DRESSING GUIDELINES NEVER CHANGE, STYLE EXPERTS

SAY THERE ARE A FEW NEW RULES CANDIDATES SHOULD ADHERE TO.

FOR INSTANCE, IT'S IMPORTANT THAT YOUR STYLE MATCHES THE

CULTURE OF THE JOB. BANKING, ACCOUNTING AND LAW, FOR

INSTANCE, TEND TO BE CONSERVATIVE, AND JOB CANDIDATES SHOULD

DRESS IN A TRADITIONAL BLACK SUIT. CREATIVE INDUSTRIES—SUCH

AS ADVERTISING, MARKETING, AND MEDIA—OFTEN HAVE A BUSINESS

CASUAL DRESS CODE, AND POTENTIAL CANDIDATES MIGHT OPT FOR

SLACKS AND A COLLARED SHIRT. STYLISTS ALSO SAY TO LEAVE LUXURY

ACCESSORIES AND CLOTHING AT HOME, SINCE A POTENTIAL EMPLOYER

COULD FIND THEM FRIVOLOUS. INSTEAD LOOK FOR AFFORDABLE YET

STYLISH ACCESSORIES FROM BRANDS LIKE TIMEX. IT HAS HUNDREDS

OF WATCH STYLES FOR MEN AND WOMEN, MANY AT UNDER A

HUNDRED DOLLARS. AS A FINAL TIP, GIVE YOUR OUTFIT A TEST-WEAR

THE NIGHT BEFORE THE INTERVIEW. IF AN ITEM DOESN'T FIT

PROPERLY, WEAR SOMETHING ELSE. FOR MORE STYLE TIPS, VISIT

TIMEX-STYLE—DOT—COM.

You should note that the Timex brand is mentioned only once in this release. This places the emphasis on the tips and makes the release more acceptable to radio newsrooms that throw away anything that sounds too commercial. Notice the dashes in the website address. This alerts the news announcer to read the URL slowly so people can remember it. The same rule is applied to telephone numbers. Oftentimes, a number or URL is repeated a second time for listeners who are in the process of grabbing a pencil and pad.

Audio News Releases

The Timex feature just mentioned is an example of a script being sent to a radio station so an announcer can read it on the air. Another approach, however, is to provide a recording of a news release or feature to the station.

An **audio news release,** commonly called an *ANR*, can take two forms. One simple approach is to hire a person with a good radio voice to record the entire announcement; he or she may or may not be identified by name. This, in the trade, is called an *actuality*.

The second approach is a bit more complex, but relatively easy to do. In this instance, you use an announcer but also include a **soundbite** from a satisfied customer, a celebrity, or a company spokesperson. This approach is better than a straight announcement because the message comes from a "real person" rather than a nameless announcer. These combination announcements are also more acceptable to stations because local staff can elect to use the whole recorded announcement or take the role of announcer and use just the soundbite.

Format — The preferred length for an ANR is 60 seconds, including a soundbite of 20 seconds or less. It is advisable to accompany any sound tape with a complete script of the tape. This enables the news director to judge the value of the recording without listening to it.

Here is the script of an ANR that includes a soundbite from a spokesperson. TVN Productions in New York produced it on behalf of its client, Hidden Valley Ranch:

WORLD'S LONGEST SALAD BAR: 60 SECONDS

(ANNOUNCER): THIS IS A TVN REPORT. WHAT IS 160 YARDS LONG, BOASTS MORE

THAN 17,000 POUNDS OF PRODUCE, AND IS FREE TO ANYONE WHO HAS AN

APPETITE FOR HEALTHY LIVING? WHY, IT'S THE WORLD'S LONGEST SALAD BAR,

OF COURSE, AND IT'S HAPPENING THURSDAY, MAY 27TH IN NEW YORK CITY'S

CENTRAL PARK TO KICK OFF MEMORIAL DAY WEEKEND. JOSIE WELLING OF

HIDDEN VALLEY RANCH EXPLAINS:

(WELLING): "RANCH DRESSING IS AS MUCH AN AMERICAN ORIGINAL AS CENTRAL

PARK AND MEMORIAL DAY WEEKEND, WHICH IS WHY WE DECIDED TO BRING

THEM TOGETHER FOR A GOOD OLD-FASHIONED MEMORIAL DAY PICNIC. IT'S ALSO

A GREAT WAY TO CELEBRATE OUR 25TH ANNIVERSARY."

(ANNOUNCER): THE SALAD BAR FEATURES COUNTLESS VARIETIES OF FRUITS, VEG-

ETABLES, GREENS AND GARNISHES, AS WELL AS 20 DIFFERENT SPECIALTY SALADS

ALL FEATURING HIDDEN VALLEY ORIGINAL RANCH DRESSING—A PRODUCT WHICH

TURNS 25 THIS YEAR. THE EVENT IS EXPECTED TO BE RECOGNIZED BY THE GUIN-

NESS BOOK OF RECORDS AS—YOU GUESSED IT—THE WORLD'S LONGEST SALAD BAR.

Notice that the above script is written in a somewhat breezy manner, reflecting the nature of the event. The World's Longest Salad Bar is a fun and oddball event.

Organizations announcing new products, however, tend to be more low-key and play it straight. The American Psychological Association (APA), for example, used ANRs to highlight the various topics of research papers at its annual convention. About 25 researchers were selected to give soundbites on topics that would be of interest to the general public. Topics included stopping brain cell loss, violence in video games, differences between men and women, high school hazing, substance abuse, and childhood mental health. The ANRs were targeted to news talk and adult consumer stations, and they reached an audience of more than 20 million listeners on a budget of only $10,000.

Production — Every ANR starts with a carefully written and accurately timed script. The next step is to record the words. In doing this, it is imperative to control the quality of the sound. A few large organizations have complete facilities for this; some get help from moonlighting station employees, but most organizations use a professional recording service.

Delivery — Once the ANR has been produced, the public relations professional must notify the news department that an ANR is available. You need to give the subject of the release and tell editors how to retrieve it. VNR-1 Communications, in a survey of 305 news-talk stations, found that almost 75 percent of respondents preferred to receive email notification about ANRs.

In terms of actually receiving the ANR, a DWJ Television survey found that the same percentage of the radio news directors preferred to receive actualities by phone. An organization can set up a dedicated phone line that has recordings of various news releases or it can contract with an organization such as Strauss Radio Strategies, which will set up and maintain an actuality line for its clients.

Another method of delivery is via satellite or the Internet. Strauss Radio Strategies, for example, also has the ability to deliver an ANR to more than 3,000 ABC-affiliated radio stations throughout the United States via a satellite network. A CD can also be mailed to stations, along with a script, but this only works if the "news" is not particularly time sensitive.

Use — Producing ANRs is somewhat of a bargain compared to producing materials for television. Ford, for example, spent $3,500 for a news release on battery recycling as part of Earth Day festivities. It got 624 broadcasts and reached more than 5 million people with the message. Despite the cost effectiveness, you should still be selective about distribution to stations that have an interest in using such material. Radio releases, like news releases, should not be shotgunned to every radio station.

Most distribution firms also monitor usage of ANRs and other mentions of a client on radio and television talk shows and news programs. Thanks to sophisticated software monitoring programs, they can compile a detailed report within 24 hours of something being aired. By using Arbitron ratings, which give estimated audience figures, public relations professionals can then calculate how many listeners were exposed to the message.

The use of audio news releases is increasingly popular with radio stations because of cost-cutting and staff cuts. Jack Trammell, president of VNR-1 Communications, conducted a survey of radio stations and found that 83 percent of the newsrooms use radio news releases (RNRs). Thirty-four percent say RNRs give them ideas for local stories. The editors look for regional interest (34 percent), health information (23 percent), and financial news (11 percent). They also like tech stories, business trends, children's issues, politics, seasonal stories, agriculture, and local interest issues.

Trammell gives some tips for successful radio and television placement:

» **Topicality.** Stories may fail to satisfy all other judgment criteria and still get airtime simply because they offer information on a hot topic. *Newsroom Maxim*: News is about issues that matter to the majority of our listeners or viewers.

» **Timeliness.** Stories should be timed to correspond with annual seasons, governmental rulings, new laws, social trends, etc. *Newsroom Maxim*: The favorite word in broadcasting is "now," followed by "today" and then "tomorrow." The least favorite word is "yesterday."

» **Localization.** Newsrooms emphasize local news. A national release should be relevant to a local audience. Reporters are always looking for the "local angle." *Newsroom Maxim*: If it's not local, it's probably not news.

» **Humanization.** Show how real people are involved or affected. Impressive graphics and statistics mean nothing to audiences without a human angle. *Newsroom Maxim*: People relate to people—and animals.

» **Visual appeal.** Successful stories must provide vibrant, compelling soundbites or video footage that subtly promotes, but also illustrates and explains. *Newsroom Maxim*: Say dog, see dog.

Public Service Announcements

Public service announcements are another category of material that public relations writers prepare for radio stations. A **public service announcement (PSA)** is defined by the Federal Communications Commission (FCC) as an unpaid announcement that promotes the programs of government or nonprofit agencies or that serves the public interest. In general, broadcasters provide airtime to charitable and civic organizations, although there is no longer any legal requirement that they do so. Thus, a PSA may be a message from the American Heart Association about the necessity of regular exercise or an appeal from a civic club for teacher volunteers in a literacy project.

Profit-making organizations do not qualify for "free" PSAs despite the "public service" nature of their messages, but an informational campaign by a trade group or foundation can qualify. For example, the Homeownership Preservation Foundation used radio PSAs to reach homeowners worried about possible foreclosures. The following 30-second and 60-second PSAs, which received a Bronze Anvil award from the PRSA, were used:

30 SECONDS

HOW ANNOYING IS DEBT? IMAGINE THE MOST ANNOYING PERSON YOU KNOW, ONLY LIKE DEBT, IT'S WITH YOU EVERY DAY. YOU KNOW THE GUM-SMACKING, LOUD-CHEWING, INCESSANT-THROAT-CLEARING, NO-TURN-SIGNAL-USING, TOO-MUCH-COLOGNE-WEARING, OPEN-MOUTH-BREATHING, HAIRY-KNUCKLES-HAND-SHAKING, 7 A.M.-LEAF-BLOWING, DUCK-TAIL-HAVING, CARELESS-CIGARETTE-FLICKING, DOUBLE-PARKING PERSON WHO COULD COST YOU YOUR HOME.

IF YOU'RE WORRIED ABOUT MISSING MORTGAGE PAYMENTS, CALL 888-995-HOPE. THERE YOU'LL GET ADVICE FROM FINANCIAL EXPERTS, FREE OF JUDGMENT, AND FREE OF COST. 888-995 HOPE. OR VISIT 995HOPE.COM.

60 SECONDS

HOW ANNOYING IS DEBT? THINK OF THE WORST DAY OF YOUR LIFE, ONLY IT'S EVERY DAY BECAUSE DEBT IS ALWAYS THERE. IT'S AS IF EVERY DAY YOU'VE OVERSLEPT TO FIND YOUR DOG HAD RUN AWAY, AND YOUR CAR WON'T START, SO YOU HAVE TO SEARCH THE NEIGHBORHOOD ON YOUR DAUGHTER'S BIKE, WHICH HAS TWO FLAT TIRES, AND WHEN YOU FINALLY MAKE IT TO WORK, YOU FIND OUT YOU'VE BEEN LAID OFF BECAUSE THE RAISE YOU GOT LAST MONTH MADE IT CHEAPER FOR YOUR COMPANY TO MANUFACTURE ITS PRODUCTS IN INDONESIA, AND THAT YOU'RE LOSING YOUR PENSION SO THAT THE OVERPAID CEO CAN ADD A NEW CABANA TO HIS COMPOUND IN TAHITI, AND WHEN YOU GET HOME YOU LEARN THAT YOUR MOTHER-IN-LAW HAS TO MOVE IN WHILE SHE RECOVERS FROM HER GALL BLADDER SURGERY, AND SINCE YOU'RE OUT OF WORK YOU'LL BE THE ONE GIVING HER THE REQUIRED DAILY SPONGE

BATH WHILE BEING TOLD HOW HER BABY SHOULD HAVE MARRIED SO AND

SO, THE ASTRONAUT BRAIN SURGEON PHILANTHROPIST WHO

RESCUES PUPPIES WITH ARMLESS ORPHANS IN HIS SPARE TIME.

KEEP YOUR HOME YOURS. IF YOU'RE WORRIED ABOUT MISSING

MORTGAGE PAYMENTS, CALL 888-995-HOPE. THERE YOU'LL GET ADVICE

FROM FINANCIAL EXPERTS, FREE OF JUDGMENT, AND FREE OF COST. 888-

995 HOPE. OR VISIT 995HOPE.COM.

This example shows the potential effectiveness of PSAs. To get the attention of public service directors at radio stations, the PSA package mimicked the stamped "past due" and "foreclosed" notices on late bills. As a result, the PSAs aired 42,000 times on stations nationwide, reaching an audience of 59 million. The foundation received more than 28,400 phone calls and more than 36,700 website hits.

> **"***In PSAs, speak to the common man.... Make it as simple as possible.***"** Christiane Arbesu, vice president of production, MultiVu

Remember, however, that such successes are the exception, not the rule. Only those PSAs that are timely, creative, and of high recording quality stand a chance of being used.

Here are a few more points to remember about PSAs:

» Only nonprofit, civic, and voluntary organizations are eligible to use PSAs. Announcements by profit-making organizations are considered ads, and stations charge regular advertising rates for carrying them.

» A survey by the Pew Research Center found that less than 1 percent of airtime is dedicated to PSAs. As a result, some nonprofits negotiate with stations to actually buy time at a discount to ensure their PSAs are aired.

» Few PSAs are aired during periods of peak listening, when a station can run revenue-producing advertisements. The Pew Research Center survey also found that almost 50 percent of all PSAs air after midnight, which is not exactly prime time.

Format — PSAs, like radio news releases, are usually written in uppercase and double-spaced. They can be 60, 30, 20, 15, or 10 seconds long. The most popular PSA length, according to a survey of stations conducted by Atlanta-based News Generation, is between 15 and 30 seconds. Sixty percent of the respondents use this length; less than 20 percent use 60-second PSAs.

Unlike with ANRs, the standard practice is to submit multiple PSAs on the same subject in various lengths. The idea is to give the station announcer flexibility in using a particular length to fill a particular time slot throughout the day. Here are some examples of varying lengths that were distributed by the National Foundation for Infectious Diseases:

10 SECONDS

PROTECT YOURSELF AND YOUR LOVED ONES THIS FLU SEASON. MORE
INFLUENZA VACCINE IS AVAILABLE THAN EVER BEFORE. TALK WITH
YOUR DOCTOR NOW ABOUT IMMUNIZATION. A MESSAGE FROM THE NATIONAL
FOUNDATION FOR INFECTIOUS DISEASES.

20 SECONDS

THE NATION'S LEADING HEALTH EXPERTS ENCOURAGE EVERYONE WHO WANTS
TO REDUCE THEIR RISK FOR INFLUENZA INFECTION TO GET VACCINATED
THIS SEASON AS SOON AS POSSIBLE. MORE INFLUENZA VACCINE IS AVAILABLE
THAN EVER BEFORE. TALK WITH YOUR DOCTOR ABOUT IMMUNIZATION FOR
YOURSELF AND YOUR LOVED ONES. A MESSAGE FROM (STATION) AND THE
NATIONAL FOUNDATION FOR INFECTIOUS DISEASES.

30 SECONDS

THE NATION'S LEADING HEALTH EXPERTS ENCOURAGE EVERYONE WHO WANTS
TO REDUCE THEIR RISK FOR INFLUENZA INFECTION TO GET VACCINATED THIS
SEASON, EVEN IF INFLUENZA HAS ALREADY BEEN REPORTED IN THE AREA.
MORE INFLUENZA VACCINE IS AVAILABLE THIS SEASON THAN EVER BEFORE.
CONTACT YOUR DOCTOR OR HEALTH DEPARTMENT AS SOON AS POSSIBLE TO
GET YOURSELF AND YOUR LOVED ONES VACCINATED. A PUBLIC SERVICE MESSAGE
FROM (STATION) AND THE NATIONAL FOUNDATION FOR INFECTIOUS DISEASES.

Adding Sound — An announcer reading a script is OK, but adding sound effects can make a radio PSA more interesting. Many PSAs have background music. A second approach is to include sound effects that reinforce the theme and subject matter. Here is a PSA from the National Heart, Lung, and Blood Institute, part of the U.S. Department of Health and Human Services, that included sound effects:

30 SECONDS

(The dramatic sound of a stock car)

Announcer: BLOCK THE FLOW OF AIR IN A STOCK CAR ENGINE, AND YOU'VE
GOT A PROBLEM ON YOUR HANDS.

(Engine starts to shut down)

IF YOU HAVE EMPHYSEMA, WHEEZING, CHRONIC BRONCHITIS OR SMOKER'S

COUGH, YOU KNOW THE FEELING. WHAT YOU DON'T KNOW IS IT COULD BE

COPD, THE NUMBER 4 CAUSE OF DEATH. BUT IT CAN BE TREATED. SO TALK

TO YOUR DOCTOR ABOUT COPD AND GET A SIMPLE BREATHING TEST. LEARN

MORE. BREATHE BETTER. GO TO WWW.LEARNABOUTCOPD.ORG.

A MESSAGE FROM THE NATIONAL HEART, LUNG, AND BLOOD INSTITUTE

OF THE U.S. DEPARTMENT OF HEALTH AND HUMAN SERVICES.

Production — Most PSA scripts are mailed or emailed to the station's director of public or community affairs. The scripts allow station announcers to make selections and to read them on the air. Many stations also have a website that includes a PSA template that allows local organizations to just fill in the blanks with answers to the standard questions of who, what, when, where, and why. This is particularly helpful when local organizations are announcing community events, such as festivals, 5K runs, and so on.

A more sophisticated approach is to record your PSAs, particularly those with music and sound effects, and use a good production house to make copies that can be distributed on CDs or a dedicated phone line or downloaded from a website. The National Foundation for Infectious Diseases and the National Heart, Lung, and Blood Institute mailed CDs of recorded announcements in both English and Spanish to stations. They also included a basic fact sheet giving more detail about the topics presented in the PSAs. In many cases, scripts are also included for the convenience of station personnel.

Use — Almost any topic or issue can be the subject of a PSA. However, stations seem to be more receptive to particular topics. A survey of radio station public affairs directors by WestGlen Communications found that local community issues and events were most likely to receive airtime, followed by children's issues. The respondents also expressed a preference for PSAs involving health and safety, service organizations, breast cancer, and other cancers.

The majority of respondents also prefer PSAs that include a local phone number rather than a national toll-free number. Because of this preference, many national groups, including the American Cancer Society and the American Red Cross, have a policy of distributing scripts to chapters that can be localized. Other studies have shown that an organization needs to provide helpful information in a PSA and not make a direct pitch for money. Radio stations tend to shun PSAs that ask people for money directly.

Some Tips — Phil Rabin, writing in *PRWeek*, gives some tips for successful PSAs—whether they are for radio or television. You should:

» Do your research so your PSA reaches the appropriate station and its primary audience.

» Keep it simple. The short length of PSAs means that you must minimize the points you want to make.

» Always send PSAs to the director of public or community affairs, not the news department.

» Send broadcast PSAs in different lengths.

» Establish an effective tracking system.

» Try to localize your PSAs; a local number is often more effective than a national toll-free number.

Another tip is to send your PSAs to the station 3 or 4 weeks before you want them to air. This gives time for distribution and for the station to evaluate what PSAs they will use from the stacks of CDs that often pile up in the office of the public affairs director. Experts also recommend that the best time to submit PSAs is in January. In contrast, the 4 months leading up to Christmas are very advertising intensive, so stations use fewer PSAs.

Radio Media Tours

Another approach in radio is the **radio media tour (RMT).** Essentially, this can be described as a spokesperson conducting a series of round-the-country, one-on-one interviews from one central location. The publicist prebooks telephone interviews with DJs, news directors, or talk show hosts around the country, and the personality simply gives interviews on the phone, which are then recorded for later use or broadcast live.

A good example of an effective RMT is one organized by Strauss Radio Strategies for the Children's Defense Fund (CDF) to discuss child health care issues. The president of CDF and four family spokespersons conducted 14 radio interviews over a period of several hours and reached an estimated audience of 6 million listeners. According to Strauss, this represented 150 airtime minutes; comparable advertising costs would have been more than $300,000. Television media tours, known as satellite media tours (SMTs), will be discussed in the next section.

Television

The fundamental factor that separates television from the other traditional media and gives it such pervasive impact is the visual element. The combination of color, movement, sound, and sight on a screen in your own living room is hard to resist. No wonder the medium is a major platform for reaching millions of people at the same time. In 2011, for example, more than 100 million watched the Super Bowl. Later that year, an estimated worldwide audience of more than 2 billion watched the wedding of Prince William and Kate Middleton.

There are almost as many television stations (1,500) in the United States as there are daily newspapers, and there are numerous opportunities for the placement of public relations materials at the local level.

There are four approaches to getting your news story on local television. First, you can send the station the same news release that you send to the local print media. If the news editor thinks the topic is newsworthy and lends itself to visual representation, he or she might tell the assignment editor to have a reporter and camera crew follow up on the news release.

A second approach is to prepare a media alert or advisory about the particular event or occasion that would lend itself to video coverage. These media alerts can be sent via email, fax, or newswire. Media alerts were discussed in Chapter 6. A third approach is to phone or email the assignment editor and make a pitch to have the station do a particular story. The art of making a pitch was also discussed in Chapter 6.

The fourth approach is to write and produce a **video news release (VNR)** that, like an audio news release, is formatted for immediate use with a minimum of effort by station personnel. The VNR also has the advantage of being a complete package that requires little effort on the part of the television station to use all or part of it.

Video News Releases

Essentially, a VNR is like a media kit prepared for print publications, which was discussed in Chapter 6. It has various components that provide the television journalist with everything he or she needs to produce a television news story.

So what exactly constitutes a VNR package? MultiVu, a video production firm, gives these four components:

» 90-second news report with voice-over narration on an audio channel separate from that containing soundbites and natural sound.

» **B-roll.** This is 2 or 3 minutes of video only, without narration, giving a television station maximum flexibility to add its own narration or use just a portion of the video as part of a news segment.

» Clear identification of the video source.

» Script, spokespeople information, media contacts, and story background information provided electronically.

VNRs are not cheap. A typical VNR, says one producer, costs a minimum of $20,000 to $50,000 for production and distribution. Costs vary, however, depending on the number of location shots, special effects, and staff required to produce a high-quality tape that meets broadcast standards. The production of VNRs can more easily be justified, however, if there is potential for national distribution and multiple pickups by television stations and cable systems. Increasingly, costs are also justified because a VNR package can be reformatted for an organization's website, be part of a multimedia news release, and be posted on the organization's YouTube channel or Facebook page.

> " *Today's VNRs are much more than just broadcast placement tools. They are being targeted to a variety of audiences through Web syndication, strategic placements in broadcast cable, and site-based media in retail outlets and hospitals.* " Tim Bahr, managing director, MultiVu

Because of the cost, you must carefully analyze the newsworthiness of your information and consider whether the topic lends itself to a fast-paced, action-oriented visual presentation. If you have nothing to show except talking heads or graphs and charts, you should think twice about producing a VNR. You should also consider whether the information will be current and newsworthy by the time one can be produced. On the average, it takes 4 to 6 weeks to script, produce, and distribute a high-quality VNR. In a crisis situation or for a fast-breaking news event, however, VNRs can be produced in a matter of hours or days.

Format — Writing a script for a VNR is a bit more complicated than writing one for an ANR, because you also have to visualize the scene, much like a playwright or a screenwriter. Perhaps the best way to illustrate this is to view the final script of a VNR, shown on page 226. There are two columns. The left one lists the visual elements of the script. The right one shows the narration and soundbites that are coordinated with the visual elements.

Production — Although public relations writers can easily handle the job of writing radio news releases and doing basic announcements for local TV stations, the production of a video news release is another matter. The entire process is highly technical, requiring trained professionals and sophisticated equipment. Consequently, the public relations writer serves primarily as an idea creator and a facilitator.

The public relations professional may come up with the idea, write a rough script (storyboard) outlining the visual and audio elements, and make arrangements for a video production and distribution service to produce the video. Such firms are listed in the Yellow Pages under "Video" and "Television." The advertisements in the public relations trade press such as *PRWeek* and *O'Dwyer's PR Report* are also good sources.

It is important to keep in mind that the video producer follows the basic **storyboard** (outline of who and what should be included) to achieve the organizational objective, but will usually shoot many minutes of scenes and interviews that will be edited to make a 90-second finished product.

Consequently, it is not necessary to write a prepared script for everyone who appears on video. It is better, and more natural, to have them talk informally in front of the camera and then use the best soundbite. The Tips for Success on page 227 offers additional information on the jargon used for writing a video script.

Here are some tips for producing VNRs that best meet the needs of TV news directors:

» Use outside experts to give credibility. A VNR with only corporate spokespeople is not a good idea.

» Avoid commercialism and hype. The VNR is a news story, not an ad. Keep corporate logos to a minimum.

» Produce the VNR with news footage in mind. Keep soundbites short and to the point. Avoid commercial-like shots with sophisticated effects.

» Never superimpose your own written information on the actual videotape. TV news departments usually generate their own written notes in their own typeface and style.

PURINA® PRO PLAN® RALLY TO RESCUE STORIES CONTEST
INTERNET VIDEO NEWS RELEASE (IVNR) SCRIPT
8/22/2011
TRT 2:00

VIDEO	AUDIO
Shots from 2011 contest finalists video montage	**VOICEOVER:** THE RESILIENCE OF A RESCUE PET AND THE BOND THAT QUICKLY FORMS WITH ITS NEW OWNER IS TRULY REMARKABLE. THIS YEAR, THE PURINA® PRO PLAN® RALLY TO RESCUE® STORIES CONTEST CELEBRATES THESE EXTRAORDINARY PET RESCUE STORIES WITH A NATIONWIDE COMPETITION HONORING RESCUE PETS AND THE ORGANIZATIONS THAT HELPED GIVE THEM NEW LIFE.
Melissa Heeter on-camera with Viola in a park setting *Title: Purina® Pro Plan® Trainer* Atlanta- or NYC-based crew to film	*Soundbite: The Pro Plan Rally to Rescue® Stories Contest honors rescue pets that have overcome tremendous odds thanks to the constant support and dedication of small pet rescue organizations. We want this contest to raise awareness about pet adoption and promote the incredible but often untold stories of pet rescue."*
Shots from 2011 contest finalists video montage Shots from file footage of the Dog Show (provided by NBC) Shots of rescue pets shots and Pro Plan dog food, pulled either from 2009 IVNR footage or other footage from CheckMark	**VOICEOVER:** STORIES FROM RALLY TO RESCUE GROUPS ALL OVER THE COUNTRY WERE SUBMITTED AND A JUDGING PANEL SELECTED THE 10 MOST INSPIRING SUCCESS STORIES AS FINALISTS. THE WINNING RESCUE ORGANIZATION, PET AND OWNER WILL WIN A TRIP TO PHILADELPHIA AND RECEIVE VIP TREATMENT AT THE NATIONAL DOG SHOW PRESENTED BY PURINA®. THE WINNING PET RESCUE ORGANIZATION ALSO WILL BE REWARDED WITH $5,000 IN PURINA® PRO PLAN® BRAND PET FOOD COUPONS TO HELP SUPPORT THEIR CONTINUED CARE FOR ANIMALS IN NEED.

FIGURE 9.2   A video news release (VNR) often starts out as an outline or general story-board. After the VNR is produced, a written script is prepared so television news directors can easily preview the VNR's content. A script has two columns—one for the visual cues and one for the script and soundbites. When outlining a VNR, a person must match the copy and the soundbites with the appropriate visuals.

» Never use a stand-up reporter. Stations do not want a reporter who is not on their staff appearing in their newscast.

» Provide TV stations with a local angle. This can be done by sending supplemental facts and figures that reflect the local situation. These can be added to the VNR when it is edited for broadcast.

» Good graphics, including animation, are a plus. Stations are attracted to artwork that shows things in a clear, concise manner.

» Avoid overproduction. Slick dissolves and flashy effects are great for music videos, but news producers equate them with advertising.

The New Trend: B-Roll Packaging

It has already been mentioned that a VNR package should include 2 or 3 minutes of B-roll, which is additional soundbites and video that television staff can use for repackaging a story. Today, television news directors generally prefer B-roll packages instead of fully scripted VNRs. In fact, even the term "video news release" seems to have fallen into disfavor according to Brian Schwartz, a former executive of Medialink, a producer of such material.

Tips for Success   The Jargon of Writing for Video

Do you know where your SOT is? Do you need a CU or a V/O for your script? The video industry has its own vocabulary, and you should be familiar with it when writing storyboards and scripts. Here are a few of the most common terms:

+ **A-roll.** Video that contains the audio portion. This may be an announcer speaking or a quote from someone being interviewed.

+ **B-roll.** Only the video portion, without sound.

+ **CU.** Close-up shot of a person or object. An *MCU* is a medium close-up.

+ **Dub.** A duplicate of an audio- or videotape.

+ **On cam.** Person or object is on camera—part of what is being videotaped.

+ **Pan.** Moving the camera (while shooting) from side to side.

+ **SOT.** Sound on tape. Usually refers to an interview.

+ **Super.** Printed material, usually words, to show the name of a person, a telephone number, or a location.

+ **V/O.** Voice-over. A story where someone off-camera, usually an announcer, reads a portion of the video story. Sometimes written as *ANNCR:V/O.*

+ **Zoom.** Changing the camera angle by going from a wide shot to a close shot, or vice versa.

One reason is that VNRs have come under fire in recent years because television stations often used them without attribution. Watchdog groups complained to the Federal Communications Commission (FCC) that stations, using video content without attributing the source, were presenting "fake news." The Center for Media and Democracy, for example, conducted a six-month probe and found that 46 stations in 22 states aired unsourced video material supplied by VNR production firms on behalf of clients.

The controversy over television's use of VNRs also put the spotlight on the public relations industry. The issue was whether public relations firms and the VNR producers are adequately labeling VNR packages to identify the sponsor or client. There was also criticism that "reporters" appearing in a VNR just said, "This is Nancy Williams, reporting from New York" and didn't add the line, "on behalf of X Company." As a consequence, the National Association of Broadcast Communicators (NABC) issued new standards for disclosure and transparency.

Given the criticism, however, video production firms have increasingly moved to just producing B-roll packages on behalf of clients. Such packages provide plenty of video files and soundbites, but are not formally scripted into a complete story. This allows television news staffs to easily pick and choose material to produce their own stories.

One example of a B-roll package was done by the Hoffman Agency, a public relations firm, on how a new surveillance product produced by Sony and A4S Security could withstand extreme conditions, providing video coverage even after the detonation of a bomb in a bus or a building. The B-roll showed a bus being blown up with 10 pounds of explosives and the surveillance device recording the interior of the bus during the explosion. Such dramatic video, accompanied by soundbites from company executives and government officials, was a hit with local and network television news directors.

Bader TV News, a production company based in New York, also produced a B-roll package on behalf of Shell about a college competition to create vehicles that would get exceptional gasoline mileage. Components of the "Shell Oil Eco-Marathon 2010 campaign" are shown in the PR Casebook on page 229.

Email advisories are usually sent to television stations notifying them that a VNR or a B-roll package is available via a satellite link or as a download from the website of a distribution firm. Web downloads can also be used for what is known as **stock footage**—standard video shots of a company's production line, headquarters, or activities that the station can store until the company is in the news. Then, as the anchor gives the news, the viewer sees the stock footage on the screen. A news story about an electric power plant, for example, may use stock footage from the utility company showing interior scenes of the facility.

Use — B-roll packages, in particular, are widely used by television stations and cable systems in smaller markets where stations have limited news staff. A survey by WestGlen Communications, for example, found that 90 percent of TV stations regularly use outside-produced video for newscasts. This optimistic statistic, however, is tempered by the reality that TV stations today receive so many video clips that only a few will ever be used.

PR casebook

B-Roll Drives Shell's Eco-Mileage Competition

Video production firms are increasingly producing B-roll packages instead of VNRs for clients because television stations want to format their own coverage. The following materials were sent to television stations via the Internet and news directors could choose one of several formats most compatible with their technical needs. According to Domenic Travano of Bader TV, "The reason behind different formats (QTime, HD, SD and Windows Media) is because of all the different set-ups broadcasters use. Unfortunately, there is no set standard in video equipment, so we try to make as many formats available to broadcasters as we can (those three being the most common)." In addition to video, it's also standard to include a script in Word document form so television news directors can determine the nature of the story.

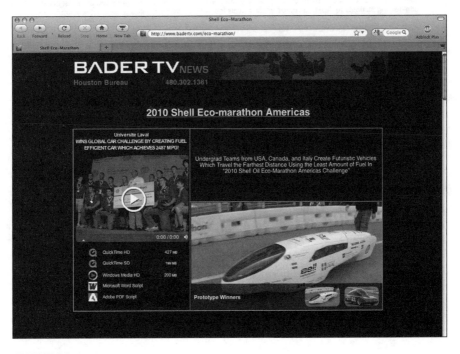

FIGURE 9.3

BADER TV NEWS
Media Information

Automotive Technology News

Undergrads Go The Eco Distance!

LAVAL UNIVERSITY WINS SHELL MILEAGE CHALLENGE
FUEL EFFICIENT ENTRY ACHIEVES 2487 MPG!

**Undergrad Teams from USA, Canada and Italy Create Futuristic Vehicles which Travel the
Farthest Distance Using the Least Amount of Fuel in
"Shell Oil Eco-Marathon 2010" Challenge**

This B-Roll package is free to use without restrictions or obligations for regularly scheduled news, business, lifestyle, sports and automotive TV news broadcasts and its corresponding websites only, covering the finals of the 2010 Shell Eco-marathon Americas: Here is the story overview:

Sunday, March 28, 2010, Houston, Texas: With a vehicle that achieved an amazing 2487 miles per gallon, students from Laval University, Quebec, won the 2010 Shell Eco-marathon Americas. The competition, hosted by the Shell Oil Company, challenges undergrad and high school teams, comprised of the brightest engineering students to design a vehicle which travels the farthest distance utilizing the least amount of fuel.

SOT Full: Rodolfo Martinez / Monrovia High School, Los Angeles, CA

Nearly 50 teams from across North America and as far away as Italy faced-off over the weekend at Houston's Discovery Green urban park. It's the first time the competition has been staged on city streets in Shell's hometown and the first time that members of the public were invited to view the event, which was held at the George R. Brown Convention Center.

SOT Full: Steven Zamora / University of Houston

SOT Full: Ted Pesyna / Purdue University (Pronounced: pes-ee-nah)

SOT Full: Nick Llanos / Loyola Marymount University, Los Angeles, California (Driver)

It was the second win in as many years for the Laval team. Shell awarded the students a $5000 prize in the "Prototype" category, which is aimed at maximum technical creativity and minimal restrictions. The school won the same award last year, but its entry performed even better, achieving 2757.1 miles per gallon.

SOT Full: Emilie Michaud / Laval University (Driver)

SOT Full: Philippe Bouchard / Laval University

Second and third prizes in the "Prototype" category went to Mater Dei High School, Evansville, Indiana, which achieved 1892.3 miles per gallon and Rose-Hulman Institute of Technology, Terre Haute, Indiana, whose entry reached 1803.3 miles per gallon. A solar powered vehicle from Politechnico di Milano, Italy also took part in the event on an exhibition basis.

SOT Full: Evan Vibbert / Mater Dei High School (Prototype)

SOT Full: Barbara Arrowsling / Rose-Hulman Institute of Technology, Terre Haute, Indiana

SOT Full: Kevin Thine / Cicero North-Syracuse High School, Syracuse, NY

FIGURE 9.4

A survey by KEF Media Associates in Atlanta, for example, found that almost 90 percent of the local TV newscasts in the top 100 markets devoted less than 5 percent of their airtime to VNR or B-roll material. In a 44-minute news hour (allowing for advertising), that represents only 2 or 3 minutes. At the same time, some stations in top markets receive more than 100 pitches a week, which graphically illustrates the stiff competition and long odds of any video's being used.

Consequently, many public relations practitioners worry about the cost and whether the potential audience reached is worth the investment. Far too many VNRs and B-rolls never get used, and even a popular one may only get 40 to 50 station airings with an audience of 2 to 3 million people.

Before deciding to produce a VNR or B-roll, you should first assess (1) the news value of the topic, (2) whether the topic lends itself to a visual treatment, (3) whether it can be recycled for use in social networking sites and blogs, and (4) whether this is a cost-effective method of reaching your target audience. A better approach, for example, could be satellite media tours, which will be discussed shortly.

Public Service Announcements

Television stations, like radio stations, use public service announcements on behalf of governmental agencies, community organizations, and charitable groups. In fact, a survey by News Broadcast Network found that the typical TV station runs an average of 137 PSAs per week as part of its commitment to public service. DWJ Television, another video producer, says that 70 percent of television PSAs are used between the hours of 1:30 A.M. and 7 A.M., with about 40 percent of this number used between midnight and 6 A.M. See the PR Casebook on page 232 for a campaign by the American Water Company using PSAs.

Many of the guidelines for radio PSAs, which were discussed previously, apply to television PSAs. They must be short, to the point, and professionally produced. Television is different, however, in that both audio and visual elements must be present. Thus, the soundbites or actualities must have someone with not only a good voice, but also an attractive appearance. As a result, many television PSAs use a well-recognized celebrity or spokesperson. North American Precis Syndicate (NAPS) distributed a 60-second PSA on behalf of Ronald McDonald House Charities, using former model Cindy Crawford. See Figure 9.5.

Some PSAs get considerable airtime. A series of PSAs on anxiety disorders got more than 100,000 airplays. A Salvation Army PSA series reached more than 43 million Americans. The National Organization on Fetal Alcohol Syndrome (NOFAS) reported a 400 percent increase in calls to its hotline in the two to three days following a PSA featuring TV star Laura San Giacomo.

The Internet, of course, has opened up new opportunities for video PSAs. The Ad Council, which produces many PSAs on behalf of national and international charitable organizations, also posts them on more than a dozen new media streams. An Ad Council PSA, featuring Mark Zupan, a member of the U.S. Paralympic rugby team, received 700 television airings, as well as 6,500 YouTube views. See Figure 9.6 on page 234 for an example of a PSA posted by UNICEF on its website and Facebook page.

PR casebook

Water Campaign Taps Media with PSAs

A public education campaign by the American Water Works Company used a variety of PSAs to generate public awareness about water conservation.

The company, celebrating its 125th anniversary, wanted to promote the benefits of drinking tap water from refillable bottles rather than disposable ones. The campaign, launched in the same week as Earth Day, used a variety of celebrities in a series of public service announcements (PSAs). They included actors Rachel Dratch, Diane Neal, and Horatio Sanz as well as national surfing champion Lakey Peterson. Each PSA directed viewers to www.SaveWaterToday.org for educational tips.

The PSAs were made available to television stations throughout the country and were posted on social media sites such as YouTube and Facebook. In addition, the company intranet and its website featured rotating videos from employees who had been with the company 20 years or more, explaining the American Water tradition.

Television stations don't usually accept PSAs from for-profit companies, but American Water also partnered with the U.S. Environmental Protection Agency (EPA) and the Student Conservation Association so its conservation message would be more acceptable to stations.

Satellite Media Tours

The television equivalent of the radio media tour (RMT) is the **satellite media tour (SMT).** This is essentially a series of prebooked, one-on-one interviews from a fixed location via satellite with a series of television journalists and, sometimes, talk show hosts.

The SMT concept started in the mid-1980s when companies began to put their CEOs in front of a television camera. The public relations staff would line up reporters in advance to interview the spokesperson via satellite feed during allotted time frames and, in this way, television journalists across the country could interview the spokesperson on a one-on-one basis. For busy executives, the satellite was a time-efficient way of giving interviews. All they had to do was visit a corporate or commercial television studio near their office.

Today, the SMT is a staple of public relations and the television industry. One-on-one interviews, as well as news conferences via satellite, are widely used. In fact, a survey by WestGlen Communications found that nearly 85 percent of the nation's television stations participate in satellite tours, including stations in the top 10 markets. Reporters like SMTs because they can ask their own questions and get an exclusive interview with a source anywhere in the world. This is in contrast to the VNR, which is a set piece, much like an ordinary news release. See the Tips for Success on page 235 for more on SMTs.

The easiest way to do an SMT is simply to make an articulate spokesperson available for an interview. Celebrities are always popular, but an organization can also use articulate experts in its subject area. Essentially, the spokesperson sits in a chair or at a desk in front of a television camera. Viewers usually see the local news

ON TAPE

TV TAKES

NORTH AMERICAN PRECIS SYNDICATE, INC.
350 FIFTH AVENUE • NEW YORK, NY 10118-0110 • (212) 867-9000

RONALD MCDONALD HOUSE

(START CINDY CRAWFORD *SOUND BITE*): "**AS A PARENT, I KNOW ONE OF THE MOST IMPORTANT TIMES TO BE WITH YOUR CHILDREN IS WHEN THEY AREN'T FEELING WELL. THAT'S WHEN THE LOVE AND COMFORT OF A FAMILY IS ESSENTIAL TO A CHILD'S WELL-BEING. FOR MANY FAMILIES, THERE'S A PLACE THEY CAN GO TO FIND THE SUPPORT THEY NEED.**" (END CINDY CRAWFORD *SOUND BITE*)

(START BILLY BUSH *SOUND BITE*): "**RONALD MCDONALD HOUSE CHARITIES' PROGRAMS PROVIDE THAT SUPPORTIVE ENVIRONMENT SO FAMILIES CAN BE TOGETHER WHILE THEIR CHILDREN ARE DEALING WITH SERIOUS ILLNESSES AND UNDERGOING TREATMENT. IT'S A 'HOME AWAY FROM HOME' FOR FAMILIES IN NEED—GIVING THEM MORE TIME FOR HUGS, KISSES AND QUIET MOMENTS TOGETHER.**" (END BILLY BUSH *SOUND BITE*)

(START NE-YO *SOUND BITE*): "**YOU CAN VOLUNTEER YOUR TIME AT A LOCAL RONALD MCDONALD HOUSE AND HELP A FAMILY IN NEED BY COOKING A MEAL OR HOSTING A MOVIE NIGHT. YOU CAN ALSO DROP YOUR EXTRA CHANGE IN AN R-M-H-C CANISTER.**" (END NE-YO *SOUND BITE*)

(START DAYANARA TORRES *SOUND BITE*): "**THESE CONTRIBUTIONS—BOTH LARGE AND SMALL—HELP MORE THAN TEN THOUSAND FAMILIES EVERY DAY—PROOF THAT A LITTLE HELP GOES A LONG WAY. TODAY IS A GREAT DAY FOR ALL OF US TO SHOW OUR SUPPORT AND HELP GIVE FAMILIES IN NEED MORE TIME TOGETHER.**" (END DAYANARA TORRES *SOUND BITE*)

(START CINDY CRAWFORD *SOUND BITE*): "**TO FIND OUT HOW YOU CAN GET INVOLVED IN YOUR COMMUNITY, VISIT R-M-H-C--DOT--ORG.**" (END CINDY CRAWFORD *SOUND BITE*)

FIGURE 9.5 This is a television script for a feature distributed by North American Precis Syndicate (NAPS) on behalf of Ronald McDonald House Charities. Including soundbites from several persons gives the feature more variety and interest. In many television PSAs, a celebrity is used as a spokesperson to attract audience interest.

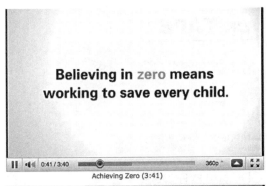

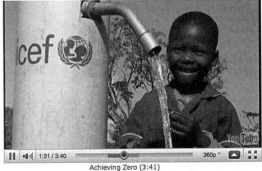

FIGURE 9.6 Television PSAs are now widely distributed via the Internet on the Facebook pages of various organizations. This PSA was produced by UNICEF.

anchor asking questions and the spokesperson on a newsroom monitor, via satellite, answering them in much the same way that anchors talk with reporters at the scene of an event.

Basically, the format is two talking heads—the news anchor and the spokesperson. An example of such an SMT is one done by Best Buy on "Black Friday," the day after Thanksgiving when stores are jammed with shoppers. Best Buy enlisted pop commentator Mo Rocca to add some lighthearted humor to the frantic day and partnered him with a personable Best Buy employee who was knowledgeable about electronic products and what was "hot" that season. In the space of 3 hours, the pair gave 23 media interviews to television stations across the country.

Although **talking heads,** as they are known in the industry, are often used for SMTs, today's most successful SMTs are more interactive and dynamic. As Sally Jewett, president of On-The-Scene Productions, told *PRWeek,* "It's important to offer reporters something beyond the talking head, especially since competition is increasing as more firms realize the benefits of SMTs."

One approach is to integrate additional video into the SMT. Video clips of an event or activity can run while the spokesperson talks off-screen. For example, Abbott Labs hired Simon Productions to do an SMT on a new product for diabetics. While the spokesperson was talking about the new product, Simon showed people using it, being checked out by a doctor, and eating the "wrong" foods.

In a survey of television news directors, WestGlen Communications found that almost 95 percent prefer that video clips accompany the interview. "Stations like to put together a background piece to air prior to the interview," says Annette Minkalis, senior vice president of WestGlen's broadcast department. She adds, "Many stations prefer B-roll and a hard copy summary three to four days in advance of the tour. Having footage in advance, as opposed to having it fed during the interview, gives stations time to prepare the story, especially in a live interview." At times, an SMT is also coordinated with the release of a VNR or B-roll package about the same topic.

Another popular approach to SMTs is to get out of the television studio and do them on location. When the National Pork Producers Council wanted to promote outdoor winter grilling, its public relations staff hired a team from Broadcast News Network to fire up an outdoor grill in Aspen, Colorado, and put a chef in a parka to give interviews, via satellite, while he cooked. In another example, the Hawaii

Tourism Board targeted television stations in New England on a cold winter day with an SMT originating from Hawaii's sunny and attractive beaches.

Organizing an SMT from a remote location, however, does involve more planning. Here are some tips from various production companies:

» Do a site survey. Figure out the logistics for sound, lighting, telephones, and satellites.

» Make contingency arrangements in case of bad weather.

» Make sure your spokesperson is adaptable and prepared to answer all sorts of questions.

Tips for Success   Guidelines for a Successful SMT

Anecdotal evidence indicates that four out of five pitched satellite media tours don't get aired. You can increase the odds if you follow these "do's" and "don'ts" compiled by *PRWeek*:

Do

+   Include a relevant angle for the stations in every market you pitch.

+   Use an interesting, visually appealing background or set. It often makes the difference between your SMT getting on the air or not.

+   Get stations involved by sending items that will help them perform and promote the interview.

+   Respect producers' wishes when they tell you they will get back to you. Incessant follow-up will only annoy those you are trying to convince.

+   Localize your SMT. If local audiences aren't going to be interested, neither are the producers airing the story.

+   Be clear in your pitch. Provide producers with the who, what, when, and why right away.

+   Use credible, knowledgeable spokespersons that project confidence and are personable.

Don't

+   Don't let the SMT become a commercial. If producers think there is the possibility of too many product mentions, they won't book it.

+   Don't be dishonest with producers about the contents of your SMT.

+   Don't pitch your SMT to more than one producer at a station.

+   Don't be conservative with the amount of talent. A boring medical SMT will pack more punch if you present a patient along with the doctor.

+   Don't surprise the producer. Newscasts are planned to the minute and unexpected events (spokesperson cancels) will not be appreciated.

» Arrange for necessary permits and permissions if using public or private property.

» Make sure the location has some tie-in with your subject.

» Make certain that the location is free from general public access to avoid background distractions.

» Be conscious of other complications, such as noise from honking horns and even air traffic.

Another aspect to consider is whether the SMT has enough news value to justify its cost. In general, a basic SMT costs $10,000 to $25,000. The Best Buy SMT cost $40,000, but it also included the cost of celebrity talent. If it is done outside a television studio, costs can rise substantially, depending on the location and logistics involved.

"At the SMT you have an attractive, knowledgeable talent and high-quality broadcast equipment. Use it to create an exciting, well-produced webisode that can be featured on your own microsite. " Douglas Simon, CEO of DS Productions

Given the cost, many organizations try to get maximum benefit by posting interviews on their website, producing audio and video podcasts, syndicating segments to YouTube and other viral news sites, embedding an interview in a multimedia news release, and even doing a webcast. Bev Yehuda, vice president of MultiVu, adds, "With your spokesperson already in a TV studio, it's easy to initiate an Internet connection and produce a video webcast."

News Feeds — A variation on the SMT is a news feed that provides video and soundbites of an event to TV stations across the country via satellite. The news feed may be live from the actual event as it is taking place (real time), or it could be video shot at an event, edited, and then made available as a package.

In either case, the sponsoring organization hires a production firm to record the event. DWJ Television, for example, was hired by Christie's to cover the auction of 56 outfits worn by women at Academy Award ceremonies. DWJ engineers managed everything from setting up cameras and lighting to troubleshooting problems for crews during the auction.

The event, which benefited the American Foundation for AIDS Research, was made available in real time to television stations around the country and the world via satellite. Stations could air the whole auction, or simply make a video clip for use in later newscasts. Stations in 9 of the top 10 markets used the news feed, which reached almost 12 million viewers.

Talk Shows and Product Placements

So far in this chapter we have concentrated on how to prepare and generate timely material for newscasts. Here we will present an overview of other placement opportunities in broadcasting, from getting people booked on talk shows to having a popular sitcom use your employer's or client's product on the show.

In these cases, your contact is no longer the news department, but rather the directors and producers of various specialty features and shows. Your most valuable communication tools are the telephone and the persuasive pitch letter (see Chapter 6).

Before using either tool, however, it is necessary to do your homework. You must be familiar with a show's format and content, as well as the type of audience that it reaches. You can obtain this information in several ways.

One method is to study the station and descriptions of its shows in a broadcast database. Directory listings can tell you program format, types of material used, and the name of the director or producer. Directories are discussed in the next chapter, but see Figure 9.1 for an example of a radio station listing.

A second approach is to watch the program or feature and study the format. In the case of a talk or interview show, what is the style of the moderator or host? What kinds of topics are discussed? How important is the personality or prominence of the guest? How long is the show or segment? Does the show lend itself to demonstrations and visual aids? The answers to such questions will help you tailor your phone calls and pitch letters to achieve maximum results.

Talk Shows

Radio and television talk shows have been a staple of broadcasting for many years. KABC in Los Angeles started the trend in 1960, when it became the first radio station in the country to convert to an all-news-and-talk format. Today, more than 1,100 radio stations have adopted the format. Other stations, of course, also include talk shows as part of their programming. In fact, it is estimated that there are now more than 5,000 radio talk shows in the United States.

The same growth rate applies to television. Seven years after KABC started the talk show format, Phil Donahue began his TV talk show. Today, there are multiple nationally syndicated talk shows and a countless number of locally produced shows. Until mid-2011, when the *Oprah Winfrey Show* ended, it attracted a daily audience of about 8 million. On the network level, three shows are the Holy Grail for publicists: NBC's *Today*, ABC's *Good Morning America*, and CBS's *Early Show*. Collectively, these three shows draw about 14 million viewers between 7 and 9 A.M. every weekday. As *PRWeek* says, "there's simply no better way to hit millions of consumers in one shot." See Figure 9.7 on next page for an example of a talk show.

The advantage of talk shows is the opportunity to tell your views directly to the American public without the filter of journalists and editors interpreting and deciding what is newsworthy. Another advantage is the opportunity to be on the air for longer than the traditional 15-second soundbite in a news program.

You may never have the opportunity to book a guest on the *Today* show, but you should be aware of such shows and their ability to reach large audiences. Talk shows and public affairs programs on local radio and television stations, as well as a proliferation of cable channels, provide excellent placement opportunities for organizational spokespersons talking on any number of topics.

FIGURE 9.7 Television talk shows are an excellent opportunity to promote products, services, and even other television shows. This is a scene from a talk show on MTV with "Dr. Oz" talking to a teen mother about a new MTV reality show about teen pregnancy and the various problems that young mothers face. The format is often an informal conversation between the talk show host and the guest.

Here are some questions to consider when thinking about placement on a talk show:

» Is the topic newsworthy? Do you have a new angle on something in the news?

» Is the topic timely? Can you tie the idea to some lifestyle or cultural trend?

» Is the information useful to the viewers? How-to ideas may be welcomed.

» Does your spokesperson have viewer appeal? A celebrity may be acceptable, but there must be a logical tie-in to your organization and to the topic to be discussed. A professional athlete might be plausible talking about running shoes but out of place in a discussion about the economy.

» Can the spokesperson stay on track? A spokesperson should have two or three key messages and avoid tangents.

» Can you keep the speaker from stressing the commercial angle? Most talk show hosts will allow a brief mention of a brand name or sponsor identification. If your speaker gets too commercial, the entire interview may be deleted—and your organization may land on the list of those who will not be invited back.

» Does the speaker fit the program? If he or she isn't a fast thinker, avoid shows full of rapid exchanges and loaded questions.

» Is the speaker an expert on the topic that will be discussed?

After you have done your homework on the format of a radio or television talk show, contact the show's producer or associate producer. If it is a network or nationally syndicated show, the contact person may have the title of talent coordinator or talent executive. Whatever the title, these people are known in the broadcasting industry as **bookers** because they are responsible for booking a constant supply of timely guests for a show.

> **❝** *We expect our hosts (spokespersons) to be able to put the products in a newsworthy context and answer unexpected questions.* **❞**
>
> Michael Friedman, executive vice president of DWJ Television

You can place a phone call briefly outlining the qualifications of your proposed speaker and why the person would be a timely guest, or you can send an email (see Chapter 6) to convince the producer to book the guest. See the PR Casebook on page 155 in Chapter 6 about how a company got on the Jay Leno show. In many cases, the booker will ask for video clips of the spokesperson on previous TV shows, and even newspaper clips relating to past interviews. As mentioned previously, the more you know about the format and the audience of the show, the better you can tailor a persuasive pitch.

It's also important to be honest about your client's expertise and personality. According to Marsha Friedman of Event Management Services in Clearwater, Florida, which specializes in booking guests, talk show producers complain that guests often bear little resemblance to their publicist's pitch. Barbara Hoffman, producer of *Doctor to Doctor*, told *O'Dwyer's PR Newsletter* that the best pitches come from publicists whose "clients are always exactly what they say they are, always prepared, interesting, on time, and always have something unusual or cutting edge to offer my program."

In general, talk shows book guests three to four weeks ahead of time. Unless a topic or a person is extremely timely or controversial, it is rare for a booking to occur on one or two days' notice. Keep this in mind as you plan talk show appearances as part of an overall public relations plan. See the Tips for Success on page 240 for more on what makes a good talk show guest.

On occasion, it's possible that a local television station will let you create your own talk show. Rex Healthcare did just that in Raleigh, North Carolina, by creating a monthly medical call-in TV show titled *Rex on Call*. The show, which featured doctors and medical researchers as guests, had a mix of health advice and took "house calls" from interested viewers. Additional viewers were reached through archived Web episodes available on the company's website.

Magazine Shows

A magazine show has a somewhat different format than a talk show, where a host interviews various guests. A magazine show, in contrast, may feature five or six stories about various issues and topics that usually include video clips and reporting by the station's news staff. Depending on the program, they can be human-interest features or in-depth investigative stories on some contemporary issue such as the high cost of medical care or the plight of the homeless in major cities. CBS's *60 Minutes* is an example of a magazine show.

On the local level, there are many human-interest magazine shows. A sampling of magazine shows in one large city featured such subjects as a 1-pound baby who survived, a treatment for anorexia nervosa, a couple who started a successful cookie company, remedies for back pain, tips on dog training, the science of karate, blue-collar job stress, and the work habits of a successful author.

Most, if not all, of these features came about as the result of someone making a pitch to the show's producers. The objective of the segment, at least from the perspective of the people featured, is exposure and the generation of new business. The tips on dog training, for example, featured a local breeder who also operated a dog obedience school. The karate expert ran a martial arts academy.

Product Placement

Television's dramatic and comedy shows, as well as the film industry, are good vehicles for promoting a company's products and services. It is not a coincidence that the hero of a detective series drives a Lexus sports coupe or that a United Airlines plane

Tips for Success   The Ideal Talk Show Guest

What constitutes a killer TV guest? Senior producer for *Your World with Cavuto* Gresham Strigel shared his thoughts with *Bulldog Reporter*, a public relations newsletter:

+   The spokesperson is personable and approachable when producers conduct pre-interviews on the phone. He or she is forthright in a nonaggressive way. "If you're wishy-washy, noncommittal, or stilted, you're not going much further."

+   Guests should have strong opinions. "We don't call certain people back because they've been trained not to say anything. The stronger your position is, and the higher up it is, the more media attention you're going to get. Nobody likes guests who play it safe."

+   Guests should be passionate about the subject. "We don't want people who are robotic—who just spit out facts. If you convey passion about what you're talking about, you jump off the screen."

+   Debate without getting personal or mean-spirited. "Smile.... Audiences like to see someone who is comfortable on-screen—someone who is happy to be there."

+   Have an engaging, outgoing personality. "Talking heads and ivory tower types don't do well on television. They're better suited to print, where their personality—or lack of one—can't turn audiences off."

is shown taking off or landing. Such product placements, called **plugs** or *plants*, are often negotiated by product publicists and talent agencies. This is really nothing new. *IPRA Frontline* reports, "In the early 1900s, Henry Ford had an affinity for Hollywood and perhaps it is no coincidence that his Model T's were the predominant vehicle appearing in pictures of that era."

Product placements, however, came of age in the movie *ET* back in the early 1980s. The story goes that M&M Candies made a classic marketing mistake by not allowing the film to use M&Ms as the prominently displayed trail of candy that the young hero used to lure his big-eyed friend home. Instead, Hershey's Reese's Pieces jumped at the chance, and the rest is history. Sales of Reese's Pieces skyrocketed, and even today, Reese's Pieces and *ET* remain linked in popular culture.

Another milestone in product placement was the James Bond films in the 1990s. Agent 007 got behind the wheel of a BMW, used a Visa card, wore an Omega watch, talked to M on an Ericsson cell phone, and drank Smirnoff vodka (shaken, not stirred). Since then, product placements in television programs and films have mushroomed into a $6.25 billion worldwide industry, with U.S. spending accounting for about half of this amount.

> **"***In the U.S., product placement in films and television has never been more widespread, accounting for $3.61 billion, or half, of global spending.***"** David Gelles and Tim Bradshaw, reporters for the *Financial Times*

There were, for example, 5,381 big product placements during prime time in 2010, up 22 percent from the previous year. The movie *Iron Man 2*, released in 2010, had 64 brand placements, including ones from Audi, Oracle, and LG. Eric Smallwood of Front Row Marketing Services explains the mania for product placement. He told the *Financial Times*, "If you're a brand and you're able to align yourself with some key actors in a movie, that's pretty powerful."

Clothing manufacturers and retailers are particularly active in product placements because studies show that today's young people get most of their fashion ideas from watching television shows. This is why upscale retailers were eager, and paid large fees, for the main characters in *Sex in the City* to be seen using their clothes, handbags, jewelry, and shoes. Coca-Cola, of course, has long been associated with *American Idol*, to the point that the backdrop is Coca-Cola red and all the judges sip Coke from branded cups. Apple has been especially prolific in product placement. Its products have appeared in more than a third of all number one films at the box office for the past 10 years.

Many major brands pay millions of dollars to have their branded products in a high-profile television series or a major film, but not all product placements are in that league. A low-profile item such as a bottle of wine or a bag of chips in a scene may only cost samples of the product to the production crew and actors for daily use or for a party. Hotels and resorts also garner exposure in location scenes if they are willing to feed the crew and provide complimentary rooms.

It's a cost-effective investment in publicity. *O'Dwyer's Newsletter* quotes Frank Zazza of iTVX productions saying that a 20-second product placement on *Desperate Housewives* would be worth about $400,000, about the same as a 30-second commercial on the show. Game shows provide an even better investment. In one episode of *The Price Is Right*, one prize was a tent, a camp table with chairs, and a lantern. The donated equipment cost Coleman about $250.

You should always be alert to opportunities for publicity on television programs and upcoming movies. If the company's product or service lends itself to a particular program, contact the show's producer directly or through an agent who specializes in matching company products with the show's needs. If you are dealing with a national television show or a film studio, you particularly need the services of a product placement firm located in Hollywood or New York. At last count, there were about 50 agencies engaged in this booming specialty area. More tips on product placement are in the box below.

Issue Placement — A logical extension of product placements is convincing popular television programs to write an issue or cause into their scripts. Writers for issue-oriented shows such as *Grey's Anatomy*, *ER*, and *Law & Order* are constantly bombarded with requests from a variety of nonprofit and special interest groups. Many social and health organizations also lobby the producers of daytime soap operas to write scripts where major characters deal with cancer, diabetes, drug abuse, alcoholism, and an assortment of other problems.

The idea is to educate the public about a social issue or a health problem in a popular television show or a movie. Someone once said, "It's like hiding the aspirin in the ice

Tips for Success — Guidelines for Product Placement on Your Favorite TV Show

Product placement in films and television shows is a specialty function that blurs the lines between marketing and public relations. *Financial Times* reporters David Gelles and Tim Bradshaw provide some basic tips.

+ Make the product prominent enough to get noticed but not so obvious that it's annoying.
+ Publicize the placement with other efforts, such as in-store promotions, sponsorships, product news releases and media kits, and program excerpts on YouTube or other viral media.
+ Consider product placement in soaps, sports programs, food shows, and reality television.
+ Keep the placement relevant to both the characters and the tone of the show.
+ Check the demographics of the viewers. Is it a prime audience for your product?
+ Limit placements to a maximum of five per show.
+ Sign long-term deals for frequent placements to ensure greater memorability.
+ Monitor social networks for good and bad comments about the placement.

Source: Gelles, D., and Bradshaw, T. (2011, March 1). "When Props Pay for Production." *Financial Times*, 12.

cream." Even the federal government works with popular television programs to write scripts that deal with the dangers and prevention of drug abuse. Remember, however, that you can only suggest themes and ideas to show producers and scriptwriters. They retain the creative independence to determine how they will write a scene.

Radio Promotions

Public relations representatives for nonprofit organizations, record companies, concert promoters, and community events committees often generate publicity and exposure through radio promotions.

Promotions are beneficial to both the station and the outside organization. For example, a concert promoter may arrange with a radio station's disc jockey to award tickets to every 10th listener who calls the station and correctly answers a trivia question on the air. Prize giveaways tend to increase the number of listeners, and the concert promoter gets publicity.

A nonprofit group sponsoring a fundraising festival may make arrangements for a radio station (or a television station) to cosponsor the event as part of the station's own promotional activities. This means that the station will actively promote the festival on the air through public service announcements and disc jockey chatter between songs.

The arrangements may also call for a popular disc jockey to broadcast live from the festival and give away T-shirts with the station's logo on them. This, too, is good promotion for the station and often attracts people to the fundraising event because the disc jockey is a well-known personality. It is a win-win situation for both the station and the nonprofit group.

Organizations that have a creative idea can often get publicity by providing newscasters and disc jockeys with something unusual to talk about. A public relations firm for Burger King, for example, came up with the idea of introducing the fast-food chain's new Breakfast Buddy sandwich by delivering the sandwiches to morning radio DJs live on the air. The announcers were asked to sample them and ask listeners to call in and win a free phone call to their "best buddy" anywhere in the United States. One delivery resulted in a 10-minute interview on one major New York show; in all, the promotion secured time on 150 stations and more than 391 minutes of announcer endorsements.

If you are handling an event or a cause that is suitable for this type of promotion, contact the director of promotions or marketing for the radio or television station. If the station is interested, negotiate the terms of the sponsorship. For example, the station may promise to air a specified number of announcements for the event in return for being listed in the organization's news releases, programs, and print advertising as a sponsor of the event.

Community Calendars

Civic clubs and other community groups can publicize upcoming events by sending short announcements to local broadcast outlets. Radio stations, in particular, operate community calendars as a service to their listeners.

To be used, however, the event must be open to the public and of general interest. A meeting of the local automobile dealers' association doesn't qualify, but a forum on the global economy sponsored by the local chapter of the World Affairs Council would be acceptable. Radio stations serving specialized audiences have variations on the community calendar. For example, a classical radio station might have an "arts calendar" that would list upcoming plays, musicals, and art shows. By the same token, a rock music station might have a "concert calendar" that lists upcoming rock concerts.

You write a calendar announcement in much the same way as you write a PSA. The announcement should be to the point. It should give the name of the event, the sponsoring organization, the date and time, location, cost, and a telephone number that listeners can call for more information.

Here is an example of a community calendar announcement for the Field Museum's map exhibition, which has been mentioned in previous chapters:

» **10 seconds:** Maps can tell us both *where* and *who* we are. The Field Museum's exhibition, "Maps: Finding Our Place in the World," allows visitors to take a look at some of the most historically valuable maps ever created. For more information, visit www.fieldmuseum.org.

» **30 seconds:** Maps can tell us both *where* and *who* we are. The Field Museum's exhibition, "Maps: Finding Our Place in the World," allows visitors to take a look at some of the most historically valuable maps ever created. Besides direction, maps can also give us clues on how a people, nation, government or organization viewed their worlds. Through contemporary, historical, flat or three-dimensional maps, this exhibition will explore a variety of themes, ranging from the history of maps to the map makers' political, cultural, or spiritual worldview. For more information, call (312) 922-9410 or visit www.fieldmuseum.org.

Community calendar items should be sent to the station via email or even fax at least 3 weeks in advance.

Film Features and Online Video

There are two other major ways to increase brand awareness and visibility for an organization. One is the development of feature-length stories that are broadcast primarily on cable channels. Short features of 2 or 3 minutes and productions that run 20 minutes or more are often used to fill gaps in cable operations that need a lot of programming to fill a 24/7 schedule. A second area, which is exploding in usage, is the production of online videos for social media.

Features for Cable

A good example is the Fireman's Fund Insurance Company's documentary *Into the Fire*, which supported a multimillion-dollar corporate philanthropy program to provide grants to fire departments and fire-service organizations.

Ketchum was commissioned to produce the documentary with the goal of raising awareness of the need for fire departments to have more resources. The target audience was affluent 34- to 65-year-old men and firefighters. The History Channel was chosen as a partner in this documentary effort because it reached the target audience. *Into the Fire*, which was produced by a high-profile director who had won Emmy awards, shared firefighters' stories in their own voices. The result was an airing on the History Channel that reached more than 2.7 million viewers. In addition, private screenings were held for Fireman's Fund agents in 29 cities, where they were encouraged to get other agents to sign up to participate in the grant program.

Such documentaries are produced and distributed by businesses, nonprofit organizations, trade associations, and professional groups. For maximum acceptability, they must be relatively free of commercial hype and must concentrate on informing or educating the viewing audience. The following are a few examples of features that have been made available to television stations and cable systems:

» *Waltzing Matilda*, a 32-minute travelogue on Australia, sponsored by the Australian Tourist Commission

» *Rethinking Tomorrow*, a 28-minute report on energy conservation, sponsored by the U.S. Department of Energy

» *Oil over the Andes*, a 27-minute account of the building of an oil pipeline, sponsored by the Occidental Petroleum Company

» *Noah Was an Amateur*, a 27-minute history of boat building, sponsored by the National Association of Engine and Boat Manufacturers

Getting such videos distributed requires some method of informing the broadcast stations of their availability. You can handle this yourself by contacting media outlets and letting them know about the subject of the video. National distribution services also market such videos. These organizations can distribute your materials by mail, Web downloads, DVDs, or satellite, depending on the preferences of the TV stations or cable systems that order them.

In addition, these distribution services have an established program that can place your films and videos with schools, clubs, special-interest groups, and civic groups. Organizations also repackage their videos into podcasts that can even be viewed on mobile phones.

Online Video

Television is no longer the only game in town for distributing well-done videos that advance an organization's products and brand. Many organizations now have a dedicated YouTube channel where they can post videos without going through traditional media gatekeepers.

Intel, for example, has a library of about 2,700 videos posted on its YouTube channel, where customers and others can search for interesting footage. Most of the videos are 4 to 6 minutes long and are part of its visual life campaign showing how Intel helps people. One 6-minute video featured two Chinese wedding photographers. On Harley-Davidson's YouTube channel, a video details the brand devotion

" YouTube is the second-largest search engine in the world. Its results also show up in Google, which owns it, so it makes a tremendous amount of sense for organizations to have addresses there. " Shel Holtz, Holtz Communication + Technology

of the Latino bikers who call themselves "Harlistas." Meanwhile, on the channel for the U.S. Navy Seals, you can learn how to tone your body through a Navy SEAL workout.

One of the most successful video campaigns in 2010 was Coca-Cola's "Happiness Machine." In the video, unsuspecting college students are surprised by a vending machine that dispenses everything from flowers to balloon animals and pizza. The video was viewed more than 3 million times and has been a catalyst for similar happiness-themed videos around the world. Coke's creative video got this large viewership because the URL was embedded, which enabled fans to share the video with other friends and even post it on blogs. Today, it's a common practice for organizations to embed URLs to help spread usage beyond the brand's channel.

Tips for Success   How to Make a Good Video

Not all videos need to be flawless, but you can improve the quality of them by following some basic guidelines. Matt Wilson interviewed several video experts for Ragan.com and came up with some tips on how to avoid major gaffes if you're producing a video for the company intranet or even posting it on YouTube or other social network sites.

Use extra lighting.   Don't just rely on room lights. It's better to invest in a small LED video light that will throw color-balanced light onto your subject at close range.

Use a good microphone.   Internal mics on most cameras don't produce good-quality sound, which is important. Learn how to record separate sound with a digital audio recorder and then sync it with the video during the editing process.

Use a tripod.   Pans and zooms are smoother if the camera is anchored to the floor. The handheld approach causes too many shaky images.

Keep videos to 3 minutes.   Audiences, particularly employees, tune out if they are longer than this.

Interview a variety of people.   Employees get tired of seeing the CEO all the time. Use a diverse group of your workforce in terms of gender, age, race, departments, and salary levels.

Avoid the talking head.   A good video should show the topic of the video, whether it's a new machine, an event, or a group of employees in a work group. Showing just the interviewee's face is boring.

Use an outline.   Don't just point and shoot. You should have a good idea of what you want to show or say and its proper sequence.

Never post raw video.   Edit your footage to ensure relevance, continuity, and length. Use production techniques such as color correction to improve the quality.

The key to a successful video is to make sure that it tells an interesting story and doesn't become just another ad. That calls for a lot of creativity. Disney Parks, for example, got high viewership by showing footage of a visit by Darth Vader, who rides in a teacup, visits Cinderella's castle, and complains about his inability to get into a "Star Wars" theme ride. Hyundai used some "dudes" who find a magic wand and conjure up a car for a wild night on the town. Amy Paquette, senior manager of global social media strategy for Cisco, says it best: "The broader goal of the YouTube portal remains telling the company's stories, not just promoting it."

Major organizations are increasingly hiring staff to manage their YouTube presence and do such tasks as filming, editing, tagging, promoting, and uploading. Jocelyn Broder, vice president of Robin Tracy Public Relations, gives some tips for creating an effective online video that gets viewership:

» Keep it real. Don't overscript, use real people, and don't overproduce it.

» Keep it genuine. Don't try to trick people or lie, because they will figure it out.

» Make people laugh. Few things spread as fast as humor online, especially if you can hit the "bored at work" crowd.

» Keep it short. The shorter and more to the point the better; 3 minutes is a good rule of thumb.

» Make them feel good. If you make viewers smile, they will be more likely to spread the video.

» Make it original. If it's not 100 percent original, execute better.

» Let it spread on its own merit. Don't push too hard or pay to spread it; it doesn't work.

» Get influencers to like it. Send the video to people who have large followings on Twitter or blogs; if they like it, they will share it.

» Use cats. If all else fails, use cats in your video. For some reason, cats almost always go viral.

Not all videos, however, require professional videographers and costly production. Today's generation records videos on smartphones and compact camcorders that are often uploaded to company intranets as part of an organization's employee communications strategy. See the Tips for Success on page 246 for some tips on how you can improve your video skills.

Summary

The Wide Reach of Broadcasting

» Radio and television are pervasive in society as major sources of news and information.

» Radio continues to thrive because of its ability to be heard almost anywhere.

» Despite the Internet, television remains the number one source of news for most Americans.

» Producing materials for broadcast requires thinking in terms of sound and visual elements.

Radio

» Radio releases are similar to press releases, but they require more concise writing and a conversational tone.

» Audio news releases (ANRs) are more interesting because they include soundbites, music, and sound effects.

» Public service announcements (PSAs) are short broadcast announcements used by nonprofit groups and public agencies.

» Radio media tours (RMTs) are a cost-effective way to reach many stations with an exclusive interview over a wide geographic area.

Television

» Television is an excellent medium of communication because it combines the elements of sight, sound, motion, and color.

» Television news releases must contain both sound and visual elements such as graphics, slides, or videotape.

» Video news releases (VNRs) are used by TV stations and cable systems. They are also posted on organizational websites and social media sites such as YouTube.

» B-roll footage, loosely scripted, is now more popular with television stations than VNRs.

» Satellite media tours (SMTs) are widely used in the broadcast industry. A popular format is setting up interviews from a location that reinforces the story.

Talk Shows and Product Placements

» A good, persuasive query or pitch is used to get placements on news programs and talk shows.

» Talk and magazine shows offer numerous opportunities for reaching mass and specialized audiences.

» Organizations can get additional exposure by using community calendars and radio promotions.

Film Features and Online Video

» Cable channels, in particular, need a lot of programming and are open to well-produced films and documentaries by various organizations.

» Online video is now a major industry. Many organizations now have a YouTube channel where they post multiple short features about their products and services.

» Online videos that get "hits" must be creative, provide entertainment, and avoid excessive commercialism.

» Videos prepared for company intranets don't need to be flawless, but they do need to also tell stories in 3 minutes or less.

Skill Building Activities

1. The U.S. Forest Service wants to warn campers that lack of rain has made forests and campgrounds more vulnerable to forest fires this summer. Write 10-, 20-, 30-, and 60-second radio PSAs on this subject.

2. The international programs office on campus wants to publicize the news that the enrollment of international students on campus will set a record of 1,000 students for fall semester. They will come from 90 nations, with China number one and India number two in terms of students. Write a 60-second audio news release (ANR) that includes a soundbite.

3. The city is sponsoring its annual jazz festival in September. Write 10-, 20-, and 30-second announcements for the community calendars of local radio stations.

4. The National Coalition of Student Health is very concerned about binge drinking on college campuses. The coalition wants to raise public awareness about the issue nationwide. Write a memo giving your suggestions on how a satellite media tour (SMT) could be organized around this subject. For example, who would you use as a spokesperson?

5. The Bally Company wants to promote exercise among busy young professionals and, of course, get visibility for its national chain of fitness centers. Write a video news release (VNR) storyboard or outline in a two-column format showing both video and copy components. What B-roll material would you include in the package?

6. Red Bull, the energy drink, is a client of your public relations firm. What TV entertainment programs might be good outlets for product placements? Recommend some popular shows and suggest how Red Bull could be used in the script or in a particular scene.

7. Select a topic that you think would make a good 3-minute video. Working individually or in a small group, work on an outline for the video and then produce it. To get you started, review the tips on page 246 about making a good video.

Media Resources

Friedman, M. (2010, April). "Making the Dream Guest for Talk Radio." *O'Dwyer's Report*, 35.

Frohlichstein, T. (2011, February). "Don't Dismiss the Boob Tube; TV Endures as Prime News Source." *The Ragan Report*, 13.

Gelles, D., and Bradshaw, T. (2011, March 1). "When Props Pay for Production: Product Placement." *Financial Times,* 12.

Morgan, D. (2010, December 9). "CBS Audience Five Times Bigger Than Facebook." Retrieved from MediaPost Publications, www.mediapost.com.

O'Dwyer, J. (2011, June 10). "FCC Cites Decline in VNRs." Retrieved from www.odwyerpr.com/blog.

Simon, D. (2010, April). "Satellite Media Tours Become Social Media Tools." *O'Dwyer's Report,* 34.

Wilson, M. (2011, June 7). "Seven Video Mistakes That Communicators Should Avoid." Retrieved from www.ragan.com.

Wong, D. (2011, March 1). "How to Pitch Video Bloggers: 5 Important Reminders." Retrieved from www.prdaily.com.

Working, R. (2011, June 16). "Brands Use YouTube to Create a Storytelling Presence." Retrieved from www.ragan.com.

Working, R. (2011, May 5). "Nine Ways to Get Your Client on the Air." Retrieved from www.ragan.com.

Distributing News to the Media 10

After reading this chapter, you will be able to:

» Use a database to find information about media outlets and bloggers

» Effectively use email to distribute news releases

» Understand the distribution power of wire services

» Organize an online newsroom for an organization

» Distribute information via mobile applications and QR codes

» Use news feature and photo syndication services

Reaching the Media

Previous chapters emphasized that an essential part of public relations writing is making sure that the right media—and the right audience—receive your material. The distribution of publicity material is a two-step process. First, you must know how to use databases that will give you accurate information about how to contact various media outlets.

A media database can answer a number of questions for you. It will give you detailed information about a print publication, a broadcast station, an online news site, and even a blog. In addition, a database will provide the name of the editor or reporter who should receive your news release or pitch and how to contact him or her via phone, email, or even tweet. If you want to know what Spanish-speaking radio stations are located within 100 miles of Dallas/Fort Worth, a good media database can answer that question, too.

The second step is to effectively use various channels of distribution for reaching key media and influential blogs. A number of distribution methods can be used. This chapter details such methods as email, online newsrooms, wire services, feature placement firms, and photo distributors. Newer distribution methods now include Twitter, mobile phone apps, and QR codes. Each method has its advantages and disadvantages, which will be discussed in the following pages.

Media Databases

Media databases vary in format and scope. However, a common denominator is that they usually provide such essential information as (1) names of publications and broadcast stations, (2) mailing addresses, (3) telephone and fax numbers, (4) email addresses, and (5) names of key editors and reporters. Many directories also give a profile of the media outlet in terms of audience, deadlines, and story placement opportunities.

Cision (www.us.cision.com) is probably the most comprehensive media database available. Its CisionPoint online media directory claims to have almost 1 million media contacts, outlets, and editorial opportunities that are updated 18,000 times a day to ensure the most up-to-date information. In addition to providing basic information, Cision includes such information as (1) how journalists like to be contacted, their topics or interests, and even their pet peeves; and (2) recent stories by a media outlet or a particular journalist so you can better tailor your pitch. A sample online listing for a magazine and a blog are shown in Figures 10.1 and 10.2.

Cision is also the publisher of *Bacon's* media directories, which are available online or in print form. There are four major directories: (1) Newspapers, (2) Magazines, (3) Radio, and (4) TV/Cable. The Newspaper/Magazine directories, for example, cover

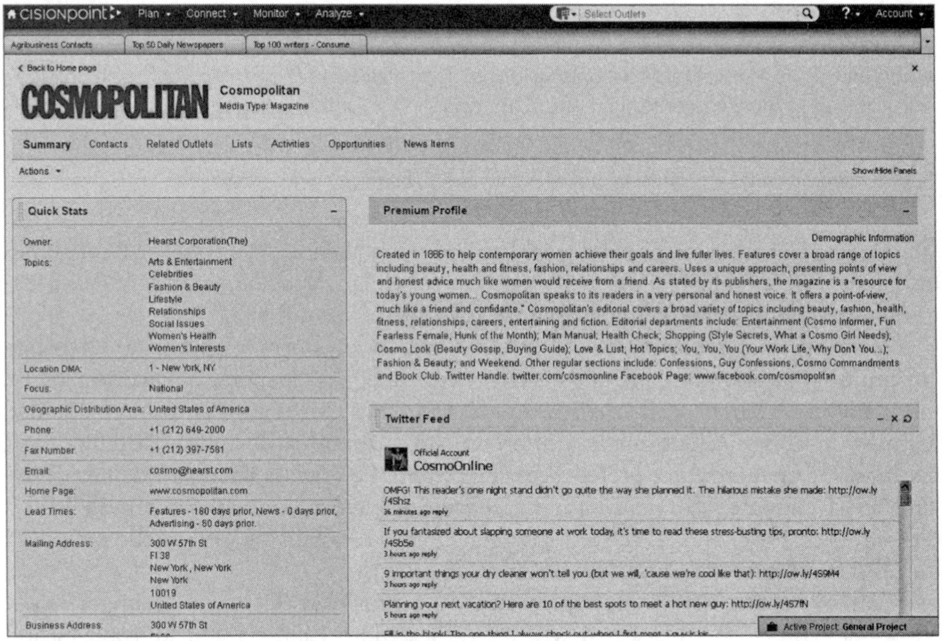

FIGURE 10.1 A comprehensive media database does more than just provide the name and address of a publication or a broadcast service. It also provides a thumbnail description of the media company, what topics are of interest to it, and how to contact various personnel. Shown here is Cision's listing for *Cosmopolitan* magazine.

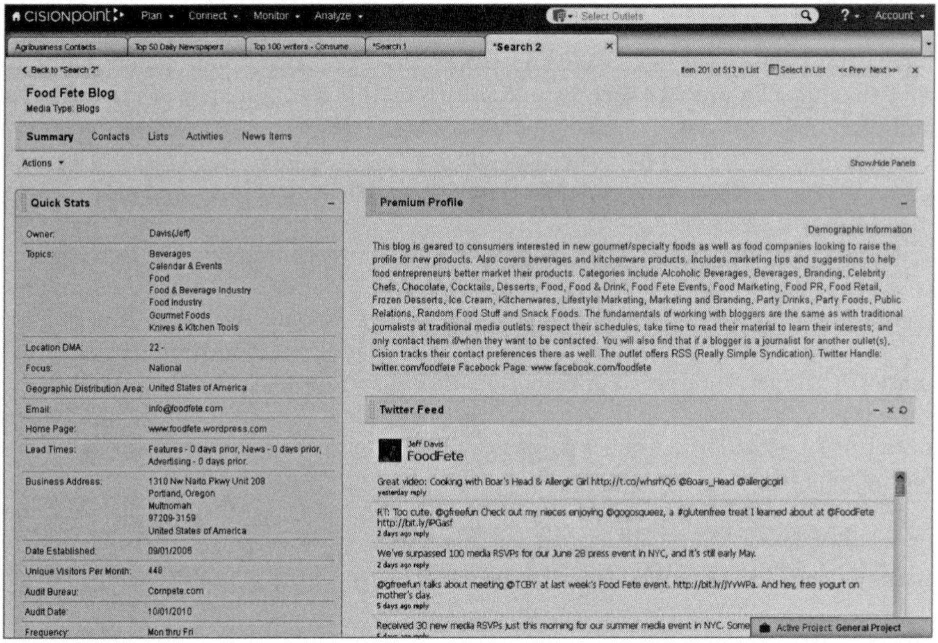

FIGURE 10.2 Bloggers, often called "citizen journalists," are now part of the media landscape and considered an important distribution channel for public relations personnel. CisonPoint, in its media database, also profiles blogs that have many followers or are influential in covering a particular topic or industry. This listing is for the Food Fete blog, which covers the gourmet/specialty food industry.

all U.S. and Canadian dailies and weeklies and more than 21,000 trade and consumer magazines. The Radio/TV directory also covers all U.S. and Canadian broadcast stations and cable systems, totaling about 40,000 broadcast outlets.

Another major directory is Burrelles/Luce (www.burrellesluce.com). It offers an online database that includes contacts at daily newspapers, magazines, radio, nondaily newspapers, and television and cable stations. It claims to have detailed listings for about 76,000 media outlets in North America, including 380,000 staff listings and their contact preferences. Electronic newswires such as Business Wire and PR Newswire also maintain databases of media contacts. Business Wire's PressCenter, for example, contains regular media contacts, as well as the details of influential writers at thousands of blogs.

A more specialized source is the Dow Jones Media Relations Manager (www.dowjones.com/mediarelations), which profiles more than 55,000 journalists and bloggers, including their interests and how to contact them. Another feature is a compilation of recent stories that the journalist has written so a publicist can get a better sense of how a journalist approaches a story and the topics that interest him or her. Armed with such information, public relations personnel can compile a "briefing" book on a journalist for the purposes of (1) preparing executives for a media interview, (2) becoming more familiar with journalists who regularly cover the organization or the industry, and (3) identifying other reporters who would be interested in particular kinds of stories. A sample listing from the Dow Jones database is on page 10 in Chapter 1.

Media databases also enable you to rapidly compile a tailored media list for your messages and to email or fax your news release directly to a journalist. For example, if you need a list of business editors in four markets at dailies with circulations above 50,000, you can compile it with a few keystrokes on your computer. Although such software has made it relatively easy to launch a thousand news releases with a few clicks, publicists should avoid this approach. It creates a blizzard of unwanted news releases comparable to spam. Indeed, the indiscriminate distribution of news releases is the major complaint that journalists have about publicists.

> *Don't fall for the 'spray and pray' method by using a media database to blast emails to anyone remotely connected with your client. You will only damage your company's reputation as well as your own.* Eric Hall, executive vice president of MyEdcals

Ruth McFarland, now retired senior vice president of Cision, says that media databases such as Bacon's should only be the starting point for thinking more strategically about what particular media outlet should be contacted. She told *O'Dwyer's PR Report*, "The paradox of PR media research is that less is more; the fewer entries you have in your database of regular contacts, the better your results will be." She continues, "Making only 10 calls to the right editors with just the right story idea will get you 10 times better coverage than sending out 100 releases and following up with 100 perfunctory phone calls or emails."

A comprehensive media database such as Cision is also a good tool for an organization to build its own media list tailored to its particular needs. One list might include only local media in the organization's headquarters city. A second list might include local media in cities where the organization has manufacturing plants. A third list might be statewide media, and a fourth list might include regional and national media. Yet another list might include trade and business media covering the industry. By segmenting media in these ways, a news release can be tailored to specific publications and audiences.

If you have compiled your own media list, however, you must update the names and email addresses of reporters almost daily. There is considerable turnover in journalists, and today's contact could be out of date next week because the reporter has changed beats or taken another job. Nothing annoys an editor or reporter more than a useless news release, but a close second is a release sent to someone who no longer works there. Fortunately, email programs usually let you know if your email "bounces."

Editorial Calendars and Tip Sheets

Not only do media databases help you find the names and addresses of media gatekeepers, several of them also tell you when to approach publications with specific kinds of stories. Trade publications and business periodicals, in particular, tend to operate on what is known as an **editorial calendar.** That means that certain issues have a special focus. Special issues are used to attract advertising, but news stories and features on the subject are also needed.

For example, a consumer magazine may have a special issue on new developments in smartphones planned for April. Companies that manufacture such devices will no doubt want to advertise in that issue. If you're in the public relations or marketing communications department of the company, this special issue should alert you that the publication is also open to news and feature stories about developments and your new products. The most comprehensive database is EdCals, which is also owned by Cision. It tracks about 500,000 editorial opportunities worldwide.

Indeed, one of your major duties for a client or an employer is to review the editorial calendars of various publications to determine stories and features that might be submitted to coincide with the editorial focus of a particular issue. It also pays to check your local daily to get a list of special supplements planned for the year. Doing this sort of homework will dramatically increase your story placements.

Another good way to find media personnel and track publications that might have an interest in your material is *tip sheets*. These are weekly newsletters that report on recent changes in news personnel and their new assignments, how to contact them, and what kinds of material they are looking for.

Public relations publications such as *Bulldog Reporter* and *PRWeek* publish profiles of journalists and bloggers. In addition, an email weekly edition of *PartyLine* (www.partylinepublishing.com) gives a roundup of new appointments and promotions in the media that helps publicists update their contact lists and find out if a particular publication is changing focus. It also gives tips on placement opportunities. One listing, for example, said that the University of the People was looking for celebrity spokespersons to join its ambassador program and gave the name of a person that publicists could contact if they had any interested clients.

Another kind of tip sheet is Help a Report Out (HARO) at www.helpareporter .com. This site is a matchmaker between expert sources and journalists who are working on a particular story. A reporter, for example, may be working on a story about renewable energy and post a query asking for information or interviews with experts in the field. If you're working for a utility or a manufacturer of solar panels, it's an opportunity to let the reporter know that your client or employer has an expert who would be a good source.

To date, more than 100,000 sources and 30,000 members of the media have registered on HARO. Experts say the most productive strategy for publicists is to (1) closely read what the reporter is asking, (2) respond immediately in the method that the reporter prefers, (3) send attachments only if requested, (4) pitch only on-topic stories, and (5) offer to help on any future stories.

Another service, which dates back to 1992, is PR Newswire's ProfNet Connect (www.profnetconnect.com). It features an opportunity for public relations professionals, members of the public, and the media to build "expert pages" that include background information, photos, videos, and abstracts of speeches indexed in major search engines.

Distribution of Materials

The vast majority of publicity materials is now distributed in digital and electronic formats. Email is now universal and so pervasive in our society that it's difficult to believe that in the not-so-distant past snail mail was the primary distribution method.

Snail mail has not disappeared from the publicist's tool kit, but today's primary distribution channels are (1) email, (2) online newsrooms, (3) newswires, (4) mobile-enabled content, and (5) feature and photo placement firms. A summary of all the channels available is on page 256.

> *With so many avenues for communications these days, PR and marketing professionals must use a mix of distribution channels to ensure their message is heard.* Vocus white paper, Five Key Ways to Distribute Your News

Email

Electronic mail, or **email,** is the oldest feature of the Internet. It was invented in 1971, but wasn't widely adopted by business until the late 1980s. Today, having an email address (or several) is practically universal. In fact, email is so pervasive in today's society that people put their email addresses on their business cards, organizations publicize their email addresses, and media personnel use email as their primary source for news releases, media advisories, and other communications.

Indeed, more than one survey has confirmed that email is the major form of communication among public relations writers, clients, and journalists. One survey conducted by the Center for Media Research, for example, found that journalists prefer communicating via email over any other medium. In fact, 98 percent of the journalists surveyed said they prefer to receive news releases via email. Another survey of journalists by Vocus, a supplier of public relations software and owner of PRWeb, found similar results.

The Vocus survey also found that most respondents prefer news releases to have links to websites so that they can easily click the links to get supplemental information. If you provide links in your news releases, Vocus notes that it is better to link journalists to a customized website that pertains to the news release. All too often, the only link on the news release is the organization's home page, and reporters have to do more clicking to find the actual material. One common solution is online newsrooms, which will be discussed in the next section.

If you do send an email news release, here are some guidelines from Vocus that will ensure maximum distribution and indexing on search engines.

- » **Keywords.** Headlines should be no longer than 80 characters and contain keywords related to the major theme of your news. It's important for search engine optimization (SEO), but it's also the first opportunity to engage your viewer. Additional keywords should be placed in the release to create content that is easily retrievable. In general, a maximum of four to six keywords should be used.

- » **Enhanced URL.** Search engines look at the keywords used in a hyperlink to a website to determine its ranking. If a hyperlink has keywords included and points to your website, then a person searching for these words is more likely to find you among the results.

» **Anchor text/embedded keywords.** Embedding hyperlinks into your release can also increase your ranking and drive traffic to your website. Make sure, however, that the hyperlink goes to a specific page directly connected to the idea or concept highlighted in the news release.

Tips for Success   Selecting a Distribution Channel

This chapter describes a number of media distribution channels. That still leaves the question, "Which channel should I use for my material?" The answer is not simple. It depends on the purpose and objectives of your message—and who you want to reach with it. In many cases, you should use a mix of distribution channels. The following are some general tips:

+ **Email.**   Good for suggesting story ideas to journalists and editors, answering media questions and queries, and sending news releases to individual reporters.

+ **Online newsrooms.**   These are comprehensive libraries of information for the journalist. Good for distributing news releases, media kits, features, corporate background information, and high-resolution photos and graphics. Distribution is enhanced by sending e-alerts and having journalists sign up for RSS feeds from the online newsroom.

+ **Newswires.**   Best for distribution of financial news to large newspapers and major broadcast outlets on a national or international basis where immediate disclosure is needed. Ideal for multimedia news releases that incorporate photos, graphics, and video. Distribution also includes Internet search engines, bloggers, and other social networking media.

+ **Mobile enabled content.**   Good for providing reporters on the go with story updates, links to websites, and answering queries. QR codes can embed a variety of information that reporters can access by scanning the code on their smartphones. Apps are good for providing tips and interactive content, primarily to consumers about products and other topics.

+ **Twitter.**   Best used for late-breaking news and posting instant updates about developments regarding a major news event, natural disaster, or accident. To a lesser degree, a good way to follow reporters and for them to contact you if they need an immediate, short answer.

+ **Feature placement firms.**   Good for reaching suburban newspapers and small weeklies. Best for feature-type material that remains relevant over a period of time and can be used in various sections of the newspaper such as food, auto, technology, lifestyle. Distribution can be done in multiple formats.

+ **Photo placement firms.**   Best for distributing high-resolution publicity photos on an international basis. Makes it possible to index images for access by search engines.

+ **Mail.**   A common method for distribution of routine materials to local and regional media. Mailing houses are effective for mailing news releases, media kits, and CDs.

+ **Fax.**   Good for sending media advisories and alerts and bypassing the stuffed inbox. Not recommended for mass distribution of news releases.

+ **CD.**   Best used for providing background material, such as corporate profiles, executive bios, and product information sheets.

» **Multimedia content.** Adding a photograph, a video, or an audio to your release will not only make your news release more consumable and graphically pleasing, but it will also ensure your news is indexed in image search engines and create more visibility for your message.

» **Social media tags.** Allowing your content to be circulated through Digg, Technorati, Delicious and other social bookmarking sites will not only increase the search engine rankings of your release, but also drive traffic to your website.

Advocates of email also say that it is less intrusive than a phone call. If reporters or editors receive the message at deadline, they can read it at a more convenient time. Email also eliminates telephone tag. Reporters and public relations personnel can easily engage in an email dialogue, posting messages on each other's computer, instead of trying to reach each other by telephone and leaving messages on voicemail.

The downside, of course, is the problem of getting noticed in a deluge of 200 or 300 emails that typically flood an editor's inbox on a daily basis. The Vocus study, for example, found that 17 percent of the respondents received over 200 email releases a week and another 33 percent received 100 to 200 releases a week. As a result, journalists often complain that mass emails from organizations and public relations firms constitute spam and are just as obnoxious as the come-ons for potions that will increase your physical attributes or improve your love life. Jennifer Martin, corporate communications manager for CipherTrust, has one solution: "Try to go through and personalize each email, and don't blind copy a press release." What she means is that you should not copy (even if it's hidden) multiple reporters at the same time.

Online Newsrooms

Sending email news releases on a regular basis is called a "push" approach to distribution. A "pull" strategy, in contrast, is to make information readily available that attracts or "pulls" journalists to your site. That's why it's a good idea to have a fully operational and up-to-date newsroom on an organization's website. See Figure 10.3 for the home page of HP's newsroom.

Indeed, an online newsroom is vital because it's often the first place journalists and even the public turn to for basic information about the organization, its products, and its services. An online newsroom link should be highly visible on an organization's home page, and it should be easy to navigate with a minimum number of clicks.

Vocus says that an online newsroom has five key components:

1. **Contact information.** The names, email addresses, and phone numbers of the primary public relations contacts for the organization should be listed and easy to find. The Center for Media Research surveyed journalists on the usefulness of company newsrooms, and 97 percent said contact information was very important. At the same time, the most frequent complaint of journalists is that such information is not included or is difficult to find.

2. **Corporate background.** The site should include a comprehensive company history, a basic fact sheet, executive profiles, and product descriptions. You can also highlight the awards of the organization, major executive presentations, and position papers. This was important to almost 90 percent of the journalists.

FIGURE 10.3 Most corporations have a "newsroom" as part of their website. With a few clicks, a journalist doing research can access everything from the organization's executive profiles to the most recent news releases. A good online newsroom, according to surveys, should provide a link to personnel in media relations who can answer questions from reporters. This figure shows the home page of HP's online newsroom.

3. **News releases and media kits.** News releases should be posted on a frequent basis and listed in reverse chronological order. Media kits should be posted in a similar way. This was important to 92 percent of the surveyed journalists. In addition, it's important to have "printer friendly" capability availability for the public and print publications. News releases available in HTML format are better for bloggers, who often cut and paste material.

4. **Multimedia gallery.** You should provide executive photos, product photos, charts, graphs, and other artwork in both low (72 dpi) and high (300 dpi) resolutions to meet the needs of visitors to the site. Materials should be downloadable in JPEG or PDF format. This was important to about 70 percent of the journalists.

5. **Search capability.** Include a search component in your newsroom to allow journalists, consumers, investors, and other visitors to easily find information by topic or date. This component was important to 95 percent of the surveyed journalists in the Center for Media Research survey.

TEKgroup International (www.tekgroup.com), which designs online newsrooms, also conducts an annual survey of journalists that asks what functions they prefer in an online newsroom. In one survey of more than 400 journalists, it was found that 70 percent of journalists often visited online newsrooms. Their reasons for visiting were mixed: to access breaking news (97 percent), to access news releases (98 percent), to access photos (92 percent), to access executive biographies (89 percent), to access company background information (97 percent), to search archives (100 percent), and to access public relations contacts (99 percent).

> *I find sites that are organized both by release date and by topical information are the easiest to navigate. The quicker I can find the information I need, the quicker I'll be able to turn the story around. It's always helpful to have a point person's contact information available for brief follow-up questions.*
>
> A journalist quoted in the TEKgroup survey

The journalists in the TEKgroup survey also indicated that almost all journalists (97 percent) preferred receiving information via a newsroom email alert or an RSS feed. Another large percentage (92 percent) preferred receiving pitched stories via a newsroom email alert. Basically, an email alert contains the company logo, a subject head, a one-paragraph summary, and a link to the full release in the organization's online newsroom. See Chapter 6 for more background on media alerts.

Journalists and bloggers who cover specific industries or companies often sign up for email alerts and RSS feeds because information is then automatically forwarded to them for their review. It saves them the trouble of taking the time to do their own searches and access multiple websites.

Online newsrooms are particularly important when there's a crisis and a need to rapidly disseminate information to the media and other important publics, such as employees, investors, and members of the community. The TEKgroup survey indicated that more than 90 percent of the journalists thought it was important to be able to access an online newsroom during a crisis. There's the expectation, however, that the organization will provide up-to-date and relevant information throughout a crisis. Indeed, one complaint about online newsrooms is that the information is not frequently updated. A website that never changes, quips John Gerstner of IntranetInsider.com, is a "cobweb." For a survey of what's included in Fortune 500 websites, see the PR Casebook box on page 260.

There's some debate whether online newsrooms should be password-protected. Many corporations, including Cisco and IBM, allow anyone to visit their newsrooms and to download materials. Thomson Financial advises, "Do not password-protect your site. You do not want to exclude anyone from spreading the word about your company." Other organizations, such as HP, believe that some areas of the pressroom should be password-protected, such as those areas offering

> *The core audience for an organization's newsroom includes shareholders, business partners, customers, donors and volunteers in nonprofits, employees, and the media.* David
>
> Henderson, author of *Making News in the Digital Era*

access to high-resolution photos and graphics. The argument is that the brand must be protected, so it's necessary to restrict access only to media representatives.

Newswires

Many organizations regularly distribute their news releases and other publicity materials, such as photos, through wire services. This is particularly true for corporate

PR casebook

Online Newsrooms: A Fortune 500 Scorecard

Most journalists say that an online newsroom should provide the names and contact information of an organization's public relations staff, but only about half of the Fortune 500 companies follow that advice. That's one finding of a study by Justin Pettigrew and Bryan Reber at the University of Georgia, who did an analysis of all Fortune 500 newsroom sites.

The percentages of Fortune 500 firms that have various newsroom components are summarized in the following table:

Updated news releases in the past 30 days	92%
Updated news releases in the past 7 days	66%
Company profile	77%
Executive biographies	74%
Company history/background	73%
Photos of executives	62%
Names of PR staff	57%
Phone numbers of PR staff	51%
Generic email address (info@ …)	51%
Email address of PR contacts	39%
Photographs of products	36%
Address of corporate headquarters	18%
Speeches by executives/experts	16%

Pettigrew and Reber say organizations, both large and small, could considerably improve their relationship with journalists by (1) providing a tool on the website for searching news releases, and (2) providing more information on how to easily reach a specific public relations staffer via phone or email. They note, "Such personal contact information would be much more useful to journalists than the more common generic information provided on the sites."

Source: Pettigrew, J., and Reber, B. (2010). "The New Dynamic in Corporate Media Relations: How Fortune 500 Companies Are Using Virtual Press Rooms to Engage the Press." *Journal of Public Relations Research* 22 (4), 404–428.

and financial news that requires immediate, timely disclosure to media over a wide geographic area to meet Securities and Exchange Commission (SEC) regulations.

The three major newswires are Business Wire (www.businesswire.com), PR Newswire (www.prnewswire.com), and Marketwire (www.marketwire.com). It's estimated that each distributes more than 200,000 news releases annually to daily newspapers, broadcast stations, trade publications, and online news services. Other major distributors are PrimeZone Media Network, PRWeb, Black PRWire, Hispanic PRWire, and USAsianWire.

To submit a news release, you send it online via a form on a newswire's website. The release is then edited and formatted before being placed on a server that posts all the releases on a daily basis, which can total several hundred. Editors and reporters can access the list on their computers and click the news releases that interest them. A reporter can edit the news release on the screen, write a headline for it, and then push another key to have it printed in the right typeface and column width.

The advantage of newswire services is the timely and immediate delivery of a large amount of material via a server that can be easily accessed by everyone in the news department. Emailed news releases, by contrast, must be processed one at a time and are usually sent to specific reporters or editors. Electronic wire services can customize the distribution of material to specific media. They can send your news release to every daily newspaper in Ohio, or you can send it to a select list of financial publications in North America, Europe, and Asia. They can also distribute full-text news releases and color photos to African American and Hispanic publications or a select list of high-tech trade magazines.

> **❝** *Our delivery platform provides our client's news releases with the long tail which allows the release to be found and highly ranked on search engines, expanding their life cycle.* **❞**
>
> Laura Sturaitis, vice president of new media development at Business Wire, as quoted in *PRWeek*

Newswires also offer clients the additional opportunity of distributing their news releases to online search engines such as Google, Yahoo!, and Bing for indexing, which also enables consumers and the general public to access the full text of news releases and other publicity materials. In recent years, as social media networks have proliferated and become part of the landscape, newswires have kept up by including bloggers and social network sites, such as Facebook and YouTube, in the distribution mix.

Indeed, news releases can be transmitted with an increasing number of bells and whistles. Although the vast majority of news releases distributed by the newswires are still in the "text only" category, multimedia news releases—which can include video and audio—often are used to launch new products and publicize major events. See Chapter 5 for a discussion of multimedia news releases.

A good example of using a newswire is Domino's launch of its Cheesy Garlic Bread Pizza. Its multimedia news release, distributed by PR Newswire, incorporated text, video, several screen shots, and links to Delicious, Digg, Technorati, Reddit, Newsvine, Google, and Yahoo! Another multimedia news release distributed by Marketwire on behalf of Zero Gravity, a company marketing suborbital flights, featured a video clip of well-known scientist Stephen Hawking in zero-gravity flight, which was downloaded 110,000 times on YouTube. For an annotated example of a newswire news release, see Figure 10.4 or refer back to the PRWeb illustration in Chapter 5 on page 138.

In other words, the news release isn't just for the press anymore. The public can also access various newswires online to read news releases and other materials that have been distributed to the media. Michael Lissauer, senior vice president of marketing for Business Wire, told *PRWeek*:

> The press release is reaching an additional audience today. Press releases were always aimed at the media, which would interpret those releases, write what they wanted to write based on those releases, that was what consumers ultimately saw. But with the advent of the Internet, the target audience can see press releases in their original form.

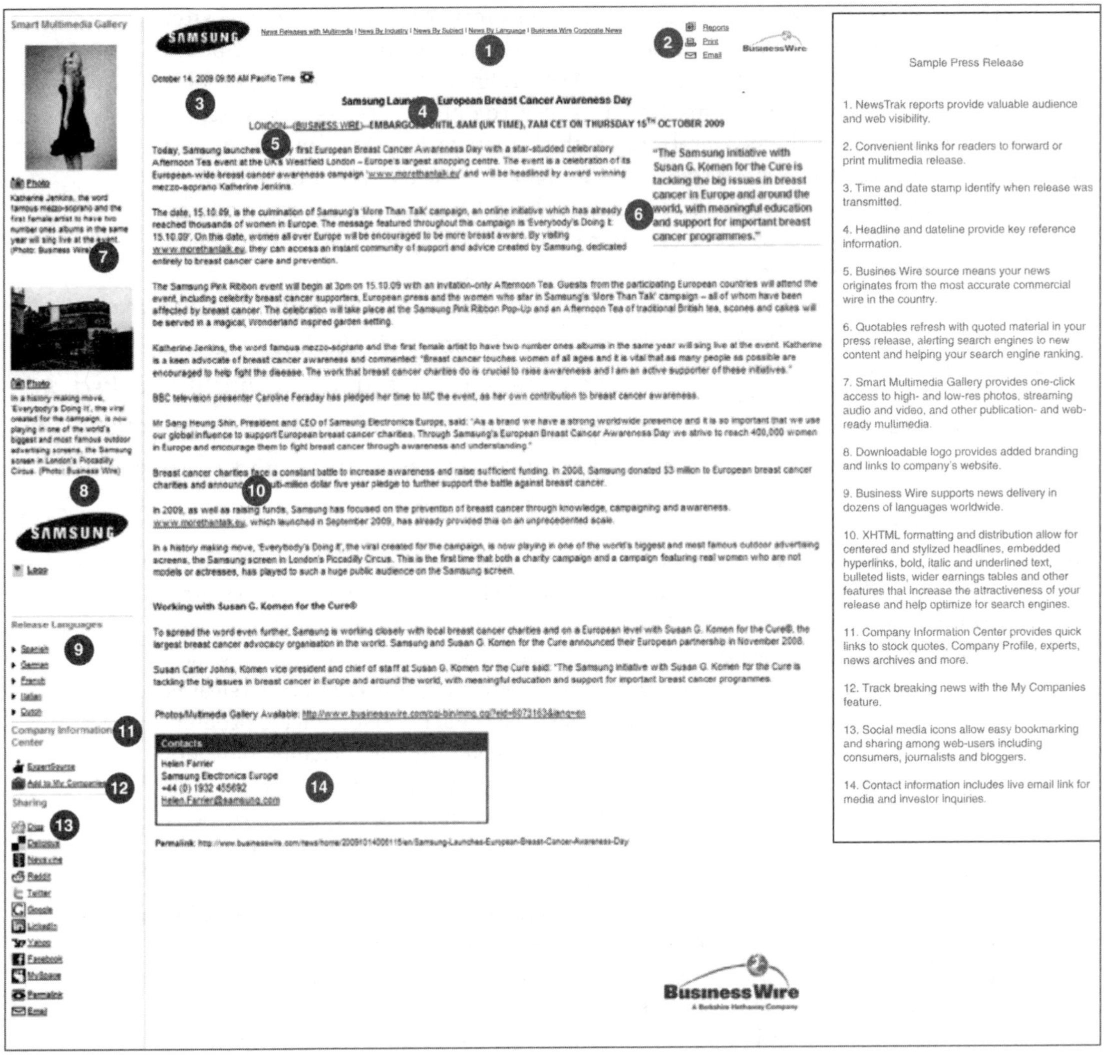

1. NewsTrak reports provide valuable audience and web visibility.

2. Convenient links for readers to forward or print multimedia release.

3. Time and date stamp identify when release was transmitted.

4. Headline and dateline provide key reference information.

5. Busines Wire source means your news originates from the most accurate commercial wire in the country.

6. Quotables refresh with quoted material in your press release, alerting search engines to new content and helping your search engine ranking.

7. Smart Multimedia Gallery provides one-click access to high- and low-res photos, streaming audio and video, and other publication- and web-ready multimedia.

8. Downloadable logo provides added branding and links to company's website.

9. Business Wire supports news delivery in dozens of languages worldwide.

10. XHTML formatting and distribution allow for centered and stylized headlines, embedded hyperlinks, bold, italic and underlined text, bulleted lists, wider earnings tables and other features that increase the attractiveness of your release and help optimize for search engines.

11. Company Information Center provides quick links to stock quotes, Company Profile, experts, news archives and more.

12. Track breaking news with the My Companies feature.

13. Social media icons allow easy bookmarking and sharing among web-users including consumers, journalists and bloggers.

14. Contact information includes live email link for media and investor inquiries.

FIGURE 10.4 Several commercial newswires send news releases directly to a publication's servers via the Web. This illustration identifies the various elements of a Business Wire "smart" news release that embeds such elements as photos, graphics, video, spreadsheets, and slideshows into the basic news release. In addition, news releases also include social media tags and keywords for maximum search engine optimization (SEO). Journalists and bloggers can access these elements with a simple click of the mouse.

Cost — Distributing news releases via a newswire is extremely cost effective in terms of reaching the vast majority of traditional and online media because most newsrooms receive at least one of the major newswires.

Business Wire, like its competition, has a fee structure based on geography. A text-only news release sent to all media in a single state such as California costs about $250. A regional distribution to the Pacific Northwest or the northeastern United States runs about $400, and national distribution to all 50 states is about $700. On an international basis, a news release distributed to only European media would cost about $3,500. Worldwide distribution is about $8,000.

Multimedia news releases, of course, cost much more because embedding audio, video, and Web links is more complex. National distribution of such a release, according to Business Wire, is about $3,000.

Mobile Applications

Organizations today must also have a mobile strategy for the distribution of information and public relations materials. The use of smartphones is growing rapidly as individuals increasingly use them for accessing email, checking baseball scores, making bank deposits, and paying bills. This means that organizations must also adapt by optimizing their websites for viewing on the small screen of a smartphone and developing useful consumer-friendly applications.

Websites — The standard webpage for an organization doesn't work on a mobile platform because it usually has too much text and graphics. Consequently, most experts recommend that a separate mobile home page be formatted that would include (1) shorter sentences, (2) abbreviations instead of complete words, and (3) simple graphics. An optimized mobile newsroom for an organization would also reformat news releases to be very basic and somewhat short. McCormick & Company, for example, reformats its major news releases and recipes into a short, narrow column that will fit a smartphone screen.

Apps — Several hundred thousand "apps" are now available and the numbers are multiplying daily as more organizations launch their own applications for public relations purposes. Indeed, it's difficult to believe that Apple first marketed apps in 2008 and by January 2011 had recorded 10 billion downloads from its App Store.

A good example of an app that provides useful consumer information is one developed by paint maker Benjamin Moore. It's called Color Capture and helps people easily find comparable color matches for a room that is already furnished. A person takes a photo of the room and uploads it to the app, which then culls through the company's database of 3,500 paints to find complementary hues. For more detailed information, the app enables consumers to directly reach the company's website. Sherwin-Williams also has a ColorSnap app. See Figure 7.4 on page 179 in Chapter 7 for an example of how apps are used in the tourism industry.

> ❝We're moving into a world that's going to be dominated by apps. You're going to have to be able to manage an app development project.❞
>
> Shel Holtz, a popular speaker and blogger about social media

Even the Chinese government has app fever. In order to soften its image abroad, the State Council Information Office has launched "China SCIO," available for free in Apple's App Store. According to the Council's website, the goal of the app is "to increase the coverage and influence" of the government's image-building efforts, and "to introduce China to the world in a better way to enhance the international image of China."

" The most important aspect of implementation of QR codes is that they really are a mobile gateway and should be treated as such. Your QR code is not just another way to get people to go to your website. They can open a new line of customer engagement and add a competitive advantage. " Stephanie Moss, editor of QRmedi.us

QR Codes — A new development in mobile technology is Quick Response codes, popularly known as QR, that are designed to be read by smartphones. They are two-dimensional matrix barcodes that can contain text or URLs to give an individual a portal to any number of apps. Shel Holtz, a social media guru, notes that "QR codes have an advantage over text messages. Scan a code and you get a video, a website, a contact card, map directions; it can even initiate a phone call."

Many journalists are constantly on the go, so a QR code giving them company or event information via their phones or mobile-enabled tablets is a good way to reach them. Jason Kintzler, CEO of PitchEngine, told *Public Relations Tactics* that a QR code could embed information on a flyer, a media kit, or other collateral so that journalists could download the material almost anywhere. "The easier we can make it for reporters, the better," Kintzler says.

In another application, *Public Relations Tactics* displayed a QR code in a story about the president of PRSA. It said, "Scan this code to watch a video interview with Rosanna M. Fiske." And, if your phone doesn't have a code reader or scanner included, the article notes that you can download one at http://m.mobiletag.com. See Figure 10.5 to see how an airport uses a QR code at shuttle bus stops.

Twitter

A good platform for distributing late-breaking news, refuting a viral rumor, or giving updates on a developing situation that has high news interest is Twitter. A tweet is limited to 140 characters, so public relations personnel often include URLs and links where reporters can get more information if they are interested.

A first step for using Twitter is to go to Twitter.com and create a profile using words that you want to be searched for. You should also add the organizational website to your profile and a link from your site back to your Twitter page. Anne Deeter Gallaher, owner of a public relations firm by the same name, wrote on Ragan.com, "This is your hub for digital information. Make it easy for people to find you and connect with you."

Experts caution, however, that you should only tweet journalists if a major news event has just occurred or when a major accident or disaster requires a constant stream of updates. Tweets are less successful as a way of pitching journalists about a story or for just telling them that a news release is now available. One study, for example, found that only 1 percent of reporters said they want to be contacted via Twitter or direct message on a social network.

If you're a publicist for a celebrity, however, another use of Twitter is to build a fan base of followers for your client. One Lady Gaga tweet to her 7.5 million

FIGURE 10.5 QR codes are increasingly used to embed text, photos, and graphics into a package that can be accessed via smartphones with scanning software. The Sonoma County Airport Express has posted a sign with a QR code at a local motel stop which links people back to its website so they can access the bus schedule. QR codes are also used in window displays showing various products and even in print articles so people can access a video or more information.

followers: "Today's cancelled Paris show is rescheduled for Tuesday, 2moro's show will happen as planned. I promise to give u the nights of ure life." Major league teams and major brands also distribute information and updates to their followers about a variety of topics. More information about Twitter is found in Chapter 12.

Feature Placement Firms

A number of distribution services specialize in preparing columns and features that are distributed as entire layouts, complete with headlines, photos, and graphics. Such materials were traditionally called *mat releases* or *camera-ready art*.

Back in the old days, editors usually received formatted stories on glossy sheets, cut out the ones they wanted to use, and then pasted the entire story or column into the layout of the newspaper. Today, features are in digital form and distributed via CDs, email, and the Web. There's also a variety of media platforms so most feature placement firms format the same feature in different ways. Family Features Editorial Syndicate (www.familyfeatures.com), for example, will prepare a feature as (1) a completely formatted feature ready for publication, (2) an unformatted text that editors can tailor to their needs, (3) an HTML, and (4) a video.

Brian Agnes, president of Family Features Editorial Syndicate, explains:

Due to the wide variety of publishing platforms for columns and mat releases (as opposed to our formatted full pages), we release our syndicated column material in unformatted fashion as Word docs, JPEGs, and PDFs. We find it encourages greater publishing frequency by allowing editors to reformat the content to suit their space needs—as releases and columns are typically used as filler material rather than occupying a fixed position in every publication.

Completely formatted features (referred to as "camera-ready") often are used by weekly and daily newspapers to fill news space inside the newspaper. According to the distribution services, the demand for camera-ready stories is booming as a result of rising costs and fewer staff writers. Thousands of newspapers, which receive the stories free, find that using such materials keeps staffing costs to a minimum and fills their inside pages. Such features are often found in the specialty sections of a newspaper, such as the auto, food, real estate, travel, and computing sections.

Feature placement firms distribute features and other information that is relevant over a period of several months. In the business, these stories are often called *evergreens*. They may include camera-ready features about food, travel, health, education, special events, and consumerism. Here are some headlines of typical feature stories, with the client in parentheses:

» "What to Do About Childhood Cancer" (National Childhood Cancer Foundation)
» "Transform Your Green Space into Livable Space" (Ace Hardware)
» "How to Protect Your House When You Go on Vacation" (Schlage Lock Company)
» "Furry Valentines With Wet Kisses" (Nestle Purina PetCare Company)

Trade groups, national charitable organizations, national membership organizations, state tourism departments, and any number of corporations use camera-ready releases to create awareness and visibility. The most successful ones emphasize consumer tips and keep commercialism to a minimum. In fact, most camera-ready features only mention the organization once or twice in the entire article. For more information on writing a food feature, see the Tips for Success on page 267.

Camera-ready features are relatively short. A one-column feature is about 225 words, and a two-column story is about 350 to 500 words. Family Features specializes in full-page features. Figure 10.6 shows an example of a full-page feature offered by Family Features that was prepared for Wild Blueberry Association. To attract editor and reader interest, camera-ready features usually also include a photo or a graphic of some kind. Radio stations receive short spots professionally voiced on CD, and TV stations often receive video features.

Cost — Several other firms also write, produce, and distribute camera-ready features. North American Precis Syndicate (www.napsinfo.com) is one of the oldest and largest in the business; other national firms include Metro Editorial Services (www.metrocreativegraphics.com) and NewsUSA (www.newsusa.com).

NAPS, for example, distributes its client features to 10,000 daily and weekly newspapers across the country and says that an organization typically will get 100 to 400+ placements. The cost for a two-column feature, which includes writing, formatting, and distribution, is about $5,550; a one-column feature is about $4,000. A camera-ready television release (four slides, plus a script) costs about $6,500 for distribution to 1,000 TV stations. According to NAPS, the client typically receives 100 to 150+ placements. NAPS also prepares and distributes radio releases to about 6,500 stations and claims clients receive about 400 to 500+ placements. The cost of a radio release is about $5,000.

NewsUSA specializes in packages of multiple releases. For example, it will send 26 different camera-ready features over the course of a year to 10,500 newspapers

+

Tips for Success   How to Write a Food Feature

Mat feature releases must be informative and appealing to consumers. In addition, they must be about somewhat "evergreen" subject matter so that they are relevant over a period of months. The following is adapted from tips provided by Family Features about how to write a food feature, but many of the suggestions are relevant to other "camera-ready" features.

Copy

+ Think like an editor.
+ Use AP style.
+ Use short, snappy headlines.
+ Use subheads to augment the headline.
+ Provide short, reader-friendly copy.
+ Use sidebars to break out copy.
+ Use subtle branding (in ingredients, Web addresses, spokesperson's tips or quotes, booklet offers, and contests).

Photos

+ Provide more than one photo, if possible.
+ Keep lighting consistent and even for all photos.
+ Provide good contrast.
+ Avoid backlighting.
+ Keep product, graphic in sharp focus.

Recipes

+ Instructions should be clear, logical, and reader-friendly.
+ Use ingredients easily found in most supermarkets.
+ List ingredients in order of use.
+ Keep measurements consistent.

FIGURE 10.6 Distributors of camera-ready features are adept at writing materials that focus on consumer tips instead of a commercial pitch. In general, the name of the sponsoring organization should be buried in the middle of the story or at the end of it. The idea is to create brand awareness and credibility, but to do so in a subtle way. This full-page, camera-ready feature on recipes for blueberries was distributed by Family Features for the Wild Blueberry Association.

for about $80,000. The same number of radio features will cost a similar amount. Of course, there is always the success story. NewsUSA prepared and distributed 23 camera-ready features for American Century Investments and received a total of 4,304 placements, representing 242 million potential readers. You should note, however, that audience size is based on the total circulation of the newspaper, not how many people actually read the feature.

Photo Placement Firms

Several firms specialize in the distribution of publicity photos and captions. Newscom (www.newscom.com) is a major resource for high-resolution photos and graphics for registered journalists and editors on any number of subjects. In fact, its website houses more than 55 million images, graphics, text, cartoons, and video from more than 100 different photo agencies, wire services, and freelance photographers.

An editor, for example, may receive an e-alert or a news release that includes a link to Newscom to retrieve a particular photo or graphic that illustrates the story. Or perhaps an editor may be looking for a particular photo that shows celebrities at a corporation's sponsored event. In most cases, Newscom will have a variety of photos available from the event, and the editor can select one that fits the publication's needs. Publicity photos provided by clients can usually be downloaded at no cost, but licensing fees must be paid for most of the photos in its inventory.

Another photo distribution firm is Feature Photo Service (www.featurephoto.com). It has 1,500 photographers worldwide; not only can they take photos for clients, but the company also writes captions and arranges for their distribution to the media. FPS offers worldwide news release and photo distribution via more than 25 news agencies worldwide. In addition, it distributes photos to 1,200 U.S. news media via Associated Press (AP) and Newscom. In addition, Feature Photo Service distributes photos to various search engines and social media aggregators. An example of a Feature Photo Service media advisory is shown in Figure 10.7.

Mail

A widely used distribution method, even in the Internet age, is still regular mail. It is often referred to as **snail mail** by dedicated users of the Internet, but newsrooms still receive thousands of news releases, CDs, and media kits via this method every day. For many weeklies in small towns across America with limited computer servers and broadband capacity, printed matter delivered by the U.S. Postal Service or by private companies such as FedEx, Airborne Express, and DHL Worldwide is just fine.

In sum, the U.S. Postal Service continues to be a cost-effective method for distributing news releases, media kits, fact sheets, position papers, and other background materials that do not contain late-breaking news. As indicated in Chapter 9, many PSAs are produced on CDs and then mailed to radio and television stations. All materials, however, must be sent via first-class mail or by overnight express. It is never acceptable to send materials by second- or third-class mail.

Fax

Many media alerts and advisories are still sent by facsimile transmission, despite the perception that a fax is an artifact of the past. A *fax* is as quick as a telephone call and has the advantage of providing a piece of paper that must be physically handled. An email, in contrast, can easily be deleted without ever opening it. Given the overloaded inboxes of every editor these days, some publicists say that a fax can often cut through the clutter and get more attention.

FIGURE 10.7 Placement firms such as Feature Photo Service (FPS) distribute a variety of publicity photos on behalf of clients. This media advisory, sent to newspaper photo editors, gives a thumbnail of the photo and the caption. Interested editors can then download the photo from a website.

Summary

Reaching the Media

» Media databases, now primarily available online, are essential tools for compiling media lists and distributing information.

» Media contacts and email addresses must be updated and revised on a regular basis; journalists frequently change jobs.

» Publicists use editorial calendars to find out what special editions or sections various publications are planning for the year.

» Tip sheets such as Help a Reporter Out (HARO) let publicists know what kind of material a reporter is seeking for a particular purpose.

Distribution of Materials

» The vast majority of news releases and other press materials are now distributed via email and through newswires.

» Email is now a popular way of communicating with reporters and editors about possible story ideas. It works best, however, when the publicist and the reporter have already established a working relationship.

» Online newsrooms, which are part of an organization's website, have become the primary source for journalists seeking late-breaking news and other information about an organization.

» Newswires are a cost-effective way of sending a news release over a large geographical area, including the world.

» Business Wire and other similar services distribute news releases to Internet search engines and social networking sites, which allows the public in addition to the traditional media to access the information.

» Advances in mobile technology now allow journalists to get news releases and other information on their smartphones via texting, QR codes, or apps.

» Feature placement services prepare and distribute camera-ready features to media outlets on behalf of clients. Such features are often found in the specialty sections of a daily newspaper such as the auto, lifestyle, technology, and gardening sections.

» Photo placement firms can take photos and videos for clients and distribute them. Some services, such as Newscom, serve as a repository for millions of photos that are available (often at a fee) for use by media outlets and other organizations.

» Mail, often called snail mail, is still widely used to distribute publicity materials.

» A fax is a good way to send media advisories and late-breaking news releases. However, it is not wise to mass-distribute routine news releases by fax.

Skill Building Activities

1. A manufacturer of sunscreen has developed a feature article about the need for protection to avoid the dangers of skin cancer. The target audience is women ages 18 to 35. Using media databases and directories available in the library or online, compile a list of magazines that reach this particular audience.

2. News releases sent by email should have a concise subject line using keywords. What subject line would you use for the sunscreen news release? You may want to review Chapter 5.

3. Check out the online newsrooms of four or five corporations or organizations. What are the contents? Are the sites

user-friendly? What would you suggest, given the discussion about online newsrooms in this chapter, to improve the sites?

4. Log on to Business Wire, PR Newswire, or MarketWire. Explore these websites and access some of the news releases filed by various organizations. Write a brief analysis of what you found.

5. QR codes are becoming popular. Chose a company or industry and write a memo outlining how the use of QR codes could be incorporated into a public relations strategy.

6. The city's water department wants to develop an app to promote water conservation and environmental awareness. Write a memo (proposal) outlining your

ideas for content and how to make the app somewhat interactive.

7. You're a writer for Family Features Syndicate and you're asked to write a 400-word feature for the National Garlic Association to promote the use of garlic. Review the Tips for Success on page 267 and write a food feature that would be formatted along the lines of the blueberry feature in Figure 10.6. In addition to writing the feature, what photos or graphics would you recommend to illustrate it?

8. Review the contents of several weekly or daily publications in your area. Try to identify articles/features that probably were distributed by a feature placement firm. Write a critique of the article(s) in terms of appeal, information, relevance, and readability.

Media Resources

Broer, J. (2011, June). "New Technologies Leave Newswires' Roles Uncertain." *O'Dwyer's*, 14.

Ciarallo, J. (2011, May 9). "Ten 'Must Have' Mobile Apps for PR." Retrieved from www.mediabistro.com.

De Souza, A. (2010, June). "Does Your Online Newsroom Deliver to Reporters?" *Ragan Report*, 17.

Gallaher, A. (2011, January 27). "Nine Easy Steps to Add Twitter to Your PR Mix." Retrieved from www.ragan.com.

Kennedy, M. (2010, November 11). "Ten Tips for Success Using Help a Reporter Out." Retrieved from www.ragan.com.

Miller, L. (2011, February). "Your Mobile Website: Keep It Fast, Easy and User-Friendly." *Ragan Report*, 24–25.

Pettigrew, J., and Reber, B. (2010). "The New Dynamic in Corporate Media Relations: How Fortune 500 Companies Are Using Virtual Press Rooms to Engage the

Press." *Journal of Public Relations Research* 22 (4), 404–428.

Porter, J. (2010, December 9). "How to Build a Better Online Newsroom." Retrieved from www.blog.journalistics.com.

Sebastian, M. (2011, May 9). "Survey: Just 1 Percent of Reporters Want to Be Contacted via Twitter." Retrieved from www.prdaily.com.

Simmons, L. (2010, November). "Smart Scanning: QR Codes Offer PR Pros New Options to Connect." *Public Relations Tactics*, 11.

Wilson, Matt (2011, January 13). "Seven Things You Need to Know about Mobile Communication." Retrieved from www.prdaily.com.

Working, R. (2011, June 13). "How to Create a Website That Reporters Will Love." Retrieved from www.ragan.com.

Zuk, R. (2010, May). "From Static to Style: Online Newsrooms in the Digital Era." *Public Relations Tactics*, 7.

Avoiding Legal Hassles

» **After reading this chapter, you will be able to:**

» Avoid lawsuits for libel or defamation

» Safeguard the privacy of employees and individuals

» Understand the rules of copyright

» Correctly use trademarks and brand names

» Understand FTC and SEC regulations

» Work with lawyers on release of information

A Sampling of Legal Problems

Public relations writers, once they have mastered the basics of persuasive writing, also have the responsibility to work within the law. You must understand basic legal concepts that provide a framework for all your writing. A false product claim in a news release or the unauthorized use of a celebrity's photograph can lead to costly lawsuits for you and your employer or client.

Here's a sampling of recent government regulatory agency cases and lawsuits that involved public relations materials and the work of PR practitioners:

» The Federal Trade Commission fined Legacy Learning Systems $250,000 for paying a marketing firm's employees to post glowing reviews of the company's new DVD series on various consumer websites.

» Tyson Foods was ordered by a federal court to stop publicizing that its chickens didn't contain antibiotics believed to cause drug resistance in humans. The judge agreed with competitors that the claim was misleading.

» Bonner & Associates and its client, the Pharmaceutical Research and Manufacturers of America, were charged with violating Maryland's lobbying disclosure laws by distributing materials under the name of a fictitious consumer-based organization set up by the pharmaceutical industry.

» The Securities and Exchange Commission (SEC) fined a former employee of Ogilvy PR Worldwide $34,000 for giving his father "insider information" that he then used to purchase stock.

» The clothing retailer Forever 21 filed a trademark lawsuit against a satire blog titled WTForever 21.

» Greenpeace filed a privacy suit against Ketchum public relations for hiring a security firm on behalf of Dow Chemical that used "unlawful means" to steal information from the environmental group.

» A Chicago man sued for invasion of privacy after he appeared in a video news release for a cholesterol-lowering drug because the company and video producer didn't tell him the actual purpose of the taping.

» An 81-year-old man sued the United Way of America for using his picture on campaign posters and brochures without his permission.

» The director of investor relations for Enron Corporation was fined and imprisoned for inflating company earnings through various news channels, including news releases.

These examples provide some idea of the legal pitfalls that a public relations practitioner may encounter. Many of the charges were eventually dismissed or settled out of court, but the organizations paid dearly for the adverse publicity and the expense of defending themselves.

Public relations personnel must be aware that they can be held legally liable if they provide advice concerning or tacitly support a client or employer's illegal activity. This area of liability is called *conspiracy*. You can be named as a coconspirator with other organizational officials if you:

» Participate in an illegal action such as bribing a government official or covering up information of vital interest to the public health and safety

» Counsel and guide the policy behind an illegal action

» Take a major personal part in the illegal action

» Help establish a "front group" whereby the connection to the public relations firm or its clients is kept hidden

» Cooperate in any other way to further an illegal action

These five concepts also apply to public relations firms that create, produce, and distribute materials on behalf of clients. The courts have ruled on more than one occasion that public relations firms cannot hide behind the defense of "the client told me to do it." Public relations firms have a legal responsibility to practice "due diligence" in the type of information and documentation supplied by a client. Regulatory agencies such as the FTC (discussed shortly) have the power under the Lanham Act to file charges against public relations firms that distribute false and misleading information.

Libel and Defamation

According to the *AP Stylebook*, "Libel is injury to reputation. Words, pictures or cartoons that expose a person to public hatred, shame, disgrace or ridicule, or induce an ill opinion of a person are libelous." Traditionally, the term *libel* was a printed falsehood and *slander* involved an oral communication, such as a speech or a broadcast mention. Today, however, the courts often use *defamation* as a collective term that involves comments made in the traditional media or even on social media.

Juries award defamation damages to the extent that the following four points can be proved by the injured party: (1) the statement was published to others by print or broadcast; (2) the plaintiff was identified or is identifiable; (3) there was actual injury in the form of monetary losses, impairment of reputation, humiliation, or mental anguish and suffering; and (4) the publisher of the statement was malicious or negligent. In one case, for example, a former employee of J. Walter Thompson advertising agency filed a $20 million defamation lawsuit after an agency news release said she was "let go" because of financial irregularities in the department she headed. The lawsuit was dismissed because she could not prove that the agency acted in a "grossly irresponsible manner."

With public figures—people in government, politics, and entertainment—the test is whether the publisher of the statement knew that it was false or had a reckless disregard for its truth. Corporations, for the most part, are also considered "public figures" because they offer products and services for purchase and comment by consumers. Consequently, corporations have little recourse when an activist group says a company is a major polluter, a consumer affairs reporter says a product is a "rip-off," or consumers pan a restaurant on Yelp! Such statements are in the realm of fair comment, which is discussed next.

The Fair Comment Defense

A possible lawsuit provides a warning of what can happen, but this does not mean that an organization has to avoid statements of fact or opinion in public relations materials. Truth is the traditional defense against libel charges, but opinions also have a degree of legal protection under the First Amendment to the U.S. Constitution, which protects the freedom of speech. This legal concept is known as *fair comment privilege*.

This defense, for example, explains why theater and music reviewers can skewer a play or concert with impunity. It also means that mainstream journalists and even bloggers are protected when they write or post comments blasting a company's policy or products even if they have some of the facts wrong. As already stated, when individuals and companies voluntarily display their wares to the public for sale or consumption, they have no real recourse against criticism done with honest intention and lack of malicious intent.

Fair comment also protects the critical comments of organizational executives, which may be included in a news release or as the result of a media interview. In one case, the owner of the New York Yankees was sued for libel by an umpire when a news release from the team called him a "scab" who "had it in" for the Yankees and "misjudged" plays. A lower court awarded the umpire libel damages, but a higher court overturned the judgment by ruling that the comments in the news release constituted protected statements of opinion.

If you ever have occasion to write a news release that makes critical comments about another individual or organization, you can use the fair comment defense. However, take several precautionary measures. Experts suggest (1) that opinion statements be accompanied by the facts on which the opinions are based; (2) that opinion statements be clearly identified with quote marks and attribution to a particular individual; and (3) that the context of the language surrounding the expressions of opinion be reviewed for possible defamation.

Avoiding Defamation Suits

A lawsuit is always expensive and often damages an organization's reputation even if the lawsuit is dismissed, so it's always wise to carefully consider your choice of words. Words, as explained in Chapter 1, have denotive and connotative meanings. In either case, an executive can invite a lawsuit by simply calling the leaders of a labor union a "bunch of crooks using Nazi tactics" during a labor dispute. Or an executive might call a news reporter "a pimp for all environmental groups." Such language, although highly quotable and colorful, can provoke legal retaliation.

In situations involving personnel, organizations often avoid potential lawsuits by saying that an employee left "for personal reasons" or to "pursue other interests," even if the real reason was incompetence or a record of sexual harassment. The main reason for using fairly innocuous language is that the individual usually hasn't been formally charged or convicted in a court of law.

It's also a good idea to avoid unflattering comments or accusations about the competition's products or services. Although comparative advertising is the norm in the United States, a company must walk a narrow line between comparison and "trade libel" or "product disparagement." Statements should be truthful, with factual evidence and scientific demonstration available to substantiate them. Companies often charge competitors with overstepping the boundary between legitimate, factual comparison and defamation.

Subway, for example, sued Quiznos because it sponsored a contest for the best homemade video showing why Quiznos sandwiches are superior to Subway's. The winning video showed a race between two wagons. The Quiznos wagon, in the form of a meaty sandwich, blasted smoke at the plain-looking Subway car, causing it to crash in defeat. The ad's creator got $10,000, and the video was shown on the Internet as well as on a giant screen in Times Square. Subway claimed that the video and others entered in the contest made "false statements" and depicted Subway in a "disparaging manner." Quiznos, of course, claimed that it was not legally liable for the content of a contest entry.

An organization, however, can offer the opinion that a particular product or service is the "best" or "a revolutionary development" if the context clearly shows that the communication is a statement of opinion attributed to someone. Then it is classified as "puffery" and doesn't require factual evidence, according to Federal Trade Commission (FTC) guidelines.

Invasion of Privacy

One area of possible liability and potential lawsuits is an organization's treatment of its employees with regards to privacy. Public relations writers and staff are vulnerable to litigation with regard to invasion of employees' privacy in at least five areas:

» Employee newsletters

» Photo releases

» Product publicity and advertising

» Media inquiries about employees

» Employee blogs

Employee Newsletters

It is no longer true, if it ever was, that an organization has an unlimited right to publicize the activities of its employees. In fact, Morton J. Simon, a Philadelphia lawyer and author of *Public Relations Law*, once wrote, "It should not be assumed that a person's status as an employee waives his right to privacy." Today, Simon's comment is still correct. A company newsletter or magazine does not enjoy the same First Amendment protection that the news media enjoy when they claim "newsworthiness" and "public interest." A number of court cases have shown that company newsletters are considered commercial tools of trade.

This distinction does not impede the effectiveness of newsletters, but it does indicate that editors should try to keep employee stories organization oriented. Indeed, most lawsuits and complaints are generated by "personals columns" that may invade the privacy of employees. Although a mention that Joe Smith collects baseball caps or that Mary Worth is now a great-grandmother may sound completely innocent, the individuals involved—for any number of reasons—might consider the information a violation of their privacy. The situation could be further compounded into possible defamation by "cutesy" editorial asides in poor taste.

In sum, one should avoid anything that might embarrass or subject an employee to ridicule by fellow employees. Here are some guidelines to remember when writing about employee activities:

» Keep the focus on organization-related activities.

» Have employees submit "personals" in writing.

» Double-check all information for accuracy.

» Ask: "Will this embarrass anyone or cause someone to be the butt of jokes?"

» Don't rely on secondhand information; confirm the facts with the person involved.

» Don't include racial or ethnic designations of employees in any articles.

Photo Releases

Ordinarily, a public relations practitioner doesn't need a signed release if a person gives **implied consent** by posing for a picture and is told how it will be used. This is particularly true for "news" photographs published in internal newsletters or posted on the organization's intranet.

Public relations departments, however, should take the precaution of (1) filing all photographs, (2) dating them, and (3) giving the context of the situation. This precludes the use of old photos that could embarrass employees or subject them to ridicule. In other cases, it precludes using photographs of persons who are no longer employed or have died. This method also helps to ensure that a photo taken for the employee newsletter isn't used in an advertisement. If a photo of an employee or customer is used in product publicity, sales brochures, or advertisements, the standard practice is to obtain a signed release.

Product Publicity and Advertising

As already noted, an organization must have a signed release on file if it wants to use the photographs or comments of employees and other individuals in product publicity, sales brochures, and advertising. An added precaution is to give some financial compensation to make a more binding contract.

Chemical Bank of New York unfortunately learned this lesson the hard way. The bank used pictures of 39 employees in various advertisements designed to "humanize" the bank's image, but the employees maintained that no one had requested permission to use their photos in advertisements. The judge agreed and ruled that the bank had violated New York's privacy law. The action is called *misappropriation of personality*, which is discussed later in this chapter.

> **"** *If I used my mother in an ad, I'd get her permission—and I almost trust her 100 percent.* **"** Jerry Della Femina, advertising executive

Written permission also should be obtained if the employee's photograph is to appear in sales brochures or even in the corporate annual report. This rule also applies to other situations. A graduate of Lafayette College sued the college for using a photo of his mother and him at graduation ceremonies, without their permission, in a financial aid brochure.

Media Inquiries about Employees

Because press inquiries have the potential of invading an employee's right of privacy, public relations personnel should follow basic guidelines as to what information will be provided on the employee's behalf.

In general, employers should give a news reporter only basic information:

Do Provide
- » Confirmation that the person is an employee
- » The person's title and job description
- » The date of beginning employment, or, if applicable, date of termination

Do Not Provide Employee's

- » Salary
- » Home address
- » Marital status
- » Number of children
- » Organizational memberships
- » Job performance information

If a reporter does seek any of this information, because of the nature of the story, several methods can be followed. First, you can volunteer to contact the employee and explain that a reporter would like to speak with him or her. If the employee agrees to speak with the reporter, this absolves the company of responsibility. Second, many organizations do provide additional information to a reporter if it is included on an optional biographical sheet that the employee has filled out. In most cases, the form clearly states that the organization may use any of the information in answering press inquiries or writing its own news releases.

A typical biographical form may have sections in which the employee can list such things as memberships in community organizations, professional affiliations, educational background, past titles and positions, and even special achievements. This sheet should not be confused with the person's official employment application, which must remain confidential. It's also important to keep bio sheets up to date; one compiled by an employee five years ago may be hopelessly out of date.

Employee Blogs

Many organizations now encourage employees to have a **blog** as a way of fostering discussion on the Internet and obtaining informal feedback from the public. In some large companies, even top executives have a blog, although public relations professionals often do most of the actual writing. In most cases, the blog is clearly identified with the creator and gives information (and images) about the employer. As John Elasser, editor of *Public Relations Tactics*, says, "Some of that content may be innocuous; other types may be embarrassing or come back to haunt the company in litigation."

Consequently, organizations should have guidelines for what rank-and-file employees, as well as public relations writers, can and cannot say on their blogs or even their Facebook pages. One consideration is the protection of proprietary information such as financial data, marketing strategies, legal proceedings, or impending changes in executive personnel. Google, for example, fired an employee blogger for leaking information about an impending raise in salaries for all employees.

Employee bloggers are also discouraged from talking about fellow colleagues or making comments about supervisors and executives. Such postings can invade the privacy of other employees and even lead to lawsuits if someone feels that he or she has been ridiculed or defamed in some way. The U.S. Equal Employment Opportunity Commission, for example, has a number of regulations protecting employees against discrimination in terms of religion, ethnic background, gender, and even their English skills. Employee statements on their own personal blogs or Facebook also have legal ramifications, which are discussed in the Tips for Success on page 279.

Tips for Success Can Facebook Get You Fired?

All employees should realize that they can get fired for (1) posting inappropriate comments on the organization's email system, (2) surfing the Internet at work, and (3) even criticizing their boss on their Facebook page.

Organizational Email

A number of court decisions have reinforced the right of employers to read employee emails. Pillsbury, for example, fired a worker for posting a message to a fellow employee that called management a bunch of "back-stabbing bastards." Other employers have successfully fired workers who used company email for posting racial slurs, harassing fellow workers, and sharing off-color jokes. Employees have also been fired for posting emails to outsiders that included proprietary information such as trade secrets. In other words, you should assume that any emails you write at work are subject to monitoring and that you can be fired for violating company guidelines.

Surfing the Net

Surfing the Internet at work for personal reasons can also get you fired. Employers, of course, are concerned about the loss in productivity when employees watch YouTube videos, update their Facebook page, and make bids on eBay. Employees surfing porn sites also pose a possible liability problem if other employees are offended and file a complaint with the Equal Employment Opportunity Commission (EEOC).

Venting on Your Facebook Page

It's wise to avoid ranting about your employer or boss on Facebook, which can also lead to being fired or getting involved in a long legal battle to keep your job. About 25 percent of employers surveyed by the Society of Corporate Compliance and Ethics had disciplined an employee for improper activities on social networking sites. According to a CNN report, "If a worker posts something negative, and a manager finds it, he or she can legally be fired, some employment attorneys say."

In one case, a Georgia school district fired a teacher for posting photos on her Facebook page of her drinking a glass of wine while on a European vacation. The teacher filed a lawsuit, but the case was still pending as of January 2011. The good news is that the National Labor Relations Board ruled that a Connecticut ambulance service company improperly fired a worker after she posted unflattering comments about her boss on Facebook. But the Board's lawyer also cautioned that employee comments may not be protected if they disparage supervisors about something unrelated to work, or if they are defamatory and don't have factual support.

Experts gave CNN some tips on how to avoid legal hassles or possibly lose your job because of what you post on Facebook or other social networking sites. They include: (1) Think before you post—imagine your post appearing in the newspaper the next day; (2) Be picky about whom you "friend"—only allow people you trust into your social network and don't necessarily accept all coworkers or even managers who ask to "friend" you; (3) Do it on your own time and computer—avoid using the company computer; (4) Watch what you post—many companies monitor social media comments that mention the name of the organization; and (5) Figure out privacy settings—make sure certain information doesn't reach everyone.

If employees mention the company in any way on a blog, most organizational policies require them to reveal their affiliation to ensure transparency. Cisco, for example, has a policy that states, "If you comment on any aspect of the company's business or any policy issue the company is involved in…you must clearly identify yourself in your postings or blog site and include a disclaimer that the views are your own and not those of Cisco."

> **"** *If someone is a fisherman and they want to talk about fly fishing outside of work, that's not our business. But if someone is going to talk about notebooks, they have to say they are from Dell.* **"** Bob Pearson, vice president of Dell computers

Copyright Law

Should a news release be copyrighted? What about a corporate annual report? Can a Dilbert comic strip be featured in the company magazine without obtaining permission from the strip's creator? What about reprinting an article from *Fortune* magazine and distributing it to the company's sales staff? Are government reports copyrighted? What about posting a video clip from Comedy Central on YouTube? What constitutes copyright infringement?

These are just some of the bothersome questions that a public relations writer should be able to answer. Knowledge of copyright law is important from two perspectives: (1) what organizational materials should be copyrighted and (2) how to correctly utilize the copyrighted materials of others. A list of guidelines on page 281 can help you sort it all out.

In very simple terms, ***copyright*** means protection of a creative work from unauthorized use. U.S. copyright law states: "Copyright protection subsists…in the original works of authorship fixed in any tangible medium of expression now known or later developed." The word *authorship* is defined in seven categories: (1) literary works; (2) musical works; (3) dramatic works; (4) pantomimes and choreographic works; (5) pictorial, graphic, or sculptural works; (6) motion pictures; and (7) sound recordings. The word *fixed* means that the work is sufficiently permanent or stable to permit it to be perceived, reproduced, or otherwise communicated.

Thus, a copyright does not protect ideas, but only the specific ways in which those ideas are expressed. An idea for promoting a product, for example, cannot be copyrighted—but brochures, drawings, news features, animated cartoons, display booths, photographs, recordings, videotapes, corporate symbols, slogans, and the like that express a particular idea can be copyrighted.

Under current law, a work is automatically copyrighted the moment it is "fixed" in tangible form. Although such a "work" doesn't have to carry a notice of copyright, many organizations take the extra precaution of using the letter "c" in a circle (©), followed by the word *copyright* and citing the year of copyright to discourage unauthorized use. A more formal step is official registration with the Copyright Office of the Library of Congress. Registration isn't necessary for copyright protection, but it is often helpful in a court case against unauthorized use by others.

A copyright, under current U.S. law, protects original material for the life of the creator plus 70 years for individual works and 95 years from publication for copyrights held by corporations. This is often called the "Mickey Mouse" law because Walt Disney Corporation lobbied Congress to extend copyright protection of its Mickey Mouse character that was due to expire.

Tips for Success   How to Use Copyrighted Material for Fun and Profit

Keep the following guidelines in mind when reproducing materials:

+ Ideas cannot be copyrighted, but the expression of those ideas is protected.

+ An entire article that is emailed to a large number of people or posted on a website or a blog requires the permission of the publication or creator of the work.

+ Using news clips to track coverage is acceptable, but distribution of clips to a large audience is a violation of copyright.

+ Major public relations materials (brochures, annual reports, videotapes, motion pictures, position papers, and the like) should be copyrighted, if only to prevent unauthorized use by competitors.

+ Although there is a concept of fair use, any copyrighted material intended directly to advance the sales and profits of an organization should not be used unless permission is given.

+ Copyrighted material should not be taken out of context, particularly if it implies endorsement of the organization's services or products.

+ Quantity reprints of an article should be ordered from the publisher.

+ Permission is required to use segments of television programs or motion pictures.

+ Permission from a recording company must be obtained to use segments of popular songs (written verses or sound recordings).

+ Photographers and freelance writers retain the rights to their works. Permission and fees must be negotiated to use works for other purposes than originally agreed upon.

+ Photographs of current celebrities or those who are now deceased cannot be used for promotion and publicity purposes without permission.

+ Permission is required to reprint cartoon characters, such as Snoopy or Garfield. In addition, cartoons and other artwork or illustrations in a publication are copyrighted.

+ Government documents are not copyrighted, but caution is necessary if the material is used in a way that implies endorsement of products or services.

+ Private letters, or excerpts from them, cannot be published or used in sales and publicity materials without the permission of the letter writer.

+ Original material posted on the Internet has copyright protection.

+ The copyrighted material of others should not be posted on the Internet unless specific permission is granted.

Not all materials, however, have copyright protection. Some material is considered to be in the *public domain* because of its age. Many literary classics and the works of great composers such as Chopin can be used without violating copyright. Materials produced by the federal government can also be used freely, but there are some guidelines regarding their use that are discussed further in the next section.

Fair Use versus Infringement

Public relations writers are in the business of gathering information from a variety of sources, so it is important to know where fair use ends and infringement begins. This also applies to **plagiarism,** which is explained in the Tips for Success below.

Fair use means that part of a copyrighted article can be quoted directly, but the quoted material must be brief in relation to the length of the original work. It may be, for example, only one paragraph in a 750-word article and up to 300 words in a long article or book chapter. Complete attribution of the source must be given regardless of the length of a quotation. In the case of using a source or a quote in an ad

Tips for Success   Don't Plagiarize: It's Unethical

Copyright infringement and plagiarism differ. You may be guilty of copyright infringement even if you attribute the materials and give the source but don't get permission from the author or publisher to reproduce the materials.

In the case of plagiarism, the author makes no attempt to attribute the information at all. As the guide for Hamilton College says, "Plagiarism is a form of fraud. You plagiarize if you present other writer's words or ideas as your own." Maurice Isserman, writing in the *Chronicle of Higher Education*, explains, "Plagiarism substitutes someone else's prowess at explanation for your own efforts." At its most basic level, plagiarism is using sentences and paragraphs from someone else's work without attribution or quote marks.

The Internet has increased the problems of plagiarism because it is quite easy for anyone, from students to college presidents, to cut and paste entire paragraphs (or even pages) into a term paper or speech and claim them as their own creation. Of course, getting away with it has become more difficult because of sophisticated tools such as Turnitin (www.turnitin.com), which can scan the Internet and find the exact sentence or paragraph that the student copied and pasted into a paper.

John Barrie, founder of Turnitin, told *The Wall Street Journal* that ". . . 85 percent of the cases of plagiarism that we see are straight copies from the Internet—a student uses the Internet like a 1.5 billion-page cut-and-paste encyclopedia." Most universities have very strong rules about plagiarism, and it is not uncommon for students to receive an "F" in a course for plagiarism. In the business world, stealing someone else's words and expression of thought is called theft of intellectual property and employees, including CEOs, are fired. In sum, don't use "cut-and-paste" as a substitute for producing your own work. If someone's sentence or paragraph is really great, at least put it in quotes and give proper attribution.

or promotional brochure, it's necessary for the original source to approve the quote and the context in which it's used.

The copyright law does allow limited copying of a work for fair use such as criticism, comment, or research. If an organization wants to reprint multiple copies of a newspaper or magazine article, however, a licensing fee must be paid directly to the publisher or through the Copyright Clearing Center (www.copyright.com). *The Wall Street Journal*, for example, has a whole department (www.djreprints.com) that arranges reprints that can be used in print, email, or PDF formats.

Government documents, as already noted, are in the public domain. Public relations personnel, under the fair use doctrine, can freely use quotations and statistics from a government document. Care must be exercised, however, to ensure that the material is in context and not misleading. The most common problem occurs when an organization uses a government report as a form of endorsement for its services or products. An airline, for example, might cite a government study showing that its on-time arrivals are the best in the industry, but neglect to state the basis of comparison or other mediating factors.

Photography and Artwork

Copyright law makes it clear that freelance and commercial photographers retain ownership of their work. In other words, a customer who buys a copyrighted photo owns the item itself, but not the right to make additional copies. That right remains with the photographer unless transferred in writing to the individual or organization that has bought the photograph.

Freelance photographers generally charge for a picture on the basis of its use. If it is used only once, perhaps for an employee newsletter, the fee is low. If, however, the company wants to use the picture in the corporate annual report or on the company calendar, the fee may be considerably higher. Consequently it is important for a public relations person to tell the photographer exactly how the picture will be used. Arrangements and fees then can be determined for (1) one-time use, (2) unlimited use, or (3) the payment of royalties every time the picture is used.

Computer manipulation of an original artwork can also violate copyright. A photo distribution agency successfully sued *Newsday* for unauthorized use of a color image after the newspaper altered the agency's original picture and claimed it as its own photo. In another situation, the Rock and Roll Hall of Fame filed a copyright suit against a freelance photographer who snapped a picture of the unique building at sunset and sold posters of his work without paying a licensing fee.

Work for Hire

Copyright automatically belongs to the creator of the work, but the "work for hire" concept provides a notable exception. If you create a work as an employee of an organization, the copyright belongs to the organization. In other words, all those wonderful news releases and brochures that you write and produce on the job belong to your employer.

It gets a bit more complicated, however, when an organization outsources work to a freelancer such as the writing of a brochure or a feature story. The U.S. Supreme

Court has ruled that freelance writers retain ownership of their work and that purchasers of it simply gain a "license" to reproduce the copyrighted work. In other words, a freelancer commissioned to write an article for the company magazine or a feature distributed to the media can also use the same information to sell articles to other publications. That's why it's important for public relations staffs to negotiate contracts with freelancers. Writers may agree to assign all copyright rights to the work they have been hired to do or they may give permission only for a specific one-time use.

Use of Online Material

The same rules apply to cyberspace as to more earthbound methods of expressing and disseminating ideas. Original materials in digital form are still protected by copyright and fair use guidelines apply for materials disseminated online. An organization, for example, may receive digital copies of media stories about the organization as a way to track its publicity efforts, but it can't automatically distribute a published article on its own website or intranet without permission from the publication where the article appeared. In many cases, the monitoring service arranges for such permissions.

An organization's public relations staff members can also be liable for copyright infringement if they upload a copyrighted photo or cartoon to the organization's website or other sites as part of a media kit or a feature news story. The following are some examples of copyright owners monitoring the Internet for possible infringement:

» Dutton Children's Books threatened a lawsuit against a New Mexico State University student for using Winnie the Pooh illustrations on his home page.

» Paramount Pictures sent warning letters to *Star Trek* fans for posting photos from the TV series on various Internet sites.

» Corbis Corporation, which has millions of photos for licensing or purchase, threatened legal action against a retirement community for using a photo of an elderly couple on its website without paying the licensing fee.

In all cases, it is the obligation of the staff to determine conditions of use and whether a licensing fee should be paid. The legal aspects are somewhat related to the concept of *misappropriation of personality* that is discussed under trademarks.

Trademark Law

What do the names Big Gulp, iTunes, Dockers, eBay, Academy Awards, Xbox, American Idol, Bubble Wrap, Frappucino, and even Ziploc have in common? Or what about "A diamond is forever," "Priceless," or "Just do it"? They are all registered trademarks protected by law. Public relations writers must know how to use trademarks in their writing. Failure to properly use a trademark frequently causes legal problems.

A **trademark** is a word, symbol, or slogan, used singly or in combination, that identifies a product's origin. According to Susan L. Cohen, writing in *Editor & Publisher's* annual trademark supplement, "It also serves as an indicator of quality, a kind of short-hand for consumers to use in recognizing goods in a complex marketplace." Research indicates, for example, that a majority of Americans say brand quality takes precedence over price considerations.

The concept of a trademark is nothing new. The ancient Egyptians carved marks into the stones of the pyramids, and the craftsmen of the Middle Ages used guild marks to identify the source and quality of products. What is new, however, is the proliferation of trademarks and service marks in modern society. Coca-Cola, Google, and Microsoft are some of the world's most recognized brands, but they are only some of more than 1 million active trademarks registered with the U.S. Patent and Trademark Office.

The Protection of Trademarks

The three basic guidelines for using trademarks are as follows:

» Trademarks are proper adjectives and should be capitalized and followed by a generic noun or phrase. For example, Kleenex tissues or Rollerblade skates.

» Trademarks should not be pluralized or used in the possessive form. Saying "American Express's credit card" is improper.

» Trademarks are never verbs. Saying "The client FedExed the package" violates the rule.

In addition, organizations take the step of designating brand names and slogans with various marks. The registered trademark symbol is a superscript, small capital "R" in a circle—®. "Registered in U.S. Patent and Trademark Office" and "Reg. U.S. Pat. Off." may also be used. A superscript "TM" in small capital letters indicates a trademark that isn't registered. It represents a company's common-law claim to a right of trademark or a trademark for which registration is pending. For example, 3M™ Post-it® Notes (see Figure 11.1).

A service mark is like a trademark, but it designates a service rather than a product, or is a logo. An "SM" in small capitals in a circle ℠ is the symbol for a registered service mark. If registration is pending, the "SM" should be used without the circle.

These symbols are used in advertising, product labeling, news releases, company brochures, and so on to let the public and competitors know that a name, slogan, or symbol is protected by law. Many news releases, for example, include a standard statement at the end that gives a brief description of the company and its trademarks. Here is one example: "Teva®, Simple®, and UGG® are registered trademarks of Deckers Outdoor Corporation."

Public relations writers play an important role in protecting the trademarks of their employers. They safeguard trademarks and respect other organizational trademarks in the following ways:

» Ensuring that company trademarks are capitalized and used properly in all organizational literature and graphics. Lax supervision can cause loss of trademark protection.

Remember,

There's only one Post-it® Note and it's from 3M. Please help us protect our trademark by including the ® when you write about Post-it® Notes or our other Post-it® products. And since a trademark is an adjective, follow it up with an appropriate noun: Post-it® Software Notes, for example. The Post-it® trademark is a name you can trust — please help us keep it that way.

Post-it®
Notes

3M *Innovation*

© 1996, 3M. "Post-it" is a registered trademark of 3M.

FIGURE 11.1 Brand names in news releases usually include trademark symbols to remind journalists that they should capitalize the first letter of the product or service in any article. The letter "R" with a circle around it indicates that Post-it is a registered trademark that is always capitalized and spelled in a specific way.

» Distributing trademark guidelines to editors and reporters and placing advertisements in trade publications. An example is the National Association of Realtors ad in Figure 11.2.

» Educating employees as to what the organization's trademarks are and how to use them correctly.

» Monitoring the mass media and news websites to make certain that trademarks are used correctly. If they are not, send a gentle reminder.

» Monitoring publications to ensure that other organizations are not infringing on a registered trademark. If they are, the company's legal department should

FIGURE 11.2 Protection of trademarks requires diligence. The National Association of Realtors places ads in consumer magazines to educate the public that "Realtor" is a trademarked name used only by individuals who have passed exams and have been certified. Anyone, however, can be a "real estate agent"

protest with letters and threats of possible lawsuits.

» Making sure the trademark is actually being used. The law no longer permits an organization to hold a name in reserve.

» Ensuring that the trademarks of other organizations are correctly used and properly noted. A good source is the International Trademark Association (www.inta.org); it has a directory of more than 3,000 trademarks and service marks with their generic terms.

» Avoiding the use of trademarked symbols or cartoon figures in promotional materials without the explicit permission of the owner. In some cases, to be discussed, a licensing fee is required.

Organizations adamantly insist on the proper use of trademarks in order to avoid the problem of having a name or slogan become generic. Or, to put it another way, a brand name may become a common noun through general public use. Some trade names that have become generic include *aspirin, thermos, cornflakes, nylon, cellophane,* and *yo-yo*. This means that any company can use these names to describe a product. An additional list of trademarked brands is provided in the Tips for Success on page 288.

The Problem of Trademark Infringement

There are thousands of companies offering a multitude of products and services, so finding a trademark that is not already in use is extremely difficult. The task is even more frustrating if a company wants to use a trademark on an international level.

The complexity of finding a new name, coupled with the attempts of many to capitalize on an already known trade name, has spawned a number of legal battles and lawsuits claiming trademark infringement. Here are some examples:

» *Entrepreneur* magazine was awarded $337,000 in court damages after filing a trademark infringement lawsuit against a public relations firm that changed its name to "EntrepreneurPR."

» Best Buy, which has trademarked "The Geek Squad," sued its online rival Newegg.com for using the term, "Geek On" in its advertising. It also threatened to sue a Wisconsin priest for putting a "God Squad" sign on his car.

» Microsoft sued Apple in 2011 for trying to trademark "app store" and Apple was suing Amazon.com for using the term. Most experts predicted that "app store" probably can't be trademarked because it's a common term used in the high-tech industry since 1985.

» Martha Stewart's attempt to trademark the name "Katonah" for a new line of home furnishings raised the ire and organized protest of a suburban New York town of the same name.

» Facebook filed an infringement lawsuit against start-up Placebook (a travel site), which forced the site to change its name.

» Anheuser-Busch filed a trademark infringement suit against a North Carolina college student for producing and selling T-shirts that said "Nags Head, NC—King of Beaches" and "This Beach is for You."

» Cisco Systems, claiming that it had already trademarked the term "iPhone," filed an infringement suit against Apple. Cisco lost, and the rest is history.

In all of these cases, organizations claimed that their registered trademarks were being improperly exploited by others for commercial or organizational purposes. Sports franchises are particularly protective of their trademarks. Teams in the National Football League and the National Basketball Association earn more than $3 billion annually just selling licensed merchandise. Major college teams also rake in millions of dollars annually by licensing their logos to be placed on everything from beer mugs to T-shirts.

Perhaps the most zealously guarded and expensive sports trademark is the Olympic rings. For the Beijing Olympics, companies paid up to $100 million for the

Tips for Success   Trademarks Require a Capital Letter

Trademarked names are like proper nouns: They are capitalized and should be followed by a generic noun or phrase. The International Trademark Association (INTA) also recommends that trademarks should never be pluralized, used in possessive form, or used as verbs. Currently, more than 700,000 trademarks are registered with the U.S. government. Here is a sampling of trademarks that are often assumed to be generic words:

Jaws of Life	Band-Aid	Chap Stick	Day-Timer	DeskJet
Frisbee	Gatorade	Hula Hoop	Handi Wipes	Muzak
Realtor	NutraSweet	Spandex	Express Mail	Rolodex
StairMaster	Teflon	MapQuest	WebCrawler	Scotch tape

Source: International Trademark Association, www.inta.org.

FIGURE 11.3 The Olympic rings logo is one of the world's most recognized brands. It is trademarked by the International Olympic Committee (IOC) and cannot be used without the hefty payment of licensing fees. The logo for the 2012 London Olympics is also trademarked and can only be used by official sponsors, who pay up to $100 million in licensing fees.

right to use the Olympic symbol in their marketing and public relations efforts. See the logo for the London 2012 games in Figure 11.3.

The following are the major guidelines that the courts use when considering cases of trademark infringement:

» Has the defendant used a name as a way of capitalizing on the reputation of another organization's trademark— and does the defendant benefit from the original organization's investment in popularizing its trademark?

» Is there an intent (real or otherwise) to create confusion in the public mind? Is there intent to imply a connection between the defendant's product and the item identified by trademark?

» How similar are the two organizations? Are they providing the same kinds of products or services?

» Has the original organization actively protected the trademark by publicizing it and by actually continuing to use it in connection with its products or services?

» Is the trademark unique? A company with a trademark that merely describes a common product might be in trouble.

Misappropriation of Personality

Another form of trademark infringement can result from the unauthorized use of well-known entertainers, professional athletes, and other public figures in an organization's publicity and advertising materials. A photo of a rock star or movie star might make a company's brochure or newsletter more interesting, but the courts call it *misappropriation of personality* if permission and licensing fees have not been negotiated.

Deceased celebrities also are protected. To use a likeness or actual photo of a personality such as Michael Jackson, Marilyn Monroe, or even Princess Diana, the user must pay a licensing fee to an agent representing the family, studio, or estate of the deceased. The estate of John Lennon, for example, generates about $45 million annually, and the estate of Peanuts comic strip creator Charles Schulz collects about $35 million annually.

In sum, you need to be familiar with what might be considered trademark infringement. Don't use stock photos of living or dead personalities or a Dilbert or Peanuts comic strip unless you have arranged permission and, in many cases, paid a licensing fee. Also, be cautious about using a known slogan as the basis for coming up with a similar slogan. One nonprofit was sued by the International Olympic Committee for having a "Reading Olympics."

Regulatory Agencies

The promotion of products and services, whether through advertising, product publicity, or other techniques, is not protected by the First Amendment. Instead, the courts have traditionally ruled that such activities fall under the doctrine of commercial speech. This means that messages can be regulated by state or federal agencies in the interest of public health, safety, and consumer protection.

Public relations writers involved in product publicity and the distribution of financial information should be aware of guidelines established by four federal agencies: (1) the Federal Trade Commission, (2) the Securities and Exchange Commission, (3) the Federal Communications Commission, and (4) the Food and Drug Administration.

The Federal Trade Commission

The **Federal Trade Commission (FTC)** ensures that advertisements are not deceptive or misleading. The agency also has jurisdiction over product news releases and other forms of product publicity, such as videos and brochures.

The FTC considers advertisements and product publicity materials as vehicles of commercial trade—and therefore subject to regulation. In fact, Section 43(a) of the Lanham Act makes it clear that anyone, including public relations personnel, is subject to liability if that person participates in the making or dissemination of a false and misleading representation in any advertising or promotional material. This includes advertising and public relations firms, which also can be held liable for writing, producing, and distributing product publicity materials on behalf of clients.

❝ There is a trend toward potential claims, including PR firms, for their role in disseminating a message that is misleading or ... has omitted material facts. ❞ Michael Lasky, partner in the New York law firm of Davis & Gilbert

The prospect of liability for communicating false or misleading information has led many public relations firms to sign contracts with clients that stipulate that clients are legally responsible for any information about their products and services that may be distributed by a public relations firm. Despite such agreements, however, the FTC contends that public relations firms can still be held liable for disseminating client messages if there is a justifiable reason for them to suspect the client may be misleading the public, either through distortion or by leaving out important information.

Ethically, a public relations professional should ensure that a client's claims can be substantiated and there's statistical evidence to support any claims. Gene Grabowski, senior vice president of Levick Strategic Communications, told *PRWeek*, "We can serve as a check for the client. And we consider that part of our job because as a communicator, you can easily get into competitive entanglements or litigious issues."

FTC investigators are always on the lookout for unsubstantiated claims and various forms of misleading or deceptive information. Some of the common words in promotional materials that trigger FTC interest include *authentic*, *certified*, *cure*, *custom-made*, *germ-free*, *natural*, *unbreakable*, *perfect*, *first-class*, *exclusive*, and *reliable*.

In recent years, the agency has also turned its attention to companies promoting their products as "green," "organic," or "eco-friendly." According to James Kohm, associate director of FTC's enforcement division, there has been a "tsunami of green marketing claims" for all kinds of products that has confused and frustrated consumers. As a result, the FTC guidelines now say companies must provide facts and data to substantiate any "green" product claims in ads, product news releases, and on packaging. See the Tips for Success below for additional guidelines on writing product news releases.

+

Tips for Success   FTC Guidelines for Publicizing Products

The following guidelines, adapted from regulations of the Federal Trade Commission (FTC), should be taken into account when writing product publicity materials:

+ Make sure the information is accurate and can be substantiated.

+ Stick to the facts. Don't **hype** the product or service by using flowery, nonspecific adjectives and ambiguous claims.

+ Make sure celebrities or others who endorse the product actually use it. They should not say anything about the product's properties that cannot be substantiated.

+ Watch the language. Don't say "independent research study" when the research was done by the organization's staff.

+ Provide proper context for statements and statistics attributed to government agencies. They don't endorse products.

+ Describe tests and surveys in sufficient detail so the consumer understands what was tested under what conditions.

+ Remember that a product is not "new" if only the packaging has been changed or the product is more than six months old.

+ When comparing products or services with a competitor's, make certain you can substantiate your claims.

+ Avoid misleading and deceptive product demonstrations.

New Guidelines for Endorsements — In 2010, the FTC also expanded its guidelines for using testimonials and endorsements. Celebrities who endorse products on television talk shows, or even social media sites (i.e. Facebook or Twitter), for example, must now disclose that they're being paid to do so. In addition, they can be fined by the FTC for making false or unsubstantiated claims during a product pitch.

Bloggers and public relations firms are also under the FTC microscope. Bloggers who endorse a product or service must disclose whether they received cash, free products, or other in-kind payments to review the product and endorse it. According to Andrew Goldstein, writing in *O'Dwyer's*, "If these disclosures are not made, the post is considered to be deceptive and false or misleading. In addition, the FTC has specified that its guidelines apply not only to the provider of the product or services...but also to the advertising or PR agency that was responsible for the endorsements."

> **"Marketers have an obligation and responsibility to the public—and to their clients and employers—to ensure they provide the most trustful and accurate information, regardless of the medium or presentation materials used.**" PRSA position statement on FTC's environmental marketing guidelines

In a 2010 case, for example, the FTC ordered Reverb, a public relations firm, to remove deceptive reviews on the iTunes store website on behalf of video game clients. The firm was charged with having its employees pose as independent, ordinary consumers who posted favorable reviews. The consent order further prohibits Reverb from continuing such a practice, which may result in a penalty of $16,000 for each instance of violating the order.

Goldstein, a partner in the law firm of Freeborn & Peters, Chicago, puts public relations firms on notice about the FTC rules regarding disclosure:

> The FTC's message here is clear; any advertisement or communications messages, including blogs or other online posts, that endorse a product or service must clearly and prominently disclose whether the endorser was hired by or received any payment, free products, or other considerations from the provider. If these disclosures are not made, the provider of the product or service and/or the PR or advertising agency responsible for the endorsements, and their owners and principals, may be held liable for deceptive and false or misleading advertising.

The Securities and Exchange Commission

Company megamergers, stock offerings in new companies, and major financial scandals have made the **Securities and Exchange Commission (SEC)** practically a household name. This federal agency closely monitors the financial affairs of publicly traded companies and protects the interests of stockholders.

SEC guidelines on public disclosure and insider trading are particularly relevant to corporate public relations staff members who must meet the requirements. The distribution of misleading information or failure to make a timely disclosure of material information may be the basis of liability under the SEC code. A company may even be liable if it satisfies regulations by getting information out but conveys crucial information in a vague way or buries it deep in the news release.

The SEC has volumes of regulations, but there are three basic concepts that you should remember:

» Full information must be given on anything that might materially affect the company's stock. This includes such things as (1) dividends or their deletion, (2) annual and quarterly earnings, (3) stock splits, (4) mergers or takeovers, (5) major management changes, (6) major product developments, (7) expansion plans, (8) change of business purpose, (9) defaults, (10) proxy materials, (11) disposition of major assets, (12) purchase of own stock, and (13) announcements of major contracts or orders.

» Timely disclosure is essential. A company must act promptly (within minutes or a few hours) to dispel or confirm rumors that result in unusual market activity or market variations. The most common ways of dispensing such financial information are through newswire services and directly contacting major financial news services such as Dow Jones, Bloomberg, or Reuters.

» Insider trading is illegal. Company officials, including public relations staffs and outside counsel, cannot use inside information to buy and sell company stock.

The courts are increasingly applying the mosaic doctrine to financial information. A court may examine all information released by a company, including news releases, to determine whether, taken as a whole, they create an "overall misleading" impression. In *Cytryn v. Cook* (1990), a U.S. District Court ruled that the proper test of a company's adequate financial disclosure was not the literal truth of each positive statement, but the overall misleading impression that it combined to create in the eyes of potential investors.

As a result of such cases, writers of financial news releases must also avoid such practices as:

» Unrealistic sales and earnings reports

» Glowing descriptions of products in the experimental stage

» Announcements of possible mergers or takeovers that are only in the speculation stage

» Free trips for business reporters and offers of stock to financial analysts and editors of financial newsletters

» Omission of unfavorable news and developments

» Leaks of information to selected outsiders and financial columnists

» Dissemination of false rumors about a competitor's financial health

The SEC also has regulations supporting the use of "plain English" in prospectuses and other financial documents. Companies and financial firms are supposed to make information understandable to the average investor by removing sentences littered with lawyerisms such as *aforementioned, hereby, therewith, whereas,* and *hereinafter.* More information about SEC guidelines can be accessed at its website (www.sec.gov).

A key SEC regulation is the Fair Disclosure regulation (known as Reg FD). Although SEC regulations already mandated "material disclosure" of information that could affect the price of stock, this regulation expands the concept by requiring publicly traded companies to broadly disseminate "material" information via news releases, webcasts, or SEC filings.

According to the SEC, Reg FD ensures that all investors, not just brokerage firms and analysts, will receive financial information from a company at the same time. Schering-Plough, a drugmaker, was fined $1 million by the SEC because the company disclosed "material nonpublic information" to analysts and portfolio managers without making the same information available to the public.

The Federal Communications Commission

The **Federal Communications Commission (FCC)** provides licenses to radio and television stations, allocates frequencies, and ensures that the public airwaves are used in the public interest. On occasion, the commission's policies and procedures directly impact the work of public relations personnel and writers who produce and distribute video news releases (VNRs) and B-roll packages on behalf of employers and clients (see Chapter 9).

According to FCC rules, broadcasters must disclose to viewers the origin of material produced by the government or corporations when the material runs on the public airways. FCC Commissioner Jonathan Edelstein told the *Washington Post*, "We have a responsibility to tell broadcasters they have to let people know where the material is coming from. Viewers are hoodwinked into thinking it's really a news story when it might be from the government or a big corporation trying to influence the way they think."

The failure of a news announcer to identify the source of a VNR or a video clip on the air is one issue, but another issue involves what is known as **pay-for-play,** which is also against FCC guidelines. In one instance, toy manufacturers paid up to $11, 000 to be part of a series of back-to-school news features that aired in 10 major U.S. cities. According to the *Los Angeles Times*, the segments featured a "toy expert" who was paid to promote the toys. Many of the stations using the "news features" failed to identify them as paid promotions.

Although the FCC only regulates and fines stations for engaging in pay-for-play tactics and failing to identify the source of video clips in news programs, public relations professionals must also ensure that their employers and clients don't participate in or initiate "pay-for-play" strategies.

The Food and Drug Administration

The **Food and Drug Administration (FDA)** oversees the advertising and promotion of prescription drugs, over-the-counter medicines, and cosmetics. Under the Food, Drug, and Cosmetic Act, any "person" (which includes advertising and public relations firms) who "causes the misbranding" of products through the dissemination of false and misleading information may be liable.

The FDA has specific guidelines for video, audio, and print news releases on health care topics. First, the release must provide "fair balance" by telling consumers about the risks as well as the benefits of the drug or treatment. Second, the writer must be clear about the limitations of a particular drug or treatment, for example, that it might not help people with certain conditions. Third, a news release or media kit should be accompanied by supplementary product sheets or brochures that give full prescribing information.

Because prescription drugs have major FDA curbs on advertising and promotion, the drug companies try to sidestep the regulations by publicizing diseases. Eli Lilly & Co., the maker of Prozac, provides a good example. The company sponsors ads and distributes publicity about depression. The Glaxo Institute for Digestive Health conducts information campaigns about the fact that stomach pains can be an indication of major problems. Of course, Glaxo also makes the ulcer drug Zantac.

Another public relations approach that has come under increased FDA scrutiny is the placement of celebrities on television talk shows who are being paid by the drug companies to mention the name of a particular drug while they talk about their recovery from cancer, a heart attack, or depression. Some programs, such as the *Today* show, have now banned such guests.

Always minimize the risk of handing over a communication that could result in regulatory action by scrutinizing not only what is being said, but how it is said, how it is presented and what, in the end, is the total picture. Mark Senak, senior vice president of Fleischman Hillard's health care practice

Working with Lawyers

You now have an overview of how various laws and government regulations affect your work as a public relations writer and specialist. A basic knowledge of the law should help you do your work in a responsible and appropriate manner, but you also should realize that a smattering of knowledge can be dangerous.

Laws and regulations can be complex. You are not a trained attorney, so you should consult lawyers who are qualified to answer specialized questions regarding libel, copyright, trademarks, government regulation, and invasion of privacy. Your organization's legal staff or outside experts on retainer are good sources of information.

At the same time, remember that lawyers can tell you about the law; they should not tell you what to say or how to say it. They are legal experts, but not experts on effective writing and communication. They don't understand that the media want information now or that "no comment" is perceived as a guilty plea in the court of public opinion.

Indeed, a major area of friction can be the clash between the legal and public relations departments. Lawyers generally prefer to say little or nothing in most situations, whereas the public relations staff perceives its role as providing a steady flow of information and news about the organization to multiple publics. The result is often a never-ending tug-of-war. At the same time, it is essential that the legal and public relations staffs cooperate in the best interests of the organization.

Great care must be taken in releasing information about litigation, labor negotiations, complex financial transactions, product recalls, and plant accidents. Numerous laws and regulations, to say nothing of liability considerations, affect what should or should not be said. Out-of-court settlements, for example, often stipulate that the amount of the settlement will not be publicly disclosed. This is why it is often important to work with legal staff to draft news releases that provide information but keep within the bounds of any legal constraints.

Your relations with legal counsel will be more pleasant and more productive if you keep abreast of new developments. To do this, you should maintain a file of newspaper and magazine articles that report on legal developments and decisions relating to public relations. This might include new regulatory guidelines, consent decrees, libel awards, trademark infringement suits, product recalls, and court decisions on employee privacy.

The following guidelines can go a long way in ensuring cooperation and mutual respect between the legal and public relations functions:

» Each department should have a written definition of its responsibilities.

» The heads of both departments should be equal in rank and should report to the organization's chief executive officer or executive vice president.

» Both departments should be represented on key committees.

» The legal counsel should keep the public relations staff up to date on legal problems involving the organization.

» The public relations staff should keep the legal staff up to date on public issues and media concerns that will require an organizational response.

» The departments should regard each other as allies, not opponents.

Summary

A Sampling of Legal Problems

» A public relations practitioner can get caught up in a lawsuit or a complaint by a government regulatory agency in any number of ways. Practitioners may be held legally liable if they provide advice or support the illegal activity of a client.

Libel and Defamation

» The concept of defamation can involve false, malicious, or negligent communication about an individual who is injured either financially or by loss of reputation.

» Libel suits can be avoided through the careful use of language.

Invasion of Privacy

» Organizations should only cover the work-related activities of their employ-

ees in newsletters. It is important to get written permission to publish photos or use employees in advertising materials and to be cautious in releasing personal information about employees to the media.

» Employees should be cautious expressing criticism about their employer on blogs and social media sites. Online communication can be monitored by the employer, and employees can be fired for revealing trade secrets or harassing fellow employees through email or websites.

» Companies also have guidelines for employee blogs. Employees, as well as public relations writers, should identify their affiliation if they are writing a blog or posting messages on social media sites if they are making comments about their employer and its products.

Copyright Law

» Copyright is the protection of creative work from unauthorized use. It is assumed that published works are copyrighted, and permission must be obtained to reprint such material.

» The "fair use" doctrine allows limited use of copyrighted material if it is properly attributed and quotation marks are used.

» Unless a company has a specific contract with a freelance writer, photographer, or artist to produce work that will be exclusively owned by that company (a situation called "work for hire"), the freelancer owns his or her work.

» Copyrighted materials cannot be downloaded or uploaded to Internet sites unless permission is given.

Trademark Law

» A trademark is a word, symbol, or slogan that identifies a product's origin. Trademarks are always capitalized and used as adjectives rather than nouns or verbs. Companies vigorously protect trademarks to prevent their becoming common nouns.

» Misappropriation of personality is a form of trademark infringement. It's the use of a celebrity's name or image for advertising or publicity purposes without permission.

Regulatory Agencies

» Public relations materials are considered commercial speech and subject to regulations by state and federal agencies charged with protecting the consumer from false, misleading, and deceptive messages.

» Public relations personnel should be familiar with the guidelines of the FTC, SEC, FCC, and the FDA for the content and dissemination of information to the public.

Working with Lawyers

» There is always a tug-of-war between public relations staff and the staff lawyers. The worldview of public relations is disclosure and transparency. Attorneys, by nature, are often hesitant to release any information regarding information that might be litigated.

» A cooperative relationship must exist between public relations personnel and legal counsel. It helps if both groups report to the same top executive and both are represented on key committees.

Skill Building Activities

1. Rosanna's, a chain of coffee shops, wants to launch a marketing and public relations program to promote its brand. Some ideas include the following: (1) establish a website that would include photos of celebrities drinking a cup of coffee; (2) develop a series of ads showing customers in store locations enjoying a cup of coffee; (3) hire a freelance writer to develop some feature stories about the origin of various coffee beans that also provide guidelines for selecting various blends sold by the chain; (4) distribute a news release giving the results of a survey that showed coffee drinkers preferred Rosanna's coffee over Starbucks; and (5) post reprints of articles that have been written about the company on its website. What are the legal concerns surrounding each of these activities?

2. You work for a company that is experiencing a downturn in its stock price. The company president suggests the

stock could go up if you write a news release about a new, highly advanced product. The R&D department, however, says the product is only in the prototype stage and may not available for another year. Does writing and distribution of such a news release violate any SEC rules?

3. You work in media relations for a company. A local reporter calls you to tell you that one of the company's employees has just been named "Citizen of the Year" by the chamber of commerce. She's on deadline and wants you to give her as much information as possible about the employee's position, home address, marital status, number of children, hobbies, and so on so she can write a good profile of this outstanding citizen. What should you do?

4. The vice president of marketing for a microbrewery wants to jump on the "green" bandwagon, so he suggests that you write a news release proclaiming that all ingredients in the beer come from organic growers. He also says that the company's beer is the only one on the market that uses organic ingredients. Before you write the release, what questions would you ask him? How would you write a release that would satisfy FTC guidelines?

Media Resources

Borzo, J. (2011, January 21). "Employers Tread a Minefield: Firings for Alleged Social-Media Infractions Sometimes Backfire on Companies." *The Wall Street Journal*, B6.

Bustillo, M. (2011, June 20). "Now That Everyone Wants to Be a Geek, Lawyers Have Been Called." *The Wall Street Journal*, A1, 12.

Chen, S. (2010, November 12). "Can Facebook Get You Fired? Playing It Safe in the Social Media World." Retrieved from www.cnn.com.

Daniels, C. (2011, April 15). "Recent Lawsuit Sheds Light on Agency Liability." Retrieved from www.prweekus.com.

Gingerich, J. (2010, December). "Legal Hurdles, Overkill Plague Today's Celeb Endorsements." *O'Dwyer's*, 12.

Gingerich, J. (2010, November). "FTC Cracks Down on 'Green' Advertising Claims. " *O'Dwyer's*, 12.

Gingerich, J. (2010, November). "Groups Ask FCC to Investigate 'Fake' News." *O'Dwyer's*, 8.

Goldstein, A. (2010, November). "PR Firm Held Liable for iTunes Product Reviews." *O'Dwyer's*, 21.

Hsu, S. (2010, November 29). "Greenpeace Accuses Dow Chemical, Sasol and PR Allies of Corporate Spying." Retrieved from www.washingonpost.com.

Senak, M. (2010, October). "FDA Increases PhRMA Communications Scrutiny." *O'Dwyer's*, 10.

Watkins, M. (2011, January 13). "Apple Trademark Push Riles Microsoft." *Financial Times*, 8.

Tapping the Web and Digital Media

>> After reading this chapter, you will be able to:

» Understand the importance of the Internet in public relations writing

» Identify uses of the World Wide Web

» Grasp the basics of webcasting

» Unleash the power of social media

» Effectively use blogs

» Identify the continuing role of traditional media

The Internet: Pervasive in Our Lives

Today's college students have grown up with the Internet, and it's difficult to imagine life without it. Many of your parents probably do not understand that the Internet is a revolutionary concept that has transformed the media almost as much as the invention of the printing press by Gutenberg in the 1400s.

For centuries, the mass media controlled the flow of information. The media traditionally have had the following characteristics: (1) they are centralized, having a top-down hierarchy; (2) they are expensive (it costs a lot of money to become a publisher); (3) they are staffed by professional gatekeepers known as editors and publishers; and (4) they feature mostly one-way communication with limited feedback channels.

Internet-based media are characterized by (1) widespread broadband; (2) cheap/free, easy-to-use online publishing tools; (3) new distribution channels; (4) mobile devices, such as camera phones; and (5) new advertising paradigms.

The astounding growth of the Internet and the World Wide Web is old news, and any figures given today are out of date almost before they are published. Nevertheless, some statistics provide a reality check regarding the power of this medium:

» The number of worldwide Internet users is more than 2 billion people. In North America alone, there are 272 million Internet users, or about 78 percent of the population of the United States, Canada, and Mexico. The use of the Internet grew 152 percent in North America between 2000 and 2011. Internet use grew 480 percent worldwide during that same time frame.

» U.S. Internet users spent an average of 74 minutes a day online in 2011, up from 64 minutes in 2010.

» The average person in the United States spent 81 minutes a day using mobile apps in 2011, up from only 43 minutes per day in 2010.

» The World Wide Web contains 255 million websites. In 2010 alone, 21.4 million websites were added.

» There are an estimated 152 million blogs worldwide.

» Facebook had about 800 million users worldwide in 2011. Those users generated an estimated 770 billion page views each month. Facebookers collectively spent 9.3 billion hours on Facebook in a typical 2011 month. That's 1,065,449 years, according to royal.pingdom.com.

» YouTube has 490 million users worldwide. Those users watched about 2 billion videos each day in 2010. Thirty-five hours of video are uploaded to YouTube every minute.

» Twitter took 18 months to sign up its first 500,000 accounts, but in 2011 about 500,000 new accounts were added each day. Twitter users send 140 million tweets each day.

» On New Year's Day 2011, 6,939 tweets per second were sent in Japan, a record rate at the time. One hundred million new accounts were created in 2010 alone. Twenty-five billion tweets were sent in 2010.

» Lady Gaga had the most-followed Twitter account, with more than 11 million followers in 2011.

» Globally, there are now more than 5 billion cell phone subscribers. In the United States, 96 percent of the population has a cell phone.

The World Wide Web

The exponential growth of the World Wide Web is due, in large part, to its unique characteristics. The Tips for Success on page 301 compares the "traditional media" and the "new media," but here are some major characteristics of the Web that enable public relations people to do a better job of distributing a variety of messages:

» You can update information quickly, without having to reprint brochures and other materials. This is an important element when it comes to major news events or dealing with a crisis.

» It allows for interactivity; viewers can ask questions about products or services, download information of value to them, and let the organization know what they think.

» Online readers can dig deeper into subjects that interest them by linking to information provided on other sites, in other articles, and from additional sources.

Tips for Success   Traditional Media versus New Media

The World Wide Web is today's new medium. Many of its characteristics can be better understood by comparing it with traditional mass media. Kevin Kawamoto of the University of Washington compiled the following chart for a Freedom Forum seminar on technology.

Traditional Mass Media

Geographically constrained: Media geared to geographic markets or regional audience share; market specific.

Hierarchical: News and information pass through a vertical hierarchy of gatekeeping and successive editing.

Unidirectional: Dissemination of news and information is generally one-way, with restricted feedback mechanisms.

Space/time constraints: Newspapers are limited by space; radio and TV by time.

Professional communicators: Trained journalists, reporters, and experts tend to qualify as traditional media personnel.

High access costs: Cost of starting a newspaper, radio, or TV station is prohibitive for most people.

General interest: Many mainstream mass media target large audiences and thus offer broad coverage.

Linearity of content: News and information are organized in logical, linear order; news hierarchy.

Feedback: Letters to the editor, phone calls; slow, effort heavy, moderated and edited; time/space limited.

Ad-driven: Need to deliver big audiences to advertisers to generate high ad revenues; mass appeal.

Institution-bound: Many traditional media are produced by large corporations with centralized structure.

Fixed format: Content is produced, disseminated, and somewhat "fixed" in place and time.

News, values, journalistic standards: Content produced and evaluated by conventional norms and ethics.

New Media

Distance insensitive: Media geared toward needs, wants, and interests, regardless of physical location of the user; topic specific.

Flattened: News and information have the potential to spread horizontally, from nonprofessionals to other nonprofessionals.

Interactive: Feedback is immediate and often uncensored or modified; discussions and debate rather than editorials and opinions.

Less space/time constraints: Information is stored digitally; hypertext allows large volumes of info to be "layered" one atop another.

Amateurs/nonprofessionals: Anyone with requisite resources can publish on the Web, even amateur and nontrained communicators.

Low access costs: Cost of electronic publishing/ broadcasting on the Internet is much more affordable.

Customized: With fewer space/time restraints and market concerns, new media can "narrowcast" in depth to personal interests.

Nonlinearity of content: News and information linked by hypertext; navigate by interest and intuition, not by logic.

Feedback: Email, posting to online discussion groups; comparatively simple and effortless; often unedited, unmoderated.

Diverse funding sources: While advertising is increasing, other sources permit more diverse content; small audiences OK.

Decentralized: Technology allows production and dissemination of news and information to be "grassroots efforts."

Flexible format: Content is constantly changing, updated, corrected, and revised; in addition, multimedia allows the integration of multiple forms of media in one service.

Formative standards: Norms and values obscure; content produced and evaluated on its own merit and credibility.

» A great amount of material can be posted. There is no space or time limitation.

» It is a cost-effective method of disseminating information on a global basis to the public and journalists.

» You can reach niche markets and audiences on a direct basis without messages being filtered through traditional mass media gatekeepers (editors).

» The media and other users can access details about your organization 24 hours a day from anywhere in the world.

A website, from a public relations standpoint, is literally a distribution system in cyberspace. Organizations, for example, use their websites to market products and services and post news releases, corporate backgrounders, product information, position papers, and even photos of key executives or plant locations.

Organizations use their websites in different ways. Here's a sampling:

» Federal Express uses its website for customer relations. It allows customers to track shipments or locate a FedEx office by keying in a zip code or address. There is also a boldface link to the FedEx newsroom for journalists.

» Apple uses its website to give video tours of the features of its iPad.

» L. L. Bean has a website that gives a history of the company and offers outdoor adventure tours for everything from biking to fly casting, in addition to providing a catalog of its products.

» Westchester Medical Center posts podcasts about stroke prevention and heart transplants. The site also establishes the medical center as the premier medical facility by describing its multiple clinics and medical services.

» IBM, a global corporation, includes a ticker-type presentation of recent IBM news. It emphasizes its social responsibility initiatives by providing a prominent link to its current corporate responsibility report.

In celebration of its centennial, IBM used its website to build a community of volunteers. The site invited visitors to pledge themselves to volunteer service: "IBM Chairman Sam Palmisano has invited all IBMers to join him in community service by pledging at least eight hours during 2011."

» Starbucks hosts a website called My Starbucks Idea on which customers and employees can "Share, Vote, Discuss, See" ideas for new products, improved in-store experience, and ways to be involved in the community. The site was modeled as a social network where users could post comments on each other's ideas.

Various surveys indicate that journalists use websites extensively to retrieve current news releases and other materials. A survey of journalists by public relations company Cision, for example, found that 96 percent of respondents visited corporate websites for background information. Eighty-nine percent said they use blogs to do online research. Two-thirds of the journalists said they turn to social network sites like Facebook or LinkedIn when they research stories.

According to *NetMarketing*, companies are sending out fewer media kits and getting fewer phone inquiries as a result of putting material on websites. As Rick Rudman, president of Capital Hill Software, told *Public Relations Tactics*, "The days of just posting press releases on your website are gone. Today, journalists, investors, all audiences expect to find media kits, photos, annual reports, and multimedia presentations about your organization at your press center." Online newsrooms were discussed in Chapter 10.

> **"***The days of just posting press releases on your website are gone. Today, journalists, investors, all audiences expect to find media kits, photos, annual reports, and multimedia presentations about your organization at your press center.***"** Rick Rudman, president of Capital Hill Software, as quoted in *Public Relations Tactics*

Writing for the Web

A surprising number of home pages are visually boring or cluttered. In order to avoid the pitfalls of having such a home page, experts offer the following advice:

» Define the objective of the site.

» Design the site with the audience in mind.

» Don't just place existing materials on the site; redesign the material with strong graphic components.

» Update the site constantly. This is the real cost of a home page.

» Don't overdo the graphics. Complex graphics take a long time to download and can cause visitors to leave the site.

» Make the site interactive; give the user buttons to click to explore various topics.

» Use feedback (an email address or computer bulletin board) to help the site evolve.

Two basic concepts are important when writing for the Web. First, there is a fundamental difference between how people read online and how they read printed documents. According to a study by Sun Microsystems, it takes 50 percent longer for an individual to read material on a computer screen. As a consequence, 79 percent of online readers scan text instead of reading word-by-word.

Second, the public relations writer needs to know the basic difference between linear and nonlinear styles of writing. Printed material usually follows a linear progression; a person reads in a straight line from the beginning of the article to the end of it. *Nonlinear* means that items can be selected out of order; a person selects a notecard out of a stack. Online reading, say the experts, is nonlinear; people seek out particular "notecards" about an organization, a product, or a service. One person clicks the tab for price and availability of a product, whereas another clicks for more information about how to use the product in a specific situation.

This technique is called *branching*. Michael Butzgy, owner of Atomic Rom Productions in Cary, North Carolina, explains in *Communication World*, "Branching allows you to send users in specific directions. The basic idea behind branching is to eliminate the need for viewers to scroll down a long linear document." In another *Communication World* article, Jeff Herrington, owner of his own Dallas public relations firm, says:

> Rather than organize information so it runs linearly from the top of the screen to past the bottom, we want to layer the information in sections that sit like index cards in a file box, one screen behind the other. The first card (or screen) of information contains within it all the links to all the cards (or screens) behind it, and so on. That way, the online user rarely, if ever, has to perform the tedious and time-consuming task of scrolling.

Helen L. Mitternight, owner of a communications firm in Annandale, Virginia, explains nonlinear writing in yet another *Communication World* article:

> Think of it as writing in chunks, with each idea or information contained in each "chunk" (or component of your writing) complete unto itself. Identify elements of your writing that contain a single unit of information and recast it into a "chunk" that can both stand alone and work with the rest of your online piece. And, even more than most writing, shorter is better. Documents written for the Web should be 50 percent shorter than their print counterparts, according to the Sun Microsystems study.

How short is "short"? Herrington says sentences should be fewer than 20 words long and a paragraph should have only two or three sentences. An entire topic should be covered in two or three paragraphs, or about the length of one screen. This approach, he says, recognizes the fact that people scan material and dislike scrolling to view other links to the topic.

Other experts offer additional tips for writing online. *Communication Briefings*, for example, says you should limit line length to fewer than 60 characters. It further states, "Long text lines are hard to read and give your website a claustrophobic 'filled-up' look that discourages visitors from remaining."

Shel Holtz, author of *Public Relations on the Net*, offers a number of writing tips:

- » **Write the way you talk.**   Injecting more personality into the copy will make it easier for people to invest the time in reading it.
- » **Limit each page to a single concept.**   Provide links to related ideas, allowing the reader to decide which information to pull.
- » **Use a lot of bullet-point lists.**   Lists are easy to scan, but they also force readers to absorb each item one at a time.
- » **Make sure each page provides the context readers need.**   You have no way of knowing whether they followed your path to get to this page.
- » **Limit the use of italics and boldface.**   Italics and bold attract attention, so use them only to highlight your key points.
- » **Don't overuse hyperlinks within narrative text.**   Each hyperlink forces the reader to make a choice between continuing to read or following the link. Collect your hyperlinks at the bottom of the page, after the narrative.

» **Make sure your hyperlinks are relevant.** Think about your audience and what they are looking for; don't include gratuitous links simply because you can.

» **Provide feedback options for readers.** Feedback can lead you to make revisions and updates that keep the writing current and relevant.

The Tips for Success below expands on what Holtz and others have said about writing for a website.

All too often, however, websites violate many of these guidelines because public relations writers don't understand the medium and simply post printed materials to a webpage without making any changes.

Ideally, at the very least, a public relations writer should edit articles, brochures, and handbooks into bite-sized chunks so the online reader isn't faced with constant scrolling. One relatively simple approach is to give the reader an executive summary of the material—in one screen or less—and then provide a link to the entire document if it isn't too long.

The ideal way, of course, is to convert the entire document to nonlinear style and make it more digestible through graphics and links. A company's annual report, for example, would get virtually no readership on a webpage if it was a replica of the 36-page printed version. However, news releases and media advisories posted to websites tend to be full-text files because such files are relatively short and reporters often download them and save them for quick referral while they are working on a story.

Tips for Success   Writing for a Website

Diane F. Witmer, in her textbook *Spinning the Web: A Handbook for Public Relations on the Internet*, says writing for the Web is much like any other writing project. You need to follow many of the same basic guidelines, but also be aware that the text will be read on a computer screen. Witmer gives 10 basic tips:

1. As with all effective public relations writing, your text must be mechanically excellent and free of any grammar, punctuation, spelling, or syntax errors.

2. Avoid "puff" words, clichés, and exaggerations.

3. Keep the sentences short, crisp, and to the point.

4. Use active verbs and avoid passive voice.

5. Support main ideas with proper evidence.

6. Keep individual paragraphs focused on one central idea.

7. Make sure each paragraph logically follows the one before it.

8. Set the reading level appropriate to the readership; use short words and sentences for young and inexperienced readers.

9. Avoid a patronizing tone by talking "with" rather than "at" the reader.

10. Avoid jargon, acronyms, and other specialized language that may confuse the reader.

Building an Effective Website

"You have 10 to 12 seconds to 'hook' an Internet surfer onto your website, or else they'll click onto something else," says consultant Gordon MacDonald in an interview with *O'Dwyer's PR Services Report*. For this reason, considerable attention is given to Web design so a site can compete with the thousands of other webpages that are readily accessible with the click of a mouse. The idea is to create a website that is attractive and easy to navigate and that offers relevant information. We have previously discussed how a website can be user friendly, so this section discusses additional aspects of creating a website for your organization.

In most cases, an organization wants a website to accomplish multiple objectives—and keeping the press informed is only one of them.

Marketing is a common objective. Indeed, the vast majority of websites in today's world are dedicated to e-commerce. Websites with a strong marketing emphasis may have several main sections that feature information about the organization and its reputation for service and reliability, a list of product lines, technical support available to customers, instructions on how to order products or services, and details on the various services available.

Another preliminary step before creating a website is to spend some time thinking about your potential audience and their particular needs. It is one thing to decide what the organization wants to accomplish; it is quite another thing to place yourself in the minds of the audience and figure out how they will use your website. Are they accessing your site to find a particular product? Are they primarily investors who are looking for financial information? Or are they looking for employment information?

Focus groups, personal interviews, and surveys often answer these questions and can help you design a user-friendly site. The San Diego Convention Center, for example, redesigned its website by forming a customer advisory board of 28 clients that used the facility. Focus group research was held to find out what they wanted to see in an updated website. According to *PRWeek*, "The Customer Advisory Board feedback enabled SDCC to jettison a great deal of the clutter that plagues many sites and focus on exactly what the target audience wanted. Gone were dense copy and hard-to-navigate pages, replaced by hot links to key portions of the site."

Indeed, paying attention to the needs of the audience helps you decide exactly what links you want to list on the home page. Intel's home page, for example, has a short list of just five categories: For Business, For Home, Products, Support, and About Intel. Under each category, there are index tabs for specific subcategories. Under the About Intel area, there are tabs for such items as corporate responsibility, company information, and technology leadership. Indeed, ease of navigation is the key to an effective site. According to *Web Content Report*, "Improved navigation ranks first on nearly every site's priority list. The goal: fewer required clicks for users to access information because your site loses users at each step in your navigation."

Jakob Nielsen, an Internet consultant, offers a list of additional design elements that enhance usability (www.useit.com):

» Place your organization's name and logo on every page.

» Provide a "search" tab if the site has more than 100 pages.

» Write straightforward and simple headlines and page titles that clearly explain what the page is about and that will make sense when read out of context in a search engine results listing.

» Structure the page to facilitate scanning and help users ignore large chunks of pages in a single glance. For example, use groupings and subheadings to break a long list into several smaller units.

» Don't cram everything about a product or topic into a single page; use hypertext to structure the content space into a starting page that provides an overview and several secondary pages that each focus on a specific topic.

» Use product photos, but avoid pages with lots of photos. Instead, have a small photo on each of the individual product pages and give the viewer the option of enlarging it for more detail.

» Use link titles to provide users with a preview of where each link will take them before they have clicked on it.

» Do the same as everybody else. If most big websites do something in a certain way, then follow along, because users will expect things to work the same way on your site.

» Test your design with real users as a reality check. People do things in odd and unexpected ways, so even the most carefully planned project will learn from usability testing.

Forrester Research says there are four main reasons why visitors return to a particular website. First and foremost is high-quality content. Then, in descending order, are ease of use, download speed, and frequent updates.

Making the Site Interactive

A unique characteristic of the Internet and the World Wide Web, which traditional mass media do not offer, is interactivity between the sender and the receiver.

One aspect of interactivity is the "pull" concept. The Web represents the "pull" concept because you actively search for sites that can answer your specific questions. At the website itself, you also actively "pull" information from the various links that are provided. In other words, you are constantly interacting with a site and "pulling" the information most relevant to you. You have total control over what information you call up and how deeply you want to delve into a subject. In contrast, the concept of "push" is information delivered to you without your active participation. Traditional mass media—radio, TV, newspapers, magazines—illustrate the "push" concept, and so do news releases that are automatically sent to media or email messages sent to you.

Another dimension of interactivity is the ability of a person to engage in a dialogue with an organization. Many websites, for example, encourage questions and feedback by giving an email address on which the user can click and then send a message.

One successful application of this is the website of the Broward County Public Schools in Fort Lauderdale, Florida. The school board was working on two new policies, and it realized that not everyone could attend meetings to discuss the proposals. Therefore, the decision was made to post the policy drafts on the board's site and allow the public to email their comments and views. Dozens of emails were received, and the suggestions were used to revise the policies.

Unfortunately, the idea of "interactive" and encouraging feedback is more buzz than reality on many websites. According to reporter Thomas E. Weber of *The Wall Street Journal*, "Many big companies invite a dialogue with consumers at their Internet outposts but are ill-prepared to keep up their end of the conversation." He explains:

> *The Wall Street Journal* zapped email inquiries to two dozen major corporate websites with email capabilities and found many of them decidedly speechless. Nine never responded. Two took 3 weeks to transmit a reply, while others sent stock responses that failed to address the query. Only three companies adequately answered within a day.

A delayed response to an email query, or no response at all, damages an organization's reputation and credibility. Ideally, an email query should be answered by an organization within 24 hours. Although it is good public relations to solicit feedback from the public, you should think twice about providing email response forms on your website if the organization isn't capable of handling the queries.

> **"*Many big companies invite a dialogue with consumers at their Internet outposts but are ill-prepared to keep up their end of the conversation.*"** Thomas E. Weber, *Wall Street Journal* reporter

Book author Diane Witmer sums it up best: "Double check that the client's staff is both prepared and able to respond quickly to email messages. If the client fails to meet the expectations of Internet users through slow or inadequate responses, the website is likely to be more harmful than helpful to the client's reputation."

Attracting Visitors to Your Site

A cliché about attracting interest is, "If we build it, they will come." If you want to attract visitors, you need to do much more than "build" a website. You also have to give a lot of directional signage so people can find it. The two major "directional" signs are hyperlinks and search engines. Most people find websites by following links, from either other websites or search engines. In fact, one study by the Georgia Institute of Technology found that 85 percent of people begin their online research at a search engine (see Chapter 1).

Hyperlinks — According to Joe Dysart, writing in *Public Relations Tactics*, "One of the Web's most powerful promotional tools is also one of its most basic: the hyperlink." In other words, sites that have a lot of links with other sites tend to get more visitors.

You should link your website to organizations or topics that have a direct or indirect interest in your organization or the industry. According to Dysart, "Some businesses, for example, exchange links with a few of their suppliers or trading partners. Others offer links to information directories, free map-making services, and the like." Another approach is to piggyback, so to speak, on already well-established websites that continually come up first in any search by keywords related to your business. If the link is not a direct competitor, you should make an inquiry about exchanging hyperlinks for the benefit of both organizations.

If your site has many links, it also increases your ranking on search engines, says Jan Zimmerman, author of *Marketing on the Internet*. Dysart says, however, that your links should not be posted on your home page. Otherwise, some of your visitors might get distracted even before they get into your site. He suggests "burying" these links within your site.

Search Engines — The essential key to the vast, sprawling universe called the World Wide Web is a **search engine.** There are multiple search engines, many of which were described in earlier chapters, but the major ones are Google (72 percent of all search traffic in 2010), Yahoo! (14 percent of all searches), and Bing (10 percent of all searches). Fredrick Marchini, in a *Public Relations Tactics* article, writes, "According to IMT Strategies, search engines create more awareness about websites than all advertising combined, including banner, newspaper, television, and radio placements."

Search engines play a large role in our daily lives for two reasons. First, most of us begin online research by typing in a few words and seeing the list of sites Google or another engine generates. Second, more than one study has shown that the average Internet user limits his or her search to the first 10 citations. In other words, if your site is mentioned in the top 10 citations—as opposed to being citation number 154 on a 27-page list—you get much greater visibility and traffic.

So how do you get into the top 10? The most common approach is using the technique of search engine optimization (SEO), which has been mentioned in previous chapters, including Chapter 5. The basic idea behind SEO is that an organization uses keywords to describe its business, products, or services—words that might be used by an average consumer. These keywords are embedded as hyperlinks in your website and materials so search engines can identify them. In addition, it's also common to have your keywords and content circulated through social bookmarking sites such as Digg or Delicious to drive traffic to your website to increase your ranking in terms of site visitors.

Another approach is paying for a higher ranking. Search engines are commercial enterprises, so they earn revenue by charging a fee to get listed on their indexes. As Aleksandra Todorova writes in *PRWeek*, "If you want your client's website to outscore the competition, the choices are to pay, or pay more."

The most expensive option is the concept of "pay for position." This is a system of purchasing, more or less in competition with others, the exclusive rights to search words that best describe your organization or products. Say your company, for example, makes basketballs; you would pay Google several cents, or even several dollars, for each click on "basketball," and Google would automatically list your organization in the top 10 results. If you are doing a three-month product publicity campaign, a pay-for-position strategy would be a good approach.

The second strategy, which is cheaper, is called "pay for inclusion." With this strategy you just pay a fee to be listed on search engine indexes. It's something like a lottery, however. You may get listed in the top 10 results on occasion or, then again, you might not. At least it's better than not being listed at all. With this approach, a lot depends on the number of visitors to your site.

A useful resource, says Todorova, for keeping updated on the latest news, tips, and trends on how to get listed on all major search engines is www.searchenginewatch.com.

Advertising — Another method of attracting visitors, of course, is a traditional advertising campaign. PepsiCo, for example, combined online, offline, and mobile media ads to promote its "Crash the Super Bowl" consumer-generated advertising for Doritos and Pepsi Max.

You may not have the budget for Super Bowl ads, but you should consider how to integrate online and offline advertising. At a minimum, include your website's URL in print and broadcast advertising. You can also do specialty advertising. If your site has an online "pressroom," for example, you may wish to advertise this fact in various trade magazines and websites that cover the journalism profession. Several studies have shown that advertising in traditional media drives Web traffic.

Another form of advertising is to place your website's URL on the organization's stationery, business cards, brochures, newsletters, news releases, promotional items, and even special event signage. In addition, employees of an organization usually have a standard signature line on their email messages that includes telephone numbers as well as website addresses.

Tracking Site Visitors

An important part of site maintenance is tracking visitors to your site, also discussed in Chapter 19. Management, given its investment, wants to know if the site is actually working. In other words, how well is it fulfilling its objectives? Is it generating sales leads? Is it selling products and services? Is it helping the organization establish brand identity? Are journalists actually using it to write stories?

Fortunately, the digital revolution allows quick and tangible ways to monitor traffic on any website. A number of different measurement terms are used, and it is often confusing as to exactly what each one means.

One term is **hit.** When the Canadian Tourism Commission launched its website, ThisIsOurVancouver.com, to battle an image problem after post–Stanley Cup rioting, it generated more than 14,000 hits, or visits, in just 10 days. Some websites report much more remarkable numbers of hits. Victoria's Secret, for example, reported that its online lingerie fashion show got 5 million hits an hour, but most of those hits didn't turn into viewers, because the servers were only configured to handle 250,000 to 500,000 simultaneous viewers.

Two other often used terms are *page view* or ***page impression.*** These terms are interchangeable and they refer to the number of times a page is pulled up. Unlike a "hit," one completed visit equals one page view. For example, the Canadian Tourism site's 14,000 hits translated to about 20,000 page views.

The term *unique visitor* occasionally is used. It basically means first-time visitors to a site. Paul Baudisch of Circle.com says it is a good metric for tracking the number of viewers, whereas page view is better for tracking brand awareness.

Armed with an understanding of these basic terms, a public relations practitioner can track various dimensions of website usage. Each individual page within a website, for example, can be tracked for first-time visitors, return visitors, and the length of time a viewer stays on a particular page. This gives you an indication of what information on your website attracts the most viewers, and it also may indicate what pages should be revised or dropped.

Return on Investment

Websites require staffing and a budget. One good way to convince management that a website is well worth the investment and contributes to the "bottom line" is to calculate its **return on investment (ROI)**. This means that you compare the cost of the website to the cost of accomplishing such functions by other means.

Hewlett-Packard, for example, says it saves $8 million a month by allowing customers to download printer drivers instead of the company mailing them out on disks. Cisco Systems says that by distributing news releases via its website—NEWS@Cisco— it saves about $125,000 annually in distribution wire costs, such as for Business Wire.

Amy Jackson, director of interactive communications at Middleberg Associates, says that calculating the ROI for your website is one of the best ways to evaluate your online success. She told *Interactive Public Relations*, "Companies who invest in developing comprehensive, well-managed online media rooms can save thousands of dollars on printing and faxing costs if the media can readily find what they are looking for on the Web."

The Basics of Webcasting

A website is enhanced and supplemented by using webcasts. Indeed, **webcasting** has become more common as bandwidth has increased and better technology has evolved. In fact, one survey found that more than 90 percent of public companies use webcasts for everything from employee training to briefings for financial analysts and news conferences launching a new product. One big advantage is that they save time and money, eliminating the cost of travel for participants.

Thomson Financial defines a webcast as "any event, live or archived, which involves the transmission of information from a person or organization to a larger audience over the Internet." The company continues, "Webcasts can be as simple as an audio-only address from a CEO or as elaborate as an audio/video webcast with a PowerPoint slide show presented from multiple locations with follow-up questions from the audience."

A good example of a media-oriented webcast was one hosted by the Chocolate Manufacturers Association (CMA) and its public relations firm, Fleishman-Hillard. It sponsored a chocolate-tasting webcast for food writers around the country who also received a "tasting kit" before the event. They could taste various chocolates as they viewed the webcast, which featured experts on chocolate. By having a webcast, the organization doubled attendance from the previous year. Lynn Bragg, CMA president, told *PRWeek*, "It's helped us connect with media and build relationships with them in a way that has increased awareness of CMA." The entire budget for the webcast was $19,500.

The value of a webcast is its delivery system—the computer. You can reach more people via a regular radio or television broadcast, but that requires the involvement of media gatekeepers making a decision to use your information, or you could buy the time at expensive commercial advertising rates. Closed-circuit television is another method, but that requires the audience to gather at a specific location to view the program.

If you do use webcasting for transmitting audio and video, either in real time or as archived material, you should be aware of two aspects. The first one is quality. People expect the same high-resolution quality from the Internet as they see on television, so top-notch lighting, staging, and production are necessary.

The second aspect is an understanding of the computer capabilities of the intended audience. Is the website easily accessible? Are there enough servers and is there sufficient broadband width available to handle the traffic? Victoria's Secret's first attempt at streaming a live fashion show of lingerie-clad models, for example, crashed because the IT infrastructure was not able to handle the traffic. You also have to be careful about using too many "cool" technologies and graphics programs that are impressive but that require a lot of broadband that older computers may not be able to handle.

Medialink offers some additional guidelines to ensure successful transfer of images on the Web or an organization's intranet:

» Minimize fast movements and significant screen shifts.

» Emphasize strong foreground images and avoid shadows.

» Tiny details are often lost through digital encoding; provide sharp, clean screens.

» Audio should be clean and without the clutter of distracting background noise.

The Value of Social Media

The first generation of the Internet, often called Web 1.0, was primarily based on information being transmitted from supplier to receiver. Although websites still serve that function, the second generation of the Internet (Web 2.0) became an interactive model, and Web users now have multiple tools to talk to each other in real time. Thus, the term *social media* has now entered the mainstream.

According to Wikipedia, "Social media describes the online technologies and practices that people use to share opinions, insights, experiences, and perspectives with each other." David Bowen, writing in the *Financial Times*, adds, "Social networks are all about a shift from vertical to horizontal communications on the Web." eMarketer, a digital marketing, media, and commerce information aggregator, predicts that by 2013, there will be more than 114 million user-generated content creators in the United States. In 2008, the number was only 82.5 million. In July 2011, the Data Center of China Internet announced that 50.7 percent of Chinese Internet content was user-generated. That means less than half of all online content in China was created by professionals.

There are various categories of social media. Blogs are the most dominant manifestation, but social networks such as MySpace, Facebook, YouTube, Twitter, and LinkedIn are also a major presence in today's world. More social networks are being created almost daily. The rise of podcasts, wikis, and virtual reality sites also powers conversation between people around the world.

This social media conversation is not organized, not controlled, and not on-message. Instead, the conversation is vibrant, emergent, fun, compelling, and full of insights. Some experts have even called social networks the world's largest focus group. The *Economist*, for example, noted that "the direct, unfiltered, brutally honest nature of much online discussion is black gold; Texas tea to companies that want to spot trends or find out what customers really think."

The rise of social networks has also changed the landscape of public relations. It means that public relations, now more than ever before, needs to be focused on *listening* in order to facilitate conversations between organizations and their constituents. One public relations counselor, in a survey conducted by the Institute for Public Relations (IPR), put it this way: "Social media has provided an opportunity to truly put the public back into public relations by providing a mechanism for organizations to engage in real-time, one-on-one conversations with stakeholders."

Such conversations, however, can't be controlled, so organizations and their public relations staffs must get used to the idea that everything an organization does is more transparent and fair game for comment. David Pogue, technology columnist for the *New York Times*, thinks this is a valuable concept. He writes, "When a company embraces the possibilities of Web 2.0, it makes contact with its public in a more casual, less sanitized way that, as a result, is accepted with much less cynicism. Web 2.0 offers a direct, more trusted line of communications than anything that came before it."

Tapping into Listservs

Listservs, started in 1984, provide a way to send items directly to listserv users or subscribers via email. The advantage of a listserv is that it eliminates the need for journalists to initiate access to a particular website. Because almost every company now has a website, it is unlikely that a reporter will make this effort unless there is a major news event involving the company.

A listserv, however, automatically sends information via email to anyone who has asked to receive information on a selected topic. It essentially serves as a mailing list for your organization. A more modern version of listserv is RSS.

Using RSS to Distribute and Manage Information

RSS (real simple syndication) is the basic tool for managing the vast amount of information available on the Internet. *PR News* explains, "Simply put, RSS enables the delivery of automatically updated information directly to your desktop based specifically on what you want to read, whether the content comes from a blog, website, social network, or digital news outlet."

Users can subscribe to any number of RSS feeds, which are offered by news organizations, corporations, professional groups, and nonprofits. The Public Relations Society of America (PRSA), for example, has a daily RSS "Trends and Issues" feed to its membership that provides links to news stories and research reports regarding the public relations industry. RSS feeds only include the headline, a short description of the article, and the link to the article.

Many organizations also have RSS feeds that automatically "push" timely information to employees or other stakeholders on a regular basis. In fact, RSS feeds often replace mass company emails that might not be read or that take up space in employee inboxes. One advantage is that more than one feed can be set up so employees are subscribed only to the feeds that are relevant to their job area. Many organizational websites have a list of RSS feeds that customers, journalists, and other publics can select to receive.

Public relations professionals also use RSS feeds to monitor blogs, bulletin boards, and websites that mention their employer or client. Instead of having to manually monitor hundreds of possible sites, an RSS feed will give you a daily summary of all mentions in one easy, digestible format.

The Explosion of Blogs

Blogs, which date back to 1998, have now practically become mainstream media in terms of numbers and influence. In the beginning, they were called *Weblogs* because they were websites maintained by individuals who wanted to post their commentary and opinions on various topics. Today, the common term is *blog*.

Although the vast majority of blogs are still the province of individuals who post their diaries and personal opinions, they are now widely recognized by business and public relations personnel as an extremely cost-effective way to reach large numbers of people. The format and mechanics of blogs make them attractive for several reasons:

» Almost anyone can create a blog with open-source software. A blog is ideal for a small business as well as a large company.

» Start-up costs are often minimal.

» The format and writing are informal, which can give an organization a friendly, youthful, human face.

» Links can be made to other blogs and webpages.

» Readers can post comments directly on the blog.

» Material can be updated and changed instantly.

» Extensive uses of syndication technologies allow aggregation of information from hundreds of blogs at once. An organization can immediately assess what customers and various publics are saying about it.

» A blog gives an organization an outlet to participate in the online dialogue already going on among other blogs and message boards.

» Blogs allow organizations to post their own points of view unfettered by the editing process of the traditional media.

Edelman, a global PR agency, is well known for its blogs. From the agency's home page, visitors can access the Speak Up section of the website (see Figure 12.1). Speak Up lists blogs by CEO Richard Edelman on general PR industry issues, by Marilynn Mobley on "Baby Boomer Insights," by Stefan Stern "On Management,"

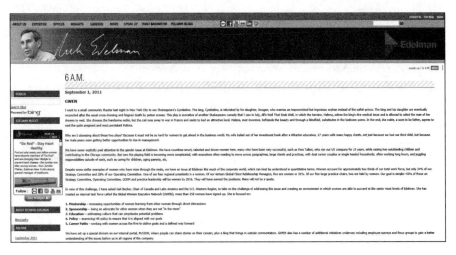

FIGURE 12.1 Richard Edelman, president and CEO of Edelman public relations, was an early adopter of the practice of executive blogging. His "6 A.M." blog receives a reported 2,000 visits per day.

and more than two dozen others by Edelman employees worldwide. Such blogging empowerment of employees by management can position the organization as an industry thought leader. See the Tips for Success on page 316 for tips on how to write a blog.

There were an estimated 450 million active English-language blogs in 2011. If non-English-language blogs are included, the estimates balloon to more than 1 billion blogs worldwide, or about one personal blog for every six people. The vast majority do not have much readership, but others have gained a large following because their postings have a reputation for credibility and for breaking major stories, which are then picked up by the traditional media. Indeed, surveys have shown that the majority of journalists regularly read blogs for story ideas and blogs heavily influence today's news coverage.

Blogs can be easily created using Blogger or Wordpress, for example. Tumblr is a blogging system that allows for easy sharing of text, photos, quotes, links, music, and videos. According to *Public Relations Tactics*, there were 2 million daily posts on Tumblr in March 2010. By March 2011, 12 million live Tumblr blogs accounted for 10 million daily posts. The *New York Times* declared that "Tumblr makes blogging blissfully easy." Giles Turnbull, writing in the U.K. newspaper *The Telegraph*, went further:

> Weblogs? Been there, done that. Facebook? It's full of kids. Twitter? That's so 2006, darling. No, the smart thing to be doing online these days is tumbleblogging, which is to weblogs what text messages are to email—short, to the point, and direct.

Tumbleblogging, *The Telegraph* reported, "represent[s] the thoughts of the tumbleblogger more or less as they happen, tumbling out of the brain, into the computer, then on to the Web."

Whether it's blogging or tumbleblogging, Susan Balcom Walton, writing in *Public Relations Tactics*, says organizations enter the blogosphere for four reasons:

» To achieve real-time communication with key stakeholders

» To enable passionate, knowledgeable people (employees, executives, customers) to talk about the organization, its products, and services

» To foster conversation among audiences with an affinity for or connection with the organization

» To facilitate more interactive communication and encourage audience feedback

Tips for Success   How to Write a Blog

A variety of sources offer numerous guidelines and suggestions about how to start a blog and maintain it. A number of sites offer tools for starting and maintaining a blog. Google offers Blogger (www.blogger.com/start), which lets anyone set up a blog in three easy steps. Another easy blogging application is Wordpress (www.wordpress.com).

Once you set up a blog, writer Sarah Fudin of *Ragan's PR Daily* offers some basic tips for getting people to notice and visit your blog:

+ **Mind your headlines.**   An easy-to-understand and enticing title is the most important part of your blog post.

+ **Make your main point quickly and clearly.**   Just like a lead paragraph in a news story, a good blog post shouldn't keep the reader guessing at the key point or points of the blog.

+ **Make a list.**   "How to" or "Top 10" lists (like this one) seem to get a lot of attention and are easily remembered.

+ **Encourage linking.**   As noted above, lists get attention and frequent links. It's also important for a blog to link out so other bloggers are apprised of your work.

+ **Make it visually pleasing.**   Graphically pleasing and easy-to-read posts maintain readers' interest, keep them coming back for more, and just communicate professionalism.

+ **Use multimedia.**   Images and videos are essential to breaking up text.

+ **Stay focused.**   Blog posts need to be succinct and focused or on topic. Don't meander from point to point.

+ **Keywords count.**   Keep keywords in mind. These are words that you might identify through Google's AdWords keyword tool.

+ **Don't ramble.**   The length of a post depends on the topic, of course. Fudin says a rule of thumb is to keep blog posts under 1,000 words. It's even better, she says, to keep them between 500 and 800 words.

+ **Be a leader.**   Don't parrot what others are saying. Cultivate an original voice. Make the reader stop and think because of the originality of your thoughts. An ideal blog post gets a conversation going.

Public relations writers are usually involved in three kinds of blogs: corporate or organizational blogs, employee blogs, and third-party blogs.

Corporate Blogs — A corporate blog, unlike an employee blog, is usually written by an executive and represents the official voice of the organization. In many cases, someone in the public relations department actually writes the blog for the executive. Some corporate blogs are now even being outsourced to public relations firms.

❝Weblogs? Been there, done that. Facebook? It's full of kids. Twitter? That's so 2006, darling. No the smart thing to be doing online these days is tumbleblogging.❞ Giles Turnbull, writing in *The Telegraph*

Larry Genkin, publisher of *Blogger and Podcaster* magazine, gives a good description of what a corporate blog should be. He says:

> In its best incarnation, corporations will use blogs to become more transparent to their customers, partners, and internally. By encouraging employees to speak their minds, companies will be able to demonstrate their heart and character. Not an easy trick for a faceless entity. This will facilitate stronger relationships and act as 'grease in the gears' of a business operation.

Although all corporate blogs should provide opportunity for the public to post comments, it's also important to provide useful and informative information that the audience can use. This was the approach Ford & Harrison, a national labor and employment law firm, took when it started a blog to address workplace issues from a legal perspective. The blog, called "That's What She Said," used graphics and humor to explore a workplace issue in terms of how much the behavior of the blog's main character would cost companies to defend in real-life lawsuits. This showcased the firm's legal expertise in a user-friendly way.

Another blog worth mention is the GM FastLane Blog, which GM describes as a "forum for GM executives to talk about GM's current and future products and services, although non-executives sometimes appear to discuss the development and design of important products. On occasion, FastLane can be utilized to discuss other important issues facing the company." GM also posted its blogger policy, which provides some good guidelines for all corporate blogs. They are:

1. We will tell the truth. We will acknowledge and correct any mistakes promptly.
2. We will not delete comments unless they are spam, off-topic, or defamatory.
3. We will reply to comments when appropriate as promptly as possible.
4. We will link to online references and original source material directly.
5. We will disagree with other opinions respectfully.

Although GM and many other major organizations have endorsed blogs, it should be noted that a blog may not be a good fit for every organization. As Ben King noted in his *Financial Times* article, "The rapid, spontaneous back and forth discourse of the blogosphere is not an easy fit with the slow, cautious approach favored by most corporate marketing departments." In other words, the organization must realize that a blog is not just another form of online advertising where the message is controlled; it's an open forum where both positive and negative comments may be posted. Michael Wiley, director of new media for GM, told *PRWeek*, "To me, this is what separates blogging from the rest of the Web."

Employee Blogs — Many organizations also encourage their employees to blog. Sun Microsystems, for example, has more than 4,000 employee blogs, accounting for about 15 percent of its workforce. More than half of them, according to the company, are "super-technical" and "project-oriented," which only appeal to fellow computer programmers and engineers. Others, such as those written by the CEO as well as managers in human resources and marketing, are more general in subject matter. Even the company's legal counsel blogs. He opened a recent post with "I really dislike the word compliance" and went on to explain why.

Many organizations are uncomfortable with employee blogs because they are concerned about liability or that proprietary information will be released. Other companies, those that have a more open system of communication and management, believe employee blogs are great sources of feedback, ideas, and employee engagement. Chapter 11 notes the potential legal ramifications of making online comments or blog posts regarding your employer. Whether the comments are on an employee blog or on a personal blog or social networking page, it is prudent to think about potential consequences before you write.

Companies do establish some guidelines for employee blogs. Cisco, for example, tells employees: "If you comment on any aspect of the company's business...you must clearly identify yourself as a Cisco employee in your postings and include a disclaimer that the views are your own and not those of Cisco." Dell also expects employees to identify themselves if they do any sort of blogging, social networking, Wikipedia entry editing, or other online activities related to or on behalf of the company. See the Tips for Success box on page 319 for IBM's list of rules for employees participating in blogs and other social media.

Steve Cody, managing director of Peppercom, a public relations firm, adds several additional important points for employee or client blogs:

» Be transparent about any former, current, or prospective clients being mentioned in the blog.

» Respond in a timely manner to individuals who post comments—pro, con, or indifferent.

» Generate as much original material as possible instead of just commenting on current news events.

» Only link to blog sites that are relevant to your post.

» Make sure that readers know that the blog represents your views and not necessarily those of your employer or client.

Third-Party Blogs — In addition to operating their own blogs and providing guidelines for employee blogs, organizations must also monitor and respond to the postings on other blog sites. The products and services of organizations are particularly vulnerable to attack and criticism by bloggers, and an unfavorable mention is often multiplied by links to other blogs and search engine indexing.

Roy Vaughn, chair of the PRSA counselor's academy, explains. "Web empowerment has made the consumer king, and it has also made long-standing corporate and individual reputations extremely vulnerable. With Web 2.0, reputations can be made or broken in a nanosecond."

A good example is the 10-day blogstorm that overtook Kryptonite Company, a manufacturer of bike locks. A consumer complaint was posted to bike forums and blogs that a Bic pen could be used to open a Kryptonite lock. Two days later, videos were posted on blogs showing how to pick the lock. Three days later, the *New York Times* and AP reported the story, and it was picked up by the mainstream media. Four days after that, the company was forced to announce a free product exchange that cost $10 million.

Tips for Success   IBM's Guidelines for Employee Blogs

IBM encourages its employees to participate in blogs and other social media. It has generated a list of 10 guidelines that has evolved over several years.

1. Blogs, wikis, and other forms of online discourse are individual interactions, not corporate communications. Be mindful that what you write will be public for a long time.

2. Identify yourself. Give your name and, when relevant, your role at IBM. When you blog about IBM or IBM-related matters, you must make it clear that you are speaking for yourself and not on behalf of IBM.

3. If you publish a blog or post to a blog outside of IBM, and it has something to do with the work you do or subjects associated with IBM, use a disclaimer such as this: "The postings on this site are my own and don't necessarily represent IBM's positions, strategies, or opinions."

4. Respect copyright, fair use, and financial disclosure laws.

5. Don't provide IBM's or another's confidential or other proprietary information. Ask permission to publish or report on conversations that are meant to be private or internal to IBM.

6. Don't cite or reference clients, partners, or suppliers without their approval.

7. Respect your audience. Don't use ethnic slurs, personal insults, obscenity, etc., and show proper consideration for others' privacy and for topics that may be considered objectionable or inflammatory—such as politics and religion.

8. Find out who else is blogging on the topic and cite them.

9. Don't pick fights. Be the first to correct your own mistakes and don't alter previous posts without indicating that you have done so.

10. Try to add value. Provide worthwhile information and perspective.

Dell has also experienced the wrath of bloggers about its customer service, which caused sales to decline, but it was a good lesson. Today, according to the *New York Times*, "It's nearly impossible to find a story or blog entry about Dell that isn't accompanied by a comment from the company."

Darren Katz, writing in *O'Dwyer's PR Report*, makes the point that "By engaging in online dialogue, companies are showing their customers that they care about their opinions, value their respect, and plan to rightfully earn their repeat business."

Consequently, it's the responsibility of the public relations department to monitor third-party blogs and even rogue websites. A list of influential blogs for your industry should be made, and such tools as Technorati, Blogpulse, and Google Search can be helpful.

You should also establish relationships with the most relevant and influential bloggers who are talking about your company. Rick Wion, interactive media director of Golin Harris, told Susan Walton in *Public Relations Tactics*, "Treat them the same as you would any other journalist. In most cases, they will appreciate the recognition. By providing materials directly in a manner that is helpful to bloggers, you can build positive relationships quickly."

A good example is how Weber Shandwick works with about 20 influential food bloggers on behalf of its food industry clients. The public relations firm regularly monitors their posts to find out what they are saying and which "hot button" issues are being discussed. This, in turn, allows the firm to build relationships with the bloggers and offer information that they can use in their blogs. See Chapter 4 for additional information on working with bloggers.

To find out more about the content of blogs, or even how to have your very own blog, see the following sites: www.blogger.com (create your own blog); www.weblogs.com (news and links about blogs); and http://blogdex.media (list of blogs and blogging news).

Making Friends on MySpace and Facebook

There are multiple online social networking communities, including the business-oriented LinkedIn, but MySpace and Facebook established early leads in popularity and continue to rank among the top social networking sites. However, use of MySpace has declined. Still, in 2011 about 80 million people visited MySpace each month. But in terms of monthly visitors, Facebook was number two among websites, behind Google, while MySpace was number 85 worldwide.

Other research studies have focused on the demographics of social networking sites. The dominant age group using social networking sites is now those 35 to 44 years old. The average age is 38. A study by the Pew Research Center showed that 59 percent of U.S. adult Internet users use at least one social network. Fifty-six percent of social network users are women.

MySpace, founded in 2003 and sold in 2011 by News Corp. to Specific Media, was the first major social networking site and registered its 100 millionth account in three years. When News Corp. bought MySpace in 2005, it paid $580 million. Specific Media paid only $35 million, providing evidence of the growing dominance of Facebook over MySpace. Nevertheless, 76 percent of MySpace users have been on the social networking site for two or more years. Facebook opened registration in 2006 and immediately became popular with college students and young professionals. In fact, a Pew Research Center report noted that 49 percent of Facebook users were between 18 and 35 years old.

Facebook has more than 800 million active users; MySpace has been in decline, with only 125 million active users, and it once lost 10 million users in one month. But 125 million users is substantial when you consider that a top-ranked television show may only bring in 13.5 million viewers.

The popularity of social networking sites such as Facebook and MySpace has been noted by advertising, marketing, and public relations professionals. They see such sites as an excellent opportunity to make "friends" in several ways. A survey of executives by Jive, a social enterprise company, for example, found that 78 percent of executives believe a social media strategy is essential to success. Other research by TNS media intelligence/Cymfony showed that marketing and public relations executives believed networking sites were vital for (1) gaining consumer insights, (2) building brand awareness, and (3) creating customer loyalty. The Jive survey confirmed this notion, as 54 percent of millennials told Jive that they rely on and make purchase decisions based on information shared in online communities.

Accomplishing these objectives, however, takes a great deal of thought and creativity, because you must shape messages that are relevant and interesting to your "friends." According to *Ragan's PR Daily*, Starbucks, Coca-Cola, and Dell collectively have more than 54 million fans. To generate such a fan or friend base often requires techniques such as humor, short video clips, music, contests, and audience participation. Chick-fil-A, the chicken sandwich restaurant whose mascots are cows, used its Facebook page to promote "Cow Appreciation Day." An image of the mascot cow wore a placard with the instructions, "Dress Like Me. Git Free Chikin." Chick-fil-A took advantage of another popular feature of Facebook by encouraging customers to upload photos for a Best Cow Costume Photo Contest. See Figure 12.2.

Coors has also expanded its traditional advertising and product publicity to embrace social networking sites. One initiative on Facebook enabled visitors (aged 21, of course) to send friends a "Code Blue" alert inviting them to meet up for a Coors Light. They could even use Facebook maps to direct their buddies to the nearest bar. Aaron, one of Coors's almost 2,000 fans, gave the site five stars: "This app is epic. I used it to set up my birthday party and it was so easy to invite everyone."

Kamila Hankiewicz, writing for *Ragan's PR Daily*, offers several tips for creating a successful Facebook presence. Among her suggestions are to post important information on Thursday because it's the best day of the week for visibility, encourage interaction with your posts, and engage followers in a one-on-one conversation. For the full list of Hankiewicz's 14 tips, see the Tips for Success on page 323.

In general, organizations use social networking sites as part of the overall media mix to execute a campaign. A good example is the PepsiCo campaign that used special events, print and broadcast publicity, a dedicated website, and Facebook, Twitter, Tumblr, YouTube, and Flickr. The campaign is highlighted in the PR Casebook on page 324.

FIGURE 12.2 Chick-fil-A is among many companies taking advantage of Facebook to communicate with stakeholders and build loyalty. The chicken sandwich company employs many of the features Facebook makes available, from uploading photos of fans in cow costumes to video invitations to events to inviting sign-up for email updates from the company.

YouTube: King of Video Clips

An extremely popular medium of communication, thanks to increased high-speed broadband capacity, are video clips. According to data from the comScore Video Matrix service, 176 million U.S. Internet users (300 million worldwide) viewed 5.6 billion online videos during May of 2011. In addition, it was found that the average online video was 5.2 minutes in length and the average online viewer watched 951 minutes of online video during the month.

Google's YouTube ranked as the top U.S. video property, with 2.1 billion views that month and an average viewer spending 311 minutes in May 2011. As early as 2007, YouTube was already streaming more than 200 million videos each day. In the same year, it was estimated that YouTube added 831,147 videos to its library. In other words, YouTube is the premier video sharing site for users to upload, view, and share video clips.

Many videos are posted by individuals, but organizations are also creating and posting online videos as part of their marketing and public relations outreach to online communities. These communities, in general, are well educated and relatively affluent. In addition, Google reports that about 40 percent of viewers are 35 years old and older, while those aged 18 to 34 constitute about 37 percent of YouTube's audience. Research shows that 95 percent of college students regularly view videos online.

Tips for Success   Making Your Facebook Page a Winner

Kamila Hankiewicz, writing in *Ragan's PR Daily* offers the following advice for making your Facebook page a success.

1. Post on Thursday because that's the best day for visibility.

2. Early morning posts get the most attention. After 11 a.m. EST, you may get lost in the crowd.

3. Include the full link when sharing stories. Hankiewicz says, "it's 300 percent more likely to get clicked on than a shortened address."

4. Use social buttons on your page, including "like" and "send."

5. Words like "today," "exclusive," and "limited time only" increase your chances of making it into your friends' "top news" feed.

6. Share good media stories on Facebook.

7. "Best," "most," "why," and "how" are among the most "shareable" words.

8. Use videos because, on Facebook, it's easy for them to go viral.

9. Tag important notes. This puts your message on up to 30 of your friends' walls. Be choosy about who you tag so your notes are not viewed as spam.

10. Try not to repeat notes. If multiple versions of the same note get tagged onto friends' walls, it'll look like spam for sure.

11. When you have a high-value link, share it and ask your friends to share and like it.

12. Encourage interaction through comments and likes.

13. Keep AIDA in mind: Attention, Interest, Desire, Action. You want your Facebook page to draw attention, stimulate desire, and spark action.

14. Create contests, encourage check-ins, and post meaningful status updates. All of these things will engage followers in a one-on-one conversation.

PR casebook

PepsiCo Uses Social Media to Build Brand Awareness and Support SXSW

South by Southwest (SXSW) is a music and technology event held each year in Austin, Texas. PepsiCo regularly partners with the conference, but in 2011 it wanted to ratchet up its involvement and provide news from the conference to those who couldn't be there in person.

Dave Aglar, vice president of digital innovation for PepsiCo's agency, Weber Shandwick, told *PRWeek*, "It is important to be closely aligned with the best thinkers in the business and make sure we are part of that culture." To that end, PepsiCo collaborated with Fast Company to create panels on cutting-edge topics and then stream the content to PepsiCoblogs.com. The goal was to keep SXSW fans informed and build buzz.

Research was used to identify which companies would be the most popular draws at the conference. Representatives from those companies were then invited to join panels on the PepsiCo stage. The panels on the PepsiCo stage as well as others throughout the conference were streamed live. Aglar said they wanted to show "how we can support up-and-coming digital trends."

The traditional media took notice as Reuters and *USA Today* both reported on PepsiCo's activity. Over five days, 65 pieces of content were streamed to PepsiCoblogs.com, generating a tenfold increase in traffic to the site.

Not only was the blog used to engage SXSW fans, but PepsiCo used all its social media channels—Facebook, Tumblr, YouTube, Flickr, and Twitter.

The success of the venture has encouraged both PepsiCo and SXSW. They report that similar efforts are likely at future conferences.

FIGURE 12.3 PepsiCo wanted to brand itself as a digitally innovative company. Among the strategies employed to reach this objective, PepsiCo streamed more than 65 pieces of content at the South by Southwest conference in Austin, Texas.

Humor was used by Old Spice to sell things like body wash and deodorant for men with the help of a YouTube video ad. With a slogan of "Smell like a man, man" the "Old Spice Guy," Isaiah Mustafa, opened each ad with "Hello, ladies" and became a sensation. And Old Spice became a household name again, especially for the young YouTube–watching crowd. The ads went viral and tallied views in excess of 30 million. The campaign, which was on traditional media as well as posted on YouTube, spawned parodies from the likes of Sesame Street's Grover. *AdWeek* reported that sales of Old Spice body wash rose as much as 107 percent in a single month during the YouTube campaign.

When Lady Gaga introduced her *Born This Way* album, the singer used online media in two ways. She linked to the popular Facebook game FarmVille and created GagaVille. The *New York Times* described GagaVille as "a special promotion that allowed FarmVille users to unlock her new songs and special virtual items like unicorns and crystals." While FarmVille/GagaVille was played on Facebook, parody ads promoted it on YouTube. The short campaign brought international publicity for FarmVille game developer Zynga as well as for Lady Gaga's album.

Not all YouTube videos, however, are humorous and entertaining. They are often used to get the attention of organizations. When some U.S. soldiers were returning from Afghanistan on a Delta Airlines flight and were charged $2,800 for extra baggage, they made and posted a protest video on YouTube. The video generated international news coverage and an apology and policy change by Delta.

Marketing specialist Chris Sturk offers six ways to use YouTube for public relations:

1. Use YouTube to kick off a campaign.
2. Respond to a crisis by putting a face on and giving a personal touch to the response.
3. Identify audiences through the social connections created by YouTube viewers.
4. Get the attention of journalists and bloggers.
5. Measure your success by using YouTube tools to determine how many views were generated from what regions of the globe.
6. Make YouTube profile pages customized to raise awareness of your organization.

Flickr: Sharing Photos

If YouTube is the king of videos, Flickr is the queen of photo sharing. The popular site allows individuals to share photos of their vacations, their children's first steps, and even their 21st birthday parties with the rest of the world. As with many social media, Facebook is elbowing Flickr with a competitive product. However, Flickr allows anyone to access your photos, whereas only your "friends" can access them on Facebook. Kate Potter of Hughes Public Relations says she got tired of people asking her why she used Flickr for the agency rather than Facebook. She replied in a blog post with seven reasons:

1. The Picnik editing tools in Flickr are easy to use.
2. Photos can be tagged with the location where they were taken.
3. A Flickr photostream can be searched using keywords or location.
4. Photos are saved at high resolution.

5. Photos can be imported to Snapfish, a photo printing website.

6. Facebook limits access to "friends," but Flickr does not.

7. Statistics are available for each photo—what was your most-viewed photo?

David Rosen, director of the Corporate-Financial Communication practice at Burson-Marsteller, cited 44 ways he thinks Flickr can be useful in public relations. His focus is on business-to-business application, but the ideas are transferable to any area of public relations practice. Five of his 44 ideas include:

1. Executive headshots

2. Images of corporate artifacts or history

3. Product shots

4. Charts or diagrams

5. Photos that demonstrate company culture

Flickr is primarily for personal use, and organizations are strongly discouraged from trying to sell products or services. Public relations personnel do, however, find creative ways to use the social networking aspect of Flickr to build awareness of an organization or brand. Here are some specific examples:

» Rotary International has a "Family of Rotary" Flickr feed. It allows Rotarians worldwide to share photos of their local club's activity. Photos are posted from Rotary Clubs as far-flung as Canada, India, and South Africa. A story by Rotary International News reported, "Using Flickr is a great way for Rotarians to promote Rotary's commitment to action-oriented service."

» Coyne Public Relations has a photostream of its own on Flickr. It provides documentation of agency activities, including the grand opening of a new office and special events such as the first "Bacon Bake-Off" and "Bagels and Books." In short, it provides prospective clients with a window into the agency and its culture.

» The Nature Conservancy invites photographers to submit their nature photos to the organization's Flickr group. The only motivator is the promise that your photo might be selected to be featured on the Nature Conservancy website. Nonetheless, the Nature Conservancy Flickr group has more than 25,000 members and houses more than 300,000 images.

The organizations just mentioned make the strong point that social media sites such as Flickr can be used for public relations purposes only if the focus is on generating participation and involvement on the part of consumers and the general public. In all these programs, the organization was basically a facilitator, connecting people to people.

Twitter

Twitter was launched in July 2006 and by mid-2011 there were about 200 million Twitter users worldwide, with about 460,000 new accounts added each day. More than 140 million tweets are sent each day, or 1 billion a week. Essentially, Twitter is a free social networking and microblogging service that allows users (known as *twits*) to post messages of up to 140 characters in length on computers and other mobile devices. Messages are displayed on the user's profile page and delivered to other users (called *followers*) who have signed up for them. In 2011 Lady Gaga had the most followers — more than 11.3 million. Justin Bieber was her closest competition, with 10.7 million followers. President Barack Obama came in third, with nearly 9 million followers.

Brands are followed on Twitter, too. Of course, it's usually the public relations department that is actually posting the tweets. Google is the most followed brand, with 3 million followers. Whole Foods has 1.9 million followers. Dell boasts 1.6 million followers. Southwest Airlines has just over 1 million followers, and Coca-Cola rounds out the top five with about 250,000 followers.

Public relations writers have to keep their company's 140-character tweets meaningful to consumers in order to maintain Twitter loyalty. *Public Relations Tactics* reported that 53 percent of people who quit following brands on Twitter said content became repetitive or boring; 41 percent said they quit the brand because its tweets became too marketing oriented. Posts that were too frequent drove 39 percent of respondents to quit following a brand, and 27 percent quit because they didn't think the company offered enough deals through its Twitter feed.

Among the goals of tweet writers is to get their messages retweeted. Dan Zarrella, author of *The Social Media Marketing Book* told *Public Relations Tactics* that 70 percent of retweets contain a link. To increase your chances of having your tweet retweeted, Zarrella suggests using nouns and third-person verbs. He says, "Highly retweetable headlines talk about someone or something doing something. A headline should never talk about all the things you did yesterday and how you did them, as past-tense verbs and adverbs both lead to far fewer retweets." For a list of most and least retweetable words, see the Tips for Success on page 328.

The following are some examples of how organizations and their public relations staffs use Twitter:

» Intuit used Twitter to launch its mobile payment app, GoPayment, during Austin's South by Southwest event. Businesses such as Dell, Whole Foods, and Coca-Cola use Twitter to provide updates to customers.

» The Los Angeles Fire Department used Twitter to communicate updates about California wildfires.

» News organizations use Twitter to distribute late-breaking news.

> **" Highly retweetable headlines talk about someone or something doing something. A headline should never talk about all the things you did yesterday..., as past-tense verbs and adverbs both lead to far fewer retweets. "**
>
> Dan Zarrella, author of *The Social Media Marketing Book* as told to *Public Relations Tactics*

Texting and Wikis

Sending text messages via a mobile or cell phone is now pervasive and universal. In fact, the public relations agency Ruder Finn reports that Americans spend an average of 2.7 hours a day on mobile media. The survey found that 62 percent of U.S. mobile phone users use their phones to instant message or text. Another survey, by RunText, a text messaging marketing firm, found that more than 72 percent of cell phone users send and receive texts. Ruder Finn reported that 58 percent of cell phone users use their phones to forward email, and 45 percent use their phones to post comments on social networking sites.

Text messaging is particularly popular among Americans in the 18 to 29 age group. RunText reported that 95 percent of cell phone users in that age range send and receive text messages. According to Nielsen, the average U.S. teenager sends about 3,000 text messages a month.

Texting — Organizations and public relations staffs use texting to reach employees, customers, and key publics. Shel Holtz, a social media expert, told Ragan.com that

Tips for Success   How to Increase Retweets

Dan Zarrella, author of *The Social Media Marketing Book*, listed the most and least retweetable words and phrases in a *Public Relations Tactics* article.

Most retweetable words and phrases:	Least retweetable words and phrases:
1. You	1. Game
2. Twitter	2. Going
3. Please	3. Haha
4. Retweet	4. Lol
5. Post	5. But
6. Blog	6. Watching
7. Social	7. Work
8. Free	8. Home
9. Media	9. Night
10. Help	10. Bed
11. Please retweet	11. Well
12. Great	12. Sleep
13. Social	13. Gonna
14. 10	14. Hey
15. Follow	15. Tomorrow
16. How to	16. Tired
17. Top	17. Some
18. Blog post	18. Back
19. Check out	19. Bored
20. New blog post	20. Listening

there are three levels of texting for organizations. One is the broadcast text, which companies often use to send a brief message to all employees at the same time. The message may be as mundane as reminding people to sign up for the company picnic or more serious, such as when updating employees about a crisis situation.

A second level of texting is by subscription. Users sign up to receive text messages from groups or organizations in much the same way that they sign up for RSS feeds. A reporter, for example, may sign up to receive text messages from a company that he or she covers on a regular basis.

The third method, says Holtz, is the "one-off," where a cell phone user can send a text message to a source to get an answer to a question. He or she may text Google, for example, to get the address and phone number of a restaurant. An employee may text HR to get a short answer to a health benefits question.

A good example of an organization using texting as a communication tool is the South Dakota Office of Tourism. Skiers visiting the state can sign up to receive daily text message alerts about snowfall and weather conditions. Email alerts to subscribers were already being used, but sending messages directly to cell phones seemed to be more logical in terms of accessibility. Wanda Goodman, public relations manager at the tourism office, told Ragan.com, "It adds a level of convenience for travelers and builds another level of connectivity with potential visitors to the state."

Randi Schmelzer, writing in *PRWeek*, gives three key points that should be kept in mind about texting:

» Text messaging is an immediate, cost-effective way for public relations professionals to communicate with a variety of publics.

» Texting should involve timely and actionable information.

» Text recipients should have the ability to opt in or out; otherwise, messages are little more than spam.

Public Relations Tactics offers these tips on how to text like a professional:

» Use proper capitalization.

» Use proper punctuation.

» Text in complete sentences.

» Avoid capitalizing all letters.

» Avoid multiple exclamation and question marks.

Wikis — Interaction between individuals working on a particular project can be facilitated by wikis. Basically, a **wiki** is a collection of webpages that enables anyone who accesses it to provide input and even modify the content. Ward Cunningham, coauthor of *The Wiki Way: Quick Collaboration on the Web*, describes the essence of wikis as follows:

» They invite all users to edit any page within the website, using a basic Web browser.

» They promote meaningful topic associations between different pages.

» They involve visitors in an ongoing process of creation and collaboration.

General Motors, for example, created a wiki site for its employees and customers as part of its centennial celebration. It encouraged individuals to contribute first-person experiences relating to the company's history via stories, images, video, and audio. The advantage of the wiki was that individuals could comment on other contributions, correct inaccurate information, and even add supplemental information regarding their experiences and viewpoints.

GM originally considered the standard coffee table book outlining the company's history, but company spokesperson Scot Keller told *MediaPost*, "We felt that a more social, more inclusive approach was appropriate, and the story is best told not by the corporation or media but by men and women who were there." As a spin-off, GM planned to package various stories and materials for distribution to other social networking communities and websites.

Wikis also are used by public relations departments and firms to keep employees and clients up to date on schedules and plans for executing campaigns. Joel Postman, executive vice president of Eastwick Communications, told Ragan.com that the firm's wiki "allows almost everyone in the agency to set up a well-organized, attractive, customized workspace for any number of tasks. Some of the more popular uses of the wiki are for event management, document version control, and maintenance of standardized documents like client 'boilerplate' and executive bios."

An example is how Eastwick used its wiki to plan a media preview for its client, Fujitsu. Every related document was kept on the wiki, including executive speeches and presentations, FAQs, bios, and the schedule. Staffers at Fujitsu could access the wiki to add their feedback on the site, and Postman said that the wiki reduced email traffic by almost 40 percent. It also reduced paper use by about 15 percent.

Podcasts: The Portable Medium

Podcasting was once described by a public relations expert as "radio on steroids." A more standard definition is provided by Wikipedia: A **podcast** is "a digital media file, or a series of such files, that is distributed over the Internet using syndication feeds (RSS) for playback on portable media players and personal computers." In other words, a podcast can be delivered to users via computers, MP3 players, tablets, and even smartphones.

So who came up with the word *podcast*, which the *Oxford American Dictionary* once designated as the Word of the Year? According to OneUpWeb, a firm specializing in making podcasts for clients, *podcast* comes from "pod" as in Apple's iPod, and "cast" from "broadcast," meaning to transmit for general or public use.

Originally podcasts were audio only, but increasingly, video podcasts are finding a home on smartphones, tablets, websites, YouTube, and other social networking sites. The three major advantages of podcasts for distributing messages are (1) cost-effectiveness, (2) the ability of users to access material on a 24/7 basis, and (3) portability. A person, for example, can listen to an audio podcast while driving to work, gardening, or even walking down a mountain trail. Simply put, podcasts have many of the same advantages as traditional radio.

Organizations use podcasts for a variety of purposes, including providing news about the company, in-depth interviews with executives and other experts, features giving consumer tips about use of products and services, and training materials for employees. Apple's iTunes Store says it offers hundreds of thousands of free podcasts. Some examples:

» Whirlpool produces a podcast series titled "American Family." Topics range from advice and discussion about traveling with kids to weight loss, stroke in women, and even snowmobiling safety. Whirlpool, as a policy, never discusses its products within the show, limiting mention of the company to the beginning and end of each transmission. The idea is to build customer loyalty and connect with women, the primary audience of Whirlpool. Dan Cook, director of interactive marketing for Whirlpool, told Ragan.com, "We cover topics that are important to the life of the everyday consumer. It's an opportunity for us to connect our brand to her."

» Purina, the pet food manufacturer, has a podcast series offering advice to pet owners. Its introduction of the series on its website gives the essence of its content: "Is it unusual for a cat to use the toilet? Is your dog bored out of its skull? Can cats and dogs suffer from heart attacks? Get answers to these questions and more in season two of Animal Advice, where veterinarians field questions from pet lovers like you." Some sample titles in the series were "Animal Safety during the Summer Months" and "Itching Dogs and Cats."

» Disney uses podcasts to promote its resorts. The short podcasts range in length from just over 1 minute to about 30 minutes and include music, behind-the-scenes looks at new attractions, and coverage of special park events.

The equipment for producing a podcast is relatively simple. You need (1) a computer; (2) a good microphone; (3) software, such as Audacity, to record, edit, and finish audio files; (4) a Web server where you can store files in a folder; and (5) a website or a blog that users can access to download the podcast. The entire podcast cycle is shown in Figure 12.4.

The hard part is creating a podcast that is interesting and relevant to the target audience. A podcast is not an infomercial, nor do you make a good one by simply reading a news release or an executive's speech into the microphone. Like radio, a podcast must be informal and conversational. Here are some other tips about podcast content:

» Keep it short. The ideal length is 10 to 20 minutes. Anything longer begins to lose audience.

» Use several stories or segments. A 3- or 4-minute interview with an executive is better than a 20-minute one. Also, no one wants to hear an announcer or host talk for 20 minutes.

» Don't use a script. A podcast should be informal and conversational. It loses vitality if it comes across as a scripted presentation.

» Select an announcer or host with a strong, animated voice and presence that won't put the audience to sleep.

» Select a name for your podcast that matches the content. Remember that users and online podcast directories usually search for a topic, not a brand name.

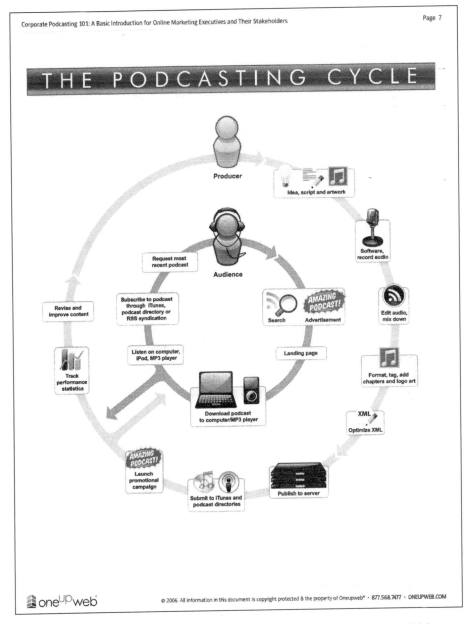

© 2006. All information in this document is copyright protected & the property of Oneupweb® · 877.568.7477 · ONEUPWEB.COM

FIGURE 12.4 The process of producing a podcast has several components, which are outlined in this chart prepared by OneUpWeb, an integrated online marketing firm.

» Be sure to include an email address or website in every podcast so listeners can respond to the content.

» Create an RSS feed for your podcast. News feeds are automatically generated if you use blog software, which also facilitates comments and feedback.

» Establish a regular schedule of producing podcasts so dedicated listeners have new material. Most experts say a podcast should be produced at least once a week.

» Drive traffic to your podcast by using other communication vehicles, such as your website, newsletters, flyers, direct mail, and advertising. Get listed on various podcast directories, such as Apple's iTunes.

Mobile Media

Two major factors are fueling the growth of podcasting and other social media: (1) the continuing evolution of smartphones and tablets and (2) affordable mobile data plans. The price of entry has gone down, which allows almost everyone to afford advanced mobile technology. Mobile phone users are able to easily download videos, surf the Internet at will, receive email and RSS feeds, post comments on blogs, and receive an extensive array of mobile-enabled content.

The growth of mobile technology—smartphones and tablets—has spurred a parallel growth in application software, or **apps,** for mobile devices. People are using these mobile media just like they once used their computers. Investment firm Morgan Stanley predicts that the mobile Web will replace desktop Web access by 2015. Apps have made this transition from fixed to mobile media almost seamless. Facebook has an app directory, as does Apple, Google, the U.S. government, and many others. For example, Facebook apps include, naturally, Facebook for iPhone, but also Pandora personalized radio, College Football Picks, Foursquare, iPhoto Uploader, and on and on.

UnwiredView.com predicted several trends in mobile applications:

» Augmented reality applications will be used for games, entertainment, and shopping experiences on mobile media.

» Integrated social features like sharing through a tweet or photo sharing or social gaming will become common.

» Cross-platform apps are a must. Apps must serve iPhones, Android, and other platforms like Windows Phone 7.

» More advertisements will appear in apps.

» Voice activation technology will become common.

Smartphones and apps are not the only potential mobile media available to public relations practitioners. The iPad dominated in 2011, accounting for 89 percent of Web traffic. Ragan's *PR Daily* asked its readers to identify their favorite iPad apps. Among them were Dragon Diction, a dictation app; News360, a news aggregation service; and Flipboard, which allows you to flip through content on Facebook and Twitter in order to "like," comment, or share content.

There is no question that application software is an important tool in the public relations communicator's toolbox. For example, when Sears Holdings, parent company of Sears and Kmart, increased its push to engage Hispanic and African-American customers, apps were part of the campaign equation.

"When we approach multicultural segments, regardless if it's Sears or Kmart, we lead with cultural insights and interests of the audiences," Sears Holdings PR director

Shannelle Armstrong told *PRWeek*. "We listen to what they want—be it from a product or message perspective." Because these two ethnic groups are highly devoted to mobile media, according to Armstrong, mobile apps Sears2go and Kmart2go were developed to make mobile shopping easier.

Apps, however, require that public relations practitioners ensure that the content on their organization's website loads quickly and is easily viewed and manipulated on a small screen. Mobile media and apps are mainstream media that are now frequently used to distribute information to journalists and the public, which was also discussed in Chapter 10.

The Continuing Role of Traditional Media

The explosion of Internet services has radically changed the way public relations professionals distribute information. It offers many new distribution and placement opportunities, but the public relations writer should always remember that the Internet hasn't yet replaced—if it ever will—traditional media.

Indeed, the traditional media are very much alive despite the impressive numbers of people who are online. The Nielsen Company, for example, reported in July 2011 that an estimated 244 million Americans have Internet access at home or work, and 195 million of them went online during April 2011. It also reported, however, that television viewing was up, thanks to access on mobile devices and computers. The average American watched more than 158 hours a month during the first quarter of 2011. In contrast, those who watch video on computer averaged only 3 hours a month and those who watch on mobile devices 4 hours a month.

It's also worth noting the following statistics for other "traditional" media:

» Daily newspaper readership, although declining, still has a strong presence. According to the Newspaper Association of America, more than 92 million U.S. adults read a daily print newspaper and more than 105 million read a print newspaper on Sunday.

» Consumer magazines remain a strong media presence. For example, *AARP the Magazine* has a circulation of about 24 million, *Better Homes and Gardens* has a circulation of about 8 million, *People* has a circulation of almost 4 million, and *Cosmopolitan* has a circulation of just under 3 million.

» Radio reaches 93 percent of the American public every day of the week, and the average person listens to radio 15 hours a week, according to Arbitron.

In other words, traditional media are still a good way for public relations professionals to reach large audiences, and they have various audience characteristics that are worth noting. For example, a 2011 media usage study by Ketchum found that among U.S. consumers who use the Internet, 93 percent watch television offline, 61 percent read print newspapers, and 82 percent listen to radio offline. The top four mainstream media used by the online population were television, Facebook, radio, and print newspapers. So, well over half of the U.S. online population still relies primarily on traditional media.

A study by *Ad Age* showed that traditional media are still relevant. It found that 90 percent of what it called "affluent" Americans (those with household incomes of

$100,000 or more, precisely the demographic with which many businesses want to connect) used television to follow coverage of the 2011 Japan earthquake, and 85 percent used television to follow coverage of the death of Osama bin Laden. Sixty-five percent used the Internet to follow the earthquake story and 45 percent used the Internet to follow the bin Laden story. Fifty-seven percent of Americans said they used newspapers to follow the Japan earthquake story, while 41 percent used newspapers to follow the death of bin Laden.

Even publicity materials in the mass media have increased credibility, because media gatekeepers, a third party, have already decided that the information is newsworthy. Two media researchers, Robert Merton and Robert Lazarsfeld, termed this the "status conferral role" of the press. Other researchers say media coverage of your organization represents an implied third-party endorsement by the press. No such status conferral occurs when anyone can post anything and everything on the Internet.

Although the Internet has no time or space constraints, this is a double-edged sword. Publicists are thrilled that the public can now access the full text of news releases instead of being presented with shortened versions (or no mention) in the news media. However, the flip side is that millions of documents are added daily to the Internet and no one has the time or ability to absorb this mountain of information.

The traditional media, in such an information glut, perform the valuable function of distilling and synthesizing information so people can easily access it at home, on a bus, or even while working out in a health club.

W. Russell Neumann, writing in *The Future of the Mass Audience,* adds:

> People will continue to rely on the editorial judgment of established news media to relay what are deemed to be the significant headlines of the world and the nation. Packaging, formatting, filtering and interpreting complex flows of information represent the valued-added components of public communications. In a more competitive, complex and intense communication environment, that value-added component will be equally important to the individual citizen, if not more so.

Another value-added aspect of traditional media content is that it drives people to the Internet. BIGresearch, for example, found that the top three media for triggering online searches were (1) magazines, (2) articles on the product, and (3) TV. Even bloggers seem to rely on traditional media for information and ideas. The Center for Media Research, for example, found that conventional forms of media often triggered bloggers' Internet searches, with magazines (cited by 51 percent of respondents) ranked the highest. Other sources of ideas, in descending order of influence, were (1) broadcast TV, (2) cable TV, (3) face-to-face communication, and (4) newspapers.

Similar surveys also indicate that ads in traditional media tend to trigger additional Internet searches. Research conducted by Clark, Martire & Bartolomeo and commissioned by Google, for example, found that 67 percent of consumers used the Internet to research products and services after first seeing them advertised in traditional media such as newspapers. And 56 percent researched or purchased at least one product they saw advertised in the newspaper in the previous month. Almost 50 percent responded to a newspaper ad by going directly online to a URL they saw in the advertisement.

Traditional media, of course, have more usage and influence with older age groups, so the choice of media often depends on the target audience. If the primary audience is seniors, for example, there is ample evidence that they are better reached through television and newspapers than websites, blogs, and social networks.

Harvard University reported that 60 percent of teenagers pay little attention to the news. The Nielsen Company reported that individuals aged 65+ watched 47 hours of television each week, whereas 18- to 24-year-olds watched only 26 hours per week. A Northwestern University survey of newspaper readership also noted that readership among 18- to 24-year-olds was declining, whereas readership among the 45+ age group was fairly stable.

Public relations professionals need to understand that "traditional" media and "new" media are not mutually exclusive categories. Most public relations programs include both in the media mix. Michael Lissauer, executive vice president of marketing for Business Wire, says it best in an op-ed for *PRWeek*. He writes, "Traditional media is alive and well and, frankly, it goes hand-in-hand with the online community." He also quotes a study from the Online Publishers Association, which found, "The power of the Web is strong, especially when combined with other media."

Summary

The Internet: Pervasive in Our Lives

» The worldwide adoption of the Internet and the World Wide Web has taken less time than the adoption of any other mass medium in history.

The World Wide Web

» The World Wide Web is the first medium that allows organizations to send controlled messages to a mass audience without the message being filtered by journalists and editors. Before the Web, the placement of advertising in the mass media was the only method by which the organization controlled the message.

» Public relations practitioners are heavy users of the Internet and the Web. They disseminate information to a variety of audiences and also use the Internet for research.

» The new media, including the Web, have unique characteristics. They include (1) easy updating of material, (2) instant distribution of information, (3) an infinite amount of space for information, and (4) the ability to interact with the audience.

» Writing for the Web requires nonlinear organization. Topics should be in an index-card format instead of a long, linear narrative. This allows viewers to click on the information most interesting to them.

» Written material for the Web should be in short, digestible chunks. Two or three paragraphs (or about one screen) should be the ideal length of a news item. Long pieces of information require too much scrolling and turn off viewers.

» Publicizing and promoting a website are necessary to generate traffic. Print and Internet advertising, email, hyperlinks, and printed material displaying the URL are some ways to promote a site.

The Basics of Webcasting

» Webcasting, the streaming of audio and video in real time over a website, is now used by the majority of organizations for everything from news conferences to employee training.

The Value of Social Media

» The second generation of the Internet, called Web 2.0, has given rise to "social media" in which most of the Internet content is consumer generated. It provides public relations professionals with the opportunity to participate in social networking sites to get feedback and also to build relationships.

» Listservs are used by organizations to send information to subscribers on a regular basis.

» RSS stands for "real simple syndication." A user may sign up for any number of RSS feeds from various organizations and news outlets. RSS also allows organizations to monitor blogs and other websites that may mention their products or services.

» Blogs have become mainstream in terms of numbers and influence. From a public relations standpoint, there are three kinds of blogs: (1) corporate, (2) employee, and (3) third party.

» MySpace and Facebook are the most popular social networking sites. Increasingly, organizations are establishing a presence on these sites. Public relations materials, however, need to be low key and creative to engage the audience.

» YouTube is the premier social networking site for posting and viewing videos.

Organizations are also heavily involved in posting video clips. The clips, however, must be creative, interesting, and somewhat humorous to attract an audience.

» Flickr is the major photo sharing site.

» Twitter is a microblogging site that has become a valuable tool for information distribution and brand-building.

» Texting and wikis are used extensively in public relations work.

» Podcasts are gaining in popularity. They can be either audio or video, but they must provide useful and relevant information in a conversational way.

» The mobile technology of the Internet will see the further development of smartphones as minicomputers. The cost of mobile-enabled content has gone down, which will enable consumers to send and receive vast amounts of information. Application software, or "apps" for mobile media like smartphones and tablets, are a growth area and can serve to complement public relations campaigns.

The Continuing Role of Traditional Media

» The traditional media are still alive and well. Despite the advent of new media, people still use traditional media in great numbers. Content in traditional media often makes people aware of new products and services and drives them to the Internet for more information.

Skill Building Activities

1. Visit the websites of five major corporations or organizations. Do an analysis and assign a grade to each of them, using the guidelines mentioned in the chapter. Some criteria might be (1) design and layout of the home page, (2) ability to easily navigate the site and find information of interest to you, (3) ability to easily read text items and download materials, and (4) ability to contact the company via email to ask a question or give feedback.

2. Find three websites that allow you to email the organization with questions or comments. How long did it take for you to get a response? From a customer relations standpoint, what is your assessment of the response?

3. A maker and distributor of yogurt wants to include the new media in its public relations efforts. What would you recommend in terms of how they might use (1) blogs, (2) RSS feeds, (3) MySpace and Facebook, (4) YouTube, (5) Flickr, (6) Twitter, (7) wikis, (8) apps, and (9) podcasts?

4. Look at print and online versions of a national daily newspaper and a popular consumer magazine. What are the presentation differences? Are there content differences? As a public relations practitioner, how would you attempt to use the strengths of each medium to promote your yogurt client? Write a short proposal describing how you would use these four media in a campaign.

5. Sign up to follow a celebrity, PR practitioner, or company on Twitter. Monitor the Twitter feed for a week. Describe how Twitter is being used as a public relations tool. How is it being used to reach out and engage stakeholders?

6. Examine the Facebook page of one of your favorite companies. You have been hired as a consultant to use the Facebook presence to build stakeholder satisfaction, engagement, and loyalty. Write a memorandum to the PR director at your selected company and outline in detail how you will leverage the existing Facebook account to achieve the desired outcomes.

Media Resources

Armstrong, L. (2009, August). "Think Before You Talk, Tweet, or Text: The Need for Technology Etiquette Guidelines." *Public Relations Tactics*, 10.

Bhargava, R. (2010, June). "How to Promote Your Business On Flickr." *The Ragan Report*, 6.

Burell, A. (2010, September). "Chick-fil-A Finds Opportune Time to Unveil Spicy Chicken Sandwich." *PRWeek*, 47.

Casey, B. (2011, May). "Intuit Hits SXSW to Bolster Awareness of GoPayment." *PRWeek*, 19.

Fertik, M., and Thompson, D. (2010, June). *Wild West 2.0: How to Protect and Restore Your Reputation on the Untamed Social Frontier*, New York: AMACOM.

Jacques, A. (2010, Summer). "2010 World Cup: A Global Conversation." *The Strategist*, 5.

Jansen, M. (2011, July 1). "5 Ways to Write an E-Newsletter People Will Read." Retrieved from www.ragan.com.

Lodge, M. (2011, June). "Exchanging Pictures Is a Snap with Latest Photo-Sharing App." *PRWeek*, 19.

Lodge, M. (2011, June). "Troubling Tweets Necessitate Firmer Social Media Guidelines." *PRWeek*, 18.

Maul, K. (2010, May). "Film Festival Outreach Places the Spotlight on Social Media." *PRWeek*, 19.

Newman, D. (2011, July 1). "12 Obvious Signs You're Addicted to Social Media." *Ragan's PR Daily*. Retrieved from prdaily.com.

Paine, K. D. (2011, May). "Measuring Influence in the Digital Age: Impressions, Likes and Followers." *Public Relations Tactics*, 16.

Paine, K. D. (2011, March). *Measure What Matters: Online Tools for Understanding Customers, Social Media, Engagement, and Key Relationships*. Hoboken, NJ: Wiley.

Ramesh, P. (2011, July 1). "PR Pros: Stop Making These Social Media Blunders." *Ragan's PR Daily*. Retrieved from prdaily.com.

Rusli, E. M. (2011, June 5). "A Force Behind Lady Gaga Inc." *New York Times*. Retrieved from dealbook.nytimes.com.

Scott, D. M. (2010). *The New Rules of Marketing and PR: How to Use Social Media, Blogs, News Releases, Online Video, and Viral*

Marketing to Reach Buyers Directly. Hoboken, NJ: Wiley.

Shuffler, J. (2011, May). "Text Messaging Service Looks to Redefine Social Connections." *PRWeek*, 19.

Stansberry, G. (2010, July). "Ten Ways to Make Your Facebook Fan Page Dynamic." *The Ragan Report,* 12.

Sutton, P. (2010, September). "Ten Reasons Why People Decide Not to Follow You on Twitter." *The Ragan Report,* 5.

Wortham, J. (2011, June 28). "The Gaga Effect Spreads to Tumblr." *New York Times*. Retrieved from bits.blogs.nytimes.com.

Zuk, R. (2009, August). "Thought Leadership on the Social Web: Six Traits that Draw People to your Ideas." *Public Relations Tactics*, 7.

Zuk, R. (2010, January). "Welcome to the DARC Side: Creating Compelling Content for your Web Site." *Public Relations Tactics*, 7.

Newsletters, Brochures, and Intranets

13

» Understand the value of print publications

» Recognize the role of editors

» Produce newsletters and magazines

» Develop online newsletters and intranet content

» Write copy for and design brochures

» Understand the role of public relations in producing annual reports

The Value of Print Publications

Several years ago, *The Wall Street Journal* announced in a page-1 headline that "Employee Newsletters Are Rapidly Becoming Obsolete." The article pointed out that organizations were switching to other communication tools—internal TV, email, and webpages—to inform employees and even external audiences.

Although organizations frequently use these communication vehicles, most professional communicators agree with Mark Twain, who once said, "The reports of my death are highly exaggerated." Indeed, newsletters and magazines in print form—as well as brochures in countless formats—are still alive and well in the age of cyberspace. In fact, the highest-circulation magazine in the United States—*AARP Magazine*—a bimonthly produced by the American Association of Retired People (AARP) for its members, has a circulation of 24 million.

Printed publications will continue to be produced in vast quantities for several reasons. Many organizations, for example, still find them to be the most efficient method of reaching their entire workforce. This is particularly true of many companies that have field staff and plant workers who have limited access to electronic communications via computer. Walgreen's *World* magazine, for example, must be in print form, because the majority of the company's 155,000 employees work in the stores and have limited access to computers on a daily basis. Readership studies have shown that 65 percent of these employees read the magazine during their 15-minute breaks or on their 30-minute lunch hour.

Gary Grates, a top executive at Edelman Worldwide, offers a second reason why print newsletters and magazines continue to thrive. He says, "A print publication is unique; employees can hold it, touch it, mark it up, pass it around, take it home, and refer back to it." He quotes another senior communication executive, who says, "There's just something about a well-written newsletter or magazine that gives you a real feel for an organization—it's not a feeling you get with email or a fax or any of the more immediate types of communication."

Indeed, one advantage of a print publication is its portability. Employees can easily pass the publication around to their family and friends in almost any situation, and a magazine often has a shelf life for long periods of time as it sits on the family coffee table or in the doctor's waiting room. The look and feel of print publications, coupled with the content, also make a powerful, positive impression on clients, prospective customers, and opinion leaders. In other words, a well-designed and well-written publication conveys the image that the organization is highly successful, well managed, and a market leader.

Although it is clear that print publications are not "obsolete," or doomed to extinction anytime soon, they are changing to accommodate digital technologies. Email, mobile apps, text messages, and the company intranet are excellent channels for giving late-breaking news and daily updates, but newsletters and magazines are better vehicles for in-depth analysis and feature articles.

Mary Hettinger, a communications specialist for Staples, told *Public Relations Tactics,* "The role for printed publications should be to expand on news with more feature-oriented articles—describing the company's goals and direction; educating employees on the business they are in so they can excel; recognizing and profiling model employees; conveying the leader's personalities; showcasing how the company is a good corporate citizen. . . ."

It should also be recognized that print publications play an important role in driving readers to content on the Web. A print story might give the highlights of the CEO's speech, but the story can also direct readers to the website, where interested individuals can view the entire speech or video excerpts. In the same vein, a story on employee benefits can provide links to more detailed information. Thus, the "traditional" media and the "new" media continue to complement each other and have an interactive relationship. This means that the editors of these publications have several roles to play.

> **The role for printed publications should be to expand on news with more feature-oriented articles—describing the company's goals and direction; educating employees on the business they are in so they can excel; recognizing and profiling model employees; conveying the leader's personalities; showcasing how the company is a good corporate citizen...** Mary Hettinger, Staples communications specialist, as reported in *Public Relations Tactics*

The Balancing Act of Editors

Editing a sponsored publication has been described as something of a high-wire act. You must produce a newsletter or brochure that advances and promotes management's organizational objectives and, at the same time, provides information that isn't boring to the audience. In addition, you have a responsibility to serve the interests of the employees or other constituents.

There is also the issue of editorial freedom. Many editors, particularly former journalists, think that they should have the right to decide what stories will be covered and in what context.

At the same time, management wants to exercise its rights as "publisher." Charlotte Forbes, senior vice president of Stromberg Consulting, sums up the management perspective. She told *PRWeek*, "Corporations need to think of a newsletter as something that can inform, educate, and hopefully drive action, as opposed to being a reporter of facts, after the fact."

Indeed, editors need to balance the needs of management, the interests of readers, and their own journalistic standards. Some never do solve the dilemma and stick to folksy stories that please many and offend none. Actually, the balancing act can be done if the editor is able to understand that all three are interrelated.

Take company strategies and goals. These are usually based on broad concepts such as human resources, corporate image, business expansion, competitiveness, productivity, marketing, and economic development. Communication goals should be based on corporate goals, so the editor may decide to support the goal of increased competitiveness by publishing at least six stories during the year about the organization's market share and what factors are involved in making the organization more competitive.

These stories, if done well, should also interest employees, because they are concerned about job security and making sure that the company remains competitive. If the company is successful, it could also mean bonuses and higher pay.

Even if management has set broad or specific goals for the year, it is usually the editor who decides how the periodical can support each goal. In this case, the editor can choose any number of journalistic treatments, including the angle of what's in it for employees. Stories about competitiveness don't have to be propaganda. They can be written with the same degree of objectivity as any article in an independent publication.

A Mission Statement Gives Purpose

The best editors, the ones who regularly win awards, seem to understand the purpose of their publication and the interests of their readers. One technique is to develop a concise, simple **mission statement** of approximately 25 words that helps both editors and management understand the purpose of the publication. The statement should cover the publication's general content, its audience, and its strategic role.

The mission of *Saudi Aramco World*, a quarterly magazine published by oil company Saudi Aramco, is to increase cross-cultural understanding. The editors also place the following statement in the magazine's masthead: "The magazine's goal is to broaden knowledge of the cultures, history and geography of the Arab and Muslim worlds and their connections with the West." The high-quality, four-color magazine is distributed free, upon request to interested readers. A cover from the magazine is shown in Figure 13.1.

Another premier publication is *Promise*, published by St. Jude's Children's Research Hospital in Memphis, Tennessee. According to Elizabeth Jane Walker, publications manager:

> The magazine serves as the hospital's external platform to educate the public about the innovative research and excellent medical care happening at St. Jude. The publication tells the public who we are—a world-class biomedical research institution as well as children's hospital that treats patients regardless of their families' ability to pay. *Promise* puts a 'face' to our work—introducing readers to individual patients who benefit directly from the research and clinical care at St. Jude.

Making an Article Schedule

It is also a good idea to prepare an annual editorial plan. An editorial plan is essentially a schedule of topics or articles you plan to cover over the course of a year. Bobby Minter of Publication Productions in New York says you need to map out what kind of articles and other material you will prepare for the entire year. This will enable you to develop story ideas that complement the organization's objectives for the year. "A long-term editorial plan establishes and maintains a stable, interactive relationship with users, and allows advertisers to place ads against relevant content," Scott Deutrom, former head of online sales at Sky Media, told *Media Week*. Deutrom was referring to content in the e-zine SkySports.com.

When *Executive Flight Guide* was launched, it included a 16-page section titled "Frequent Flyer." Charlene Seoane, publisher of "Frequent Flyer," told *PRWeek* that the magazine's editorial plan would include themed issues, guest articles, regional profiles, "on the road with" a frequent flyer, "guilty pleasures" on the road, and sections focusing on women travelers, security topics, and fitness and lifestyle. Of course, when Seoane and her staff put together their editorial plan, the various components might be assigned to certain months. For example, an "on the road with" feature might focus on a corporate traveler vacationing with family in July, whereas the feature might normally focus on corporate travelers in global business cities.

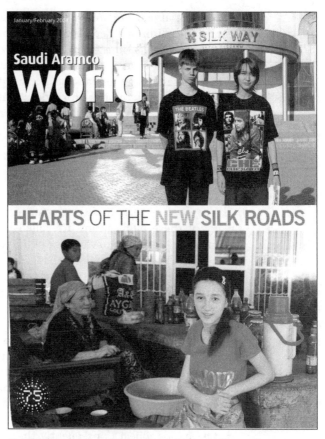

FIGURE 13.1 *Saudi Aramco World* is a high-quality company publication that is sent to opinion leaders, libraries, and educators around the world. The well-designed, four-color magazine focuses on in-depth articles about the culture and history of the Muslim world. Aramco is an international consortium of oil companies that operates in the Middle East. The magazine's headquarters are in Houston, Texas.

Source: © 2008 Aramco Services Co., Houston

Editorial plans are relevant for public relations writers in two ways. First, they enable the editor of an employee publication to plan what topics and articles will be covered in a year's time. Such an overview ensures that important upcoming events are marked for coverage for a specific issue and that all aspects of the organization get coverage during the year. Second, an editorial plan for a consumer or trade publication enables you to pitch story ideas that are relevant to the content or theme of a particular issue. Using editorial calendars as a guide to place stories in various media outlets was discussed in Chapter 10.

Newsletters and Magazines

The content of periodicals, in broad terms, is news and information. That is why many of these publications are called *newsletters*—they essentially are messages from the organization to various publics who want news and information.

Civic and professional groups use newsletters to inform their members of upcoming meetings and events. Nonprofit organizations send donors and prospective contributors information about their programs and needs and recognize the efforts of current volunteers.

Muse News, the four-color newsletter of the Health Museum (www.thehealth museum.org) in Houston, Texas, is an example of the multi-audience publication. *Muse News* is sent to key groups who can influence the attendance and financial support of the museum, which include educators, families with children, donors, scouts, homeschoolers, corporations, health professionals, and anyone interested in the health and medical sciences.

Such a broad audience requires the publication to have creative design elements that have wide appeal. Consequently, the publication often uses bright colors and interesting covers. In a typical edition of the magazine, the cover photo and headline refrred to a story about a fun and educational "Teddy Bear Check-Up" event. Other brief stories gave information on (1) educational programs, (2) membership benefits, (3) a calender of upcoming exhibits, (4) a list of recent donors, and (5) a back page listing hours of operation and the current board of directors and advisors. The museum's outreach and innovative approach have been recognized with a PRSA Bronze Anvil award.

Meeting Audience Interests

Every sponsored periodical is unique, but some general guidelines can be applied. The International Association of Business Communicators (IABC) and Towers, Perrin, Forster & Crosby, a consulting firm, surveyed 40 companies and 45,000 employees to determine what topics employees were most interested in. The top five choices were (1) the organization's future plans, (2) personnel policies and procedures, (3) productivity improvement, (4) job-related information, and (5) job advancement information. In sum, the study clearly indicated that today's employees are more concerned about the health and direction of their companies than they are about the fact that someone in the accounting department just celebrated a wedding anniversary or won a bowling tournament.

Michael C. Brandon, director of internal communication for Northern Telecom in Nashville, Tennessee, puts it more bluntly. He writes in IABC's *Communication World* that today's employee communications need to do more than make employees feel good. He continues:

> Communicators can no longer permit bowling leagues, birthdays and babies to dominate the pages of the company newsletter. Instead, employee communication must deliver business information critical to the organization's success. The most critical information employees need is about the organization's objectives. If employees are to maximize effectiveness, management must strive for alignment between the organization's goals and the individual objectives of the employees.

Another survey of employees at one corporation by Dallas consultant Tom Geddie indicates that editors should always start with the assumption that employees want answers to the "what's-in-it-for-me" questions. The number one information concern for 30 percent of employees was the internal work environment and how their work was important to the company. Another 22 percent wanted to know about the company's financial health and the prospects for continued employment. The Tips for Success on page 346 gives some additional ideas for newsletter stories. How to package this content in an attractive, eye-appealing form is discussed next.

Design

More than one communications expert has pointed out that a publication's design should reinforce the content and also reflect the organization's personality. The idea is that content and design should work together to achieve a complete message.

Consequently, periodicals have distinct "personalities" that reflect their organizations. *Guide Dog News,* the newsletter of Guide Dogs for the Blind (www .guidedogs.com), features stories about people and their guide dogs, naturally, but it also highlights donors, fundraising events, and reports about research into eye diseases. The color layout includes simple, sans serif headline and body type, and lots of large photographs. The publication, shown in Figure 13.4, projects the warmth and friendliness of a program that connects blind people and companion guide dogs.

In contrast, *Merchant Intelligence*, published by Wells Fargo Bank, is a four-page quarterly newsletter with simple headlines, lots of white space—even between lines of body copy—one photo per page, and color headlines. *Merchant Intelligence* is aimed at the commercial business clientele of the bank. The content includes jargon that is useful in the business and banking worlds, but it would hold little meaning or interest for lay readers. It thereby reflects the nature of the financial and insurance business.

Format

Newsletters are easy to produce, are cost-effective, and can reach any number of small, specialized audiences. Word processing programs such as MacWrite and Microsoft Word make it possible for almost anyone to produce a simple newsletter with mastheads, a two- or three-column format, and clip art or scanned photos. The use of desktop publishing software such as Adobe Creative Suite will be discussed shortly.

The most popular format for a newsletter is letter-size, 8.5 by 11 inches. Organizations from large corporations to the local garden club use two- to four-page newsletters to reach employees, customers, and members. Although this format is workable, it has greater design limitations than the larger tabloid format, which is 11 by 17 inches. This format, often called a *magapaper*, allows a great deal of flexibility in design and can incorporate more graphic elements.

The magazine, usually in an 8.5- by 11-inch format, often is an organization's top-tier publication. Magazines are the most expensive to produce because they are printed on glossy paper, have up to 56 pages, and include multiple displays of graphics and full-color photographs. For example, *Vermont Life,* the official promotional magazine of the state of Vermont, once reported an annual budget of about $2 million to *Folio* magazine.

+

Tips for Success Story Ideas and Packaging Tips for Newsletters

Periodicals carry a variety of feature articles and news stories. Here are some ideas from *Communication Briefings* for your newsletter or magazine.

+ Feature a day in the life of an employee. Describe what the person does and how his or her work ties into the organization's goals.

+ Select a current issue affecting the organization and give an in-depth analysis of the situation.

+ Interview long-term employees or managers. Have them discuss how things have changed, and link the changes to the organization's strategy and industry developments.

+ Offer "how-to" tips on writing memos, choosing a health plan, or even selecting a child-care center.

+ Show how the functions of each department affect the others. Follow a typical customer going through all the channels to show the importance of teamwork.

+ Profile customers. Describe how a customer problem was solved. Use quotes from the customer and the employee problem solver.

+ Interview 10 employees about their opinions on key issues or events. Use short quotes under pictures of the employees, along with their names and job titles.

Jim Ylisela, writing for *The Ragan Report,* offered the following ideas for putting together a story package.

1. The first step is to conceive and communicate to the writer the purpose of the story.

2. Sidebars, or short complementary stories or factoids, can bring depth to a subject.

3. Photographs should be compelling and capture action.

4. When numbers are involved, simplify and treat them graphically.

5. Ylisela calls elements such as pull quotes, fact boxes, or summary paragraphs the "finishing touches" of a good story package.

Magazines concentrate on in-depth stories about people and industry trends. Stories, unlike the shorter articles found in newsletters and newspapers, are much longer and tend to be more thoroughly researched. In sum, you have the option of the standard newsletter, the magapaper, or the magazine. It all depends on the purpose of the publication, the kind of messages you want to send, and the target audience. Budget is a major consideration.

Layout

Layout is a plan showing the arrangement of the material in the publication—the size and location of such items as stories, regularly appearing columns, headlines, photographs, and artwork.

There is no exact rule for any of these items. The most important stories, of course, should be placed on the front page. If a story is fairly long, it can be continued on a later page. This offers two advantages. First, you can give several stories visibility on the cover if you continue stories on other pages. Second, continuing a story on an inside page encourages the reader to go beyond the first page. Another rule of thumb is to place important stories on the inside right page of a publication, because this is where people look first when they turn the page.

Most periodicals have a layout that is somewhat standardized, so that each issue of the publication has the same look and feel. This is called a *template*. A template starts with the **masthead,**or the name of the publication. It is always in the same type font and has the same graphics. Other items that may remain the same in every issue are the location of the major story on the front page, boxes giving a list of stories inside the issue, or the placement of a standard column or update of late-breaking news items.

The idea behind a template is that the readers rapidly learn where to find specific kinds of information in the publication. Readers of *Time* magazine, for example, know that the first pages are brief developments from around the world and the section on pop culture and movies is at the end of the issue. Although the basic layout of a periodical should be the same from issue to issue, each issue will vary, depending on the length of the articles, the availability of good illustrations, and the relative importance of the stories.

Keep the following ideas in mind as you do the layout for a newsletter or magazine:

» Use white space. Don't think you need stories or illustrations covering every single part of the page.

» Vary paragraph length. If your copy looks as dense and forbidding as the Great Wall of China, your readers will be intimidated. Make paragraphs seven lines long or less to create even more white space.

» Break up longer stories with boldface subheads.

» Create bulleted lists. Any sentence containing a sequence of three or more items is a good list candidate. Listing also frees up more white space.

» Use only two or three typefaces, to give consistency to your periodical. The variety comes in using different type sizes, not a different type family.

» Keep articles relatively short for maximum interest.   If *USA Today* can summarize a world crisis in four paragraphs, you can cover the company picnic in the same amount of space.

» Inside pages should balance one another.   If you use a strong graphic on one page, you should balance it with a large headline or a graphic on the facing page.

» Use headlines that give information, not just labels such as "Company Picnic" or "New Vice President." (See the section on headline writing.)

A summary of how to create great publications is offered in the Tips for Success on page 349.

The traditional method of layout, which is still helpful in this age of computers, is to work with a blank template and sketch out where stories, headlines, and artwork will be placed. This method helps you conceptualize the entire issue and how the various stories you have planned might be incorporated. This can be done with a sheet of paper and a pencil, or you can call up the template on the computer and sketch out the contents electronically.

Desktop publishing is a common term used for computer-assisted publication design. The term *layout* is really more accurate than *publishing* because software programs don't "publish" anything; what they do is allow a person to provide a commercial printer with electronic files that, when linked together, provide the text, artwork, photos, and design of your publication.

Today, practically all newsletters, magazines, and brochures are produced through software programs. The biggest advantage, according to most surveys, is keeping control over the stages of publication preparation, from the writing of copy to camera-ready output.

Desktop software allows you to manipulate text and artwork in a number of ways. You can (1) draw an illustration and then reduce or enlarge it, (2) use different type fonts and sizes, (3) vary column widths, (4) shade or screen backgrounds, (5) add borders around copy, (6) import graphics and photos from other sources, and (7) print out camera-ready pages that can be photocopied or printed on an offset press.

Several levels of desktop publishing software are available. They range from the very basic level, Microsoft Word or Apple's iWork word processing program templates, to Adobe's Creative Suite at the most sophisticated end of the spectrum. In between, Microsoft Publisher or Apple Pages gives you increased capability to design newsletters, brochures, and banners using an extensive library of layout templates and clip art.

Although desktop publishing has made it possible for public relations writers to do their own layouts and to prepare materials in a more attractive manner, experts caution that you need more than writing skills. You also need design and layout skills to come up with a camera-ready layout that meets professional standards. As one public relations practitioner observed, "These skills are not necessarily found in a single person under normal circumstances."

Consequently, public relations writers often work closely with professional designers who are responsible for putting all the components of a publication together. Good communication and understanding between an editor or writer and the

Tips for Success   How to Create Great Publications

Newsletters and brochures should be designed to convey information in an attractive, uncluttered way. Here are some general guidelines.

Copy

+ Less is better. Write short, punchy sentences. Keep paragraphs short.
+ Write in terms of reader benefits and "What's in it for me?"
+ Use positive language and active voice.
+ Summarize the message in two or three key points.
+ Use bullets to list key points.
+ Use headlines that convey key messages.
+ Use informative subheads to break up copy blocks.
+ Include facts and figures.
+ Use testimonials or quotes from customers or credible experts.

Type

+ The best type size for text is 10 or 11 point with 2 points of leading. If the target audience is senior citizens, increase the type size to 12 or 14 point.
+ Use serif type for text. It is easier to read. Headlines can be set in sans serif type.
+ Use a minimum number of fonts and type families. A three-ring circus of type is poor design and just confuses people.
+ Use boldface sparingly. Use for subheads and a few key words only. Don't use for an entire paragraph.
+ Use italic type for emphasis sparingly, if at all.
+ Avoid all caps in headlines. Caps and lowercase is more readable.

Layout

+ Don't cram the page with copy; allow for plenty of white space.
+ Organize layout from left to right and top to bottom. Most people read in this sequence; don't confuse them with another arrangement.
+ Avoid large blocks of reverse type (white on black). It's difficult to read.
+ Facing pages should be composed as two-page spreads; that's how readers see them.
+ Use graphics and photos to balance blocks of copy.
+ Make photos and illustrations as large as possible. Whenever possible, use action-oriented photos.

Color

+ Use black ink for stories. If you use a second color, apply it as a highlight to frame a story, a quote (set in larger type), or an entire page.
+ Headlines can utilize color, but the ink should be on the dark side.
+ Avoid using extensive color on low-quality paper. Reproduction and clarity of images suffer.
+ Eliminate complex screens. A color or graphic behind a block of copy often makes the type difficult to read.

designer are important. Heather Burns, a communications consultant, gave several suggestions in an interview with Ragan.com:

» Include the designer at the beginning of the content development process so there is an understanding of the entire production process and what kinds of stories are being planned.

» Discuss the publication's purpose, strategy, and target audience so the designer has a framework in which to work.

» Write creative and interesting copy. Burns says, "If the writer gives the designer something fun to read, it's a lot easier for the designer to design something fun to look at."

» Don't confuse effective design with creative design. A design may be very creative from an artistic standpoint but not very effective if words get lost and readers can't easily find the information they want.

Photos and Illustrations

Photos and artwork were discussed extensively in Chapter 8. Many of the concepts presented there also apply to sponsored periodicals.

All publications need strong graphic elements to attract a visual generation of readers. Photos must be tightly composed or cropped for impact, and a good photo should be used in as large a format as possible. A common criticism of organizational periodicals is that they use tiny photos awash in a sea of type. Another major criticism is dull and boring pictures. *Communication Briefs* gives a list of photos to avoid:

» "Look here!" Someone pointing to something somewhere in the distance.

» "Grip and Grin." Two people shaking hands, jointly holding a giant check or trophy and grinning at the camera.

» "Firing Squad!" Several people standing in a line and staring at the camera while holding their arms straight at their sides or even worse, using them as a fig leaf to cover their crotch.

» "Work!" A group of people gathered around a computer, pretending they are working on something while trying not to smile at the camera.

In addition, *Communication Briefs* says the best order is photo, headline, and text. Never place a photo at the bottom of the story. Justin Allen, writing for Ragan.com, makes another suggestion: "For every photo of execs shaking hands at expensive dinners and parties, include three photos of 'regular' workers hard at work."

Computer-generated graphics and imported clip art are commonly used in periodicals. Clip art is available in Microsoft Office, on CDs, or through Google Images (http://images.google.com) or other websites, such as iStockphoto (www.istockphoto.com). In addition, if you see something in another publication or book, you can use a scanner to import it into your computer. (Be certain not to violate copyright laws, which were discussed in Chapter 11.) A better use of scanners is to import graphic designs commissioned by the organization.

Headlines

Writing good headlines takes practice. The headline is an important component of any story for two reasons: (1) it attracts a reader to the article and (2) it's often the only thing they will read. According to *Communication Briefs*, 70 to 90 percent of readers look at headlines. Subheads attract 60 to 90 percent of the readers, and photos also rank high, with the same percentage. About 40 to 70 percent will read a lead paragraph, but only 5 to 10 percent of the potential readers read the text of a story. In today's culture of information overload, headlines are the real workhorses of effective communication.

There are several rules or guidelines for writing a good headline. Mark Ragan, in Ragan.com, writes "Headlines should answer the questions: Why should I care? Why should I spend my time reading this article? How have you, the writer, helped me do my job?" He lists five basic rules:

» Use strong, active verbs.

» Readers want to know "What's in it for me?" so use that angle in the headline.

» Avoid acronyms; they slow down the readers and tax their brains.

» Use how-to headlines to help readers remember the key points.

» When appropriate, speak to readers informally by using "we" or "you."

The major mistake headline writers make is using headlines that are labels and don't say anything. Ragan gives the example of a headline from a major insurance company newsletter. It said, "Regional Structure and Focus Strengthened." Ragan, after reading the story and finding out what was actually being said, changed the headline to: How Restructuring Will Change Our Lives. Here are several other revised headlines from Ragan's story. The rewritten headline appears in boldface type:

> **The better the headline, the better your odds of beating the average and getting what you've written read by a larger percentage of people.** Brian Clark, founder of *Copyblogger* newsletter

UNICARE educates Kmart employees about insurance options

How We Matter: Our lower premiums helped Kmart's laid-off workers

E-Learning providing benefits on several Xcel Energy fronts

Online learning can cut your training time in half

Figure 13.2 gives some headlines from various newsletters and magazines. Notice the variety of styles, the use of smaller explanatory heads, and the active voice. A secondary headline in smaller type, following the main headline, is often helpful to give a key point for just the headline reader. The secondary headline is also often used in news releases (see Chapter 5).

You should also note that there are two styles of formatting. One format is known as *downstyle* because only the first word and proper nouns are capitalized, just as in a sentence. The second, which is more traditional, is capitalizing all

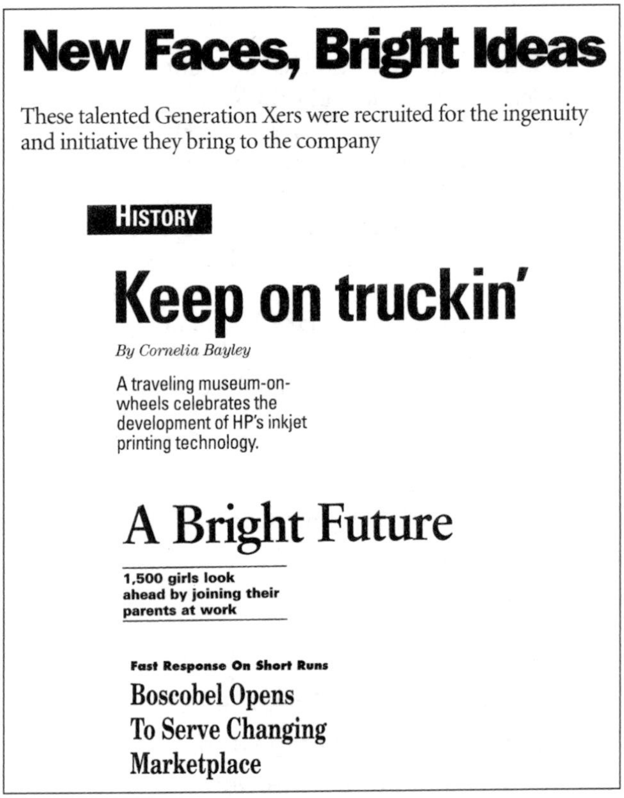

New Faces, Bright Ideas

These talented Generation Xers were recruited for the ingenuity and initiative they bring to the company

HISTORY

Keep on truckin'

By Cornelia Bayley

A traveling museum-on-wheels celebrates the development of HP's inkjet printing technology.

A Bright Future

1,500 girls look ahead by joining their parents at work

Fast Response On Short Runs

Boscobel Opens To Serve Changing Marketplace

FIGURE 13.2 Most people read headlines, but rarely entire articles. Therefore, it is crucial for headlines to convey a key message. Here are some sample headlines from various publications. Notice that kicker heads and secondary headlines combine to give the essence of the story. They also are written in active, present tense.

major words in the headline. For example, "GM to Build Diesel Engines in Thailand." In the downstyle format, this would be, "GM to build diesel engines in Thailand." In general, article posts on the Internet use downstyle heads.

In writing headlines that require two or more lines, you should avoid splitting ideas between lines. Here is one humorous example:

Pastor Leaves for Good

Friday Services at Prison

After writing a headline, it is always a good idea to review it for context, use of the correct word, and whether it conveys the right impression. Here are several somewhat humorous headlines found in the nation's newspapers by the *Columbia Journalism Review*:

Harrisonburg Man Killed When Deer Crashes His Motorcycle

Church Member Donates Organ to St. Aloysius

Woman Gets Shot on Lottery Show

Local High School Dropouts Cut in Half

Red Tape Holds Up New Bridge

Panda Mating Fails; Veterinarian Takes Over

Writing headlines requires that you know the width of the space allocated for each headline. In a word processing software program, you simply set the margins and keystroke the headline you want. If it doesn't fit the space allocated to it in your mock-up or in the desktop publishing layout, you can easily enlarge or reduce it until it fits. Selection of type fonts will be discussed shortly.

Lead Sentences

The most important element, after the headline, is the lead sentence or paragraph. All too often, they turn off readers by being vague, mundane, and a tired old cliché.

Examples are "It's spring—a time of renewal—when the snow melts and the flowers bloom," or "A handful of member cooperatives are conducting public hearings that comply with provisions of the Energy Policy Act of 2011."

Contrast these leads with leads found in the mainstream press, where they either arouse reader interest or state the essence of the story. A curiosity or human-interest lead from the *New York Times* about a trend in retail window dressing, for example, was "'One size fits all' no longer applies to mannequins." Other stories require a straight news lead that tells readers the crux of the story without having to read much further. An example from *The Wall Street Journal* is "General Motors said it will invest $445 million to build a diesel engine plant in Thailand and upgrade an existing assembly facility."

Jim Yisela, writing for Ragan.com, believes that leads should do one or more of the following:

» **Go for one sentence.** Move the reader into the next paragraph for more information.

» **Keep it short.** One- or two-word openings can have punch.

» **Tell a story.** An anecdote can set a tone and draw in the reader.

» **Tease the reader.** Pique the reader's curiosity.

» **Make news vivid.** Use strong verbs to provide information that matters.

For more information on writing leads, see Chapters 5 and 7.

Online Newsletters

Many organizations supplement their print publications with online newsletters. These are also known as **e-zines** (the hyphen is optional), and their primary advantage is the instant dissemination of information. The Natural Resources Defense Council "publishes" *NRDC Online*. See Figure 13.3.

FIGURE 13.3 In this issue of its NRDC Online, The Natural Resources Defense Council addressed the worldwide demand for coal and its impact on the environment. A "Take Action Now" link urged readers to send their members of congress a message requesting protection of clean air regulation. And a member of the "Green is Gray" over-60 activist group cited the importance of the Clean Air Act.

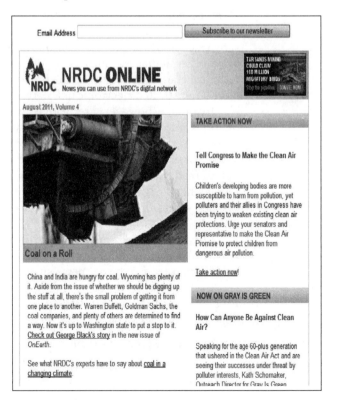

Unlike print publications that go through a number of production steps, editors of an e-zine do everything on the computer. With one mouse click, the newsletter is instantly sent via email or an organization's intranet to everyone on the "subscriber" list. The second advantage is cost. An average printed newsletter might cost one dollar or more per individual copy including postage, whereas an e-zine typically costs less than 10 cents per "copy."

An online newsletter, however, should not just be a replica of the printed newsletter in digital form. The home page, or cover, of an online newsletter should be formatted to provide some photos and give a brief description of stories that a reader can access with a click. In general, the stories are much shorter than found in a print publication so readers can read them within one screen, with no scrolling.

Online publications also have a more informal writing style than regular print publications. You can be more conversational and use less formal English than is expected in print. This is not to say, however, that you can forget about crafting well-written sentences. Every word, particularly in a short story, still counts, so it's important to keep sentences short and to the point. The difference in format between a print and online newsletter is illustrated in Figure 13.4.

Intranets

Many corporations also have intranets for communicating with their employees. Essentially, an **intranet** works on the same principles as the Internet, but it is a private network within an organization for the exclusive use of employees and perhaps some other audiences, such as suppliers. Because they are closed systems and the technical standards are set by the organization, intranets are able to produce much more sophisticated electronic newsletters.

Intranets, however, are primarily a daily newsletter or bulletin board that provides information about policies, news events, and general announcements. Consequently, most news items are brief and somewhat conversational. Longer news stories are highlighted on the home page, but an employee usually clicks a link to read the entire story. Some tips for intranet design are given on page 356. Increasingly, organizations are also mobile-enabling their intranets so employees can access it from their phones or other mobile devices anywhere they are located.

Microsoft, for example, has an intranet portal dubbed MSW, for Microsoft Web. To keep content current and appealing, Microsoft's intranet features a mix of information from external news sites, blogs, and user-submitted photos. The executive communications section on the intranet is among the most popular sections, Microsoft's Christine Bennett told the *Ragan Report*. MSW communicators might package video of a town hall meeting with a link to a pertinent blog, and a form to submit questions to the CEO.

" *Your employees demand a clean, white home page with absolutely no scrolling. This is a fact, supported by dozens of employee focus groups...* **"** Toby Ward, writing in *The Ragan Report* about the layout of an intranet site

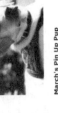

FIGURE 13.4 Print and online newsletters have different formats. On the left is the print version of the newsletter for Guide Dogs for the Blind. The online version is on the right. The home page, or cover, of the online version serves as a preview of stories in the issue, with links to the actual story or video.

FIGURE 13.5 Many organizations rely on dedicated in-house websites or intranets. Cisco's intranet home page is a typical format for most large organizations.

An especially appealing aspect of an intranet is its potential for collaboration and social networking. Microsoft allows employees to share pictures on an intranet feature called "Snapshot." Microsoft SharePoint is an off-the-shelf product that allows work collaboration and sharing. But many intranets offer their own version of a collaboration feature. Such sharing features of an intranet can connect employees in far-flung branches to those in the organization's headquarters, providing an easy solution for global companies. See Figure 13.5 for an example of an intranet page from Cisco.

Tips for Success   Lessons in Good Intranet Design

Writing copy for an intranet requires the same journalistic skills as writing for a traditional newsletter. Toby Ward, founder and CEO of Prescient Digital Media, offers eight tips in *The Ragan Report* for presenting your stories and announcements in an intranet format.

1. Let business objectives and needs drive intranet design.
2. Don't mistake an intranet for a website.
3. Make sure elements on your intranet load and transfer quickly.
4. Get design input from users—management and employees.
5. Soft colors are better than dark, bold colors.
6. Use photos, not clip art.
7. Use white space. Don't fill up every bit of screen real estate.
8. Keep links to a minimum.

Brochures

Writing brochures, like producing newsletters and magazines, requires the coordination of several elements. These include message content, selection of type, graphics, layout, and design. It also requires working with designers and printers.

Brochures are often called *booklets*, *pamphlets*, or *leaflets*, depending on their size and content. A pamphlet or booklet, for example, is characterized by a booklike format and multiple pages. An example is the corporate annual report, required by the Securities and Exchange Commission (SEC), which is discussed shortly. A leaflet, however, is often described as a single sheet of paper printed on both sides and folded into three panels. There are also handbills and flyers, which are printed on one side only and are often found on bulletin boards and a surprising number of telephone poles. For the purposes of this section, however, the term *brochure* will be used.

Brochures are used primarily to give basic information about an organization, a product, or a service. Organizations mail them or hand them out to potential customers, place them in information racks, hand them out at conferences, and generally distribute them to anyone who might be interested. Whenever an organization needs to explain something to a large number of people—be they employees, constituents, or customers—a brochure is the way to do it.

Planning

The first step in planning a brochure is to determine its objective. Such items are always prepared to reach a specific audience and to accomplish a definite purpose, so the following questions should be asked:

» Who are you trying to influence and why? Be as specific as possible in identifying who you must reach.

» What do you want the piece to do? Be clear about the desired effect. Do you want to impress, entertain, sell, inform, or educate?

» What kind of piece do you need to get your message across? Should it be a simple flyer, a pocket-sized brochure, a cheaply produced leaflet for widespread public distribution, or an expensive four-color brochure for only key customers or opinion leaders?

Factors such as budget, number of copies needed, and distribution method must be considered. In addition, you should think about the method of printing. There are various levels of printing quality that you can use, depending on the answers to the above three questions. Authors Beach, Shepro, and Russom refer to four levels in their book, *Getting It Printed*:

» **Basic:** This is quick copy, such as flyers, simple business forms, and one-color leaflets. Copy shops are commonly used for large numbers of copies. A computer printer may even be acceptable for these brochures.

» **Good:** This is material that requires strong colors, black-and-white photos, and exact alignment or registration of graphic elements.

» **Premium:** This requires a full-service printer, expensive paper, and high-end graphic elements.

» **Showcase:** Everything from design to paper and specialty inks is first class. Best for portraying an organization as well managed and successful.

Writing

Once you have a general idea of what format you will use to communicate with your audience, you need to think about how that format will shape your writing. If you decide that a simple flyer is needed, you will have to be concise and to the point. Flyers, for example, contain the basic five Ws and one H—and not much more, because the type must be large and the space (usually 8.5 by 11-inches) is limited. However, a simple brochure that has three to six panels folded to a pocket-sized format (4 by 9 inches) or that will be mailed in a standard #10 business envelope can contain more detailed information. See the Tips for Success below for information on how to format a basic brochure.

+

Tips for Success   Basic Brochure Design 101

The most common brochure format is the basic bi-fold brochure constructed by folding an 8.5- by 11-inch sheet of paper twice to create three panels on each side. Christa Hartsook, communications specialist for the Agricultural Marketing Resource Center at Iowa State University, offers the following basic brochure guidelines.

Front Cover

Don't just name your product on the front cover, or your logo. Instead, develop a theme that captures attention and interest. Use your theme as a headline for your front cover and repeat it throughout the brochure. Include a customer or reader benefit, clearly stated or implied.

Back Cover

Don't put anything on the back cover other than contact information. This is the panel that people are least likely to read, so if you put an important message there, it will be lost.

Inside Front Panel: First Panel You See When the Brochure Is Opened

This is the most important panel. Use it to summarize why the customer should choose you. It is a good location for a glowing testimonial. Although this is the most important panel, write it last. If you craft the inside spread first, you will have a better idea of what you want to summarize on the inside front page. The inside front panel is also a great place for your phone number, email, or website URL.

Inside Three Panels

When the brochure is fully open, there are three full panels to write a description of your business and what it does. Carry the brochure theme over into your inside panels. Use images, subheads, captions, and body copy that continue your front cover theme throughout the brochure.

Hartsook also recommends that you edit and condense your original copy to make it more succinct and descriptive. A good brochure, she says, is like a conversation, not a manuscript.

Whatever the format, you should keep it in mind as you write copy. The most common mistake of novice public relations writers is to write more than the proposed format can accommodate. A second major mistake is to try to cram everything in by reducing type size or margins instead of editing, thus creating a mass of dense type that nobody wants to read. Indeed, the most difficult concept to learn is that less is best. Copy should be short and should have plenty of white space around it. This means ample margins, space between major subsections, and room for graphics.

The concepts of good writing, elaborated in previous chapters, are the same for brochures. Short, declarative sentences are better than compound sentences. Short paragraphs are better than long ones. Major points should be placed in bulleted lists or under subheads. If statistics are used, try to portray them as an infographic, discussed in Chapter 8. It is always a good idea to pretest brochure copy on members of the target audience to be sure that it is understandable and that you have included all the necessary information.

Research — Gathering information for use in a leaflet or brochure may involve anything from asking a few questions to conducting a major survey. In most cases, the needed information can be found within the organization.

Keeping in mind the subject and purpose of the proposed publication, start by talking to the people in the organization who know the most about the subject. Tell them what you want to accomplish, and ask for information that will enable you to prepare a clear explanation of the subject. Often, all the information needed can be obtained from one source.

A good way to decide what to include in a brochure is to put yourself in the position of a member of the prospective audience. Ask every question that this person might have about the subject. The answers can constitute sections of the publication. You can even use the questions as subheads. Many successful brochures have consisted entirely of Q&As.

Putting It Together — Brochures vary so widely that no general guide is applicable. Each has a different audience, a different purpose, and a different format. It is imperative to use words that your readers will understand. If you have to explain a technical topic, check with the experts once you have put the story into everyday English to be sure you've got it right. For any but the briefest publications, you will need to prepare an outline. This should cover all the main points to be included, and it should list the illustrations to be used.

As you write and plan the layout of the publication, remember to include visual variety in your pages. Illustrations, blocks of copy, and headlines not only serve the direct purpose of communication, but can also make the pages attractive and interesting. Some writers recommend preparing a complete layout before starting to write. Others prefer to develop the layout after the writing is finished. A practical compromise is to prepare a rough layout before writing and then to revise it as the writing progresses.

Format

Before deciding on the format of print materials, get samples of items like those you want to produce. Note how they were done, and be guided by them. There are several

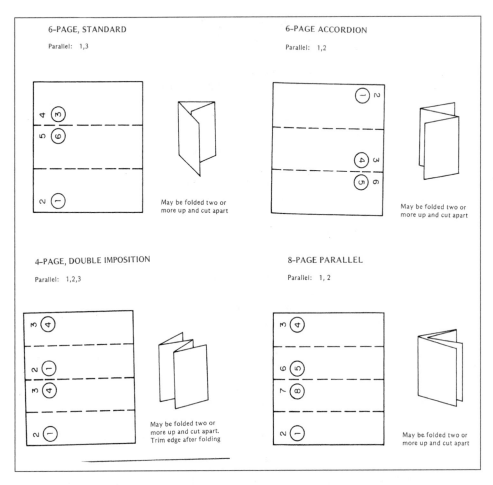

FIGURE 13.6 These diagrams show how a single piece of paper, printed on both sides, can be folded into four, six, or eight panels (or pages). Each panel has its own number. The circled "1" is the cover, and the "2" is the reverse panel. The illustration is from Baum Folder Company in Sidney, Ohio.

basic formats, which have already been mentioned. The most basic brochure is six or eight panels, folded, which is illustrated in Figure 13.6.

Brochures with multiple pages, however, need to be bound. The binding may be **saddle-stitched,** which means the pages are stapled together on the centerfold. Magazines such as *Time*, for example, are usually bound in this way. If the booklet is large, it may be stapled on the side (*side-stitched*) or spiral-bound. Another alternative is perfect binding, which is a glued binding with the brochure cover wrapped around the binding. Magazines such as *Cosmopolitan* are perfect bound.

Preparing a Layout — The layout is the plan for the finished piece. It may be rough or comprehensive, but it must be accurate enough for the designer who assembles the parts to do exactly what you want. One approach is to make a *dummy*—a blank-paper mock-up of the finished product. It should be made of the paper to be used in the printed piece and should be the same size. If the piece is to be a booklet, the dummy should be stapled just as the finished booklet will be. If it is to be a brochure, the dummy should be folded the same way. A shortcut, of course, is to do just a computer-generated layout.

With the dummy in hand, you can now plan where everything is to go. For a leaflet, the layout will be complete—it will indicate what is to go on each page. For a small booklet, the layout will also be complete, but if there are many pages, you will need to design only the cover and sample pages of the body.

The layout indicates both type and illustrations. Thus, a page layout might show various blocks of copy, headlines, and the location of illustrations for that page. For very simple jobs, you may make the layout yourself; however, most printers are able and willing to do this for you, especially on big jobs.

Paper

The weight of the paper may range from very light (such as bond) to very heavy (such as cover stock). There is also a range of weights within these classes. Usually, the heavier the paper within a class, the more it costs. Thus a 100-pound cover is more expensive than a 50-pound cover. These weights are based on the actual weight of 500 sheets of that paper in the standard sheet size. For your purposes, you need only remember that heavier paper (the higher the number) is bulkier, stronger, and more expensive.

The intended use will guide you in selecting the weight of paper. A simple one-page flyer might be printed on 20- or 24-pound bond. If you want it to be more substantial, you could use a 65-pound paper. Brochures are usually printed on fairly substantial paper. This makes them look more impressive and last longer. You must consider, however, the total bulk of the item. Brochures on thick paper are more expensive to mail, and the paper doesn't fold very well in a brochure that has several panels.

There are seven types of paper, according to Media Distribution Services (MDS), that you are most likely to use:

» **Bond** for lightweight directories, letters, business forms, newsletters, and quick printing.

» **Text** for a textured look on annual reports, announcements, books, and calendars.

» **Coated** for a smooth, high-quality look on brochures, magazines, and posters. Coated, or glossy, paper is ideal for photographs and color printing.

» **Book** for an antique or smooth finish on trade and textbooks. Less expensive than text paper.

» **Cover** for a stable, durable quality to complement text and coated papers for covers and booklets.

» **Tag** for good bending and folding qualities. Good for pamphlets that have several folds.

» **Bristol** for a softer surface than tag or index paper. Good for high-speed folding, embossing, or stamping.

There are a number of variations on these basic types, and printers have entire shelves of paper samples from a wide range of manufacturers. Printers are experienced in what papers work best for various jobs, and you should ask them for their recommendations. Paper usually represents 35 to 50 percent of the printing cost for most jobs, so you should take care in selecting paper that is appropriate to your budget and needs.

Another option is recycled paper. Increasingly, organizations are using such paper for newsletters, stationery, office forms, and brochures. In fact, one survey of public relations people indicated that 90 percent had selected recycled paper for printing documents. The main reason for selecting recycled paper was concern for the environment. A large percentage of respondents also thought that it benefited the organization's image.

Type Fonts

There are several ways in which to classify type, but the simplest is to organize the various faces into three groups: serif, sans serif, and decorative.

» **Serif types**, such as Times Roman, Caslon, or Century Schoolbook, are the most readable because the serifs help guide the eye along the lines of type.

» **Sans serif types**, such as Helvetica or Arial, are popular. Some of the earlier types in this group were hard to read in body copy but quite satisfactory in headlines. The newer designs seem to work well for text copy, too.

» **Decorative typefaces**, such as Script and Old English, should be used with great care. They look elegant on certificates and invitations, but they should not be used for large blocks of text. Only use them when the importance of design exceeds that of legibility.

Type Families — Microsoft Word has a variety of type choices and variations. Among the possibilities are Times New Roman, Helvetica Neue, New Century Schoolbook, Avant Garde, Georgia, Zapfino, Century Gothic, and Palatino. A large number of decorative typefaces are available that have shading, stripes, and ultramodern designs. Typefaces are constantly being introduced. For example, Jonathan Hoefler and Tobias Frere-Jones operate H&FJ type foundry. Two of the popular typefaces they have designed are Archer and Gotham, which was used and made famous by Barack Obama during his 2008 presidential campaign.

One note of caution: People often are so impressed with the variety of typestyles available that they try to use too many in a given publication. Novice enthusiasts tend to go overboard, and the result is a mishmash of conflicting styles that almost guarantees reader confusion.

Printers' Measurements — The beauty of word processing programs such as Microsoft Word is that they offer a variety of type fonts that are scalable to any size. In computer layout, you can select one typestyle and size for the headline and another type and size for the body text. If a headline or text copy doesn't quite fit the layout, a few clicks of the mouse will reduce it until it fits. Of course, you have to consider readability, which is discussed shortly.

We are so used to just clicking on a type size such as 14, 16, 24, 36, etc., that some historical background is needed. Printers have always measured type size in *points;* long ago, the standard was 72 points to the inch. In other words, a 72-point headline is 1-inch high. A 36-point headline is ½-inch high. And, of course, copy set in 18-point type is ¼-inch high.

Many printers still measure the length of a typeset line by **picas.** There are 6 picas to an inch, so a 24-pica line is 4 inches wide. Note, however, that many experts say column widths should be no more than 12 to 14 picas and no fewer than 8 picas. Picas are also used to measure the depth of a block of copy. Thus, a story that is 42 picas deep will measure 7 inches.

Desktop publishing software has eliminated the need to be totally conversant in points and picas, but you should be familiar with the terms and what they mean when you are talking with a printer.

Readability — Legibility is affected by the typeface. Times Roman is more legible than Old English. Readability is affected by the legibility of the type and by letter spacing, line spacing, the length of the lines, the color of paper and ink, the kind of paper, and the total amount of reading matter involved. A brochure could be effective with headlines in 18- or 24-point Times Roman, but using this size type for body text in a 16-page booklet would not work.

The only purpose for printing anything is to get it read. Accordingly, any print material should be planned with readability in mind. Select a legible type and, if necessary, use letter spacing to spread headlines. Use line spacing to improve the readability of lowercase body copy. Keep the length of lines short enough that each can be read as one unit. As a general rule, try to use type no smaller than 10 point for text copy. If your target audience is over 50 years old, you should probably use 12-point, or even 14-point, type.

Ink and Color

Technological advances in printing now make it easy and economical to use color in all kinds of publications. The use of color, either by choosing colored paper or various inks, not only makes the publications more attractive, but studies show that it improves reader comprehension and willingness to read the material.

Mario Garcia, a nationally known graphic designer, told *Public Relations Tactics,* "The color is the first thing people notice when a publication lands on their desk. People attach meaning to the publication based on the colors they see."

In many respects, color also conveys the image and values of the organization. If the organization is somewhat conservative and traditional, it's best to stick with soft pastels and earth colors. Garcia, for example, used champagne and sky blue shades when he redesigned *The Wall Street Journal.* This approach also is more pleasing to an older and more traditional audience, which the newspaper serves. In contrast, *USA Today,* with a younger audience and considerable reliance on newsstand sales, uses a lot of bright colors throughout its pages to attract readers.

> **" The color is the first thing people notice when a publication lands on their desk. People attach meaning to the publication based on the colors they see. "** Mario Garcia, graphic designer, to *Public Relations Tactics*

Color can be used in photos, graphics, headlines, background screens (text boxes), and even body type. Black, however, is the most often used color for body text in newsletters, magazines, and brochures. There are two reasons for this. First, black provides the strongest and clearest contrast on white or pastel paper. In other words, black type is much easier to read than text in hot pink or another vivid color. Second, printers typically have presses set up for black ink, so the cost is less than that for using multiple colors.

With any ink, however, you must consider the color of the paper on which it will be printed. No color will read well against a dark-colored stock. Black ink on dark green paper, for example, makes the copy almost impossible to read and causes eye strain. Consequently, the best choice is white paper or something in a pastel or neutral shade.

Listen to the advice of your designer and printer. They are much more knowledgeable about how inks and paper go together for maximum effectiveness and readability. A printer's input is particularly important if you plan to use full-color photography.

Finding a Printer

A variety of printers and printing processes are found in every city. You should meet with several of them to discuss your particular needs and their capabilities. Look at samples of their work. Find out what various services cost. It is particularly important to find out what software publishing programs they use and what format is preferred for submission of copy and artwork.

Printers today are computerized, and the most common software programs used are InDesign, Quark Xpress, and PhotoShop. Therefore, if you are submitting digital files to them via email or on a CD, they should be compatible with the printer's system. The computers of most commercial printers, for example, can't read files created on programs such as Microsoft Publisher or PrintShop. You also have to ask whether a printer's system is PC- or Mac-based.

You should get bids from several printers to get the most value for your money. Printers, in order to give you a cost estimate, will ask you to give them all the specifications of the publication you are planning. See the Tips for Success on page 365 for a list of specs that printers will need.

Annual Reports

The most expensive and time-consuming publication prepared by an organization is the annual report. Although it is called a "report," it really is a major brochure complete with photos, charts, text, and color that can run up to a hundred pages.

Much of the information in such a report is mandated by the Securities and Exchange Commission (SEC) as a way to ensure corporate accountability to shareholders. All this legal and financial material, of course, is a fairly dry accounting of how the company did in a previous year, so corporate annual reports often use bar graphs, pie charts, and color to make the report readable and interesting to the average reader.

Many companies also use the annual report as a marketing tool to build stockholder loyalty, attract new investors, recruit employees, recognize current employees, and even increase their customer base. As Bob Butter, associate director of Ketchum's global practice, told *PRWeek*, "The annual report is still a company's most rounded corporate capability presentation."

If you work on an annual report, you'll primarily be involved with the nonfinancial part. The report may consist largely of tables, but it is more interesting if it contains items such as a letter from the CEO or details about the products or services and the people who make or perform them. The report might also include information on new product innovations, expansion into new markets, and how the corporation is engaging in social responsibility and environmental matters.

Another approach is what might be called "storytelling," incorporating short features about employees and their work or customers who have benefited from the organization's products and services. Johnson & Johnson's 2010 report, for example, humanized the company by linking products to researchers who developed them or to consumers who benefited from them.

FedEx (see Figure 13.7) set the tone for its narrative on the cover of its 2011 annual report. The cover read simply, "Momentum/Moment." The first page of the

> ❝ *The annual report is still a company's most rounded corporate capability presentation.* ❞
>
> Bob Butter, associate director of Ketchum's global practices, to *PRWeek*

Tips for Success   How Much Will It Cost?

Printers need detailed specifications before they can tell you how much your publication will cost. Media Distribution Services in New York says you should be prepared to provide the following information when you contact a printer:

+ Size of piece
+ Print quantity
+ Number of colors
+ Type and quantity of photos and illustrations
+ Number of folds
+ Whether there are "bleeds"
+ Type of binding
+ Quality and weight of paper
+ Whether there will be die cuts or embossing
+ Delivery deadlines

It's also a good idea to show printers a "dummy," or sample of what your piece will look like, so they can see what you require. This preliminary "look-see" will help the printer spot potential problems.

report reinforced the theme: "Momentum around us: Powerful, long-term trends in global trade revolve around FedEx." The chairman's letter then outlined how the company had a defining moment in 2011 with, among other successes, double-digit revenue growth.

FIGURE 13.7 One of public relations writers' key roles in developing an annual report is to help determine an appropriate theme that catches the attention of the reader and can be threaded throughout the publication. FedEx, in this report, boasted about growth in spite of tough economic times. Its "Momentum/Moment" cover headline served as a catalyst for FedEx to tell its story inside regarding how 2011 was a defining moment for the corporation contributing to its forward momentum in 2012 and beyond. FedEx® is a registered trademark of Federal Express Corporation.

Most annual reports are still prepared in print form and mailed to investors and stockholders. Traditionally, companies were required by the SEC to automatically mail the annual report to all stockholders, which may be several million for some corporations, such as GM. But in 2008, the SEC ruled that corporations are required to mail reports only to those stockholders who request one. The change in requirements was, in part, due to the widespread availability of the annual report on an organization's website.

The readers of annual reports are of two sorts: the nonexpert individual and the sophisticated financial analyst. The amateur is interested mainly in the quality of the management, earnings, dividends, stock appreciation, and the outlook for the industry. The experts—who advise investors or manage large holdings—want much more information, which they feed into their computers. This difference in information needs presents the organization with a problem. A few hundred people want great masses of data, whereas thousands don't want the details.

A common solution is to design an annual report that gives the financial highlights in easy-to-read charts and graphs at the beginning of the report. This section is, in fact, often labeled "Financial Highlights." Merck, a pharmaceutical firm, took this approach in its 2010 report. The corporation posted two versions of its annual report in PDFs on its website. A dense, black-and-white SEC form 10-K version without illustrations provided all the elements required by analysts and regulators. But a colorful, 18-page highlight version offered only the very most basic information in a highly visual format. Coca-Cola took a similar track, even referring to the 10-K version as the "annual report" and the visual highlights version as the "annual review."

Planning and Writing

An annual report usually covers every aspect of the organization. Consequently, every department head may want input, and each may have different ideas. The task of the public relations people involved is to coordinate, plan, consult, write, design, and produce the report. Tact, perseverance, and determination to get the job done are essential. In fact, Ragan Research notes that "The majority of editors, with the most crucial print document that their organizations put out, dread annual report time like the flu season."

Work on the report may start six months before the date of issue. A first step is to establish a budget. Glossy, four-color reports can be expensive, so it is important to know how many copies you will need. With a budget established, you can start planning the report. First, you should look at the last report; compare it with those of other organizations—especially those in the same industry; criticize it; think of ways to make it more informative, more understandable, and more useful. One useful tool is focus groups with analysts and stockholders to find out what they want to see in your upcoming annual report.

When you have enough information, you can start consulting with key executives and establishing a theme for the report. Basically, the objective is to inform, but a theme makes the report more interesting and focused. Usually, it focuses on some aspect of the business that the company wants to showcase that particular year. The theme of many corporate annual reports, after the Enron scandal and intense public scrutiny of executive misdoing, was corporate responsibility and accountability. Other examples of themes were "Innovating, Discovering, Connecting" (Merck), "This is the New GM" (General Motors), "Lean Forward" (Harley-Davidson), and "Advancing Our Global Momentum" (Coca-Cola).

When the theme is established, it is time to think of design—how the report will look, what will be included, how the various elements will be treated.

Design, to a large degree, depends on what the corporation wants to communicate. If it wants to project an image of success and dominance in the marketplace, the report may be a dazzling display of glossy paper, color, and state-of-the-art graphics. However, if the company did not do so well the previous year, there is a tendency to use only one or two colors, simple graphics, and plain paper, so stockholders don't think the company is wasting money. Beth Haiken, vice president at the PMI Group, says it best in a *PRWeek* interview: "In a good year, more color, photos, or unique design features won't seem out of place. In a bad year, lean and clean is best."

Trends in Content and Delivery

Annual reports change with the times. They are considered the most important single document a public company can produce, so a great amount of attention is given to content, graphics, and overall design. The objective is to ensure that the annual report reflects corporate culture and external economic conditions.

Several key themes in corporate annual reports are apparent:

» **Candor and frankness.** Global competition has caused the shrinkage of corporate profits and major dislocations in many industries. Consequently, many corporations are more candid in their annual reports. Johnson & Johnson, for example, told annual report readers, "2010 will be remembered as a year in which our company was severely tested on numerous fronts."

» **Corporate governance and accountability.** All corporations are under intense public scrutiny because of major scandals in financial reporting and executives receiving benefits in the millions of dollars. Consequently, many companies are being more transparent in their annual reports.

» **Websites.** Most companies now make their annual reports, often with video excerpts from the annual meeting, available online. One advantage is savings on postage and paper costs, but this doesn't mean that the print version is going out of fashion. There are several reasons for this. First, financial analysts and portfolio managers still request a printed annual report to review prior to meeting with the company's management. Second, a printed report has a beginning, middle, and an end that makes it an easy-to-follow narrative that avoids the disjointed pages and links of a website. Third, a printed report represents a tangible item that often projects the human side of an organization better than looking at the same material in digital form.

» **More emphasis on marketing.** Today, the annual report is also used as a marketing tool to increase consumer loyalty and build the company's image. General Motors, for example, featured a glossy color picture of its "World-Class Lineup" of automobiles in its 2010 annual report.

» **Readability.** Annual reports are becoming more magazine-like, with summary headlines, easy-to-understand charts and graphs, simple question-and-answer sections, and more conversational prose. This reflects the growing trend of distributing the annual report to a variety of publics—customers, current and prospective employees, suppliers, community opinion leaders, and others.

» **Environmental sensitivity.** In an effort to portray themselves as environmentally conscious, many organizations use recycled paper and soy-based inks for annual reports. In addition, annual reports are becoming shorter, saving more trees.

» **Corporate social responsibility (CSR).** The public now expects corporations to be good citizens and to make a contribution to society. Consequently, corporations now include a summary of their CSR activities in their annual reports, or even take the step of producing another major brochure that exclusively focuses on CSR. A good example is Coca-Cola's sustainability report (Figure 13.8).

» **Global approach.** Corporations now have global operations, and the annual report functions as a capabilities brochure that markets a company on a worldwide scale. Some companies even translate parts of their annual report into several languages. The chairman's letter in Nike's annual report was translated into French, Spanish, and Chinese.

FIGURE 13.8 Many corporations are now publishing extensive brochures, or even magazines, about their corporate social responsibility (CSR) activities as a complement to their traditional annual reports. This is the cover of the CSR report for Coca-Cola, which the company calls its "Sustainability Review." It is a 50-plus-page review of the beverage company's work in sustainable agriculture, energy efficiency, sustainable packaging, water stewardship, and corporate values.

Summary

The Value of Print Publications

» Printed materials, such as newsletters, magazines, and brochures, are still important communication channels in the Internet age.

» Two strengths of print publications are that they can feature in-depth stories and they can reflect the "face" of the organization. Other strengths include portability and an extended shelf life.

The Balancing Act of Editors

» An editor must balance management expectations, employee needs, and journalistic standards.

» A publication's format and content should reflect the organization's culture, goals, and objectives.

» Today's employees want periodicals that address their concerns about the economic health of the organization and their job security.

» Every publication should have an overall mission statement. An annual editorial plan outlines the kind of stories and features that will support the organization's priorities.

Newsletters and Magazines

» The newsletter is the most common organizational publication. Magazines usually are the most expensive publication and are often sent to both internal and external audiences.

» Headlines should be written in active voice and provide key messages.

Online Newsletters

» Online newsletters sent on an organization's intranet system often contain more color, graphics, and photos. Newsletters sent via email tend to use fewer graphics and have stories 10 to 12 lines long.

» Desktop publishing is widely used for preparing newsletters, magazines, and brochures. Desktop publishing requires the preparation of extensive electronic files that show the links between copy, graphics, photos, headlines, and layout.

Intranets

» Many corporations are using intranets to communicate with employees.

» Intranets are most effective when they are uncluttered and the home page is limited to one screen.

Brochures

» Writing and designing a brochure requires you to know its purpose, the target audience, and the most cost-effective format.

» A brochure requires simple sentence construction, informative headlines, liberal use of subheads, and short paragraphs.

» The most common mistake of novice writers is to write too much copy for the space available. A brochure page crammed with type is a turnoff.

» Factors such as cost, distribution, and estimated life span of the brochure help determine the format of the printed piece and the kind of writing required.

» It pays to prepare a dummy or mock layout of the brochure before you begin writing.

» A printer needs to know all the specifications of a planned piece before he or she can give you a cost estimate.

» There are various grades of paper, each designed for specific kinds of jobs.

- » There are various type classes and families. Stick to fonts that are highly readable. Use decorative type and italics sparingly.
- » Black ink is the most popular and readable color. Use spot color to make your publication more attractive.
- » Although you may be able to write and design a simple flyer or brochure, experts recommend hiring a professional graphic designer for bigger jobs.

Annual Reports

- » Annual reports require considerable planning, resources, and design expertise. They are probably the single most expensive document that an organization produces.

Skill Building Activities

1. Collect three or four copies of an organization's employee newsletter or magazine. Write a critique of the publication regarding its content and design, using the guidelines and advice given in this chapter. If you were the editor, what changes would you make in the content or design?

2. You have just been hired as the editor of a new monthly magazine for the local hospital. The magazine will be mailed to potential donors, doctors, community leaders, and employees. Write a 25-word mission statement for this publication. Then prepare a 12-month editorial plan, giving your ideas about the type and content of stories that you would publish each month.

3. Your manufacturing company has just received a $750,000 contract to produce and install solar panels for a new office building being built in your city. This contract ensures full employment at your plant and the recruitment of another 50 workers. What headline would you write for the employee newsletter?

4. Collect some brochures produced by various organizations. Based on the guidelines suggested in this chapter, write a critique of each brochure from the standpoint of content, format, and design. Mention what you like about each brochure, and what you would change.

5. Write and design a simple brochure for a campus organization. Use the format of a 4-inch by 9-inch brochure with six panels. See the Tips for Success on page 358 for some guidelines.

6. Review the online newsletters of five national organizations and write a critique of them. What did you like and dislike about their format and content? If you had to start an online newsletter, what did you learn from your review that would help you?

Media Resources

Davis, E. (2010, February). "Read This! Make Your Headlines Stand Out." *Public Relations Tactics*, 17.

Hampp, A. (2010, October). "Gap to Scrap New Logo, Return to Old Design." *Advertising Age*, 12.

Jansen, M. (2011, July 1). "Five Ways to Write an E-newsletter People Will Read." Retrieved from www.ragan.com.

Kent, C. (2011, February 21). "How Western Union Used Mobile to Reach Its Global Workforce." Retrieved from www.ragan.com.

Kent, C. (2010, October). "Two Keys to a Terrific Intranet: Searching and Sharing." *The Ragan Report,* 28–29.

Miller, L. (2010, March). "Microsoft Ups Intranet Use by Offering Superb External Content." *The Ragan Report,* 13–14.

Miller, L. (2010, January). "3 Ways to Make Your Annual Report Greener (Cheaper, Too)." *The Ragan Report,* 25–27.

Ragan, M. (2010, June). "How to Write Headlines that Scream 'Read Me!" *The Ragan Report,* 3.

Spurlock, B., and O'Neil, J. (2009, Spring). "Designing an Employee-Centered Intranet and Measuring Its Impact on Employee Voice and Satisfaction," *Public Relations Journal 3* (2). Retrieved from www.prsa.org.

Ward, T. (2010, October). "Employees Prefer Intranet Homepage with No 'Fold.'" *The Ragan Report,* 24.

Wilson, M. (2011, June 21). "Discovery Health: The World's Best Intranet." Retrieved from www.ragan.com.

Writing Email, Memos, and Proposals

14

》 After reading this chapter, you will be able to:

- 》 Manage communication overload
- 》 Use email professionally
- 》 Write effective memorandums

- 》 Develop business letters
- 》 Understand the basics of writing proposals

The Challenge of Communication Overload

The public relations writer doesn't always communicate with a large, impersonal audience. He or she also communicates on a more personal level through email, memos, letters, phone calls, and face-to-face communications.

Public relations personnel typically spend a large percentage of their working day engaging in interpersonal communications. They are constantly sending, receiving, and replying to email, texting, summarizing the results of client or management meetings, answering voicemail, sending memos to colleagues, writing proposals, and preparing position papers. All this takes organization, efficiency, and communication skills.

It takes a lot of time to simply read all the messages that inundate us, but it also takes ample time to organize, write, and send all those messages. In many cases, public relations writers are major contributors to information clutter, because their jobs involve the writing and dissemination of so many messages.

The problem is best expressed by Richard E. Neff, a consultant in Belgium, who writes in *Communication World*, "Writers waste too much time producing texts that waste even more time for readers." The solution, he says, is to "write smart, simple, and short." Neff continues, "When people write letters and reports that are clear enough and simple enough and accurate enough and short enough—the time it saves the reader is immense." To be sure that your messages are pertinent, consider the following:

- 》 **Completeness.** Whether you are writing a 10-line memo or a 32-page annual report, you must be certain that it contains the information needed to serve its purpose. Ask yourself why you are writing and what your reader wants or needs to know. If more information will aid the reader's understanding, provide it—but don't give your reader a mass of irrelevant material. Preparing an outline will help ensure your message is on target and complete.

» **Conciseness.** *Less is better.* Conciseness means brevity. Your objective is to be as brief as possible, because people don't have the time or the patience to read through long messages. This means that you need to carefully select words that convey ideas and thoughts in a concise manner. If you can summarize a message in a 140-character tweet, why not transfer that skill to other media?

» **Correctness.** You must be accurate in everything you write. If an item in the mass media contains an error, the blame may be spread among many people. An error in a personalized communication, however, reflects solely on you and your abilities. Be sure that what you prepare is accurate, and you will get credit for being a professional.

» **Courtesy.** These are *personal* communications. Personal names are used extensively, and both senders and receivers have considerable interest in the material. You might think it advisable to make the messages as personal as possible, but don't go overboard. The writing should be polite, but not effusive, personal, but not overly familiar.

» **Responsibility.** Be prudent and think about how your communication will be perceived by the recipient. A letter, a text message, a tweet, or email is a highly visible record of what you say, so be careful about setting the right tone. Do you come across as flippant, arrogant, or defensive? Or do you come across as helpful, sympathetic, and concerned? You are representing your employer or client, so your communications must be in accordance with the organization's policies and procedures.

> **" When people write letters and reports that are clear enough and simple enough and accurate enough and short enough—the time it saves the reader is immense. "** Richard E. Neff, writing in *Communication World*

These general guidelines are helpful in all communications, but now we will discuss the specific techniques of how to write emails, memos, letters, and proposals in an efficient and professional manner.

Email

Electronic mail (email) inboxes are getting backed up at an astounding rate. In 2010, 107 trillion emails were sent to 2.9 billion email accounts worldwide, 25 percent of which were corporate accounts, according to global online monitoring company Pingdom. Research by the Radicati Group, a market research firm, showed that in 2011 the average number of corporate emails sent and received per person on a daily basis was 105.

By 2015, the volume is expected to increase to 125 per person per day. But the pace of growth in the number of emails organizations must deal with is slowing in large part because of other technologies such as instant messaging and social networks, according to the firm. Nonetheless, the Radicati Group predicts that between 2011 and 2015 the growth of corporate email accounts will outpace that of individual email accounts due, in large part, to the increasing availability of Cloud-based email services.

Despite the concerns of psychologists and productivity experts, email no doubt will continue to thrive because of its multiple advantages for cost-effective communication on a global scale. As a professional communicator, however, you need to recognize its limitations and to use it efficiently to get your message through the thick forest of information clutter. In many situations, you should bypass email by using text messaging, Twitter, wikis, and RSS feeds. These were discussed in the last chapter.

Purpose

According to a survey of communicators in Fortune 500 corporations, email (1) reduces the cost of employee communications, (2) increases the distribution of messages to more employees, (3) flattens the corporate hierarchy, and (4) speeds decision making.

Email has other advantages. It is a good way for public relations writers to send media advisories and news releases to the media, disseminate employee newsletters, and even chat with colleagues around the world. Email is also effective from the standpoint of (1) keeping up with events, (2) making arrangements and appointments, and (3) reviewing or editing documents. Increasingly, however, organizations are also using wikis for group editing, scheduling, and overall logistics.

Email is not suitable for all person-to-person communications. It is primarily an informal memo system. At times, it is best to send a more formal letter on organizational stationery. A job recommendation or a letter to a disgruntled customer makes a better impression on paper than in an email message, which seems less official and permanent. Writing the personal letter will be discussed shortly.

Also, experts say that email should never be a substitute for face-to-face communication. More than two-thirds of the respondents in the Rogen International survey say that face-to-face communication is the preferred channel of communication for delivering important information. The study notes, "The good and the bad should be delivered face-to face: Seventy-one percent preferred good news to be delivered that way, as did 81 percent for bad news."

According to *PR Reporter:*

Similarly, face-to-face should be used for discussing issues of workplace performance or personal confrontation. When it comes to job performance, employees need to be able to probe for answers and clarify responses, which is lost in email dialogue. For other discussions around potential conflicts or misunderstandings, face-to-face is crucial because email messages can be misunderstood; readers can perceive angry tones, abrupt manners, and even humor incorrectly.

In other words, you should think of email as one of your communication tools—just not the only one. Email is a somewhat sterile, mechanistic form of interpersonal communication that can convey routine information very well, but you should also make the time to use the telephone and talk face-to-face with colleagues and customers.

Content

Both style and substance are important to effective email. Michael Hattersley, writing in *Public Relations Tactics*, noted, "Although one can be quite informal in a personal conversation or even in a meeting, you never know where an email will end up. Make sure it represents you as you want to be seen. Every written communication should be flawless and represent your best work."

In other words, you can be somewhat informal in an email message, but that does not mean you can be sloppy about grammar, punctuation, spelling, and sentence structure. It also means that you need to think twice about writing something that would be embarrassing to you if the sender decided to forward it to others.

Today's technology means that no email message is secure or confidential. If you are using email at your place of work, be aware that management has the ability and legal right to read your email messages, even if you erase them. More than one employee has been fired for posting messages that have included crude jokes about ethnic minorities and negative comments about supervisors. Newer kinds of surveillance software can even log all your keystrokes even if you don't send a message or if you erase that rant about your "stupid" boss.

> **"Although one can be quite informal in a personal conversation or even in a meeting, you never know where an email will end up. Make sure it represents you as you want to be seen. Every written communication should be flawless and represent your best work."**
>
> Michael Hattersley, writing in *Public Relations Tactics*

Here are some other suggestions about the content of your email messages:

» Use language that falls halfway between formal writing and spontaneous conversation.

» Blunt words and statements assume more importance in electronic form than in a telephone conversation. Temper your language.

» TYPING IN ALL CAPITAL LETTERS MAKES PEOPLE FEEL LIKE YOU'RE SHOUTING AT THEM. See what I mean? Furthermore, it makes your email harder to read.

» Keep messages short. Remember that many people now read email on their smartphones.

» Give deadlines at the beginning of the message or even in the subject line.

» Send messages without attachments whenever possible. An attachment dramatically decreases the odds that your message will be read.

» Use standard English and abbreviations. Don't use a lot of cryptic symbols as shorthand. Kids, not businesspeople, use acronyms like IMHO (In My Humble Opinion).

» Copy only necessary people when responding to a group message. Avoid the "reply to all" syndrome.

» Double-check who will receive your message before sending it.

» Break out points or questions as numbered items. It helps recipients answer them in sequence.

» When sending email messages to the media, use blind copy distribution so that the recipients don't know it is a mass mailing. Use of bcc distribution is also best when emailing to groups of people who may not know each other. It protects their privacy.

» Don't be an email junkie. Don't clutter up mailboxes with inane chitchat or forward jokes to large groups; it's irritating to receivers.

» Although email is a form of one-to-one communication, it is not a substitute for phone conversations and meetings. They are important for maintaining personal relationships.

» Always reread an email message before sending it. Will the tone or choice of words offend the receiver? Are you coming across as friendly and courteous, or brusque and pompous?

» Have a spell-checker automatically review every outgoing email and proofread it yourself. Poor spelling reflects on your professionalism and the organization's credibility.

» Respond to relevant, work-related email messages in a timely manner.

Format

Everyone knows how to send an email. All you have to do is sit down in front of the computer, connect to the Internet, and start typing. Right? Although this method may be all right for quick notes among friends, you should be aware that everyone is getting flooded with emails, and your missive is one of many that appear in an inbox. Consequently, it is important to know some techniques that can improve the readership of your email. It's also necessary to mind your manners, and the Tips for Success box on page 378 can help.

Subject Line — An email format, after the address, includes a subject line. This is the opportunity to say succinctly what the message is about. The growing reliance on mobile devices for accessing email only increases the importance of concise subject lines. Think of the subject line as a form of headline, which was discussed in Chapter 5, when sending emails to journalists. If you are announcing an event, don't just do a label line such as "Spring Concert." You have about 40 characters to give more detail. For example, you might say "Tickets Available for May 5 Concert."

If you need a decision or response, say so. The subject line, in this case, might say, "Your plans for attending Spring Concert?" or even "You're invited to a Spring Concert on May 5." When you provide context and more description, the recipient knows exactly what is being discussed or requested.

A report by the Center for Media Research noted, "Though the research showed that, overall, shorter subject lines correlate with higher open rates and click rates, subject line word order, word choice, and brand and audience awareness are also critical success factors."

Salutation — An email is somewhat informal, so it is unnecessary to include the sender's full name, title, organization, and address as you would in a business letter. It is also unnecessary to say, "Dear..." Just begin with the person's first name. There is some debate, however, about using first names of people you haven't met. Many people are put off by an email that assumes a familiarity that doesn't exist. You need to exercise some judgment; if the email is business oriented, such as to a customer, you might use a more formal designation, such as "Hello, Ms. Smith." You can also say "Dear Ms. Smith," but that term doesn't quite fit the format of an email, which is more like a memo. If the email is being distributed to a group, use an opener such as "Team" or "Colleagues."

First Sentence or Paragraph — Get to the "bottom line" right away, so the recipient knows immediately what the key message is and what you want him or her to do with it. Avoid starting email messages with such phrases as "I wanted to inform you . . ."

Body of Message — Think of an email as a memo, which is discussed in the next section. Most experts say the best email messages are short. How short? A good rule

+

Tips for Success   Mind Your Email Manners

Microsoft Office Online has a column authored by the "crabby office lady." In one issue, she listed the top 10 cyber-discourtesies that are "driving all of us nuts."

+ **Avoid the "Reply to All" button.**   In most cases, your personal reply to an email doesn't require you to share your thoughts with everyone on the mailing list. Greta, in accounting, probably could care less if you are attending the company picnic.

+ **Skip the CAPITAL letters.**   By using uppercase letters, it essentially means that you are yelling at the recipient. Save the capital letters unless you really want to shout and seek assistance.

+ **Save the fancy stationery.**   You don't need pastel backgrounds, smiley faces, and a fancy letterhead to send an email. Keep it simple and uncluttered.

+ **Give your response first.**   When you reply to an email, make sure your reply is the first thing the recipient reads.

+ **Keep forwards to a minimum.**   Everyone has already heard the joke.

+ **Don't be a cyber-coward.**   If you have something to say that is highly personal, scary, sad, angry, tragic, vicious, shocking, or any combination of the above, say it in person.

+ **Keep the 500KB image file to yourself.**   Most email accounts have limited capacity. Don't send your vacation photos to everyone in your address book. Use Facebook or Flickr to post your photos.

+ **Fill out the subject line.**   People get plenty of emails every day; if you can't take the time to fill out the subject line, I don't need to take time to open it.

+ **Avoid HTML format.**   The most easily accessible email format around the globe is plain text.

+ **Count to 10 before hitting the Send button.**   Think twice, or even wait 24 hours, before sending that clever, scathing message to someone and possibly the rest of the world. A "flaming" email often starts more fires than you can put out.

of thumb is one screen. That is about 20 to 25 lines, single-spaced. It is also recommended that there be no more than 65 characters per line. Others recommend that you keep the length of lines even shorter, because people can read material faster in a narrow column (left half of page) than as an entire screen of type.

When appropriate, you can use boldfacing, underlining, and bullets to highlight key pieces of information. The idea, as stated in Chapter 13, is to help the viewer scan the message for the important points. As previously noted, don't use ALL CAPITAL letters, however. It is also a good idea to include other email addresses or websites so a viewer can easily click on them to get more information.

Closing — Sign off with a brief word such as "Regards," "Best," or even "Cheers." You can also use the standard closing "Sincerely" if you're so inclined. Include your name, title, organization, email, phone, and fax numbers or Twitter handle in a standard signature. This enables the recipient to contact you directly if he or she wants additional information. It is also a handy reference if the recipient prints out the message and files it.

Memorandums

A memorandum—*memo* for short—is a brief written message, usually a page or less in length. In the past, it was photocopied and distributed to employees through the organization's mail system. Today, the standard method of delivery is email for most routine memos. On occasion, however, memos are still distributed in hard copy if they contain important information about employee benefits, major changes in policy, or other kinds of information that an individual should retain for his or her records.

Purpose

A memo can serve almost any communication purpose. It can ask for information, supply information, confirm a verbal exchange, ask for a meeting, schedule or cancel a meeting, remind, report, praise, caution, state a policy, or perform any other function that requires a written message.

Many public relations firms require staff to write a memo whenever there is a client meeting, or even a telephone conversation, because it creates a record and "paper trail" of what was discussed and what decisions were made.

It should be noted, however, that hard copies of memos are often distributed even if they were sent via email. The reason is that people don't always pay close attention to the multiple emails they receive, and they often overlook or unintentionally delete some before they are read. Consequently, many organizations continue to distribute and retain hard copies of their most important memos even if they are sent via email.

Content

A memo should be specific and to the point. The subject line, as in email messages, should state exactly what the memo is about. If it is about a meeting, the subject line should state: "Department meeting on Thursday at 3 P.M." If it is a summary of decisions made at a meeting, you could use: "Decisions made at last staff meeting."

The first sentence or paragraph of a memo should contain the key message that would be of most interest to the reader. All too often, first sentences don't provide any meaningful information. *Communication Briefings* asked readers to choose the best opening statement for a memo. Which one of the choices below would you choose?

1. "Kevin Donaldson and I recommend that we cancel the Carstairs account."
2. "Kevin Donaldson and I met yesterday to discuss the Carstairs account."
3. "Kevin Donaldson and I recommend that we cancel the Carstairs account for these reasons."
4. "I've been asked to reply to your request for more information on the Carstairs account."
5. "You'll be glad to know that we finally got the results on the Carstairs account."

Both 1 and 3 are better than the other choices because they are specific about a course of action. Number 3 is the preferred choice because it includes "for these reasons"—a phrase that explains why. All the others are too vague and don't give the reader much useful information.

Format

Every memo should contain five elements: (1) date, (2) to, (3) from, (4) subject, and (5) message. This format should be used in email and hard copy memos. Here is an example of a simple memo:

Monday, May 1

To: Public Relations Committee
From: Susan Parker
Subject: Meeting on Monday, May 15

We will meet in the conference room from 3 to 4 P.M. to discuss how to publicize and promote the company's annual employee picnic. The president wants to encourage the families of all employees to attend, so please come prepared to offer your ideas and suggestions.

Letters

Many college students, used to the informality of email, have no idea how to compose a business letter. A business letter, actually printed on paper and sent via the postal service, requires a more systematic approach to writing and formatting a message. It is written primarily to individuals when a more "official" or formal response is required. Job applicants, for example, make a much better impression with prospective employers by sending a handwritten thank you note instead of an email or text message thanking the employer for the interview. As Max Kalehoff, vice president of Clickable, says, "If well-written, a handwritten letter can deliver extraordinary impact."

As a public relations writer, you will write two kinds of letters. One is the single, personal letter to a specific individual. This is the most personal form of letter writing, because a one-to-one dialogue is established between the sender and the recipient. A letter is perceived as more permanent than email and often serves as an official record of a dialogue involving employment, an issue about company policy, or even an answer to a consumer complaint.

The second kind of letter is less personal, because it is often a form letter about a specific situation sent to large numbers of people, such as stockholders, customers, or even residents of a city. These form letters might be considered direct mail (discussed Chapter 16), but they go beyond the common description of direct mail as a form of advertising to sell goods or services, or even to solicit funds for a charitable organization. Form letters, often written by public relations staff and signed by the head of the organization, usually give background or an update on a situation affecting the organization and a particular public.

A good example is a form letter signed by the president of Coca-Cola to stockholders about the recall of some of its products in Belgium and France due to quality concerns. Various negative news reports had caused the stock value to drop, so the president wrote the letter to let the stockholders know what the company was doing to solve the problem. He assured the stockholders that "your company remains totally committed to maintaining the quality of our products, the strength of the brand and the trust of our customers and consumers, as we continue to seize the vast opportunities before us to build value for you."

Whether you are writing a personalized letter or a form letter, here are some general guidelines about their purpose, content, and format. Other tips are given on page 382.

Purpose

A letter may be used to give information, to ask for information, to motivate, to answer complaints, to soothe or arouse, to warn, to admit, or to deny. In short, a letter can carry any sort of message that requires a written record. It is a substitute for personal conversation, although it is not as friendly as face-to-face conversation. It does have the advantage, however, of allowing the writer to get facts in order, develop a logical and persuasive approach, and phrase the message carefully to accomplish a specific purpose.

Answering a complaint letter is a good example. The specific purpose is to satisfy the customer and retain his or her product loyalty. Although many organizations use standard form letters to answer customer complaints, a more personal approach that specifically deals with the complaint is usually more effective. This is not to say that every letter must be written from scratch. There are often key sentences and paragraphs that can be used or modified that fit the situation. Most letters, for example, will include language (1) thanking the customer for writing, (2) apologizing for any inconvenience, and (3) explaining how the product will be replaced or providing a coupon for future purchases.

Content

The most important part of any letter is the first paragraph. It should concisely state the purpose of the letter or tell the reader the "bottom line" so the reader knows immediately the objective of the letter. This is the same principle that was discussed in Chapter 5 for the first paragraph of a news release.

From a writing perspective, a declarative statement is best. Instead of writing, "I am writing you to let you know that our company will be contacting you in the near future about your concerns regarding product reliability," you can simply say, "A company representative will contact you about our product reliability."

The second and succeeding paragraphs can elaborate on the details and give relevant information. The final paragraph should summarize key details, or let the recipient know you will telephone if something needs to be resolved through conversation.

Writing a business letter requires clear thought and thorough editing to reduce wordiness. Every time you use the word "I" to start a thought, think about how to remove it. At the same time, take every opportunity to use the word "you" in a letter. It places the focus on the receiver and his or her needs instead of those of the sender.

Tips for Success   How to Write Efficient Letters

A personal letter is a labor-intensive effort. Here are some ways to increase your efficiency and still keep the personal touch.

+ Produce courteous and effective printed forms for repetitive correspondence, such as requests for printed material or acknowledgments of inquiries.

+ Develop standard replies for often-asked questions or often-solicited advice where this is a part of the organization's routine business.

+ Develop standard formats for certain kinds of common correspondence to enable inexperienced writers to handle them easily and effectively.

+ Prepare a correspondence guide containing hints and suggestions on keeping verbiage and correspondence volume down to reasonable and effective levels.

+ Place a brief heading on the letter after the salutation, indicating the letter's subject. The heading will give the reader an immediate grasp of the letter's substance and will also facilitate filing.

+ Use subheads if the letter is more than two pages long, thereby giving the reader a quick grasp of how the subject is treated and where the major topics are discussed.

+ To personalize printed materials, attach your card with a brief, warm message.

+ If a letter requires a brief response, it is acceptable to pen a note on the original letter and mail it back to the sender. Retain a photocopy for your files.

The tone of a letter is an important consideration. Readers don't like to be scolded, chastised, or pacified. Try to write positive statements instead of negative ones. Instead of saying, "You didn't follow up with the client," it is better to say, "You need to improve your follow-up with the client." If you are apologizing for something, say so. Don't just say "I'm sorry ... " Be specific in your apology.

Format

As a general rule, letters should be written on standard business stationery. The letterhead should have the name, address, and telephone number of the organization. Additional information can include email address, fax numbers, and website.

Letters should always be word processed. Usually they are single-spaced. Each paragraph should be indicated, either by indention or by a line space. One page is the preferred length. A two-page letter is acceptable but, if the letter runs longer than that, consider putting the material in another format, such as a brochure that is included in the letter.

> *If you can't get your point across in one page, you probably haven't done enough preparatory work.* Communication Briefings

The date the letter was written should be at the top left on the letterhead. Next comes the full name, title, and complete address of the recipient. It is formatted in the same way as an address on an envelope. The next element is the salutation or greeting. The usual approach is to write "Dear Mr. —" or "Dear Ms. —." The latter avoids the "Miss" or "Mrs." dilemma and is common in business correspondence. You should not use a first name, such as "Dear Susan," in a greeting unless the person already knows you.

On occasion, you will need to write a letter to an organization on some routine matter and you won't know the name of the recipient. This often occurs when you are requesting information or inquiring about a billing. It is increasingly inappropriate to use the time-worn "Dear Sir," now that more than half the workforce is female. A better approach is to put your letter in the form of a memo. For example, a letter about a bill might be addressed, "To: Manager, Accounting Department."

The body of the letter should be about four or five paragraphs. It's wise to use short sentences and keep every paragraph to about four or five sentences. One common problem that inexperienced writers have is writing compound sentences that get quite convoluted and difficult to understand.

Closing a letter is easy: You can write "Yours truly," or "Sincerely." Then leave a few lines for your signature, followed by your word processed name. You can also add your direct phone line or email address so the recipient can easily contact you.

There is one more crucial step. Once you have the final draft, use a spelling and grammar checker to correct any errors. You also need to personally proofread your letter because a spell-checker program doesn't catch wrong words that are spelled correctly. You may want to write "site" but write "cite" instead. Sending a letter with obvious mistakes is sloppy and unprofessional. Many employers, for example, automatically discard any letter or résumé from a job applicant that has grammar or spelling errors.

Proposals

Proposals are a management technique to pitch new services, programs, or policies. Any number of outside suppliers and vendors write proposals to provide goods and services to an organization. Non-profit organizations also regularly write grant proposals to foundations and other funding organizations.

As a public relations writer, you should be familiar with how to organize and write a proposal for at least two purposes: (1) to present a new public relations initiative to management for approval, and (2) to help the organization or client get support or funds from other organizations or groups. Staff members at public relations firms are constantly writing proposals to get new business, and that particular area will be discussed in the next section.

Purpose

The purpose of a proposal is to get something accomplished—to persuade management to approve and authorize some important action that will have a long-lasting effect on the organization or its people. By putting the proposal in writing, you let management know exactly what is proposed, what decisions are called for, and what the consequences may be. A verbal proposal may be tossed around, discussed briefly, and then discarded. In contrast, when the idea is in writing and presented formally, it forces management to make a decision.

Before writing a proposal, author Randall Majors says you should ask yourself questions like these:

> » What is the purpose of the proposal?
> » Who will read the proposal?
> » What are the pertinent interests and values of the readers?
> » What specific action can be taken on the basis of the proposal?
> » What situation or problem does the proposal address?
> » What is the history of the situation?
> » How much and what kinds of information will make the proposal persuasive?
> » What format is most effective for the proposal?
> » How formal in format, tone, and style should the proposal be?

❝ Make sure your proposal answers these basic questions: 'Why should my audience members care?' and 'What's in it for them?' ❞

Communication Briefings

Organization

A proposal may be presented in a few pages or multiple pages, depending on the size of the organization and the scope of the proposal. *Communication Briefings* suggests that proposals are more compelling if the writer includes four major components:

- » **Show a need.** The opening should be tailored to your readers' needs. If you are seeking funds for a special event, for example, tell how such an event will enhance the organization's reputation, improve employee morale, or increase customer loyalty.
- » **Satisfy the need.** Suggest how the event would be organized to meet the needs of the audience and the organization.
- » **Show benefits.** Stress how the event would improve employee morale, increase media coverage, or improve reputation among key publics.
- » **Call for action.** Ask for a decision. Be specific about the resources and budget that you require to execute the project.

An informal proposal, one that is project oriented, might include the four components listed above in the following organizational structure:

- » **Introduction:** State the purpose of the proposal.
- » **Body:** Provide background to the problem situation, criteria for a solution, the proposed solution, a schedule for implementation, personnel assignments, budget, and some background on the proposal's authors.
- » **Conclusion:** Request approval or the signing of a contract.

A template for a major proposal includes the following components:

- » **Transmittal:** A memo, letter, or a foreword that summarizes why the proposal is being made.
- » **Table of contents:** A list of all items in the proposal.
- » **Tables and exhibits:** A list of illustrative elements and where they can be found.
- » **Summary:** A condensation of the proposal, which gives readers the basic information and enables them to appraise the idea before they go on to the details.
- » **Introduction:** Gives the scope, the approach, how information was obtained and evaluated, limitations and problems to help the reader understand the idea and weigh its impact.
- » **Body:** A complete, detailed statement of what is proposed.
- » **Recommendation:** A clear, concise statement of just what is suggested and how it is to be implemented.
- » **Exhibits and bibliography.** Items substantiating the statements in the proposal and assuring the readers that the proposal is based on thorough study of the problem or the opportunity.

The Foundation Center says that typical fundraising proposals include (1) an executive summary, (2) a statement of need, (3) a project description, (4) a budget, (5) organization information, and (6) a conclusion. Public relations writers, on occasion, also author position papers for organizations. See the guidelines in the Tips for Success on page 386 for how to write a position paper.

Tips for Success   How to Write a Position Paper

Organizations, on occasion, prepare a report about an issue relating to the organization or the industry. Such reports are called *white papers,* *briefing papers,* or *position statements.* The three reasons for writing and distributing a position paper are (1) as background information when executives and public relations personnel talk to the media, (2) as a method of advancing an organization's perspective and point of view on a trend or issue, and (3) as a marketing technique for establishing the organization as a "thought leader" in the industry.

> **"A white paper is not—and should not be—an overt marketing vehicle for the company."** Joel Postman, EVP of Eastwick Communications.

Several vendors in the public relations industry, for example, regularly produce white papers on various trends and issues. One example is Cision, which publishes media databases and provides monitoring services. One of its white papers was titled "Staying Afloat in a Sea of Social Media: An Intelligent Approach to Managing and Monitoring Social Media." BurrellesLuce, a similar firm, issued a paper titled "Gearing Up for Web 3.0: What Public Relations Practitioners Can Expect."

Here are some tips for writing a position paper:

+ On a cover page, use a title that tells exactly what the paper is about.

+ Keep it short. A position paper should be five pages or less. If the paper is 10 pages or more, use a table of contents or an index.

+ Include an "executive summary" at the beginning of the paper, which is a succinct summary of the report's findings or recommendations. It enables busy readers to rapidly understand the crux of the position paper.

+ Place any supporting materials or exhibits in an appendix at the end of the report.

+ Use subheads, boldface, or underlining throughout the paper to break up blocks of copy.

+ Use simple graphs, bar charts, and pie charts to present key statistical information.

+ Use pull-out quotes from key executives or experts to highlight key messages.

+ Be concise. Don't use excessive words. Check for repetitious information.

+ Check for clarity. Is it clear what you want to say or communicate?

+ Avoid overt marketing and promotion for the organization's services or products.

+ Give appropriate websites and other sources for readers who want more information on the topic.

+ Post the position paper on your website and make it printer-friendly.

Proposals by Public Relations Firms

Public relations firms usually get new business through the preparation of a proposal offering services to an organization. In many cases, a potential client will issue a request for proposal, known as an **RFP,** and circulate it to several public relations firms. Trade publications such as *PRWeek* or *Jack O'Dwyer's Newsletter* or even websites including the RFP database (www.rfpdb.com) regularly list RFPs.

An RFP—especially those that come from government entities—may have quite specific requirements that bidding agencies must meet. A typical public relations proposal might include the following sections:

1. the background and capabilities of the firm
2. the client's situation
3. goals and objectives of the proposed program
4. key messages
5. basic strategies and tactics
6. general timeline of activities
7. proposed budget
8. how success will be measured
9. a description of the team that will handle the account
10. a summary of why the firm should be selected to implement the program

See Figure 14.1 on page 388 for a cover and table of contents of a proposal by a major public relations firm.

A good example of an RFP is one issued by Visit Florida, the state's tourism agency. It was seeking a public relations firm to develop its social media strategy to support its global brand. Visit Florida wanted a digital plan with "clear, measurable, and aligned" objectives to build a network of websites and promote Florida through participation in a variety of social media to generate "engaged and enthusiastic brand advocates." The RFP further noted that the social media plan was to include "a description of how Visit Florida and its public relations firm will respond quickly and appropriately, as trusted sources of Florida tourism, to rapidly developing situations such as the 2010's Deepwater Horizon oil spill." See the PR Casebook on page 389 for the RFP on Zipcar.

When a public relations firm is asked to prepare a proposal for service, this will usually include going through the written proposal in a somewhat formal presentation to the client. The presentation enables the firm to project its enthusiasm for the project, make a persuasive case for its recommendations, and answer any concerns or questions

Many organizations, before asking for an RFP, will narrow their list of possible providers by issuing a request for information (RFI). This asks public relations firms to provide information about their capabilities, experience, and expertise. A public relations firm should respond to an RFI by giving the following types of

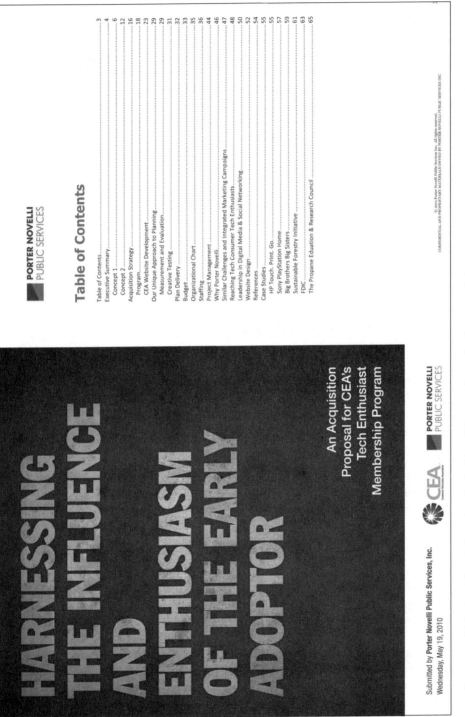

Table of Contents

Table of Contents 3
Executive Summary 4
Concept 1 6
Concept 2 12
Acquisition Strategy 16
    Program 18
    CEA Website Development 23
Our Unique Approach to Planning 29
    Measurement and Evaluation 29
    Creative Testing 31
Plan Delivery 32
Budget 33
Organizational Chart 35
Staffing 36
Project Management 44
Why Porter Novelli 46
Similar Challenges and Integrated Marketing Campaigns 47
Reaching Tech Consumer Tech Enthusiasts 48
Leadership in Digital Media & Social Networking 50
Website Design 52
References 54
Case Studies 55
    HP Touch. Print. Go. 55
    Sony PlayStation Home 57
    Big Brothers Big Sisters 59
    Sustainable Forestry Initiative 61
    FDIC 63
    The Propane Eduation & Research Council 65

PORTER NOVELLI
PUBLIC SERVICES

© 2010 Porter Novelli Public Services Inc. All rights reserved.
CONFIDENTIAL AND PROPRIETARY. MATERIALS OWNED BY PORTER NOVELLI PUBLIC SERVICES INC.

HARNESSING
THE INFLUENCE
AND
ENTHUSIASM
OF THE EARLY
ADOPTOR

An Acquisition
Proposal for CEA's
Tech Enthusiast
Membership Program

Submitted by **Porter Novelli Public Services, Inc.**
Wednesday, May 19, 2010

PORTER NOVELLI
PUBLIC SERVICES

FIGURE 14.1 Global public relations firm Porter Novelli frequently replies to requests for proposals (RFPs), as do all public relations firms, large and small. This is a response cover sheet to an RFP that Porter Novelli prepared for a potential client.

PR casebook

Zipcar Picks Weber Shandwick through RFP Process

Zipcar is a car-sharing company—a concept also known as "cars on demand." In fact, Zipcar's theme is "wheels when you want them." The company began in Cambridge, Massachusetts, more than a decade ago. Now the company claims: "Zipcar is the world's leading car-sharing network with more than 560,000 members and over 8,000 vehicles located in major metropolitan areas and college campuses throughout the United States, Canada, and the UK." The company is publicly traded on NASDAQ and was looking for public relations agency representation.

+ Zipcar began the proposal process by asking 10 public relations firms to reply to a request for information (RFI). An RFI typically asks general questions about an agency's expertise in the area of interest to the soliciting company. Following response to the RFI, Zipcar winnowed the number of agencies down to four and sent those four a request for proposal (RFP). Public relations agencies often generate business through the RFI and RFP process.

+ Zipcar had previously worked with several small firms in different countries. According to *PRWeek*, Zipcar decided to consolidate its public relations work "and boost its investment, as it plans for long-term growth and expansion."

+ Rob Weisberg, chief marketing officer for Zipcar, told *PRWeek* that Weber Shandwick's pitch "was head and shoulders above the rest." He told *PRWeek* he particularly liked the agency's plan to "leverage and generate brand advocates called 'Zipsters.'" As a result, Weber Shandwick was selected as Zipcar's global agency of record (AOR). The global PR firm is handling corporate PR, consumer PR, and social media for the car-sharing company. The RFI and RFP process paid off for Weber Shandwick *and* Zipcar.

FIGURE 14.2 A proposal usually includes a somewhat formal presentation to management to enable a joint discussion of the ideas presented and any concerns or questions can be answered. The public relations and marketing team of the Belgrade (Serbia) Beer Fest are shown here making a presentation to the city council to get approval for their plans and budget.

information: (1) number of employees, (2) standing in the industry, (3) range of resources, (4) primary areas of expertise, (5) current clients, (6) examples of successful campaigns in the same field or industry, and (7) unique characteristics of the firm that differentiate it from other firms.

Summary

The Challenge of Communication Overload

» Information overload is pervasive in our society. You can help reduce clutter by keeping your messages simple, short, and to the point. In addition, limit messages to only those who are in your key audiences. Don't shotgun information to the entire planet.

Email

» Email bulge is overwhelming many organizations and individuals. Use wikis, text messaging, RSS, and applications such as Twitter to reduce the flow.

» Email is rapid and cost-efficient. It is not, however, a substitute for personal one-on-one communication.

» Email is less formal than a letter, but more formal than a telephone call. You can increase the effectiveness of your email messages by (1) providing key information in the subject line, (2) keeping them to 25 lines or less, and (3) using proper grammar, spelling, and punctuation.

Memorandums

» Memos should be one page or less and state the key message immediately. A memo has five components: (1) date, (2) to, (3) from, (4) subject, and (5) message.

Letters

» Business letters are personalized communication that should be well organized, concise, and to the point. They can prevent misunderstandings and provide a record of an agreement or a transaction.

Proposals

» Proposals must follow a logical, well-organized format. They are prepared to generate new business, convince management to make a decision about a contract or approve money and

resources for a project, or request funding for a business or nonprofit.

Proposals by Public Relations Firms

» Staff at public relations firms must constantly write proposals for new business.

» Organizations often issue a request for proposal (RFP) that invites selected firms to prepare a detailed pitch.

Skill Building Activities

1. The chapter provided a number of suggestions about how to write and format emails. Write a short essay about the guidelines that you find relevant and will incorporate into your future emails.

2. It is suggested that wikis can often take the place of sending emails back and forth among individuals working on the same project. Do some research on wikis and how you might use this application in classroom group projects or in your work setting. See also the discussion on wikis in Chapter 12.

3. You're the public relations manager for a department store. Write a letter to an irate customer who has complained that the clerks were too busy socializing among themselves to give her any service or assistance.

4. Your student organization needs $5,000 to sponsor a week of activities to focus

on the dangers of binge drinking on campus. Write a proposal for presentation to the executive board of the student council, which has authority to allocate the funds for such projects.

5. Do an online search of RFPs for public relations projects. Look at the details of the requests. Write a short essay identifying the RFPs for which *your* public relations firms would submit proposals. Why do you think your firm is uncommonly equipped to develop a public relations campaign in support of this or these RFP(s)?

6. Write a business letter to accompany your résumé when you begin your public relations job hunt. Think of yourself as a business entity. What strengths would you bring to your dream public relations position? Convince the reader that you have the skill set to contribute immediately to his or her firm or organization.

Media Resources

Berry, T. (2011, January 13). "Ten Old New Rules for Business E-mails." Retrieved from http://smallbiztrends.com.

Clark, B. (2011, January 27). "The Three Key Elements of Irresistible Email Subject Lines." Retrieved from www.copyblogger.com.

Egan, M. (2011, March 17). "E-mail Overload? Three Ways to Tame Your In Box." *The Christian Science Monitor*.

Glei, J. (2011, January 11). "Email Etiquette for the Super Busy." Retrieved from http://the 99percent.com/tips.

Giving Speeches and Presentations 15

» After reading this chapter, you will be able to:

» Identify speaking opportunities

» Write or ghostwrite a speech

» Identify audience needs and organizational objectives of the speech

» Prepare dynamic visual aids for presentations

» Participate in panels

» Coach and place speakers

The Challenge of the Speaking Circuit

Speakers and audiences are a fundamental part of human communication around the world. An executive of Ruder Finn, a public relations firm, once estimated that—in the United States alone—companies, organizations, and clubs convene more than a million meetings daily, all of them focusing on speakers in seemingly endless succession.

Indeed, speechwriting and presentations are important tools in public relations to reach key publics on an interpersonal level. Such activities are being given even more emphasis today as organizations strive to enhance their reputations, build brand awareness, convey a commitment to transparency, and portray responsibility to society. Michael Witkoski, writing in *Public Relations Tactics*, notes, "It's easy to understand the demand for good speechwriting. More than ever, we recognize the importance of giving large organizations a human face, desirably a face that is trustworthy, competent, friendly, and coherent."

During your career, you will be asked to write speeches for executives; prepare visual aids, such as PowerPoint or Prezi presentations; conduct speaker training; get executives on the agenda of important conferences; organize speaker's bureaus; publicize speeches. You might even give a few speeches and presentations yourself. This chapter will give you the basics of doing all of these activities.

The Basics of Speechwriting

Researching the Audience and Speaker

If you are given a speechwriting assignment, the first step is to find out everything possible about the audience. Who? Where? When? How many people? What time of day? Purpose of meeting? Length of speech? Purpose of talk? Other speakers on the program? To find answers to these questions, you should talk with the organizers of the event or meeting. Don't accept vague answers; keep asking follow-up questions until you have a complete picture.

A good example of defining the audience is when an EDS corporate executive was asked to give the keynote address for a meeting of the Association of American Chambers of Commerce of Latin America in Lima, Peru. Beth Pedison, executive speechwriter of EDS, analyzed the intended audience the following way:

> **Intended Audience:** 400 top Latin American and Caribbean business executives, government leaders, and Chamber representatives. Because the audience came from diverse industries, countries, and company sizes, their familiarity with information technology varied widely. We didn't want to talk down to those who were technologically savvy, or talk over the heads of those who were not technologically proficient. English was the business language for the conference and the speech, although almost everyone in the audience spoke English as a second language. Therefore, we needed to keep sentence structures simple, and avoid the use of colloquialisms, contractions, or U.S.–centric language.

You also need to learn everything you can about the speaker. Listen to the speaker talk—to other groups, to subordinates, to you. See how his or her mind works, what word phrases are favored, and what kinds of opinions are expressed. In addition to listening, it is also a good idea to go over material that the client has written or, if written by others, that the client admires in terms of style and method of presentation.

Brenda Jones, 2010 Theodore C. Sorensen Speechwriting Award winner, described her work with Congressman John Lewis when he was asked to deliver the keynote for the 60th anniversary of the National Trust for Historic Preservation:

> My job was to craft an address set in Nashville, which is almost a second home to my boss. His experiences there are the foundation for all that he accomplished as a participant and leader in the civil rights movement and as a member of Congress. Because my boss is a trained minister, he likes to discuss philosophy... to prick an individual's conscience and inspire them to do what is right.

Laying the Groundwork

Ideally, a writer should have lengthy conversations with the speaker before beginning to write a rough draft of the talk. In a conversational setting, you and the speaker should discuss the speech in terms of objective, approach, strategy, points to emphasize, scope, and facts or anecdotes the speaker would like to include. Admittedly, this isn't always easy. Pete Weissman, a speechwriter in the White House and at Coca-Cola, told *The Strategist*, "The executives I write for are busy. They speak often, they're traveling and running a business—making sure that we have time to sit down with them and understand their point of view and what they'd like to accomplish is always a challenge."

This is how Marie L. Lerch, director of public relations and communication for Booz Allen & Hamilton, described her work with the company's chairman for a diversity awards speech to company employees:

> The central message, "Do the Right Thing," has been Mr. Stasior's core theme throughout his tenure as chairman. I worked with him to adapt that theme to the issue of diversity; researched quotes and other materials that would add color and emphasis to the message; and interviewed him to flesh out his ideas and words on the subject. With notes and research in hand, I developed a first draft of the speech, which Mr. Stasior and I revised together into its final form....

Indeed, before you start writing a speech, you should have a thorough understanding of three aspects of the speech—the objective, the key message, and the strategy/approach. This approach is highlighted in the PR Casebook on page 396 about a speech by the CEO of the Grocery Manufacturers of America.

> **" The executives I write for are busy. They speak often, they're traveling and running a business—making sure that we have time to sit down with them and understand their point of view and what they'd like to accomplish is always a challenge. "** Pete Weissman, speechwriter, in *The Strategist*

Objective — First you must determine the objective. What is the speech supposed to accomplish? What facts, attitude, or opinion should the audience have when the speech is concluded? Is the objective to inform, persuade, activate, or commemorate? This is a start, but objectives are usually stated in more specific terms.

When the CEO of Novelis, the world's largest rolled aluminum company, gave a major presentation at an industry conference about a new manufacturing process, the speech had three objectives: (1) position Novelis as a technology leader and innovator in the industry; (2) create a demand in the automotive, construction, and electronics industries for the new technology and product; and (3) generate coverage in the trade and mainstream media.

Key Messages — Objectives provide the framework of a speech, but they must be supported by key messages that are given emphasis throughout the speech. A speech can have only one key message, but it may also have two or three. The major point is that people hear a speech and can remember only two or three points. Consequently, as a speechwriter, you want to ensure that they remember what you believe is most important in terms of organizational objectives. When asked for his advice on crafting a compelling speech, Reverend Jesse Jackson reportedly told a speechwriter, "Go to the point and to the passion."

Strategy — This can be described as the setting and tone of the speech. Novelis, for example, decided to have the CEO make the announcement of the new technology in a major presentation at the 11th World Aluminum Conference in Montreal. The setting was ideal, because the entire aluminum industry was there, and the conference was being covered by the trade and mainstream media. By having the CEO give the speech, the new product announcement received much more attention than a low-level product news release would.

The tone of a speech depends on the audience being addressed. A friendly audience may appreciate a one-sided talk, with no attempt to present another side of an issue. For example, a politician at a fundraising dinner of supporters does not bother to give the opposition's views.

Many speaking engagements, however, take place before neutral audiences (Rotary, Lions, Kiwanis, and any number of other civic or professional organizations) where the audience may have mixed views or even a lack of knowledge about the topic.

In such a case, it is wise to take a more objective approach and give an overview of the various viewpoints. The speech can still advocate a particular position, but the audience will appreciate the fact that you have included other points of view. From the standpoint of persuasion, you also have more control over how the opposition view is expressed if you say it instead of waiting for an audience member to bring it up. By including an opposing viewpoint and acknowledging its validity, you can neutralize audience opposition to your perspective.

Hostile or unfriendly audiences present the greatest challenge. They are already predisposed against what you say, and they tend to reject anything that does not reinforce their opinions. Remember the old saying, "Don't confuse me with the facts—my mind is already made up." The best approach is to find some common ground with the audience. This technique lets the audience know that the speaker shares or at least understands some of their concerns.

Writing the Speech

Writing the speech is a multistep process involving a finely honed outline and several drafts. Weissman says the four key elements of any public speaking equation are audience, message, media, and speaker.

Outline — After gathering the material you need, you must prepare an outline. The outline for a speech has three main parts: the opening, the body, and the closing.

The opening is the part of the speech that must get the audience's attention, establish empathy, and signpost to the conclusion. In the opening, it is wise to tell the audience what the topic is, why it is important to them, and the direction you plan to take in addressing it.

The body of the speech presents the evidence that leads to the conclusion. The outline should list all the key points. In this section, you will use quotes from experts in the field, facts and figures, and examples that drive home your point.

The conclusion summarizes the evidence, pointing out what it means to the audience.

The outline should be submitted to the speaker, and, once it has been approved, you can go on to the next step.

PR casebook

A Systematic Approach to Speechwriting

Writing a speech for someone requires the writer to understand the intended audience, the objectives of the speech, and the key messages that must be delivered. Melissa Brown, a freelance speechwriter in St. Joseph, Michigan, compiled the following outline in consultation with her client.

The assignment: Write a speech for the president of the Grocery Manufacturers of America (GMA) on the topic, "The Changing Challenges Facing the Food Industry."

The audience: The International Food and Lifestyles Media Conference, Cincinnati.

Speech objectives:

+ Give food writers useful, research-based information on the lifestyles of American consumers, thus positioning GMA as a good source of statistics/information.

+ Neutralize misinformation presented by opponents of biotechnologically developed food products, presenting the industry's side of the story and exposing the lack of credentials of a major voice in the opposition.

+ Provide information on the good work the industry has accomplished in addressing environmental issues, in particular, packaging and solid waste.

+ Demonstrate to GMA board that GMA is speaking out on the issues that affect their businesses.

+ Frame the arguments other food industry spokespeople can use in other opportunities, within their companies and with the press.

Key messages:

+ The profile and purchasing habits of the American consumer have changed significantly.

+ We enjoy the safest and most abundant food supply in the world, despite what you hear from a small but vocal group of opponents.

+ The grocery industry has surpassed government regulations and everyone's expectations in the rapid progress made on environmental issues.

Word Selection — A speaker talks *to* listeners, not *at* them. Your choice of words can either electrify an audience or put it to sleep. As someone once said, "The best idea in the world isn't worth a damn if it cannot be expressed well." Here are some tips about wording when you write a speech:

» **Use personal pronouns.** "You" and "we" make the talk more conversational and let your listeners know you are talking to and identifying with them.

» **Avoid jargon.**   Every occupation and industry has its own vocabulary of specialized words. Don't use words and acronyms that are unfamiliar to your audience. You may know what "ROI" means, but many in the audience may not.

» **Use simple words.**   Don't say "print media" when you mean "newspapers." Don't say "possess" when "have" means the same thing.

» **Use round numbers.**   Don't say, "253,629,384 Americans"; say "more than 250 million Americans."

» **Use contractions.**   Instead of "do not," say "don't." Say "won't" instead of "would not." It makes your speech more conversational.

» **Avoid empty phrases.**   Don't say "in spite of the fact" when "since" or "because" works just as well. Another common one is saying "In spite of the fact that" when "though" or "although" is better.

» **Use bold verbs.**   Instead of saying "profits went up," use a more descriptive verb such as "exploded" or "skyrocketed."

» **Don't dilute expressions of opinion.**   It blunts the crispness of your talk if you start sentences with "Of course, it's only my opinion" or "It seems to me... ."

» **Avoid modifiers.**   Words such as "very" or "most" should be deleted.

» **Use direct quotes.**   You can say, "My colleague, Allen Knight, says ..."

» **Vary sentence length.**   In general, short sentences are best. However, occasionally break up a series of short sentences with some longer ones.

» **Use questions.**   Questions often get the audience more involved. "Does anyone know the average family income in the United States?"

» **Make comparisons and contrasts.**   "An extra 3 cents in gasoline taxes would provide enough money to build another 400 miles of four-lane highway next year."

» **Create patterns of thought.**   It's all right to restate a phrase to create a pattern of emphasis. Hillary Clinton once used this phrase in one of her speeches: "if women are healthy and educated, their families will flourish. If women are free from violence, their families will flourish. If women have a chance to work... their families will flourish." Repetition in triplets, as Clinton did, reinforces a theme and helps the audience retain the information.

Drafts — The next step is to write a rough draft for the speaker. Keep in mind the time constraints on the speech. If the speech is supposed to be about 20 minutes, your draft should be about 2,500 words—or 10 pages, double-spaced. It takes about 2 minutes to read a page to an audience, so a 10-minute talk would only be about five double-spaced pages.

The speaker should use this draft to add new thoughts, cross out copy that doesn't seem to fit, and rewrite sentences to reflect his or her vocabulary and speaking style.

Don't feel rejected if the first, second, or even third draft comes back in tatters. It is only through this process that the speech becomes a natural expression of the speaker's personality.

This is the ideal process. The most successful speakers take the time to work with their speechwriters. Unfortunately, too many executives fail to understand this simple concept.

A report prepared by Burson-Marsteller public relations gives several reasons why businesspeople have trouble explaining themselves to the public. The report noted:

> All too often the chief executive expects a speech to appear magically on his desk without any contribution on his part. He feels too busy to give the speech the attention it deserves. In the end, he becomes the victim of his own neglect. He stumbles through a speech that, from start to finish, sounds contrived. And then he wonders why nobody listened to what he said.

Coaching — In addition to writing the speech to reflect the speaker's thoughts and personality, there may be a need for coaching. Whether the speech is memorized, partially read, or read entirely, it should be rehearsed enough times for the speaker to become familiar with it and to permit improvements in its delivery. Tone of voice, emphasis given to certain words or phrases, pauses, gestures, speed—all are important.

Some speakers prefer to have certain phrases underlined and to have detailed cues in the script, such as "pause," "look at audience," and "pound on lectern." Others don't want such cues. It is purely a matter of individual preference.

Format is also a matter of personal preference. Some people prefer double-spacing; others want triple-spacing. A few like to have the speech typed entirely in capital letters, but most prefer the normal upper- and lowercase format that is used to present most material that is to be read. Some speakers like to have capital letters used in the words that are to be stressed. All of these formats are acceptable.

The speaker should be sufficiently familiar with the note cards or prepared text to permit abridgment on short notice. Such advance thinking is particularly important for a speaker at a luncheon meeting. All too often, the meal is served late or the group takes an excessive amount of time discussing internal matters or making general announcements, leaving the speaker far less time than originally planned.

The same thing can happen at an evening banquet. The awards ceremony takes longer than expected, and the speaker is introduced at 9:15 P.M., 3 hours after everyone has sat down to dinner. In this instance, the greatest applause is for the person who realizes the hour and makes a five-minute speech.

The Basics of Giving a Speech

Writing a speech focuses almost exclusively on content. Giving a speech is all about delivery. You can have a wonderful script, but the words are enriched and become more powerful in the hands of an excellent speaker. Consequently, it is important to know the components of how to give an effective speech. In addition, see the Tips for Success on page 399 for guidelines on how to introduce a speaker.

Know Your Objective

Knowing your objective, as previously noted, is the most important requirement of all. There is no point in making a speech unless it accomplishes something. In preparing a speech, the first step is to determine what you want the audience to know or do. What attitude or opinion do you want the audience to have after listening to the speech?

A speech may inform, persuade, activate, or celebrate. It may also amuse or entertain. That particular kind of speech will not be considered here, but this does not rule out the use of *some* humor in the other kinds of speeches.

An informative speech is one that tells the audience something it does not know or does not understand. An informative speech might tell the audience about how the new local sewage system works, the results of the latest United Way campaign, the expansion plans of a major local corporation, or budget problems facing the state's system of higher education.

An activating speech is designed to get the listener to do something. Direct and specific action is suggested and urged. A basic principle of persuasion is that a speaker should provide an audience with a specific course of action to take: write to a congressional representative, vote for a candidate, purchase a product, or take steps to conserve energy.

A celebratory speech is designed to honor some person or event. Such speeches are often trite and boring, but they don't have to be. If a person is being honored for

Tips for Success   How to Introduce a Speaker

On occasion, you will be asked to be an emcee or to introduce a speaker at a meeting or gathering. This is also a speech, which requires thought and preparation in order to be as brief as possible. A good introduction, for example, should be between 30 seconds and 2 minutes.

Introducing a speaker serves two primary purposes, according to Mitchell Friedman, a San Francisco public relations counselor and speech trainer. "First," he says, "it functions as a transition from one part of the program to another. Second, your introduction offers valuable cues to the audience as far as what they should expect from the speaker and the topic."

In order to write an introduction, you should contact the speaker in advance and get a copy of his or her professional background. Second, you should ask the speaker about his or her objectives for the presentation, the value of the topic to the audience, and any other thoughts about the forthcoming talk.

Like any speech, the introduction should have an opening, a body, and a conclusion. Friedman says, "The opening should grab the attention of the audience by establishing the importance of the subject… ." The body needs to emphasize the importance of the topic, the relevance of the topic to the audience, and establish the credentials of the speaker to address the topic. The conclusion is a brief comment to make the speaker feel welcome and to lead the applause as the speaker steps up to the podium.

Friedman cautions that a good speech introduction does not summarize the speech and, even more important, it doesn't include every detail of the person's background. Indeed, the biggest mistake made in speech introductions is giving the speaker's background in agonizing detail. A final note from Friedman: "It is not typically an occasion to make a joke at the expense of the speaker or to embarrass him or her."

Again, for emphasis: Keep your introduction short—30 seconds to 2 minutes—and everyone, including the speaker, will be grateful.

lifetime professional achievement, why not start out with an anecdote that best exemplifies the feats being honored? This is much better than a chronological account of the person's life as if it were being read from an obituary.

Events such as grand openings, anniversaries, and retirements usually have friendly, receptive audiences. In such cases, you can be more emotional and get away with some platitudes, which will probably be warmly received. When you prepare such a speech, however, keep it brief. Five minutes should be ample, because you are probably one of many speakers.

Structure the Message for the Ear

The average speech has only one brief exposure—the few minutes during which the speaker is presenting it. There is no chance to go back, no time to let it slowly digest, no opportunity for clarification. The message must get across now or never.

You may be an accomplished writer, but you must realize that speaking is something else again. As American lawyer and raconteur Louis Nizer once said, "The words may be the same, but the grammar, rhetoric, and phrasing are different. It is a different mode of expression—a different language."

One major difference is that you have to build up to a major point and prepare the audience for what is coming. The lead of a written story attempts to say everything in about 15 to 25 words right at the beginning. If a speaker used the same form, most of the audience probably wouldn't hear it. When a speaker begins to talk, the audience is still settling down—so the first few words are often devoted to setting the stage: thanking the host, making a humorous comment, or saying how nice it is to be there.

> *The words may be the same, but the grammar, rhetoric, and phrasing are different. It is a different mode of expression—a different language.* Attorney Louis Nizer

You should also be aware that people's minds wander. As your speech progresses, you must restate basic points and summarize your general message.

One platitude of the speaking circuit, but still a valid one, is to "tell them what you are going to tell them, tell it to them, and then tell them what you have told them." In this way, an audience is given a series of guideposts as they listen to the talk.

Some concepts used by writers are, of course, transferable to speaking. The words you use should be clear, concise, short, and definite. Use words that specify, explain, and paint pictures for the audience. In addition, avoid delivering a speech in a monotone voice. That puts audiences to sleep.

Tailor Remarks to the Audience

Because every speech is aimed at a specific audience, you must know as much as possible about yours. Who are they? Such factors as age, occupation, gender, religion, race, education, intelligence, vocabulary, residence, interests, attitudes, group memberships, knowledge, politics, and income may bear on what they will find interesting. But you must also keep in mind, in today's 24/7 Internet world, that a speech may travel beyond its present audience.

Professional speechwriter Pete Weismann put it this way in *The Strategist*:

Another challenge is the number of audiences that will hear a speech. It's not just the 300 or 400 people in a ballroom at a New York hotel. It's basically everyone with an Internet connection. So the speaker and the speechwriter need to think about how that message will be perceived from Beijing to Bombay. The barriers around an audience no longer exist. You have to be mindful of how your message will be perceived by other cultures and perspectives.

Of course, it remains key to prepare for your primary audience while keeping unintended audiences in mind. A talk before a professional group can also end up being more relevant if you prepare for it by doing some audience analysis and basic research. Talk to members of the profession. Get an idea of the issues or problems they face. If you don't know anyone in the profession, at least read five or six issues of the group's professional journal or visit its website. This will give you some insight and perhaps even provide you with some quotations from leaders in the field.

In summary, most audiences have a core of common interests; this should help you prepare a speech that will appeal to them. A talk to the stockholders of a corporation should be considerably different from one to employees or to a consumer group. See the Tips for Success below for more tips on tailoring your message for the audience.

Give Specifics

People remember only a small part of what they hear. You must therefore make sure that they hear things they can remember. A vague generality has little or no chance

Tips for Success   Keep Your Audience in Mind

+ **Know your listeners.**   You can hardly know too much about the members of your audience: age, gender, occupation, education, socioeconomic status, and any other facts— and especially why they are listening to this speech.

+ **Use their language.**   Use terms and expressions that are familiar. Similes, metaphors, and anecdotes are valuable only if they are pertinent.

+ **Use visuals.**   Your audience will remember much more if you show *and* tell than if you only tell.

+ **Use humor carefully.**   Avoid side comments and jokes that may offend the opposite sex or various racial and ethnic groups.

+ **Watch your facts.**   Be absolutely certain that you are giving listeners information that is reliable. Check and double-check your information.

+ **Focus on the benefit.**   Any speech must tell listeners why they will gain from the ideas being expressed.

of being understood, let alone remembered. The speech must be built around specific ideas phrased in clear and memorable language.

A vague statement—for example, "We ought to do something about gun control"—has no chance of being effective. If it was more specific—"We should ban all handguns and make it an offense to be in possession of one"—it would offer the audience an idea that is definite and understandable.

In most cases, the person who is asked to speak is perceived as an expert on a given subject. Consequently, the audience wants the benefit of that person's thinking and analysis. Listeners don't want platitudes or statements that are self-evident. An economist should offer more than the flat statement that the economy is in trouble; he or she should explain why it is in trouble and what the solution might be. Beth Haiken, vice president of public relations for PMI Group, says it best. She told *PRWeek*, "Never ever announce a problem without also announcing a solution for it."

Keep It Timely and Short

Regardless of the nature and the objective of a speech, it must be interesting *now*. It must include up-to-date facts and information; don't talk about a situation that is no longer current or has no immediate interest for the audience. If the topic is an old one, it is imperative that you talk about it in a new way. For example, everyone knows that dinosaurs are extinct, but their demise retains current interest as scientists argue over the reasons for it.

If the speech is one of several in a general program, it is wise to learn what others will be talking about. This will provide a context for your talk and add interest by reference to the other topics and speakers. It will also help you avoid saying the same thing as other speakers.

Another dimension of timeliness is the length of the speech. In general, shorter is better. For a luncheon meeting, the talk should be about 20 minutes long. As previously mentioned, this is about 10 pages, double-spaced. It is a typical practice in many organizations to put the speaker on after a half-hour of organizational announcements and committee reports.

The time of day is very important. A morning speech generally finds the audience most alert and receptive. At the end of the afternoon, with the cocktail hour only minutes away, a speaker is at an extreme disadvantage. The latter situation calls for more skill on the part of the speaker; he or she must be more enthusiastic, more forceful, and more attention-getting than his or her morning counterpart.

The guidelines generally refer to run-of-the-mill luncheon and dinner meetings. If you are giving a major speech at a conference, you often have 30 to 60 minutes to present.

Gestures and Eye Contact

Gestures, posture, and eye contact can make or break a speech. One classic study by Dr. Albert Mehrabian in the 1960s found that 93 percent of all communication occurs not through words, but through vocal and nonverbal performance, such as gestures, posture, and attire.

In other words, gestures play a major role in establishing credibility. Gestures should agree with the vocal message to be effective. If you are making a major point, you might

FIGURE 15.1 The art of public speaking requires the speaker to be animated, enthusiastic, and use gestures to make an important point. Here, President Barack Obama illustrates the effectiveness of combining powerful words and actions.

raise your hand for emphasis. See the photo of Barack Obama in Figure 15.1 for an example of how a successful speaker uses gestures. Other experts say that you can "reach out" to an audience by extending your arms outward with the palms up.

Nervous gestures, however, are distracting to the audience. Don't play with your hair, fiddle with a pen, fondle your necklace or tie, or keep moving your leg or foot. Remember your facial expression; smile at the audience, express interest and attention instead of boredom. Audiences pick up on nonverbal cues and assess the speaker accordingly.

Posture is also a gesture. Speakers should stand straight up, leaning slightly forward. Don't hunch over the podium; it conveys a lack of passion for the subject and implies that you are not completely certain of what you are saying.

Eye contact is crucial. Don't read a speech with your eyes glued to the lectern or keep looking at the screen behind you with your PowerPoint slide. It is important to look up at the audience and establish eye contact. Experts recommend that you look at specific people in the audience to keep you from superficially gazing over the heads of the audience. Eye contact, according to research studies, is the major factor that establishes a speaker's rapport and credibility with an audience.

The SPEAK model summarizing the key points of nonverbal communication is provided in the Tips for Success on page 404.

Just as you learned in elementary school, actions speak at least as loud as, if not louder than, words. *PRWeek* managing editor Gideon Fidelzeid made that point in an editorial in the trade magazine. He wrote: "So what makes a great communicator? It helps to speak well, but that must be balanced by having enough restraint to allow certain moments to communicate for themselves.... Great speeches can get you elected.... But it's action post-oratory that brings communications full circle." In other words, speakers must walk the talk.

Visual Aids for Presentations

The chapter so far has focused on the techniques of writing and giving a speech or presentation. We now turn our attention to the use of visual aids to enhance and improve the speaker's effectiveness.

First, it is commonly recognized that visual aids can enhance learning, productivity, and message absorption. Consider the following findings:

» Sight accounts for 83 percent of what we learn.

» When a visual is combined with a voice, retention increases by 50 percent.

» Color increases a viewer's tendency to act on the information by 26 percent.

» Use of video increases retention by 50 percent and accelerates buying decisions by 72 percent.

» The time required to present a concept can be reduced by up to 40 percent with visuals.

Research at the Wharton School of Business also shows the benefits of visual aids. In its research, it was found that audience members perceived presenters who used visuals as more effective than those who did not. In addition, almost two-thirds of those who were shown visuals were able to make a decision right after the presentation. Using visuals also cut meeting time by 24 percent.

Tips for Success   Nonverbal Communication Speaks Volumes

A speaker doesn't communicate to an audience with voice alone. The audience also receives a great deal of nonverbal communication from the speaker. Veteran speaker Jack Pyle, writing in *PR Reporter*, offers the SPEAK method to help you appear confident and become a better communicator:

S = Smile.   It's one of your best communication tools, always helps make a good first impression, and helps make others want to listen to you.

P = Posture.   How you stand or sit makes a big difference. Your physical stance tells others how you feel about yourself. Confident people stand tall and sit straight.

E = Eye contact.   A person who is believable and honest "looks you right in the eye." Don't stare, but look at a person's face for at least 3 seconds before moving on to look at another person. If you are talking to a group, give your message to one person at a time.

A = Animation.   Show your interest in your subject with your energy and animation. Be enthusiastic. Animate your voice by speeding up and slowing down, talking louder and softer at times. Make your face animated. "A" is also for attitude. Make sure you feel good about yourself and what you are doing.

K = Kinetics (motion).   Use your arms to make gestures that support your words. Use two-handed, symmetrical gestures, and hold your hands high when gesturing—at about chest level.

This is not to say that every speech or presentation requires a visual aid. In many cases, such as a banquet or a formal meeting, the speaker uses no visual aids. Nor does the president of the United States need them when presenting the annual State of the Union Address to Congress. More often than not, however, most of us find ourselves giving presentations to a variety of audiences who need visual aids to keep their attention as well as to increase their retention of the information.

It is important to understand the advantages and disadvantages of each visual aid technique to determine what will be the most effective in a given situation. Indeed, visual aids are planned for a specific situation and audience. If you are giving a workshop or seminar where the objective is to inform and educate an audience, a PowerPoint presentation may be the best approach. If, however, you are conducting a brainstorming session where audience interactivity is the objective, perhaps an easel with a blank pad of paper to record ideas is the only visual aid required.

PowerPoint

The leading presentation software is Microsoft's PowerPoint. *USA Today* business writer Kevin Maney said it best when he wrote several years ago, "PowerPoint users are inheriting the earth. The software's computer generated, graphic-artsy presentation slides are everywhere—meetings, speeches, sales pitches, websites. They're becoming as essential to getting through the business day as coffee and Post-it notes."

Indeed, Microsoft estimates there are about 300 million PowerPoint users in the world, and about 30 million presentations are given every day. In fact, about 1 million presentations are going on somewhere in the world as you are reading this. Such a robust market has generated some imitators, such as Google Presentations, which is part of Google Docs, a suite of online applications.

But the ubiquity of PowerPoint has earned it some detractors. "Death by PowerPoint" is a critique that has become common in board (or should I say bored?) rooms. The *New York Times* quoted U.S. military leaders as saying "PowerPoint makes us stupid" and "Some problems in the world are not bullet-izable." But communication blogger Shel Holtz argues that PowerPoint's darker image simply means "people need to be taught the right and wrong uses of PowerPoint." In short, PowerPoint and similar presentation programs are useful tools, as long as they're used correctly.

Most users like PowerPoint because it allows you to make relatively attractive slides of information by simply following the directions and using any number of available templates. By clicking on a variety of options, an individual can write the title and body text in a variety of fonts, select background and text colors, add photos and clip art, and even do multicolored charts and graphs. Experienced users also add sound clips, animation, and video files to their slide presentations through the increased use of such creative programs as Photoshop, Illustrator, and Flash.

PowerPoint is a very versatile software program from the standpoint of preparing information that can be used in a variety of ways. Here are some of the ways it can be used:

» **Use your computer monitor.** A desktop or laptop is ideal to show the presentation to one or two individuals. The laptop presentation is popular on media tours when you are talking one-on-one with an editor or a financial analyst.

- » **Harness your laptop to a computer projector.** If you are reaching a larger audience, you can project a PowerPoint presentation on a large screen in a meeting hall.
- » **Post the PowerPoint presentation on the Web.** You can post an entire slide presentation to the organization's website or the company intranet.
- » **Print pages.** You can distribute copies of your entire presentation to the audience. The software also allows you to do thumbnails of each slide on the left column and give a place for individuals to take notes on the right side of the page.
- » **Create CDs and DVDs.** Many organizations put PowerPoint presentations on CDs or DVDs so they can be easily sent to media reporters, customers, and field personnel for their viewing and background. A low-tech version of this is to place a spiral-bound copy of a PowerPoint presentation in a media kit as a kind of extended fact sheet giving reporters key points about the organization or product.

Whatever the medium of presentation, there are some rules about the composition of a PowerPoint slide that you should keep in mind.

One key rule is not to make your slide too detailed or cluttered with too much clip art or the use of fancy borders. Another common mistake is to include too much copy. Peter Nolan, writing in *Public Relations Tactics*, says, "The last thing any presenter wants is to have the audience reading a heavy text slide rather than paying attention to what is being said. Presentation slides should support the speaker with a few key words or easily understood graphics."

> 〝 *The last thing any presenter wants is to have the audience reading a heavy text slide rather than paying attention to what is being said. Presentation slides should support the speaker with a few key words or easily understood graphics.* 〞 Peter Nolan, writing in *Public Relations Tactics*

A good antidote to Nolan's concern is the four-by-four rule. Use no more than four bullets, and no more than four or five words for each bullet. Some experts advise that there should be no more than 10 lines of copy on a slide; others say no more than 20 words. This is not to say that every slide should look like the previous one; that gets boring. Transitional slides, from one topic or major point to another, may only consist of one or two words or perhaps a photo or clip art. In general, remember the motto about text—less is better. Some experts recommend photos; they are more interesting than standard clip art.

A standard rule is a minimum of 24- to 28-point type for all words. Anything smaller will be difficult to see from the back of the room. Also, be aware that you should have at least a 2-inch margin around any copy. PowerPoint has text boxes, which helps the amateur format the right amount of space around the text. Several examples of basic layouts, done with PowerPoint, are shown in Figure 15.2.

Color is also an important consideration. PowerPoint has hundreds of colors available in its palette, but that doesn't mean you have to use all of them. Multiple colors for the background and the text only distract the audience and give the impression of an incoherent presentation. It also leads to a common complaint about PowerPoint presentations—people spend too much time focusing on the slides and not enough time focusing on the message.

In other words, keep it simple. You should use clear, bold fonts for colors that contrast with the background. As for background, dark blues convey a corporate

FIGURE 15.2 PowerPoint slides are the workhorse of the speech and presentation circuit. The most effective slides, however, should be simple and relatively uncluttered. These slides, taken from a presentation by the Arthur W. Page Society, a group of senior communication executives, make the point. The first slide (a) shows how basic concepts can be displayed in colorful and graphic terms. The second slide (b) shows how data can be prepared in simple bar chart form for easy readability. The third slide (c) shows how text can be formatted with color and boldfacing.

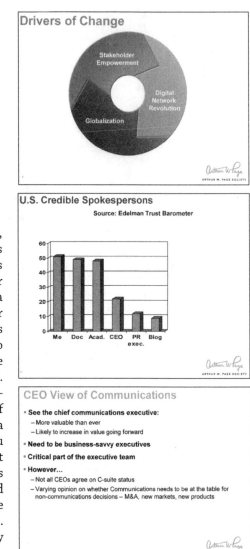

approach, greens work well when feedback is desired, and reds motivate the audience to action. Yellows and purples are not recommended for most business presentations. In general, black is the best color for text, but remember the contrast rule. Black type on a dark blue or red background won't be readable. Other experts simply recommend that you use earth tones and middle-range colors for a slide's background so there is maximum contrast between the color of the text (black or another dark color) and the background.

Art Samansky, president of a public affairs consultancy, makes another comment about the use of PowerPoint in presentations. His advice: "Slides, like a magician's wand, are only a prop. You are the act. If you are merely reciting the material on the slides, you might as well email your audience a copy and save all precious time and travel expenses." Put another way, don't read your slides to the audience; everyone in the audience with a third-grade education can read for themselves. Slides should only provide a track or outline of key points you want to elaborate upon to the audience.

Prezi

An increasingly popular alternative to PowerPoint and similar slide-based technologies are zooming presentation technologies such as Prezi. Prezi presentations, or Prezis, are nonlinear. PowerPoint slideshows are linear. Prezis can be created and downloaded on a medium such as a flash drive and loaded onto a computer or they can be stored and played directly from prezi.com if a room has Internet access.

Prezi was founded in Budapest in April 2009 and moved to San Francisco in November 2009. One technology blogger wrote, "For PowerPoint haters, Prezi surely offers hope.... Prezi differs radically from PowerPoint in that it requires an alternative mental model: Information is displayed in a nonlinear fashion."

FIGURE 15.3 Prezi is one of several zooming presentation applications available online. This image is part of the Prezi introduction presentation, "What is Prezi?"

Critics and fans alike note that Prezi is more difficult to use than PowerPoint because you begin with a "blank canvas" rather than slide templates, and its zooming nature can lead overzealous adopters to almost give audience members vertigo.

While adoption has been relatively slow, for the design and tech savvy, zooming technologies such as Prezi provide a real alternative to slide-based presentations. See Figure 15.3 for an example of a simple zooming presentation element.

Other Speech Formats

A speech is controlled by the speaker. He or she knows what is going to be said. The subject matter is complete and well organized. The speech has been well rehearsed, and the speaker has polished his or her remarks to give a solo performance without interruption.

The environment changes, however, when the speaker participates in activities such as panels and media interviews. Here someone else is directing the action, and a speaker's comments can't always be scripted in advance. Even so, these opportunities are valuable aids to public communication and should be used whenever possible.

Panels

A panel usually consists of a moderator and several people, each of whom makes a brief opening statement 5 to 7 minutes in length. The rest of the time is spent on answering questions from the audience.

The moderator may solicit audience questions in several ways. One common method, if the audience is relatively small, is simply to recognize people who stand up and ask a question. In larger audiences, a portable microphone may be brought to the audience member so everyone can hear the question. Another method is to have the audience submit questions on distributed forms. The moderator then goes through the written questions and tries to select those that would be of most interest to the audience.

Individual panelists are asked to comment on questions, or the question may be addressed to the entire panel. In either case, it is your responsibility as a panelist to give a short answer (one minute or less) so that other panelists will also have an opportunity to comment. It is unfair for any panelist to monopolize the forum by giving long-winded answers. Furthermore, such behavior has the tendency to alienate audience members.

Panels are good vehicles for getting audience involvement, and they are a standard feature at most conventions. The key to a good panel, however, is an effective moderator. He or she must control the panel by policing the time that a person takes to give an opening statement, politely cutting off long-winded answers to a single question, and making sure all panelists have an equal opportunity to express their views.

Speaker Training and Placement

Giving talks and speeches is an important part of an organization's outreach to its key publics. A talk by an executive or an employee is a highly personal form of communication and adds a human dimension to any organization. It's a form of face-to-face communication, and it offers the chance for interaction between the speaker and the audience.

Speech giving should be an integral part of an organization's overall public relations program. Indeed, public relations personnel are often involved in training speakers and seeking appropriate forums where key publics can be reached.

Executive Training

Today, the public is demanding more open disclosure and accountability from organizations, which is forcing many executives to take the speaker's platform and become company **spokespersons.** *PR Reporter*, in one survey of executives, found that more than half spend 10 hours or more each month meeting with outside groups. In addition, the majority average 20 speeches a year, about two-thirds spend time on press conferences, and another third appear on TV. A study by global PR agency Burson-Marsteller found that CEOs of large companies are asked to speak to external audiences more than three times a week, on average.

As a consequence, more executives are taking courses designed to improve their public speaking skills. The rush into speech training for executives has created a major boom for consultants who train employees at all levels to represent their firms in public forums or media interviews.

Because the costs of such training sessions often run into thousands of dollars, organizations with limited budgets may not be able to afford them. Therefore, the public relations department is often given the responsibility of training executives in media interview and speech skills. Video recording is often done to help an executive see how he or she comes across giving a speech. It's a powerful educational tool that almost always has more impact than telling a person how to give an effective speech.

Speech training can be divided into two parts: what to say and how to say it. Public relations personnel are most effective at helping crystallize messages. Both you and the speaker should review the context of the speech from the standpoint of location, expected audience, and what information would be interesting to them.

Another consideration is what you want to say that will advance organizational objectives—to position the organization or industry as a leader, to plant the perception that the organization is successful, or maybe to show that the organization is environmentally conscious and a good community citizen. All speeches should have one to three key messages.

There are entire courses and many textbooks on how to give a speech. The ideal speaker is one who knows about the subject, whose voice and appearance will make a good impression, and who is comfortable standing in front of an audience.

Public relations manager Charlene Jacobs, writing in *Public Relations Tactics*, offered tips on training spokespersons for interviews:

1. Be prepared. Spokespersons should be familiar with key organizational messages before interview requests arrive.

2. Interview the interviewer. Preparation and research for a specific interview should include asking the reporter the nature of the story and what issues he or she wants covered. This way the spokesperson can have command of pertinent information.

3. Practice Q&As. After identifying the purpose of the interview, develop tough questions the reporter might ask and go over those questions with the spokesperson in practice sessions. This will help executives, who aren't accustomed to being interrogated, not lose their cool if a journalist gets aggressive in questioning.

4. Reassure spokespersons. Identify both positive and negative aspects of their performance. Let them know that "I don't know, but I'll find out" is an acceptable answer.

5. Do a postmortem. After the interview, review the outcome with the spokesperson so that each interview becomes a learning opportunity. Let the spokesperson see coverage of the interview, so he or she can assist in identifying points of success and points that need improvement in future interviews.

Speaker's Bureaus

Top executives aren't the only ones who give speeches. Many organizations effectively use technical experts, middle managers, and even rank-and-file employees on a systematic basis to extend the organization's outreach to potential customers, the industry, and the community.

Steve Markman, head of a conference and management firm, makes the case in an article for *Public Relations Tactics*. He writes:

Companies need to expose their expertise and technologies to prospective customers and clients. What is a proven method of accomplishing this objective? Speaking at public forums produced by other organizations—at conferences, seminars, and forums held by independent event organizations, associations, professional and industry trade groups, and academic institutions and think tanks. There is much evidence that speaking at public forums often results in the attainment of business, by providing increased awareness of the company in general and specific subjects in particular, to an audience of potential customers or clients.

In every organization, there are individuals who are capable of giving speeches and presentations. In many cases, it is part of their job description. Members of the technical staff, for example, are often asked by professional groups to share their research or talk about the development of a particular product. In other situations, a community group may want a general talk about how the company is dealing with a sluggish economy.

One way of systematically organizing a company's outreach is to set up a **speaker's bureau**. This is more than just a list of employees who are willing to speak. It is also a center that trains speakers; produces supporting audiovisual aids; and even develops key messages about the organization, product, or service that should be included in any presentation.

Ideally, a speaker's bureau will have a list of employees who are expert on a variety of subjects. A person in finance may be an expert on worker's compensation, and an engineer in product development may have expertise with lasers. Markman warns, however, that a speech or presentation to a group should avoid being a "sales pitch." He says, "A presentation that turns out to be a sales pitch will ensure low evaluations by the audience and a one-way ticket home . . . ."

Placement of Speakers

Once executives and employees have been trained, your job is finding opportunities for them to speak. An organization usually publicizes the existence of a speaker's bureau by preparing a simple pamphlet or brochure and sending it to various clubs and organizations in the community that regularly use speakers. Another method is to place advertisements about the speaker's bureau in local newspapers. The public relations department regularly fields calls from organizations that need speakers on select topics. At other times, you have to be more proactive and contact the organization to offer the services of a speaker on a particular topic. One of the most difficult jobs in any club is that of program director, and most welcome any suggestions that make their lives easier.

Once a speaker has been booked, the manager of a speaker's bureau usually handles all the logistical details. He or she briefs the speaker on (1) the size and composition of the audience, (2) the location, (3) availability of audiovisual equipment, (4) the projected length of the presentation, (5) directions to the meeting, and (6) primary organizational contacts.

The placement of the organization's top executives, however, tends to be more strategic. Top executives often get more requests for speeches than they can ever fulfill, so the problem is selecting a few of the invitations that are extended.

The criteria, at this point, become somewhat pragmatic and cold-hearted. Public relations staff is charged with screening the invitations on the basis of such factors as the venue, the nature of the group, the size of the audience, and whether the audience is an important public to the organization. If most or all of these factors are positive, the executive will generally consent to give a speech.

Toyota, for example, has even developed a "grading sheet" to screen speech requests. Ron Kirkpatrick, manager of executive communications at the automaker, uses four questions:

1. Will the speaking forum advance the goals/strategies of the company?
2. Will it attract media coverage?
3. Is the audience highly influential?
4. Can we get extended reach through the host group's website, newsletter, etc.?

If a group doesn't make the cut, Kirkpatrick is diplomatic. He writes in Ragan. com, "We usually tell them that our executive's busy travel schedule won't allow them to accept the invitation. And that's pretty much true. Our executives travel so extensively that getting a speech on their calendars is a huge challenge."

At other times, public relations managers are proactive in seeking placement opportunities. If the CEO wants to become a leader in the industry, for example, the public relations staff actively seeks out speech opportunities before prestigious audiences that can help establish the executive as the spokesperson for the industry.

Several years ago, UPS organized an executive communications program that actively promoted its top executives as business leaders through speeches at national and regional business and trade events. Matthew Arnold, writing in *PRWeek*, quotes Steve Soltis, head of the UPS executive communications unit: "The whole program was created for the express purpose of using senior management as a component of brand building. Using them as leaders, creating the platform for our values and strategies."

Burson-Marsteller recently compiled the 10 top-valued podiums for CEOs. The top five corporate conferences, in descending order, are sponsored by The World Economic Forum, *The Wall Street Journal*, *Forbes*, *Fortune*, and the World Business Forum.

Publicity Opportunities

The number of people a speech or a presentation reaches can be substantially increased through publicity.

Before the Event — Whenever anyone from your organization speaks in public, you should notify the appropriate media in advance. This often takes the form of a media advisory, discussed in an earlier chapter.

An advisory is simply a short note that gives the speaker's name and title, the speech title, and details about time and place. In a brief sentence or two, describe why the speech is important and of interest to the medium's audience. If it is available and it is a major policy speech, you can also send an advance copy of the speech to selected reporters. Make sure they realize they should not report the speech until after it is given. This request to the media is called an "embargo" and is often invoked in the case of an important speech being delivered at a specific time. Media relations was discussed in Chapter 4. If the speech is a major event, you will also make arrangements with a vendor to do a live webcast of the speech so reporters and others not attending the event can view it in "real time." See Chapter 12 for more details on how webcasts are done. You may also make arrangements for the speech to be videotaped.

Reporters attending the speech should be seated near the podium, and arrangements should be made for accommodating photographers and television camera technicians. Reporters should also be provided with a media kit that gives the background of the organization and the speaker and a copy of the speech. See Chapter 4 for more about organizing news conferences.

After the Event — After a speech is given, you must prepare news releases about what was said so that the speech can be reported in appropriate publications. The Tips for Success below offers guidelines for converting a speech into a news release. Video clips must be sent to television stations via the Internet or satellite, and radio stations must receive audio clips. Preparing material for broadcast outlets was discussed in Chapter 9.

Tips for Success   The Speech as News Release

The audience reach of a speech is multiplied many times when a news release is distributed that summarizes the speaker's key message. A speech news release follows many of the same structural guidelines outlined in Chapter 5, but there are some specific concepts that you should keep in mind.

"The key to writing stories about speeches is to summarize the speech or to present one or two key points in the lead sentence," says Douglas Starr, a professor of journalism and public relations at Texas A&M University.

In an article for *Public Relations Tactics*, Starr says a speech news release should follow a particular format. He says, "Answers to the questions—who said what, to whom—must be in the lead of every speech story. Answers to the questions—where, when, how, why—may be placed in the second paragraph."

The most common mistake inexperienced writers make is to tell readers that a *speaker spoke about a topic* instead of saying what the *speaker said about the topic.* An example of the first approach is "Susan Jones, president of XYZ Corporation, spoke about environmental regulations." A better approach would be, "Susan Jones, president of XYZ Corporation, says rigid environmental regulations are strangling the economy." See the difference?

The second sentence or paragraph of a speech news release usually describes the event where the speech was given, the location, the attendance, and the reason for the meeting. It is unnecessary, however, to give the title of a person's speech or even the theme of the convention or meeting. They are meaningless to the reader.

The third and subsequent paragraphs may contain speaker quotes, additional facts or figures, and other relevant information that helps provide context for the speech. When attributing quotes, "said" is the preferred verb. However, some writers vary this by using the terms "stated," or "added." Starr suggests you stay away from such attribution terms as "discussed," "addressed," and "spoke," because they don't say anything.

The speech also can be shortened and excerpted as a possible op-ed article in daily newspapers or trade publications. (How to write and place op-ed articles was discussed in Chapter 7.) Reprints, or excerpts of the speech, also can be posted on the organization's websites or sent through an organization's intranet to employees.

An example is AMD. Its president, Hector Ruiz, gave the keynote address at Comdex, a major trade show for the high-technology industry. This was a major platform for AMD and Ruiz to establish leadership in the industry, so the company spent considerable time and effort to ensure that the speech got wide coverage and distribution.

The company arranged for a webcast at the time of the speech, but it also placed the speech on the AMD website for later viewing. The webpage also included a photo of Ruiz giving the speech and a short summary of the key points. In addition, there was a link for "Read a transcript of the keynote address" and "Read what they're saying," which displayed press comments on the speech.

If a speech is particularly important, it can be printed as a brochure and mailed to selected opinion leaders. You can also ask a member of the U.S. House of Representatives or the U.S. Senate to insert the speech into the *Congressional Record*.

Summary

The Challenge of the Speaking Circuit

» Writing and giving speeches are outstanding public relations opportunities for organizations to increase their visibility and reach key publics.

The Basics of Speechwriting

» Speechwriting requires clear objectives, effective organization of relevant key messages, knowledge of the audience, and a close working relationship with the person who will be giving the speech.

» A speech is a powerful communication tool. It must be prepared for listeners, not readers. It must fit the audience, be specific, get a reaction, have a definite objective, and be timely.

The Basics of Giving a Speech

» Nonverbal communication is important in a speech. Speakers should be enthusiastic, make eye contact with the audience, and use gestures that support their words.

» The recommended length of a speech at a luncheon or dinner meeting is 20 minutes. Such a speech would be 10 pages, double-spaced.

» Speeches should have one to three key messages.

Visual Aids for Presentations

» Audiovisuals dramatically increase the ability of audiences to retain and understand information.

» PowerPoint can create attractive slides that can be used in a variety of formats—paper copies, computer display, webpages, CDs, and DVDs.

» Prezi is a zooming rather than slide-based visual aid.

» Computer projectors are now widely used by most organizations.

» The key to successful visual aids is brief copy and large type.

Other Speech Formats

» Other presentations—panels and media interviews—follow the same basic principles as speeches. However, they also involve special preparation for dealing with opposition, interruptions, and hostile questions.

Speaker Training and Placement

» Executive and staff speech training is often the responsibility of the public relations professional.

» A speaker's bureau is a good way to organize an effective program of community outreach.

» Top executives of an organization must be selective about what speech invitations they accept. Factors such as the sponsoring organization, the size of the audience, and whether the venue advances organizational objectives must be considered.

» A speech provides opportunities for the public relations professional to generate additional publicity by (1) inviting the press to cover it, (2) preparing news releases, (3) distributing audio and visual clips, (4) converting the speech to an op-ed piece, (5) reprinting it in a brochure, and (6) posting excerpts on a webpage.

Skill Building Activities

1. Interview a fellow classmate or colleague about a current issue or topic that he or she wants to talk about and about which he or she has some knowledge. Write a five-minute speech, which is about three pages, double-spaced, for that person on the subject. Get feedback on the first draft and then do a final draft that the person would present to the class.

2. Attend a speech given to a campus or community organization. Write a critique of the speaker and assess his or her effectiveness according to the guidelines for speaking outlined in this chapter.

3. While you are at the speech (see Exercise 2), take notes on what the speaker said and write a news release about what the speaker said.

4. Select an organization that regularly has a speaker for its weekly or monthly meeting. Prepare a short memo that would help the president of the university prepare for a talk before the group. Include some brief background on the organization, a profile of the membership, the time and place of the meeting, the format of the entire meeting, and the amount of time that a speaker should talk.

5. Prepare a 10-minute PowerPoint presentation on some topic of interest to you and then present it to your classmates or colleagues. Remember to employ the rules about brevity on slides. In addition, prepare a handout using a thumbnail of the slide on the left and spaces on the right for the audience to write notes while you are speaking.

Media Resources

Campbell, J., and Walton, S. B. (December 2009). "A Guide for the 24/7 Spokesperson: Rules to Remember When the Microphone is Always On." *Public Relations Tactics*, 10, 13.

Dean, F. (October 2010). "Worst. Speech. Ever. Essential Don'ts for Speechwriters." *The Ragan Report*, 20.

Dean, F. (July 2010). "Writing Funny Speeches: The Dos and Don'ts." *The Ragan Report*, 20–21.

Garland, L. (March 2010). "Speechwriting under Less than Ideal Circumstances." *The Ragan Report*, 15–16.

Jacobs, C. (December 2009). "Beyond Traditional Media Training: How to Prepare Spokespeople for Interviews." *Public Relations Tactics*, 12.

Jacques, A. (Spring 2011). "Writing for Leaders: The Art of Crafting Executive Speeches." *The Strategist*, 28–29.

Rackleff, R. (2010, November 9). "6 Memorable Ways to Close a Speech." Ragan.com.

Starks, C. (July 2010). "How to Unify and Engage Your Audience." *The Ragan Report*, 23–24.

Watkis, J. (July 2010). "Effective Speech Openings in 3 Simple Steps." *The Ragan Report*, 25.

Using Direct Mail and Advertising

16

» After reading this chapter, you will be able to:

» Understand the basics of direct mail

» Create a direct mail package

» Understand the basics of public relations advertising

» Identify types of public relations advertising

» Create a print ad

» Work with an ad agency

» Use other advertising channels

The Basics of Direct Mail

Letters and accompanying material mailed to large groups of people is a form of marketing called *direct mail*. Although many consumers and the media often refer to it as *junk mail*, it has a long history. According to Media Distribution Services, one of the first examples of "direct mail" was in 1744, when Benjamin Franklin mailed a list of books for sale to a selected list of prospects. Not exactly Amazon.com, but a start.

Since then, the use of direct mail to sell ideas, goods, and services has skyrocketed. Billions of direct mail pieces are produced each year in the United States, primarily to sell products and solicit donations for a variety of charities. Indeed, according to some estimates, the average person receives 41 pounds, or more than 800 pieces, of direct mail annually. In fact, the U.S. Post Office estimates that almost two-thirds of the mail you receive is advertising.

Although the major use of direct mail is to sell goods and services, it also is an effective public relations tool. Direct mail, for example, is used by political candidates to inform voters about issues and also to ask for their votes. It is used by charitable groups to educate the public about various social issues and diseases and to solicit contributions. It is used by cultural organizations to announce a concert series or new exhibition or to seek volunteers.

> **"Direct mail has maintained its large ad share even with the introduction of new, fast-growing ad markets such as the Internet."** Center for Media Research

Corporations often use direct mail to notify consumers about a product recall, inform investors about a merger or acquisition, or apologize about poor service or shoddy goods. Community groups use direct mail to let their members and other interested people know about forthcoming events or their stand on important issues. In other words, whenever a number of people can be identified as a key public, it is logical to reach them with direct mail.

While we will discuss direct mail as primarily a print product, it is important to recognize that direct mail tactics are also combined with or used via email. Oftentimes, direct marketing is used as a synonym for direct mail. In fact, *Direct Marketing News* reported, "Response increases across the board when direct mail and email are combined in a multichannel campaign."

Advantages of Direct Mail

Direct mail is a controlled communication medium, just like newsletters, brochures, and websites. It allows you to have total control over the format, wording, and timing of a message to audiences as broad or narrow as you wish. Indeed, the three major advantages of direct mail are (1) the ability to target your communication to specific individuals, (2) personalization, and (3) cost-effectiveness.

Targeted Audience — An appropriate mailing list is the key to using direct mail as an effective public relations tool. At the most basic level, a mailing list may be a compilation of an organization's members, past contributors, employees, or customers. Organizations compile mailing lists on all sorts of audiences. In public relations, for example, you may compile a mailing list of community leaders or civic organizations.

You can also rent mailing lists from some membership organizations and media outlets. If you want to send a letter to all dentists in your area, you might contact the American Dental Association. If your purpose is to reach affluent or brand-conscious individuals, it would be logical to rent a list of BMW and Mercedes-Benz owners from the state department of motor vehicles. You can also rent the subscription lists of various newspapers and magazines if you feel that the demographics of the subscribers fit your particular purpose. For about $150, for example, List Services Corp. will provide 1,000 subscribers to *Forbes* magazine with average incomes of $232,000.

Advances in marketing research, including demographics and psychographics, make it possible to reach almost anyone with scientific precision. Thanks to vast data-collection and data-crunching networks, it is now possible to order mailing lists based on people's spending habits, charitable contributions, and even their favorite beer. Every time you purchase groceries with a store discount card, buy a book from Amazon.com, conduct a search on Google, or order something from a catalog, your name and address go into a marketing database that is often sold to other organizations.

Personalization — Direct mail, more than any other controlled or mass medium, is highly personalized. It comes in an envelope addressed to the recipient and often begins with a personalized greeting such as "Dear Jennifer." In addition, through computer software, the name of the person can be inserted throughout the letter. Specialized paragraphs can also be inserted in the direct mail letter to acknowledge past charitable contributions or make reference to localized information or contacts. The technology, which will be discussed shortly, also allows handwritten signatures and notes to make the basic "form" letter as personable as possible.

Cost — Direct mail, according to Media Distribution Services, is relatively inexpensive when compared to the cost of magazine ads and broadcast commercials. Typically, a rented list of consumers costs about $490 for 1,000 names, or 49 cents per name, according to DirectMail.com. You can get these names and addresses on labels or, more commonly, have a computer program print them directly on mailing envelopes.

Direct mail is cost-efficient from a production standpoint. In many cases, it is produced in one color (black), with perhaps a second color for emphasis of key points. Graphics are not elaborate, and the whole emphasis is on economical printing. Postage is a consideration. First class is the most expensive, but it is more reliable and timely than the cheaper third class (often called "standard mail"). First class also ensures that mail is forwarded or returned without additional cost to the sender. Nonprofit postage rates, available to qualified organizations, are the cheapest. You can cut postage costs by presorting letters by zip code and mailing at least 200 pieces at one time.

Disadvantages of Direct Mail

The major disadvantage of direct mail is its image as "junk mail." All such mail, whether it is a first-class letter from a political party or a flyer from the local pizza parlor, is put into the same category of "useless" information that just clutters up a person's mailbox.

Indeed, *U.S. News & World Report* estimates that nearly half of it goes directly to the garbage without even being opened. Even if it is opened, it is estimated that only 1 or 2 percent of the recipients will act on the message. Despite such odds, U.S. consumers purchased $244 billion worth of merchandise in a recent year by responding to direct mail sales pitches. Studies show that, on average, every dollar spent on direct mail advertising brings in $12 in sales—a return more than twice that generated by a television ad. Nonprofit agencies that rely on direct mail for much of their fundraising also say that the ROI (return on investment) makes direct mail a major component of their communication strategy.

Information Overload — It has already been noted that the average person receives more than 800 pieces of direct mail annually. Although it is argued that a person reads direct mail in isolation from other messages and distractions, there is the problem of clutter and the inability of people to cope with so many messages on a daily basis. Consequently, it is important to know how to write and format a direct mail piece that gets opened, read, and acted upon.

Creating a Direct Mail Package

The direct mail package has five basic components: (1) mailing envelope, (2) letter, (3) basic brochure, (4) reply card, and (5) return envelope. On occasion, a sixth component is added—"gifts" such as address labels, greeting cards, and even calendars that are designed to entice a person to open the envelope and at least read the message.

Mailing Envelope

The envelope is the headline of a direct mail package, because it is the first thing the recipient sees. If this doesn't attract the reader's interest, a person will not "read on" by opening the envelope.

According to Media Distribution Services, there are several ways to make an envelope attractive and appealing. It can be visually enhanced through the creative use of paper stock, windows, tabs, teasers, and other design options. Heavy, glossy paper can give the envelope the appearance of value and importance. Windows can provide teasers and other information that cater to the question, "Why should I open this?"

Sometimes, envelopes carry a preview of what's inside. UNICEF, in one of its fundraising letters, used the envelope teaser, "Enclosed: The Life or Death Seed Catalog." The Sierra Club simply marks its envelopes "Urgent" in big, red letters.

In contrast, some envelopes provide little or no information. The U.S. Postal Service awarded Mlicki, an Ohio branding agency, with its Marketing Achievement in Innovation and Leadership (MAIL) Award. The award recognized a direct mail campaign that garnered a 10 percent response rate and was designed as a dossier. The envelope was stamped "classified" to get the attention of prospective customers. But the sender of the mail was clearly identified in the return address on the front of the envelope. The idea is to arouse the curiosity of the reader so he or she will open the envelope. Organizations sometimes resort to trickery. They make the envelope look like it is an official letter from a government agency or there is the misleading teaser that you are the winner of a large prize.

In general, public relations writers should avoid misleading teasers and envelope designs that mislead readers or cause mistaken impressions. This causes credibility problems at least, and may border on being unethical. Your direct mail envelope should always have the name of the organization and the return address in the upper-left corner. Teasers should provide honest information.

Research has also found that a regular stamp is better than metered postage at getting attention, and a commemorative stamp is the most effective. Such stamps are attention getting, and it makes the direct mail envelope look more important. Of course, a name and address printed on the envelope is better than an adhesive label.

The Letter

For maximum effectiveness, the cover letter should be addressed to one person and start with a personal greeting, "Dear Ms. Smith." Some letters skip the personal salutation and just use a headline that will grab the reader's attention. A headline or a first paragraph is the most-read part of a letter, so it must be crafted to arouse the reader's interest. Some studies show that it takes a reader about 1 to 3 seconds to decide whether to read on or pitch the letter in the trash.

Headlines and First Paragraphs — A sales pitch for a product or service often has a headline that emphasizes a free gift or the promise of saving money. Nonprofit groups and public action groups, however, often state the need in a headline. The National Resources Defense Council, for example, used a headline in red that said, "Stop Big Oil's Attack on the Arctic Refuge . . . And Alaska's Imperiled Polar Bears."

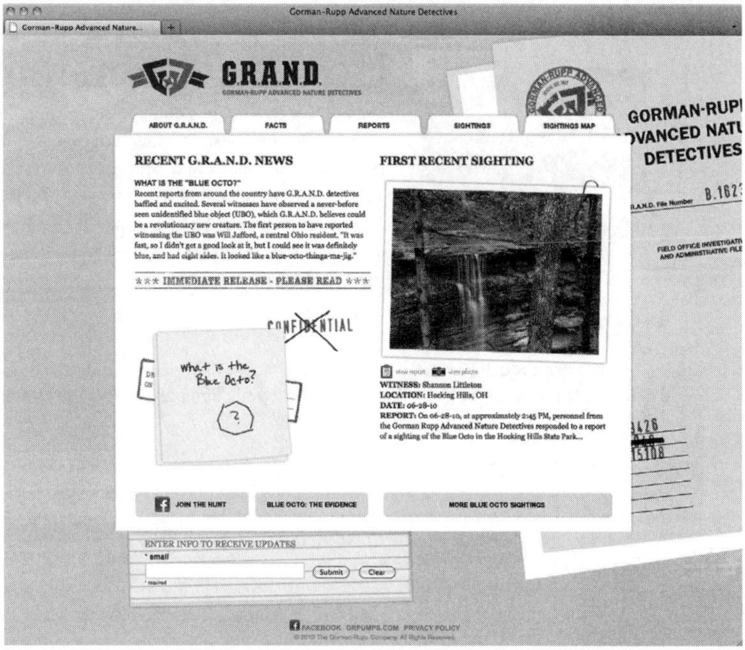

FIGURE 16.1 Mlicki won a U.S. Post Office award for its successful direct mail campaign for Gorman-Rupp. The direct mail envelope got attention with the promise that it held "classified" information about Gorman-Rupp's new product, the Blue Octo, an industrial pump. Inside the envelope was a nontraditional direct mail letter. Instead of the standard letter format, the envelope held what looked like a file folder with notes about the elusive Blue Octo.

You can use a straight lead for the beginning paragraph, or a human-interest angle. The straight lead is to the point. The Sierra Club began one letter from the executive director with the following: "I am writing to ask for your immediate help to ensure victory for the most ambitious government plan to protect endangered wilderness in our nation's history—the Wild Forest Protection Plan." Strong emotional appeals are also used. Human Rights Watch started one letter with the sentence, "Imagine the brutality of being raped and seeking help through your government and the only response is silence."

The award-winning Mlicki campaign was promoting an obscure industrial water pump named the Blue Octo. The campaign for manufacturer Gorman-Rupp used humor to get the attention of prospective pump purchasers. The campaign brought the Blue Octo to life and encouraged reporting of spottings, much like Bigfoot sightings. The headline on the letter designed as a dossier or file folder was "Gorman-Rupp Advanced Nature Detectives," or G.R.A.N.D. Inside the file was an adhesive note that looked handwritten and offered a website "For more information." The letter looked like a declassified report on the sighting of the elusive Blue Octo. Of course, it provided basic statistics about the pump. For a nontraditional but clever treatment of a direct mail letter, see Gorman-Rupp's Blue Octo letter in Figure 16.1.

Typeface and Length — Most direct mail letters are written on the organization's letter-size stationery. There is no rule about length, but experts recommend a maximum of two to four pages. A typewriter-style font for the text, such as Courier, makes the letter appear more personal than a fancier typeface. Several devices are used to make the letter easy to use. One is short sentences and paragraphs. Another is putting key words and phrases in boldface or even larger type. Some organizations emphasize key messages with a yellow highlighter, use red ink, or underline them. An example from the Marine Mammal Center is shown in Figure 16.2.

How *could* someone?

She was just five months old, a feisty sea lion pup practicing what sea lions do best – fishing. But this time the fish she swallowed had a hook in it. She was yanked violently from the sea and left dangling from the end of a fishing rod. Then someone aimed a high-powered crossbow and fired a metal arrow point-blank, directly into her neck.

Dear Friend,

The distress call came in just after dawn. It could have come from almost anywhere, but this time it was Morro Bay: "Female California sea lion pup, hooks with fishing lines in her body … a crossbow arrow just below her neck!"

Immediately, the volunteers and staff of The Marine Mammal Center swung into action. We rescued "Arrow," as we named the emaciated pup, and rushed her to our hospital near San Francisco. Our veterinary staff gave her antibiotics and tube-fed her. We flushed her wounds, and when she was stabilized we removed the hooks and arrow while she was under anesthesia.

Without the intervention of The Marine Mammal Center, Arrow would be dead today. Instead, *after three months of expert medical care and round-the-clock monitoring, we released Arrow back into the ocean – fully recovered!*

Every year, The Marine Mammal Center rescues hundreds of sea lions, otters, seals, dolphins, porpoises – even whales. Many are victims of gunshot wounds, fish hooks, fishing nets, or boat propellers.

At one time, these animals were left to die on beaches. Or were destroyed as threats to human health and safety. But since 1975, when The Marine Mammal Center was founded, these beautiful and intelligent creatures have been given a second chance to survive in their natural ocean environment.

Financed by individuals and families across the nation, and run strictly not-for-profit, *The Marine Mammal Center rescues and assists in the recovery of thousands of animals.* In fact, we recently rescued our 13,000th! And the challenges of our life-saving work grow greater every day.

The Marine
Mammal Center   1065 Fort Cronkhite · Sausalito, CA 94965 · 415.289.SEAL · www.marinemammalcenter.org

♻ Recycled & Recyclable

FIGURE 16.2 Direct mail is a major tool for fund-raising by nonprofits. This letter by the Marine Mammal Center in Sausalito, CA, effectively engages the reader with a story about the center's rescue of a sea lion pup. It goes on to tell about the center's multiple efforts every year to rescue marine mammals who have been victims of gunshot wounds, fish hooks, fishing nets, or boat propellers. Donation forms and a return envelope were included in the direct mail piece.

Information on how to write a fundraising letter is found in the accompanying Tips for Success. Other tips for planning a direct mail package are provided in the Tips for Success on page 424.

Postscript — The most effective direct mail letters always end with a postscript, or P.S. Many experts say this is the second most-read part of a letter, after the headline and beginning paragraph. It gives the writer an opportunity to restate the benefits or make a final pitch for support. CARE ended a fundraising letter with the postscript "I hope you'll consider sending a gift to support CARE's World Hunger Campaign. Let's show poor children and families we care. May we count on you?"

Brochures

Chapter 13 discussed the writing and production of brochures, and one popular use is their insertion into direct mail packages. Typically, the brochure describes a product, service, organization, or company. It supports the mailing's offer, adding credibility to the overall message. An effective brochure must be brief but at the same time provide useful information. A brochure insert for the Environmental Defense Action Fund, for example, gave "20 Simple Steps to Fight Global Warming."

Media Distribution Services offers the following elements that can increase a brochure's interest:

» **Testimonials.** List them in one place or sprinkle them throughout the text.

» **Questions and answers.** A good format. Your questions should address motivations, not just product features. They should seem natural, not contrived.

+

Tips for Success   How to Write a Fundraising Letter

A large percentage of fundraising for charitable institutions is conducted through direct mail. The purpose of the letter, of course, is to elicit a response—a donation. Writers of fundraising letters have learned to use the following approaches:

+ Use an attention-getting headline.

+ Follow the headline with an inspirational lead-in on why and how a donation will be of benefit.

+ Give a clear definition of the charitable agency's purpose and objectives.

+ Humanize the cause by giving an example of a child or family that benefited.

+ Include testimonials and endorsements from credible individuals.

+ Ask for specific action and provide an easy way for the recipient to respond. Postage-paid envelopes and pledge cards are often included.

+ Close with a postscript that gives the strongest reason for the reader to respond.

» **List of benefits.** Lists, when highlighted by large numerals or bullet points, make an attractive visual reference.

» **Guarantee.** A guarantee seems even stronger when printed in more elaborate type or framed in a box.

» **Models, colors, options.** Customer product choices can be pictured or described with words.

» **Benefit tables, comparisons.** These help readers identify your offer's advantages quickly.

» **Call-outs.** These are free-floating captions arranged around a picture or text. Short sentences emphasize key points.

Most brochures used in direct mail are designed to fit into a standard #10 business envelope. This means the brochure should be about 4 by 9 inches in overall dimension. It may be two or three panels. See page 360 in Chapter 13 for more on various brochure layouts.

Tips for Success How to Do a Direct Mail Package

Here are several techniques that have proven effective in direct mail over the years:

+ **Define the audience.** Know exactly who you want to reach and why they should respond. The more you know about the demographics of the members of your audience and their motivations, the better you can tailor a letter to them. Don't waste time and money sending your material to people who can't or won't respond.

+ **Get the envelope opened.** There is so much junk mail nowadays that many letters go directly into the trash without ever being opened. Put a teaser headline on the outside of the envelope that makes the recipient want to know what's inside. The opposite approach, which also raises curiosity, is to use a sender's address but not the name of the organization. Using stamps instead of a postal permit number also increases envelope opening.

+ **Keep the idea clear and pertinent.** State the offer or request in the first two or three sentences. Tell what the advantages or benefits are—and repeat them throughout the letter. At the end of the letter, summarize the message. You cannot be too clear.

+ **Make it easy for people to respond.** Tell the recipient exactly what to do and how to do it. Include a postage-paid reply card or envelope. Design forms that require only a check mark to place an order or make a pledge.

+ **Pretest the campaign.** Conduct a pilot campaign on a limited basis. Prepare two or three different appeals and send them to a sampling of the target audience. By doing this, you can find out what appeal generates the greatest response before doing an entire mailing.

Reply Card

If you want a response from the reader, the best way to get it is to provide a reply card. The card, printed on index-card stock so it is more rigid, should contain all the information you and the reader require to process an acceptance to attend an event, make a pledge to the organization, or order merchandise.

Additional care should be used to prepare the reply form. Exactly what information do you need to process it? Typical reply cards give a space for the respondent to give his or her name, address, city, and zip code. In addition, you may want the person's telephone number and email address. This information is valuable for updating lists in future mailings to the same people.

If the person is making a charitable donation or buying a product, you need to provide categories for payment by either check or credit card. The credit card information you need is (1) name of credit card, (2) name of person listed on the credit card, (3) the card number, and (4) expiration date.

It is important to ensure that the space allowed is large enough to accommodate requested information. A short line may not be sufficient for a person to write his or her complete address clearly. In general, reply cards should be at least 4 by 6 inches, and many of them are 4 by 8 inches.

Return Envelope

Although reply cards can offer a self-addressed return address on the reverse side, an envelope with a return address is usually provided. This ensures privacy, and an envelope is definitely needed if you are requesting a check or credit card information. Commercial operations often provide a postage-paid envelope, but nonprofits generally ask respondents to provide their own postage. This reduces costs, and more money can be spent on the cause itself. A nonprofit may provide a postage-paid envelope, but encourage supporters in the letter to help defray costs by covering the postage-paid designation with a stamp, thereby avoiding the mailing cost for the nonprofit.

Gifts

Many nonprofit and charitable organizations use direct mail packages that include a gift of some kind. Most common are address labels, greeting cards, and calendars. The theory is that the inclusion of such material cuts through all the competing solicitations and gives the person a "reward" for opening the envelope.

The inclusion of such items, however, considerably raises the cost of direct mail, and it's no guarantee that people will make a contribution out of "guilt" or even "gratitude." Indeed, there is some evidence that such "gifts" can increase the ire of individuals, because they don't like charitable causes spending so much money on direct mail—money that could go to the cause itself.

Oxfam, the humanitarian aid agency, took this tact on one mailing. The beginning of the letter announced in big, bold letters the following: "Enclosed: No address labels to use, No calendars to look at, No petitions to sign, and No pictures of starving children. What you will find is a straightforward case for one of the most effective humanitarian aid agencies anywhere in the world."

The Basics of Public Relations Advertising

The American Marketing Association defines advertising as "any paid form of non-personal presentation of ideas, goods, or services by an identified sponsor." Melvin DeFleur and Everett Dennis, authors of *Understanding Mass Media*, go even further and state, "Advertising tries to inform consumers about a *particular* product and to persuade them to make a *particular decision*—usually the decision to buy the product."

They are describing the most common forms of advertising—national consumer advertising (the ad in *Time* magazine about a new car model) and retail advertising (the ad in the local paper telling you where to buy the car).

However, advertising can serve other purposes besides just persuading people to buy a product or service. Todd Hunt and Brent Ruben, authors of *Mass Communication: Producers and Consumers*, say other purposes of advertising might be to build consumer trust in an organization (institutional advertising), to create favorable opinions and attitudes (goodwill or public service advertising), or to motivate people to support a cause or a political candidate (issue or political advertising).

These kinds of advertising can be placed under the umbrella of public relations advertising. In fact, the American National Advertisers and Publishers Information Bureau suggest several characteristics that distinguish public relations advertising. The following list uses the word "company," but the concept is applicable to any organization, including nonprofits, trade groups, and special-interest groups:

» It must educate or inform the public regarding the company's policies, functions, facilities, objectives, ideals, and standards.

» It must create a climate of favorable opinion about the company by stressing the competence of the company's management, accumulated scientific knowledge, manufacturing skills, technological progress, and contribution to social advancement and public welfare.

» It must build up the investment qualities of the company's securities or improve the financial structure of the company.

» It must sell the company as a good place in which to work, often in a way designed to appeal to recent college graduates or people with certain skills.

In other words, public relations advertising does not sell goods or services directly. Instead, its primary purpose is to inform, educate, and create a favorable climate of public support that allows an organization to succeed in its organizational objectives. Of course, an indirect by-product of this may be the selling of goods and services.

Advatages of Advertising

Advertising, like direct mail, is paid and controlled mass communication. This means that the organization completely bypasses the newsroom gatekeepers and places its messages, exactly as written and formatted, with the medium's advertising department. Thus a primary reason for advertising as a communications tool is that control of the message remains with the sender.

Some other advantages of advertising are its selectivity and the advertiser's control of the impact and timing.

Audience Selection — Specific audiences can be reached with advertising messages on the basis of such variables as location, age, income, and lifestyle. This is done by closely studying the audience demographics of newspapers, magazines, and broadcast shows. BMW, for example, advertises in magazines such as the *New Yorker* and *National Geographic*, which have highly educated and affluent readers. The neighborhood deli, however, might advertise only in the local weekly that serves the immediate area. Online ads provide an additional means of targeting your audience.

Message Control — Gatekeepers frequently alter or truncate the news or features they receive. Sometimes the changes do little harm, but occasionally the changes ruin an idea or eliminate an important point. Your communications plan may involve informing the public about subject A before you say anything about subject B, but if a gatekeeper changes the order or eliminates one story, the sequence is destroyed. With advertising, however, you can be sure that your message is reproduced in the exact words you choose and in the sequence you have planned.

Impact — With advertising, you can make your messages as big, frequent, and powerful as you choose. Media gatekeepers, by definition, are looking for newsworthy, timely material. An organization, however, might want to send a message to a large audience that doesn't meet the standards of traditional news values. The editor may discard your information or run it in a brief story buried on page 9. With advertising, however, you can have a much larger impact by simply buying the entire page.

Timing — If timing is an important factor, advertising can guarantee that your message will be timely. Prompt response to a public issue, a fixed sequence of messages, continuity of communication—all can be maintained through advertising. To the gatekeeper, your message may be just as usable on Tuesday as on Friday; but for your purpose, Tuesday may be a day too early and Friday is too late. You can't be sure about the timing unless you pay for it.

Disadvantages of Advertising

Although institutional advertising can be effective in getting key messages to specific audiences, there are some disadvantages.

Cost — Paid space is expensive. Ads in multiple media, which are necessary for message penetration, can cost thousands of dollars in the trade press and millions in the consumer press. The most extreme example is the Super Bowl. A 30-second TV commercial cost $3 million in 2011. Compared to that, a similar commercial on the Academy Awards costs about $1.7 million. Likewise,

> *Half the money I spend on advertising is wasted. The trouble is, I don't know which half.* John Wanamaker, founder of department store chain bearing his name

a 1-minute commercial on a prime TV entertainment show can run $250,000 to $500,000. The average cost for a 30-second spot on broadcast television is $110,000. An international publication such as *The Wall Street Journal* charges about $265,000 for a one-page black-and-white ad and $345,000 for a color ad.

The high cost of buying space for advertising has led many companies to shift more of their marketing communications budgets to the Internet, product publicity, and direct mail. Online ads often are paid for per click through, which can be more cost efficient. But online ads may not create the same level of awareness that traditional mainstream media ad buys might. See the Tips for Success below for creating an effective online ad.

Credibility — Public relations executives are fond of saying, "Advertising raises awareness, but publicity published as news stories creates credibility."

Because they are controlled messages, advertisements are generally less believable than publicity that appears in the news columns or on broadcast news shows.

Tips for Success   Effective Online Ad Elements

Internet advertising reached $7.3 billion in the first quarter of 2011, which was a 23 percent increase over the same period in 2010. Facebook, as the leading social networking site, was projected to exceed $4 billion in advertising revenue. MediaCollege.com is an educational website focused on electronic media. The experts at MediaCollege.com offer these 10 tips for successful online ads:

+ **Target your ad.**   Make sure your ad is on a site that will reach your intended audience.

+ **Get attention.**   Animation and colors are great attention-getters, as long as they're not overdone to the point of being gaudy.

+ **Experiment.**   Systematically change ads to see which generates the most click-throughs or queries.

+ **Call to action.**   As with any persuasion, an online ad is best when it directs the target to do something.

+ **Make it obvious.**   Viewers shouldn't have to scratch their heads or guess what the ad is promoting.

+ **Be honest.**   Don't try to trick your audience into clicking into your ad.

+ **Be specific.**   Focus the message as tightly as possible. Online ads are not the place for complex messages.

+ **Involve the audience.**   Something as simple as a click-through to additional information or more complex like a game will draw attention.

+ **Sex sells.**   Like it or not, having good-looking people in your ads will draw attention.

+ **Keep the file size down.**   Experts recommend that banner ads should not exceed 15KB.

The public perceives that news reports have more credibility because journalists, who are independent of the organization, have evaluated the information on the basis of truth and accuracy.

Indeed, a widely perceived value of publicity is the concept that a third party, the medium, has endorsed the information by printing or broadcasting it. Advertisements have no such third-party endorsement, because anyone with enough money can place an advertisement, provided it meets the acceptance standards of the medium.

Types of Public Relations Advertising

The majority of public relations advertising is done in magazines, with television and newspapers in second and third place, respectively. The advantage of magazines is a highly defined readership in terms of income, education, occupation, and specific interests.

There are several types of public relations advertising. At times, the distinctions between categories can become blurred; however, for the purposes of this discussion, we will deal with five basic types: (1) image building, (2) investor and financial relations programs, (3) public service messages, (4) advocacy, and (5) announcements.

Image Building

The purpose of image-building advertising is to strengthen an organization's reputation, change or reinforce public perceptions, and create a favorable climate for selling the organization's goods and services.

A good example of an image-building campaign is one by Toyota, which wants to project its image as an integral part of the American economy. One magazine ad, showing an assembly plant, was headlined "Our blue-sky scenario: more U.S. manufacturing jobs, cleaner U.S. manufacturing plants." The copy was as follows:

> Since 1986, Toyota has been building vehicles and creating manufacturing jobs in the U.S. Today, with our eight manufacturing plants, sales and marketing operations, research and design facilities, and through our dealers and suppliers, Toyota's U.S. operations account for more than 190,000 jobs. And with two new state-of-the-art manufacturing facilities being built to strict environmental standards, we're continuing our commitment to responsible growth as an employer, and a neighbor.

After a Gulf of Mexico oil spill, British/Dutch oil company BP tried to rebuild its image. Among the many image ads it ran was one titled "We'll Get It Done. We'll Make This Right."

Nonprofits and civic groups also engage in image advertising. An example of image building advertising by a oil company is the Chevron ad in Figure 16.3.

Investor and Financial Relations

A different type of public relations advertising is targeted to the financial community—individual and institutional investors, stock analysts, investment bankers, and stockholders. Such advertising often has the objective of informing and reassuring

FIGURE 16.3 Organizations such as manufacturing or energy companies often use image building advertising to inform consumers and community members of policies and activities. This ad from Chevron announces the company's devotion to community relations.

investors that the company is well managed, worthy of investment, and has bright prospects for the future.

Such advertising is used extensively during proxy fights for control of companies, when a company is undergoing some major reorganization, or when a company believes it is being unfairly attacked by consumer groups or regulatory agencies. A variety of these ads appear in financial publications, notably *The Wall Street Journal*.

Taco Bell took out print ads in the *New York Times* and *The Wall Street Journal* when the company was named in a lawsuit alleging its products were not as advertised. The headline read "Thank you for suing us" with the subhead, "Here's the truth about our seasoned beef." The copy went on to reveal the restaurant's "secret" recipe as evidence to back up its claim. When the suit was dropped, the restaurant chain ran another full-page ad in national newspapers. This time the headline read, "Would it kill you to say you're sorry?" The copy assured investors and consumers that Taco Bell had not changed its recipe in response to the lawsuit. See the initial ad in Figure 16.4.

Other forms of financial advertising are somewhat routine. You can use an ad to announce a new corporate name, the acquisition of another company, or a new CEO. Such ads help fulfill SEC requirements, discussed in Chapter 11, for full and timely disclosure. Releasing news to the media may be adequate, but many corporations also use advertising to ensure wide distribution.

Public Service

Public service advertisements provide information, raise awareness about social issues, and give how-to suggestions. A number of nonprofit and charitable organizations, as well as governmental agencies, use such advertising for public education.

FIGURE 16.4 Corporations use public relations advertising to repair their image or counter claims made by opponents. In the case of Taco Bell, it did both in a series of two ads targeted at claims made in a lawsuit. Two ads used humor to get the reader's attention. This "Thank You for Suing Us" ad appeared in several national newspapers to provide Taco Bell's "secret" recipe for its beef taco filling. Taco Bell was being sued for false advertisement. The lawsuit was dropped and Taco Bell ran an ad with an equally attention-grabbing headline that suggested those who filed the then-dropped lawsuit should apologize.

Thank you for suing us.

Here's the truth about our seasoned beef.

The claims made against Taco Bell and our seasoned beef are absolutely false.
Our beef is 100% USDA inspected, just like the quality beef you buy in a supermarket and prepare in your home. It is then slow-cooked and simmered in our unique recipe of seasonings, spices, water, and other ingredients to provide Taco Bell's signature taste and texture.

Plain ground beef tastes boring.
The only reason we add anything to our beef is to give the meat flavor and quality. Otherwise we'd end up with nothing more than the bland flavor of ground beef, and that doesn't make for great-tasting tacos.

So here are the REAL percentages.
88% Beef and 12% Secret Recipe.

In case you're curious, here's our not-so-secret recipe.
We start with USDA-inspected quality beef (88%). Then add water to keep it juicy and moist (3%). Mix in Mexican spices and flavors, including salt, chili pepper, onion powder, tomato powder, sugar, garlic powder, and cocoa powder (4%). Combine a little oats, caramelized sugar, yeast, citric acid, and other ingredients that contribute to the flavor, moisture, consistency, and quality of our seasoned beef (5%).

We stand behind the quality of our seasoned beef 100% and we are proud to serve it in all our restaurants. We take any claims to the contrary very seriously and plan to take legal action against those who have made false claims against our seasoned beef.

Greg Creed

Greg Creed
President, Taco Bell

TacoBell.com
Facebook.com/TacoBell

TACO BELL

Here are some other examples of public service campaigns by public service agencies and nonprofits and sponsored by the Ad Council:

» Feeding America urges U.S. citizens to contribute to or use its community food bank.
» The American Association of People with Disabilities informs people about the 20th anniversary of the organization and how to get involved with disability groups.
» The U.S. Army works at high school dropout prevention by encouraging students to stay in school and graduate.
» United Way gives parents, grandparents, and other caregivers easy tips to boost childhood learning and development during routine activities.
» Autism Speaks educates parents about the growing rates of autism and the value of early detection.
» The American Heart Association introduces a new CPR technique that is "Hands-Only."

The Ad Council prepared public service ads for these national nonprofit groups. The Council, in cooperation with volunteer advertising agencies, does this as a public service. A good example of an Ad Council campaign, about hunger prevention, is shown in Figure 16.5. Ads were prepared for newspapers and magazines, TV stations, radio stations, and transit signage. Go to www.adcouncil.org to see a full list of current campaigns.

FIGURE 16.5 The Ad Council partnered with Feeding America to develop public service announcements for several media. This ad demonstrates the power of a headline. Its "Hunger Reads the Morning Paper, Too" gets your attention, and then the fact that 1 in 6 Americans is hungry feeds you the facts.

Corporations also do public service kinds of advertising to generate goodwill. In most cases, it is related to their products and services. For example:

» The Pacific Gas & Electric Company provides helpful hints on how to save energy and money.
» The Coca-Cola Company, in collaboration with the National Park Foundation, America's State Parks, and the National Recreation and Park Association, encourages families to go play in their favorite parks and vote for "America's Favorite Park."
» Microsoft gives parents tips about how to teach their children about online security.

Advocacy/Issues

Although it can be argued that advocacy is an element in all public relations advertising—whether it's the American Cancer Society telling you to stop smoking or a company telling you it's all right to buy its stock—the term "advocacy advertising" has a more exact meaning.

It usually means advertising to motivate voters, to influence government policy, or to put pressure on elected officials. A good example is the campaign by the Humane Society of the United States to put public and legislative pressure on the Canadian government to stop the killing of baby seals for their fur.

Allstate Insurance has also run a series of advocacy ads that call for more legislation to curb the dangerous driving habits of teenagers. The company would like to see legislation banning anyone under the age of 18 from using cell phones or any text-messaging device while driving. In addition, the insurance company advocates graduated driver licensing laws that place limitations on new drivers.

The headline for one Allstate ad was, "Two Out of Three Teens Admit to Texting While Driving: Some of Them Will Never Be Heard From Again." The lead sentence in the text continues, "Car crashes are the leading cause of death among American teens. Is any text message worth the risk?" The ad concludes, "Tell your congressional representatives that you support the STANDUP Act. Go to allstate.com/STANDUP."

If 9 fully loaded jumbo jets crashed every year, something would be done about it. Every year, more than 4,000 teens die in car crashes. Allstate insurance issues ad that advocated more restrictions on teen drivers

Announcements

Announcements can be used for any number of situations. The primary purpose is to inform the public promptly about something that might interest them. This might be the recalling of a product, apologizing for a failure of service, announcing a community event, or even expressing sympathy to the families who lost loved ones in a plane crash. Here are some other examples of announcement ads:

» Taco Bell reassures customers that its meat is 100 percent USDA inspected following the filing of a class action lawsuit.
» State Farm Insurance tells residents of a disaster area how to file claims.

» The High Museum of Art in Atlanta announces a special exhibition of folk art.

» The Clinton Foundation announces a National Cholera Education and Awareness campaign in Haiti.

Creating a Print Ad

Print advertisements have several key elements. They are headline, text, artwork, and layout. Although broadcast advertising is not covered here, the basic format follows guidelines that were given for VNRs and PSAs in Chapter 9. You have to write copy for the ear, keep it short, and adopt a conversational style. For television, you need strong graphic elements.

Headline

Advertising expert John Caplets says, "The headline is the most important element in most ads—and the best headlines appeal to the reader's self-interest or give news."

Headlines should be specific about a benefit, or they can be teasers that arouse interest. Here is a headline about a specific program: "The Phoenix Mutual Insurance Retirement Income Plan." Caplets thought this was all right, but he created a headline that sold much more successfully: "To Men Who Want to Quit Work Some Day." This was accompanied by an illustration of a smiling senior citizen fishing in a mountain stream.

Caplets offers the following suggestions for writing an advertising headline:

» Include the interests of the audience.

» Use words such as "introducing," "announcing," "new," or "now" to give the headline a newsworthy appeal.

» Avoid witty or cute headlines unless they include reader interest and appear newsy.

» Present the headline positively. Don't say "Our competitors can't match our service" when you can say, "Our service surpasses that of our competitors."

Text

The headline is followed by one or several copy blocks. These are sentences and short paragraphs that inform and persuade. In general, copy should be limited to one or two major points. Sentences should be short and punchy and use active voice. A declarative sentence is much better than one that includes a dependent or an independent clause.

The copy should evoke emotion, provide information of value to the reader, and suggest a way that the reader can act on the information. You might include a toll-free telephone number, an email address, or the URL of the organization's website. A review of the ads featured in this chapter will give you some idea about copywriting.

Artwork

An ad can consist of just a headline and copy, but the most effective ones usually have a strong graphic element. This may be a striking photo, a line drawing, or a computer-generated design. Visual elements play a crucial role in motivating a reader to even look at the ad.

Artwork and graphics are doubly important if the ad is on the Internet. In this case, text is secondary and graphics are primary. Websites were discussed in Chapter 12, but the guidelines also apply to advertising. The graphics can't be too complex because of possible downloading problems, but the ad does need to be interactive, with "click here" buttons to involve the reader.

Layout

The headline, copy, and graphic elements need to be integrated into an attractive, easy-to-read advertisement. A layout can be a mock-up of the planned ad, or it can be a detailed comprehensive that includes the actual type and artwork that will be used.

A number of tips about layout were given in Chapter 13. Many of them are also applicable to preparing an advertisement. In general, avoid all-capital letters or large blocks of copy. Use serif type for body copy, avoid large blocks of reverse type (white on dark color), and use plenty of white space. See the Tips for Success features on page 428 and below for more tips on creating an effective ad.

+

Tips for Success   Getting the Most from Your Ads

A successful advertisement grabs the reader's attention. *Communication Briefings* offers the following suggestions provided by Direct Response in Torrance, California:

+ **Busy layouts often pull better than neat ones.**   One split-run test showed busy layouts outpull neat ones by 14 percent.

+ **Vary shapes, sizes, and colors.**   People will get bored, and turn the page, if there is no variety.

+ **Color will attract attention.**   But it may not be cost-effective. Consider using color when the product itself demands it.

+ **Putting something odd into a picture will attract attention.**   David Ogilvy's Hathaway Shirts campaign used a model with an eye patch. That odd little detail made the campaign a classic.

+ **Too many extraneous props divert attention.**   A curtain material company ran an ad with a cute teddy bear in it. The company got more calls asking about the bear than it did about its product.

+ **Photographs are more convincing than drawn illustrations.**   Photos can increase responses by over 50 percent.

+ **Before-and-after pictures are very persuasive.**   The technique is a great way to show the benefit of your product.

Working with an Ad Agency

Most public relations advertising is prepared with the assistance of an advertising agency. The agency has employees who are experts in all phases of creating the ads and purchasing space in the selected media.

In an integrated marketing communications campaign, personnel from a public relations firm and an advertising agency often work together on a campaign. Fleishman-Hillard public relations, for example, works with BBDO on anti-tobacco campaigns for the New Jersey Department of Health and Senior Services. In addition, BBDO has also worked on integrated campaigns with Golin/Harris (for Visa), Edelman Worldwide (for KFC), and Porter Novelli (for Gillette and M&Ms).

The key to a successful relationship is keeping the communication channels as open as possible.

Sara Calabro, a writer for *PRWeek*, gives some pointers for working with an ad agency:

» Do clarify the respective responsibilities of each agency from the outset and communicate openly and frequently throughout the campaign.

» Do always view an integrated account from the perspective of how public relations can complement advertising and vice versa.

» Do consider the compatibility of team members' personalities when selecting a partner agency.

Other Advertising Channels

Other forms of advertising that can be used as a tactic in a public relations program are (1) billboards, (2) transit panels, (3) buttons and bumper stickers, (4) posters, (5) T-shirts, and (6) promotional items. See the PR Casebook on page 437 to see how the U.S. Census Bureau employed nontraditional advertising techniques to reach university students.

Billboards

Most outdoor advertising consists of paper sheets pasted on a wooden or metal background. The 24-sheet poster is standard, but there are also painted billboards, which use no paper. Outdoor advertising reaches large audiences in brief exposures. Accordingly, advertising for this medium must be eye-catching and use few words. Ten words is a rule-of-thumb limit for outdoor copy. When design and copy are approved, the individual sheets that make up the whole advertisement are printed and then pasted to the billboard.

Location is vital in this medium—and prices are based on the traffic that is exposed to the site. Occasionally, nonprofit organizations can obtain free or heavily discounted usage of outdoor space that is temporarily unsold. Displays are usually scheduled in monthly units, and occasionally there are gaps in the schedules, which may lead to discounted rates.

PR casebook

U.S. Census Bureau Targets Millennials

The U.S. Census Bureau is charged with counting every citizen once a decade. During the 2010 Census, the government turned to the Public Relations Student Society of America (PRSSA) and its annual Bateman Case Study Competition for help in counting college students. According to Philip Volmar, writing in *Public Relations Tactics,* "One of the nation's most transient populations is college students, and the Bureau lists these mobile Millennials as part of its 'hard-to-count' category because students are often moving or too distracted with schoolwork to fill out the Census form."

Teams from the University of Georgia, Loyala University, and Roger Williams University came in first, second, and third, respectively, in the competition. Each team developed ways to raise awareness among college students about the importance of being counted. They used handbills, yard signs, logos on milk cartons, and public service announcements—all tactics that fall broadly into the public relations advertising category.

"We saw the incredible potential in PR students to develop campaigns that not only reach students, but also their communities at large," Stacy Gimbel, a public affairs specialist for the Bureau, told *Public Relations Tactics.* "Working with college students to share our message with their own communities was an important tactic for us," Gimbel said.

The winning University of Georgia campaign was called "iCount" and asked the university's hometown, Athens, this question: "Is your silence worth $1,697?"—the amount of money lost locally for each person who doesn't participate in the Census.

All three campaigns targeted non-English-speaking groups—Latinos in Georgia, Latinos and Vietnamese in New Orleans, and Portuguese in Rhode Island, which required translating campaign materials into the languages of these publics.

The University of Georgia team also won the 2011 PRSA Silver Anvil for its campaign.

Transit Panels

This category includes the small posters placed in subway and commuter rail stations, the cards used in buses and rail cars, the highly visual ads often seen at bus stops, and the large ads on the sides and backs of buses. All types of transit advertising require eye-catching graphics, but the copy can be longer than for outdoor posters. The person waiting for a train or holding a strap or a bar on a bus or rail car has some time to absorb a message. Cards in transit vehicles often carry coupons or tear-off notes allowing readers to ask for more information or respond to some sort of offer.

Buttons and Bumper Stickers

Buttons are widely used in political campaigns and at special events. They are also useful in fund-raising, when they are distributed to people who make donations. In San Francisco one year, money was raised for the ballet by selling "SOB" ("Save Our Ballet") buttons to pedestrians in the downtown area.

In general, buttons have a short life span. They are worn by convention delegates or by sales representatives during a trade show. Buttons are sometimes sold at events as a wearable "ticket" to demonstrate that you've paid an entry fee or that you support the sponsoring cause. Outside of these areas, people don't generally wear buttons unless they are highly committed to a particular cause.

Bumper stickers are another specialty item. They are often used to support political candidates and social issues, but they can also be used to promote a special event or a scenic attraction or membership in an organization. Magnetic bumper stickers are a popular alternative to adhesive ones because they don't mar the finish on a car.

Posters

Posters are used in a variety of settings to create awareness and remind people of something. Many companies use posters on bulletin boards to remind employees about basic company policies, benefits, and safety precautions.

Government agencies often use posters as part of public information campaigns about preventing AIDS, getting flu shots, or having pets neutered.

Museum exhibits and art shows lend themselves to poster treatments. The poster, often a piece of art itself, can promote attendance and can also be sold as a souvenir of the show.

To be effective, a poster must be attractively designed and have strong visual elements. It should be relatively large, convey only one basic idea, and use only a few words to relate basic information. A poster is a very small billboard.

Posters, if done properly, can be expensive to design and produce. Therefore, you need to assess how the posters will be used and displayed. Costs can be controlled, often by buying ready-to-use posters from printers and having the organization's name or logo imprinted on them. Local chapters of national organizations, such as the American Cancer Society, also get posters from the national organization that can easily be localized.

T-Shirts

T-shirts have been described as "walking billboards," and some people, including sociologists, lament the fact that people are so materialistic that they willingly become walking ads for products, services, and social or political issues. Why people do this remains unknown, but the fact is that they do spend their own money to advertise things with which they may or may not have any direct connection.

Because so many people are willing to serve as billboards, you may find an opportunity to use this medium, which is particularly convenient for causes such as environmental protection. Often such groups make sizable incomes from the sale of T-shirts.

Corporations don't usually sell T-shirts, but they do distribute them to attendees at conferences, sales meetings, picnics, and other events. In these situations, the T-shirts contribute to a feeling of belonging to a team.

Almost every town and city in America has at least one shop where you can order T-shirts. You can specify just about anything you can imagine—slogans, corporate logos, symbols, and so on. The process is simple and fast, and the costs are low. At some time, almost any organization may find T-shirts useful.

Promotional Items

An inexpensive item with the organization's logo or name on it often accompanies public relations events. Angela West, public relations manager for the Promotional Products Association International, writes in *Public Relations Tactics*, "Whether you're conducting a media relations program, staging a press conference, or hosting a special event, promotional products are a valuable public relations tool."

Promotional items may include pens, coffee mugs, key chains, paperweights, mouse pads, vinyl briefcases, plaques, and even T-shirts. An organization may include such an item in a media kit, although most reporters complain they have enough pens and coffee mugs to last a lifetime. At other times, promotional items are made available at press parties and trade shows.

The main consideration, says West, is choosing products that bear a natural relationship to the product, service, or message being promoted. A press kit for the Kansas Wheat Commission, for example, might include a cookbook with wheat-based recipes together with an apron and press release about commission activities.

Summary

The Basics of Direct Mail

» Direct mail, used primarily in marketing to sell goods and services, also can be an effective public relations tool to inform, educate, and motivate individuals.

» The three major advantages of direct mail are (1) ability to reach specific audiences, (2) personalization of message, and (3) cost.

» A major disadvantage of direct mail is the perception that it is "junk mail," which reduces its acceptance as a credible tool of communication.

Creating a Direct Mail Package

» The direct mail package has five components: (1) envelope, (2) letter, (3) brochure, (4) reply card, and (5) return envelope.

» Advances in technology and market research allow you to rent or buy a mailing list that is compiled with scientific precision.

» Nonprofit and advocacy groups often use a compelling human-interest angle to start direct mail letters.

» Direct mail envelopes, experts say, attract more attention if they use commemorative stamps instead of metered postage.

» The headline and first paragraph, as well as the postscript, get the most readership in a direct mail letter.

The Basics of Public Relations Advertising

» Advertising, the purchase of paid space and time in a mass medium, can be a useful tool in a public relations program.

» Public relations advertising does not sell products directly, but it can create a supportive environment for the selling of products and services by enhancing public perception of an organization.

» The major advantages of advertising are (1) ability to reach specified audiences, (2) control of the message, (3) frequency of the message, and (4) control of the timing and context.

» Advertising has the disadvantages of (1) high cost and (2) lower credibility than publicity that appears in news columns.

Types of Public Relations Advertising

» There are five kinds of public relations advertising: (1) image building, (2) financial, (3) public service, (4) advocacy/issues, and (5) announcements.

Creating a Print Ad

» Writing an effective ad requires considerable skill and imagination. You must think about the headline, text, artwork, and layout and how they all relate to each other.

» Effective advertising copy is short and punchy. Copy must be oriented to the self-interest of the reader, viewer, or listener.

Working with an Ad Agency

» A successful working relationship with an advertising agency requires frequent and clear communication.

Other Advertising Channels

» Other channels of public relations advertising include (1) billboards, (2) transit panels, (3) buttons and bumper stickers, (4) posters, (5) T-shirts, and (6) promotional items.

Skill Building Activities

1. Collect a variety of direct mail pieces from various nonprofit organizations and have a class or group discussion about their content and format. What techniques did you like? What turned you off?

2. Based on the guidelines mentioned in this chapter, write and design a fundraising letter packet (envelope, letter, and reply card) for a nonprofit in your community.

3. Find at least three samples of ads illustrating the five areas of public relations advertising: image building, investor/financial relations, advocacy, public service, and announcements. Critique the ads. What do you believe did or didn't work in the ads?

4. An organization of which you are a member (for example, club, religious group, Greek organization) needs your help in raising awareness of an issue it supports. Write copy for a print issue advertisement and suggest some of the other advertising channels, such as T-shirts or promotional items, that may support a public relations strategy.

5. Write a short essay on the difference between public relations advertising and marketing advertising.

Media Resources

Bachman, K. (2009, May 20). "Printed Direct Mail Declining." *AdWeek*. Available at: http://www.adweek.com/news/advertising-branding/printed-direct-mail-declining-105820

Grensing-Pophal, L. (2011). *Direct Mail in the Digital Age*, North Vancouver, BC: Self-Counsel Press.

Klein, K. (2011). *Fundraising for Social Change*, Hoboken, NJ: Jossey-Bass.

Ward, D. (2010, November 1). "Print Ad Placement Quickly Becoming Front-Page News." *PRWeek* p. 21.

Wayman, J. (2011, July 1). "There's a Place for Both New and Traditional Channels in Cause Engagement." *PRWeek* p. 17.

Organizing Meetings and Events

» After reading this chapter, you will be able to:

» Know the logistics of planning a meeting

» Plan a banquet, reception, or cocktail party

» Understand the multiple aspects of organizing a convention

» Understand the components of participating in a trade show

» Creatively think about promotional events that attract attention

» Organize open houses and plan tours

A World Filled with Meetings and Events

Meetings and events are vital public relations tools. Their greatest value is that they let the audience participate, face-to-face, in real time. In this era of digital communication and information overload, there is still a basic human need to gather, socialize, and be part of a group activity.

Individuals attending a meeting or event use all five of their senses—hearing, sight, touch, smell, and taste—so they become more emotionally involved in the process. Marketing and public relations professionals, for example, often use events to foster more brand awareness and loyalty.

Meetings and events, of course, come in all shapes and sizes. A committee meeting of a civic club or an office staff may only include four or five people. Corporate seminars may be for 50 to 250 people. At the other end of the scale is a trade show, such as the Consumer Electronics Show (CES) in Las Vegas, which attracts 130,000 attendees over a 3-day period. Promotional events to launch a new

" Events deliver face time between consumers and brands. They also introduce consumers to new products. " Yung Moon, associate publisher of *Self* magazine, as reported in *PRWeek*

441

product or to increase brand awareness of a current product or service are also done on a frequent basis. Glenfiddich scotch, for example, took a cask of scotch around to various cities and had people write their dreams and aspirations on it.

However, effective meetings and events don't just happen. Detailed planning and logistics are essential to ensure that defined objectives are achieved whether you're organizing a committee meeting or a national conference. This chapter discusses various types of meetings and events that require attention to detail and good communication skills.

Staff and Committee Meetings

Staff and committee meetings are part of any organization, from the local garden club to the multinational corporation. Indeed, through such meetings, employees or group members have a chance to express their views and participate in decision making.

There are two major complaints about meetings: They are time consuming and they are often ineffective. A survey of office workers by PolyVision Corporation, for example, found that men spend 4.3 hours a week and women spend 2.26 hours a week in meetings. The study also found that 75 percent of the respondents said their meetings could be more effective. In another study, the Wharton Center for Applied Research found that middle managers spent an average of 11 hours a week in meetings and concluded that about 30 percent of these meeting could have been better handled through one-on-one talks, by phone, or via email.

This is not to say that meetings should be banned. It does say, however, that meetings should be held only if other communication channels are not appropriate for accomplishing the purpose of the meeting. "Is this meeting really necessary?" is always a good question to ask before scheduling a meeting. If the answer is "yes," consider the following guidelines for having an effective staff or committee meeting:

> » **Limit attendance.**   Only those who are directly involved should be invited.
> » **Distribute the agenda in advance.**   Let people know what will be discussed or decided, so they can think about the issues before the meeting. Experts recommend that you prioritize the agenda and plan to cover only two or three items.
> » **Use a round table.**   Everyone has equal positional status and equal access to each other. The next best alternative is a square table.
> » **Set a time limit.**   The agenda should clearly state the beginning and ending time of the meeting, so people can plan their day. A meeting should run a maximum of 60 to 90 minutes. The longer the meeting runs, the less effective it is.
> » **Manage the meeting.**   The chairperson must make sure the meeting stays on track. Do not allow an individual or the group to go off on tangents.
> » **Budget time.**   Set a time limit for discussion of a specific agenda item. Do not spend an excessive amount of time on an item that shortchanges other items on the agenda.
> » **Know Robert's Rules of Order.**   It may be unnecessary in an informal, friendly meeting, but knowledge of parliamentary procedure is helpful to manage discussion and conclude it with a vote.

» **Close with a brief overview.** At the end of the meeting, summarize what has been accomplished, what will be done, and who will do it. Remember that meetings are held to make decisions, not just to discuss things.

» **Distribute a summary memo.** The chair or secretary should distribute a summary of the meeting within a day after the meeting. This helps remind people what was decided.

Group Meetings

Having meetings seems to be part of human nature. There are literally thousands of civic clubs, professional societies, trade associations, and hobby groups that have meetings that attract millions of people every year. In addition, many of these organizations sponsor workshops and seminars on a regular basis.

Planning

The size and purpose of the meeting dictate the plan. Every plan must consider these questions: How many will attend? Who will attend? When and where will it be held? How long will it last? Who will speak? What topics will be covered? What facilities will be needed? Who will run it? What is its purpose? How do we get people to attend? A checklist for planning a club meeting is provided in the Tips for Success on page 444.

Location — If the meeting is to be held on the premises of the organization, the room can be reserved by contacting whoever is responsible for such arrangements. If the meeting is to be held at some outside location, you will have to talk to the person in charge. In a hotel or restaurant, that person is the catering manager. In a school, it may be the principal; in a church, the minister or priest.

The meeting room must be the right size for the expected audience. If it is too large, the audience will feel that the meeting has failed to draw the expected attendance. If it is too small, the audience will be uncomfortable. Most hotels have a number of meeting rooms ranging in size from small to very large. If you hold your meeting in a hotel or in a restaurant with many banquet rooms, make sure your meeting is listed on a board or sign so guests know where to find the meeting.

Seating — A variety of seating arrangements can be used, depending on the purpose of the meeting. A monthly club meeting, for example, often features a luncheon or dinner. In this case, attendees are usually seated at round tables of six or eight, where they first have a meal and then listen to a speaker.

Seminars, designed primarily for listening, usually have what is called "theater" seating. Rows of seats are set up, all facing the speakers. Such meetings may be held in theaters or auditoriums (Figure 17.1). A workshop or a small seminar may use what is called "lunchroom" seating. This uses long tables with chairs on one side so that attendees can take notes or set up laptop computers.

Occasionally, large meetings are broken into discussion groups. Typically, the audience starts in one large room, where a speaker gives information and states

Tips for Success How to Plan a Meeting

Every meeting requires its own specialized checklist, but here is a general "to-do" list for a local dinner meeting of a service club or professional association.

In Advance

+ What is the purpose of the meeting? Business? Social? Continuing education? Combination?

+ What date and time are best for maximum attendance?

+ What size audience do you realistically expect?

+ Select the restaurant facility at least 4 to 6 weeks in advance.

+ Confirm the following in writing: date, time, menu, cocktails, seating plan, number of guaranteed reservations, and projected costs.

+ Enlist the speaker 4 to 6 weeks in advance. If the speaker is in high demand, make arrangements several months in advance. Discuss the nature of the talk, its projected length, and whether audiovisual aids will be used that require special equipment.

+ Publicize the meeting to the membership and other interested parties. This should be done a minimum of 3 weeks in advance. Provide complete information on speaker, date, time, location, meal costs, and reservation procedure.

+ Organize a phone committee to call members 72 hours before the event if reservations are lagging. A reminder phone call is often helpful in gaining last-minute reservations.

On the Meeting Day

+ Get a final count on reservations, and make an educated guess as to how many people might arrive at the door without a reservation.

+ Check the speaker's travel plans and last-minute questions or requirements.

+ Give the catering manager a revised final count for meal service. In many instances, this might have to be done 24 to 72 hours in advance of the meeting day.

+ Check room arrangements 1 to 2 hours in advance of the meeting. Have enough tables been set up? Are tables arranged correctly for the meeting? Does the microphone system work?

+ Prepare a timetable for the evening's events. For example, cocktails may be scheduled from 6:15 to 7 P.M., with registration going on at the same time. Dinner may be from 7 to 8 P.M., followed by 10 minutes of announcements. At 8:10 P.M., the speaker will have 20 minutes to talk, followed by an additional 10 minutes for questions. Your organizational leaders, as well as the serving staff, should be aware of this schedule.

+ Set up a registration table just inside or outside the door. A typed list of reservations should be available, as well as name tags, meal tickets, and a cash box for making change. Personnel at the registration table should be briefed and in place at least 30 minutes before the announced time.

+ Decide on a seating plan for the head table, organize place cards, and tell VIPs as they arrive where they will be sitting.

+ Designate three or four members of the organization as a hospitality committee to meet and greet newcomers and guests.

After the Meeting

+ Settle accounts with the restaurant, or indicate where an itemized bill should be mailed.

+ Check the room to make sure no one forgot briefcases, handbags, eyeglasses, or other belongings.

+ Send thank-you notes to the speaker and any committee members who helped plan or host the meeting.

+ Prepare a summary of the speaker's comments for the organization's newsletter and, if appropriate, send a news release to local media.

FIGURE 17.1 Corporate meetings and conferences are a way of life. The typical setup is an auditorium where attendees sit in theater-style seats and a speaker uses a podium on the stage. Large video monitors project PowerPoint slides.

a problem. The audience then moves into another room, or set of rooms, where round tables seating 8 or 10 people are available. A discussion leader is designated for each table. After the problem has been discussed, the leaders gather the opinions and the audience returns to the first room, where reports from each group are given to the entire assembly.

Facilities — A small meeting may not need much in the way of facilities, whereas a large and formal one may require a considerable amount of equipment and furnishings. Following are things that should be considered—and supplied if needed. You should check everything an hour or two before the meeting:

- » **Meeting identification.** Is it posted on the bulletin board near the building entrance? Are directional signs needed?
- » **Lighting.** Is it adequate? Can it be controlled? Where are the controls? Who will handle them?
- » **Screen or monitors.** Are they large enough for the size of the audience?
- » **Projectors and video equipment.** Are they hooked up and working? Whom do you contact at the facility if you have technical difficulties?
- » **Seating and tables.** Are there enough seats for the audience you are expecting? Are they arranged properly?
- » **Speaker's podium.** Is it positioned properly? What about a reading light? Is there a PA system? Is it working?
- » **Wi-Fi.** Can the room's wireless network support all the users who may be tweeting, checking their messages, or downloading material from various websites?
- » **Water and glasses.** For speakers? For audience?
- » **Audience and speaker aids.** Are there programs or agendas? Will there be notepaper, pencils, and handout materials?
- » **Name tags.** For speakers? For all attendees?

Invitations — For clubs, an announcement in the newsletter, a flyer, or an email should be adequate. For external groups—people who are not required to attend but

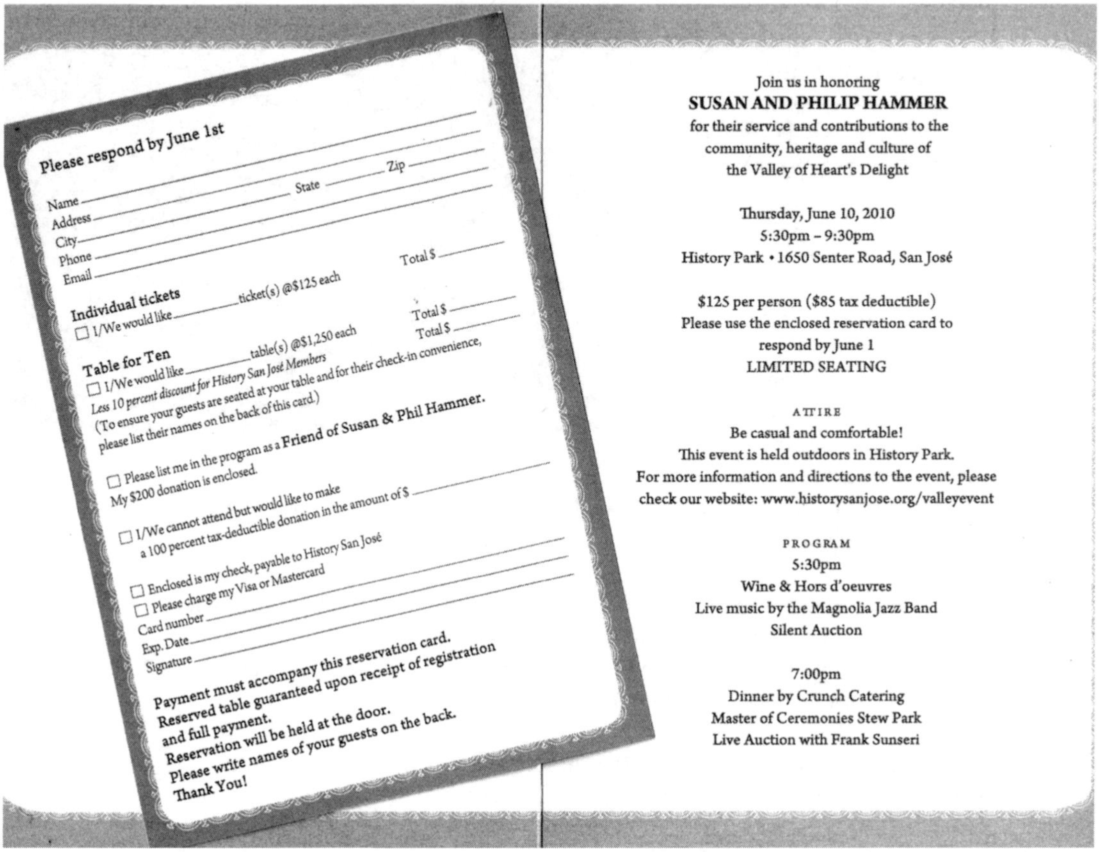

Please respond by June 1st

Name
Address
City State Zip
Phone
Email

Individual tickets
☐ I/We would like ____ ticket(s) @$125 each Total $

Table for Ten
☐ I/We would like ____ table(s) @$1,250 each Total $
Less 10 percent discount for History San José Members Total $
(To ensure your guests are seated at your table and for their check-in convenience, please list their names on the back of this card.)

☐ Please list me in the program as a **Friend of Susan & Phil Hammer.**
My $200 donation is enclosed.

☐ I/We cannot attend but would like to make a 100 percent tax-deductible donation in the amount of $

☐ Enclosed is my check, payable to History San José
☐ Please charge my Visa or Mastercard
Card number
Exp. Date
Signature

Payment must accompany this reservation card.
Reserved table guaranteed upon receipt of registration and full payment.
Reservation will be held at the door.
Please write names of your guests on the back.
Thank You!

Join us in honoring
SUSAN AND PHILIP HAMMER
for their service and contributions to the community, heritage and culture of the Valley of Heart's Delight

Thursday, June 10, 2010
5:30pm – 9:30pm
History Park • 1650 Senter Road, San José

$125 per person ($85 tax deductible)
Please use the enclosed reservation card to respond by June 1
LIMITED SEATING

ATTIRE
Be casual and comfortable!
This event is held outdoors in History Park.
For more information and directions to the event, please check our website: www.historysanjose.org/valleyevent

PROGRAM
5:30pm
Wine & Hors d'oeuvres
Live music by the Magnolia Jazz Band
Silent Auction

7:00pm
Dinner by Crunch Catering
Master of Ceremonies Stew Park
Live Auction with Frank Sunseri

FIGURE 17.2 Invitations to fundraising events are usually sent by mail and have reply cards that collect such vital information as names, mailing addresses, email addresses, and credit card information. This invitation and the reply card from History San Jose (CA) are well organized and provide all the information necessary to register for the event.

whose presence is desired—invitations via the mail, email, or an online invitation service are necessary. They should go out early enough for people to fit the meeting into their schedules—3 to 6 weeks is a common lead time. See Figure 17.2 for an example of an invitation reply card to an event.

The invitation should tell the time, day, date, place (including the name of the room), purpose, highlights of the program (including names of speakers), and a way for the person to RSVP. This may be a telephone number, an email address, a reply card mailed back to the event's organizers, or even an online registration service that handles everything from making the reservation to processing the credit card information to pay for the event. Using an online reservation service for conferences and conventions is discussed later in the section. A map showing the location and parking facilities is advisable if the facility is not widely known.

Registration

If everyone knows everyone else, registration can be somewhat informal. If the group is large it is customary to have a registration desk or table at the entrance. Here the names of arrivals are checked against lists of those who have registered for the event and, in many cases, paid for it. In the case of a civic club that holds regular monthly meetings, the arrivals often sign in on a plain sheet of paper and no one checks the membership roster.

Greeting — A representative of the sponsoring organization should be at the entrance of the room. If the number attending is not too large, a personal welcome is in order. When hundreds of people are expected, this isn't possible, but the chairperson should greet the audience in his or her opening remarks.

Name Tags — Name tags are a good idea at almost any meeting. You should use label-making software to prepare name tags for everyone with advance reservations. Names should be printed in bold, large block letters so that they can be read easily from a distance of 4 feet. If the person's affiliation is used, this can be in smaller bold letters.

For people showing up without advance registration, you can have felt-tip pens available for on-the-spot name tags. However, a nice touch is to have someone at the registration desk make these tags so that they look neat and consistent. Most tags are self-adhesive. Plastic badges with clamps or a chain are popular for large meetings such as conventions.

Program

At any meeting, the word "program" has two meanings. It is what goes on at the meeting, and it is the printed listing of what goes on.

The meeting must have a purpose. To serve that purpose, it is necessary to have a chairperson who controls and directs the meeting, introduces the speakers, and keeps discussions from wandering. It is necessary to have speakers who will inform, persuade, or activate the listeners.

The printed program that is handed out to the audience in a workshop or seminar tells them what is going to happen, when, and where. It lists all the speakers, the time they will speak, coffee breaks, lunch breaks, and any other facts attendees should know about the meeting. Because speakers may have last-minute changes in their plans, the programs should not be printed until the last possible moment.

Speakers — Speakers should be selected early—several months in advance, if possible. They should be chosen because of their expertise, their crowd-drawing capacity, and their speaking ability. It is a good idea to listen to any prospective speaker before tendering an invitation, or at least to discuss your intention with someone who has heard the person speak before. Many prominent people are not effective speakers.

When a speaker has agreed to give a talk, it is essential to make sure that he or she has all the information needed to prepare remarks and get to the meeting. This was also discussed in Chapter 15. Barbara Nichols, owner of a hospitality management firm in New York City, gave this comprehensive checklist to *Meeting News* regarding what speakers should be told about your meeting:

» The meeting's sponsor and who is expected to attend

» Meeting purpose and objectives

» Presentation location, including meeting room, date, and hour

» Topic and length of presentation

» Anticipated size of the audience

» Session format, including length of time allowed for audience questions

» Names of those sharing the platform, if any, and their topics

» Name of person who will make the introductions

» Speaker fee or honorarium

» Travel and housing arrangements

» Meeting room setup and staging information

» Audiovisual equipment needed

» Dress code (business attire, resort wear, black tie)

» Request to speaker for presentation outline, handout material

» Signed release to record or videotape the remarks

» Arrangements for spouse, if invited

Meals — Club meetings and workshops often occur at a mealtime. In fact, many meetings include breakfast, lunch, or dinner.

Early morning breakfast meetings have the advantage of attracting people who cannot take the time during the day to attend such functions. A full breakfast, served buffet style, is a popular choice, because it allows people to select what they normally eat for breakfast. People attending a half-day or full-day workshop often partake of a self-served continental breakfast—rolls, juice, and coffee—during the registration period just prior to the start of the meeting.

Luncheons are either sit-down affairs with a fixed menu or buffets. A 30- to 45-minute cocktail period may precede a luncheon, usually during registration, as guests arrive. A good schedule for a typical luncheon is registration, 11:30; luncheon, noon; adjournment, 1:30. In rare instances, the adjournment can be as late as 2 P.M., but it should never be later than that.

Dinner meetings are handled in much the same way as luncheons. A typical schedule is registration and cocktails, 6 P.M.; dinner, 7 P.M.; speaker, 8 P.M.; adjournment, between 8:30 and 9 P.M. Speakers, as mentioned in Chapter 15, should talk about 20 minutes.

You will need to have an accurate count of people who will attend a meal function. The hotel or restaurant facility needs a count at least 24 hours in advance to prepare the food and set up table service. The standard practice is for the organization to guarantee a certain number of meals, plus or minus 10 percent. If fewer attendees than guaranteed show up, you still pay for all the meals.

Banquets

Banquets, by definition, are fairly large and formal functions. They are held to honor an individual, raise money for a charitable organization, or celebrate an event, such as an organization's anniversary.

A banquet or even a reception may have 100 or 1,000 people in attendance, and staging a successful one takes a great deal of planning. The budget, in particular, needs close attention. A banquet coordinator has to consider such costs as (1) food, (2) room rental, (3) bartenders, (4) decorations and table centerpieces, (5) audiovisual requirements, (6) speaker fees, (7) entertainment, (8) photographers, (9) invitations, (10) tickets, and (11) marketing and promotion.

All of these components, of course, must be factored into establishing the per ticket cost of the event. You are not just paying $50 to $150 for the traditional rubber chicken dinner, but for the total cost of staging the event. If the purpose is to raise money for a worthy charitable organization or a political candidate, tickets might go for $150 to $250. The actual price, of course, depends on how fancy the banquet is and how much you are paying for a speaker. See the Tips for Success on page 450 for a checklist on how to prepare a budget for a banquet or other special events.

Featuring a well-known personality as a banquet speaker usually helps ticket sales, but it also is a major expense in your budget. Karen Kendig, president of the Speaker's Network, told *Public Relations Tactics* that the going rate is $3,000 to $10,000 for "bread-and-butter" business-type talks, and $15,000 or more for entertainment and political celebrities. Sarah Palin and Al Gore, for example, charge $100,000 for a speech. A number of firms, such as the Washington Speaker's Bureau in Alexandria, Virginia, and the Harry Walker Agency in New York, represent celebrity speakers.

Such fees cannot be fully absorbed in the cost of an individual ticket so, in addition to sending out individual invitations, there usually is a committee that personally asks corporations and other businesses to sponsor the event or buy a table for employees, clients, or friends. A corporate table of eight, for example, may go for $25,000 or more, depending on the prestige and purpose of the event. The inside details of an upscale charity event in New York are outlined in the PR Casebook on page 451.

Working with Catering Managers

When organizing a banquet, you usually contact the catering or banquet manager of the restaurant or hotel at least 3 or 4 months before your event. He or she will discuss menus, room facilities, availability of space, and a host of other items with you to determine exactly what you need.

Hotels and restaurants have special menus for banquets, which are often subject to some negotiation. If you plan a banquet during the week, for example, the restaurant or hotel might be willing to give you more favorable rates because weeknights aren't ordinarily booked. However, if you insist on having a banquet on Friday or Saturday night—which is the most popular time—you can expect to pay full rates.

A banquet usually has a fixed menu, but you must also make a vegetarian dish available to those who request it. In general, a popular choice for a meat entree is chicken or fish. Pork may be objectionable on religious grounds, but beef has become

Tips for Success   Making a Budget for a Banquet

All events have two sides of the ledger: costs and revenues. It is important to prepare a detailed budget so you know exactly how much an event will cost. This will enable you to also figure out how much you will need to charge so you at least break even. The following are some of the items that you need to consider.

Facilities

+ Rental of meeting or reception rooms
+ Setup of podiums, microphones, audiovisual equipment

Food Service

+ Number of meals to be served
+ Cost per person
+ Gratuities
+ Refreshments for breaks
+ Bartenders for cocktail hours
+ Wine, liquor, soft drinks

Decorations

+ Table decorations
+ Direction signs

Design and Printing

+ Invitations
+ Programs
+ Tickets
+ Name tags
+ Promotional flyers

Postage

+ Postage for invitations
+ Mailing house charges

Recognition Items

+ Awards, plaques, trophies

+ Engraving
+ Framing
+ Calligraphy

Miscellaneous

+ VIP travel and expenses
+ Speaker fees
+ Security

Transportation

+ Buses
+ Vans
+ Parking

Entertainment

+ Fees

Publicity

+ Advertising
+ News releases
+ Banners
+ Postage

Office Expenses

+ Phones
+ Supplies
+ Complimentary tickets
+ Staff travel and expenses
+ Data processing

PR casebook

A Fundraising Gala: The Nitty-Gritty

The New York Women's Foundation hosted its first autumn benefit in midtown Manhattan, according to *New York Times* writer Laura Lipton. The organizers considered time, place, menu, centerpieces, entertainment, guest list, seating arrangement, and so much more. "To produce the few hours of gaiety, five chairwomen and a brigade of behind-the-scenes workers had spent months vetting every detail, from the hors d'oeuvres to the guests of honor. Such considerations are crucial for a gala to succeed amid scores of other parties, all for organizations seeking benefactors for their good works," Lipton wrote.

The chairwomen set a budget of $175,000 and a theme of "Stepping Out and Stepping Up." They hired CMI Event Planning and Fundraising to handle the details of invitations, catering contracts, and helping the chairwomen keep on top of the details. Cathy McNamara of CMI told Lipton, "We're the professional nags."

One of the chairwomen described how she spent Labor Day writing personal notes in 70 to 100 invitations. "'The New York Women's Foundation is extremely important to me. Please help support these extraordinary women,'" she said she wrote. "Then I might put, 'Say hi to your husband' or 'Hope you're well.'"

The foundation guaranteed 300 guests for the caterer, with an upper end of 350. As the event drew nearer, the chairwomen met to test and select appetizers (the mini hamburgers), select floral arrangements (coppery bowls were selected, but woven green reeds in one arrangement were rejected), and choose napkin colors (olive green was given the nod).

Lipton described the evening of the benefit: "At Gotham Hall, a grand, lofty space that was once the headquarters of a bank, guests sipped martinis and applauded the speeches. A mambo performance by a dozen school-age dancers momentarily transfixed the room." While the competition among benefits is strong and the economy in which this event found itself was weak, the organizers counted it as a success when 280 guests contributed $675,000 to the foundation through the event.

---

more popular in recent years. Offering the choice of two entrees requires the extra work of providing coded tickets for the waiters, and the hotel or restaurant may charge more for the meal. Get the catering manager's advice before ordering multiple entrees.

When figuring food costs, many amateur planners often forget about tax and gratuity, which can add 25 percent or more to any final bill. That $25 chicken dinner on the menu is really $32 if tax and gratuity are added. In addition, there are corkage fees if you provide your own liquor or wine. In many establishments, corkage fees are set rather high to discourage you from bringing your own refreshments. At one banquet, for example, the organizers thought it was a great coup to have the wine donated, only to find out that the hotel charged a corkage fee of $20 per bottle.

Logistics and Timing

Organizing a banquet requires considerable logistics, timing, and teamwork. First, you have to establish a timeline for the entire process—from the contacting of catering managers to the sending out of invitations and lining up of a speaker. Second, you need a detailed timeline for the several days or day of the event to ensure that everything is in place. Third, you should have a timeline for the event itself, so that it begins and ends at a reasonable time. A good example of timing for the night of an awards banquet is shown below.

CONSERVATION AWARDS BANQUET
JW MARRIOTT HOTEL
WASHINGTON, DC
WEDNESDAY, MAY 13

Crew Agenda

3:30 – 5:00 p.m.	Program agenda review – participants and staff only. Live run-through of C. Ghylin's remarks. (Grand Ballroom)
5:00 – 6:00	Private pre-reception for honorees, judges, Chevron staff. Honoree photo session including E. Zern and J. Sullivan. (Suite 1231)
6:30 – 7:15	Greetings and reception, open bar. Photo opportunities available. (Grand Ballroom Foyer)
7:15 – 7:30	Close bar, enter Grand Ballroom.
7:30 – 7:35	C. Ghylin: Welcome and opening remarks.
7:30 – 8:20	Dinner served.
8:20 – 8:25	C. Ghylin: Introduces special guests at head table, introduces E. Zern.
8:25 – 8:30	E. Zern: Welcome, honoree toast, introduces judges, completes remarks.
8:30 – 8:35	C. Ghylin: Introduces J. Sullivan.
8:35 – 8:45	J. Sullivan: Remarks.
8:45 – 8:50	C. Ghylin: Introduces slide presentation.
8:50 – 9:25	Slide presentation. (C. Ghylin remains at podium) (a) Introduces/explains honoree category; (b) Comments on professionals. Introduces/explains honoree category. (c) Comments on citizens. Introduces/explains organizations' honoree category.
9:25 – 9:40	C. Ghylin: Comments on organizations. Invites J. Sullivan and E. Zern for plaque presentation. Plaque presentation.
9:40 – 9:45	C. Ghylin: Final remarks.
9:45 p.m.	America the Beautiful.

FIGURE 17.3 This is the timeline for an awards banquet. Compiling a timeline and going over it with the master of ceremonies help keep the event on schedule.

In addition, you need to work out the logistics to ensure that registration lines are kept to a minimum and that everyone is assigned to a table. Table numbers must be highly visible. If the group is particularly large (1,000 or more), you should provide a large seating chart so people can locate where they are sitting. Another more personalized approach is to have staff inside the hall directing people to their seats.

Receptions and Cocktail Parties

Banquets are often preceded by a "cocktail hour" before people sit down for dinner. A reception, however, is a stand-alone event primarily organized for people to talk and "network" over drinks and appetizers. It's a cost-effective way to celebrate an organization's or individual's achievement, to introduce a new chief executive to the employees and the community, or simply to allow college alumni to get together.

In any event, the focus is on interaction, not speeches. If there is a ceremony or speech, it should last a maximum of 5 to 10 minutes. A reception can last up to 2 hours, and the typical format is a large room where most people will stand instead of sit. This facilitates social interaction and allows people to move freely around the room. Such gatherings, like any other event, require advance planning and logistics.

It is important, for example, that food be served in the form of appetizers, sandwiches, cheese trays, nuts, and chips.

> **" Don't make a lengthy presentation part of an event. You'll lose the attendees' attention. "** Erica Iacono, reporter for *PRWeek*

People get hungry, and food helps offset some of the effects of drinking. The bar is the centerpiece of any reception, but you should make sure there are plenty of non-alcoholic beverages available, too. Urns of coffee, punch, and tea should be readily available in other locations around the room.

There are two kinds of cocktail parties. One is the *no-host bar*, which means that guests buy their own drinks and the host provides the room, any decorations, and the appetizers. A variation on the no-host bar is to provide attendees one or two drink coupons, but they buy any additional refreshments. Most receptions, however, have a *hosted bar*, meaning that drinks are free. This is the norm when an organization is having a cocktail party or reception for journalists, customers, or community leaders.

A reception, like a meal function, requires you to talk with the catering manager to order finger food and vegetable or cheese trays. If you have a reception over the traditional dinner hour, you should also order heavier hors d'oeuvres such as shrimp, sausages, or even petite lamb chops because many attendees will also make it their dinner. As a rule of thumb, there should be one bartender per 75 people. For large events, bars are situated in several locations around the room to disperse the crowd and shorten lines.

It is also important to find out how the facility will bill you for beverages consumed. If the arrangement is by the bottle, this often leads to the problem of bartenders being very generous in pouring drinks, because more empty bottles means higher profits for the caterer.

Starting a cocktail party is easy—just open the bar at the announced time. Closing a party is not so easy. The only practical way is to close the bar. The invitation may indicate a definite time for the reception to end, but don't rely on this.

A vocal announcement will do the job. The smoothest way is to say, "The bar will close in 10 minutes." This gives guests a chance to get one more drink.

Conventions

A convention is a series of meetings, usually spread over two or more days. The purpose is to gather and exchange information, meet other people with similar interests, discuss and act on common problems, and enjoy recreation and social interchange.

Most conventions are held by national membership groups and trade associations. Because the membership is widespread, a convention is nearly always "out of town" for many attendees, so convention arrangements must give consideration to this.

Planning

It is necessary to begin planning far in advance of the actual event. Planning for even the smallest convention should start months before the scheduled date; for large national conventions, it may begin several years ahead and require hundreds or thousands of hours of work. The main components in planning a convention are (1) timing, (2) location, (3) facilities, (4) exhibits, (5) program, (6) recreation, (7) attendance, and (8) administration. There's an entire industry of specialists in event planning, which may appeal to you as a career.

Timing — Timing must be convenient for the people who are expected to attend. Avoid peak work periods. Summer vacation is appropriate for educators, and after harvest is suitable for farmers. Preholiday periods are bad for retailers, and midwinter is probably a poor time in the northern United States but may be very good in the South. Here, as in every area dealing with the public, it is imperative to know your audience and to plan for their convenience.

Location — As real estate agents say, "it"s location, location, location." A national convention can be anywhere in the country, but one in Fairbanks, Alaska, would probably not be well attended. A convention in Las Vegas or New Orleans could be a great success because the glamour of the location might outweigh the cost and time of travel. Many organizations rotate their conventions from one part of the state, region, or country to another to equalize travel burdens.

Another factor in choosing a location is availability of accommodations. A suitable number of rooms must be available to house the attendees. In addition, enough meeting rooms of the right size must also be available. Timing enters into this, because many such accommodations are booked months, or even years, in advance. Large cities usually have large convention facilities and numerous hotels, but early reservations are necessary for such popular cities as San Francisco, New York, New Orleans, Las Vegas, and San Diego. Once a tentative location has been selected, you must find out if the convention can be handled at the time chosen. Early action on this can forestall later changes. Be sure to get a definite price on guest rooms as well as meeting rooms.

Small conventions are often held in resorts, but accessibility is a factor. If the visitors have to change airlines several times or if the location is hard to get to by automobile, the glamour may fail to compensate for the inconvenience.

Facilities — For every meeting or session of the convention, it is necessary to have a room of the right size and the equipment needed for whatever is to occur in that room. The convention might start with a general meeting in a large ballroom, where seating is theater fashion and the equipment consists of a public address system and a speaker's platform with large video monitors.

After opening remarks, the convention might break into smaller groups that meet in different rooms with widely varying facilities. Your responsibility is to ensure that the presenter in these sessions has the equipment needed. One speaker may require a computer projector and wireless access to the Internet. Another may just need a pad of paper on an easel, while someone else needs a DVD player. In one room the speaker may request round table seating, while another presenter wants theater seating. To get everything right, you must know exactly what is to happen, who is going to participate, and when.

Exhibits — The makers and sellers of supplies that are used by people attending conventions frequently want to show their wares. This means that the convention manager must provide space suitable for that purpose. Most large convention centers have facilities that can accommodate anything from books to bulldozers. There is a charge for the use of these rooms, and the exhibitors pay for the space they use.

The exhibit hall may be in the hotel where the convention is being held or in a separate building. For example, McCormick Place is an enormous building on the Chicago lakefront. It is an easy taxi trip from the Loop, where conventions are usually based and where the visitors sleep. Eating facilities, ranging from hot dog stands to elaborate dining rooms, are to be found in almost any such building. Exhibits are covered in more detail when trade shows are discussed.

Program

A convention program usually has a basic theme. Aside from transacting the necessary organizational business, most of the speeches and other sessions will be devoted to various aspects of the theme. Themes can range from the specific, such as "New Developments in AIDS Research," to the more general, as in "Quality Management and Productivity." Some groups use an even broader theme, such as "Connections" or "At the Crossroads."

With a theme chosen, the developer of the program looks for prominent speakers who have something significant to say on a particular topic. In addition, there may be a need for discussions, workshops, and other sessions focusing on particular aspects of the general theme.

The printed program for the convention is a schedule. It tells the exact room, time, topic, and speakers for every session. Large conventions often schedule different sessions at the same time. Attendees then choose which session they prefer. Large, bulky programs may look impressive, but they are cumbersome to carry and expensive to produce. A better approach is to design a program schedule small enough to fit in a pocket or handbag.

In recent years, the traditional printed program has gone digital. Organizers are now using apps to list all the program details so attendees can conveniently access their smartphones or tablets for all the information they need. Flash drives and microsites are also used to distribute information about sessions, special events, speaker bios, PowerPoint presentations, and even lists of restaurants near the convention center.

It is important to realize, however, that not all convention attendees have gone digital and not everyone has a smartphone or a tablet. Consequently, it's still prudent to make summarized versions of program details in hard copy for those who want them.

> " *While participants are sitting in a classroom, they can scroll through updates and Twitter feeds to find out what else is going on in other sessions....* " Greg Lorentz, CEO of Meeting Professionals International, talking about the use of apps and other mobile devices at conventions and trade shows in a *New York Times* article.

Recreation — Recreation is a feature of practically all conventions. This may range from informal get-togethers to formal dances, cocktail parties, golf tournaments, sightseeing tours, and shopping. Sometimes recreational events are planned to coincide with regular program sessions. These are patronized by spouses and by delegates who would rather relax than listen to a speaker. Evening receptions and dinners at interesting venues such as an art gallery or museum are often planned for both attendees and their significant others.

Attendance — Getting people to attend a convention requires two things: (1) an appealing program and (2) a concerted effort to persuade members to attend. Announcements and invitations should go out several months in advance to allow attendees to make travel plans. A second and even a third mailing or email blast is often done in the weeks preceding the convention. Reply forms should be provided, accompanied by online hotel reservation forms. Many corporations and organizations now use specialty firms such as cvent (www.cvent.com) that prepare digital invitations and provide event management tools. The Tips for Success on page 457 discusses the use of online reservation services.

Administration — Managing a convention is a strenuous job. The organization staff is likely to see very little of the program and many delegates with problems. Among the things that must be done are arranging for buses to convey delegates from the airport to the convention (if it is in a remote location) and to take them on tours. Meeting speakers and getting them to the right place at the right time is another task.

People arriving at the convention in a large city must be met, registered, and provided with all the essentials (name tags, programs, and any other needed materials). Special arrangements should be made for the media. A small convention may interest only a few people from trade publications, but larger conventions may draw attention from the major media. In this case, a newsroom should be set up with telephones, computers, Internet access, tables, and other needed equipment. A refreshment area is also a good idea.

Tips for Success   Online Invites Make It Easy to RSVP

The digital age has made event planning more precise. A number of companies now offer event planners the ability to send invitations via the Internet and to track response rates.

Email invitations are used for any number of organizational meetings and corporate events, including a college student having a party to celebrate his or her 21st birthday. Evite, for example, has almost become a household name and sends more than 700,000 invites daily. Another firm, Paperless Post, offers a more "formal" invitation that resembles those found in a stationery shop.

Email invitations, according to cvent (www .cvent.com), a firm offering such services, should have eye-catching graphics, an effective subject line, and relevant content, such as the five Ws and one H.

> *"Even if you add every conceivable extra to your stack of online invitations, the cost of each remains tiny, measured in nickels, while the unit price of printed counterparts is often measured in dollars."*
>
> Randall Stross, writing in the *New York Times*

Most individuals just concern themselves with generating a list of yes, no, and maybe responses, but professional and trade groups bundle the email invitation with software that enables attendees to pay registration fees online. According to cvent, event planners can achieve up to three times the standard response rate by integrating email, direct mail, and phone campaigns.

Meeting planners like the capabilities of software programs and online systems that allow them to manage an entire event online. StarCite and cvent, for example, offer a variety of meeting management services—from gathering hotel bids to sending electronic invitations and tracking registrations online. Software can even compile data on why individuals aren't coming to the event, which may help in planning future meetings. Once someone does register, the site also allows him or her to book hotel, airline, and car reservations at the same time.

Electronic tracking is also helpful for figuring out exactly how many hotel rooms are needed; bad estimates, cancellations, and no-shows can add up to substantial hotel cancellation fees. Other management tools allow groups to track the flow of registrations. If registrations are lagging, it's a signal to do another round of emails and direct mail to bolster attendance. You can even track attendance at various sessions. If breakfast sessions, for example, aren't well attended, it might be wise to plan fewer early morning meetings next year.

Although email invitations are economical and efficient, they are most appropriate for business-related meetings and events. It's still considered tacky to send an email invitation to your wedding or to a major fund-raising dinner for a community cause. In these instances, mailed invitations and replies are the norm. If you use a mailed invitation, you can still provide an email address or phone number for people to respond if they don't want to fill out the reply card.

Trade Shows

Trade shows are the ultimate marketing event. According to *Tradeshow Week* magazine, about 6,000 trade shows are held annually in the United States. They range in size from more than 100,000 attendees to those in very specialized industries that attract fewer than 1,000 attendees. It is estimated that about 65 million people attend trade shows on an annual basis.

The Consumer Electronics Show (CES), sponsored by the Consumer Electronics Association, illustrates the power and influence of a trade show. The show, open only to industry professionals, attracts 130,000 to the Las Vegas Convention Center every January. Almost 3,000 companies show their new consumer products, taking up about 2 million square feet of exhibit space. For exhibitors, the CES event is the coming-out party for many new products such as advanced 3D TVs, tablets, smartphones, and hundreds of other high-tech gizmos (see Figure 17.4).

❝For people to pay attention at a trade show, you need real news.❞ David Rich, senior vice president of the George P. Johnson marketing company, as reported in *PRWeek*

FIGURE 17.4 Trade shows attract millions of people annually. They provide an opportunity to see new products from a number of companies, generate sales leads, and attract media coverage. The Consumer Electronics Show (CES) in Las Vegas attracts 130,000 industry professionals every January; in 2011, almost 3,000 companies filled about 2 million square feet of exhibit space.

Exhibit Booths

Although food and entertainment costs are high, the major expense at a trade show is the exhibit booth. At national trade shows, it is not unusual for a basic booth to start at $50,000, including design, construction, transportation, and space rental fees. Larger, more elaborate booths can easily cost between $500,000 and $1 million.

Any booth or exhibit should be designed for maximum visibility. Experts say you have about 10 seconds to attract a visitor as he or she walks down an aisle of booths. Consequently, companies try to outdazzle each other in booth designs.

Another tactic that attracts attention, of course, is to have a celebrity. Intel, for example, hired soccer star Mia Hamm to demonstrate features of its new processors by working out on an Intel-equipped fitness machine. Polaroid did one better by appointing Lady Gaga a creative director and having her demonstrate some of the company's new imaging products at its booth on the first day of CES (see Figure 17.5). Her appearance, of course, stole the show and generated reams of media coverage for Polaroid.

Not every company has the resources to hire Lady Gaga, but here are some points to keep in mind if you get involved in planning an exhibit booth:

» Select the appropriate trade shows that have the best potential for developing contacts and generating future sales.

» Start planning and developing your exhibit 6 to 12 months in advance. Exhibit designers and builders need time to develop a booth.

» Make the display or booth visually attractive. Use bright colors, large signs, and working models of products.

FIGURE 17.5 Companies compete to attract visitors to their trade show booths, and Polaroid pulled out all the stops by having Lady Gaga appear to demonstrate products at the CES meeting in Las Vegas. The company stole the show on opening day and generated considerable media coverage.

» Think about putting action in your display. Have a video or slide presentation running all the time.

» Use involvement techniques. Have a contest or raffle in which visitors can win a prize. An exhibitor at one show even offered free foot massages.

» Give people an opportunity to operate equipment or do something.

» Have knowledgeable, personable representatives on duty to answer questions and collect visitor business cards for follow-up.

» Offer useful souvenirs. A key chain, a shopping bag, a luggage tag, or even a copy of a popular newspaper or magazine will attract traffic.

» Promote your exhibit in advance. Send announcements to potential customers and media kits to selected journalists 4 to 6 weeks before the trade show.

Most organizations feel that the large investment in a booth at a trade show is worthwhile for two reasons. First, a trade show facilitates one-on-one communication with potential customers and helps generate sales leads. It also attracts many journalists, so it is easier and more efficient to provide press materials, arrange one-on-one interviews, and demonstrate what makes the product worth a story. Second, a booth allows an exhibitor to demonstrate how its products differ from the competition's. This is more effective than just sending prospects a color brochure. It also is more cost-effective than making individual sales calls.

Hospitality Suites — Hospitality suites are an adjunct to the exhibit booth. Organizations use them to entertain key prospects, give more in-depth presentations, and talk about business deals.

The idea is that serious customers will stay in a hospitality suite long enough to hear an entire presentation, whereas they are likely to stop at an exhibit hall booth for only a few minutes. Although goodwill can be gained from free concerts and cocktail parties, the primary purpose of a hospitality suite is to generate leads that ultimately result in product sales.

Pressrooms and Media Relations

Trade shows such as CES and MacWorld attract many journalists. About a thousand reporters, for example, descend on MacWorld every year. Consequently, every trade show has a pressroom where the various exhibitors distribute media kits (now mostly on CD or flash drives) and other information to journalists. Pressrooms typically have phone, fax, and Internet facilities for reporters to file stories back to their employers.

An important part of your job is to personally contact reporters several weeks before a trade show to offer product briefings and one-on-one interviews with key executives. The competition is intense, so you have to be creative in pitching your ideas and showing why your company's products or services merit the journalist's time when multiple other companies are also pitching them. If you can arrange as many preshow interviews and briefings as possible, you are more likely to be effective and successful.

A survey by Access Communications, for example, found that more than 90 percent of journalists assigned to a trade show want to hear about the company and product news before the show even starts. Michael Young, senior vice president of Access, told *PRWeek*, "Journalists have limited bandwidth at the show. They can only do so much, so they want to know what the news is before getting there." In other words, your media relations work starts before the show; it continues throughout the show, and then you have to do follow-up with reporters to provide additional information.

Sarah Skerik, director of trade show markets for *PR Newswire*, provides some additional tips for working with the media during a trade show:

» Plan major product announcements to coincide with the show.

» Include the name of the trade show in your news releases, so journalists searching databases can log on using the show as a keyword.

» Include your booth number in all releases and announcements.

» Make it easy for journalists to track down key spokespeople and experts connected with your product by including cell phone numbers, Twitter hashtags, and email addresses in your materials.

» Have your spokespeople trained to make brief presentations and equip them with answers to the most-likely-asked questions.

» Consider a looped video to run in the booth, with copies available to the media.

» Provide photos that show the product in use, in production, or in development.

» Provide online corporate logos, product photos, executive profiles, media kits, and PowerPoint presentations to those journalists who cannot attend or who prefer to lighten their suitcase by having everything in digital format.

Promotional Events

Promotional events are planned primarily to promote product sales, increase organizational visibility, make friends, and raise money for a charitable cause. They also include the category of corporate event sponsorship, which is discussed in the Tips for Success on page 462.

The one essential skill for organizing promotional events is creativity. Multiple "ho-hum" events compete for media attention, and even attendance, in every city, so it behooves you to come up with something "different" that creates buzz and interest.

Grand openings of stores or hotels, for example, can be pretty dull and generate a collective yawn from almost every journalist in town, let alone all the chamber of commerce types that attend such functions. So how do you come up with something new and different for the same old thing? First, you throw out the old idea of having a ribbon cutting. Second, you start thinking about a theme or idea that fits the situation and is out of the ordinary.

The reopening of the Morgan Hotel in San Antonio is a good example. The hotel featured a new restaurant named

"Events bring you face-to-face with your customer and can often serve as qualifying tools in reaching decision makers. Most often, the individuals that attend events are there by choice." Jennifer Collins, Event Planning Group, as quoted in *PRWeek*

Oro (meaning "gold" in Spanish), so the theme for the opening night reception was gold—complete with gold flowers, gold curtains, and even bikini-clad women who were coated with gold paint and served as living mannequins.

Using Celebrities to Boost Attendance

You can also increase attendance at a promotional event by using a television or film personality. The creative part is figuring out which personality fits the particular product or situation. A national conference on aging for policymakers, government officials, and health care experts attracted attendees because former senator and astronaut John Glenn was a major speaker. Unilever wanted to reach a Hispanic audience through a series of events promoting its Suave and Caress brands, so it tapped famous stylists Leonardo Rocco and Fernando Navarro, who gave hair and beauty

+

Tips for Success   Corporate Sponsorships Require Strategic Thinking

Many corporations, in order to cut through the media clutter and establish brand identity, sponsor any number of events that, in turn, are covered by the media. In North America alone, about $10 billion is spent by corporations on sponsorship of various events. According to the *Economist*, about two-thirds of this total is sponsorship fees for sporting events.

The Olympics is the World Series of corporate sponsorships. Companies such as Coca-Cola, General Electric, Visa, and Samsung are among the top 12 official sponsors of the Olympics. In fact, Coca-Cola has been an official sponsor since 1928 and marked its 80th anniversary at the Beijing Olympics in 2008. If your employer or client is thinking about sponsoring an event, here are some questions you should consider:

+   Can the company afford to fulfill the obligation? The sponsorship fee is just the starting point. Count on doubling it to have an adequate marketing and public relations campaign to publicize the event and your particular event.

+   Is the event or organization compatible with the company's values and mission statement?

+   Does the event reach the organization's target audiences?

+   Are the event organizers experienced and professional?

+   Will the field representatives be able to use the event as a platform for increasing sales?

+   Does the event give the organization a chance to develop new contracts and business opportunities?

+   Can you make a multiple-year sponsorship contract that will reinforce brand identity on a regular, consistent basis?

+   Is there an opportunity to get employee involvement and raise morale?

+   Is the event compatible with the personality of the organization or its products?

+   Can you do trade-offs of products and in-kind services to help defray the costs?

FIGURE 17.6 The Avon Walk for Breast Cancer is a promotional event that takes place in multiple cities and has more than 20,000 participants. Its global ambassador, Reese Witherspoon, often walks in many of these events and helps attract media coverage. Planning such walks and getting city permits require considerable advance planning.

advice to women attending the events. The Avon Walk for Breast Cancer, shown in Figure 17.6, uses actress Reese Witherspoon as its global ambassador, who participates in many of the walks in major cities.

A celebrity, or "personality" as such a person is called in the trade, is not exactly the most creative solution to every situation, but it's a time-honored way to increase the odds that the media will cover your event, because "prominence" is considered a basic news value.

A personality, however, can be a major budget item. Stars such as Oprah Winfrey, Jennifer Lopez, and Jon Stewart typically charge $100,000 for an appearance. If you don't have that kind of budget, you'll have to make do with what the business calls the "up and coming" or the "down and going." Claire Atkinson, writing in *PRWeek*, explains:

> For $5,000 to $10,000, you'll get young TV stars. For $10,000, you can get Ivana Trump to open your restaurant. The cost of a personal appearance by Shirley MacLaine is $50,000. Members of the cast of *Friends* charge $25,000. Supermodels Claudia Schiffer and Naomi Campbell command between $10,000 and $15,000 per appearance. And soap opera stars tend to get between $5,000 and $10,000, as do lesser TV stars. . . .

On occasion, if the event is for a charity that the celebrity supports as a personal cause, he or she will reduce or waive an appearance fee. You should note, however, that the organization is often expected to pay for the celebrity's transportation (first-class, of course), hotel suite, and room service. In addition, an organization also pays the cost of assistants, hairstylists, valets, and other accompanying personnel. Such arrangements can greatly increase your costs, even if the celebrity is "free."

One source for finding celebrities for promotional events is the Celebrity Source (www.celebritysource.com). It matches requests with the 4,500 names in its database and handles all the details of negotiating fees, expenses, and transportation logistics for your organization. The value of a firm such as Celebrity Source or Celebrity Access (www.celebrityaccess.com) is that it has regular contact with a celebrity's business agent and publicist. An organization trying to figure out whom to contact for a particular celebrity, let alone how, may have less success.

On its website, Celebrity Source gives some tips on what the firm needs to know in order to select the right celebrity for your event. The following is a good checklist for you if you are thinking about using a celebrity:

» What exactly do you want the celebrity to do?
» Whom do you want to appeal to by having a celebrity? Is it the public, the media, or the sponsors?
» What do you want to accomplish by having a celebrity participate? Sell tickets or add glamour?
» What are the demographics of your audience or attendees?
» What is your budget?
» What is the maximum that you're willing to spend for the right celebrity?
» Are you prepared to pay for first-class expenses for the celebrity and at least one staff person?
» Do you have access to any perks or gifts that will help motivate the celebrity to say "yes"?

Planning and Logistics

You should be concerned about traffic flow, adequate restroom facilities, signage, and security. Professionally trained security personnel should also be arranged to handle crowd control, protect celebrities or government officials from being hassled, and make sure no other disruptions occur that would mar the event. Apple, for example, experienced security and crowd control problems in Beijing when it offered the iPad2 at its local store. People lined up for hours to purchase the new product, but scalpers tried to break the line and Apple decided to close the store. The people in line were outraged, and a melee started that caused injuries to a number of people.

Liability insurance is a necessity, too. Any public event sponsored by an organization should be insured, just in case there is an accident and a subsequent lawsuit charging negligence. If your organization doesn't already have a blanket liability policy, you should get one for the event.

Charitable organizations also need liability insurance if they are running an event to raise money. This is particularly relevant if your organization is sponsoring an event that requires physical exertion, such as a 10K run, a bicycle race, or even a hot-air balloon race.

Participants should sign a release form that protects the organization if someone suffers a heart attack or another kind of accident. One organization, which was sponsoring a 5K "fun run," had all participants sign a statement that read, in part: "I know that a road race is a potentially hazardous activity. . . . I assume all risk associated with running in this event, including, but not limited to, falls, contact with other participants, the effects of the weather, including high heat/or humidity, traffic and the conditions of the road."

> 66 *Security at public events is a significant aspect that should get as much attention as lighting, sound, or signage.* 99 Matt Glass, managing partner at Eventage, as reported in *PRWeek*

Promotional events that use public streets and parks also need permits from various city departments. If you are sponsoring a run, you need to get a permit from the police or public safety department to block off streets, and you need to hire off-duty police to handle traffic control. Permits for the Avon Walk for Breast Cancer, for example, are arranged months in advance, because there are many requests for "runs" and cities have imposed a limit on how many will be permitted each year.

A food event, such as a chili cook-off or a German fest, requires permits from the public health department and, if liquor is served, a permit from the state alcohol board. If the event is held inside a building, a permit is often required from the fire inspector.

You must also deal with the logistics of arranging cleanup, providing basic services such as water and medical aid, registering craft and food vendors, and posting signs. Promotion of an event can often be accomplished by having a radio station or local newspaper cosponsor the event.

Open Houses and Plant Tours

Open houses and plant tours are another kind of special event. They are conducted primarily to develop favorable public opinion about an organization. Generally, they show the facilities where the organization does its work and, in the case of plant tours, how the work is done. A factory might have a plant tour to show how it turns raw materials into finished products. A hospital open house could show its emergency facilities, diagnostic equipment, operating rooms, and patient rooms.

Open houses are customarily one-day affairs. Attendance is usually by invitation, but in other instances, the event is announced in the media, and anyone who chooses to attend may do so. See Figure 17.7 on page 466 for a flyer announcing a community open house for a city/university library. If you're having a community open house, you also have to think about entertainment and activities for the attendees.

Many plants offer tours daily or regularly while the plant is in operation. These tours are most common among producers of consumer goods such as beer, wine, food products, clothing, and small appliances. These daily tours are geared to handle only a few people at any one time, whereas open houses generally have a large number of guests and normal operations are not feasible during the tour.

Dr. Martin Luther King, Jr. Library –
Check It Out!

FREE

FREE

FREE

Grand Opening Celebration
Saturday, August 16
10 a.m. – 4 p.m.
4th & San Fernando, downtown San José

- *Entertainment on 2 stages for the whole family*
- *Games, crafts, children's activities, story times*
- *Book bingo*
- *Mystery tea*
- *Formal dedication ceremony at 10 a.m.*
- *Commemorative gifts*
- *Contests with prizes*
- *Tours and demonstrations*
- *A day of fun and surprises*

You've never seen a library like this one!

(408) 277-4000
www.newkinglibrary.org

*Lots of free parking in downtown City garages
Metered on-street parking is free on Saturday*

To arrange for an accommodation under the Americans with Disabilities Act, please call (408) 277-4000 or (408) 998-5299 (TTY) at least 48 hours prior to the event.

The Bay Area's **NBC11**

FIRST5 SANTA CLARA COUNTY

T48 TELEMUNDO

The Mercury News The Newspaper of Silicon Valley MercuryNews.com

Dr. Martin Luther King, Jr. Library

A collaboration between the City of San José and San José State University

Printing Donated to the King Library

FIGURE 17.7 This flyer, in multiple colors, was distributed to various community groups to promote the grand opening of a new city/university library on the grounds of San Jose State University. It gives the basic five Ws and also entices the public with a list of activities for the day. The reverse side of the flyer gave the basic information in Spanish and Vietnamese to reflect the multicultural nature of the city. The outstanding programs and materials received an American Library Association (ALA) award.

Because the purpose of an open house or a plant tour is to create favorable opinion about the organization, it must be carefully planned, thoroughly explained, and smoothly conducted. The visitors must understand what they are seeing. This requires careful routing, control to prevent congestion, signs, and guides. All employees who will be present should understand the purpose of the event and be coached in their duties.

A detailed checklist for planning an open house is provided in the Tips for Success on page 468, but the following are the major factors to consider in planning an open house:

» **Day and hour.** The time must be convenient for both the organization and the guests.

» **Guests.** These may be families of employees, customers, representatives of the community, suppliers and competitors, reporters, or others whose goodwill is desirable.

» **Publicity and invitations.** These materials should be distributed at least a month before the event.

If a plant tour is a continuing daily event, the availability of the tour should be announced by signs near the plant and possibly by advertising or publicity. For any open house or plant tour, consider the following points:

» **Vehicles.** Parking must be available, and there should be a map on the invitation showing how to get there and where to park.

» **Reception.** A representative of the organization should meet and greet all arriving guests. If guests are important people, they should meet the top officials of the organization.

» **Restrooms.** If you are expecting a large crowd, arrange for portable toilets to supplement the regular facilities.

» **Safety.** Hazards should be conspicuously marked and well lighted. Dangerous equipment should be barricaded.

» **Routing.** Routes should be well marked and logical (in a factory, the route should go from raw materials through production steps to the finished product). A map should be given to each visitor if the route is long or complicated.

» **Guides.** Tours should be led by trained guides who have a thorough knowledge of the organization and can explain in detail what visitors are seeing on the tour.

» **Explanation.** Signs, charts, and diagrams may be necessary at any point to supplement the words of the guides. The guides must be coached to say exactly what the public should be told. Many experts can't explain what they do, so a prepared explanation is necessary.

» **Housekeeping and attire.** The premises should be as clean as possible. Attire should be clean and appropriate. A punch press operator doesn't wear a necktie, but his overalls need not be greasy.

» **Emergencies.** Accidents or illness may occur. All employees should know what to do and how to request appropriate medical assistance.

Tips for Success How to Plan an Open House

Preplanning

Initial Planning

+ Select and research the date.
+ Set up your committees or areas of responsibility.
+ Determine your budget.

Open House Announcement

+ Notify employees and recruit their assistance.
+ Invite staff and families, if appropriate.
+ Develop your mailing list.
+ Design and print invitations.
+ Arrange advertising.
+ Prepare and distribute press releases/ posters.
+ Create radio/TV spots.

Food and Beverages

+ Decide on the menu.
+ Arrange for catering or volunteer servers.
+ Arrange for cleanup.

Equipment/Decorations

+ Determine the equipment available from your organization.
+ Arrange for necessary rentals, such as tables, chairs, or an outdoor tent.
+ Arrange for table linens, plates, and silverware.
+ Plan flowers in strategic locations.

Specialty Advertising

+ Arrange for giveaways that increase your organization's visibility, such as balloons, T-shirts, and mugs.

Media Relations

+ Invite the media personally and by mail.
+ Develop and distribute press releases announcing the event.
+ Arrange for media coverage on the day of the open house.
+ Arrange for a photographer to cover the event (photos can be used for publicity or internal communications).

Day of Event

Reception

+ Set up a staffed reception table with a sign-in book.
+ Distribute information on your organization and giveaways.
+ Have staff explain the activities to guests.

Tours

(Some preparation required in planning process)

+ Develop a floor plan for tours to ensure consistency.
+ Arrange a regular tour schedule, such as every 30 minutes.
+ Offer an incentive (such as a T-shirt) to those who complete the tour.
+ Brief tour guides on the key points to cover and how to field questions.
+ Arrange for visuals such as a display or demonstrations during the tour.

Activities/Entertainment

This depends on the nature of your event but could include:

+ Health education displays or screenings.
+ A road race.
+ Games, a magician, or a storyteller for the children.
+ A local band.
+ A short questionnaire to evaluate community response to the event and issues related to your organization.

Ceremony

+ Arrange a focal point for your open house, such as a ribbon cutting, awards ceremony, music/ dance performance, or brief message from the company president.

Summary

A World Filled with Meetings and Events

» Meetings are an important tool in public relations because they let the audience participate and interact in real time, using all five senses—hearing, sight, touch, smell, and taste.

» Events and meetings don't just happen. They must be planned with attention to every detail. Nothing can be left to chance.

Staff and Committee Meetings

» Before scheduling a staff or committee meeting, ask, "Is this meeting really necessary?" You can make meetings more effective if you distribute an agenda in advance, adhere to a schedule, and keep people from going off on tangents.

Group Meetings

» Club meetings and workshops require you to consider such factors as time, location, seating, facilities, invitations, name tags, menu, speakers, registration, and costs.

Banquets

» Banquets are elaborate affairs that require extensive advance planning. In addition to the factors necessary for a club meeting, you have to consider decorations, entertainment, audiovisual facilities, speaker fees, and seating charts.

Receptions and Cocktail Parties

» Cocktail parties and receptions require precautions about the amount of alcohol consumed and the availability of food and nonalcoholic drinks. Possible liability is an important consideration.

Conventions

» Conventions require the skills of professional managers who can juggle multiple events and meetings over a period of several days. A convention may include large meetings, cocktail parties, receptions, tours, and banquets.

Trade Shows

» Trade shows are the ultimate marketing events and attract millions of attendees annually. Exhibit booths may cost from $50,000 to $1 million.

Promotional Events

» A celebrity at your promotional event will attract crowds and media attention, but appearance fees can be costly.

» A promotional event may be a "grand opening" of a facility or a 10K run sponsored by a charitable organization. It is important to consider such factors as city permits, security, and liability insurance.

Open Houses and Plant Tours

» Open houses and plant tours require meticulous planning and routing, careful handling of visitors, and thorough training of all personnel who will be in contact with the visitors.

Skill Building Activities

1. Select a community group that has just completed a conference, an annual awards banquet, or a convention. Interview the organizers to follow the steps that were taken in planning and organizing the event. You should consider timelines, budget, contracts with hotels and other vendors, speaker arrangements, invitations, registration packets that were prepared, publicity

tools, and problems that occurred that should be considered in planning future events.

2. The School of Business at your university has scheduled its annual awards banquet. It will be held in 6 months. It usually attracts about 500 alumni and members of the local business community. Traditionally, a speaker with a national reputation is asked to give the major address at the banquet. In addition, outstanding students will be recognized. Prepare a detailed outline of what must be done to plan the banquet, including a timeline or calendar of what must be done by specific dates.

3. A new sports bar is opening in a month. What "grand opening" or special event would you organize to attract media coverage?

4. Second Harvest food bank desires more corporate involvement and sponsorship of its activities to provide food for the unemployed and the poor. Do some brainstorming. What would you suggest to various local corporations in terms of (1) what's in it for them, and (2) what kind of events or activities they could sponsor to generate more donations to the food bank?

5. Your organization has decided to sponsor a 10K run as a community event to raise money for a park that will cater to special-needs children. Write a memo detailing what needs to be done to organize this event.

Media Resources

Craven, G. (2011, January 12). "CES 2011: Social Media Transformed the Trade Show." Retrieved from http://.blog.ogilvpr.com.

Lipton, L. (2008, October 5). "What Goes On Behind the Scene: It's Tough Enough to Put On a Charity Bash—And Then the Economy Goes South." *New York Times*, Sunday Styles, 1, 10.

McPherson, S. (2010, January). "A 12-Month Guide How to Enhance Your Company's Trade Show Performance." *Public Relations Tactics*, 11, 14.

Stross, R. (2010, March 22). "They're Not Waiting for an Invitation to Evite's Party." *New York Times*, B12. "Superstar's Role Gets CES Crowd Gaga over Polaroid." (2010, May). *PRWeek*, 82.

White, M. (2011, May 10). "Lightening the Paper Load: At Conferences, Apps Can Replace Piles of Handouts." *New York Times*, B5.

Planning Programs and Campaigns

18

> >> After reading this chapter, you will be able to:

» Recognize the importance of having a plan

» Understand the steps necessary to organize a campaign plan

» Identify the eight basic elements of a plan

» Present a plan for management approval

The Value of a Written Plan

The primary focus of this book has been on the tactical aspects of public relations—news releases, feature placements, publicity photos, video clips, online newsrooms, satellite media tours, media relations, newsletters, speeches, and so on—that require considerable writing skill and creativity.

Now that you have mastered multiple "media techniques," it is important to devote a chapter to the key concepts of campaign management and public relations programming. Basically, we are now talking about the coordination of multiple "tactics" as part of an overall program to achieve organizational objectives.

A written plan is imperative for any public relations campaign. It improves the campaign's effectiveness. By using multiple communication tools together, you ensure a greater overall impact. Put another way, a plan is a blueprint. It explains the situation, analyzes what can be done about it, outlines strategies and tactics, provides a timeline of activities, and tells how the results will be evaluated.

Laurie Wilson, author of *Strategic Program Planning for Effective Public Relations Campaigns*, offers some insight about the relationship of a program plan to the actual process of writing and distributing materials to key audiences. She says:

> Each communication tactic is planned before it is created. The copy outline requires for each communication tactic the identification of the key public, the desired action by the public to contribute to the accomplishment of the plan's objectives, and the

message to be sent to that public to motivate its action. Each of these elements draws the information as it is specified in the strategic plan.

This chapter provides a brief overview of how to write a comprehensive public relations program. With this skill, you will become much more than a public relations writer—you will also become a public relations manager.

Developing a Plan

The first step in developing a plan is to consult with the client or your management. This serves two purposes. First, it gets these people involved. Second, it is likely to give you the basic information you need to start making a plan.

In talking with the people who will pay for the campaign, you strive to identify the problems and opportunities confronting the organization. In some cases, these will be apparent to all. At other times, one party will have ideas that have not occurred to the other. Out of this discussion should be an agreement as to the general nature of the situation and a preliminary establishment of the campaign's objectives. All of this, of course, is subject to change when more information is gathered.

> **"**PR planning is a bona fide social science that distinguishes strategic PR from the seat-of-the-pants practice of which many in the field are often guilty.**"** Fraser Seitel, author of The Practice of Public Relations

A good example is the California Avocado Commission. It faced the problem of selling Haas avocados on the East Coast. Sales were not good, and, with a bumper crop of 600 million avocados, the California growers realized that they had a problem. Some informal research found that New Yorkers were not acquainted with avocados that turned jet black when ripe; they thought the fruit was rotten. The objective, then, was to inform consumers that Haas avocados are supposed to have black skins and that they have excellent flavor. The campaign succeeded because it was based on sound information and analysis.

Gathering Information

You cannot know too much about the subject you intend to promote. Don't be satisfied with a cursory investigation—dig and keep on digging until you have the whole story. There are several sources from which you can get the facts and figures that will enable you to plan an effective campaign:

» **Organization.** Much basic information should be available within the organization. Ask for marketing research that has been conducted about the product or service. Talk to sales representatives who deal with customers. Get an overall picture of the organization's successes and failures. Find out why things have happened or how they have been done.

» **References.** Go through all the information in your files. Consult other files. Use libraries and online databases. Review Chapter 1; many sources of information are cited there.

» **Questions.** Ask colleagues for their ideas. Review the experiences of others in similar situations. Read any case histories you can find. The trade press is a good source.

» **Analysis of communications.** Field reports from representatives of the organization, inquiries on telephone hotlines, and consumer complaints should be checked and studied.

» **Brainstorming.** Get a group of colleagues together to kick around ideas and suggestions. Many of the ideas won't be practical or realistic, but some may contain the kernel of a creative idea that can be further developed into a strategy. A typical brainstorming session among colleagues is shown in Figure 18.1.

» **Focus group interviews.** Assemble a group of people who are representative of the audience you want to reach. These interviews are not quantitative research, but they may point to a need for detailed research in a specific area.

» **Surveys.** In many situations, you will need to conduct a survey to ascertain the attitudes and perceptions of target audiences. Doing a survey takes a lot of time and money. If the organization does not have the relevant data on hand, you must either do the survey yourself or use a survey research firm.

» **Media databases.** To plan your tactics, you need to know which channels of communication will be most efficient. A number of media directories, including *Bacon's* and *BurrellesLuce*, provide profiles of various media outlets and their audiences.

FIGURE 18.1 Planning a public relations program requires brainstorming sessions like this one, at which participants discuss the characteristics of the audience and work to come up with innovative and creative tactics that will accomplish the organization's objectives.

» **Demographics.** The *Statistical Abstracts of the United States, American Demographics*, and the comprehensive *Simmons Index* provide insights into the characteristics of an audience. *Simmons*, in particular, will give you detailed information on consumer buying habits and consumers' major sources of information. Another good resource is surveys by various organizations about lifestyles, public opinion, and consumer behavior. Many of these survey results are posted on websites and reported in the media.

Analyzing the Information

Having gathered all pertinent information and perhaps conducted a survey or several focus groups, your job is to analyze all the facts and ideas. You must consider the reliability of what you have found. If there are contradictions, you must eliminate erroneous elements and confirm the credibility of what remains.

Now, with reliable information in hand, you can start to draw conclusions. The situation, with its problems and opportunities, and the reason for it should be apparent. The objectives should be obvious, and the strategy, after careful thought, should start to take form.

At this point, you should prepare an outline of your findings and discuss them with management or the client. You can say, "These are the facts that I have, this is the situation as I see it, these are the objectives I think we should select, and this is the strategy I suggest." This discussion may result in an approval in principle. If it does, you can start writing a program or campaign plan that will outline the strategies and tactics required to address the problem or opportunity.

> **" Before goals and tactics are drafted, PR Directors must thoroughly understand their organization's business plan. "** David B. Oates, principal at Stalwart Communications, San Diego

Elements of a Plan

There is some variation regarding the elements of a basic program or campaign plan. Organizations designate these elements in different ways, combining or dividing them as seems appropriate. Nevertheless, any good plan will cover eight elements: (1) situation, (2) objectives, (3) audience, (4) strategy, (5) tactics, (6) timing, (7) budget, and (8) evaluation. These elements are described in the following sections and summarized in the Tips for Success on page 475.

Situation

An organization's situation can be determined by summarizing the organization's relations with its public or publics. This tells why the program is needed and points out the need or the opportunity. This may be the most important part of the plan. Unless a client or management is convinced that a campaign is necessary, it is not likely to approve spending money on it.

Tips for Success Components of a Public Relations Plan

A basic public relations plan is a blueprint of what you want to do and how you will accomplish your task. Such a plan, be it a brief outline or a comprehensive document, will enable you and your client or employer to make sure that all elements have been properly considered, evaluated, and coordinated for maximum effectiveness:

+ **Situation.**   You cannot set valid objectives without understanding the problem. To understand the situation, (a) discuss it with the client to find out what he or she expects the program to accomplish, (b) do your own research, and (c) evaluate your ideas in the broader perspective of the client's business plan.

+ **Objectives.**   Once you understand the situation, it should be easy to define the objectives. To determine if your stated objectives are the right ones, ask yourself: (a) Do they really solve or help to solve the problem? (b) Are they realistic and achievable? (c) Can success be measured in terms meaningful to the client?

+ **Audience.**   Identify, as precisely as possible, the group of people to whom you are going to direct your communications. Is this the right group to approach in order to solve the problem? If there are several groups, prioritize them according to which are most important for your particular objectives.

+ **Strategies.**   The strategy describes how, in concept, the objective is to be achieved. Strategy is a plan of action that provides guidelines for selecting the communications activity you will employ. There are usually one or more strategies for each target audience. Strategies may be broad or narrow, depending on the objective and the audience.

+ **Tactics.**   This is the body of the plan, which describes, in sequence, the specific communications activities proposed to achieve each objective. Discuss each activity as a separate thought, but relate each to the unifying strategy and theme. In selecting communication tools—news releases, brochures, radio announcements, and so on—ask yourself if the use of each will really reach your priority audiences and help you accomplish your stated objectives.

+ **Calendar.**   It is important to have a timetable, usually outlined in chart form, that shows the start and completion of each project within the framework of the total program. A calendar makes sure that you begin projects—such as brochures, story placements, newsletters, or special events—early enough that they are ready when they are needed.

+ **Budget.**   How much will implementation of the plan cost? Outline, in sequence, the exact costs of all activities. Make sure that you include such things as postage, car mileage, and staffing. In addition, about 10 percent of the total budget should be allocated for contingencies.

+ **Evaluation.**   Before you begin, you and the client or management must agree on the criteria you will use to evaluate your success in achieving the objective. Evaluation criteria should be (a) realistic, (b) credible, (c) specific, and (d) appropriate to the client's expectations.

A need often is a remedial situation. For example:

» BP, after the oil spill in the Gulf of Mexico, had to restore public confidence about its commitment to clean up the spill and be socially responsible.

» Wal-Mart, under attack from labor unions about employee benefits and community groups that didn't like "big box" stores, was forced to change policies and begin new "green" initiatives to improve its corporate image and reputation.

» Domino's Pizza had to regain the confidence of its customers after two employees in North Carolina, as a prank, posted a YouTube video showing them making a pizza with unsanitary ingredients.

Most public relations situations, however, are not problems that must be solved in a hurry. Instead, they are opportunities for an organization to increase public awareness, advance its reputation, or attract new customers or clients. Here are some examples:

» Murphy-Goode winery conducted a social media campaign to attract young adults to its brand by sponsoring an online contest to hire a social media expert. See the PR Casebook on page 477.

» Friskies PetCare Company increased brand awareness by sponsoring a national canine Frisbee competition.

» The New York State Canal System launched a campaign to make citizens more aware of the historic canal system as a first-class tourist destination.

» McCormick & Company launched a multiple social media initiative to increase use of its various spices and rubs during the summer grilling season.

Objectives

Neither employers nor clients are likely to approve a campaign without clear objectives. Many campaigns will have two or three objectives, but others might have just one objective. The key, however, is to thoroughly understand what you are trying to accomplish. See the Tips for Success on page 480 on how public relations campaigns often assist an organization's marketing efforts.

It's also important that you don't confuse objectives with the "means" rather than the "end." Novices, for example, often set an objective such as "Generate publicity for the new product." Publicity, however, is not an end in itself. The real objective is to create awareness among consumers about the availability of the new product and to motivate them to purchase it.

There are basically two kinds of objectives: informational and motivational.

Informational Objectives — A large percentage of public relations plans are designed primarily to increase awareness of an issue, an event, or a product. Here are some informational objectives:

» To inform people about the nutritional benefits of eating strawberries

» To tell people that cigarette smoking is a major cause of cancer

» To generate awareness about a new computer tablet on the market

» To inform the public that water conservation is needed

PR casebook

Winery Creates a "Goode" Job through Social Media

A public relations plan contains eight basic elements. The following is an outline of a plan that Murphy-Goode winery implemented using social media to reach millennial (aged 21–31) wine consumers. The innovative campaign received a Silver Anvil award from PRSA.

Situation

The winery, noting the social media phenomenon, decided that it could expand awareness of its brand by creating a social media–based campaign employing a social media expert who would receive $10,000 a month, be elegantly housed, and be charged with living "the Wine Country Lifestyle" of the Napa Valley in California. The idea of a dream job ("A Really Goode Job") coincided with a time when jobs were hard to find among young people, who were also social media savvy.

Objectives

» Increase brand awareness and exceed media coverage of competitive brands.

» Move from 1 million media impressions in the previous year to at least 300 million impressions as a result of the campaign.

» Increase traffic to website.

» Increase email database.

  • Increase distribution.

  • Create dialogue with millennial generation social media users

  • Establish image as young, hip brand and social media leader in the wine industry

Research

Market research indicated that almost 50 percent of millennials said they are drinking more wine and that wine education was important. The Internet was a key communications tool for them, but they didn't want traditional sales messages. Instead, they preferred to get their information from peers. It was determined, however, that peer messages were highly influenced by traditional media, which were then spread into the digital community through websites, emails, Facebook, YouTube, and blogs.

Target Audience

Millennials were the target audience because it was a demographic that could replace aging consumer bases. In addition, the nature of a highly unusual dream job involving wine and the social media would be attractive to them —a group that highly valued technology, unconventional careers, and Internet-based brand recommendations. The possibility of a great job, in an age of economic recession, would create an irresistible opportunity.

Strategy

The strategy was to conduct an online contest in which individuals would apply for the "Goode Job" through submitting applications via YouTube or the winery's website. After the application deadline, the campaign would count down to the final 50 candidates, the top 10, and then the winning candidate for the job. This strategy would garner myriad brand ads at no cost and dramatically increase traffic and direct sales opportunities. An online poll about favorite applicants encouraged consumer participation and interest while adding to the winery's email database.

Tactics

The winery created a webpage that could take applications and display applicant videos in large numbers.

The "Really Goode Job" page was linked to the winery's regular website. The site explained the job, the winery, the brand personality, wines, and the application process. It also directed visitors to wine sales pages, posted news releases, and provided contact information.

The launch event was in San Francisco. Applicants were encouraged to attend so they could meet the winemaker and learn more about the job. Pre-event news releases and media advisories were distributed, along with Internet flash mob notices. Over 200 people waited in line, which created great visuals for television stations. Coverage in the mainstream media spread virally to all social media.

Calendar

The program was a 3-month activity, from April through July.

Budget

$200,000 for staffing and collateral materials

Evaluation

All objectives were met or exceeded:

- » Media coverage was triple what was expected.
- » Major media coverage included CNN, Fox News, the *Today Show*, MSNBC, the *New York Times,* the *Los Angeles Times,* Associated Press (AP), and Reuters news service.
- » About 2,000 people applied for "A Really Goode Job." About half posted video applications on YouTube.
- » There was a fourfold increase in the winery's email database.
- » Traffic to the Murphy-Goode website increased from several hundred hits a month to over 433,000.
- » Product orders increased 60 percent.
- » Media coverage exceeded coverage of all competing brands for the year.
- » The winery established itself as a social media leader in the wine industry.

Although informational objectives are legitimate and are used by virtually every public relations firm and department, it is extremely difficult to measure how much "awareness" was attained unless before-and-after surveys are done; these are expensive and time consuming. In addition, awareness doesn't equal action. Consumers may become aware of your new product, but that doesn't necessarily mean that they will buy it.

Motivational Objectives — Motivational objectives are more ambitious, and also more difficult to achieve. However, they are easier to measure. Basically, you want to change attitudes and opinions with the idea of modifying behavior.

Some motivational objectives might be:

- » To increase the consumption of "healthy" foods, such as strawberries
- » To reduce cigarette smoking
- » To increase the sales of the new tablet computer
- » To reduce the amount of water used in a household

Notice that motivational objectives are more "bottom-line oriented." The effectiveness of the public relations plan is based on making something happen, whether increasing sales or changing public support for some issue.

By contrast, informational objectives merely inform or educate people. Take the informational objective of making people aware of cigarette smoking as a major cause of cancer. This might be achieved, but people who are "informed" and "aware" often continue to smoke. A better gauge of the American Cancer Society's success in its efforts would be an actual increase in the number of people who have stopped smoking or a decline in cigarette sales.

In setting objectives, you must be sure that they are realistic and achievable. Furthermore, they must be within the power of the campaign alone to attain. Sometimes the unwary set objectives such as "to increase sales," without realizing that sales may be affected by such things as product quality, packaging, pricing, merchandising, advertising, sales promotion, display, and competitive activity.

In establishing objectives, you must state exactly what you want the audience to know (a new product is now on the market), to believe (it will cut utility bills), and to do (ask for a demonstration). Objectives must be measurable. At some point the people who pay for the campaign are likely to ask, "What did you accomplish?" Many practitioners rely on general feedback—random comments and isolated examples that indicate public reaction. True professionals give facts and figures.

Evaluation is covered in detail in Chapter 19; at this point, however, you must start thinking about setting objectives that can be measured with figures. In an

Tips for Success   How Public Relations Helps Fulfill Marketing Objectives

A public relations program, particularly product publicity, can make a substantial contribution to fulfilling an organization's marketing plan:

+ It can develop new prospects for new markets, such as inquiries from people who saw or heard a product release in the news media.

+ It can provide third-party endorsements—via newspapers, magazines, radio, and television—through news releases about a company's products or services, community involvement, inventions, and new plans.

+ It can generate sales leads, usually through articles in the trade press about new products and services.

+ It can pave the way for sales calls.

+ It can stretch the organization's advertising dollars through timely and supportive releases about it and its products.

+ It can provide inexpensive sales literature for the company, because articles about it and its products can be reprinted for prospective clients.

+ It can establish the organization as an authoritative source of information on a given subject.

+ It can help sell minor products. Some products are too specialized for large advertising expenditures, so exposure to the market is more cost-effective if product publicity is utilized.

informational campaign, it is easy to state an objective such as: "To increase the number of people who believe that carpooling is a good way to save energy." A motivational objective in this situation could be "To increase the number of people who use carpooling." However, it would be far better to put it this way: "To increase carpooling by 50 percent."

As you think about these numerical goals, you should realize that there must be a base point for such measurements. To know how many people have been convinced by your campaign, you must consult public opinion surveys about public attitudes toward carpooling and then do additional surveys after the campaign to see if there has been any change.

Audience

Public relations programs should be directed toward specific and defined audiences or publics. If you define the audience as the "general public," you are not doing your homework.

In most cases, you are looking for specific audiences within a "general public." Take, for example, the Ohio vaccination program for children under the age of 2. The primary audience for the message is parents with young children. A secondary audience is pregnant women. This knowledge should provide guidance on the selection of strategies and tactics that would primarily reach these defined audiences.

Increasing the use of carpooling is another example of an objective for which you can define the audience more precisely than saying "the general public." The primary audience for the message on carpooling is people who drive to work. A secondary audience might be parents who drive their children to school. Sunkist, for example, sponsored a program encouraging kids to have a lemonade stand during the summer months to raise money for charity. Its primary audience for the campaign was women aged 25 to 35 with families because they usually supervised the activities of their children and were more inclined than men to support community activities.

Another common mistake is defining the mass media as an audience. In 9 out of 10 cases, media serve as channels to reach the audiences that you want to inform, persuade, or motivate. On occasion, in programs that seek to change how mass media reports an organization or an issue, editors and reporters can become a primary "public" or audience.

Gaining a thorough understanding of your primary and secondary audiences, which are directly related to accomplishing your objectives, is the only way that you can formulate successful strategies and tactics.

Strategy

Strategy is the broad concept on which the campaign will be based. Strategy must be keyed directly to the objective, and it must be formed with a thorough knowledge of what the primary audiences perceive as relevant and in their self-interest.

The vaccination program for children, for example, was based on the idea that parents love their children and want them to be healthy. Thus, the strategy was to tell parents how important vaccinations are in keeping their children out of danger. In fact, the theme of the campaign became "Project L.O.V.E." with the subhead "Love Our Kids Vaccination Project."

The program to increase carpooling was based on research showing that commuters were interested in saving time and money. Thus, the strategy was to show how people using designated carpool lanes could cut the time of their commute. A second strategy was to show how much money a carpooler would save annually in gasoline, insurance, and maintenance costs.

> **A PR campaign or program is a series of coordinated, unified activities and messages, driven by a single strategy, delivered to relevant publics by a variety of means.** Doug Newsom and Jim Haynes, authors of *Public Relations Writing*

The strategy for Sunkist was to use country artist Billy Dean as a spokesperson to generate awareness about the program, build relationships with key supermarket retailers, and generate stories in local media about kids setting up lemonade stands in the community to raise money for charity.

These examples illustrate two basic concepts about strategy. First, the strategy must reflect the audience's self-interests. Second, the strategy must be expressed in simple terms as a *key selling proposition*. It must be reiterated throughout the campaign in various ways, but the concept should remain clear and simple. Every campaign has one to three key messages, which are expressed in every activity—whether it's a news release, a feature article, a media interview, or a promotional event.

Indeed, one of the criteria for an effective public relations program is whether the audience was exposed to your key copy points and absorbed them. One way of determining this is a content analysis of media mentions, which will be discussed under evaluation and in the next chapter.

Tactics

This is the "how to do it" portion of the plan. In public relations, it often is called the "execution" part of the plan. Tactics are the actual materials that are produced in a public relations campaign by one or several public relations writers.

The children's vaccination project, for example, used a variety of tactics, including:

» Posters in child-care centers and doctors' offices

» PSAs on radio stations that had audiences of childbearing age

» Articles in newspapers and magazines catering to parents

» Pamphlets sent to child-care service providers

» Booklets mailed to every new mother explaining vaccination and the schedule of shots

» Letters to doctors reminding them to ask about vaccinations when a child has a checkup

» Corporate and hospital sponsorship of two-week-long "Shots for Tots" promotional events

» Endorsements by government leaders and child-care experts

» Information advertisements in community newspapers

» Stories about the L.O.V.E. Project on television and in the city's daily newspaper

The campaign on carpooling also used a variety of tactics. One tactic was to enlist the support of drive-time DJs on popular radio stations, who promoted carpooling as part of their early-morning and late-afternoon banter between songs. Billboards along major highways were also used. There was also a concentrated effort to distribute posters and pamphlets that businesses could post and distribute to employees. Editors of employee newsletters and magazines were given background information on carpooling for possible stories. Another successful tactic was the compilation of a kit for employers telling them how to organize carpools for their employees.

> **"Today, our clients clamor for a blog, a Facebook page, a YouTube channel, or a Twitter handle, convinced that they hold the solution to their problem. Yet the faulty logic still holds true. An individual tactic—no matter how popular—cannot substitute for a solid PR strategy."** Holly Potter, vice president of public relations for Kaiser Permanente

The Sunkist campaign used the following tactics: (1) kick-off concert in Nashville with Billy Dean, (2) heartwarming feature stories about kids and their lemonade stands raising money for charity, (3) distribution of a media kit to food editors, (4) distribution of camera-ready features about the program and tips on how kids can set up a lemonade stand, (5) an appearance by Billy Dean at the Little League Baseball world series for a barbecue and concert, and (6) a partnership with supermarket chain Harris Teeter to do a promotion about the program in all 400 of its stores.

Calendar

Three aspects of timing must be considered: (1) when the campaign is to be conducted, (2) the sequence of activities, and (3) the reach and frequency of the message.

A campaign must be timely; it must be conducted when the key messages mean the most to the intended audience. Some subjects are seasonal; hence publicists release information on strawberries in May and June, when a crop comes to market. A software program on doing your own taxes attracts the most audience interest in February and March, just before the April 15th deadline.

At times, the environmental context is important. A campaign on carpooling might be more successful if it follows a price increase in gasoline or a government agency report that traffic congestion has reached gridlock proportions. A charitable campaign to provide for the homeless is more effective if the local newspaper has just run a five-part series on the human dimensions of the problem.

Other kinds of campaigns are less dependent on seasonal or environmental context. The L.O.V.E. vaccination program, a Red Cross drive for blood donations, and even the selling of a new e-reader could be done almost any time during the year. The pre-Christmas season, however, is a favorite time for companies to introduce new products.

The second aspect of timing is the scheduling of activities during a campaign. A typical pattern is to have a concentrated effort at the beginning of a campaign when a number of activities are implemented. This is the launch phase of an idea or concept and, much like a rocket, takes a concentration of power just to break the awareness barrier. After the campaign has achieved orbit, however, it takes less energy, and fewer activities are needed to maintain momentum.

You must also think about advance planning. Monthly publications, for example, often need information at least 6 to 8 weeks before an issue. If you want something in the August issue, you have to think about placing it in May or June. A popular talk show may work on a schedule that books guests 3 or 4 months in advance. The main idea is that you must constantly think ahead to make things happen in the appropriate sequence.

A brochure may be needed on March 29, but you must start the brochure long before that date. To determine the starting date, you must know every step in the production process and how long it will take.

This activity, as well as the scheduling of other public relations tactics, should not be trusted to your memory or to jottings on your desk calendar. It is important that the entire public relations team working on the program has a single source of information, such as a wiki, for the schedule of the entire campaign.

The easiest way to keep everything on schedule is to prepare a working calendar for detailed planning and internal use. The brochure example, cited earlier, might look like this:

Activity	Date Due	Responsibility
Outline brochure	January 11	J. Ross, G. Jones
Write copy	January 18	J. Ross
Photos and artwork	January 25	A. Peck and N. Lopez
Design and layout	February 8	A. Peck and N. Lopez
Final client approval	February 15	B. Boss
Printer prep and proofs	February 28	Ace Printers. G. Jones, supervising
Printing and binding	March 10	Ace Printers. G. Jones, supervising
Delivery	March 15	United Parcel Service. G. Jones, supervising

Other entries planned using this kind of format might be preparing news releases, drafting speeches, writing pitch letters, scheduling spokespeople on radio talk shows, arranging media tours, and commissioning a camera-ready feature article. You can also map activities by listing the activities at the left of a chart, with days or weeks across the top. Lines or bars show graphically when various steps are being worked on. This is often called a *Gantt chart*; an example is shown in Figure 18.3.

The main idea is that you should have a systematic means of tracking activities throughout the public relations program so everything stays on schedule. If a brochure or a media kit is delayed, it can delay other activities, such as a media tour or

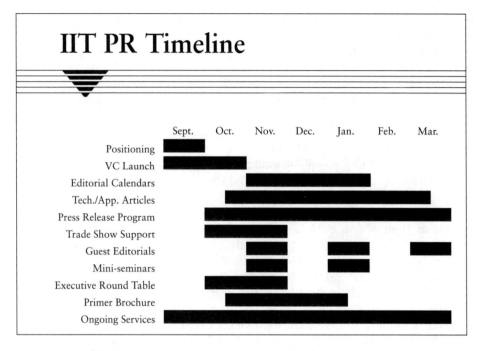

FIGURE 18.3 Planning requires precision scheduling. This is a simplified Gantt chart showing the various activities and tactics in a public relations program. Some tactics, such as news releases, are ongoing; others are phased in during the campaign.

a news conference, that are dependent on having the materials available. All activities in a public relations program are interrelated for maximum effectiveness.

The third element of calendaring is a timeline that ensures that the message reaches every possible audience and the message is repeated frequently. *Reach* is the number of different people exposed to a single message. *Frequency* is the number and pattern of messages presented to a particular public in a given amount of time. In a Gantt chart, for example, multiple news releases about the same subject, but perhaps different angles, will be done throughout the campaign.

Budget

A budget can be divided into two categories: staff time and out-of-pocket (OOP) expenses. Staff and administrative time usually takes the lion's share of any public relations budget. In a $100,000 campaign done by a public relations firm, for example, 70 percent or more will go to salaries and administrative fees.

A public relations firm has different hourly rates for the level of personnel involved. The head of the agency, who would oversee the account, might bill at $200 per hour. The account supervisor might bill at $120 per hour, and the account executive at $100 per hour. Account coordinators, those who do a lot of the clerical work, might bill at $55 per hour.

A public relations firm, when submitting a plan, has usually constructed a budget based on the number of estimated staff hours it will take to implement a plan. The other part of the budget is out-of-pocket expenses, which includes payments to various vendors for such things as printing, postage, graphics, video production, travel, phone, fax, photocopying, and so on.

You can do a reasonable job of estimating out-of-pocket expenses by making a few phone calls. You would call a printer, for example, to get an estimate of how much 10,000 copies of a pamphlet would cost. If you are doing a media tour, you would decide what cities would be visited and then find out the cost of airline fares, hotels, meals, and ground transportation costs. The Internal Revenue Service even has a guide to daily living expenses in major cities around the world.

One method of doing a budget is to use two columns. The left column, for example, will give the staff cost for writing a pamphlet or compiling a media kit. The right column will give the actual OOP costs for having the pamphlet or the media kit designed, printed, and delivered. Internal public relations departments, where the staff is already on the payroll, often compile only the OOP expenses.

Budgets should also have a line item for contingencies—that is, unexpected expenses. In general, allow about 10 percent of the budget for contingencies.

Evaluation

Evaluation refers directly back to your stated objectives: It is the process by which you determine whether you have met your objectives.

If you have an informational objective, such as increasing awareness, a common procedure is to show placements in key publications and broadcast stations that reached the intended audience. Related to this is a content analysis of whether the news coverage included your key messages. A more scientific approach is to do a benchmark study of audience knowledge and perceptions before and after the campaign. In many cases, "before" activity has already been documented through marketing studies, so all you have to do is a post-campaign survey.

Motivational objectives, such as increased market share or sales, are much easier to determine. The Ohio campaign had the objective of increasing vaccinations—and it succeeded by raising the vaccination rate by 117 percent in public clinics over a 2-year period. A campaign by Ketchum on behalf of prune producers caused a 4 percent increase in sales after several years of decline.

Increased sales, however, may be the result of other factors, such as the economy, the additional use of advertising, or a reduction in prices. Because of this, it is often wise to limit your objectives to something that can be related directly to your activities. For example, you might get feature placements in various magazines that also give a website for more information. Success could then be declared when there have been 50,000 visitors to the site.

Chapter 19 expands on methods of evaluation in public relations.

Submitting a Plan for Approval

The eight elements of a plan, which have just been discussed, become the sections in a written plan submitted to management or a client for approval. How to write proposals is covered in Chapter 14, but here's the general organization of a public relations plan:

» Title page (date, program name, client or organization, and team members)

» Executive summary (overview of the plan)

» Table of contents (name and page number of each section)

» Statement of principles (the planner's approach to the situation, i.e., integrated with marketing, alignment of campaign with overall organizational goals, etc.)

» Capabilities of the team or public relations firm submitting the plan

» The eight sections of the program plan, from situation to evaluation

» Conclusion (summary of why this is the best plan and request for approval)

Before you submit your written plan to a client or management for final approval, you should review it with a critical eye. You might even ask some knowledgeable person whose opinion you respect to read the plan and then discuss it with you. Check these points:

» Is the situation clearly stated?

» Is the audience the right one? Is it clearly defined?

» Are the objectives attainable and measurable?

» Is the strategy logical and effective?

» Is the message persuasive and memorable?

» Are the tactics sound and effective?

» Is the timing right?

» Are the costs reasonable and justified?

» Will the proposed evaluation really measure the results?

» Is the plan practical and appropriate?

» Is the plan logical, strong, and clearly written?

» Should any additions or deletions be made?

In addition to these suggestions, the Tips for Success on page 488 provides a thumbnail of what makes a winning campaign.

Your responsibility is to make the proposed plan as sound as you can make it, based on your professional expertise. You should remember, however, that any plan is a work in progress, and your client or management may suggest changes. They may not think a particular idea is very good, or they may decide to reduce the cost by eliminating a component.

In many cases, such feedback from the client or management sharpens and improves the plan. At other times, if you think the proposed changes would seriously impact the effectiveness of the plan, you have to express your rationale in a diplomatic manner and persuade them that your initial idea is the better one.

Tips for Success   Do You Have a Winning Campaign?

There are thousands of public relations campaigns every year. Some fail, some are moderately successful, and some achieve outstanding success. Each year, about 650 of these campaigns are submitted for the Public Relations Society of America's Silver Anvil award, which recognizes the very best in public relations planning and implementation. Of this number, about 45 are chosen for excellence.

Catherine Ahles and Courtney Botsworth of Florida International University analyzed the campaigns that have received Silver Anvil awards and identified some common characteristics of outstanding public relations campaigns:

+ **Budgets.** There's no question that big budgets help a winning campaign, but it's more important to have a budget that is efficiently used. Most winning campaigns are in the $100,000 to $199,000 range and use innovative tactics to stretch dollars over large geographic regions.

+ **Research.** According to Jennifer Acord, regional manager for public relations for Avon Products, "The best campaigns use research to develop the objectives, create the strategy, and provide clear benchmarks for evaluation." Literature searches and competitive analysis were the most frequently used techniques. About half of the campaigns used demographic profiles of audiences. About 40 percent of the campaigns pretested messages on the target audience before launching a full campaign.

+ **Benchmarking.** A campaign's outcome must be measured against some benchmark in terms of the target public's attitudes or behavior so you know if the campaign "moved the needle" in terms of creating awareness, increasing sales, or even changing attitudes and perceptions.

+ **Objectives.** "The most important aspect of a campaign is the objective," says Gerard F. Corbett, former vice president of Hitachi America Ltd and 2012 president of PRSA, "Four out of five Silver Anvil campaigns sought to change behavior in some way, and almost that percentage had awareness- and visibility-based objectives. There are four elements to writing a good objective, says Ahles. They are specifying (1) a clear tie to the organization's mission and goals, (2) the nature of the desired change, (3) the time frame for the change, and (4) the amount of change sought.

+ **Measuring results.** It is important, in a winning campaign, to evaluate the impact of a program and the actions taken by the target audience. Too many Silver Anvil entries fail to do this. Instead, they emphasize media clips and the number of meetings held. There is nothing wrong with press clips as one index of success, but Silver Anvil judges say the winning campaigns also devote attention to documenting behavior change.

+ **The X factor.** There are many good, solid campaigns, but the X factor is that ounce of daring and creativity that lifts the campaign to the extraordinary level. According to Corbett, "It's the chemistry that makes the program gel. It could be an out-of-the-box idea; it could be the people involved or the manner in which the campaign was implemented. Or it could be many factors woven together like a resilient fabric."

Summary

The Value of a Written Plan

» A program or campaign has multiple facets that must be considered and coordinated.

» A plan is a blueprint of an entire program or campaign.

Developing a Plan

» A plan is based on becoming thoroughly familiar with the organization and its business goals.

» It is necessary to conduct research in the form of a literature search, market studies, and surveys to determine the proper audience and the exact message.

Elements of a Plan

» A program plan has eight elements: (1) situation, 2) objectives, (3) audience, (4) strategies, (5) tactics, (6) calendar, (7) budget, and (8) evaluation.

» Objectives can be informational or motivational, depending on the desired results.

» Creating publicity is not a valid objective; it is a means to an end.

» For public relations purposes, audiences must be clearly defined. In most cases, a specific audience is defined by income, interests, geography, lifestyle, and a host of other variables.

» A strategy is a broad conceptualization that gives direction to a public relations program. A good strategy is based on research and reflects audience self-interests. It can also be expressed as the program's key selling proposition.

» Tactics are the "how to do it" part of the program plan. They list the communication tools and activities that will be used to support the strategy.

» Timing of activities and messages is important. They must occur within a broader context of public interests and must be scheduled in advance.

» A detailed budget is an integral part of a public relations plan. Staff and administrative expenses usually consume more of the budget than out-of-pocket expenses.

» Working a plan means that you must have a detailed calendar of activities and who is responsible for carrying them out.

» A program is evaluated as a success if it meets the set objectives of the campaign. Objectives must be measurable for evaluation methods to be effective.

Submitting a Plan for Approval

» The client or employer must approve a plan and its budget before any work can be done.

» A written plan may start with an executive summary and then outline the steps that will be taken to execute the program.

Skill Building Activities

1. The Almond Advisory Board, a trade group of almond growers, is gearing up for a major marketing effort to increase almond consumption by the American public. Write two informational and two motivational objectives for this campaign.

2. The Purple Cow Ice Cream Company has a strong market in the northwestern United States where it is located, but it wants to expand brand recognition and sales in other markets. The company doesn't have the money for a

national advertising campaign, so it has hired your public relations firm to plan and execute an effective social media and networking strategy. The budget is $100,000. Prepare a plan for Purple Cow that would take place over a period of 6 months. Your plan should include (1) background of the situation, (2) objective(s), (3) publics to be reached, (4) strategies, (5) tactics, (6) timeline, (7) budget, and (8) evaluation method. You should use the media techniques and tools that you have learned throughout this book.

Media Resources

Hendrix, J., and Hayes, D. (2009). *Public Relations Cases*, 8th edition. Belmont, CA: Thomson/Wadsworth.

Newsom, D., and Haynes, J. (2008, February.) "Writing the PR Plan: Defining Success for Your Organization." *Public Relations Tactics*, 16–17.

Potter, H. (2010, Summer). "Integrating Social Media into PR Plans." *The Strategist*, 40–41.

Seitel, F. (2010, May). "PR Planning = Social Science." *O'Dwyer's*, 57.

Smith, R. (2009). *Strategic Planning for Public Relations*, 2nd edition. Mahwah, NJ: Lawrence Erlbaum Associates.

Vega, T. (2011, March 8). "Taking Photos of Breakfast and Giving Meals to Children: Kellogg Promotes National Breakfast Day at Grand Central," *New York Times*, C4.

Wilcox, D., and Cameron, G. (2012). *Public Relations: Strategies and Tactics*, 10th edition. Boston: Allyn & Bacon.

Williams, P. (2010, September). "How to Write a Strategic Communications Plan." *The Ragan Report*, 28–29.

Wilson, L., and Ogden, J. (2008). *Strategic Program Planning for Effective Public Relations Campaigns*, 4th edition. Dubuque: Kendall-Hunt.

Measuring
Success

19

》 After reading this chapter, you will be able to:

» Understand the importance of measuring a program's success

» Write measurable campaign objectives

» Track the production and distribution of publicity materials

» Know the number of people who read your message

» Calculate how many absorbed the key message

» Measure changes in audience attitudes

» Track changes in audience behavior

» Evaluate the effectiveness of newsletters and events

» Write a measurement report

The Importance of Measurement

The final step in any public relations program or campaign, as the last chapter indicated, is measurement and evaluation.

Bill Margaritis, senior vice president of worldwide communications for FedEx, told *PRWeek*, "Measurement helps us prioritize and execute our programs; it's a road map to our activities. It also helps build alignment with business objectives, and gives executive management a sense of confidence that we are using a quantifiable process in which to invest our money and time."

You Mon Tsang, CEO of Biz360, a measurement firm, is blunter about the need for evaluation. He is quoted in *PRWeek*, saying, "It's almost inconceivable to invest money in a significant program like communications without understanding the results. How would any other department justify its investments without understanding what they are getting out of it?"

Another important reason for conducting measurement and evaluation, and perhaps the most compelling argument, is that clients and management are demanding more accountability. Today's public relations programs are

> **❝** *Measurement is a process that requires you to compare results against something—either with your competition or with your results over time. You note the change, analyze the reasons, and improve your program accordingly.* **❞** Katie Paine, president of KDPaine & Partners, a measurement firm

highly sophisticated and expensive, so organizations want to be sure that they are getting good value for their money. In addition, public relations personnel often compete with advertising and marketing for budget, so it is important to document how public relations activity is a cost-effective use of funds.

Consequently, here are some general questions that you should honestly ask yourself upon completion of a public relations program:

» Was the program or activity adequately planned?

» Did recipients of the message understand it?

» How could the program strategy have been more effective?

» Were all primary and secondary audiences reached?

» Was the desired organizational objective achieved?

» What unforeseen circumstances affected the success of the program or activity?

» Did the program or activity stay within the budget?

» What steps can be taken to improve the success of similar future activities?

Answering these questions requires a mix of measurement methods, many borrowed from advertising and marketing, to provide complete evaluations. To evaluate a public relations program fully, you must use more systematic research methods to document message exposure, accurate dissemination of the message, acceptance of the message, attitude change, and changes in overt behavior.

You can track message exposure and dissemination by counting media mentions and blog postings, but you also need to do a content analysis to determine if key messages were included. Indeed, the most common factor in judging the success of a campaign is whether there is an increase in public "awareness" about the key message being disseminated. These methods, however, emphasize the output of public relations staffs instead of the outcomes that result from their work. Tudor Williams, writing in the online newsletter *NetGain*, explains:

> For many years, organizations were content to measure the outputs of communication, how many newsletters were published, how many 'impressions' or column inches were created, or the size of the audience reached. But in a world where accountability matters, it is the outcomes that are important, the extent to which we were successful in achieving our goal. The output is but the means to achieve successful outcomes, not success itself.

Williams, when he discusses outcomes, is talking about a higher level of measurement that focuses on the effects of news releases, brochures, newsletters, and online efforts. Changes in audience awareness and understanding, as well as changes in attitudes and preferences and even behavior, are all "outcomes" that are more difficult to measure, but are more meaningful to the "bottom line." The chart in Figure 19.1 shows the three levels of measurement and evaluation.

Increasingly, public relations departments and firms are using various research tools to measure outcomes. Indeed, in one *PRWeek* survey more than half of the

FIGURE 19.1 There are three levels of public relations measurement. The most basic is measuring media placements. At the second level, there is more concern about comprehension and retention of the message on the part of the audience. At the advanced level, the emphasis is on opinion and behavior change. Each level requires different measurement tools.

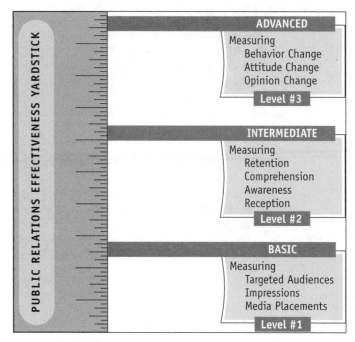

respondents said they used "outcomes" measurement to evaluate changes in attitudes and behavior as their most valuable form of measurement. It's ironic, however, that other surveys show that public relations personnel still use media mentions (clippings) as their most frequent measurement method. See the Tips for Success on page 494 for a list of measurement tools.

The following pages discuss the measurement and evaluation of "outputs," as well as "outcomes." The first step, however, is determining and writing your program objectives.

Program Objectives

Before any public relations program can be properly evaluated, it is important to have a clearly established set of measurable objectives. These must be part of

66 You have to budget for measurement up front. Not on the back. How much? Figure 5 percent of your total PR spend, including fees and pass-through costs. 77 David Rockland, managing director of research for Ketchum

the program plan, discussed in the last chapter, but some points need reviewing.

First, public relations staff and management should agree on the criteria that will be used to evaluate success in attaining the objectives. Does the client or employer want to evaluate the program on the number of media mentions or want you to show that you actually increased sales or market share? A frank discussion about objectives and client or management expectations—before a program is launched—can make a big difference in how you structure your campaign to achieve specific outcomes.

Second, don't wait until the end of a public relations program to determine how it will be evaluated. Albert L. Schweitzer of Fleishman-Hillard public relations in St. Louis makes the following point: "Evaluating impact/results starts in the planning stage. You break down the problems into measurable goals and objectives, then after implementing the program, you measure the results against goals."

In other words, it is not wise to have nonspecific objectives that you will be unable to measure at the end of your program. "Increase awareness of product X," for example, is not a measurable objective because it lacks two basic elements: (1) a change in something, and (2) a time frame. Thus, a much better—and more measurable—objective would be "Increase awareness of Product X from 25 percent to 50 percent by the end of 2012." For an example of how objectives were measured in a Frito-Lay campaign, see the PR Casebook on page 495.

Measurement of Production/Distribution

One elementary form of evaluation is simply to give your client or employer a count of how many news releases, feature stories, photos, and such were produced in a given time period.

This kind of measurement is supposed to give management an idea of your productivity. However, this approach is not very meaningful, because it emphasizes

Tips for Success   Media Clippings Remain Most Popular
                        Measurement Tool

BenchPoint, a measurement firm, conducted a global survey of public relations and communications professionals for the European Measurement Summit in Berlin, which was held in 2009. The respondents, coming primarily from Europe and the United States, ranked the effectiveness of measurement tools as follows:

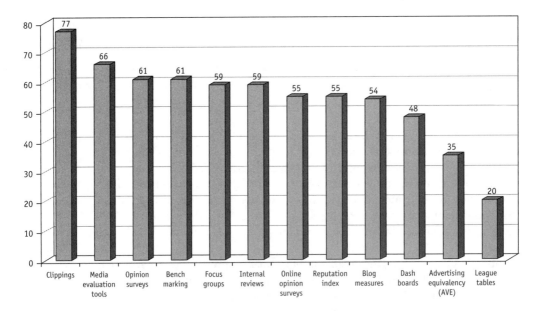

PRCasebook

A Frito-Lay Campaign Meets Its Objectives

Campaigns are evaluated on the basis of how well they achieve their objectives within a specific time frame.

Ketchum, a major public relations firm, had six months to conduct a campaign for Frito-Lay, which was introducing a new product line of SmartFood snacks for women. Research had found that women feel guilty about eating chips, so the new line was designed for the "conflicted pleasure seeker" who wanted both pleasure and wellness. The following is a summary of how each of the campaign objectives was evaluated:

Executive Summary

In six months, the program generated 195+ million positive media impressions, more than doubling the goal, with 100 percent key message penetration.

Introduce campaign's sharable entertaining content for women

32 posts on online entertainment sites including *E!* and *People*

23 campaign-focused stories in news outlets including *Ad Week* and *Fast Company*

Roundups on *CNN's Morning News* and Better TV syndicated segment about companies targeting women

Forge a relationship with the target and let her know Frito-Lay "gets" her

73 posts from women bloggers about the screening event and campaign

65 additional posts about webisodes

Stimulate waves of positive conversations and recommendations woman-to-woman

Real-time, positive conversations about the campaign and new products

250+ tweets from Twitter members

5,000+ @AWomansWorld Twitter followers

Raise awareness that Frito-Lay has new products just for her

20 publications positively reviewed SmartFood

Life & Style, *OK!*, and *In Touch* mentioned Baked! Lay's and Flat Earth

Good Morning America featured SmartFood in two segments about best snacks for women

Business goals

Snack aisle trips went up 1.8 percent among women.

SmartFood earned $3.8 million by the end of the year.

quantity instead of quality. It also encourages the public relations writer to send out more news releases than necessary, many worthless as news, in an attempt to meet some arbitrary quota. In many cases, it's better to skip writing the 15 routine news releases and spend the same amount of time pitching a story to one or two major newspapers with national circulation.

Closely aligned to the production of materials is their dissemination. Thus, it may be reported that a news release was sent to "977 daily newspapers, 700 weekly newspapers, and 111 trade publications." Such figures are useful in terms of tabulating how widely a news release or feature is distributed, but sending out vast quantities of news releases just to impress management with big numbers doesn't fool anyone.

Large mailings are not just the fault of publicists. Many organizations, including far too many public relations firms, think sending a news release is a relatively cheap proposition involving only postage or a group email. Why not do a blanket mailing to increase the odds that the material will be used? Such mass mailings, as discussed in Chapter 10, really irritate journalists, who then form the impression that public relations people are basically incompetent.

As a professional public relations practitioner, you should document distribution but not succumb to sending out reams of news releases just to impress the boss or the client. A better approach is to use targeted mailings that generate a high percentage of media placements.

Measurement of Message Exposure

The most common way of evaluating public relations programs is the compilation of print stories, broadcast mentions, and the number of visitors to your website. In fact, *PRWeek* surveyed public relations firms and found that 81 percent primarily used media mentions as their major tool to evaluate program success.

Monitoring services can be hired to review large numbers of print and online publications. They digitally "clip" all the articles/mentions about your client or employer. Major firms that offer such services include Cision (*Bacon's*), BurrellesLuce, Vocus, and Factiva. Major newswires such as Business Wire and PRNewswire also offer services that monitor print media, online publications, and thousands of blogs. VMS, a video monitoring service, covers all 210 U.S. television markets. Clients can be notified within minutes of a television news story and even view the video clip.

Most major services offer customers any number of ways to slice, dice, and compile media mentions according to their needs and budget. They can provide clients tabulations giving the name of the publication/program, date, frequency, and circulation/viewership. Clients can also have the monitoring service evaluate clips on such variables as article size, advertising cost equivalent, audience, editorial slant of the article, subject, number of keyword mentions, type of article, byline, and how an organization's overall mentions compare with those of major competitors. Other aspects of media analysis will be discussed shortly.

The main purpose of compiling media mentions is to find out if your material was used by the media. It gives the organization a way to determine if the public was exposed to its message. Miller High Life, for example, reported that it generated more than 5,000 newspaper, television, radio, and online stories about its 1-second ad during the Super Bowl on local NBC affiliates. Jay Leno even mentioned it on his *Tonight Show*. In addition, the website attracted 500,000 visitors and more than 3 million viewed YouTube videos about the unusual commercial.

The volume of media mentions is still popular among public relations firms and clients, but its importance and value are declining as a meaningful measurement of campaign effectiveness. Today, public relations managers and senior management are placing more emphasis on who is reached and what they do with the message.

Media Impressions

Another popular way of measuring output is to compile the circulation of the publications where your news release, feature story, interview, or product mention appeared. In the case of a broadcast mention on a radio program or television show, you use the audited average of listeners or viewers for that particular show.

This is known as compiling *gross impressions*, *media impressions*, or just ***impressions***. Geri Mazur, director of research for Porter Novelli International, told *PRWeek*, "At a most basic level, clients expected to know how many impressions or how many bodies their message touched." For example, if a story about an organization appears in a local daily with a circulation of 130,000, the number of media impressions is 130,000.

A story appearing in 15 or 20 publications can easily generate several million media impressions. Korbel Champagne Cellars, for example, generated about 1,000 media placements with its "perfect marriage proposal" contest for a total of about 90 million "impressions" by adding up the circulation of each publication and the viewing audience of various broadcast programs.

Total media impressions are used in advertising and publicity to illustrate the penetration of a particular message. However, high numbers of media impressions only report total circulation and potential audience size, not how many people actually read, heard, or viewed that particular story.

Advertising Value Equivalency

The numbers game is also played by converting stories in the news columns or on broadcast news and talk shows into the equivalent of advertising costs. For example, a 10-inch story in the local daily would be worth the same as an ad of the same size. And a 30-second story on a TV newscast would be worth an ad of the same length.

Some practitioners like the concept of **advertising value equivalency (AVE)** because it is a form of return on investment (ROI). It shows management that the public relations staff is earning its salary by generating more "income" than it costs to pay the staff's salary.

Mark Scott of HomeBanc Mortgage Company told *PRWeek*, for example, that AVE helps him "justify his PR budget to the CEO and head of marketing." The ad equivalency of HomeBanc's news coverage one year was $810,000, using a metric supplied by Burrelle's Information Services. According to Scott, salaries and expenses were about $200,000, so "the ROI is about four times the expense—and that looks pretty good to the corporate bean counters."

Some public relations practitioners even multiply the AVE figures with the rationalization that publicity is worth more than advertising because it is more credible and influential. In general, three is a common multiplier. If such a multiple were applied to HomeBanc's $810,000, it would mean that the news coverage was worth about $2.4 million. More recently, photos of President Obama visiting a pub and drinking a Guinness beer during a trip to Ireland were touted by a publicist in the UK as being worth $32 million in worldwide publicity for stout beer.

The concept of using AVE and exercises in multiplication, however, is condemned by most professional public relations groups such as the Public Relations Society of America (PRSA), the Global Alliance of national public relations groups, the International Public Relations Association (IPRA), and the Institute for Public Relations (IPR). In a policy paper, the IPR called the use of multipliers "unethical, dishonest, and not at all supported by the research literature."

> **"** *The PR practitioner who says, 'We got 500 hits, which generated 250 million impressions with an AVE of $2 million!' is a thing of the past* **"** Andre Manning, head of global communications, Royal Philips Electronics

Indeed, the whole idea of advertising equivalency is highly suspect, because you are comparing apples and oranges. First, you control the exact wording, graphics, and placement of your message in an ad. By contrast, news releases and features are subject to the whims of media gatekeepers who decide what is published and in what context. There is no guarantee, as there is in advertising, that your message will be communicated in the way you wish.

Second, a mystery remains as to what is actually being counted. If a 10-inch article in the local daily mentions your company along with several competitors, is this equivalent to 10 inches of advertising space? Also, when there were riots in Vancouver after the Canucks' loss in the Stanley Cup finals, the city received considerable negative coverage that certainly was not worth "millions in publicity."

Third, the practice of equating news stories and publicity with advertising is not particularly good for promoting effective media relations. Editors often suspect that all that publicists seek is "free advertising," and this impression is reinforced when public relations people take great pains to convert story placements to comparable advertising costs.

Although there are public relations departments and public relations firms that still use AVE, the practice is fading among professionals. The winning campaigns in PRSA's Silver Anvil awards, for example, rarely use AVE as a major criterion to demonstrate the success of their programs. Instead, they use outcomes such as increased sales, awareness, change in attitudes or behavior, and contributions to overall organizational objectives. These measurements will be discussed shortly.

Systematic Tracking

Measuring the volume of media mentions is a start, but a more systematic content analysis can now be done thanks to the computer and various software programs.

In addition to getting the traditional information about a publication's name, date, frequency, and circulation, it is now possible to do a more complete analysis of news coverage. BurrellesLuce, for example, offers media analysis that includes (1) article size compared to available space in the publication; (2) whether the article was positive, negative, or neutral; (3) mention of key messages, products, brands, and competitors; (4) the number of keyword mentions; (5) the type of article; (6) the byline of the article; (7) degree of coverage in top markets; and (8) coverage by region. Other services, such as Factiva, Vocus, Biz360, and CARMA, offer similar media analysis capabilities.

Such detailed analysis is a good diagnostic tool to tabulate details about the coverage and what audiences were exposed to it. You might find out, for example, that your new product or policy is getting a lot of negative news coverage. See Figure 19.3 for a chart summarizing editorial slant. Or you may find out that only newspapers in the West are using the information, leaving other key markets without any penetration.

Such an analysis may also show that 45 percent of your company's news releases are management and personnel stories, but that these releases account for only 5 percent of the stories published about the company. By contrast, stories about new product developments may constitute only 10 percent of the news releases but account for 90 percent of the press coverage. Given these data, a logical step might be to send out fewer personnel stories and more product development articles.

A systematic tracking system also identifies which publications receiving the news releases are using them. Your mailing list may include 500 different periodicals, but by the end of a 12-month period you may find that only half of these used your releases in any way. Given this information, you would be wise to prune your mailing list. Computer analysis of press clippings also is a valuable way to determine whether key messages are being included in print and broadcast stories.

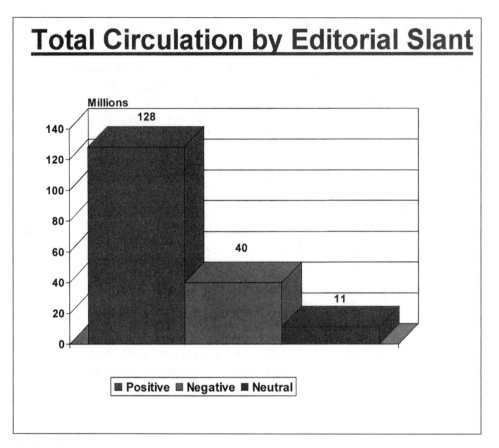

FIGURE 19.3 Thanks to software programs, media mentions can be analyzed on multiple levels—by region, page, mention of key messages, type of article, etc. This chart, originally in color, summarizes the news slant of all your coverage by the total circulation of the publications where stories appeared. As the chart shows, a large percentage of the stories were positive.

Monitoring the Internet

Measuring the reach and effectiveness of your messages on the Internet is getting more sophisticated by the month. One earlier approach was the cyberspace version of media impressions, which was the number of people reached via the organization's webpage. Each instance of a person accessing a site is called a *hit* or a *visit*.

In a national campaign to increase awareness of autism, for example, the Centers for Disease Control and Prevention reported 540,000 unique visitors and more than 50,000 materials downloaded from its website. Even a campaign by the National Potato Board did pretty well. Its Mr. Potato Head site attracted almost 10,000 visitors who spent an average of 5.5 minutes at the site, reviewing an average of 6.6 pages about the health benefits of potatoes.

Blogs, social media sites, and online publications can also be monitored using the metric of site visits, but such data is less valuable than knowing about the content and tone of what is being said. Consequently, public relations professionals use free online sites such as Technorati, Blogpulse, Google Alerts, and Google Analytics to compile mentions regarding their organization or client. You can receive all this information on a daily basis via RSS feeds, which were discussed in Chapter 12. You can also pay companies such as Radian6, Collective Intellect, Attensity360, Lithium, or a score of other commercial providers to monitor the entire Internet for you and give you a daily report.

Radian6 (www.radian6.com) is a good example of a comprehensive social media monitoring service. According to its website, it monitors more than 150 million public sites and sources including blogs, forums, online news publications, public photos, videos, and every tweet. In addition, its "dashboard" approach can give a client instant information about a variety of metrics:

» Overviews of the brand in terms of the number of posts, the opinions expressed, and the brand's share of the conversation about a particular topic or issue.

» The current perception of the organization and its products or services and a tracking of perceptions over a year's time.

» Identification of influential people in the brand's industry in terms of who's talking about the brand online and who their followers are.

The metrics of measurement are readily available at social networking sites. There's Facebook Insights, for example, which gives you information about why and when your fans' activity increases or decreases. You can also track exposure to your message and who found it compelling enough to pass it on to others through bookmarking sites such as Digg and Delicious.

YouTube, for example, can provide data beyond just the number of viewers and how many times a video was downloaded. A feature called YouTube Insight gives account holders who have

> **"Measurement has become more sophisticated. You can now measure share of voice, share of mind, and even understand impact of product sales."** Jim Tsokamos, president of the Americas for MS&L Group

uploaded videos to the site a range of statistics, charts, and maps about their audience. The data available through Insight include age, gender, and geographic location, as well as the identities of the Internet sites that viewers came from and where they went after watching the video.

Insight product manager Tracy Chan told the *Los Angeles Times*, "Marketers and advertisers use the data to decide how to target their next round of ads or where bands should tour." She was referring to Weezer, an alternative rock band, which found out that 2.2 million people watched its YouTube video and that 65 percent of the audience was men under age 18 and between the ages of 35 and 45.

Other metrics on the Internet are more difficult to quantify. Social networking sites, for example, are all about listening, participating, and engaging the audience, not necessarily delivering key messages. Ed Terpening, vice president of social media at Wells Fargo, told a Dow Jones seminar, "We care a lot about participation and engagement. That's our number one metric."

One dimension is called the "conversation index," which is the ratio between blog posts and comments. It helps measure whether a blogger is doing a lot of writing with very little response on the part of readers or whether the audience is engaged and contributing to the conversation. Obviously, blogs that generate a lot of "conversation" are more important to organizations in terms of feedback and dialogue. The Tips for Success below gives the most popular metrics for measuring social media.

In sum, the ability to measure the effectiveness of social media is continuing to evolve. Richard Houghton, president of the International Communications Consultancy Organization (ICCO), is quoted by Ruth Pestana in a *PRWeek* article saying that the major obstacles to measurement are:

1. Lack of budget.
2. Lack of measurement expertise or understanding among PR professionals.
3. Agencies and measurement providers' preference for selling their own measurement systems to differentiate themselves from competitors. There are now more than 200 measurement "products" on the market.
4. Fear of what the results might say. The campaign, despite the money spent, might be a flop.

Requests and 800 Numbers

Another measure of media exposure is to compile the number of requests for more information. A story in a newspaper or an appearance of a spokesperson on a broadcast

Tips for Success How to Measure the Impact of Social Media

Katie Paine, CEO of KDPaine & Partners and a pioneer in public relations measurement, wrote in *The Ragan Report*, "Measurement is not counting. Or monitoring. It is not the number of followers, friends, rankings, or scores." Instead, she wrote in *PRWeek* that better evaluation of social media impact can be achieved by calculating the percentage increase in other factors such as:

+ number of downloads, registrations, qualified leads, or online sales
+ engagement as measured by the number of repeat visitors, time on site, comments, retweets, links, and references from your blog posts or tweets
+ improvement in Google page rank
+ desirable conversations or recommendations versus the competition
+ share of desirable positioning on key issues versus competitors
+ posts containing one or more key messages
+ share of visibility for your thought leaders

show often provides the impetus for driving people to a website to download more information, request a brochure, or even order the product.

In many cases, a toll-free 800 number is provided. The American Association of Clinical Endocrinologists, through Fleischman-Hillard, conducted a public information campaign about thyroid disorders and got 10,000 requests for its "Thyroid Neck Check" brochures. In addition, the organization's website increased its "hits" from 4,000 to 12,000 immediately after the launch of the information campaign.

The readership of product publicity features, discussed in Chapter 7, is often monitored by offering readers an opportunity to call or go online to get more information. In this way, for example, Air New Zealand has measured the value of sending travel features to daily newspapers throughout the United States. Such monitoring often shows top management that product publicity generates more sales leads than straight advertising.

Cost per Person

The cost of reaching each person in the audience often is calculated as part of the evaluation process. The technique is commonly used in advertising in order to place costs in perspective. Although a 30-second commercial during the Super Bowl costs about $3 million, most advertisers believe it is worth the price because an audience of more than 100 million is reached for about three cents per household. This is a relatively good bargain, even if several million viewers probably visited the bathroom while the commercial played.

Cost-effectiveness, as this technique is known, also is used in public relations. Cost per thousand (CPM) is calculated by taking the total of media impressions (discussed earlier) and dividing it by the cost of the publicity program. Skytel, for example, spent $400,000 to publicize a new product and obtained 52 million impressions, about seven-tenths of a cent per impression. You can do the same thing for events, brochures, and newsletters. Nike produced a sports video for $50,000 but reached 150,000 high school students, for a per-person cost of 30 cents.

Event Attendance

Speeches, meetings, presentations, tours, grand openings, and other such activities have one important thing in common: They all involve audiences who are exposed to a message.

A first step in evaluating these activities is to count the number of people who come to an event. Port Discovery, a new children's museum in Baltimore, conducted a public relations program to let citizens know about its grand opening. Thanks to the efforts of its public relations firm, Trahan, Burden & Charles, Inc., almost 9,000 visited the museum in its first week—double the number expected.

Although numbers are impressive, you also can measure audience attitudes by observation and surveys. A standing ovation at the end of a speech, spontaneous applause, and complimentary remarks as people leave, even the "feel" of the audience as expressed in smiles and the intangible air of satisfaction that can permeate a group of people, will give you an idea as to the success of an event.

A more scientific method is the survey. People leaving an event can be asked what they think in a 30-second interview. At a meeting, attendees can be asked to fill out a short questionnaire or answer a short email questionnaire after the event. A simple form might ask respondents to give their opinion on (1) the location, (2) the cost, (3) the facilities, (4) the program, (5) individual speakers, (6) how they learned about the event, and (7) suggestions for future events.

Measurement of Audience Awareness

Audience exposure to a message, as just reviewed, depends primarily on whether the media distributed the message with some degree of accuracy. Audience awareness, however, is somewhat more complicated to measure because you have to find out how many people actually read or viewed the message and, to a degree, remembered it. Indeed, most public relations campaigns have the primary objective of creating awareness among key publics. See the Tips for Success below for other objectives of a campaign.

The tools of survey research are needed to determine how much public awareness there is about a new product or service and what people remember about it.

Tips for Success   A Major Goal of Campaigns: Create Awareness

What factors are important in judging the effectiveness of a public relations program? A survey of corporate communicators and marketers conducted by CDB Research & Consulting and Thomas L. Harris & Associates found that 99 percent of the respondents rated "increase in awareness" as the most important factor. Other factors included the following:

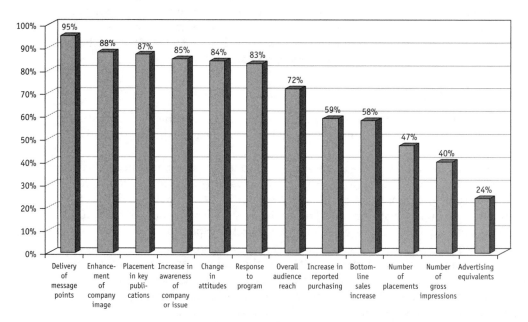

Such research, for example, found that Apple achieved a phenomenal 99 percent public awareness about its new iPhone before it was even available for purchase.

A good case study of measuring audience awareness is a public relations program conducted by Washington Mutual, a Seattle-based financial services institution. It had become one of the largest banks in California through acquisitions, but was entering the market with virtually no name recognition. It hired Rogers & Associates to conduct a program using the introduction of the newly designed $20 bill as the centerpiece. The idea was to give 20 consumers in seven major markets a chance to enter a wind cube filled with the new $20 bills and give them 20 seconds to grab as many of the swirling bills as they could.

Shortly after this event, a survey was conducted that showed that 80 percent of consumers surveyed in new markets were familiar with the Washington Mutual name. This percentage was up from virtually zero name recognition a month before the promotional event.

Another way of measuring audience awareness and comprehension is the day-after recall. Under this method, participants are asked to view a specific television program or read a particular news story and are then interviewed to learn what messages they remembered.

Ketchum, on behalf of the California Prune Board, used this technique to determine if a 15-city media tour was conveying the key message that prunes are a high-fiber food source. Forty women in Detroit were asked to watch a program on which a prune board spokesperson would appear. The next day, they were asked what they remembered about the program. Ninety-three percent remembered the spokesperson and 65 percent, on an unaided basis, named prunes as a source of high fiber.

Measurement of Audience Attitudes

Closely related to audience awareness and understanding of a message is whether the audience actually changes its attitudes and opinions about the product, service, or idea.

One way to measure changes in attitude is to sample the opinions of the target audience before and after the campaign. This means conducting **benchmark studies**—studies that graphically show percentage differences in attitudes as a result of increased information and persuasion. Of course, a number of possible intervening variables may also account for changes in attitudes, but a statistical analysis of variance can help pinpoint to what degree the attitude change is attributable to your efforts.

Sears, for example, used a benchmark study to prove that its efforts at getting a positive story about the company on *The Oprah Winfrey Show* actually increased sales and influenced consumer attitudes. With the help of Delahaye/Medialink, Sears gauged the attitudes of consumers before and after they saw Oprah Winfrey announce the retailer's donation of $20,000 worth of Christmas gifts to families in need.

Following the show, according to a monograph published by Lawrence Ragan Communications, "a measurement survey showed a fivefold increase in perceptions that Sears does good things for the community and the environment. The respondents who said they agreed with the statement, 'Sears is a quality company' increased from 58 to 65 percent." In addition, consumers expressing intent to shop at Sears increased from

The capability to comprehensively monitor global media coverage is a strategy large companies need to protect reputation and shareholder value. " Ad copy from Factiva (Dow Jones & Reuters), a media monitoring company

59 to 70 percent, and estimated spending levels rose 39 percent per shopper, or about $13 million in incremental sales.

Such companies as ExxonMobil, General Electric, and Wal-Mart regularly use benchmark surveys to measure their reputation on a continuing basis. Surveys showed, for example, that Microsoft's corporate reputation dropped after the U.S. Justice Department filed an antitrust suit against the company. As a result, Microsoft considerably beefed up its public relations efforts and Bill Gates announced the formation of the Gates Foundation, now the largest foundation in the world. Benchmarking showed that the image of Microsoft improved among the public despite the antitrust case against it.

Benchmark surveys are only one way to measure attitudes and opinions. You can also do evaluations on a less sophisticated level by keeping a record of telephone calls and emails received from customers. This is very important in the area of consumer affairs. If a pattern can be ascertained, it often tells the company that a particular product or service is generating many questions and complaints. Armed with such knowledge, the organization can take steps to solve the problem and maintain customer loyalty.

Measurement of Audience Action

The ultimate objective of any public relations effort, as has been pointed out, is to accomplish organizational objectives. David Dozier of San Diego State University says it succinctly: "The outcome of a successful public relations program is not a hefty stack of news stories.... Communication is important only in the effects it achieves among publics."

In other words, you should never say that the objective is to generate publicity. This is simply a tactic to achieve a specific outcome. Greenpeace's objective, for example, is not to get publicity, but to motivate the public to (1) become aware of environmental problems, (2) understand the consequences of not doing anything about them, (3) form attitudes and opinions favorable to conservation, and (4) take some action such as writing elected officials or even sending a donation to Greenpeace.

Changing audience behavior or motivating them to purchase a product or service is difficult to accomplish through public relations efforts, because people are complex and make decisions on the basis of many factors. At the same time, however, audience action is relatively easy to measure. All you have to do is look at sales figures or increase in market share.

A campaign that measured audience action was one for Hungry Jack instant potatoes, pancake mixes, and syrups. The objective of the public relations firm, Carmichael Lynch Spong, was to increase the brand equity of Hungry Jack by sponsoring a national contest, "Who Is Your Hungry Jack?" to find hardworking, dependable, and adventurous "Hungry Jacks."

The program, mostly through radio promotions, had a goal of 10,000 entries and received 22,000 entries. In addition, the contest promotion helped increase market share between 10 and 20 points in targeted markets. Following the campaign launch, there was a 23 percent sales increase in instant potatoes and a 9 percent sales increase for pancake mixes.

The ballot box also can provide convincing proof. Beaufort County in South Carolina had a bond referendum providing for a 1 percent sales tax to raise $40 million over 2 years to improve a local highway. There was strong opposition to the sales tax, so the local citizens' committee supporting the measure hired a public relations firm to conduct a campaign to persuade the voters. The theme "Vote Yes, Highway 170, the Wait Is Killing Us," was used and a series of activities was organized. This included forming a grassroots coalition with speaker events and letter writing, recruiting third-party endorsements, and getting media support. The result: The bond issue passed with 58 percent of the vote.

Evaluation of Newsletters and Brochures

If you are an editor of a newsletter or an employee magazine, it is wise to evaluate its readership on an annual basis. This will help you ascertain reader perceptions of layout and design, the balance of stories, kinds of stories that have high reader interest, additional topics that could be covered, the publication's credibility, and whether the publication is actually meeting organizational objectives.

Systematic evaluation, it should be emphasized, is not based on whether all the copies are distributed or picked up. This is much like saying that the news release was published in the newspaper. Neither observation tells you anything about what the audience actually read, retained, or acted on. If all newsletters or printed materials disappear from the racks in a few days, it may simply mean that the janitorial staff is efficient.

The following discussion focuses on periodical publications, but the same methods can be used to evaluate leaflets, booklets, and brochures distributed to external publics. Informal questioning of readers, monitoring of email, and requests for more information can all show whether the material is being read or needs improvement.

There are a number of ways in which a newsletter, newspaper, or magazine can be audited. These include content analysis, readership interest surveys, readership recall of articles actually read, application of readability formulas, and use of advisory boards or focus interview groups.

Content Analysis

Select a representative sample of past issues and categorize the stories under general headings. You may wish to cover such subjects as management announcements, new product developments, new personnel and retirements, employee hobbies and interests, corporate finances, news of departments and divisions, and job-related information.

A systematic analysis will quickly tell you if you are devoting too much space, perhaps unintentionally, to management or even to news of a particular division at the expense of other operations. For example, you may think that you have a lot of articles about employee personnel policies and job advancement opportunities, only to find, on analysis, that less than 10 percent of the publication is devoted to such information.

By analyzing organizational objectives, doing a content analysis, and surveying reader interests, you may come to the conclusion that the publication could be improved.

Readership Surveys

The purpose of readership surveys is to obtain employee feedback on the types of stories they read and what they think of the publication. Such surveys can be done online, but the wisdom of doing so depends on the organization and whether its employees have regular access to the Web.

These are relatively simple surveys that can be posted for employees on an organization's intranet, or to a wider audience using a Facebook page or a full-service Web survey company. A cheaper approach is to use freeonlinesurvey.com. You can provide a list of topics or statements and have employees mark each one as "very important," "somewhat important," or "not important." Another way is to have them select numbers 1 through 5 to show the degree of agreement with a statement.

A readership interest survey becomes even more valuable if you can compare it to a content analysis of your publication. Substantial differences are a signal to change the editorial content of your publication.

Article Recall

The best kind of readership survey is done when you or other interviewers sit down with a sampling of employees to find out what they have actually read in the latest issue of the publication.

Employees are shown the publication page by page and asked to indicate the articles they have read. As a check on the tendency for employees to tell you that they have read the publication from cover to cover (often called a "courtesy bias"), you also ask them how much of the article they read and what the article was about. The resulting marked copies of the publication are then content-analyzed to determine what kinds of articles have the most readership.

The method just described is much more accurate than a questionnaire asking employees to tell you how much of the publication they read. You do not get accurate data when you ask questions such as "What percentage of the newsletter do you read? All of it? Most of it? Some of it?" In this case, employees know that the company expects them to read the publication, so you get a preponderance of answers at the high end of the scale. Very few people will want to admit that they don't read it at all.

Advisory Boards and Focus Groups

Periodic feedback and evaluation can be provided by organizing an employee advisory board that meets several times a year to discuss the direction and content of your publication. Between meetings, members of the advisory board would also be able to relay employee comments and concerns to the editor. This is a useful technique in that it expands the editor's network of feedback and solicits comments that employees may be hesitant to offer the editor face to face.

A variation of the advisory board is to periodically organize several focus groups where a diverse group of employees talk about what kinds of information and stories would help them do their jobs more effectively. The purpose is to share information, generate new ideas, and work to make the publication more valuable as an instrument for obtaining organizational objectives.

Writing a Measurement Report

When you have finished evaluating a campaign, you must report the results to management. In some cases, it may be necessary to report on individual events or activities immediately after they have occurred. At other times, an annual evaluation report is done at the time next year's budget is being reviewed. Whatever the case, it's your opportunity to convince management that what you have done is worthwhile and your forthcoming activities deserve funding.

To prepare the report, you should refer to the original plan and state what you accomplished under each heading. Answer the following questions:

» **Situation.** Was the situation properly appraised? While the program was under way, did you learn anything that forced changes? What happened, and what did you do?

» **Audience.** Was it properly identified? How effectively did you reach the audience in terms of numbers, response, and feedback?

» **Objectives.** Did you achieve what you planned to achieve? Provide figures. You should have set numerical goals; now tell how well you did in reaching them.

» **Strategy.** Did it work? Did you have to modify it? Should it be continued or changed?

» **Tactics.** Did all the tools accomplish what they were supposed to accomplish? Were changes made? Why? Here again you can give numbers: news items published, feature stories published, printed items distributed, response of readers or viewers, TV and radio appearances, and so on.

» **Timing.** Was everything done at the right time? Should changes be made next year?

» **Costs.** Did you stay within the budget? If not, why not? This is the point at which you set the stage for the next budget and perhaps explain why more money would have permitted greater accomplishments.

Summary

The Importance of Measurement

» Measurement is absolutely essential. You must tell what was done, how well it was done, and what good it did.

» Results should be quantified instead of making broad statements.

Program Objectives

» Evaluation and measurement start with having a set of program objectives that are realistic, credible, and measurable.

» Public relations staff and the client or employer should mutually agree on objectives and how they will be measured at the end of the program.

Measurement of Production/Distribution

» Counting the number and distribution of news releases and features puts an emphasis on quantity instead of quality.

Measurement of Message Exposure

» The most common form of measurement in public relations is the compilation of media mentions, or what is called "clippings." It is an indication that an audience was exposed to the message.

» Monitoring services can be hired to monitor print, broadcast, and online mentions of your client or employer's name, products, and services.

» Today's software can give metrics such as message reach, tone of coverage, and how many times a key message is mentioned.

» Impressions are the total circulation of a publication or the audience of a broadcast outlet. They do not tell you how many people actually read or heard your story.

» Advertising equivalency, the idea of converting publicity in the news columns to comparative advertising rates, is highly suspect as a legitimate form of measurement.

» It is important to monitor the Internet to find out what bloggers, chat groups, and social networks are saying about your organization, products, and services.

» The metrics of measuring the effects and impact of social media on brands and organizations are still evolving. It's important, however, to consider participation and engagement as criteria.

» Social networking sites such as FaceBook and YouTube are now providing statistics about the gender, age group, geographic location, and other demographics of individuals who sign up as "friends" of a company or a brand.

» Requests for brochures and calls to 800 numbers give you an indication of people's exposure to a message.

» Cost per person is a way to analyze the cost of reaching your audience.

» Attendance at an event is a form of measurement because it shows audience exposure to the message. Through surveys at a meeting, you can also ascertain attitudes and opinions about the meeting.

Measurement of Audience Awareness

» Surveys are needed to tell whether an audience actually got the message and understood it.

Measurement of Audience Attitudes

» Benchmark surveys done before and after a campaign can help you to ascertain whether audience attitudes and opinions have changed.

Measurement of Audience Action

» Actual behavioral change, although difficult to accomplish, is relatively easy to measure. You can use sales figures, market share, or even voting results.

Evaluation of Newsletters and Brochures

» Newsletters and brochures should be evaluated on a frequent basis. Some techniques include content analysis, readership surveys, and article recall.

Writing a Measurement Report

» After a campaign is over, it is important to give a final evaluation report to the client or employer. This report becomes a record of accomplishment and a source of ideas for future programs.

Skill Building Activities

1. The chapter points out that objectives must be measurable. Assume you're writing a 12-month public relations plan for Purple Cow Ice Cream Company. Write objectives that could be used to measure (1) production/distribution, (2) audience

exposure, (3) audience awareness, (4) audience attitudes, and (5) audience behavior. In addition, write a brief description of what kinds of "results" you would place in each of these categories.

2. Compile the articles about your college or another organization of choice that appear in the local daily newspaper over a period of several weeks. Find out the cost of advertising per column inch and multiply it by the number of column inches found. Given the dollar value of the publicity, do you think the coverage was worth this amount? Why or why not?

3. Content analysis of media stories is important to document the nature of the coverage. Select a company or organization in your community and follow it in the local daily. Is the coverage neutral, positive, or negative? What is the subject of the stories? What percentage of the stories quote a company spokesperson? Do you think key messages from the organization were in the story? Write a brief analysis.

4. Many commercial firms monitor online content. Visit the website of such companies as Radian6, Collective Intellect, Lithium, and Attensity360 and write a comparative analysis about the kind of services they offer.

5. Use Google Alerts to track a national company or nonprofit over a period of several weeks. Perform a content analysis of what you receive. What aspects can be quantified? What aspects of the coverage are difficult to quantify, such as tone and level of conversation?

6. Perform a content analysis of a company or organizational newsletter. Place articles, including the number of column inches, into general categories. Given your findings, do you think the organization is accomplishing such objectives as (1) building employee loyalty and morale, (2) informing employees of opportunities for advancement, and (3) informing employees about policies and procedures?

Media Resources

Bartholomew, D. (2011, January 10). "Social Media Metrics: 5 Things to Learn in 2011." Retrieved from www.ragan.com.

Burke, J., Krall, J., Marklein, T., Paine, K., and Sugovic, M. (2010, March). "What Metrics Are Most Important When Measuring Social Media Efforts?" *PRWeek*, 51–52.

Daniels, C. (2010, September). Social Media Survey. *PRWeek*, 31-35.

Huyse, K. (2010, December 15). "How to Use Google Analytics URL Builder to Track Online Campaigns and Show Value." Retrieved from http://overtonecomm .blogspot.com.

Lasica, J., and Bale, K. (2011, January 13). "Top 20 Social Media Monitoring Vendors for Business." Retrieved from http://www .socialmedia.biz.

Manning, A., and Rockland, D. (2011, Spring). "Understanding the Barcelona Principles (Measurement)." *The Strategist*, 30–31.

Paine, K. (2011, February). "Stop Confusing ROI with Results and Measurement with Counting." *The Ragan Report*, 29.

Paine, Katie Delahaye. *Measuring Public Relationships: The Data-Driven Communicator's Guide to Success.* Berlin, NH: KD Paine & Partners, 2007.

Pestana, R. (2011, June 22). "Breaking Down Barriers to Measurement." Retrieved from www.prweekus.com.

Stacks, D., and Michaelson, D. (2010) *A Practitioner's Guide to Public Relations Research, Measurement, and Evaluation.* Barnes & Noble Nook.

Wright, A. (2010, August 24). "Mining the Web for Feelings, Not Facts." *New York Times*, B1, 7.

Glossary

Actuality A recorded statement by an identified person used in a radio newscast. See *Soundbite*.

Advertising value equivalency (AVE) Converting news articles to how much it would cost to advertise in the same space.

App (application) Commonly used term for an application on a mobile-enabled device.

Application story In feature writing, a story that tells how to use a new product or how to use a familiar product in a new way. Similar to a *case study*.

Audio news release (ANR) News release distributed to radio stations via CD, telephone, or website.

Backgrounder A compilation of information about an organization, a problem, a situation, an event, or a major development. It is given to media to provide a factual basis for news to be published or broadcast.

Benchmark studies Surveys of public attitudes and opinions before and after a public relations campaign.

Blog A website maintained by an individual to post comments, link to other sites, and engage in dialogue with readers.

Boilerplate Standard news release copy, usually in paragraph form, that provides basic information about a company, including stock symbols and URLs.

Booker The contact person for a broadcast talk show who is responsible for arranging guests.

Brainstorming Sessions designed to generate creative ideas in which the participants are encouraged to express any idea that comes to mind.

Branding The use of symbols to market organizations or products.

B-roll Only the video portion of a tape, without an announcer. It may include additional soundbites that broadcast editors may include in a newscast.

Camera-ready News releases and features already formatted in column format. Editors insert the material into the layout and prepare the page for offset printing. Camera-ready copy also is called a *repro proof*.

Caption The brief text under a photo that informs the reader about the picture and its source.

Case study In feature writing, a story that demonstrates the value of a product or service by detailing how it works and by providing specific examples that are often supported with statistics or customer testimonials.

Channeling The use of a group's attitudes and values in order to create a meaningful message.

Clip art Line art and other graphic designs that can be used in public relations materials. Clip art is available on CD and online.

Corporate profile(s) A fact sheet that focuses exclusively on an organization's identity, particularly its nature and objectives, main business activity, size, market position, revenues, products, and key executives.

Cropping The editing of photographs by cutting off portions of the original.

Desktop tour A series of meetings at the desks of editors and reporters at various media outlets for the purpose of building a relationship.

513

Earned media Refers to story placements in the media that public relations sources "earned" because they were newsworthy. The contrast is "paid media," which is advertising.

Editorial calendar A listing of topics and special issues that a periodical will feature throughout the year.

Email Electronic mail. Personal messages to individual receivers transmitted on the Internet.

Evergreen A news release or feature that has no particular time element. The subject matter can be used by media outlets at almost any time.

E-zines Electronic newsletters distributed via the Internet or organizational intranets. Sometimes called *E-pubs*.

Fact sheet A brief outline of who, what, when, where, why, and how. Sent to journalists so they have a quick review of basic information.

Fair comment privilege A legal concept derived from the First Amendment right to freedom of speech that allows for the public airing of opinion. To protect against libel, however, experts suggest that (1) opinion statements be accompanied by the facts on which the opinions are based; (2) opinion statements be clearly labeled as such; and (3) the context of the language surrounding the expressions of opinion be reviewed for possible libel implications.

Fam trip Familiarization trip. Refers to journalists who go on a trip at the invitation of an organization to become acquainted with a situation, product, or service.

FAQs (frequently asked questions) A variation on the traditional fact sheet in which information is presented in a question-and-answer format. Often used on the Internet.

Feature story A story, generally longer than a news release, that focuses on a human interest or provides background about a service or product in an entertaining way.

Federal Trade Commission (FTC) A federal regulatory agency that scrutinizes advertising and publicity products for fairness and accuracy.

Food and Drug Administration (FDA) A federal regulatory agency that oversees the advertising and promotion of prescription drugs, over-the-counter medicines, and cosmetics.

Historical piece In feature writing, a story that stresses the continuity between past and present to garner reader interest.

Hits A term used in relationship to the number of people that click on a particular page on the World Wide Web.

Hometowners Stories custom-tailored to a particular newspaper or broadcast station by focusing on the local angle in the first paragraph of the news release.

Hype Exaggerated publicity about a product, service, or celebrity. Often characterized by flowery adjectives and inflated claims.

Implied consent The unwritten and unstated consent employees give their employers to use their photographs in such items as the employee newsmagazine and newsletters. Implied consent does not extend to advertising or promotion, which requires *written* consent.

Impressions Relates to the circulation of a publication or the audience size of a particular radio or television program. If a story or ad appears in a newspaper with 100,000 circulation, this constitutes 100,000 impressions.

Infographics Computer-generated artwork used to display statistics in the form of tables and charts.

Intranet A private network within an organization for the exclusive use of employees. Intranets are based on the same principles as the Internet.

IT An acronym for *information technology*, which encompasses hardware, software, and how computer systems operate.

JPEG An acronym for Joint Photographic Experts Group, which deals with a common method to compress photos and send them via the Internet.

Junket A common term for when journalists go on a trip to visit a site such as a manufacturing facility to see a new product, or to attend an out-of-town promotion for a new product or service

Lead The first sentence or paragraph of a news release or feature story.

Letter to the editor (LTE) A concise letter intended to rebut an editorial, clarify information mentioned in a news story or column, or add information that might not have been included in an original story.

Listserv An Internet site that automatically emails messages to individuals who subscribe to the service.

Magapaper An organizational publication that has a newspaper-type layout but incorporates the design elements of a magazine.

Masthead The place on the layout of a newsletter, newspaper, or magazine where the name of the publication appears. This is usually at the top of the first page.

Media advisory A notification to assignment editors informing them of a newsworthy event that could lend itself to photo or video coverage. Also called *media alert*.

Media gatekeepers The people within media who decide what information is newsworthy and what is not. Factors that influence the final decisions of media gatekeepers include timeliness, prominence, proximity, significance, unusualness, human interest, conflict, and newness.

Media kit A packet of materials distributed by mail, CD, or online to media outlets that contains news releases, photos, backgrounders, and fact sheets about a new product or service.

Misappropriation of personality The use of a person's image, particularly that of a popular personality, without permission.

Mission statement A brief statement of purpose for a newsletter or magazine.

Mug shot A slang term for a head-and-shoulders photo of an individual.

News release A news story prepared by an organization and sent to media outlets. Also called a *press release*.

Op-ed Opposite the editorial page. A page that contains the views and opinions of individuals who are not on the staff of the newspaper.

Page impression The number of times a webpage is pulled up by individuals. The term is used in relation to tracking "traffic" on the Internet.

Pay for play Payment in the form of providing a media outlet cash, advertising placements, or products in exchange for news coverage.

Personality profile In feature writing, a story that focuses on a person of public interest to stimulate reader awareness of that person and/or the organization, product, or service the person represents.

Photo news release (PNR) A photograph with a long caption beneath it that tells an entire story.

Pica A printer's term for measuring the length of typeset lines. There are 6 picas to the inch.

Pitch Jargon for making an appeal to an editor or journalist to do a story on your product or service.

Plagiarism A form of theft in which an author appropriates the writing or ideas of another author and claims them as his or her own.

Plugs Refers to mentions of organizations, products, and services in movies and broadcast entertainment shows.

Podcast An audio or video program that can be downloaded from the Internet via an iPod, MP3 player, or RSS feed.

Press kit See *Media kit*.

Press release See *News release*.

Product tie-in The appearance of a branded product or service in a movie or TV series as part of a contracted agreement between the organization and the producers. Such a contract may call for the organization to actively promote the movie or TV series in its product advertising.

PSA (public service announcement) These short messages, usually by a nonprofit agency or governmental agency, are used on radio and television stations as a public service at no charge.

Pseudoevent A term coined by historian Daniel Boorstin to describe events and situations staged primarily for the sake of generating press coverage and media interest.

Public service announcement See *PSA*.

Publics The potential or actual audiences for any given public relations message. Often defined by income, age, gender, race, geography, or psychographic characteristics.

R&D Acronym for Research and Development.

Radio media tour (RMT) A spokesperson conducting a series of interviews with various broadcast outlets from a central location.

Research study In feature writing, a story that uses information derived from surveys, polls, or scientific studies to garner reader interest and to demonstrate the value of a product or service.

Retouching The alteration of a photograph by the traditional means of airbrushing or, more frequently now, by the electronic manipulation of a digital image.

Return on investment (ROI) A comparison of total costs to reach an audience divided by the amount of business that is generated.

RFP (request for proposal) Organizations seeking public relations assistance often issue an RFP requesting public relations firms to prepare a proposal outlining their recommendations and capabilities.

RSS Acronym for *real simple syndication*. Materials are aggregated according to subscriber interests and sent directly to their computers.

Saddle-stitched Refers to the binding of a magazine, where the pages are stapled together at the centerfold.

Satellite media tour See *SMT*.

Search engines Software programs that allow users to search for topically identified resources and information on the Internet. Popular examples include Google, Yahoo!, and Bing.

Securities and Exchange Commission (SEC) A federal regulatory agency that requires that any information affecting the value of a security be made known to the owners and to the SEC.

(SEO) search engine optimization Refers to the selection of keywords that search engines such as Google would index in terms of a particular topic.

Service journalism The practice of publishing "news you can use," for example, stories featuring consumer tips, professional advice, etc.

SMT (satellite media tour) A media event that involves arranging for news anchors around the country to interview a spokesperson in a television studio via satellite.

Snail mail First-class mail delivered by the U.S. Postal Service.

Social media Online networks that allow people to share opinions and perspectives with each other.

Soundbite A statement or quote from an individual, which is inserted into audio and video news releases.

Speaker's bureau An organization's effort to provide spokespersons to civic clubs and other organizations at no cost. Commercial speaker's bureaus serve as agents to book celebrity speakers who charge for an appearance.

Spokesperson A term commonly used in the media to describe a public relations person who provides information or a quote in a news article.

Stakeholders The groups impacted by an organization's decisions. These potentially include employees, consumers, neighbors, suppliers, environmental groups, and investors.

Stock footage Standard video shots of an organization's production line, headquarters, and activities that a television station can store until the company is in the news.

Storyboard A written outline of an audio or video news release. For video, a description of scenes, plus dialogue, is prepared.

Talking head Refers to a television broadcast or a video news release in which the screen is dominated by a person who is talking.

Template The standardized format of a newsletter or magazine, so each issue has the same look and feel.

Video news release (VNR) A short publicity piece formatted for immediate use by a television station.

Webcasting The delivery of a broadcast (live or delayed) over the Internet. When it is done in real time, it is also called *streaming*.

White paper An organization's analysis of a particular issue or the potential of a market for a specific product or service. Other terms used are *briefing paper* and *position statement*.

Wiki An interactive website that allows multiple persons to access content, make changes, and edit each other's input.

Index

60 Minutes, 240
A4S Security, 228
AARP Magazine, 340
Abbott Labs, 234
ABI/Inform Complete, 16
Abundant Forests Alliance, 180
Academic Search Premier, 16
Academy Awards, 71, 84, 427
Academy of Country Music
    Awards, 194
Achievers, 35
Active audience, 40
Active verbs, 22
Actuality, 216
Ad agencies, working with, 436
Ad Council, 231
Adobe Creative Suite,
    206–207, 348
Advertising
    advantages and disadvantages
      of, 436–429
    audiences for, 427
    billboards, 436
    buttons and bumper stickers,
      437–438
    cost of, 427–428
    credibility, 428–429
    defined, 426
    impact of, 427
    influence of
    message of, 427
    posters, 438
    privacy issues in, 425
    promotional products, 439
    purposes of, 426
    sponsored books
    timing of, 427
    transit panels, 437
    on t-shirts, 438
    types of, 429–434
    of websites, 310, 428
Advertising Research
    Foundation, 191
Advertising value equivalency
    (AVE), 498–499
Advocacy and issue
    advertising, 433
Aglar, Dave, 324
Agnes, Brian, 266

Ahles, Catherine, 488
AIG, 95
Air New Zealand, 50, 503
Akron Children's Hospital 4
Alaska Division of Tourism, 175
Allen, Justin, 350
AlliedSignal, 69
Allure magazine, 50
Amato, Melanie, 66
Amazon.com, trademark
    issues, 288
AMD, 414
America's State Parks, 433
American Academy of
    Ophthalmology, 62
American Association for Public
    Opinion Research, 78
American Association of Clinical
    Endocrinologists, 503
American Association of
    Orthodontics, 62
American Association of People
    with Disabilities, 431
American Association of Retired
    People, 340
American Cancer Society, 50,
    480, 438
American Century
    Investments, 286
American College of
    Gastroenterologists, 62
American Dental Association, 50
American Fly Fishing Trade
    Association (AFFTA), 83
American Girl, 174
American Heart Association, 432
*American Heritage Dictionary
    of the English Language*, 7
American Idol, 241
American Kennel Club, 77
American Legion, 74
American Library Association
    (ALA) award, 466
American Medical Association, 67
American Petroleum Institute
    (API), 93
American Psychological
    Association (APA), 217
American Revolution, 45

American Society of
    Newspapers, 166
American Society for the
    Prevention of Cruelty to
    Animals (ASPCA), 48, 51
American Veterinary Medical
    Association, 222
American Water Works
    Company, 231
Ameritech, 62
Anheuser-Busch, 288
Anne Taylor Loft, 112
Announcements, in advertising,
    433–434
Annual reports, 364–369
    content and delivery, 368–369
    planning and writing, 367–368
Apple I work, 348
Apple iTunes Store, and podcasts,
    331, 333
Apple Pages, 348
Apple Computer, 6, 38, 68, 73, 95,
    101, 122, 464
    apps, 263
    product placement, 241
    trademark issues, 288
    website, 302
Application story, 170
Apps, 333
Arbitron ratings, 218
Aristotle 4, 32
Arizona Republic, 66
Arketi Group, 88, 93
Armstrong, Shannelle, 334
Arnold, Matthew, 412
Arth, Marvin, 124
Arthur W. Page Society, 54, 407
Associated Press (AP), 269
*Associated Press Stylebook and
    Briefings on Media Law*, 8
Atkinson, Claire, 463
Atlanta City Chamber of
    Commerce, 70
Audience analysis
    benchmark studies, 505
    for persuasive writing, 40–42
    See also Measurement
Audio news release, 216–218
    delivery, 217

format, 216
production, 217
use, 217–218
Australian Tourist
    Commission, 105
Authorship, 280
Autism Speaks, 432
Avon Walk for Breast Cancer, 463
Awards, 83–84

Backgrounders, 173
Bacon's Media Directories, 9
Bader TV News, 228
Baidu, 14
Baker, Sherry, 54
The Band Perry, 194
Bandwagon, 49
    propaganda technique, 52
Banfield Pet Hospital, 177
Bank of America, 130
Banquets
    costs, 449
    logistics and timing, 452–453
    tips, 450
    working with catering
        managers, 448
Bar chart, 205
Barrie, John, 282
Baskin-Robbins, 79–80
Bateman Case Study
    Competition, 437
Bath, Scott, 61
Baudisch, Paul, 310
Baum Folder, 360
Beaufort County, 507
Becca, 50
Belgrade (Serbia) Beer Fest, 390
Belongers, 35
Benchmark studies, 505
BenchPoint, 494
Benjamin Moore, 263
Bennett & Company, 88
Bennett, Christine, 354
Best Buy, 234
    trademark issues, 288
Bias, avoiding, 28–29
Bieber, Justin, 50
    use of Twitter, 327
Billington, James, 64
Bing, 14, 261, 309
Biz360, 499
Black PRWire, 260
Blogdex.media, 320
Blogger, tool, 315
Bloggers, working with, 93

Blogger.com, 320
Bloglines, 93
Blogpulse, 320, 501
Blogs, 314–320
    corporate blogs, 317–318
    employee blogs, 278, 318
    pitching to, 161
    third party blogs, 318–320
    tips for writing, 316
BMW, 427
    product placement, 241
Body
    of email, 378–379
    of a feature, 178–180
    of news release, 128–129
Boggs, Rich, 103
Boilerplate, 130
Bonner & Associates, 272
Bookers, 239
Booklets. See Brochures.
Boorstin, Daniel, 70
Borders, 73
Boston Beer Company, 173
Botsworth, Courtney, 488
Bowen, David, 312
BP, 112, 476
Bradshaw, Tim, 241
Bragg, Lynn, 311
Brainstorming, 72
Branding, 45
Brandon, Michael C., 345
Breast Cancer Awareness Week, 63
Briggs & Stratton, 77
Brochures
    cost of design of, 365
    format of, 359–360
    ink and color choice for,
        363–364
    layout for, 360–361
    paper choice for, 361–362
    planning for, 357–358
    printing of, 364
    research for, 359
    tips for putting together, 359
    typeface for, 362–362
    tips for design, 358
    writing for, 358–359
    See also Print Publications
Broder, Jocelyn, 247
Brodeur, 93
B-roll, 224, 227–229
Brookings Institute, 183
Brooks, Kelly, 152
Broward County Public
    Schools, 307

Brown, Melissa, 396
Brown, Adam, 93
Bruegger's Bagels, 63
Bulldog Reporter, 9, 10, 99
Bunching, 303
Burger King, 243
Burns, Heather, 350
Burrelles, 156
BurrellesLuce, 9, 252, 497, 499
    white paper, 386
Burson-Marsteller, 34–35, 63, 398
Business Wire, 117, 133, 137,
    178, 208, 252,260, 497
    news release of, 121
Butter, Bob, 365
Butterball Turkey, 62
Butzgy, Michael, 303

California Academy of Sciences,
    152–153
California Association of
    Winegrowers, 77
California Avocado
    Commission, 472
California Pharmacists
    Association (CPhA), 83
California Prune Board, 505
California Strawberry Advisory
    Board, 42
Camera-ready
    art, 265
    features, 167
Campbell Soup Company, 130
Canadian Tourism
    Commission, 310
Caplet, John, 434
Captions
    photo, 203–204
Card stacking, 53
CARE, 423
CARMA, 499
Carmichael Lynch Spong, 183
Carver, Benedict, 90
Case study technique, 47
Case study, 169–170
Cat in the Hat, 64
Catalysts, 38
Celebrity Access, 464
Celebrity Source, 464
Centers for Disease Control, 500
Chabria, Anita, 54, 74
Champagne Wine Information
    Bureau, 104
Champagnes Week, 104
Chan, Tracy, 501

Chanel No. 5, 50
Channel, of communication, 33
Channeling, 40
Charts, 205
Cheapflights.com, 76
Chemical Bank of New York, 277
Chevron, 35
Chevron, advertising, 430
Chiagouris, Larry, 76
Chik-fil-A, Facebook use, 322
Children's Defense Fund
    (CDF), 223
Chocolate Manufacturers
    Association (CMA), 311
Chopin, 282
Christie's, 236
Churnalism.org, 118
Cisco Systems, 173, 311
    employee blogs, 280, 318
    intranet, 356
    newsroom, 259
    trademark issues, 288
Cision, 156, 160, 213, 251, 497
    white paper, 386
CisionPoint PR, 9
CisionPoint, 251
Clinton Foundation, 434
Clip art, 206–207
Clorox, 71
CMI Event Planning and
    Fundraising, 451
Coca-Cola, 66, 433
    annual report, 367, 368
    CSR, 369
    letter to stockholders, 381
    online video, 246
    product placement, 241
    slogan of, 45
Cocktail parties, 453–454
Cody, Steve, 318
Cognitive dissonance theory,
    35–36
Cohen, Susan, L., 284
Collins, Thomas, 53
Comdex, 414
Communication
    theories of, 34–40
Communication Briefings, 10
Communication Briefings, 19
Communication World, 11
Community calendars, 243–344
Company profiles, 145
Computers
    choosing, 5–7
    components, 6–7

cost, 6
    importance of, 5
comScore Video Matrix, 322
Concise Oxford English Dictionary, 7
Conflict in news, 67
Conspiracy, 272
Consumer Electronics Show
    (CES), 442, 458
Contact information, in news
    release, 122–123
Contests, 74–75
Contract, with photographer, 201
Conventions
    administration, 456
    attendance, 456
    exhibits, 455
    facilities, 455
    location, 454
    program, 455
    recreation, 456
    timing, 454
Cook, Dan, 331
Copyright
    of art and photography, 201,
        203, 283
    defined, 280
    fair use versus infringement,
        282–283
    online material, 284
    tips for, 281, 281
    work for hire, 283–284
Copyright Clearing Center, 283
Copyright Office of the Library
    of Congress, 280
Corbis Corporation, 284
Corley, Carol Ann, 83
Corporate Communications
    International (CCI), 87
Corporate profiles. *See* company
    profiles
Corporate social responsibility
    (CSR), 369
Cosmopolitan magazine, 251
Cost per thousand (CPM), 503
Council of American Survey
    Research, 78
Courtesy bias, 508
Covenant House, 47
Coyne Public Relations, 326
Craolya, 150
Crisis communication
    media relations, 112–114
CRO, 83
Cropping, of photos, 202
Cunningham, Ward, 329

Cury, James, 68
cvent, 457
Cytryn v. Cook, 293

The Daily, 13
Daily Beast, 13
Dallas Museum of Art, 74
Danny Brown, 12
Darden, Michael, 61
Data Center of China Internet, 312
Databases
    electronic, 16–17
    for research, 18
Dateline, of news release, 124
Dean, Billy, 482
DeBeer's
    slogan of, 45
Deckers Outdoor Corporation,
    286
Deeter, Anne, 264
Defamation, 274
DeFleur, Melvin, 426
Del.icio.us, 137, 267
Delahaye/Medialink, 505
Delicious, 501
Dell, 204
    employee blogs, 318
    third party blogs, 320
DeLorme, Denise E., 89
Delta
    YouTube use, 325
Dennis, Everett, 426
Department of Child and
    Family Services of New
    Hampshire, 70
Derelian, Doris, 17
Desktop publishing, 348
Desktop tour, 103
Deutrom, Scott, 343
Diagrams, 206
Diffusion and adoption, 37–38
Digg, 124, 137, 257, 501
Digital press kit. *See also*
    Electronic press kit (EPK),
    151–153
Direct mail
    advantages and disadvantages
        of, 418–419
    audiences of, 418
    brochures in, 423, 424
    costs of, 419
    creating packages for, 419–423
    gifts in, 425
    information overload from, 419
    personalization of, 418–419

purposes of, 417–418
reply card in, 425
return envelope in, 425
tips on, 424
Direct mail letter
envelope for, 420
headline and lead paragraph of, 420–421
post script of, 423
tips for writing, 423
typeface and length, 421–423
Disney Parks, video, 247
Disney, podcasts, 331
District of Columbia Housing Authority, 77
Ditka, Mike, 61
Dollywood, 104
Domino's Pizza, 261, 476
Donahue, Phil, 237
Donatella Versace, 50
Donovan, Ryan, 208
Douglis, Phil, 195–196
Dow Chemicals, 73
Dow Jones Media Relations Manager, 10, 156, 252
Dow Jones Media Manager, 9
Dowler, Helen, 190
Downstyle, 351
Dozier, David, 506
Dr. Pepper/Snapple Group, 65
Drama, in persuasive writing, 47
Dratch, Rachel, 232
Dremel, 177
Due diligence, 273
Duncan, Arne, 64
Duracell, 62
Dutton Children's Books, 284
Dysart, Joe, 308–309

Early majority, 38
Early Show, 237
Earned media 2, 90
Eastwick, 330
Economist, 13
EdCals, 254
Edelman Trust Barometer, 24
Edelman Worldwide, 12
Edelman, 314
Edelman, Richard, 314
blog, 315
Edelstein, Jonathan, 294
Editorial board, meetings with, 107–108
reasons for, 107

tips for, 108
value of, 108
Editorial calendars, 156, 253–254
Editorial plans, 343
Edwards, Lauren, 130
Elasser, John, 278
Electronic Arts (EA), 152
Electronic press kit. See also Digital press kit, 151–153
Elements of Style, 7
Eli Lilly & Co., 295
E-mail (electronic mail)
body of, 378–379
closing, 379
content, 376–377
first sentence or paragraph, 378
news distribution, 255–257
purpose, 375
subject lines of, 377
salutations, 377–378
tips, 378
Email advisories, for VNRs, 228
Emotional Appeals, in persuasive writing, 51
Employee blogs, 278, 318
privacy issues of 278–280
Employee newsletters, privacy issues of, 276
Endorsements
celebrity, 43, 50
in persuasive writing, 50–51
Enlyten, 50
Enron Corporation, 273
Entrepreneur magazine, 287
Environmental Defense Action Fund, 423
Environmental Protection Agency (EPA), 232
ER, 242
ET, 241
Ethical considerations, in photo retouching, 202–203
Ethos, 32
Euro RSCG Worldwide PR, 76
European Measurement Summit, 494
Evaluation. See Measurement
Event or exhibit announcements, 143
Events
banquets, 449–453
characteristics of
cocktail parties, 453–454
conventions, 454–456
corporate sponsorships, 462

invitations, online, 457
open houses, 465–468
plant tours, 465–468
promotional, 461–465
receptions, 453–454
trade shows, 458–461
value of, 441
Evergreens, 266
Exclusives, offering, 111
Executive Flight Guide, 343
Executive quotes, tips for, 130
Exhibits
at conventions, 455
at tradeshows, 459
ExxonMobil, 52, 64, 506
e-zines, 352

Facebook Insights, 501
Facebook, 12, 112, 320–321
and employees, 279
infringement issues, 288
tips for creating, 323
Fact sheets
defined, 143
types and examples of, 143–146
Factiva, 16, 497, 499
Fair comment privilege, 274
Fair Disclosure Regulation (Reg FD), 293
Fam (familiarization) trips, 105
Family Features Editorial Syndicates, 265, 268
Family Features, 168
FarmVille, 325
Fax, for news distribution, 269
Fear arousal, 51
Fearn-Banks, Kathleen, 112
Feature Photo Service, 117, 192, 208, 268, 269
Feature placement firms, 265–268
Feature story
body, 178–180
contrasted with news releases, 165
defined, 165
examples of, 179, 181
headline of, 175–177
lead of, 127–128, 177–178
parts of, 175–180
photos and graphics in, 180
placement of, 182–183
planning of, 166–167
summary of, 180

Feature story (*Continued*)
  tips for writing, 176
  types of, 169–175
  value of 165–166
  writing and releasing, 167–168
Feder, Barnaby, 207
Federal Communication
    Commission (FCC), 294
Federal Express, website, 302
Federal Trade Commission (FTC),
    290–292
FedEx, annual report, 366
Fedler, Fred, 89
Feeding America, 431
Ferguson, Fred, 176
Fernandez, Lauren, 95
Festinger, Leon, 35
Fidelzeid, Gideon, 403
Field Museum of Chicago,
    community calendar
    announcements, 244
  fact sheet, 143
  media kit, 10
Film features, 244–245
Financial Times, 13
Fireman's Fund Insurance
    Company, 244
First Act, 61
First Amendment, 274
Fisher Nuts, 175
Fixed, 280
Flash, 405
Fleishman-Hillard, 35, 43, 311
Flickr, 325–326
Food and Drug Administration
    (FDA) 294–295
Food Fete blog, 253
Food, Drug, and Cosmetic Act, 294
Forbes, Charlotte, 342
Ford, use of audio news
    release, 217
Ford & Harrison, 317
Ford Motor Co., 74, 105
Forever 21, 273
Formula PR, 155
Foundation Center, 385
Frame strategist, 37
Framing, 36–37
Franklin, Benjamin, 417
Frequency, 485
Friedman, Marsha, 239
Friedman, Mitchell, 399
Frito-Lay, 42, 495
Fudin, Sarah, 316
Fujitsu, 330

Gallup Applied Science, 203
Gandy, O. H., 88
Gantt chart, 484–485
Garcia, Mario, 363
Gates Foundation, 506
Gebbie Press All-In-One Media
    Contacts Directory, 9
Geddie, Tom, 345
Gelles, David, 242
General Electric, 506
General Mills, 93
General Motors (GM)
    annual reports, 367–369
    Fastlane Blog, 317
    wiki use, 330
Genkin, Larry, 317
Gerstner, John, 259
Get It Printed, 357
Gillette, 49, 82
Gilman Ciocia, 60
Gimbel, Stacy, 437
Glaxo Institute for Digestive
    Health, 295
Glenfiddich, 442
Glittering generalities, 53
Global Green, 62
Global Positioning System
    (GPS), 173
Gobbledygook, 23–34
Goggle News, 124
Gold's Gym, 170
Goldberg, Betsy, 100
Goldsborough, Julie Story, 17
Goldstein, Andrew, 292
Good Morning America, 237
Goodman, Wanda, 329
Goodwin, Peter, 76
Google Adwords, 136
Google Alerts, 93, 501
Google Analytics, 501
Google Blog Search, 93
Google Blogger, 316
Google External Keyword, 136
Google Images, 207, 350
Google Presentations, 405
Google Search, 320
Google Trends, 136
Google, 14, 260, 309
    employee blogs, 278
    on Twitter, 327
Gorman-Rupp, 421
Gossett, Steven, 175
Grabowski, Gene, 291
Graham, Andrea, 106
Graphs, 205

Grates, Gary, 341
Great Data Now, 177
Great Date, 169
Greenpeace, 80–81, 273
Grey's Anatomy, 242
Grocery Manufacturers of
    America (GMA), 396
Gross impressions, 497
Group meetings
    facilities, 445
    greetings for, 447
    invitation, 445–446
    location, 443
    meals, 448
    name tags, 447
    programs, 447
    registration for, 447
    seating, 443
    speakers for, 447
Groupon, 78
Grove, Teri, 107
Grunig, James, 40
Guide Dog News, 354
Guide Dogs for the Blind, 344, 355
Guinness Book of World
    Records, 79
Gunderson, Amy, 159

H.J. Heinz Company, 61
Hacker, Diana, 7
Haddix, Carol, 167
Haiken, Beth, 368
Hair Battle Spectacular, 80
Hall, Julie, 80
Hallahan, Kirk, 37
Hamm, Mia, 459
Hammons, Rich, 61
Hankiewicz, Kamila, 321, 323
Hanson, Arik, 118
HAPPO, 12
Harden & Partners, 47
Harley-Davidson, 368
    online video, 245
*Harry Potter and the Deathly
    Hallows*, 73
Harry Walker Agency, 449
Hartsook, Christa, 358
Hattersley, Michael, 376
Hauss, Deborah S., 204
Hawaii Tourism Board, 234
Hawking, Stephen, 261
Haywood, Dave, 84
Headline
    of feature, 177–175
    of news release, 122–124

Heath, Robert, 4, 53, 55
Heckel Consumer Adhesives, 66
Heinrich, Aaron, 93
Helitzer, Melvin, 159
Help a Reporter Out (HARO),
    156, 157, 254
Henry, Reg, 63
Herradura, 155
Herrington, Jeff, 304
Hersey Company, 174
Hersey, 74
Hersey's Reese's Pieces, product
    placement, 241
Hettinger, Mary, 341
Hewlett-Packard (HP), 130, 191,
    168, 169, 208, 311
    electronic media kits,
        152–153
    fact sheet, 145
    online news room, 258, 259
Hicks, Nancy, 77
Hidden Valley Ranch, 79
    audio news release, 216–217
    media alert, 148
Hierarchy of needs, 38–40
Higbee, Ann, 108
High Museum of Art, 434
Hispanic PRWire, 260
Historical piece, 174–175
The History Channel, 245
History San Jose (CA), 446
Hit, of a website, 310, 500
Hoefler, Jonathan, 361
Hoffman agency, 228
Hoffman, Barbara, 239
Hollywood Chamber of
    Commerce, 84
Hollywood Walk of Fame, 84
Holtz, Shel, 264, 304, 328, 405
Home Depot, 62
Homeownership Preservation
    Foundation, 218
Hometowners, 64
Homewood Suites, 170
Honeywell Corporation, 47
Hoover Institution, 183
Hosted bar, 453
Houghton, Richard, 502
Hovland, Carl, 52
HP Labs, 76
Huff, Diana, 36
Huffington Post, 13
    pitch, 155
Huffy Sports Company, 177
Human interest stories, 66–67

Human Rights Watch,
    direct mail, 421
Humanizing the issue, 47
Hungry Jack, 506
Hunt, Todd, 426
Hype, avoiding, 28
Hyperlinks, 308
Hyundai, video, 247

IBM, 197, 199
    employee blog guidelines, 319
    newsroom, 259
    website, 302
ICI Pharmaceuticals, 63
Illustrator, 405
Image building, 429
Imagery, 22–23
IMG, 93
Imperial Stars, 81
Implied consent, 276
Impressions, 497
Influentials, 38
Infographics, 205
Informal lead, 127
Innovators, 38
Inside Children 4
Intel, 75, 195, 197, 204, 495
    online video, 245
    website, 306
Inter Science Talent Search, 75
International Advertising
    Festival, 79
International Association of
    Business Communication
    (IABC), 11, 344
International Civil Rights Center &
    Museum, 72
International Music Products
    Association, 61
International Olympic Committee
    (IOC), 289
International Trademark
    Association, 287
Internet
    prevalence of, 299–300
    See also World Wide Web
Interviews, press
    preparing for, 94
    tips, 96–98
Into the Fire, 244
Intranets, 354–356
Intuit, 327
Invasion of privacy
    employee blogs, 278–280
    employee newsletters, 276

media inquiries about
    employees, 277–278
photo releases, 276–277
product publicity and
    advertizing, 277
Inverted pyramid structure,
    128–129
Investor and financial relations
    advertising, 429–431
iPad 2, 6, 39, 68, 333
iPhone, 68
IPRA, 54
Iron Man 2, 241
Isserman, Maurice, 282
Issue placement, 242–243
Issues and Trends, 10
iStockphoto, 350

J. Walter Thompson, 274
Jack O'Dwyer's Newsletter, 10
Jackson, Amy, 311
Jacobs, Charlene, 410
James Bond films, 241
Jargon, 23–24
JetBlue, 112
Jewett, Sally, 234
Jobs, Steve, 42, 71, 95, 101
Joe Boxer Corporations, 105
Johnson & Johnson, annual
    report, 365, 369
Jones, Brenda, 393
Journal of Public Relations
    Research, 11
Journalism, correcting errors
    in, 110
Journalists, working with,
    92–93
Jowett, Garth, S., 52
Junk mail. See Direct mail
Junkets, 105–107
    ethical issues of, 106–107

Kalehoff, Max, 381
Kalm, Nick, 159
Kansas City Health Department,
    43
Kansas Wheat Commission, 439
Katz, Darren, 320
Kauffmann, Peter E., 95
Kawamoto, Kevin, 301
Keller, Scott, 330
Kelley, Charles, 84
Kendig, Karen, 449
Kennedy, Mickie, 92
Kenneth Cole, 61

Ketchum, 61, 71, 245, 486, 495, 505
Key selling proposition, 482
Kidman, Nicole, 50
Kimberly-Clark, 49, 61, 74
King, Ben, 317
Kintzler, Jason, 264
Kirkpoatrick, Ron, 412
Klepper, Michael, 158
Knightley, Keira, 43
Knoth, Audrey, 63
Koch, Jim, 173
Kodak, 43
Kohm, James, 291
Konami Digital, 155
Korbel Champagne Cellars, 148, 497
Kraft Foods, 79
Kryptonite Company 319

L.L. Bean, website, 302
Lady Antebellum, 84
Lady Gaga, 264, 325, 459
    use of Twitter, 327
Laggards, 38
Lake, Matt, 91
Lancaster, Hal, 71
Lanham Act, 273, 290
*Late Show with
    David Letterman*, 83
Law & Order, 242
Lawrence Ragan
    Communication, 505
Lawry Seasoned Salt, 42
Lazarsfeld, Robert, 335
Lead paragraph
    errors in, 124–126
    of feature, 177–178
    guidelines for, 128
    of news release, 124–128
    types of, 127–128
Lead sentence, of email, 378
Leaflets. *See* Brochures
Lee, Ivy, 117
Legacy Learning
    Systems, 272
Legal issues
    avoiding, 275
    conspiracy, 272
    copyright, 280–284
    defamation, 274
    examples of, 272–273
    invasion of privacy, 276–280
    libel, 274
    regulatory agencies, 290–295

trademark infringement, 284–290
    working with lawyers, 295–296
Lennon, John, 290
Leno, Jay, 155
Lerch, Marie L., 394
Letter of agreement,
    with photographer, 201
Letterhead, of news release,
    121–122
Letters
    content, 382–383
    format, 383
    purpose, 381
    tips, 382
    types, 381
Letters to the editor (LTEs),
    185–187
Levy, Ron, 100
Lexis/Nexis, 16
Libel, 274
Line drawings, 206–207
LinkedIn, 12
Lipinski, Lynn, 155–156
Lipton, Laura, 451
Lissauer, Michael, 261, 336
List Services Corp., 418
Listservs, 12
Litman, Gregg, 118
Logos, 32
Los Angeles Fire Department, 327
Lowe's, 175
Lunch dates, with journalists,
    111–112

M&M Candies, product
    placement, 241
MacDonald, Gordon, 306
MacWrite, 345
Madonna, 50
Magapaper, 346
Magazine shows, 239–240
Magazines
    format, 346–347
    placement of feature in,
    182–183
    See also Print Publications
Mail, for news distribution, 269
Majors, Randall, 384
Maney, Kevin, 405
Marchini, Fredrick, 309
Margaritis, Bill, 491
Marine Mammal Center, 51, 422
MarketingProfs, 12
Marketwire, 93, 137–138, 208, 260

Markman, Steve, 410–411
Marriott Corporation, 171
Martin, Dick, 92
Martin, Jennifar
Martinez, Pedro, 82
Martinson, David, 54
Maslow, Abraham H., 38
Master Card
    slogan of, 45
Masthead, 347
Mat releases, 265
Mateas, Margo, 159
Mattel, 35, 75, 113
McCafferty Interests, 183
McCaffrey, Lindsey, 27
McCormick & Company, 135,
    263, 476
    fact sheet, 147
    news release, 125, 134
McCormick Place, 455
McDonalds, slogan of, 45
McFarland, Ruth, 253
McGuire, Craig, 137, 152
McNamara, Cathy, 451
Measurement
    advertising value equivalency,
    498–499
    advisory boards and focus
    groups, 508
    of article recall, 508
    of audience action, 506–507
    of audience attitudes, 505–506
    of audience awareness,
    504–505
    content analysis, 507
    of cost per person, 503
    establishing objectives, 493–494
    of event attendance, 503–504
    importance of, 491
    of the Internet, 500–502
    levels of, 493
    of media impressions, 497–498
    of message exposure, 497
    of newsletters and
    brochures, 507
    of production and distribution,
    494–496
    purposes of, 491
    readership surveys, 508
    requests and 800 numbers,
    502–503
    of social media, 502
    systematic tracking, 499
    tools, 494
    writing, 509

Media advisory (media alert), 146
    examples of, 148–149
Media alerts. *See* Media advisory
Media databases, 251–253
Media distribution services, 365
Media gatekeepers, 90
Media impression, 497
Media kits
    compiling, 150–153
    defined, 150
    electronic, 151–153
    examples of, 150–153
See also Press kits
Media relations
    areas of friction, 90–93
    checklist for, 108–109
    in crisis situations, 112–114
    editorial board meetings,
        107–108
    etiquette for, 110–112
    fam trips, 105
    importance of, 87–88
    junkets, 105–107
    media tours, 103–104
    as mutual dependency, 88–90
    news conferences, 99–102
    press interviews, 94–98
    previews and parties, 104–105
    at trade shows, 104
Media tour, 83
    described, 103
    to generate coverage, 103
    as a relationship builder,
        103–104
    PR role in, 104
MediaOnTwitter, 160
Medicare, 46
Meet the Press, 83
Meetings
    characteristics of
    group, 443–448
    planning for, 444
    shortcomings of, 442
    staff and committee,
        442–443
    value of, 441
Mehrabian, Albert, 402
Memoranda (memos)
    content, 379–380
    format, 380
    purpose, 379
Merchant Intelligence, 345
Merck, annual reports, 367, 368
Merton, Robert, 335
Message, of communication, 33

Messages
    clarity, 44
    persuasive themes, 44
Metro Editorial Service, 266
Meyers, Peter, 14
Mickey Mouse Law, 281
Microsoft MSW, 354
Microsoft Office, 205, 207, 250
Microsoft Publisher, 348
Microsoft search engine (MSN), 12
Microsoft SharePoint, 356
Microsoft Word, 345, 348, 361
Microsoft, 433, 506
    trademark issues, 288
Middleman, Ann, 76
Milana, Paolina, 137
Miller High Life, 497
Minkalis, Annette, 234
Minter, Bobby, 343
Misappropriation of personality,
    277, 289–290
Miss America, 70
Miss Universe, 62
Mission statements, 341
Mitternight, Helen L., 304
Mobile applications, news
    distributions, 263–264
Mobile media, 333–334
Mobley, Marilynn, 314
Morgan Hotel, 461
Morton, Linda, 64
Morton's, 146
Mossberg, Walt, 6, 68
Mothers Against Drunk Driving
    (MADD), 50
MTV, 238
Multimedia news release
    example of, 138
    tips for creating, 137
MultiVu, 224
Murphy-Goode, 476, 477
Muse News, 344
Mustafe, Isaiah, 325
MySpace, 320–321

Naked Juice, 197–198
National Association for Broadcast
    Communicators, 228
National Association of Potato
    Growers, 166
National Association of
    Realtors, 287
National Bagel Day, 63
National Education Association
    (NEA), 64, 66, 196

National Football League, 71, 288
National Foundation for
    Infectious Disease, use of
    PSAs, 220–222
National Heart, Lung and Blood
    Institute, use of PSAs,
    221–222
National Investors Relations
    Institute (NIRI), 102
National Labor Relations
    Board, 279
National Organization on
    Fetal Alcohol Syndrome
    (NOFAS), 231
National Park Foundation, 433
National Pork Producers
    Council, 234
National Potato Board, 500
National Public Radio (NPR), 13
National Recreation and Park
    Association, 433
National Resource Defense
    Council (NRDC), 37, 65, 353
    direct mail, 420
National Safety Council, 50
National Turkey Federation,
    34, 39
The Nature Conservatory, 326
Navistar, 155
Neal, Diane, 232
Neff, Richard E., 373
Neumann, W. Russell, 335
New York Fashion Week, 93
New York State Canal
    System, 476
New York Times Stylebook, 8
New York Times, 13, 63
New York Toy Fair, 75
New York Women's
    Foundation, 451
New York Yankees, 271
Newegg, 288
News
    creating, 70–71, 73
    external sources, 70
    internal sources, 69
News conferences, 99–102
    appropriateness, 99
    handling, 102
    invitations, 100–101
    location for, 99–100
    post conference, 102
    scheduling, 99
    teleconferences, 102–103
    webcasts, 102–103

News distribution
  choosing a channel, 256
  via e-mail, 255–257
  editorial calendars, 253–254
  via feature placement firms,
    265–268
  via newswire, 259–263
  via fax, 269
  via mail, 269
  media databases, 251–253
  via mobile applications,
    263–264
  via online newsroom, 257–259
  via photo placement firms,
    268–269
  via Twitter, 264–265
  tip sheets, 254
News feature. *See* Feature story
News feeds, 236
News release
  audio, 216–218
  body of, 128–129, 136
  contact information on,
    122–123
  dateline of, 124
  headline of, 122–124
  importance of, 118–119
  lead paragraph of, 124–128
  letterhead of, 121–122
  multimedia, 137–139
  newsworthiness, 120
  organization description in,
    129–131
  online, 133–136
  parts of, 120–121
  planning, 119–120
  speeches as, 413
  about speaking engagement, 413
  tips for writing, 129,
    130, 132
  types of, 133–139
  value of, 118–119
  video (VNR), 224-231
News USA, 70, 266
NewsCom, 192, 268–269
Newsday, legal issues, 283
Newsletters
  constituencies of, 344
  format, 345–346
  online, 352–354
  tips, 346
  See also Print Publications
Newsmagazines, as a source, 13
Newspaper Association of
  America, 166

Newspapers
  placement of features in, 183
  as source for current events, 13
  See also Print Publications
NewsUSA, 268
Newsweek, 13
Newswires, 259–263
Nichols, Barbara, 447
Nielsen, Jakob, 306
Nike
  annual report, 369
  cost per person advertising, 503
  slogan of, 45
  swoosh of, 45
Nikon, 75
Nizer, Louis, 400
Noah Was an Amateur, 245
No-host bar, 453
Nolan, Pter, 406
North American Precis Syndicate
  (NAPS), 178–179, 181,
    215, 266
  PSA use, 231, 233
Novartis Animal Health, 42
Novelis, 395
Numbers, guidelines for
  using, 26
NYU Stern, media advisory, 149

O'Donnell, Victoria, 52
*O'Dwyer's Communications and
  New Media*, 11
O'Dwyer's Daily News Briefings, 10
O'Dwyer's, 11
Oakland Tribune, 47
Obama, Barack, 403
  use of Twitter, 327
Obama, Michelle, 64
Obici, Amedeo, 174
Ochman, B. L., 135–136
Ogilvy PR Worldwide, 273
Oil Over the Andes, 245
Old Spice, 325
Olympic Paints and Stains, 42
Olympics, trademark, 288–289
Omega, product placement, 241
OMG!, 76
OneUpWeb, 332
Online news release 133–136
Online newsrooms, 257–259
Online video, 245–247
  tips for, 246, 247
Op-ed columns, 183–185
  format of, 185
  placement of, 183–184

purpose and motivation of, 183
  tips for writing, 184
Open houses, 465–468
Opera Company of Philadelphia, 80
Oprah & Friends XM, 61
Oprah Winfrey Show, 237
Optometric Association, 62
Oxfam, 425
*Oxford Pocket Dictionary and
  Thesaurus*, 7
Oxygen Media, 80

Pacific Gas & Electric
  Company, 433
Page impression, 310
Page view, 310
Paid media, 90
Paine, Katie, 502
Pamphlets. *See* Brochures
Panasonic, 197
Paper
  folds of, 360
  types of, 361–361
Paquette, Amy, 247
Paragraphs
  guidelines for writing, 20–21
Paramount Pictures, 284
Parties for the press, 104–105
PartyLine, 254
Passive audience, 40
Pathos, 32
Pay-for-play, 294
Payola, 112
Pedison, Beth, 393
People magazine, pitch, 155
PepsiCo, 75, 310
  use of social media, 321, 324
Perry, Kimberly, 194
Perry, Neil, 194
Perry, Reid, 194
Personal appearances, 83
Personality profiles, 173–174
Persuasion
  communication and, 33
  ethics of, 53–54
  and propaganda, 52–53
  rhetoric, 32
  techniques of, 55
Persuasive speaking, 51–52
  tips for, 41
Persuasive Writing
  audience analysis for, 40–42
  content and structure of,
    46–47
  examples in, 49

reasons for failure, 36
as spur to action, 46
tips for, 41
types of appeals, 44
PETCO, 72
Peter Webb Public Relations, 66
Peterson, David, 95
Peterson, Lakey, 232
PetSmart, 78
Pettigrew, Justin, 260
Pew Research Center, 88
Pharmaceutical Research
and Manufacturers of
America, 272
Philips Norelco, 177
Phipps, Jennie, 185
Photo news release (PNR), 203
Photo placement firms, 268–269
Photo releases, 276–277
Photo session planning, 201–202
Photography
captions, 203–204
copyright issues of, 201, 203
cropping and retouching, 202
distribution of, 207–208
in feature articles, 180
keeping files of, 207
outdoor, 199
See also Publicity photos
PhotoShop, 202, 405
Picas, 363
Pie chart, 205
Pilsbury, 279
Pitch, 154
Pitchmaking, 154
to bloggers, 161
by email, 157–159
follow-up to, 160–161, 163
opening lines in, 157–158
researching for, 154–156
by telephone, 159–160
to television station
tips for, 157, 162
using Twitter, 160
Pitt, Brad, 62
Plagiarism, 282
Plain folks, propaganda
technique, 52
Plans, in public relations
audience, 481
budget, 485–486
components of, 475
evaluation of, 486
importance of, 471–472
information analysis, 474

information gathering, 472–474
information objectives of,
476–479
marketing objective, role in, 480
motivational objectives,
479–481
objectives, 476–481
situation of, 474
strategy in, 481–482
submission of, 487
tactics in, 482–483
timing in, 483–485
written, 471
Plant tours, 465–468
Planters, 150–151, 174
Plugs, 241
Podcasts, 330–333
Pogue, David, 154, 156, 157, 312
Polaroid, 459
Political correctness, semantics
of, 46
Politically correct language
(PC), 29
Politico, 13
Polls, 76–77
for persuasive writing, 40–42
Port Discovery, 503
Porter Novelli, 388
Porter, Jeremy, 162
Position papers. *See* White papers
Post-it Notes, 285–286
Postman, Joel, 330
Potter, Kate, 325
PowerPoint (Microsoft), 205,
405–407
PR Daily News Feeds, 10
PR Job Watch, 12
PR News Group, 12
PR News, 10
PR Newswire, 117, 137, 252, 260
PR Reporter, 10
PR Week, 63, 87, 88, 92
PR Writer. *See* Publicist
Present tense, 22
Press kits
compiling, 150–153
defined, 150
electronic, 151–153
examples of, 150–153
See also Media kits
Press Release. *See* News release
Pressroom, 460–461
Previews for press, 104–105
Prezi, 407–408
PrimeZone Media Network, 260

Print ads
artwork, 434–435
headlines, 434
layout, 435
text, 434
tips for, 435
Print publications
audience interests,
344–345
design, 354
editorial plan for, 343–344
format, 345–347
headlines, 351–352
layout, 347–350
lead sentences, 352–353
mission statement for,
342–343
photos and illustrations, 350
tips, 349
value of, 340–341
See also Brochures; Magazines;
Newsletters; Newspapers
Priskies PetCare Company, 476
PRNewswire, 208, 497
Procter & Gamble, 79
Product demonstrations,
77–79
Product placement, 240–243
history of, 241
tips for, 242
Product specification
sheets, 145
ProfNet Connect, 254
ProfNet, 157
Prominence, 62–64
Promise, 343
Promotional events
celebrities, use of, 462
planning and logistics, 464
Propaganda and Persuasion, 52
Proposals
for features, 167
purpose, 384
organization, 384–385
from public relations firms,
387–390
tips, 386
ProQuest Newsstand, 16
Protests, 81–82
Proximity, 64–65
PRWeb, 137, 260
PRWeek, 10, 11
on Facebook, 12
Pseudoevent, 70–71
Public domain, 282

Public Relations
  components, 1
  definition, 92
  evaluation of, 491.509
  framework, 1–3
  legal issues in, 272–290
  planning for, 472–487
Public Relations Association
    of Indonesia, 53
Public Relations Quarterly, 4
Public Relations Review, 11
Public Relations Society of
    America (PRSA), 10
  ethics code, 107
  RSS feed, 313
Public Relations Strategist, 10
Public Relations Tactics, 10, 11, 24
Public service advertising,
    431–432
Public service announcement (PSA)
  characteristics of, 218
  defined, 218
  distribution of, 223
  effectiveness of, 218–220
  format of, 220–221
  production of, 222
  sound added to, 221
  for television, 231
  tips for producing, 222–223
  use of, 222
Publicist, 59
  audience of, 4–5
  media gatekeeper, 60
  objectives of, 4
  skills of, 3
Publicity photos
  action in, 196–197
  camera angles for, 197–198
  captions for, 203–204
  color in, 199
  composition of, 194–195
  cropping and retouching
    of, 202
  distribution of, 207–208
  ethical considerations
    regarding, 202–203
  finding photographers for,
    200–201
  importance of, 191
  lighting and timing of, 196–197
  photo session for, 201–202
  scale of, 197
  subject matter of, 193–194
  technical quality of, 192–193
  tips for shooting, 192, 200

Publicity, 59
  brainstorming, 72
  conflict in, 67
  contests, 74–75
  creating news, 70–71, 73
  human interest, 66–67
  newness of, 68
  obstacles to, 59–60
  prominence of, 62–64
  proximity of, 64–65
  significance of, 65–66
  special Events, 72–74
  stunts, 79–81
  timeliness of, 60–62
Publics, 34
Purina, 331
Putka, Gary, 88
PWR New Media, 190

Queensland Tourist Authority, 79
Query, for feature story, 168
Quick response codes (QR codes),
    264, 265
Quiznos, 275

Rabin, Phil, 222
Radio
  audio news release for (ANRs),
    216–218
  audience of, 212–213
  community calendars on,
    243–244
  importance of, 212
  news release for (RNRs),
    213–215
  promotion on, 243
  public service announcements
    on, 218–223
  tips for using
Radio media tours (RMT), 223
Radio news release (RNR),
    213–215
  tips for writing, 213
Rafe, Stephen, 97
Ragan Report, 10, 12
Ragan, Mark, 351
Ragan.com, 12, 118
Ragan's Daily Headlines, 10
Rallies, 81–82
Reach, 485
Read Across America, 64
Reber, Bryan, 260
Receiver, of communication, 33
Receptions, 453–454
Red Crescent, 45

Red Cross, 45
Redundancy, 25
References, 7–12
  blogs, 11–12
  dictionary, 7
  discussion groups, 12
  encyclopedia, 7
  media directories, 9
  professional publications, 9–11
  stylebook, 7–9
Regulatory agencies
  Federal Trade Commission
    (FTC), 290–292
  Securities and Exchange
    Commission (SEC), 292
  Federal Communication
    Commission (FCC), 294
  Food and Drug Administration
    (FDA) 294–295
Renderings, 206
Reporter Connection, 157
Request for information
    (RFI), 387
Requests for proposals
    (RFP), 387
Rescigno, Richard, 154, 157
Research, 1, 13–17
  electronic databases, 16–17
  search engines14–16
  studies, 171
  types, 14
Rethinking Tomorrow, 245
Retouching, of photos, 202
Return on investment (ROI), 311
Reverb, 292
Rex Healthcare, 239
Rex on Call, 239
RFL Communications, 73
Rhetoric 4
*Rhetorical and Critical
    Approaches*, 53
Rich, Judith, 71
Robertie, Renee, 70
Rocca, Mo, 234
Rock and Roll Hall of Fame,
    copyright issues, 283
Rogers & Associates, 505
Rogers, Everett, 37
Ronald McDonald House
    Charities, 231, 233
Rosen, David, 326
Rotary International, 326
Rowling, J.K., 73
Royal Caribbean, 106
Ruben, Brent, 426

Rudman, Rick, 303
Ruiz, Hector, 412
Ruiz, Manny, 139

Safeway Select Bank, 66
Salutaions, of email, 377–378
Salvation Army, PSA use, 231
Samansky, Art, 407
San Diego Convention
    Center, 306
San Diego Zoo, 66
San Giacomo, Laura, 231
San Jose State University, 466
Sanz, Horatio, 232
Satellite media tours (SMT), 83,
    232–236
    content of, 234
    cost of, 236
    format of, 232–234
    origin of, 232
    tips for producing, 235–236
Saudi Aramco World, 342–343
Saudi Aramco, 342
Save Darfur Coalition, 81
Sawyer, Joel, 95
Scale models, 206
Schering-Plough, 294
Schmelzer, Randy, 329
Schneider Associates, 80
Schubert Communications, 132
Schulman, Mark A., 78
Schultz, Charles, 290
Schweigert, Julie, 160
Schweitzer, Albert L., 493
Scott, Hilary, 84
Scott, Mark, 498
Seaport Village, 74
Search engine optimization
    (SEO), 124, 255, 309
    need for, 136
Search engine, 14–16, 309
Searchenginewatch.com, 309
Sears Holdings, 333
Sears, 505
Securities and Exchange
    Commission (SEC), 292, 364
    regulations, 260
Self-interest, appeals to, 43–44
Semantics, 45–46
Sender, of communication, 33
Sentences
    guidelines for writing, 19
    poor structure, 24
Seoane, Charlene, 343
Service journalism, 166

Sex in the City, 241
SGI, 101
Shaquille O'Neal, 50
Shedd Aquarium 121
    electronic media kit, 152
    fact sheet, 143–144
    news release of, 122
Shell, 229
Sherwin-Williams, 263
Shipley, David, 184
Shorenstein, Marissa, 95
Sierra Club, 52
    direct mail, 420, 421
Sigal, L. V., 88
Significance, 65–66
Silver Anvil Award, 437, 477, 488
Simmons Study of Media
    and Markets, 17
Simon, Morton, J., 276
Sjytel, 503
Slander, 274
Slogans, 45
Smallwood, Eric, 241
SmartFood, 495
Smirnoff, product placement, 241
Smokey the Bear, 45
Snail mail, 269
Social Media
    blogs, 314–320
    defined, 312
    Facebook, 320–321
    Flickr, 325–326
    listservs, 313
    MySpace, 320–321
    real simple syndication
        (RSS), 312)
    texting, 328–329
    Twitter, 326–327
    value of, 312–312
    wikis, 329–330
    YouTube, 322–325
Social media release (SMR). See
    multimedia news release
Social Reality, 130
Society of Corporate Compliance
    and Ethics, 279
Society of Professional
    Journalists, ethics code, 107
Soltis, Steve, 412
Sonoma County Airport
    Express, 265
Sony, 228
Soundbite, 34, 216
Source credibility, 42–43
South by Southwest (SXSW), 324

South Dakota Office of
    Tourism, 329
Southwest Airlines, 130
    use of Twitter, 327
SPEAK model, 404
Speakers
    introducing, 399
    placement of, 411–412
    researching, 393
    training of, 409–410
Speakers' bureaus, 410–411
Special events, 72–74
Speeches
    audiences of, 393
    brevity of, 402
    coaching and rehearsal of, 398
    drafting of, 397–398
    introducing speakers, 399
    message of, 394
    news releases about, 413
    objective of, 394
    outline of, 395
    panels, 408
    publicity before, 412–413
    settings for, 395
    strategy of, 395
    types of, 399
    visual aids for, 403–408
    word choice for, 396–397
Speechmaking
    brevity of, 402
    focusing on audience, 400–401
    focusing on objectives,
        398–400
    focusing on specifics, 401–402
    gestures and eye contact,
        402–403
    SPEAK model for, 404
    structuring the message, 400
Speechwriting
    demand for, 392
    groundwork for, 393–395
    process of, 395–398
    researching the audience and
        speaker, 393
Spelling, 23
Spin doctors, 53
Spitzer, Eliot, 61
Spokesperson, 409
Spokesperson, 94
    ethics of, 95–96
    tips, 98
SRI International, 34
St. Jude's Children's Research
    Hospital, 343

Staff and committee meetings, 442–443
Standard Rate and Data Services, 213
Stanton, Edward, m 4
Starbucks, 197
　website, 302
StarCite, 457
State Council Information Office, of China, 263
State Farm Insurance, 433
Statistics, 47–49
Step Reebok, 103
Stereotypes, avoiding, 28–29
Stern, Stefan, 314
Stewart, Joan, 107
Stewart, Martha, 288
Stock footage, for VNRs, 228
Stone, Glen, 151
Storyboard, for VNRs, 225
Stratacomm, 155
The Strategist, 71
Strategy 2
Strauss Radio Strategies, 217, 223
Structure, of news release, 120–121
Student Conservation Association, 232
Stunts, publicity, 79–81
Sturk, Chris, 325
Styli-Style, 79
Subheads, 123
　use in features, 180
Subject lines,
　of email pitches, 158–159
　of emails, 377
Subway, 275
Summary lead, 127
Sun Microsystems, 318
Sunkist, 482, 483
Super Bowl, 71, 427
Surveys, 76–77
　conducting, 78
　online, 76
　persuasive use of, 49
　for research, 171–172
Survivors, 34
Sustainers, 34
Swatch, 101
Symbols, 45

Taco Bell, 431, 433
Tactic, 2
Talk shows
　advantages, 237

guests on, 238–239
product placement on, 240–243
tips for appearances on, 241
Talking heads, 234
Technorati, 11, 93, 137, 257, 320, 501
TEKgroup International, 258
Teleconferences, 102–103
Telephone pitch, 159–160
Television
　magazine shows on, 239–240
　prevalence of, 223
　public service announcements on, 231
　satellite media tours on, 232–236
　soundbites for, 34
　talk shows on, 237–239
　video news releases (VNRs) for, 224–231
Template, 347
Terpening, Ed, 501
Testimonials
　in persuasive writing, 49–51
　propaganda, 52
Texting, 328–329
Third-party endorsement, 50
Thomas Rankin Associates, 166
Thomson Financial, 259
Time magazine, 13
　layout, 347
Timeliness, 60–62
Timex, 216
Tip sheets, 254
Today show, 83, 237
Todorova, Aleksandra, 309
Tokyo Electric Company, 101
The Tonight Show, 155
Top ten lists, 77
Towers, Perrin, Forster & Crosby, 344
Toyota, 47, 412
Trade Shows
　exhibit booths, 459
　hospitality suites, 460
　pressrooms and media relations, 460–461
Trademarks
　capitalization of, 288
　defined, 284
　genericization of, 287
　infringement of, 287–289
　misappropriation of personality, 289–290

protection of, 285–287
　of sports teams, 288
Traditional media, continuing role of, 334–336
Traditional news release, 133
Trahan, Burden & Charles, 503
Trammell, Jack, 218
Transfer, propaganda technique 43
Travano, Domenic, 229
Trial Lawyers of America, 67
Trip Advisor, 49
Tsang, You Mon, 491
Tucker, Kerry, 17
Tumblr, 315
Turnbull, Giles, 315
Turnitin, 282
TVN Productions, 216
Twain, Mark, 340
Twitter, 205, 206, 326–327
　chats, 12
　groups, 12
　for news distribution, 264–265
　pitches, 160
　tips for, 328
Tyson Foods, 272

UNICEF, 234
United States Army, 432
United States Census Bureau, 437
United States Equal Employment Opportunity Commission (EEOC), 278, 279
United States Navy Seals, online video, 246
United States Potato Board, 35
　direct mail, 420
United States Chamber of Commerce, 67
United Way of America, 273, 432
Unique visitor, 310
Unusualness, 66
UPS, 412
USAsianWire, 260
Use, 228–231
Usenet, groups, 12
Uses and gratification theory 34–35

VALS, 34
Vaughn, Roy, 319
Vermont Life, 346
Victoria's Secret
　webcasts, 312
　website visitors, 310
Video clips, 139

Video news release (VNR)
  components 224
  costs, 224
  format, 225
  production, 225
  tips for creating, 225, 227
Visa, product placement, 241
Visit Florida, 387
Visit, to a website, 500
Visual aids, for speeches, 403–408
VMS, 497
Vocus, 9, 156, 497, 499
Vogel, David, 114
Volmar, Phillip, 437
Vonn, Lindsey, 43

Walk Disney Corporation, 281
Walker, Jane, 343
Walker, Jerry, 200
The Wallstreet Journal, 13
  reprint department, 283
Wall Street Journal Stylebook, 8
Wal-Mart, 64, 476, 506
Walton, Susan Balcom, 159,
  203, 316
Waltzing Matilda, 245
Wanta, Wayne, 191
Ward, David, 75
Ward, Toby, 356
Washington Mutual, 505
Washington Speakers Bureau, 449
Washington University, 183
Wasserman, Maya, 160
Water Pik, 171
Weblogs.com, 320
Webcasting, 311–312
Webcasts, 102–103
Weber Grills, 78
Weber Shandwick, 93, 320, 389
Weber, Thomas E., 308

Weber-Stephens Products, 105
Websites
  attracting visitors to,
    308–310
  effective building of, 306–307
  interactive elements of,
    307–308
  organizational use of, 302
  for research, 15
  ROI of, 311
  tips for, 305
  tracking visitors to, 310
  writing for, 303–305
Webster's New College
  Dictionary, 7
Weidlich, Thom, 190
Weisberg, Rob, 389
Weissman, Pete, 394, 401
Wells Fargo, 354
West, Angela, 439
Westchester Medical Center,
  website, 302
Whetsell, Tripp, 155, 157
Whirpool, 331
White papers, 386
Whitmore, Steve, 94
Whole Foods, 327
Wikipedia, 7
Wikis, 329–330
Wild Blueberry Association,
  266, 286
Wiley, Michael, 317
Williams, Tudor, 492
Wilson, Laurie, 471
Wilson, Matt, 246
Wion, Rick, 320
Wirthlin Group, 118
Witkoski, Michael, 392
Witmer, Diane F., 305, 308
Word choice, 21–22

Word Works, 207
Wordpress, 315, 316
Words
  choice of, 19, 21, 25
  commonly confused, 26
World magazine, 340
World Wide Web
  characteristics of, 300–302
  as a journalistic tool, 302–303
  organizational use of, 302
  versus new media, 301
  See also Internet; Websites
Writer
  role of, 2
Writing
  avoiding errors in, 23–28
  focus of, 19
  preparing for, 5–13
  purpose of, 17
  tips for, 20, 27
  for websites, 303–205, 305

Yahoo!, 12, 14, 16, 76, 171–172,
  261, 309
Yamamoto, Mike, 166
Yehuda, Bev, 236
YELP, 49
Ylisela, Jim, 346
YMCA, 83
Young, Michael, 461
YouTube Insight, 501
YouTube, 322–325, 501

Zarrella, Dan, 327, 328
Zazza, Frank, 241
Zero Gravity, 261
Zimmerman, Jan, 309
Zinio.com, 16
Zipcar, 389
Zupan, Mark, 231

Photo Credits

Chapter 1, p. 6, BAO-Images Stock Connection Worldwide/Newscom; p. 10, Dow Jones & Co.; p. 11, top left, PRWeek, Haymarket Media, Inc.; p. 11, top right, PRSA; p. 11, bottom, Courtesy of Jack O'Dwyer; p. 12, Reprinted by permission of Lawrence Ragen Communications, Inc; p. 24, PRSA.

Chapter 2, p. 39, Shen Hong/Xinhua/Photoshot/Newscom; p. 43 Fabrice Coffrini/AFP/Getty Images/Newscom.

Chapter 3, p. 64, Mike Theiler/UPI/Newscom; p. 68, Brian Kersey/UPI/Newscom; p. 74, Courtesy of JSH&A; p. 81, mm7/ZUMA Press/Newscom; p. 82, Fernando Leon/ABACAUSA.COM/Newscom; p. 84, Jim Ruymen UPI Newspictures/Newscom.

Chapter 4, p. 94, Splash News/Newscom; p. 101, Kenichiro Seki/Xinhua/Photoshot/Newscom; p. 105, Eva Zeno, PRX, Inc.; p. 106, Agencia el Universal GDA Photo Service/Newscom.

Chapter 5, p. 121, Courtesy of BMI; p. 122, Copyright John G. Shedd Aquarium; p. 125, Courtesy McCormick & Company; p. 134, Courtesy McCormick & Company; p. 135, Courtesy McCormick & Company; p. 138, PRWeb, Inc.

Chapter 6, p. 144, Copyright John G. Shedd Aquarium; p. 146, Courtesy of Morton's; p. 147, Courtesy of McCormick & Company; p. 149, Courtesy NYU Stern School of Business; p. 151, Kraft Foods, Inc.; p. 153, top, California Academy of Sciences; p. 153, bottom, Courtesy of Hewlett-Packard.

Chapter 7, p. 168, The UPS Store; p. 171, Boggiatto Produce, Inc.; p. 172, Reprinted with Permission from Yahoo! Inc. YAHOO! and the YAHOO! logo are trademarks of Yahoo! Inc; p. 179, Courtesy of the North American Precis Syndicate; p. 181, Courtesy of the North American Precis Syndicate.

Chapter 8, p. 191, Courtesy of Hewlett-Packard; p. 194, Lionel Hahn/AbacaUsa/Newscom; p. 195, Bob Goldberg Feature Photo Service/Newscom; p. 196, Courtesy of Jeff Weikert; p. 197, Robyn Beck/AFP/Getty Images/Newscom; p. 198, Jonathan Kirn Feature Photo Service/Newscom; p. 199, Bob Goldberg Feature Photo Service/Newscom; pp. 205, 206, Created by Sebastian Lann, Founder of InfographicsArchive.com.

Chapter 9, p. 213, Cision USA; p. 226, Courtesy of Purina; pp. 229, 230, Bader TV; p. 233, Courtesy of the North American Precis Syndicate; p. 234, Courtesy of UNICEF; p. 238, Sony Pictures TV/Splash News/Newscom.

Chapter 10, pp. 251, 252, Cision USA; p. 258, Courtesy of Hewlett-Packard; p. 262, Courtesy of Business Wire; p. 265, p72/ZUMA Press/Newscom; p. 268, Wild Blueberry Association; p. 269, Graham Carlow/Feature Photo Service for IBM.

Chapter 11, p. 28, Courtesy of 3M; p. 287, Courtesy of National Association of Realtors® p. 289, Staff/MCT/Newscom.

Chapter 12, p. 315, Courtesy of Richard Edelman; p. 322, Courtesy of Chick-Fil-A; p. 332, OneUpWeb digital; p. 324, WpN/Photoshot.

Chapter 13, p. 343, ©2008 Aramco Services Co., Houston; p. 353, Reprinted with permission from the Natural Resources Defense Council; p. 355, Courtesy of Guide Dogs for the Blind; p. 356, Courtesy Cisco Systems, Inc; p. 360, Baum Folder Company; p. 366, Courtesy Federal Express; p. 369, Courtesy Federal Express.

Chapter 14, p. 388, Courtesy Porter Novelli; p. 390, Nenad Aksic/Belgrade Cultural Network; p. 389, Regina H. Boone/MCT/Newscom.

Chapter 15, p. 403, Jason Moore/ZUMA Press/Newscom; p. 407, Courtesy Arthur W. Page Society; p. 408, Courtesy of Prezi.

Chapter 16, p. 421, Mlicki, Inc.; p. 422, Drakes Bay Fundraising drakesbaynet.com; p. 430, Courtesy of Chevron; p. 431, Courtesy of Taco Bell; p. 432, Ad Council/Feeding America Hunger Prevention Campaign.

Chapter 17, p. 445, vario images GmbH & Co.KG/Alamy; p. 446, Courtesy of History San Jose; p. 458, Robyn Beck/AFP/Getty Images/Newscom; p. 459, AJM/AAD/ starmaxinc.com/Newscom; p. 463, Stefan/ splash News/Newscom; p. 466, Martin Luther King, Jr. Library at San Jose State University.

Chapter 18, p. 473, Konstantin Chagin/ Shutterstock; p. 477, Mark & Audrey Gibson Stock Connection Worldwide/Newscom.

Chapter 19, p. 495, Daniel Sicolo/Design Pics/ Newscom.